Sybase
DBA
COMPANION

BRIAN HITCHCOCK

Prentice Hall PTR
Upper Saddle River, NJ 07458
http://www.prenhall.com

C000006734

Library of Congress Cataloging-in-Publication Date
Hitchcock, Brian.
   Sybase DBA companion / Brian Hitchcock.
     p. cm.
   Includes index.
   ISBN 0-13-652389-7 (alk. paper)
   1. Relational databases   2. Sybase.
QA76.9.D3H553   1997
005.75`8--dc21
                                    97-6036
                                    CIP

Editorial/Production Supervision: Craig Little
Acquisitions Editor: Mark Taub
Buyer: Alexis Heydt
Marketing Manager: Dan Rush
Cover Design: Scott Weiss
Cover Design Direction: Jerry Votta
Cover Illustration: Don Martinetti, D.M. Graphics
Art Director: Gail Cocker-Bogusz
CD Design: Cynthia L. Mason

 © 1997 Prentice Hall PTR
Prentice-Hall, Inc.
A Simon & Schuster Company
Upper Saddle River, NJ 07458

Prentice Hall books are widely used by corporations and government agencies
for training, marketing, and resale.

The publisher offers discounts on this book when ordered in bulk quantities.
For more information, contact: phone: 800-382-3419; fax: 201-236-7141; e-mail: corpsales@prenhall.com
or write:
Prentice Hall PTR
Corporate Sales Department
One Lake Street
Upper Saddle River, NJ 07458

Printed in the United States of America

10 9 8 7 6 5 4 3 2

ISBN 0-13-652389-7

Prentice-Hall International (UK) Limited, London
Prentice-Hall of Australia Pty. Limited, Sydney
Prentice-Hall Canada Inc., Toronto
Prentice-Hall Hispanoamericana, S.A., Mexico
Prentice-Hall of India Private Limited, New Delhi
Prentice-Hall of Japan, Inc., Tokyo
Simon & Schuster Asia Pte. Ltd., Singapore
Editora Prentice-Hall do Brasil, Ltda., Rio de Janeiro

Contents

❄ Chapter 10   Performance and Tuning 389

Preface

This book discusses the issues that anyone involved with supporting SQL Server needs to be aware of. Here we cover the following topics that describe what is and is not discussed in the text:

Purpose of this Book

Who Is This Book For?

What You Need to Know to Use This Book

What You Will Learn From This Book

Conventions

Terms

PURPOSE

This book is intended for those persons who need to support SQL Server System 11, System 10, Version 4.9.2, and any combination thereof.

WHO IS THIS BOOK FOR?

Clearly, the Database Administrator (DBA) is one person for whom this book is intended, but so is the manager who is trying to plan the growth of the system and the financial officer who will have to pay for staff and hardware to support the system. The experiences described here will benefit DBAs with less experience while the checklists and procedures will save the experienced DBA time.

It is assumed that the reader is familiar with the Sybase SQL Server and the commands used to control the server. The book does not provide a complete syntax for any of the server commands and, as such, is not intended as a beginning training text. The Sybase courses are very good for this purpose, and this book is an excellent companion to the course material, as it expands on, explains, and underscores the practical impacts of many things described in the course and the manuals.

WHAT YOU NEED TO KNOW TO USE THIS BOOK

This book is written based on experiences with the Sybase SQL Server running on Sun hardware using Solaris 2.x. The descriptions of the server and the procedures will work with the Sybase SQL Server on other UNIX operating systems. Every attempt has been made to make the discussion relevant to any Sybase SQL Server installation. When needed, commands or procedures that are specific to Solaris are identified as such.

You probably won't use and don't need to use all of the material presented all at once. Certain sections will be immediately relevant to your current situation. When a crisis hits you can use the other sections as checklists of things to review as a way to isolate and fix the problems your system is experiencing.

WHAT YOU WILL LEARN FROM THIS BOOK

The DBA who is responsible for the administration of a Sybase SQL Server will find the information directly applicable to their job. While portions of the discussions relate directly to the Solaris UNIX environment, the commands used are described in sufficient detail so that the equivalent commands for virtually any UNIX platform can be readily identified.

This book is designed for use in the real world. Procedures are laid out to be followed step by step. Sufficient detail is included to ensure the procedures can be used on a variety of systems by all members of the DBA staff from the most senior to the latest recruit. Further, these procedures make the process of training a new person much easier.

Real-world observations are included throughout the text and are denoted by the symbol. These observations are included to motivate the reader to pay attention to the subject and apply what is presented to their own systems. Viewed another way, these observations provide stark evidence of the price you may well pay if you choose to avoid the advice presented. Without these observations it is easy to dismiss the instruction as too detailed and perhaps even paranoid.

Disasters do happen and real people get fired over them.

The manuals included with the Sybase SQL Server (including the CD-based products SyBooks and AnswerBase) are excellent and cover the topic of a single server very well. This is their purpose and their duty. However, as you encounter the different versions of SQL Server and have to deal with installing and upgrading these versions, there are new problems that just aren't addressed in the manuals. This books covers these issues in detail and as such provides a bridge between the manuals with their single-versioncentric view of the world to your multiversion environment. While the manuals are invaluable for documenting and describing all the options for a given command, they won't even begin to help you understand the large database environment.

As your business grows and expands, you will need to be familiar with the System 11 family of Sybase products. Whether you upgrade your existing servers from 4.9.2 or System 10 to System 11, or install a new server at System 11, you will face the hurdles of upgrading and installing. System 11 has many new features and the upgrade process is more involved than simply installing another Emergency Bug Fix (EBF). This book covers the upgrade process in detail, and covers the important differences between the 4.9.2, System 10, and System 11 Versions of the Sybase SQL Server.

As with the many other Sybase products available, there are an endless number of permutations of hardware, operating system software, middleware, and so forth, that you may have in your environment. We make no attempt to address the issues that would arise in any given multivendor environment. We cover in great detail the issues relevant to administering a Sybase multiserver environment running UNIX. While the examples are taken from a Solaris environment, care has been taken to make these examples useful in any UNIX environment. Wherever possible, we avoid the use of commands or tools that are available only in the Solaris environment. Further, the function of the Solaris commands used is covered in sufficient detail so that it should be easy to determine the equivalent commands or options in the UNIX environment you are using.

This book does not cover any theory of databases, nor does it compare the functionality of any competing products. We assume you have (or were hired into an environment that already has) the selected Sybase SQL Server. If you are in the process of selecting the Database Management System (DBMS) for your environment, this book will assist you in determining what you need to have in place to maintain a large, multiversion Sybase system, but it will not provide any comparisons to other DBMS vendors or their products. We assume you are at a point where you need information relevant to administering a Sybase environment, not in need of a survey of DBMS products.

CONVENTIONS

Sybase SQL Server commands are shown in the text in the following font:

```
disk init
```

Sybase SQL Server command syntax is shown in the following font;

sp_helpdb database_name

sp_helpuser sa

sp_addsegment segment_name, server_device

sp_addsegment myseg0, server_device_1

Stored procedures that are supplied by Sybase as part of the SQL Server product are always referred to as

```
sp_<stored_procedure_name>
```

```
sp_helpdevice
```

Stored procedures that are not supplied (or supported) by Sybase that are described in Chapter 14, are referred to as

`p_<stored_procedure_name>`

`p_devspace`

The names of databases, segments, tables and columns are shown in the following font;

master database

system segment

syslogins table

segmap column

Operating system (OS) commands are shown in the following font;

`prtvtoc`

Real-world experiences that you need to think about are introduced by
:-). When you can find further information on the CD-ROM, you'll see
.

TERMS

There are many terms that are used in the description of the Sybase SQL
Server and its environment. Listed below are some terms that will be used
throughout the book. These terms are defined here to provide a standard
set of definitions for the discussions that follow.

server—Within this book a "server" is a Sybase Server, and almost all
the time it refers to a SQL Server. Occasionally the term "server"
may refer to a Sybase Open Server such as the Backup Server that
is part of the System 11 SQL Server.

server machine—This refers to the CPU, memory, disks, and network
interfaces that form the computer that actually executes the SQL
Server.

server logical device (tape or disk)—This is a "device" as seen by the
SQL Server. Note that SQL Server knows only about devices that
are assigned to it and there isn't necessarily any direct correlation
between a SQL Server device and a physical disk, for example.

server device—This is the same as a server logical device.

spindle—This is another term for a physical disk.

physical device—This refers to a physical disk or tape drive as opposed to a "logical" device, such as a partition of a physical disk that is assigned to a server device.

SQL Server user "sa"—This is the SQL Server login that has ultimate authority and is used by the DBA.

server machine SA—This is the person who installs, maintains, and repairs the hardware and operating system software that supports the SQL Server and its associated products.

database system—This is the entire collection of server machines, SQL Servers, networks, clients, backup systems, and so forth, that work together to support your business.

fail over—This is the process of moving from a primary to a stand-by SQL Server. Also, the process of moving from a server device to its mirror.

VERSIONS OF SQL SERVER

While there are many differences between SQL Server 4.9.2, System 10, and System 11, almost all the material presented here applies to all versions. With the exception of the material that is specific to installing or upgrading one of the specific versions, all the other topics are applicable to all versions. Whether you are running 4.9.2, System 10, or System 11, you need to be concerned with the issues and solutions regarding documenting a server, capacity planning, assigning segments to server devices, partitioning disks, and recovery. Further, few environments support only one version of SQL Server. The typical environment will support multiple versions at the same time with new servers being installed and some 4.9.2 or System 10 Servers being upgraded to System 11.

Acknowledgements

This book is dedicated to the Sun Service SOtool Development, Support and ENS groups. Their names are listed here, but their accomplishments are too numerous to detail: Cindi Beckett, George Brandetsas, Keri Brettell, Rebecca Burgess, Arindam Chakraborty, Linda Halloran, Frankie Lau, Jessica Tsai, Xiang Wang and Joon Yong. Most importantly, they kept going when all seemed hopeless. Deepak Alur and Sharon Gilbreth had the foresight to stay away from the latest implementation, but they helped make it happen nonetheless. While the organization as a whole was focused on new and more sexy projects, this team had to keep an aging, mission-critical system going, upgrading in parallel and making it all work. Linda Halloran has put up with a great deal from me. She can always see through my wild schemes and brings them down to earth and to a successful conclusion. She and I are the veterans of many campaigns. When the time comes, I'll miss working with her.

Here, then, are the people who really helped make this project happen. They helped by providing the environment I needed to learn the many things contained in this book.

Keri Brettel deserves special mention. She is a loyal ally and can be a fearsome enemy. She supported my efforts during these two years and that support was critical to keeping the project alive. Now that the backend response times are truly subsecond, she deserves much of the credit for not letting the project die. She has endured an incredible amount in her time, and I hope, in some small way, seeing this project through to a successful completion will provide her with some comfort.

Thien Nguyen and Xuan Van put up with my endless requests for machine upgrades and more disks. They refer to me now as Brian "wantsmoredisks" Hitchcock. I depend on them to make all these systems perform.

Bret Butcher took the time to help me get set up to work from home, and helped while I was learning to write scripts.

Ron Sha believed in me, bought machines for me, and, most of the time, put up with my requests for more hardware. I had to wait a long time to have a good manager, but it was worth it.

Mich Akamatsu, Tim Hickey, and Tim Weil statistically at least, have probably added 10 years to my life expectancy. They don't realize it, but through their efforts, I was able to relax and get this done.

Sheryl Diane believed that I could and should write again. She provided many suggestions that led to the completion of this project. I hope that her projects will provide her a similar amount of personal satisfaction. I also hope she feels properly "awarded" for her efforts. Projects like this require the dedication of many, and most don't realize how helpful they were.

Scott and Jade Vu, after many challenges, are living proof that you can survive the assaults of those without morals and continue with your own life. Their success is inspirational. In every generation there are survivors.

Amy, Jody, Terry, Sienna, and Jackie—I can see their eyes, their smiles, and hear their laughter. I know that someday someone will appreciate them as I do, on a more intimate and ongoing basis.

Helen Ruth made all of this possible through her support over many years.

Eric Robert and Christopher Noah continue to progress and at the same time allow me to write. They both learned to pilot their own Pentium class cruisers during this project and I'm sure the proceeds will help them journey into yet unimaginable worlds. Christopher also learned to say "No!" during the same period. Milestones all. Once, while gazing into the bedtime darkness, after I told him I had more writing to do, Eric focused on me and told me, "this is your second book—your second Sybase book." His command of the facts of the situation is irrefutable. I only hope this inherited compulsion for accuracy will help him more than it burdens him.

Francis Griswold provided emotional support. It takes someone who has been there to really understand what you have to get done.

Patrick and Robert Eric, I hope, are having as much fun as I am. They are loved, and that is a powerful advantage in the modern world.

Mark Taub actually asked me to write again.

Donna and Jerry provided tax advice regarding what to do with royalties.

Finally, with regards to the previous life, all I had to do was walk out of the darkness, into the sun. And, in retrospect, institutionalized sadism is its own reward.

Psycho, East of Glenn's Ferry, Idaho, October 1996

SQL Server
Overview

INTRODUCTION

Sybase SQL Server is a high-performance Relational Database Management System (RDBMS). As such, it supports many features needed to serve many concurrent users and to guarantee that mission-critical business data is not lost. This book covers multiple versions of the Sybase SQL Server, each of which is described briefly below. Note that this same format is followed in the introduction of many of the chapters that follow. In this way you will see how the material discussed in each chapter is relevant to the various versions of the SQL Server. You will see references to the "server" and to SQL Server which are the same thing. Do not confuse the term "server" used here for any other sort of server such as a file server, network server, or other application programs.

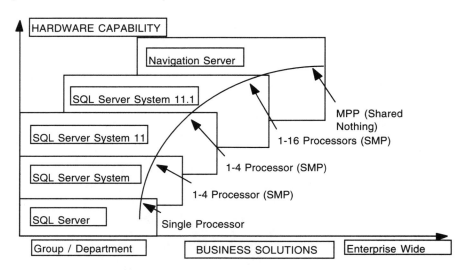

Figure 1–1. SQL Servers and Business Solutions

SQL SERVER VERSIONS

We cover the latest three versions of SQL Server; Version 4.9.2, System 10, and System 11. As shown in Figure 1–1, these SQL Server versions overlap quite a bit. Many of the features found in SQL Server 4.9.2 are carried through System 10 into System 11. Note that as SQL Server moves through this series of releases, the focus is changing to stay in step with the changing hardware and operating system changes that have occurred over the same time period. SQL Server System 11.1 is the next major release of the Sybase SQL Server. Since this release is not yet available, the specific features can"t be covered in this book. Navigation Server, now marketed as Sybase MPP (Massively Parallel Processing), is a product which uses multiple SQL Servers, each running on independent server machines to satisfy very complex queries against very large data sets. Navigation Server is beyond the scope of this book.

A brief description of the major features of each of the three SQL Server versions is given below followed by a general look at the features of SQL Server in general. This high-level view of SQL Server features will lead into the more detailed description of how these general features have changed in the three versions of the SQL Server. The new features of each version are also described.

SQL Server 4.9.2

This is the oldest version of the Sybase SQL Server that is discussed here. While there were even older versions, the 4.9.2 Server is the oldest version that is still being used by many sites. You will hear of SQL Servers 4.9.1 and 4.9.2, but note that the only difference between these subtypes of the 4.9 Server is the EBF level. EBF (Emergency Bug Fix) is simply a Sybase term which really means an update to the actual server executable binary. You will most likely encounter a 4.9 Server as a 4.9.2 Version. You may see references to the 4.9.2 or 4.9 Server which for this book will mean the same thing.

The 4.9.2 Server supported all the basic features of a RDBMS system. The versions of the server that followed built upon this feature set, and with few exceptions, the features of the 4.9.2 Server are found in the very latest server.

SQL Server System 10

The SQL Server System 10 release was originally supposed to be the 5.0 release of Sybase SQL Server. But, with Oracle, Sybase's arch-rival [although you should not discount the imminent and omnipresent threat from Microsoft (see below)], on the verge of releasing their newest RDBMS product family called Oracle 7.0, the marketing geniuses at Sybase decided that everyone in the database market place would be fooled if they jumped from 5.0 to 10.0 and the System 10 version of Sybase SQL Server was born. The reason that the SQL Server was now marketed as a "system" was that several related products were developed and released in the same period of time. It's too bad that the technical capabilities of the product didn't do as well as the marketing had promised. While it took several years, the scalability issues surrounding System 10 became critical and had a very negative impact on the company. The good news is that this actually led to a much more robust and much more thoroughly tested product when System 11 was released.

Features introduced with System 10 included cursors, many modifications to comply with ANSI SQL specifications, user roles, increased security and auditing and many detailed changes to the way queries were examined and processed by the query optimizer. Backup Server was introduced as a separate OS level process that handles all SQL Server dumps and loads. With System 10, the SQL Server can't make any backups or loads without Backup Server. Two new system databases were introduced. The first, *sybsystemprocs*, stores all the system stored procedures such as **sp_who**. The second, *sybsecurity*, stores all the information needed to support the new auditing features of System 10.

SQL Server System 11

System 11 is the latest major release of the Sybase SQL Server. It has only one focus and that is to make Sybase SQL Server scalable across multiple processors. This scalability means SQL Server now takes full advantage of the computer resources that you have available. This also means that as the demands on your SQL Server increase you can apply more computing hardware and see very tangible benefits. For example, if your user load doubles, you can, with System 11, apply twice the processors and maintain the same overall response time as you had previously. Obviously, you, as a DBA, have never seen performance that pleases any of your users, and the scalability of System 11 means you can double the processors to increase the speed of the server for the existing number of users.

System 11, as with System 10, is a product family. While the primary focus was on improving the scalability of the SQL Server, new versions of the other products like Replication Server were also released. Together, the products of the System 11 family provide a new level of performance that should provide your users with much improved performance.

Overall the System 11 release is all about performance on multiprocessor systems. Note that this implies that if you are running on a single- processor system, you will not be able to take advantage of the scalability which enables higher performance. For the vast majority of RDBMS systems, the performance benefits of going to multiprocessor hardware are far too appealing to prevent this migration.

As with most other things in life, this major improvement in server performance comes at a price, and not just in the cost of those extra processors. The Sybase System 11 SQL Server supports a level of performance monitoring and tuning that was unthinkable with previous versions. This cuts both ways. You, as the DBA for System 11 will probably need to work very carefully to deal with the virtually unlimited tuning possibilities now available to you. For example, where previous versions of the server supported approximately 30 server configuration parameters, the System 11 SQL Server has over one hundred and with the ability to create and tune things like named caches and multiple buffer pools, the tuning possibilities (as well as the opportunities for screwing up) are truly endless. The flip side of this is that you, as the DBA, can now become even more mysterious and invaluable than ever before. Imagine your users trying to figure out how you messed up the thirty-first of 102 named caches. You will be able to withdraw even further into a world of the truly arcane. But, more importantly, System 11 represents the best thing to happen to your job security since you learned about SQL.

Microsoft SQL Servers 4.2 and 6.0

While this book covers the Sybase SQL Server, you need to understand a very confusing aspect of the development of the Sybase product family. Once upon a time, in a galaxy not so very far away, Microsoft and Sybase agreed to some sort of arrangement whereby they shared various core technologies of the server code. Sybase developed and marketed the Sybase SQL Server for many platforms, most notably the various flavors of UNIX, and Microsoft sold Microsoft SQL Server for NT. As with so many high-tech fairy tales, there was some sort of falling-out. While the details of all this are probably fascinating, and probably not really understood by any single multicellular creature stalking the planet, the only thing you really need to know is that up through SQL Server 4.9.2, the Sybase and the Microsoft versions were virtually identical and were based on the same development effort, with the obvious exceptions for the different operating system platforms each product was designed to operate on.

Once the "arrangement" had been undone, Microsoft starting developing its own version of the server which resulted in Microsoft SQL Server 6.0 for NT. With this release, Microsoft's SQL Server began to diverge from the Sybase SQL Server in several major areas. This corresponded approximately with the release of the Sybase SQL Server System 10 family of products. The good news for you is that as Microsoft continues to suck up all forms of life on the planet, you, as an experienced Sybase SQL Server DBA, are in a great position since you already know most of what you need to support the Microsoft SQL Server. You should not worry about the outcome of this "ideological" conflict—either way you have job security and that is what this is all about.

Unless you see the specific phrase "Microsoft SQL Server," the terms server and SQL Server will refer to the Sybase version of SQL Server.

Future Versions of SQL Server

The specifics of any future software release remain vague until the software is generally available and there has been some user experience with the product. Still, several major features have been discussed for future versions of SQL Server. Trying to figure out when each of these features will really be available is problematic. You can ponder these future features, but you shouldn't count on any of them appearing at any time in the future. The details of these "coming attractions" are not described here but are delayed until the end of this chapter. Understanding the details of these expected features requires covering the features of System 11 first.

RDBMS Concepts

You need to understand the major features of any Relational Database Management System (RDBMS). Then we can discuss the way Sybase SQL Server implements these RDBMS features. For now we cover the generic RDBMS from a high-level perspective. The concepts described here are presented from the DBA perspective, that is what you need to know to get your job done, look good, and keep the users happy.

Relational

The definition of what is relational has been used to justify a lot of Ph.D.s, but a working definition is that all data is stored in tables (see Figure 1–2). Also, all operations applied to a relational system return tables as the result. For example, if you retrieve all the customers who live in California, the result will be a table of data. Tables have rows and columns. By storing data in the rows and columns of tables, it is very easy to relate the data in one table to the data in another table. This ability to relate data in tables means you can access the data in many different ways. Another key concept is that the user makes a request for data, but the way that request is satisfied is not specified. The database engine, the core software that stores and retrieves that data, is free to perform its tasks in any manner. The way the data is stored is not relevant to how you ask for data.

psycho_books

title	title_id	published	made_money	year_published
DBA_Handbook	1	yes	no	1995
DBA Companion	2	yes	no	1996
CSP Training	3	no	no	NULL

select * from psycho_books where year_published != NULL

title	title_id	published	made_money	year_published
DBA_Handbook	1	yes	no	1995
DBA Companion	2	yes	no	1996

select title, year_published from psycho_books

title	year_published
DBA	1995
DBA	1996
CSP	NULL

Figure 1–2. Relational Tables

Structured Query Language (SQL)

Since the data in a relational database is stored in tables, and since you can relate these tables in many different ways, you can access data in multiple tables in a variety of ways. The Structured Query Language, SQL has become a standard way of accessing relational data. This is another reason that relational databases have become popular. You can learn SQL and have a good chance of accessing data stored in relational databases from many different vendors. While it is far from perfect, SQL makes working with relational data much easier than if each vendor had their own independent method of accessing the data in their databases. Without SQL it would be much more difficult to connect many different vendors" RDBMS products on the network. When you send SQL command(s) to the server you are sending a "query" to the server. Note that a query refers to any SQL command, even commands that add new data to the database. While the SQL language is worthy of much discussion, the very basic SQL data manipulation commands that you need to be aware of are as follows.

Select

This is the command to read data from a table or tables.

Insert

This command allows you to add data to a table.

Update

This command allows you to change existing data in a table.

Delete

This command allows you to remove data from a table.

While SQL is very useful, each vendor has, of course, added their own proprietary and incompatible extensions to the language. The vendors will tell you that they had to add these extensions to make up for failings in the SQL standard, but we know better. The extensions are the way each vendor tries to differentiate their RDBMS product in the marketplace. Hence, while SQL is a standard, you must be aware of each vendor's extensions to the language. As business moves to incorporate many and varied databases on the network, the need to move data between heterogeneous platforms is becoming commonplace. This also means that you will be dealing with the incompatible extensions to SQL more and more often.

Database Objects

Within the RDBMS, there are many objects that store data and support manipulation and validation of that data. Other objects (see Figure 1–3), are described next.

Table

The most basic database object is the table. Data is stored as rows in a table. The columns of a table are the fields and each field stores the data for one attribute of the object being described by the table.

title	title_id	published	made_money	year_published
DBA_Handbook	1	yes	no	1995
DBA Companion	2	yes	no	1996
CSP Training	3	no	no	NULL

table -- fields (title, title_id, published, made_money, year_published)
-- each row describes a title
rule -- published field valid values Y, N
default -- if made_money = NULL then made_money = N
stored procedure -- update year_published to year_published + 1
-- updates all rows at once

trigger -- on insert, compute new_total for books published
-- fires whenever a row is inserted

index -- create index on title_id
-- index entries are
1, pointer to row where title_id = 1

NULL -- year_published is not known for title_id =

Figure 1–3. Database Objects

Rule

This object specifies the allowable values or format of the data in a column. For example, all employee numbers must be six digits in length.

Default

This object specifies the value to be used for a field if no value is specified when the data is added to the table. For example, if the employee salary is not specified when a new employee is entered into the employee table, assign the default salary of $0.00.

Stored Procedure

While SQL is fine, the default way to use SQL is to send each SQL statement to the SQL Server. As the complexity of your application and the number of server users grows, the number of SQL statements flying around the network becomes huge. Stored procedures allow you to create a batch of SQL statements that are stored in the server. By sending just the name of the stored procedure, the server will execute all the commands of the procedure. This reduces network traffic. The server also stores each procedure in compiled form which means the server does not have to compile the SQL statements of the procedure each time they are executed. Being precompiled and reducing network traffic make stored procedures a very good method of improving the performance of your applications. It also means the stored procedure in the server is available to all server users. Instead of having business rules coded into each application, you can code the business rules into stored procedures. All applications can use these stored procedures and thereby use the same business rules. This reduces maintenance since there is one central store of procedures that contains all the business rules.

Trigger

A trigger is a stored procedure that is executed in response to an event in the database. Typical examples would be a trigger that is executed when a table is updated. Such a trigger could be used to validate the data changes that the update made.

Index

As the tables that hold data grow, it can take a long time for the server to find any one piece of data in the table. An index is a separate data struc-ture that contains an ordered set of key values. Along with the key values, the index also stores a pointer to the actual row of data. The key values are some subset of the data stored in each row in a table. By creating an index, the server can scan the index looking at the key values and then find the pointer to the actual row of data. Since the index is an ordered set of key values, the server can find any given key value much faster. Since the key values are typically a small subset of each row of data, the index can be much smaller than the actual table. The server can very quickly find a specific key value in a small, ordered set of key values. An example would be finding the name of the employee with employee number 1002. Without an index, the server would need to scan through the entire employee table looking to the one row where employee number is equal to

1002. With an index built on the key value of employee number, the server can move quickly to key value 1002 and then use the pointer to the actual row of data to retrieve the employee name.

NULL Values

The working definition of a NULL value is a value that is unknown. For example, when you enter a new employee and a badge number has not yet been assigned, what do you enter for the employee badge number? The topic of NULLs and what they mean is another excuse for lots of Ph.D.s. The whole subject of NULLs is very controversial and will never be settled. You still need to deal with them and what they mean for your business. While NULLs seem harmless enough in this example, you just update the badge number when the badge number is issued Consider another example. Your business tracks customers orders. Due to negotiations with your biggest customer, the actual terms of a large order are not known. If you enter the order in your database, you could insert NULL for the amount of the order. But, what will the server do when you ask for a total amount for all orders outstanding? What does the NULL order amount mean to the server and to the business? If you don't insert the order information, than the database doesn't reflect the fact that you are in negotiations for a potentially very large order that other parts of the business need to know about.

Transactions

You will often see a transaction described as the "unit of work" for a RDBMS. This does not capture the real importance of transactions from the DBA point of view relative to the business you are supporting. A transaction has no meaning or value outside of the business process it supports. Within the Sybase RDBMS world a transaction is the basic unit of recoverability. That means that a transaction is guaranteed to either complete or fail as a unit. Now, from the business perspective, a transaction must also represent the smallest change in the business data that can be completed without putting that data into a state that does not make any business sense. A good example is updating your bank account. You would probably be upset if the database tracking you account recorded a deposit you made as one transaction and then recorded the update to your account balance as a separate transaction. From a database point of view, either transaction would be guaranteed to complete or fail entirely. But, from a business perspective, it makes no sense at all to call either of these "transactions" a "unit of work". In fact, the business rules will dictate that any transaction contain both the recording of a deposit and the updating of the account balance.

The point here is to explain that while the concept of a transaction is very important to the operation of any RDBMS, the only way any transaction has any value is in terms of the business that the RDBMS supports. This also means that while you will spend countless hours worrying about the transactions in your system, it is up to those persons who develop the queries submitted to the server to ensure that each and every transaction that the server executes is indeed a valid unit of work to the business. You must also realize that this also means that while you may recover a database completely, recovery is only in terms of transactions, and if those transactions don't follow the rules of the business, then you may completely recover a system that only knows that a deposit was made, but the account balance will not be correct.

Within the RDBMS, you will be constantly examining the performance and security of the database(s) in terms of transactions, but you must understand that for all the technical aspects of transactions, they only have meaning, and you only get paid, if those transactions have some relation to the business that all this is supporting. And, if you want to continue to get paid, you need to ensure, as best you can, that the users and their applications that use the server understand that you can only guarantee that transactions are indeed the basic unit of work in the RDBMS, but they must be correctly correlated to the business process.

The database system uses transactions as a way to define a change to the business data, a change that takes the business data from one valid state to another. Hence, as long as any transaction completely succeeds or fails, the business data is in a valid state (see Figure 1–4). When a transaction completes, it is said to have been committed. This means that the changes made by the transaction have been made a permanent part of the database. The server is designed to guarantee that all committed transactions will be recovered in the event of a server or server machine problem, assuming that all recommended backup and recovery procedures are followed. A transaction that fails for any reason is said to have rolled back. This means that all changes made by the transaction are backed out leaving the database in the same state it was in when the transaction began.

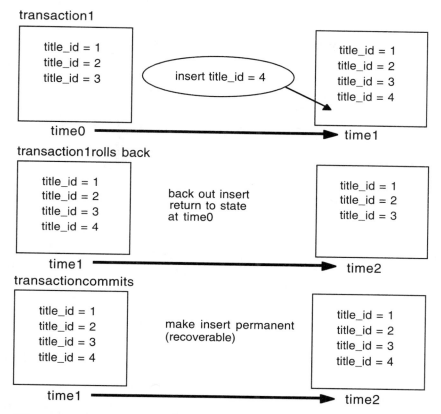

Figure 1–4. Transactions

Recoverability

One of the critical differences between a commercial grade database system and any others is that it provides the features necessary to guarantee recoverability of the business data it contains. Of course, this assumes that these features are used properly and that various factors outside the database, such as a tape being destroyed, are controlled by other means. Still, the commercial database system makes it easy to make database dumps to ensure that all business data can be recovered, and that when that data is recovered, the database is in a state that represents a valid business state, see Figure 1-5. This brings us back to transactions, in that the database only guarantees the recoverability of data changes that were

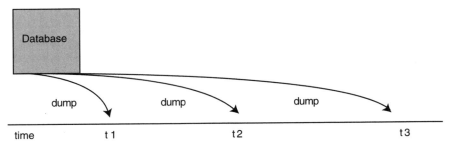

database dumps can be loaded to restore database to state at time
database dump was made

Figure 1–5. Recoverability

made by complete transactions. The database provides the mechanisms to
ensure that the database can be restored to a state whereby all the
completed transactions are reflected in the data.

Locking

Along with the concept of the database containing a set of data that
represents a valid state of the business comes the idea that any time you
examine the database you should see a valid state of the business. This
means that while a transaction is being applied to the database, but hasn't
yet completed, those changes should not be seen by other users of the
system. To prevent this from happening, the server will maintain locks on
pieces of the database that are being modified (see Figure 1-6). Any other
request to examine or change that same piece of the database will wait
until the modifications are complete before proceeding. The process that is
granted a lock on a portion of the database is said to be holding a lock and
this lock will block other processes from gaining access to that portion of
the database. Locking is the way the database makes sure that one user
doesn't see the changes made by any other transaction until that transaction is complete.

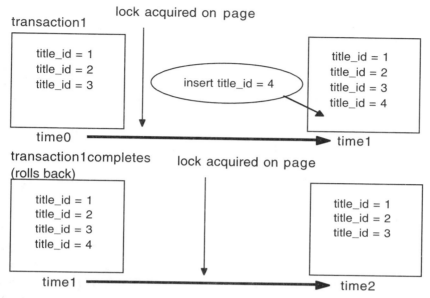

Figure 1–6. Locking

Multi-user

The ability to handle multiple concurrent users is also of vital importance to a commercial database system. This is another feature that separates a commercial grade database system from the PC -based database systems that are designed for single-user desktop applications. In order to support a business application, the RDBMS must allow multiple concurrent users and the database must support the various mechanisms needed to ensure that the database moves from one valid business state to another as any one of the many concurrent user transactions completes. The database uses locking to provide this functionality. Note that this level of data consistency is configurable on different systems. As we will see, System 11 supports what is called "dirty reads" which means, if the server is configured in this manner, a user is allowed to see changes made by other incomplete transactions. This is done to improve user transaction throughput.

RDBMS Concepts and SQL Server 4.9.2

We discuss how the various components of a generic RDBMS are implemented in SQL Server. These components are described as implemented in the 4.9.2 Version of SQL Server. The 4.9.2 Version serves as the baseline server implementation. The features of SQL Server System 10 and System 11 are described as additions on top of those of Version 4.9.2.

Server

The SQL Server is one OS-level process that can support multiple databases. In fact, when installed, the SQL Server actually consists of one or more databases. The server itself does not exist without the *master* database which stores information on server users and the configuration of the server and the databases within the server. Later versions of the SQL Server have added several more databases that are part of the server. Note that you can install more than one SQL Server on a single host computer, but this is not typical. Since a single SQL Server can support multiple databases the need for multiple servers on one machine does not come up often. Some third-party software may require multiple servers on the same machine. For example, a third-party application may be bundled with a SQL Server. The application may require that a separate SQL Server be dedicated to the support of this single application. In such a situation you may need to install more than one SQL Server on a single server machine.

Note that the server maintains information regarding users and their passwords. Further, the fact that a server user account exists does not mean a user has any access to any databases. Access to databases is set up for each user after the user login is created at the server level. This means there are server users and database users and sometimes this can get confusing.

General Structure

The SQL Server runs on a server machine, using memory for the server executable, creating cache in memory to store data while it is being read or modified, and using the physical disks to store the database. The server

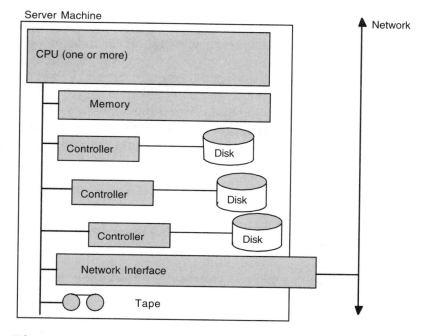

Figure 1–7. Server Machine

also uses the network interface hardware of the server machine to communicate with the network. Tape drives on the server machine are used to make backup copies of the server files and databases.

Server Machine

The server machine (see Figure 1–7) is the hardware and Operating System (OS) software that support the SQL Server. The major components of the server machine are described below.

CPU

The CPU is the physical processor that runs all the code executing on the server machine. When the CPU is part of a Symmetric Multiprocessing (SMP) hardware platform, the SQL Server can make use of multiple CPUs.

Memory

The SQL Server runs in the memory of the server machine. When the SQL Server is installed and configured, some amount of the memory available on the server machine is assigned to the SQL Server. When the server starts up, it takes control of all this memory. Since the SQL Server is taking control of a large portion of the server machine's memory, it is vital that the kernel be configured to allow this. Part of the server installation process involves checking and, if needed, changing the kernel parameters that control shared memory.

Network

The SQL Server was designed around the network. This means that all connections to the SQL Server must be done over the network. You cannot connect to the server machine and then directly access the SQL Server. You must connect over the network even if you are running on the same server machine as the SQL Server to which you want to connect.

Controllers

Disks are connected to controllers. Disk controllers are connected to the server machine. The disk controllers actually read and write the data to and from disk. There are a number of disks that each controller can support before throughput will suffer. You must not overload the controllers on your server machine. You must verify for your hardware platform how many disks can be attached to a single controller. Note that there are many recent developments in disk hardware that allow many more physical disks to be controlled by fewer disk controllers than ever before. You must investigate the situation for your own hardware platform. The only requirement is that the controller not be a bottleneck for disk access.

Disks

These are the physical disks that are physically attached to the server machine. SQL Server will use portions of these disks to store the database and the files needed to install and maintain the server.

Tape Drives

The server machine should have a tape drive to make backup copies of the database and system files on the server machine. SQL Server can make backup copies of the databases in the server to both disk files and to tape. At some point, you must make copies to tape. With backups on tape you can recover the server and its contents after a hardware failure. There are many ways that the server machine can fail so that backups made to disk files would no longer be available.

There has been rapid progress made recently in the number of options available for backing up files of all types, especially for installations that have many individual systems. Many vendors offer hardware and software solutions that can back up the files of multiple systems over the network. For routine backups this can be a very effective approach since all your systems can be backed up by a single system working over the network. However, these systems are generally controlled by a single organization and will backup each system once during the entire back up cycle. Such systems may not, in general, be able to respond to the unique back-up needs of any single system for either technical or political reasons. If you need to perform a recovery or some unusual maintenance, you may need to take multiple backups of a database during the same day. If the routine backups are being made over the network, you may only get a backup once a day. Further, you may well need to make a backup when the network is down. In such situations you will need to have a tape drive on the individual system.

Finally, current 32-bit based UNIX systems can't deal with a disk file larger than 2 Gb. Many databases are larger than 2 Gb and this means you won't be able to make a database dump to a single disk file. In this case, you need to make the database dump directly to tape. Note that, with SQL Server System, 10 and 11 you can use the Backup Server to dump a database to multiple disk files. If you are using a 4.9.2 system, or you don't have enough disk space to accommodate large database dumps, you need a tape drive to make the database dump.

Server Machine Memory Usage

The memory installed in the server machine is used for several purposes including the SQL Server (see Figure 1–8).

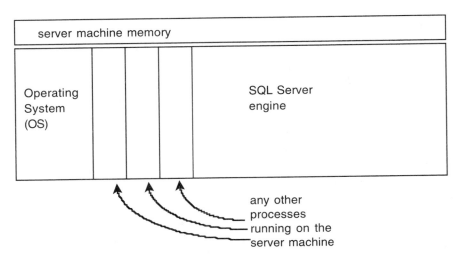

Figure 1–8. Server machine memory

OS

The server machine doesn't help you much without the operating system. The operating system and the computer hardware are both vital parts of the server machine. You must be aware of the details of both the hardware and operating system used on the server machine. This information is vital to ensuring that the version of SQL Server that you are running is appropriate for the server machine. The server machine's operating system is constantly being updated with what are called patches that fix bugs and add functionality. Each version of SQL Server may require a different set of patches for a given operating system.

Other Processes

This refers to any other process that is running on the server machine. All such processes take up memory, disk, and CPU resources that can affect SQL Server. You need to be aware of all the processes running on the server machine when you install and configure the server. For most production business applications, the SQL Server should be the only major process running on the server machine.

SQL Server

The SQL Server runs on the host computer as a single process. All user access to the SQL Server is done through that process. Within the single process the SQL Server maintains multiple threads which are "lightweight" processes. SQL Server manages all aspects of user connections and sharing of resources among the users. This is more efficient in that the OS level sees only one process and within the SQL Server the multiple user connections can be switched in and out faster than if each of them were a completely independent OS level (heavyweight) process. The SQL Server is said to be multithreaded. Note that while each server user is handled by the SQL Server process, the number of simultaneous user connections is limited by the configuration of the kernel. Specifically, the number of file descriptors that are allowed for a single process will limit the number of user connections that can be made to the server.

SQL Server versions represent major changes in the functionality of the server. The server versions covered in this book are 4.9.2, System 10, and System 11. Within each server version there are minor changes that are released to fix bugs within the server. Each of these minor releases is called an Emergency Bug Fix (EBF). The name is not accurate since they are released regularly to fix problems on the many platforms that support SQL Server. You need to be aware of what EBF you are running, especially when dealing with Sybase Technical Support.

SQL Server uses various server machine resources (see Figure 1–9). The server uses the CPUs to execute the server binary. The server stores the databases on disk and uses the server machine network interface to communicate with clients. The server also makes database backups to disk files or tape drives on the server machine.

Engines

When you are executing the SQL Server binary, you are running an engine. When you are running Sybase on a hardware platform that has multiple processors the engine that represents the SQL Server process can be run by any of the available processors. When you configure the server, you select how many engines will be running when the server is running. Based on this configuration information, the server will start up multiple engines. Each engine is a SQL Server process and each engine can be run

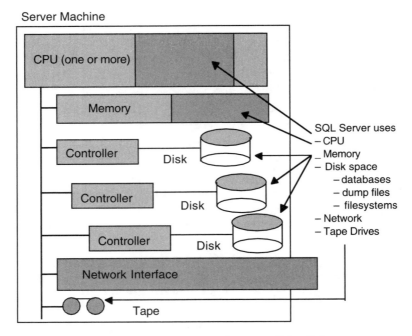

Figure 1–9. SQL Server on Server Machine

on multiple processors. Usually there isn't any point to running multiple engines unless you have multiple processors. When multiple processors are available there isn't much point to running more engines than the number of processors and, the rule of thumb is to configure SQL Server to run N-1 engines where N is the number of processors available to run Sybase. Note that if you have any other processes on the same machine, you may not want to start up one engine for each processor. Also, SQL Server was designed so that even when multiple engines are running, one of those engines has to handle all the network I/O for the entire server.

Don't try running N-1 engines if your server machine has only a single processor. Running zero engines will not only reduce server performance; it will also eliminate performance altogether. On the other hand, running zero engines would make a great performance baseline. Anything you do with more engines will be an 'infinite' performance improvement.

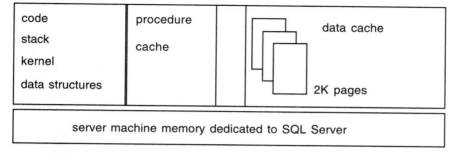

Figure 1–10. SQL Server Memory Usage

SQL Server memory usage

The portion of the server machine's memory allocated to SQL Server is further subdivided into portions for various components of the SQL Server (see Figure 1–10). Note that the server machine memory that is allocated to SQL Server is allocated when the server starts up. Once the server is running, the server can not acquire more server machine memory.

Data Structures

Within the memory allocated to the SQL Server, a portion is used for the actual server code, the server kernel, the stack, and the data structures needed by the server. The details of this area of server memory are not important. You simply need to be aware that some portion of the server memory is allocated for these purposes.

Procedure Cache

After a portion of server memory is allocated to server data structures, a portion of the remaining server memory is allocated to stored procedures. The size of this fraction is configurable. You specify the percentage of the remaining server memory that will be allocated to the procedure cache. This is the area of server memory that will be used to store the execution plans of the stored procedures.

Data Cache

Portions of the server memory have been allocated to server data structures and to the procedure cache. The server memory that is not yet allocated is what is left to be used as data cache. Data cache is where the SQL server works with the data in the databases. The data in the databases is stored on disk. All data that the server will read, write, or change is moved into the data cache in server memory before any manipulation can take place. Similarly, when the server needs to save data it will move the data in cache back to disk.

Network

All Access over Network

The SQL Server is designed and built around the network (see Figure 1–11). As such, the server assumes all client connections will be done over the network. Clients are users connecting to the server and other SQL Servers that need to query the server. Even if the server and the client both run on the same physical computer, the client and server can only communicate over the network. There is no way for you to access the server without going over the network to the machine and port number that were specified when the server was started. This combination of machine and port number tell the server software where to listen for client connections. You will have to be familiar with the interfaces file which gives a name to each server that you can communicate with on the network.

Interfaces File

Since SQL Server does all of its interactions with users over the network, the way in which these interactions are established is very important. You will find that many of the user problems you are called in to cure will relate to users who can't get access to the SQL Server. The server runs on a port of the server machine. The details of ports are beyond the scope of this book. What is important is that the users need to connect to the server by making a connection to the port. There can be many servers on the network and there will be many users as well. Each server machine has a unique network address (IP address). The interfaces file acts as a file that relates servers and the combination of server machine address and port number that each server is running on (see Figure 1–12). The way you use the interfaces file is to specify the name of the SQL Server you are trying

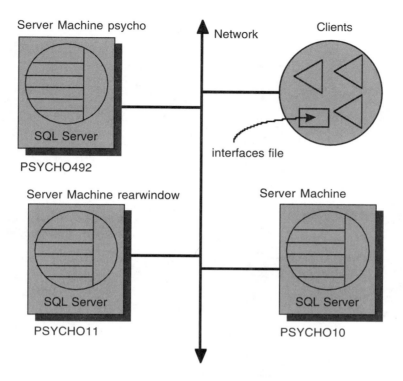

Figure 1–11. SQL Server Network Based

```
#

PSYCHO492
     query tcp sun-ether psycho 1025
#

PSYCHO10
     query tcp sun-ether psycho 1025
#

PSYCHO11
     query tcp sun-ether psycho 1025
```

Interfaces file entries shown in SunOS format for clarity. Interfaces file entries for Sun Solaris are different, see Chapter 12 Operational Details of SQL Server for details of both the SunOS and Sun Solaris versions of the interfaces file.

Figure 1–12. Interfaces File (SQL Server 4.9.2 on SunOS)

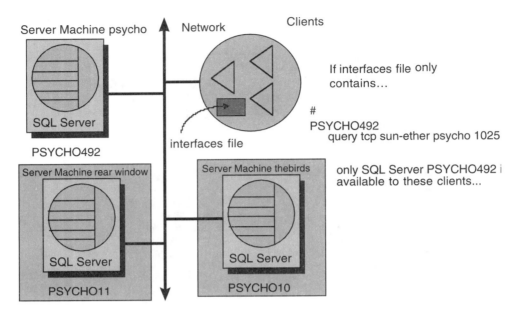

Figure 1–13. Interfaces File Limits User Access

to connect to. The application you are using will then use one of several methods to access the interfaces file. Your application will locate the server name in the interfaces file. Along with the server name, the server machine name and port number will also be found. Your application can then find the network address of the server machine and connect to the server machine on the port number specified in the interfaces file. Note that all access to any SQL Server is done through this mechanism. Even if you are running your application on the server machine you must go through the interfaces file. Your application will only know about the interfaces file that you specify in the setup of your application. This means you can have many interfaces files each of which contains the information needed to connect to some number of SQL Servers. You can control which users, through their applications, can access which servers.

You need to realize that if a remote server is not listed in the interfaces file that a client is using, that remote server is not available to the client (see Figure 1–13). The interfaces file that a client has controls which servers a client can access. As far as the client is concerned, any server that isn't in the interfaces file doesn't exist.

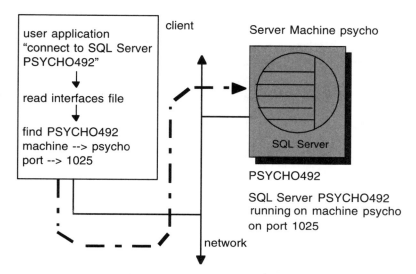

Figure 1–14. Interfaces File Function

Interfaces File Functionality

You must understand how the client uses the interfaces file to connect to a server (see Figure 1–14). When the client issues the commands to connect to a server, the clientís interfaces file is read. If the interfaces file canít be found, then the client canít access any servers at all. Once the interfaces file is read, the requested server name is located. In the interfaces file, each server name is associated with a server machine name and port number. This information tells the client where the server machine is on the network. This also tells the client which server machine port the server is running on. With this information, the client can go out over the network to the server machine and attempt a connection to the port number specified. If the remote server is running on that port, the client connection can proceed.

Users

Users are created at the server level. Server users are then added to a database, and only then can a user of a database be granted permissions to the data or the database objects in the database, see Figure 1-15. Note that the server maintains passwords for the server users, but not for the database users.

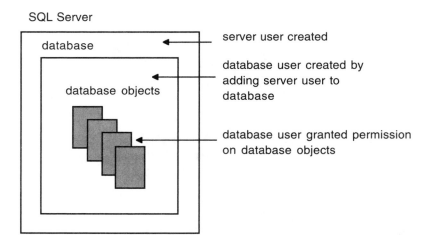

SQL Server

database

database objects

server user created

database user created by
adding server user to
database

database user granted permission
on database objects

Figure 1-15 SQL Server Users

Some applications prefer to have all the application users access the SQL Server through one server login. This makes it easier to administer the application, but it can cause problems for you on the SQL Server side. The server reports many things about each server user. If all the server users are the same server login, it becomes impossible to identify who the individual user is who is causing the performance problems. Simplifying the administration of users may result in trouble later on when you need to troubleshoot performance problems.

You must also be sensitive to the security impacts of multiple users accessing a SQL Server through a single server login. Many organizations require that each server user have an individual server login. You must carefully balance the need for security with the resources available to manage multiple server logins. If you do not have sufficient resources to keep track of all the user logins, you may end up with a server where many server users are using a few server logins.

Devices

All of the components of the SQL Server are stored on disks attached to the server machine. While the OS level files make up the software components of the server, all the structures of the databases and the data they contain are stored on portions of disk called server devices (see Figure

Server Machine

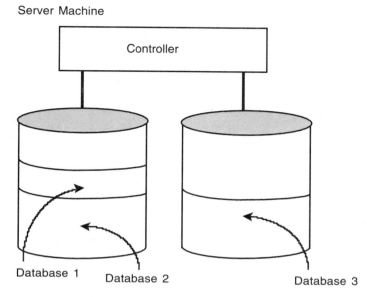

Figure 1-16 SQL Server Devices

1–16). Sybase SQL Server can create a server device in a file system at the OS level, or by using a raw partition of the physical disk. Sybase will not support your server if you use file system server devices because the server relies on a committed transaction being written to disk immediately to ensure recoverability. File system server devices would move data through the OS file system buffering system. This means the server doesn't know whether a committed transaction was really written to disk or just to the file system buffer. If the machine were to crash and the transaction had only been written to buffer but not to disk, the transaction would be lost and when the server recovered the database, the transaction would be lost. You must, with very few exceptions, use raw partitions for server devices.

Each of the physical disks of the server machine can be partitioned, or broken up, into a set of partitions (see Figure 1–17). Any one of these partitions can then be used to store data. Each partition can be used for either a file system or a raw partition. In the case of the raw partition, the OS basically relinquishes all responsibility for a raw partition. For Sybase this means the server takes over management of all raw partitions. You must be careful to keep all file systems on disk partitions that are not being used for raw partitions and vice versa. Note that the only difference between the

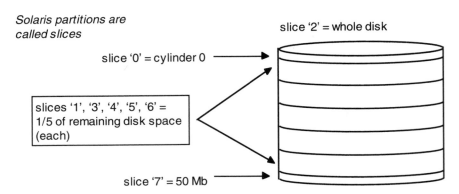

Figure 1-17 Disk Partitions

same piece of disk being a file system or a raw partition is the way that portion of disk is accessed. At the OS level, there is the block mode of access and the character mode. The block mode is the mode used for file systems where blocks of data are setup before being written to disk. The character mode moves data to the disk without buffering. You must be very sure that you are accessing each partition as you intended. It is very easy to get this wrong and the server will not raise any errors. The many aspects of server devices are covered in great detail in a Chapter 8.

The term server device also refers to dump devices which are OS level file system files or tape drives. Database backups are made and loaded through these dump devices (see Figure 1–18).

Databases

A single SQL Server can support multiple databases. Generally, one or more databases is set up to store logically (until the developers get involved) related information for an application. Multiple applications may use databases managed by a single SQL Server. You can configure various options for each of the databases, such as how recovery is handled, read-only status, and so forth. The SQL Server requires the *master, model* and *tempdb* databases, the system databases, in order to function (see Figure 1–19). The *master* and model databases are not for storage of user data but support the operation of the server. As such they should be protected and backed up with care. All other databases are user-defined databases that you create after the server is installed.

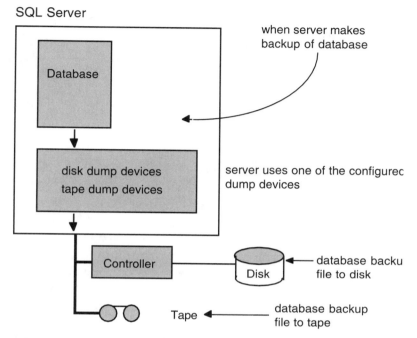

Figure 1–18. Other Server Devices

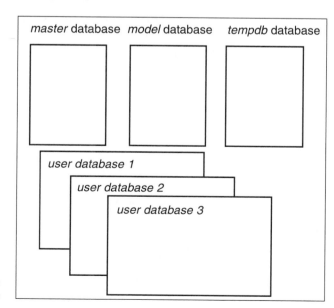

**Figure 1–19.
SQL Server Databases**

master Database

The *master* database is created when the SQL Server is installed. The *master* database is the heart, soul, and brains (if your server has any) of the server. The system tables that define the configuration of the server, its users, devices, and so forth, are all stored in the *master* database. You should not allow server users to store data in the *master* database. You need to back up the *master* database regularly. The *master* database is the most important database in the server.

model Database

Like the *master* database, the *model* database is also created when the server is installed. The *model* database contains a template of the database structure that the server uses whenever it creates a database. This template can be changed and any changes will then be applied to all databases that are created after that point. If there are elements of your databases that are common to all the databases on a server, you may want to install those elements in the *model* database before creating the databases.

Tempdb Database

The *tempdb* database is a temporary database. It is created when the server is installed. The *tempdb* database is used by the server as a work area for performing sorts and other operations that require multiple processing steps. The *tempdb* database is not backed up and the server does not support recovering the *tempdb* database. You can, and often will need to, expand the *tempdb* to provide enough space for all the intermediate work that the server users need to do. Note that each time the server starts up, the *tempdb* database is cleared. Server users can also explicitly create temp tables in *tempdb* to store the results of queries.

User Databases

These are the databases that you create to store data that supports user applications.

Transact-SQL

This is the Sybase version of the SQL language. While the whole idea of SQL is to provide a common interface between user and data, each

RDBMS vendor has their own version of SQL. Each vendor adds extensions to the standard to support functionality that is not part of the current standard version of SQL. This provides developers with more features but also means the SQL they generate is not guaranteed to be portable to any other vendor's version of SQL, o, for that matter, to the same vendor's previous version of SQL. This means you must be careful when using the vendor's extensions to the SQL standard. Sybase has many such extensions and they call their version of SQL Transact-SQL. Note that this level of incompatibility can be more confusing than it initially appears. Some years ago, Sybase was able to tout stored procedures and triggers as a unique feature of Transact-SQL. Now, other RDBMS vendors have added extensions to their versions of SQL that support the same functionality and in the case of stored procedures and triggers, even use the same names. However, this does not mean a stored procedure written in Sybase Transact-SQL will be portable to any other vendor's RDBMS, even though the other vendor's version of SQL supports stored procedures.

 Open systems, standards, the end of proprietary interfaces — the best thing to happen to my job security in a long, long time.

Objects

Within the SQL Server there are many relational database objects such as tables, columns, rules, defaults, and user-defined datatypes (see Figure 1–3). In addition there are stored procedures and triggers which are executable database objects. A stored procedure is a set of Transact-SQL commands that are stored within the server. Since this set of SQL commands is stored inside the server, it can be executed by name. This means a great deal of server processing can be initiated by simply sending the name of the stored procedure to the server and there will be a great deal less network traffic. Further, the stored procedure is protected by the server security mechanisms. This means you can limit who can execute these procedures and you can require that all server access be done through stored procedures. This allows you to know all the queries that can be executed against the server and you can then tune the server for those queries. This also means you can store business rules in these stored procedures and all applications that access the server will have to use those same rules. This is much easier than trying to maintain the business rules in the code of each and every application. Finally, the server will generate an execution plan for each stored procedure when it is first executed and from then on, subsequent executions will not need to be compiled. All of this means that stored procedures are a very good way to get maximum performance out of the server.

Triggers are stored procedures that are executed (fired) in response to a select, update, insert or delete against a table. Triggers are created for a table in the database and will execute (fire) any time any row of the table is affected by a query. Triggers are often used to enforce referential integrity. Referential integrity means that information in one table is related to information in another table. A good example of this is orders and order details. The order table will contain a row for each order. One or more fields of each row will define the order number. This same order number will be used as part of each row in the order_detail table. The order_detail table will record the line item details of each order. Now, if you want to maintain the business integrity of these tables, changes made to one may need to be applied to the other. If you want to change an order number, you need to also change the related rows of the order_detail table. This is referential integrity. You can maintain referential integrity through the use of triggers. As changes are made in one table, a trigger will be fired that will also change the data in any dependent table(s) as well. This functionality would otherwise have to be coded into each application. As with stored procedures, triggers allow this logic to be coded once and used by all queries that affect the table, and this allows the central maintenance of business rules.

Sybase SQL Server supports clustered and nonclustered indexes. In the Sybase SQL Server a clustered index means the rows of data in a table are physically stored in the order of the clustered index key, and this also means there can only be one clustered index for each table. Each table can have multiple nonclustered indexes. An interesting feature of a nonclustered index is that the leaf level (lowest level) of the index contains pointers to the actual rows of table data, and these pointers are ordered by the key of the nonclustered index. Any query that only needs to access the columns of the table that make up the nonclustered index key can be satisfied simply be accessing these pointers. When this is the case, the query is said to be "covered" by the nonclustered index and such queries can be satisfied much more quickly than queries that need to access the same number of rows of the actual table data. For a covered query, the nonclustered index is really a clustered index of the columns of the table that make up the nonclustered index key. This can be used to even greater advantage when tuning the server by separating the table data from the nonclustered indexes onto separate physical disks so that queries that are covered can be using one disk while all other queries use another disk.

 Are you old enough to remember when stored procedures and triggers made Sybase unique? Ah, for the good old days when marketing was as simple as "we've got triggers."

Users

Each database contains information about the server users that are allowed to use the database, as well as each server user's permissions on each and every database object in the database. This means there are server users and database users (see Figure 1–15).

Database users are created by adding server users to a database. Only then can a user of a database be granted permissions to the data or the database objects in the database. Note that the server maintains passwords for the server users, but not for the database users.

The server maintains permissions so that database users can be configured to have various levels of access to the data and various abilities to modify that data. The many levels of the protection hierarchy can become confusing. It is best to develop and maintain as simple a server security scheme as possible. One way to do this is to create groups within a database and assign permissions to each group, see Figure 1-20. Then, as new server users are added to a database, the database user can be assigned to one of the existing groups and will then have all the database permissions of that group.

Operations

The care and feeding of the SQL Server involves many tasks.

Administration

sa

Within the SQL Server the server user 'sa' has complete control. Any data or database object (stored procedure, trigger, etc.) can be examined

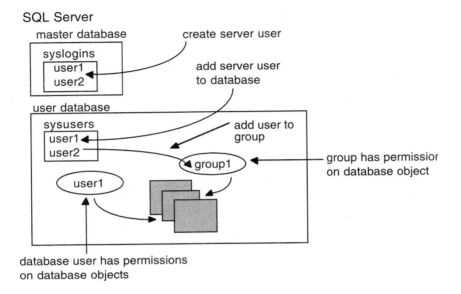

Figure 1-20. SQL Server Groups

by the server user 'sa'. Typically, most database objects are owned by 'sa'. This simplifies many server administration tasks such as dropping users and so forth. Note that any objects that aren't owned by sa are still accessible to the sa user because the sa user can become any server user.

dbo

Another important server user is the database owner. Technically, the server does not allow a given server user to be both a database user and the database owner. The database owner is the server user that created the database, unless the dbo designation has been transferred to another server user. It is typical to have all databases owned by the server user 'sa' (dbo is sa). This simplifies the administration of the server. However, some organizations prefer to separate the administration of the server and the data in the server. In such a case, you would have each user database owned by the individual responsible for maintaining the data within the database.

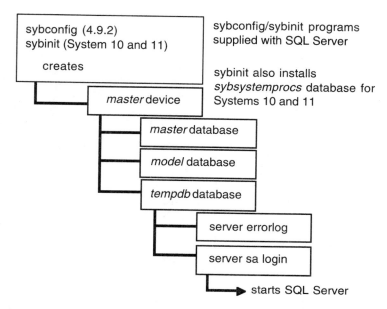

Figure 1–21. SQL Server Installation (4.9.2)

Installation

You install the SQL Server using a program provided by Sybase. The installation process will create the *master, model* and *tempdb* databases on the master device. The master device is a portion of disk space that you designate. The installation process will install the many system stored procedures that you will need to monitor and maintain the server, create the sa server user, start the server, create the server errorlog and so forth (see Figure 1–21). Note that sybconfig is the program used to install a 4.9.2 SQL Server while sybinit is the program used to install a System 10 or 11 SQL Server.

isql

Sybase supplies a utility called isql (interactive SQL) which you use to connect to the server (see Figure 1–22). isql is a character based interface and is not sophisticated. On the other hand, isql is always there and you will use it extensively during installation, configuration and operation of the SQL Server. Using isql you can connect to a server and execute any Transact-SQL or server administration command.

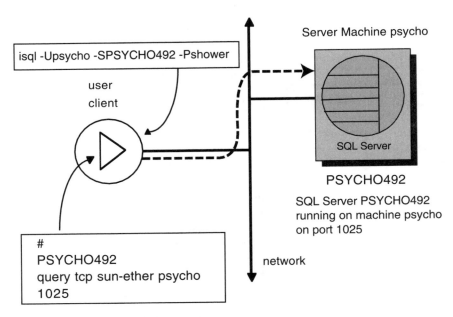

isql -Upsycho -SPSYCHO492 -Pshower

user
client

Server Machine psycho

SQL Server

PSYCHO492

SQL Server PSYCHO492
running on machine psycho
on port 1025

network

#
PSYCHO492
query tcp sun-ether psycho
1025

Figure 1–22. Sybase Utility `isql`

Environment Variables

There are several OS level environment variables that you must know about. DSQUERY is the default name of the SQL Server that a client will access. If a client does not specify a server name when connecting (through isql for example), the client will be connected, by default, to the server name stored in the client's environment variable DSQUER (see Figure 1–23).

The server machine environment variable DSLISTEN is used if a server name is not specified, by the server process when it starts up. The server process will use DSLISTEN as the default server name when starting up. The server will then look in the interfaces file on the server machine to determine which port number the server should start up on. Note that this means both the clients and the servers need a local interfaces file. This shouldn't surprise you. Every server can also be a client to another server. All clients need to have an interfaces file and that includes servers.

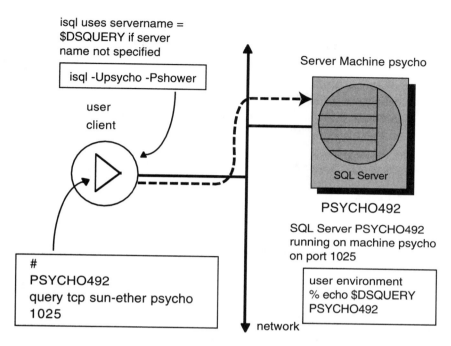

isql uses servername =
$DSQUERY if server
name not specified

isql -Upsycho -Pshower

user
client

Server Machine psycho

SQL Server

PSYCHO492

SQL Server PSYCHO492
running on machine psycho
on port 1025

#
PSYCHO492
query tcp sun-ether psycho
1025

user environment
% echo $DSQUERY
PSYCHO492

network

Figure 1–23. DSQUERY Environment Variable

The environment variable SYBASE specifies where the Sybase home or installation directory is located. This environment variable is used by clients and servers. If the complete path for the interfaces file is not specified, the client or server assumes the interfaces file is in the directory specified by SYBASE.

Starting/shutdown

Starting the SQL Server is done by executing a shell script that executes the SQL Server executable with various options (see Figure 1–24). Stopping the SQL Server is done one of two ways. If you can gain access into the server, you can issue the **shutdown** command (see Figure 1–25). If you cannot access the server, you can kill the OS level process that is the SQL Server (see Figure 1–26).

on server machine
execute the OS level file RUN_PSYCHO492

```
psycho% $SYBASE/install% more RUN_PSYCHO492

#! /bin/sh
# Server name:     PSYCHO492
# dslisten port:
# master name:     /dev/rsd1h
# master size:     15360

DSLISTEN=PSYCHO492; export DSLISTEN

/dba/sybase/bin/dataserver -d/dev/rsd1h -
e/dba/sybase/install/errorlog_PSYCHO492
```

Figure 1–24. Starting SQL Server

on server machine

use isql to log into SQL Server

```
psycho% isql -Usa -SPSYCHO492 -Pshower
```

use SQL Server command shutdown

```
1> shutdown
2> go
```

if there are other server users

```
1> shutdown with nowait
2> go
```

Figure 1–25. Stopping SQL Server

on server machine
use ps command to see which process is SQL Server

```
psycho% ps -ef I grep sybase
--> find process owned by OS user sybase that is the SQL Server
```

use OS level kill command

```
psycho% kill -9 <server_process_id>
```

use kill with care -- only when you must stop SQL Server
and you can't get into the server any other way

Figure 1–26. Killing SQL Server Process

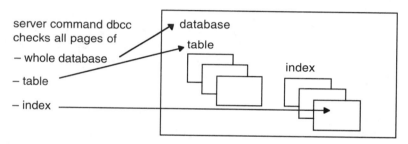

server command dbcc
checks all pages of

– whole database

– table

– index

Figure 1–27. SQL Server dbcc Utility

Database Consistency Checks (dbcc)

The SQL Server relies on the data structures within the databases for its core functionality. Any corruption in a data page or in the links between pages can crash the server or result in widespread corruption of the data in the server. You must periodically run **dbcc** checks to identify and correct any corruptions that exist in the databases. There is no way around this. If you do not perform **dbcc** runs regularly, you may not be able to recover your database even from backups. Sybase supplies the **dbcc** commands to perform this task (see Figure 1–27). You must decide which **dbcc** commands to use and how often to use them. It is desirable, but often not practical, to run a full set of **dbcc** runs before each database dump.

Transactions

Within SQL Server, by default, each SQL command that you send to the server is a separate transaction. If you want to treat multiple SQL statements as one transaction, you must first tell the server to begin a transaction, and when all the SQL statements have been sent, you must also tell the server that the transaction is complete. This has implications for the way you write your applications and the way you submit SQL statements to the server. You must be aware of how the server is interpreting your SQL queries. If you access the server through an application that batches up multiple SQL statements and sends them to the server as one transaction, that means all those SQL statements will either succeed or fail as one transaction. If you access the server directly and submit those same SQL statements and don't tell the server to treat the whole set as one transaction, each SQL statement will be treated as a separate transaction. If one of them fails for some reason, only that one SQL statement will be affected. The previous SQL statements will have been executed and you will have to determine how to back out all the changes made by the previous statements.

Transaction Log

Each database, including the system databases, has a transaction log. The transaction log is the mechanism that SQL Server uses to guarantee the recovery of all completed (committed) transactions within the server. This also explains why it is so important to be dumping (making copies of) the transaction log at regular intervals. As a transaction makes changes to data in cache, the affected data before (before image) and after the changes (after image) is recorded in the transaction log (see Figure 1–28). At this point in the process, the transaction log is also in cache. When the transaction commits, the transaction log records in cache are flushed out to disk. This ensures that the transaction records are on disk to support recovery. This minimal set of transaction data allows the server to completely reconstruct each and every change that has gone on in the database. When a database is recovered, the server will read these transaction logs and reconstruct, as needed, any of the changes that were made to the database after the database dump was made. In this way, the server can completely reconstruct the state of the database right up to the point of the last available transaction log. This also means that if any of the transaction logs are missing from the sequence of logs dumped since the last database dump,

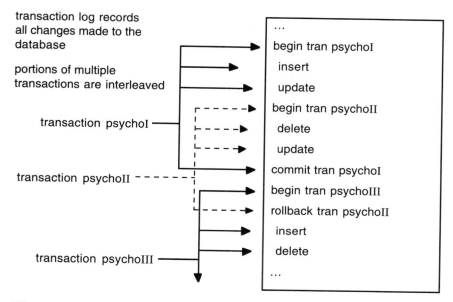

Figure 1–28. Transaction Log

the database can't be recovered past the time of the interruption of the sequence.

Many of the performance issues that will be discussed later revolve around the need for each and every transaction to go through the transaction log.

Page

The way SQL Server specifies chunks of memory and disk space is not consistent. There are several terms that come up but the most common is that of a page. Within SQL Server a page is 2K bytes or 2048 bytes. Confusingly, the server will sometimes refer to a 2K page as a block. This means that all data within the SQL Server is stored, moved, and accessed in 2K-byte pieces. Note that the terms "page" and "data page" are used synonymously. Further, the term data page does not mean the page is strictly data. A data page simply refers to a page of server data. A data page may contain index data, stored procedure commands, or actual user table data.

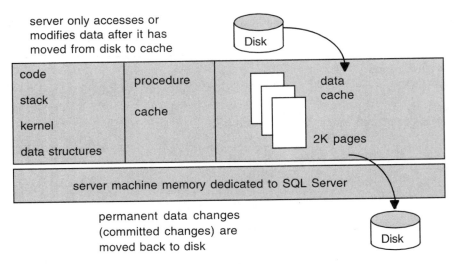

Figure 1–29. SQL Server Cache

Cache

The SQL Server performs all of its operations on database data in memory called cache. Cache is simply a part of the memory that SQL Server runs in. Cache is where all database data is located when it is being created, read, changed, or deleted (SQL insert, select, update, delete) (see Figure 1–29). Obviously, the databases within SQL Server are stored on disks attached to the host computer, but you must understand that nothing happens to the database while it is on disk. When any operation is to be performed on the data within a database, the data pages that are affected are moved from disk into cache memory. After the data is in cache, the server will perform the necessary operations and any changes are made to the data in cache. When any such changes are complete and made permanent (i.e., a transaction completes), the server will record all the information needed to reconstruct the data before and after the change in the transaction log. As the cache fills up with data, data that has not been used recently will be moved back out to disk. Only when the data is moved back to disk are the changes that have been made in cache recorded on the disk. Clearly, the size of the server cache has performance implications since every piece of data that is accessed, let alone changed, must move through the cache.

LRU/MRU

LRU/MRU refer to the way the server decides what data should be in cache (memory) and which data should move back to disk. The server

server needs data page 5, page 5 is already in cache

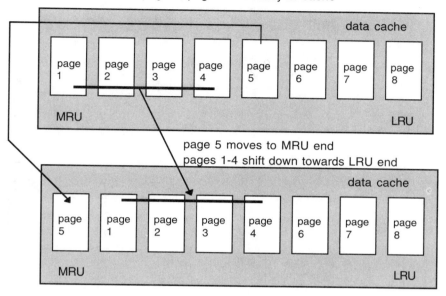

Figure 1–30. Server Needs Page Already in Cache

moves any page of data that it needs to access into cache before it can work with it. If cache were unlimited, this would not be such an issue. As cache fills up, the server must decide which pages of data should remain in the limited space in cache and which pages should be moved from cache back to disk. The server uses the Least Recently Used (LRU) solidus Most Recently Used (MRU) algorithm to make these decisions. This algorithm is based on the assumption that a data page that has just been used will probably be needed again, and, conversely, pages that haven't been accessed in a while are less likely to be needed again, at least in the short term.

When the server needs to access a data page it looks for the page in cache. If the page is already in cache, the server moves the page to the MRU end of the cache. The other pages already in cache move down toward the MRU end of the cache (see Figure 1–30). If the data page is not in cache, the server will bring the page in from disk and place it at the MRU end of the cache. The other pages in cache must then move towards the LRU end of the cache (see Figure 1–31). If the cache is full before the latest page is moved into the MRU end of the cache, the page that was at the LRU end of the cache must be moved out of cache, back to disk.

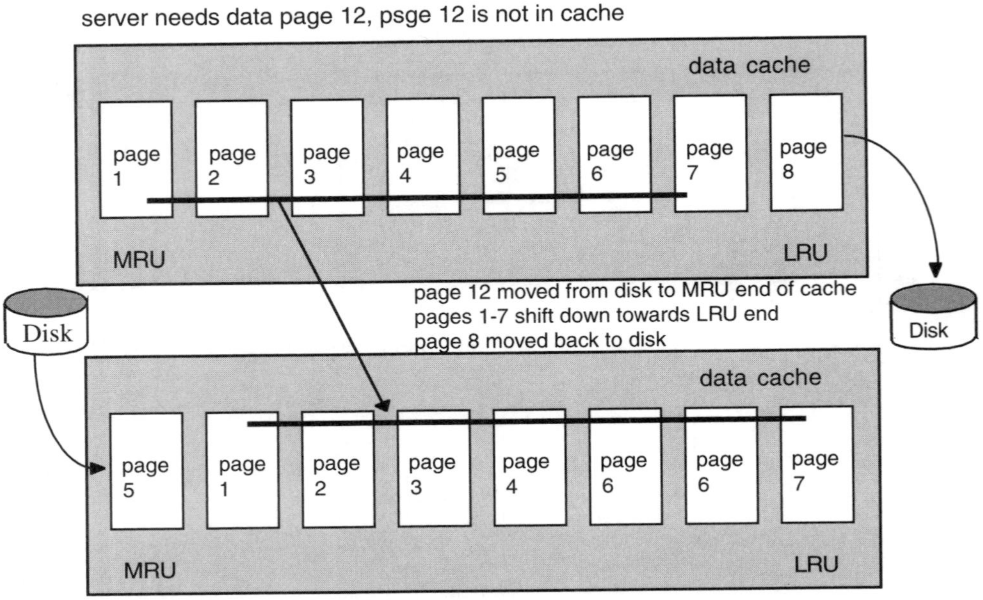

server needs data page 12, psge 12 is not in cache

Figure 1–31. Server Needs Page Not in Cache

Logical versus Physical I/O

When the server moves a data page that is already in cache to the MRU end of the cache (as in Figure 1–30), this is a logical I/O. When the server has to move a page to or from disk (as in Figure 1–31), this is a physical I/O. Physical I/O takes much longer to complete than logical I/O. From a performance standpoint, physical I/O is much more expensive than logical I/O. Anytime the server can find the needed page in cache, that is a logical I/O. Anytime the server has to read a page from disk or write a page to disk, that is a physical I/O. Performance tuning boils down to minimizing the total amount of I/O needed to complete a given query. This means that minimizing physical I/O is the point of most performance tuning.

Shuffling Pages in Cache

If the server can find the pages it needs in cache, the pages in cache simply move around within cache. It is only when the server needs a page that is not in cache that a page currently in cache must move out to disk.

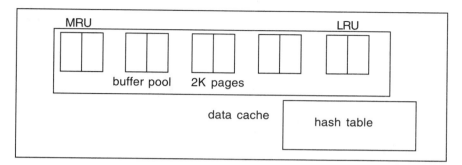

Figure 1–32. Cache Buffer Manager

Buffer Manager

The buffer manager keeps track of all the pages currently in cache. It does this by maintaining a hash table that has the page *id* for each page in cache (see Figure 1–32.). It is much faster for the server to scan the hash table than it is to scan each of the pages in cache looking for the needed page.

Locking

The server supports multiple concurrent users. Each user submits SQL queries that will ask the server to access pages of data. Multiple users will often need to access the same data. This leads to a problem. Each user expects to see that database as an accurate representation of the business as a point in time. Each user expects that each order, for example, has either been made by a customer, shipped, paid for, or some other valid business status. The user does not expect that data that is present when the query executes will just disappear the next moment. With multiple concurrent users, you can easily have the situation where one user has inserted a row of data representing a new order, but this transaction is not complete. Another user reads that same new row and thinks the order has been placed. If the customer then decides not to place the order (items turn out to not be in stock, etc.) the transaction placing the order will be rolled back and the row removed from the table. If the second user reads the data again, the order is not there. If the order had been placed and then deleted that would be a different situation. The order entry application should track such a business event. In this case, the order was never really entered, but to the other users, it appeared to have been placed.

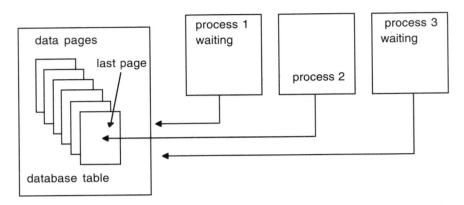

Figure 1–33. Locking

The SQL Server deals with this by supporting locking. This means the server will grant a lock to the first transaction that is inserting the row representing the new order. Until that transaction is complete, no other query can update the data representing the new order (see Figure 1–33), although other queries can still read the data. Since SQL Server supports page level locking, but not row-level locking, this means that one query that is updating a single row prevents (blocks) any other queries from updating any rows on that same data page. Once the transaction completes, the lock will be released and other queries can access the data. If the transaction completed by committing, that means the new order was inserted and the order officially exists. If the transaction completed by rolling back, that means the process of placing the order did not complete and the new order is removed before any other query can view it.

The problem with locking is more acute for the Sybase SQL Server. Multiple users will often want to access rows of data that are stored in the same page. There can easily be many rows of data in a single 2K-page. The Sybase SQL Server only supports locking down to the page level and does not support row-level locking. This means that, for our example, the query that was inserting just one row will need to acquire a page lock on the page where the new row is being inserted. This means that once the page lock has been granted, no other query can have any access to any row of that page. The performance impacts of this are debatable and are often debated. Page-level locking means that if a query wants access to only one row of a table, the query needs to acquire a lock on the entire page of data that contains the row. For applications where many small rows of data are

server machine

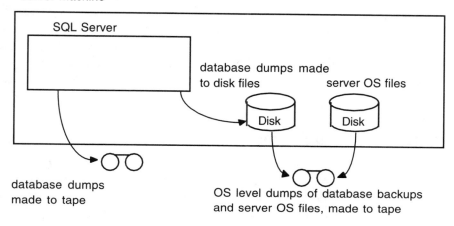

Figure 1–34. Database Backups

stored on a single page, which describes classic On-line Transaction Processing applications where performance is paramount, page-level locking can result in serious blocking and throughput problems.

Backup

Part of the normal operation of the SQL Server is making backups of the databases in the server. There are several components to this process. Figure 1–34 shows the various kinds of backups you need to make on a regular basis.

Database Dumps

A single SQL Server can support multiple databases, but each database is backed up and recovered as a single unit. This means that for any database in the server, including the system databases, you must make individual database dumps. This also means that you have to dump only the databases that you need to be able to recover. Data that is supplied from some other source may not need to be backed up and such data could be placed in a separate database within the server. This means you can reduce the number and size of the database dumps to just the data that you really need to protect.

The SQL Server will create a dump file, to disk or to tape, for any database in the server. The dump file can be read only by SQL Server. The database dump contains all the database objects in the database. A database dump usually takes enough time so that you can't, as a practical matter, make a database dump while users are connected to the server. You generally make database dumps during off-hours, often during the very early morning hours.

Transaction Log Dumps

The server will also make a backup of the transaction log. These backups can be made to disk files or to tape just like database backups. Whenever the server executes a query that makes changes to the database, the server will document those changes in the transaction log. The transaction log is a separate table from the rest of the database and is used only for transaction log records. The transaction log records the original values (before image) and the changed values (after image) for each transaction. The server stores these transaction log records separately so that when needed, the server can read the transaction log as quickly as possible, without having to sort out which records belong to the transaction log and which records belong to some other part of the database.

Since the transaction log only records the changes made by each transaction, the transaction log is much more compact relative to the size of the database. This means it is much faster to dump the transaction log. This also means you can dump the transaction log while users are connected (see Figure 1–35). You need to do this because a database dump only has the state of the database at the time of the database dump. All changes made to the database after the database dump are not captured. The transaction log dump does capture all the changes made since the database dump. This provides the mechanism by which the server can recover all changes made to the database since the last database dump.

Each transaction log dump makes a copy of the current contents of the transaction log and then deletes all records of completed transactions. The transaction log records are deleted up to the point of the oldest open transaction (see Figure 1–36). An open transaction is a transaction that has neither committed nor rolled back. This frees up space for more transaction log records. The server must record every transaction to assure recoverability. This means the transaction log must have some free space or the

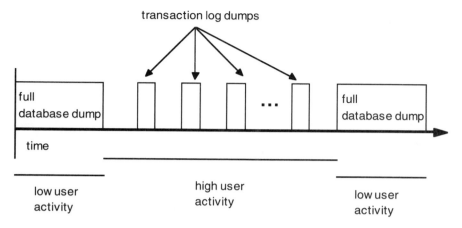

Figure 1–35. Database Backups

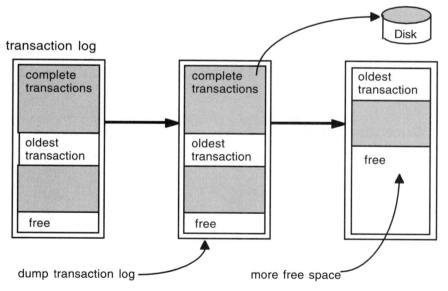

Figure 1–36. Transaction Log Truncation

server will stop processing transactions. Any database that is supporting a mission-critical application should be dumping the transaction log frequently during the period in between full database dumps.

All applications are mission-critical – just ask the users of those applications.

OS-Level Dumps

While database and transaction log dumps are a vital part of your server backup process, you also need to perform backups of the files on the server machine at the operating system level. These backups will make a copy of the Sybase software, any database or transaction log dumps made to disk files, scripts that you use to install and configure the server, and so forth.

Recovery

The process of recovering a database or a server assumes that you have been making backups before the server has a problem. The recovery process is not possible if the backup process is not operating before hand.

Database Loads

Loading a database dump will completely overwrite the existing database. You can only load a database if there are no server users in the database. Loading a database dump only recovers the database to the state it was in at the time the database dump was made.

Transaction Log Loads

In the event of a database problem that requires recovery, you would load the most recent database dump. Then you would apply, in the order in which they were made, each of the transaction log dumps that has been created since the full database dump that has been loaded. You would then load the current contents of the transaction log (see Figure 1–37). This allows you to recover the database right up to the time the failure occurred. Without transaction log dumps you can only recover the database to the time of the most recent full database dump. You can

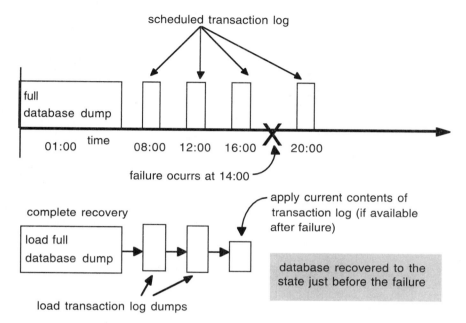

Figure 1–37. Database Loading Complete Recovery

only load transaction logs in the same order as they were dumped. The transaction log dumps form a complete set of dumps from the time that database was last dumped up to the time of the server problem. If any one of the set of transaction log dumps is missing, the process of loading transaction log dumps will stop at the point of the first missing transaction log dump.

The complete set of transaction log dumps represents a record of all the changes made to the database since the last full database dump. Loading a transaction log dump causes the server to replay all the transactions that are documented in the transaction log dump. This takes the database to the state it was in at the point in time when the same transaction log dump was made. This explains why you can't continue loading transaction log dumps after one is missing. The transaction log records each of the changes made to the database, but without the complete series of those changes, the changes in any one transaction log don't make sense. The transaction log records only the changes made by a transaction. If a transaction log dump is missing, the server can't load the

incomplete recovery 1 – no transaction log dumps made, or dumps lost

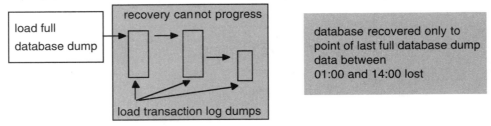

incomplete recovery 2 – current contents of transaction log not available

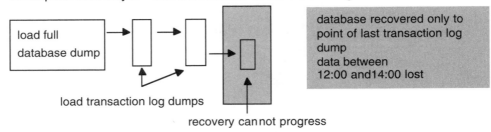

incomplete recovery 3 – intermediate transaction log dump missing

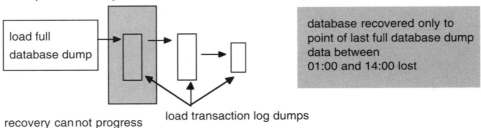

Figure 1–38. Database Loading Incomplete Recovery

next transaction log dump because the server has no way of knowing what states the database went through in the transaction log that is missing (see Figure 1–38).

Mirroring

The SQL Server supports device mirroring. This means that for any single server device, the server will maintain a complete copy of the server device on another disk (see Figure 1–39).

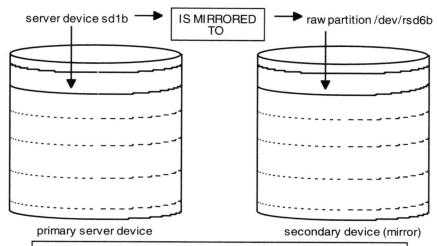

Figure 1–39. Server Device Mirroring

Function

Recall that a server device is a portion of a physical disk that has been assigned to the server. Mirroring is another form of backup. If the server detects a problem with the primary server device, the server will take the primary server device off-line and will switch the mirror to become the primary server device. This means the server can continue processing without interruption. With mirroring, the failure of a server device (disk) does not stop the server. Without mirroring, any server device failure will stop all processing that uses any database that is on the failed device. If the failed device is the master device, the entire server stops.

Priorities

You should mirror all the server devices so that all parts of all the databases in the server are protected. If this isn't possible, you should mirror the master device. The transaction logs of the critical databases on the server should be mirrored next. This ensures that the transaction log will be available for recovery in the event of a server device failure. After that, the databases should be mirrored in order of importance.

Sybase versus OS Level

The Sybase SQL Server supports mirroring of server devices. Mirroring can also be done at the Operating System (OS) level. This means that all the disks, not just those used by the SQL Server, can be mirrored. OS-level mirroring is better in that any disk can be mirrored. Also, the OS-level mirroring can detect more disk problems than the SQL Server level mirroring. On the down side, OS-level mirroring pushes the responsibility for mirroring back to the server machine system administrator. This person may or may not be trained to support this, and may not have the proper perspective on what should and shouldn't be mirrored.

Scalability

Scalability is a term that refers to the ability of the server to support increased numbers of users and/or user load as the hardware supporting the server is scaled up. For example, assume a server is handling 100 concurrent users with a given response time running on a hardware platform with a single CPU. Then, if the server is scalable, we should be able to add a second CPU and either handle 200 users with the same response time, or handle 100 users with the response time cut in half.

Engines

The process that is executing the SQL Server executable on the server machine is called a server engine. You can start up multiple engines. Each engine is an execution of the server binary and each engine is a separate OS-level process. All engines share the server machine memory and disks (see Figure 1–40). When the server machine hardware was typically a single processor, there wasn't much to discuss. More than one engine would have been terrible. Each engine would be a full OS-level process and as they were swapped on and off the single processor, the SQL Server would have come to a full stop. This would not have improved performance.

With the advent of multiprocessor hardware platforms, you can improve server performance by running multiple engines. The optimal number of engines for a given number of processors has never been debated but no one answer applies to all situations. The only thing that will work for your individual system is to monitor performance with a given set of engines and then change the number of engines. Only through this trial and error process can you determine the optimal number of engines for your hardware platform.

server machine

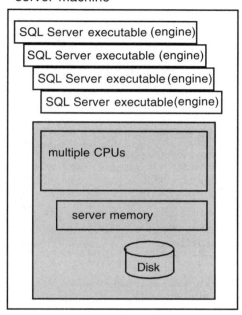

each engine is a separate
OS level process executing
on the server machine

OS schedules engines onto
available processors

SQL Server schedules server
user tasks onto available
engines

all engines share server
memory and disk(s)

Figure 1-40 SQL Server Engines

Contention Limits

As a practical matter, SQL Server has not been able to scale much beyond four processors. The reasons for this lack of scalability are described in the next sections.

Network I/O

The SQL Server allows only engine 0, the first engine that is started, to handle all network I/O for all the engines that are running. This limitation does not exist in System 11. When a user connects to the server, or sends a query, the server receives these events as network I/O. When the server returns results to a user, this too is network I/O. This means that as the number of users and concurrent queries goes up, the server is waiting for network I/O before it can do other things. Since all network I/O has to go through engine 0, all other engines have to wait for engine 0 to be available before the other engines can complete their network I/O (see Figure

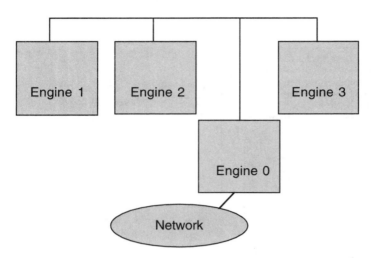

Figure 1-41 Network I/O Contention

1–41). This also means that adding more engines wonít help because that just means more engines waiting for engine 0. This feature of the server limits scalability.

Transaction Log

Each database in the server has a transaction log. All changes made to a database are recorded in the transaction log. This means that almost all queries that affect that database will need to write to the transaction log. The transaction log is a simple table. All new entries to the transaction log are made to the last page of the table. Since SQL Server locks that entire last page, there is contention among the concurrent transactions. All but one of these transactions must wait to acquire the lock on the last page (see Figure 1–42). Running more server engines won't help. More engines just mean more transactions that must wait for the same last page of the transaction log.

Cache

The server accesses all data in cache (memory). This means that all data pages that the server needs must be moved into cache before the server can access them. There are two aspects of this process that limit scalability.

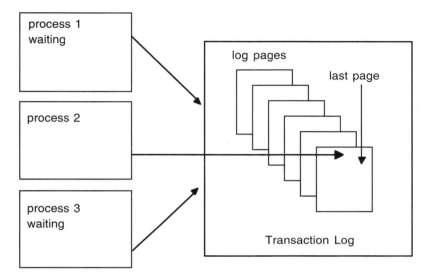

Figure 1–42. Transaction Log Contention

First, when the server needs a data page, it will look to see if the required page is already in cache. The way the server does this is to check the hash table. The buffer manager maintains the hash table which records the pages that are in cache. It is much faster for the server to scan the hash table than to look at the pages in cache. As the number of server engines rises, the number of processes needing to look for a page in cache rises as well. With a single hash table, there are limited resources to keep track of whom is doing what to the cache. More engines only makes this problem worse (see Figure 1–43).

Second, consider what happens as more and more engines are trying to access more and more pages of the database. One query needs to have access to one page of a table and that page is in cache. Another query needs to scan a large table. The number of pages in this table will not fit in cache. As the server brings the pages into cache from disk, the pages move from the Most Recently Used (MRU) end of the cache to the Least Recently Used (LRU) end and are moved back to disk. As this happens, the one page needed by the previous query is also forced out of cache (see Figure 1–44). On-Line Transaction Processing (OLTP) generally requires short queries that access a few pages over and over. An example of an OLTP system would be order entry. You want the server to respond to this kind of query quickly to support your business. Decision Support

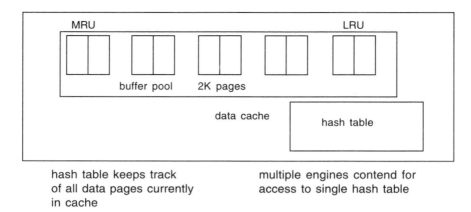

Figure 1–43. Cache Contention

Systems (DSS) usually require long-running queries that need to access many pages. An example of a DSS system would be a reporting system that scans the orders table and reports on total sales for some period. A long-running query that needs more pages than cache can handle, can flush the OLTP pages out of cache. After each DSS query runs, all the pages needed for your OLTP queries must be moved back into cache from disk. This involves physical I/O which slows the server down. Adding more engines doesn't help as more queries will be trying to access a wider range of data pages.

Inserts

When the server inserts a new row into a table, the new row is added to the end of the table, on the last data page. (Certain indexing schemes prevent this). When this happens, as in the case of the transaction log, you have contention as multiple queries wait to acquire the lock on the last data page. More engines will only make this worse (see Figure 1–45).

Performance

Query Optimizer

The server uses the query optimizer to evaluate the "cost" of performing each query that is submitted. The cost refers to the total I/O activity and overall processing that will be needed. This includes examining how many

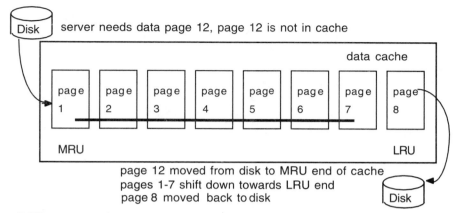

Figure 1–44. DSS and OLTP Cache Contention

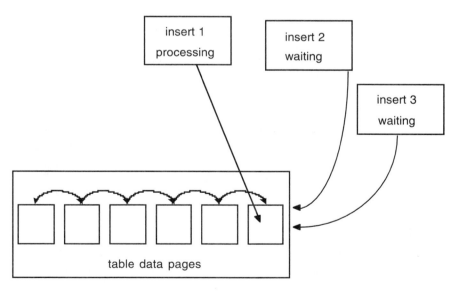

Figure 1-45 Insert Contention

tables, as well as the number of rows in those tables, will have to be examined to satisfy the query, what indexes are available to speed the retrieval of a small set of rows, what the possible join strategies are, and so forth. The query optimizer must examine all this and decide how best to process the query. In general, this all boils down to minimizing the number of physical I/Os needed to move data into cache from disk. While the optimizer is concerned with the number of logical I/Os, which is the processing needed to retrieve data from pages already in cache, physical I/Os are much more expensive. The query optimizer is affected by many things, and since the server relies on the query optimizer to examine each and every query that is submitted to the server, you must ensure that the server is maintained in such a way that the query optimizer can do its job. This means updating the statistics on each table in the server. The query optimizer needs these statistics to determine how many rows of a table will be returned for each part of a query. If these statistics are not available or out of date, the optimizer may make very poor decisions and server performance will suffer.

Stored Procedures

Note that the very fact that the query optimizer has to evaluate each and every query makes stored procedures more beneficial. Stored procedures are examined by the query optimizer only when they are compiled which normally happens only when the stored procedure is created. After compilation, the query plan for the stored procedure is stored and will be used again whenever the stored procedure is executed. This also means that the SQL of the stored procedure is stored in the SQL Server. The stored procedure can then be executed by a single command sent from the client (see Figure 1–46). Each client can now send one command over the network rather than each sending all the SQL each time. This reduces network traffic.

Indexes

By using indexes, you can help the server find needed data faster. The types of indexes that SQL Server supports are described next.

Clustered

When you create a clustered index on a table, the server will physically order the rows of the table in the order of the key you specify for the

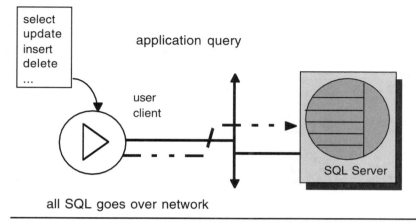

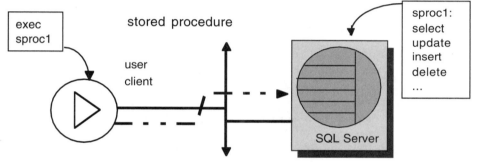

Figure 1–46. Stored Procedures

clustered index, see Figure 1-47. For example, assume you create an employee table with a clustered index on employee number. The employee number is the key of the clustered index. The server will physically arrange the rows of the table on disk in order of employee number. When you need to insert a new row, the server will examine the employee number of the new row and physically place the new row in the proper place among the existing rows of data.

Some applications assume that each new employee number will be one greater than the maximum existing employee number. If this is the case, when you insert a new row, you will always be inserting on the last page of the table. This leads to contention and slows the server down as only one query at a time can acquire the lock on the last page. Some

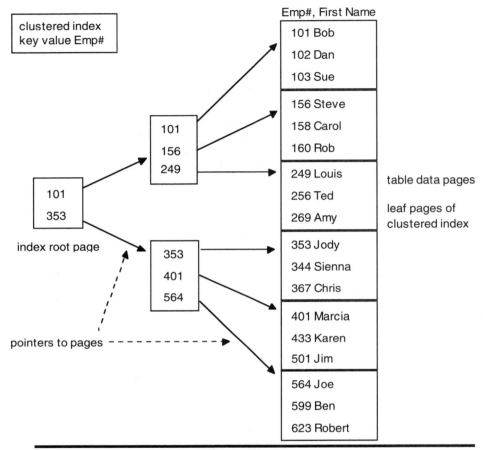

Figure 1–47. Clustered Index

applications deal with this problem by adding a field to each row of data that contains a random number generated by the server. The server then builds the clustered index, not on the employee number, but on the random number. The server then stores the rows of data in order of the random number, not the employee number. When the server needs to insert a new row, the location of the new row is spread randomly among the existing rows. This reduces the contention for the last page. This is an example of how proper use of indexes can help solve performance problems. It also demonstrates that the optimal index for a table changes from query to query. The issue of index design and server performance is complicated and requires ongoing monitoring.

A clustered index is very useful when a query needs a range of data and that range of data is based on the key of the clustered index. For example, find the employees that have employee numbers between X and Y. The server can use the clustered index to find the row of the table with employee number X. The server can then read into cache the sequence of pages on disk that have the rows up to employee number Y. This is much faster than having to find each data page at a time, once for each employee number.

There can be only one clustered index per table. The server must perform additional work when it inserts a new row because it may have to shuffle all the other rows around on disk to make room for the new row. If you decide to create a clustered index on an existing table you will need enough disk space to completely copy the table. This space is needed as the server will indeed create a complete copy of the table sorted in the order of the new clustered index key.

Nonclustered

A table can have multiple nonclustered indexes. The rows of the table data are not stored in the order of the key of a nonclustered index. Rather, the key values themselves are stored in order of the key values. Along with each key value is stored a pointer to the actual row of table data (see Figure 1–48). When the server needs to access a certain row of data it uses the key values in the index to locate the pointer to the actual row data. The server then uses the pointer to move to the actual row data to retrieve the data needed. Note that if the data that the server needs is contained in the key value, the server doesn't need to move to the actual row data. Queries that can be satisfied by the data in the key values of a nonclustered index are said to be covered by the index. Covered queries can be satisfied very quickly. For a covered query, the nonclustered index is a clustered index made up of the key values for the index.

Nonclustered indexes require the server to continually update the index as new rows are added or the key values of existing rows are changed. If you create multiple indexes on a table, one change to that table may require the server to update many pages of all the indexes. The optimal balance between the benefits of nonclustered indexes (faster access) and the overhead maintaining the indexes is complicated.

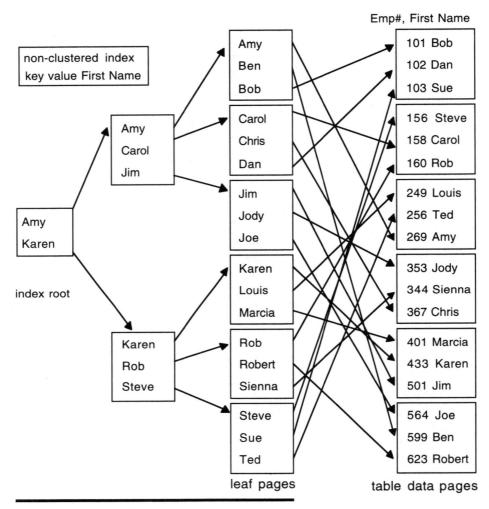

Figure 1-48. Non-clustered Index

Segments

The server create database objects on disk. As these objects grow and need more space, the server will use additional space on disk. If nothing is configured ahead of time, the server will add space for new portions of all database objects on the same disk. You can improve server performance be

no segments - all objects can exist on all disks

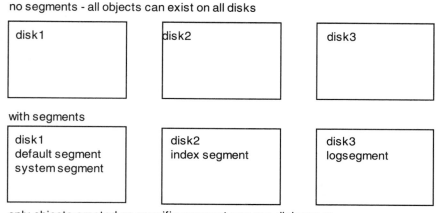

only objects created on specific segment can use disk space
all other objects use default segment
transaction log uses logsegment

Figure 1–49. Segments

separating database objects onto separate locations on disk (see Figure 1–49). For example, you could place the data and the indexes for a heavily accessed table on different physical disks. The server could then look for table data on one disk while another query was looking through an index on the other disk. The way you configure this is using segments. A segment is simply a name assigned to a set of space on one or more server devices. You then create database objects on a specific segment. If done properly, only the objects created on such a segment can use the disk space of the segment.

Replication

The whole topic of replicating data is not covered in this book. Sybase has a product, Replication Server, that, in conjunction with the SQL Server, will support replication of data between multiple sites. The topic of replication in general and Replication Server in specific is very complicated. It is important that you be aware of the product as there are links between SQL Server and Replication Server that will be discussed. For example, when you upgrade SQL Server there are things you must be aware of if you are using Replication Server.

Replication Server works by scanning the transaction log of the primary database. A component of Replication Server called the Log Transfer Manager (LTM) scans the transaction log. When transactions occur that affect data in a primary table, the LTM passes the transaction log records of these transactions to the Replication Server. The Replication Server keeps track of where the data needs to be sent , that is the replicate table in the replicate database. Replication Server then uses the transaction log records to apply the same transaction to the replicate table (see Figure 1–50).

SQL SERVER SYSTEM 10

With the arrival of Sybase SQL Server System 10, significant changes were made to enhance features in several areas of the server.

Backup Server

Before System 10, all database and transaction log dumps and loads were handled by the SQL Server directly and therefore any dump or load directly affected the throughput of the server. With System 10, the process of dumping or loading was moved outside of the SQL Server to a separate Backup Server (see Figure 1–51). You must note that the Backup Server is a separate OS-level process just like the SQL Server. As such the Backup Server needs to be started up and monitored and must have an interfaces file entry known to the SQL Server. Also, while the Backup Server is a separate product, it is bundled with the SQL Server and, in fact, you can not make any form of SQL Server dump or load without the Backup Server installed, running, and configured to communicate with the SQL Server.

Compatibility

The System 10 databases are not compatible with those of SQL Server 4.9.2. This means that you cannot load a 4.9.2 database dump into a System 10 database. Further, all the databases in the server are at the same version, that is if the server is at System 10, then all the databases within the server are System 10 databases. In order to upgrade a 4.9.2 Server to System 10, you must go through the upgrade process which will make changes to the system databases and all the user databases in the 4.9.2 Server. Once the

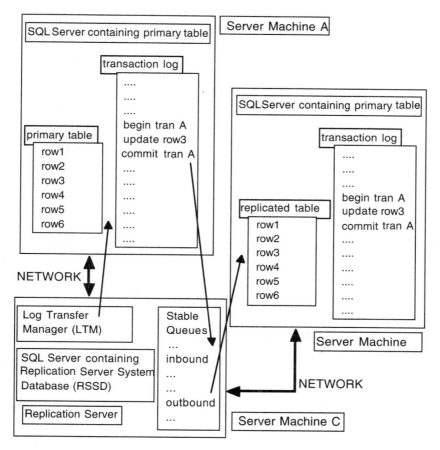

Figure 1–50. Sybase Replication Server

upgrade is done, you cannot use any of the previous database dumps that were made at the 4.9.2 Version level.

The only other way to migrate from 4.9.2 to System 10 would be to install a System 10 Server and create databases of the same size as those on the 4.9.2 Server and then re-create all the database objects one at a time manually or with scripts you have created. At that point you would have to copy the data in the 4.9.2 Server database tables out to files using the bcp utility and then use the System 10 version of bcp (the version of bcp that came with the System 10 software you used to install the System 10 Server) to load each of the files into the same table on the System 10 Server. In most cases, you will want to upgrade the 4.9.2 Server to System 10.

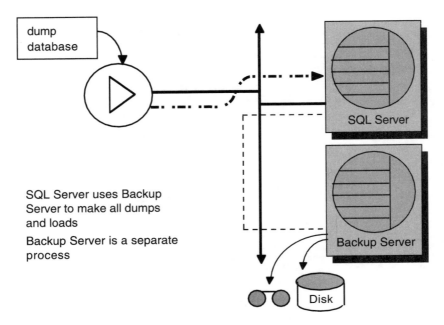

dump database

SQL Server uses Backup Server to make all dumps and loads

Backup Server is a separate process

SQL Server

Backup Server

Disk

Figure 1-51. Backup Server

Roles

System 10 introduced the concept of roles. Each server user can be assigned various roles that affect what the user can do within the server. The roles and their functions are described next.

sa_role

This role allows the user to perform sa activities such as creating a database. Note that you would expect the **sa_role** to have all the same functionality of the server user sa but this is not the case. The **sa_role** cannot add a server user or change a server user password.

sso_role

This is the System Security Officer (SSO) role. Server users with **sso_role** can add server users and change passwords. A user with **sso_role** can also reset the sa password if everyone forgets it.

SQL Server System 10

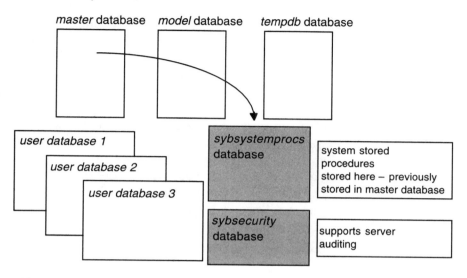

Figure 1–52. System 10 System Databases

operator_role

This role is needed for anyone who needs to dump a database.

As a practical matter, for most servers, you, as the DBA, will need **sa_role**, **sso_role**, and **operator_role**. The usefulness of these roles is limited. Only the largest sites are going to have enough people assigned to any one server to justify completely separate individuals to add server accounts.

New System Databases

System 10 requires a new system database called *sybsystemprocs* to store all the system stored procedures. Previously, these system stored procedures, such as **sp_who**, were stored in the *master* database. System 10 supports various auditing functions which use tables stored in the *sybsecurity* database. The system databases for the System 10 SQL Server are shown in Figure 1–52.

Security

System 10 supports the locking of server user accounts. This means you can simply lock an account rather than have to drop the user from the server. This can prevent some problems that come up when you drop a server user and reuse the server user **id**. This can cause confusion later on, especially when database dumps are moved between servers. By simply locking an account, the server user **id** is not reused.

System 10 also introduced the auditing features which use a dedicated database called *sybsecurity*. This new feature allows you to configure the auditing to track various levels of database object usage and so forth. This feature can be useful for tracking security issues but is not a performance monitoring tool. Also, use of this feature will impact server performance, and, if the auditing database has any problems, the whole server stops.

SQL SERVER SYSTEM 11

Sybase SQL Server System 11 support many new features, some of which can be challenging to implement properly. We discuss the highlights of these new features here to illustrate the continuing evolution of SQL Server. Chapters 2 through 6 cover the details of these new features. All these new features were designed to cure the scalability problems that became apparent with System 10. Scalability refers to the ability of the SQL Server to make efficient use of more processors on SMP computing platforms. As the hardware vendors began to support multiple processors, it became apparent that there were performance bottlenecks in the Sybase server that prevented the server from making efficient use of the additional processors. Hence, as multiprocessor platforms have become common place, the System 10 Server performance was relatively fixed.

Note that if you are running on a single-processor hardware platform, many, if not all, of the performance benefits that System 11 provides may not be effective. System 11 is designed to provide a direct improvement over System 10, but only on multiprocessor hardware platforms. Applications where performance is not CPU bound may not see any performance improvement with System 11. Scalability equates to better performance only if the additional engines are all busy.

Multiple Processors

Previous to System 11, even when multiple engines were running on multiple processors, one of the engines was required to handle all of the network I/O (see Figure 1–41). This meant the server couldn't really use additional processors efficiently because those extra processors would often be waiting for network I/O to be completed. System 11 removes this restriction.

Named Caches

Previous to System 11, the SQL Server worked with a single cache. This cache was what remained of the machine memory assigned to the server after the server itself was loaded and space was reserved for all the needed memory structures for user connections, server devices, and so forth. A fraction of the cache was further dedicated to storage of stored procedures. The remaining cache, the data cache, was the memory where SQL Server would perform all the manipulation of data in the server. All data that the server needed to satisfy queries would be copied from disk into cache. When the cache was full, the oldest data pages were copied back out to disk and the needed data pages were copied over these old pages in cache. This approach works well as long as the cache is large enough to hold most, if not all, of the frequently needed data pages. However, if a single query needed to load a large number of data pages into cache, this meant that virtually all the data already in cache had to be moved out to disk. This causes a lot of physical I/O that can slow down the server. System 11 allows you to designate portions of cache with a name and then to assign database objects to a named cache (see Figure 1–53). This means that a database table or index can be loaded into cache and it will remain there. Even if a query requires lots of data pages be moved into cache, this activity canít overflow the assigned cache, so the contents of other named caches are not forced out of cache.

Configurable I/O size

System 11 allows you to configure the block size of various I/O operations from 2K to 16K bytes (one to eight 2K pages) (see Figure 1–54). For certain types of operations, such as bulk loading of data, this can result in much more efficient processing. Previous versions of the server required that all I/O be done in 2K blocks.

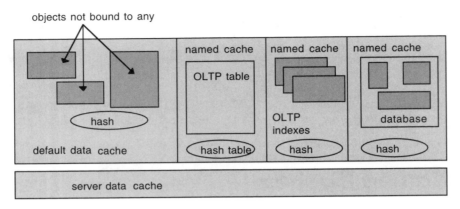

Figure 1–53. System 11 Named Caches

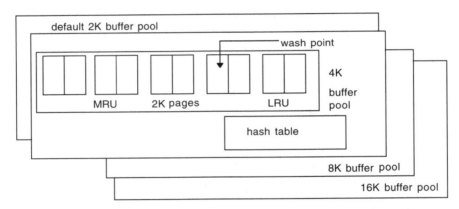

Figure 1–54. System 11 Named Caches and Large I/O Buffer Pools

Transaction Log

Since each and every transaction in the server must record its changes in the transaction log, the log was always a source of contention as all the concurrent processes would have to wait for their turn to have exclusive access to the transaction log. System 11 creates a transaction log in cache for each user (see Figure 1–55). When the userís transaction log is full or when the userís transaction commits, the log cache is flushed to the normal transaction log on disk. This greatly enhances the serverís ability to

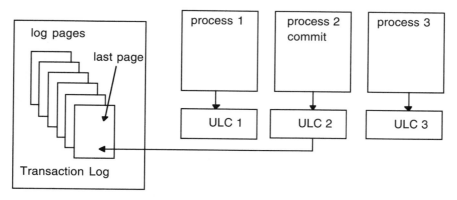

Figure 1–55. System 11 User Log Cache

handle concurrent users. Coupled with multiple processors, this allows the server to scale up very well to large numbers of users without contention for the transaction log that in previous versions of the server would have slowed server performance to such an extent as to virtually eliminate the benefit of having multiple processors.

Partitioned Tables

As with the transaction log, multiple concurrent users who are adding data to a table may contend for a given data page of the table. This is especially true for the Sybase SQL Server since it does not support locking below the data page level. This means that even if all the concurrent users were trying to access a different row in the database, all users who were accessing rows in the same data page would have to wait their turn to have exclusive access to the data page. Unless the table had a clustered index, any new data rows would be added to the last page of the table which would also generate contention. System 11 supports partitioning of tables which simply means that new rows can be added to the table at multiple points, not just the last data page (see Figure 1–56).

Server Monitoring and Tuning

System 11 provides a wealth of new configuration and performance monitoring options that were not previously available. This is just as good as it is bad. You can now observe and tweak hundreds of previously

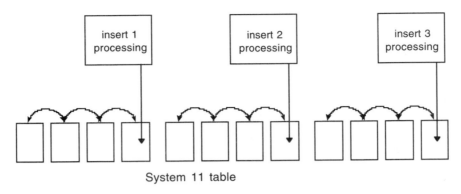

System 11 table

Figure 1–56. System 11 Table Partitioning

unknown (publicly anyway) parameters. You can also devise new and dia-bolical ways to completely destroy your server. This means that you have new power and new responsibilities.

 Look at the bright side – with all these new ways to tune the server, there is no way your boss or your users will have a clue what you are up to. If you are ever cornered, you can always try this - "Well, clearly the choice of free buffer wash point was suboptimal". No self-respect-ing techno-geek is going to dare challenge you with a line like that!

 Look at the dark side – imagine being called in to fix a server that has been configured by some demented DBA (that's redundant!) and has recently been sucked under a commuter train and having to explore, under pressure, 300 configuration parameters, countless named caches, and partially filled table partitions. Of course, this also means that job security is here for everyone.

Compatibility

As was discussed for System 10 compatibility, database dumps from the System 11 Server can't be loaded into a System 10 or a 4.9.2 SQL Server. However, unlike System 10, the System 11 Server can load a data-base dump from a System 10 Server. This means it is possible to upgrade from System 10 to System 11 by making database dumps of the System 10 databases and loading them into databases of the same structure on the System 11 Server. After each database is loaded, the System 11 Server will upgrade the database.

SQL Server Future Releases

Many features have been rumored to be included in future releases of SQL Server and the related products of System 11. We describe those features that are most often promised by Sybase itself. As always, the timing of the release of any given version is completely unknown.

Scalability

To further improve the scalability of SQL Server, the server will be able to assign engines to specific tasks. Along with the ability to create named caches, supported by the System 11 logical memory manager, this means you will be able to assign one of more engines to deal with access to a set of objects in a set of named caches. This supports true mixed-workload environments where the OLTP and Decision Support System workloads can be assigned to independent SQL Server engines. Along with this, the server would support priorities for various tasks within the server. You could assign an application to run on a set of engines, with a specified priority using dedicated portions of cache.

Performance

A resource governor would be provided to limit the resources that can be used by any given transaction, query or batch job. The resource governor could be configured to limit resource usage based on total I/O, total time elapsed, total amount of data returned, and so forth. The configuration of the governor would be dynamic, allowing changes during your business cycle to support different requirements during a given day, week, or other business interval. The governor would also support various options for what action to take when a specified resource limit was violated.

Operational

The ability to perform routine server maintenance functions in parallel will be supported. This means dbcc, sort operations, index creation, and recovery operations would be parallelized to make use of the multiple server engines and physical CPUs available.

Recovery would be improved to support point-in-time recovery, and would support partial user access to the database during recovery. The details of this are vague, but again, this could lead to some very interesting operational scenarios. Enhancements to the capabilities of the Backup Server are also mentioned. This would include object-level recovery and the ability to recover a partition of a table. The integration of SQL BackTrack to improve the backup and restore functionality of the server is also rumored, but it isn't clear if this would be an integration of the DataTools product or some other arrangement. The ability to implement user-defined roles would be supported along with enhanced security features to control access by those roles.

Decision Support

Further support for Decision Support Systems (DSS) would be provided. DSS these days is synonymous with data warehouse efforts. This means support for true parallel query processing, including integration with the cost-based query optimizer and further tuning features. These features would build on the Logical Memory Manager features already in System 11. Parallel query support would include parallel support of table and index scans, sorts, joins, and computing aggregates.

Distributed Database

This relates primarily to replicating data using Sybase Replication Server. New features would include simplified mechanisms to configure primary and replicate data which is often referred to as the publish and subscribe model. Features would support the resynchronization of mobile databases. The Replication Server product itself would be more customizable and would support events and new data types as well as transactions.

Pure Speculation

If the preceding feature descriptions were based on the consistency of the available rumors, then the following possible new features are based on even less real information. Row-level locking is always being hinted at. The speculations as to whether or not Sybase will move to this are rampant. There are a number of System 11 improvements that would not have been necessary if row-level locking had been implemented. Contention over the last page of the transaction log, or the last page of a table, would not be an issue if row-level locking were supported. Of the many features that may or may not be supported in future releases of the SQL Serve, row-level locking is the most speculative, debatable and interesting of them all. Further enhancements may also include features specific to the recovery of Very Large Databases (VLDB). Complex data types would be supported. SQL Servers running on separate server machines could be clustered so that their combined computing power could be user to satisfy complex queries.

SUMMARY

From SQL Server 4.9.2 to System 11 there have been many major changes in the way the server operates, and the parameters you can configure and tune. Still, the server operates in pretty much the same basic way it always did. Also, despite the endless obsession with the latest features, the issues for the Sybase SQL Server DBA remain very much the same. You must understand how the server supports and affects your business. No matter how fancy your configuration file, the point here is to support the business. With each new release and the ever-increasing complexity of the server, it becomes easier than ever to lose sight of the real goal which is to provide your business with the data needed to stay in business.

 The fact the every new server release allows you to send your kids to a nicer college, even farther away from home, is just a secondary consideration. Nature abhors both a vacuum and a simple database server.

POINTS TO REMEMBER

There are three versions of SQL Server currently in use. Version 4.9.2, System 10, and System 11 share many features. System 10 added features such as the Backup Server and server auditing. System 11 improves the scalability of the SQL Server on multiprocessor platforms.

Each server version has many differences. Remember that many of the new features of each new version may not help your individual server. You should be aware of the major new features of each server version, but you must resist the impulse to start applying all the new features just because they are available.

System 11 supports many new features, but you don't have to use most of them immediately. The few new features that you must use will be set up for you automatically. The scalability of System 11 will only help applications that are CPU bound and are running on SMP hardware and software platforms.

System 11
Features

Despite all the new features, and all the performance enhancement that they may promise, it is vital keep two points in mind. First, all these new features are designed to help SQL Server scale up across multiple CPUs. If the server machine hardware you are using doesn't support multiple processors, or you haven't installed them, you may not see any performance improvement from upgrading to System 11. Also be aware that you must be sure that the OS you are running also supports multiple CPUs. You can't take this for granted it is possible to have a multiprocessor hardware platform running a version of the OS that doesn't take advantage of the multiple CPUs that are physically present.

Second, you do not have to use any of the features that will be discussed in the following chapters. You need to be aware of these features, but you do not have to make use of any of them until you are ready to. Further, you shouldn't start using the new features just because they exist. You must have a good reason for using them. We discuss the new features of the Sybase System 11 SQL Server in groups. The groups are scalability, named caches, configuration and DBA features. This means that the first features discussed are the ones that contribute most to the improved scalability of System 11. Within each of these groups, the new features are discussed in order of importance. The features at the beginning of each group are the ones that you will use the most often or are the most important to improve server performance. The features at the end of the list are those you will use less often, and, for most users, will not contribute significantly to improved server performance.

System 11 introduces many new features. Some of these features involve a great many details in their use and implementation. We discuss the most important aspects of these new features and how they will impact your work with the SQL Server. However, there are many more details that are documented in the Sybase manuals.

We will discuss these new features in the following order.

System 11 Features

Scalability

System 11 Multiple Network Engines (MNE)
System 11 transaction log
Lock management and System 11

Named Caches

Buffer manager and named caches
Buffer manager and large I/Os
Query optimization and the System 11 buffer manager
Query optimization improvements

Configuration

Configuring SQL Server 11

DBA Features

Database dumps
sp_sysmon
System tables
Table partitioning

If You Do Nothing

There are many new features supported by SQL Server System 11. You should not start using them just because they are there. You must carefully examine your server to determine which, if any, of the new features will help your server. You must also be careful to ensure that any new features used are worth the administrative effort to configure and maintain.

With this in mind, we list the new features that have been discussed. We then discuss whether you have to be concerned with each of the new features immediately. We discuss which features you have to worry about (marked with a *), and which ones you can ignore until you need them. You will see that of all the new features discussed, only two of them (query optimization improvements and database dumps) have any immediate direct impact on the server. The others are important, but until you need to use them, you don't have to worry about them. This doesn't mean these features aren't useful and significant. It simply means you don't have to start using them until you are sure you know what you are doing. Note that if you are upgrading from 4.9.2 to System 11 you do need to be careful that the last-chance thresholds are enabled (see Chapter 12 for more details).

System 11 New Features

Scalability

System 11 Multiple Network Engines (MNE)

The server will automatically enable this behavior as soon as you start a second server engine.

System 11 Transaction log

The server automatically creates the default 2K User Log Cache (ULC) for each user. You don't need to configure the size of the ULC until you have a very good reason to do so.

Lock Management and System 11

The server creates a set of spinlocks for each server engine. Other locking improvements (isolation levels and promotion) don't need to be configured until you are sure you need to change them from their defaults.

Performance

Buffer Manager and Named Caches

The server automatically creates the default data cache which will function just as the data cache did in previous server versions.

Buffer Manager and Large I/Os

The server automatically creates the default data cache with the default 2K buffer pool. The entire default data cache will be one buffer pool with 2K buffers.

Query Optimization and the System 11 Buffer Manager

Until you are aware of a performance problem that would be solved by using larger I/Os, you can leave this alone.

Query Optimization Improvements*

The System 11 server processes subqueries differently from previous versions. Existing stored procedures, views, and triggers, especially those that contain subqueries, will not use the new behavior unless they are dropped and recreated. If you don't drop and recreate these objects, their performance may actually be worse than with the previous server version. This applies only to servers that have been upgraded to System 11.

Table Partitioning

Very few, if any, tables in your server will benefit from this feature. You need to be very sure you need this before you implement it.

Operational

Configuring SQL Server 11

You do need to be aware of how to use the configuration file to clear the server configuration, and so forth, but you don't have to create any files, and so forth. When you install the System 11 server (or upgrade to System 11), the <servername>.cfg file will be created for you. Each time you make a configuration change using **sp_configure**, the server will update the <servername>.cfg file for you. Each time you restart the server, it will use the latest version of the <servername>.cfg file. You can manage the server configuration the same way you did with previous versions.

Database Dumps*

Due to the off-line status of databases after a database load, you must change any existing scripts that load a database. You must included the on-line database command in these scripts. If you don't do this, the database will not be usable.

sp_sysmon

You should certainly use this to monitor server performance and decide which other new features to use. Until you are ready to carefully examine your server and monitor its performance over time, you don't need to worry about this feature

System Tables

You should be aware of them and you may want to dump their contents as part of a complete server configuration backup. You don't need to do anything with them until you have a specific need.

THINGS THAT SYSTEM 11 STILL DOESN'T DO

There are several features that Sybase System 11 still doesn't provide. Row-level locking has been rumored for a long time but is still not supported. While System 11 does support a new 'max rows per page' option on the create table command, this is a weak imitation of true row-level locking.

A resource governor would be very welcome and has been discussed but is not in the 11.0 release.

The removal of all restrictions on update-in-place has also been discussed but has not been supported in the 11.0 release. While some of the restrictions have been removed, there are still some significant ones left.

SUMMARY

The System 11 SQL Server has many features that are aimed at improving the scalibility of the server on multi-processor platforms. For a single-processor platform, there will be little if any performance improvement over previous server versions. It is very easy to misuse the increased flexibility of System 11 and end up hurting your server and complicating your working life with no discernible benefit.

3

System 11 Scalability

SYSTEM 11 MULTIPLE NETWORK ENGINES (MNE)

Previous versions of SQL Server supported multiple engines. Each engine is an operating system-level process that is executing the SQL Server binary. However, until System 11, the way the SQL Server used multiple engines was not very sophisticated. The main problem was that all network communication had to go through one engine. This limited scalability. As you added more engines running on more processors of the server machine, all engines still had to wait for network activity on engine 0. System 11 supports multiple network engines which means any of the engines that are running can handle network I/O activity. This allows you to configure and effectively use more engines than with previous server versions. This results in improved scalability for SQL Server. As more processors are added to a SMP server machine, more engines can be started, and none of them is slowed down waiting for network activity through engine 0.

SQL Server Engines

Each SQL Server process (executing the SQL Server data server binary) at the OS level is an "engine." All the engines running for a given server share locks and other server resources. Each engine is associated with one OS-level process no matter how many engines or CPUs are available. All the engines, together, form the SQL Server on the server machine. Server engines communicate with each other through shared memory. Also, engines use "spinlocks" to control which engine is using portions of shared memory at any given time. Spinlocks are also called semaphores. When an engine needs a shared memory structure that is currently locked by another engine, the waiting engine is said to "spin," while it continually checks the lock to see if the structure is available.

When you start the server, the server spawns additional engines up to the number of "online engines" the server is configured for. You must understand that the number of engines running is not the same thing as the number of physical CPUs available on the server machine platform. While the server can be configured so that the number of server engines exactly equals the number of physical processors, this is not generally the best way to configure the server for performance. You use **sp_configure "max online engines"**, **<numberofengines>** to establish the number of engines that the server will start. This has not changed from previous versions of the SQL Server.

Note that with System 11, SQL Server will not allow you to configure more server engines than there are processors on the server machine. The output below is for a server machine that has two processors.

```
1> sp_configure "max online engines"
2> go
 Parameter Name       Default     Memory Used    Config Value    Run Value
max online engines      1            147              1              1

(return status = 0)
1> sp_configure "max online engines", 2
2> go
```

Parameter Name	Default	Memory Used	Config Value	Run Value
max online engines	1	147	2	1

Configuration option changed. The SQL Server must be rebooted before the change in effect since the option is static.

```
(return status = 0)
1> sp_configure "max online engines", 3
2> go
Msg 5846, Level 16, State 1:
Server 'PSYCHO', Procedure 'sp_configure', Line 329:
Illegal value '3' specified for configuration option 'max online
engines". The legal values are between '1' and '2'.
Msg 5849, Level 16, State 1:
Server 'PSYCHO', Procedure 'sp_configure', Line 329:
Verification failed for parameter 'max online engines'.
(return status = 1)
```

System 11 and Network I/O

In SQL Server 4.9.2 and System 10, all network I/O had to go through engine 0 no matter what else any of the other engines was doing (see Figure 3–1). This meant that all network I/O queued up waiting for eng 0 to be available even if the other engines were not heavily loaded. This also limited scalability since adding more CPUs would not help where network I/O was the limiting performance factor. Since SQL Server is built upon the client/server network connection, network I/O is always a performance factor.

Figure 3–1. Pre-System 11 Network I/O

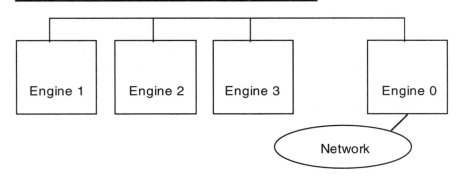

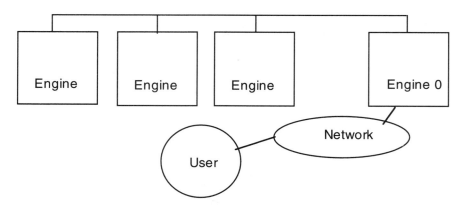

Figure 3-2 System 11 Initial Network I/O

System 11 SQL Server will assign the network I/O load among the available engines so that network I/O requests are assigned to the engine with the fewest connections at that time. Note that from then on, any one user connection may have its processing assigned to any available processor, but all network I/O needed for the duration of that user connection will continue to be assigned to the same engine that the user connection was initially assigned to. The user connection or task is said to be affiniated to a given engine and all network I/O will be assigned to the network affiniated engine for the duration of the connection. Note that when any user connection is first established, the user connection is initially affiniated to engine 0 (see Figure 3–2), and then affiniated to another engine for the duration of the connection (see Figure 3–3). Most SMP platforms support network affinity migration (Sun Solaris, DEC, RS6000, AIX, HP), but you should check your particular platform version to be sure you can take advantage of this performance improvement.

This is great, but note that it doesn't guarantee that an engine with few user connections isn't doing some very intense work. An engine with one very intensive user connection may be given network I/O while another engine sits with hundreds of users connected but actually idle at that time. Overall, the way System 11 handles network I/O is an improvement, but it will not solve all potential network I/O load balancing problems.

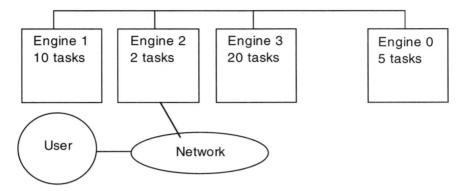

Figure 3-3. System 11 Network I/O Migration

Server Engines and User Connections

With previous SQL Server versions the total number of server user connections was limited by the number of file descriptors. The operating system placed a limit on the number of file descriptors allowed for any single operating system process. Since only engine 0 could handle network I/O in 4.9.2 and System 10, the maximum number of file descriptors for engine 0 was also the total limit on user connections to the server. With System 11 and MNE, the number of file descriptors still applies, but only to each MNE. Double the number of MNEs and the server can handle twice as many user connections without overrunning the OS limit on file descriptors for a single process.

For example, assume the OS limit on file descriptors for a single process is 1024. For a single engine, the maximum number of user connections is 1024. This number will really be a few less than this as some connections are used by SQL Server itself. For MNE, with three engines, the maximum server user connections are now 3 x 1024 = 3072, even though the per process limit on file descriptors is still 1024.

Optimal Number of Engines

You do not want more engines running than there are processors on the server machine. Further, you don't want more engines than the number of server machine processors that you want to dedicate to the SQL Server. If you do have too many engines relative to the number of processors, then the OS must swap out one engine to let another engine run on one of the processors. Swapping operating system-level processes is very costly. Process swapping can actually reduce server performance below the performance attained when a smaller number of engines are running. More engines is not always good.

Configuring MNE for optimal performance, that is, determining how many engines to run, requires determining existing server engine usage. Note that this is not the same thing as monitoring the physical processor usage levels. Processor (CPU) usage as seen at the operating system level often shows 100 percent engine usage for an engine that may only be looking for work. You must obtain baseline performance of existing engines, and then add more engines and observe performance. You must remember that more engines may require more memory be assigned to the SQL Server. Always start with a small number of engines and verify that you really need more. Once added, verify that you can see the benefit of more engines. The issue of determining the optimal number of engines to run on your server machine is discussed in Chapter 10.

For most situations the discussion is about increasing the number of engines. You must also understand that if you have a hardware failure, or if or if you need to run non-SQL Server OS level processes on the server machine, you may need to reduce the number of engines to obtain optimal performance. Also, if you are moving to another platform, even if it is the same type, you must check that the new platform has all the necessary resources and configuration to support the same number of engines. If the new platform doesn't have the same amount of memory or has a different number of physical processors, you may not want the same number of engines running.

Engine Scheduling in SQL Server

SQL Server dynamically assigns user tasks to available engines and requires that all network I/O for a given user connection be done by the engine that was network affiniated for the connection. As tasks within the SQL Server require an engine to continue processing, the server will schedule tasks onto available server engines. However, this does not mean that the server has any control over how server engines are scheduled onto the available physical processors. The server machine operation system schedules server engines onto the physically available processors. This hasn't changed between 4.9.2, System 10, and System 11.

Uniprocessor Server Machine Platforms

With all of the advantages of System 11 and MNE, you must realize that if the server is running on a single processor system, none of this will help the performance of the SQL Server. Similarly, the OS platform may not support SMP to the point that additional processors are actually usable for multiple server engines. You must be sure your OS/hardware platform can really exploit these capabilities before you spend the time needed to understand and configure the server for MNE.

SYSTEM 11 TRANSACTION LOG

System 11 supports several new features that improve the way the server handles access to the transaction log. Also improved is the way in which the log is moved between disk and cache. These features reduce the performance bottlenecks relating to the transaction log that were present in previous versions of the server.

The SQL Server uses a transaction log for each database to record all the changes made to the database. The transaction log is the way the server guarantees recovery of committed transactions. However, one transaction log for each database limits scalability. All records that are added to the transaction log are added to the last page of the log. All server activity in a database that needs to write to the transaction log has to access the last page of the transaction log. For multiple concurrent users in a pre-system 11 server this meant that there was always contention as all but one process had to wait for access to the last page of the transaction log, (see Figure 3–4). This became a critical problem as multiple engines running on SMP hardware became widely used. Multiple engines should help performance, but with the transaction log bottleneck, only one engine could have access to the transaction log at a time.

User Log Cache

System 11 addresses this problem by creating a user log cache (ULC) for each server process. Each server process that generates transaction log records will have those records stored in the user log cache for that process

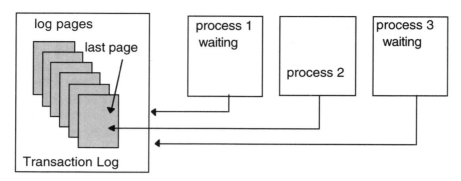

Figure 3–4. Pre-System 11 Transaction Log

(see Figure 3–5). The server will flush a user log cache to the transaction log as needed. Once flushed, the transaction log records that were in the user log cache are part of the normal database transaction log.

While this may not improve performance for a single-processor system, this is a significant improvement in scalability for multiprocessor systems. Multiple engines running on multiple processors can now work in parallel on user queries and not contend over the transaction log. You do not need to configure the server to support user log caches; this is the default behavior in System 11.

The user log cache is flushed to the transaction log when needed. This will occur when the current transaction is complete, when the transaction begins activity in another database, when the user log cache has filled up, and when a checkpoint occurs.

When multiple-user queries commit, there can still be contention over the last page of the transaction log. However, up until the time of these commits, the queries can be processed without contention over the transaction log. Many queries normally generate transaction log records at multiple points before the transaction completes. This means that each query can wait until the transaction completes before accessing the transaction log. This greatly reduces the number of times that a set of concurrent queries will wait for the last page of the transaction log. Further, nothing is written to the user log cache until at least one row is changed. This means that long-running transactions that retrieve lots of data before determining what data to change won't need to access the user log cache until they begin changing data.

Many times users, or their applications, can create problems for the DBA by beginning their session with a "begin tran" which is then moved

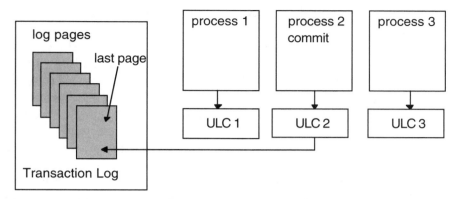

Figure 3–5. System 11 Transaction Log and User Log Cache

into the transaction log. With user log cache, the begin tran is placed in the user log cache but will not move to the transaction log until the transaction completes. This prevents almost all the situations where a user connects to the server, begins a transaction, and leaves for Tahiti. This leads to a situation where you can't truncate the transaction log beyond this point without killing the user process or restarting the server. The transaction log then fills and all server activity, except for selects, comes to a halt.

Since the user log cache will be flushed when it becomes full, whether the transaction has completed or not, the size of the user log cache is very important. You can configure the size of the user log cache, but this can only be configured for the server level. All user log caches are the same size throughout the server. The user log cache has a default size of 2K and can't be less than this. Further, you can't configure the user log cache to be greater than 2 Gb. The syntax is

sp_configure "user log cache size", 4096

 Can you imagine wanting each and every transaction to have 2 Gb of cache? Further, who is going to really try 33K or 1093K user log caches? Can it really be an advantage to be able to configure things down to this level (1K) over such a wide range (2K to 2 Gb)?

You need to consider several factors when estimating the optimal size for the user log cache. Recall that this size is specified at the server level. The same user log cache size will be applied to all users of the server no matter what they are doing. You would like the user log cache to be no bigger than the largest transaction that any user will submit. Of course, this is hard to determine. If the user log cache is much larger than the average transaction however, you are wasting memory. The memory dedicated to the user log cache can't be used for anything else. If the average transaction completes and is flushed from the user log cache well before the cache is filled up, the unused portion of the cache is wasted memory for most transactions. On the other hand, if the user log cache is smaller than the average transaction, the server will have to flush the cache frequently as it fills up. These frequent cache flushes then cause multiple server engines to contend for the transaction log. This is the very situation you are trying to avoid. Overall, you need to size the user log cache for the size of the typical transaction, not for the rare long running query. You will have to experiment to really determine the optimal size for the user log cache.

Transaction Log Buffer Pool

In previous versions of the server, everything, including the transaction log, was moved around in 2K pages. With System 11 and large I/Os, this restriction has been removed. The server can be configured so the transaction log is moved in 2K up to 16K blocks at a time. As with the user log cache, the size of the transaction log buffer is server wide. All transaction logs for the server will be configured to the same size. The default log I/O buffer size is 4K. Note that the errorlog shows what size buffer pool is being used for the transaction log for each database.

However, this alone has no affect. The server may be configured for 4K log I/O buffer size, but this is only used if there is a 4K buffer pool available in the cache where the transaction log is bound. You need to think about each of the transaction logs in your server. All those that are not bound to a named cache will use the default data cache. You need to create a 4K buffer pool in the default data cache for these transaction logs. For those that are bound to a named cache, you need to create a 4K buffer pool in each of these named caches.

If a 4K buffer pool is not available, the server will use the default 2K buffer pool. A buffer pool for the transaction log must be created using **sp_poolconfig**. The size of the log I/O buffer is established by reading the *sysattributes* table when booting. If there is a transaction log bound to a named cache that does not have a buffer pool for the log I/O size in *sys attributes*, the log I/O size will revert to the default of 2K. The log I/O size can also be changed dynamically while the server is running using

sp_logiosize. The best size for your server will need to be determined be experimenting and monitoring.

Oldest Outstanding Transaction

When there is a transaction in the transaction log that has not completed, the transaction log cannot be truncated beyond the open transaction. If this goes on long enough, the transaction log fills up and the server can't support anything but select operations for that database. Before System 11, you had no direct way to determine which user process was responsible for the open transaction that was causing the problem. You had little choice but to restart the server to kill such transactions. System 11 has a new system table, *syslogshold*, which records the oldest active transaction, and how long it has been active, for each database in the server. Note that the server doesn't consider a transaction to be active until it causes a change in a table, since, up to that point, the transaction hasn't produced any transaction log records.

Transaction Log Issues

Transactions that fill up the user log cache will still need access to the last page of the transaction log even though they have not yet completed. If many of the queries fill the user log cache, then the server will need to flush multiple user log caches at the same time. This means all these transactions will need to access the last page of the transaction log. The bottleneck will simply reappear.

Using a larger log I/O size may hurt more than it helps because the server does not wait to fill the log buffer before flushing it to disk. If the server deals with many short transactions, then the log buffer will be flushed as each short transaction completes. Having a large log I/O buffer size in this case would cause the server to move much more data than needed each time a transaction committed.

There is no system stored procedure to query the *syslogshold* table. You can create a stored procedure that will examine the *syslogshold* table, but a simple select will tell you what you need to know (see the example below). You also need to realize that just identifying the server user that is holding the oldest open transaction doesn't help much. The kill command still can't kill a user process for all states. You may well identify the user and still have to restart the server to get rid of them.

Why wasn't this part of the system stored procedures? I guess this was left as an "exercise" for the DBA. Is it legal to kill a user in your state?

Examples—User Log Cache Command Syntax

Examine Current User Log Cache Size

```
1> sp_configure 'user log cache size'
2> go
 Parameter Name     Default   Memory Used   Config Value   Run Value
user log cache size  2048          0            2048          2048

(return status = 0)
```

Configuration File Entry for Current User Log Cache Size

```
[User Environment]
     number of user connections = 50
     stack size = DEFAULT
     stack guard size = DEFAULT
     systemwide password expiration = DEFAULT
     permission cache entries = DEFAULT
     user log cache size = DEFAULT
     user log cache spinlock ratio = DEFAULT
```

Changing User Log Cache Size

```
1> sp_configure "user log cache size', 2060
2> go
 Parameter Name     Default   Memory Used   Config Value   Run Value
user log cache size  2048          0            2060          2048
```

Configuration option changed. The SQL Server must be rebooted before the change in effect since the option is static.

```
(return status = 0)
```

Server Errorlog After Changing User Log Cache Size

```
00:96/05/30 15:34:34.35 server  'iso_1' (ID = 1).
00:96/06/12 10:13:08.41 server  The configuration option 'user log
cache
size' has been changed by 'sa' from '2048' to '2060'.
00:96/06/12 10:13:08.47 server  Configuration file
'/export/home/sybase/11.0.1/VERTIGO11.cfg' has been written and the
previous version has been renamed to
'/export/home/sybase/11.0.1/VERTIGO11.017'.
```

Configuration File After Changing User Log Cache Size

```
[User Environment]
      number of user connections = 50
      stack size = DEFAULT
      stack guard size = DEFAULT
      systemwide password expiration = DEFAULT
      permission cache entries = DEFAULT
      user log cache size = 2060
      user log cache spinlock ratio = DEFAULT
```

After Restarting Server (User Log Cache Size Change Is a Static Configuration Parameter)

```
1> sp_configure 'user log cache size'
2> go
```

Parameter Name	Default	Memory Used	Config Value	Run Value
user log cache size	2048	0	2060	2060

```
(return status = 0)
```

Examine Transaction Log Buffer I/O Size of Current Database

```
1> sp_logiosize
2> go

The transaction log for database 'master' will use I/O size of 2
Kbytes.

(return status = 0)
```

99

Examine Transaction Log Buffer I/O Size for All Databases in Server

```
1> sp_logiosize 'all'
2> go
Cache name: default data cache
  Data base                         Log I/O Size
  master                               2 Kb
  model                                2 Kb
  psycho_db                            2 Kb
  sybsecurity                          2 Kb
  sybsystemprocs                       2 Kb
  tempdb                               2 Kb

(return status = 0)
```

Change Transaction Log Buffer I/O Size From 2K to 8K

```
1> use psycho_db
2> go
1> sp_logiosize
2> go
The transaction log for database 'psycho_db' will use I/O size of 2
Kbytes.
(return status = 0)
1> sp_logiosize '8'
2> go
Unable to change the log I/O size. The memory pool for the specified
log I/O size does not exist.
(return status = 0)
```

Create The Needed 8K Buffer Pool In The Default Data Cache

```
1> sp_helpcache
2> go
```

Cache Name	Config Size	Run Size	Overhead
default data cache	0.00 Mb	28.77 Mb	1.47 Mb

Memory Available For Named Caches	Memory Configured To Named Caches
28.77 Mb	0.00 Mb

There is 28.77 Mb of memory left over that will be allocated to the default cache

─────────────── **Cache Binding Information:** ───────────────

Cache Name	Entity Name	Type	Index Name	Status

```
(return status = 0)
1> sp_poolconfig 'default data cache', '2M', '8K'
2> go
00:96/06/12 10:31:46.39 server  Configuration file
'/export/home/sybase/11.0.1/VERTIGO11.cfg' has been written and the
previous version has been renamed to
'/export/home/sybase/11.0.1/VERTIGO11.018'.
(return status = 0)
1> sp_cacheconfig 'default data cache'
2> go
```

Cache Name	Status	Type	Config Value	Run Value
default data cache	Active	Default	0.00 Mb	28.77 Mb
		Total	0.00 Mb	28.77 Mb

Cache: default data cache,   Status: Active,   Type: Default
    Config Size: 0.00 Mb,   Run Size: 28.77 Mb

IO Size	Wash Size	Config Size	Run Size
2 Kb	512 Kb	0.00 Mb	26.77 Mb
8 Kb	408 Kb	2.00 Mb	2.00 Mb

```
(return status = 0)
```

Create, Again, the Needed 8K Buffer Pool in The Default Data Cache

```
1> sp_logiosize '8'
2> go
Log I/O size is set to 8 Kbytes.
The transaction log for database 'psycho_db' will use I/O size of 8
Kbytes.
(return status = 0)
```

New Entry in sysattributes Due to logiosize Changing from Default 2K

```
   2    0 T           NULL                          8
                 NULL        NULL        NULL        8
        NULL

        NULL

        NULL

        NULL
```

Edit Configuration File to Reset User Log Cache Size to Default at Next Server Restart

```
[User Environment]
     number of user connections = 50
     stack size = DEFAULT
     stack guard size = DEFAULT
     systemwide password expiration = DEFAULT
     permission cache entries = DEFAULT
     user log cache size = DEFAULT
     user log cache spinlock ratio = DEFAULT
```

NOTE: You can't use DEFAULT with **sp_configure** but you can in the configuration file.

Restart Server—Server Uses Modified Configuration File

```
00:96/06/12 10:42:43.47 server   Recovering database 'psycho_db'.
00:96/06/12 10:42:43.48 server   Recovery dbid 6 ckpt (10248,19) old-
est tran=(10248,18)
00:96/06/12 10:42:43.51 server   1 transactions rolled back.
00:96/06/12 10:42:44.11 server   The transaction log in the database
'psycho_db' will use I/O size of 8 Kb.
00:96/06/12 10:42:44.15 server   Database 'psycho_db' is now online.
```

Examine Transaction Log I/O Size

```
1> sp_configure 'user log cache size'
2> go
```

Parameter Name	Default	Memory Used	Config Value	Run Value
user log cache size	2048	0	2048	2048

```
(return status = 0)
```

Examine syslogshold

```
1> select * from syslogshold
2> go
```

dbid	reserved	spid	page	xactid	masterxactid
11	0	0	11971	0x000000000000	0x000000000000

starttime	name
Jan 1 1900 12:00AM	$replication_truncation_point

```
(1 row affected)
```

> NOTE: This entry is present because dbid=11 is the RSSD database for Sybase Replication Server. The RSSD database is being replicated and hence this row in *syslogshold*.

Begin tran and syslogshold Table

```
1> begin tran psycho
2> go
1> use master
2> go
1> select * from syslogshold
2> go
```

dbid	reserved	spid	page	xactid	masterxactid
	starttime			name	

```
(0 rows affected)
```

> NOTE: Just a begin tran doesn't show up because it doesn't fill the user log cache.

Long-running tran and syslogshold

```
1> select * from syslogshold
2> go
   dbid      reserved       spid       page         xactid          masterxactid
   11           0             0         11971    0x000000000000   0x000000000000
        starttime                              name
   Jan 1 1900 12:00AM              $replication_truncation_point

(1 row affected)

1> use cmsdb
2> go
1> begin tran psycho
2> go
1> update service_orders set so_number = so_number + 1
2> go

1> use master
2> go
1> select * from syslogshold
2> go
   dbid      reserved       spid       page         xactid          masterxactid
   11           0             0         11971    0x000000000000   0x000000000000
   5            0             1         77107    0x00012d33000e   0x000000000000
        starttime                              name
   Jan 1 1900 12:00AM              $replication_truncation_point
   Jan 12 1996 10:48AM                        psycho

(2 rows affected)
```

> NOTE: dbid = 5 is the database where the long running transaction is running and spid = 1 is the server user that started the transaction.

Identify the User Process from the spid in syslogshold

```
1> select * from sysprocesses where spid=1
2> go
```

spid	kpid	enginenum	status	suid	hostname
1	341639182	0	sleeping	1	psycho

program_name	hostprocess	cmd	cpu	physical_io
isql	13925	UPDATE	17	14325

memusage	blocked	dbid	uid	gid
3	0	5	1	0

tran_name	time_blocked	network_pktsz
psycho	NULL	512

```
(1 row affected)
```

Transaction Has Finished, but Still Open

```
1> begin tran psycho
2> go
1> update service_orders set so_number = so_number + 1
2> go
(20598 rows affected)
1> use master
2> go
1> select * from syslogshold
2> go
```

dbid	reserved	spid	page	xactid	masterxactid
11	0	0	11971	0x000000000000	0x000000000000
5	0	1	77107	0x00012d33000e	0x00000000000

starttime	name
Jan 1 1900 12:00AM	$replication_truncation_point
Jan 12 1996 10:48AM	psycho

```
(2 rows affected)
```

Roll Back Long-running Transaction

```
1> use cmsdb
2> go
1> rollback tran psycho
2> go
1> use master
2> go
1> select * from syslogshold
2> go
```

dbid	reserved	spid	page	xactid	masterxactid
11	0	0	11971	0x000000000000	0x000000000000

starttime	name
Jan 1 1900 12:00AM	$replication_truncation_point

```
(1 row affected)
```

LOCK MANAGEMENT AND SYSTEM 11

Locking is used by the server to ensure that each multiple transaction sees a consistent view of the data. Locking prevents one transaction from changing a single row of data while another transaction has already started a table scan that will read that same row. System 11 supports dirty reads, configurable lock promotion, and the parallel lock manager. There are many details to the hierarchy of lock promotion configuration, and syntax, which are covered in the Sybase documentation.

Dirty Reads

Normally, the server will not allow one transaction to read changes made but not yet committed by another transaction. System 11 allows you to configure the server to allow just such "dirty" reads to occur. Dirty here refers to a data page that has been changed, but whose changes have not been committed. Allowing dirty reads can improve performance. Queries that only need to read data no longer have to wait for transactions that are changing the data. The trade off is that the data that is read may not yield correct results since it may be changing as other transactions commit or roll back.

Allowing dirty reads is called "isolation level 0". The default server configuration is isolation level 3 which ensures that each transaction sees a consistent set of data during its execution. You can set the isolation level for either the entire user session or for an individual statement.

There are hazards to allowing dirty reads. First, the results of a query may not be accurate. Calculating the average employee's salary may not be accurate if some of the data is changing while the average is being computed. You must determine if the trade off between performance and accuracy is worthwhile. You must ensure that your users understand that their query results may not be accurate. In order for the server to handle rows changing while a transaction is in progress, tables must have a unique index. If a unique index is not present, the server may not be able to complete a query that tried to read data that has changed, and the query may be aborted. See the server documentation for all the details of how the server handles this situation.

Configurable Lock Promotion

Before System 11, any time a process needed to lock more than 200 pages of a table, the server would escalate to a table lock. This meant that no other process could access that entire table. For large tables, this was another bottleneck for multiple server engines. With System 11 you can configure the lock promotion for the server, database and table levels. Now, the lock promotion is specified to occur as a percentage of the pages in the table. Further, a low and high watermark (LWM/HWM) can be configured. If the percentage computed falls below the LWM, the LWM will be used to determine when to escalate to a table lock. Similarly, the promotion to a table lock will occur when the HWM is reached if it is lower than the percentage configured for lock promotion.

Parallel Lock Manager

In previous versions of the SQL Server, there was one set of locks for all server engines. This obviously limited the scalability of the server. In System 11 each server engine has its own set of lock structures. The size of the cache for each engine is configurable as well. Multiple locks replace the single lock of previous server versions for managing the lock structures themselves. System 11 also allows configuring the time the server waits before looking for deadlocks. This means that a blocked process will wait before the server starts checking for a deadlock situation. If the blocks clear up in time, the process can start up again. This saves the server from examining every blocked process for a potential deadlock situation. Previously, any time a server process was blocked the deadlock search began immediately.

4

System 11
Named Caches

BUFFER MANAGER AND NAMED CACHES

Introduction

The SQL Server can read or write only data when the associated data page is in memory (cache) of the server machine. For all selects, inserts, updates and deletes, the server must bring all the affected data pages from disk into memory. This requires reading from the physical disk and is called a physical I/O. If the data page needed is already in

109

cache, then the server only needs to move that page within memory and that is called a logical I/O. Since a logical I/O doesn't involve any moving parts, it is much faster than a physical I/O. Physical I/O also leads to more contention as multiple processes need to access the same physical disk drive. The SQL Server tries to keep the most-often requested data pages in cache to improve performance. Clearly, the more memory available on the server machine that is assigned to the SQL Server, the better. More server memory means more cache and more data pages will be found in cache. The ability of the server to find a data page in cache will also depend on the types of queries that are being executed. Short transactions typical of OLTP will need relatively few pages. Most OLTP applications have a few tables that are accessed by most, if not all, transactions. Long-running queries for reporting or DSS in general will often require massive amounts of data. This means that it is harder to keep all the needed data pages in cache for DSS.

Overview of Pre-System 11 Usage

In previous versions of SQL Server, there was only one data cache. All data pages that the server needs are loaded from disk into this area in the server machine memory. All changes the server makes to any data page are made to the page in cache. To save changed data pages, the server wrote the changed page from cache to disk. All server operations (**select, insert, update, delete**) against a data page require that the data page be in cache before the operation can begin. When SQL Server is configured, some total number of megabytes of server machine memory are dedicated to the server process. From this memory, space is allocated for various server data structures for server users and server devices, the SQL Server stack, code, and kernel areas. After this, the configured percentage of the server memory is allocated to the stored procedure cache. The memory remaining after all of this is the data cache (see Figure 4–1).

The data cache is managed by the buffer manager (see Figure 4–2). Note that a buffer is a pointer to a data page. Within the data cache there are several important structures. The hash table is where the server keeps track of the pages that are in cache. When looking for a certain data page, it is much faster for the server to examine the hash table than it is to scan all the pages in cache. The data pages in cache are a doubly linked list of pages. Whenever the server needs to access a data page, it moves the page to the end of this list of pages. The page that has been accessed most recently is at the most recently used (MRU) end of the list. As each

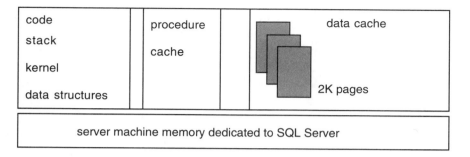

Figure 4–1. Pre-System 11 Data Cache

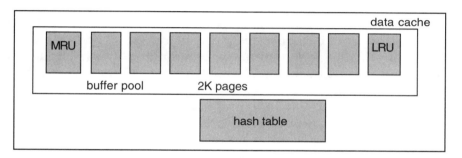

Figure 4–2. Pre-System 11 Buffer Manager

subsequent page is accessed, it too is moved to the MRU end of the list. This means that the page that was at the MRU end of the list must be moved. This page is moved over in place, in the direction of the other end of the list. When the cache is full, the page that has been in cache the longest, without being accessed again is at the other end of the list. This end is the least recently used (LRU) end of the list. Once cache is full of data pages, there will be a data page filling every spot in the list from the MRU end to the LRU end. Now, when the server needs to access the next data page, one of two things will happen. If the needed page is already in cache, the server moves that page from wherever it is in cache to the MRU end of the list, a logical I/O. All the other pages shuffle down toward the LRU end of the list as needed to make room. If the next page needed is not in cache, it must be read in from disk, a physical I/O. This means there isn't room in the cache for this newest page. The server will take the data page that is at the LRU end of the list and write it out to disk. All the other data pages move one spot over toward the LRU end of the list and the new page is moved from disk to the MRU end of the list.

With all this background, you need to observe the impacts this structure has on scalability, that is, the ability to keep adding more server engines and improve performance and/or workload. With only a single data cache, all server activity must go through this cache. OLTP activity will most likely need a relatively small number of data pages. If these are always in cache, the OLTP activity will require very little physical I/O. DSS queries, on the other hand, will often require more data pages than the data cache can hold. You need to realize what this means. When a single DSS query executes, the server will need to bring in more data pages than the cache can hold. This means the first page the DSS query needs will start at the MRU end of the list and will move all the way to the LRU end of the list before the query is satisfied. This also means that any other data page that was in cache previously will be pushed down to the LRU end of the list and written out to disk. Hence, a single DSS query can flush all of cache and thereby push out all the data pages that were supporting OLTP queries. As the next OLTP queries come along, they must wait while the required pages are read in to cache from disk. This slows all the OLTP queries until all the needed pages are back in cache. This process will slow the overall performance of the server. And, this process will be repeated each time a DSS query is executed.

Adding more engines wonít help since additional engines wonít affect this process. Further, having only one hash table will cause contention as more engines have to contend for access to the same hash table.

In System 11, the buffer manager supports multiple named caches and large I/Os. This means you can create named caches and assign database objects to them (see Figure 4–3). This allows you to isolate portions of cache for OLTP and DSS queries. Each named cache also has its own hash table which can reduce contention as you add more server engines. Large I/Os means the server can move data in larger chunks, up to 16K per I/O. In previous server versions, all I/O was done one 2K page at a time.

Named Cache

By default, when the System 11 SQL Server is installed, there is one cache, the default data cache. In previous server versions this cache was also called the data cache. In System 11, as with previous versions, the buffer manager takes care of the data cache portion of server memory. With System 11 you can create named caches. A named cache is simply a

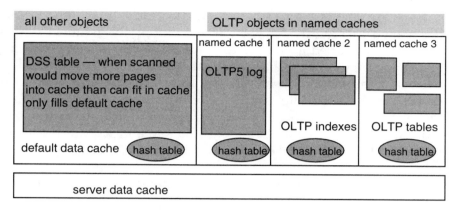

Figure 4–3. System 11 Named Caches

portion of the default data cache. You need to realize that each named cache you create reduces the size of the remaining default data cache. A named cache allows database objects to be assigned to a portion of server memory so that activity in other caches does not move the object out of memory. Frequently used lookup tables could be assigned to a named cache. A table needed for DSS queries could be assigned to another named cache. A DSS query that needs to scan a large table will only use the MRU-LRU page chain in the one named cache. The table scan will not be able to move the lookup table out of its own cache. This allows OLTP and DSS queries to access their own database objects without interfering with each other's cache access strategy.

You create each named cache or edit the configuration file to create them for you. You must have **sa_role** to create a named cache. Note that creating and changing any named caches require a server restart before the changes take effect. For each named cache you specify the size, name and the status. The status can be mixed (default), log-only or data-only. The status determines what database objects can be stored in the cache. Mixed cache can contain both data and transaction log pages. Log-only cache is for holding transaction log records only. Data-only cache is for data pages that are not part of the transaction log. After a named cache is created, it doesn't hold anything. Until one or more database objects are assigned to the named cache, it will not be used at all. You can assign a table an index or even an entire database to a named cache. If no database object is ever assigned to a named cache, the overall data cache available for storing other database objects will effectively be reduced by the size of the named cache.

113

Database objects are assigned to a named cache by binding the object to the named cache. Any database object that is not assigned to a named cache will be placed in the default data cache. If you bind an entire database to a named cache, then all the database objects in the database are bound to the named cache. This process of binding objects to named caches can become quite complex. You can assign a database to a named cache. You can then assign individual objects of that same database to other named caches. You can assign a table and its indexes to separate named caches. You can even assign a table and its clustered index to separate named caches.

Note that when you bind an object to a named cache, the server records this as a row in the system table *sysattributes*. Further, this is the only place where the binding is recorded. You can't tell what objects are bound to which named cache from the configuration file or from the output of **sp_configure**. If the server is running, you can use **sp_helpcache <cachename>** to see which objects are bound to a given named cache. However, if the server is not running, you have one of two situations to deal with. First, assume the server must be recovered. This could be due to a server crash, or if you are building a new server. Assuming that you have all the information needed to reconstruct the server and load the database dump, things will be fine. Since the system table *sysattributes* is stored in each user database, the details of which object are bound to which cache will be restored by recovering each user database. In the second case, you need to recover but you don't have all the dumps needed, and so forth. In this case, either you can't recover a user database at all, or you can only recover it to some time before the failure. Even if the data can be re-created, you won't have any way to re-create all of the object bindings. The bindings that are in the database dumps that you used for recovery will be restored. Any object bindings that have been created after that point will be lost. Therefore, you need to have the contents of *sysattributes* as part of the server configuration. Without this information, you can't completely rebuild the configuration of the server. However, the *sysattributes* table contains lots of other information that does not relate to object bindings. The best way to capture the information stored in *sysattributes* is to dump the output of the sp_helpcache command. This output will document all objects bound to all caches within the server. If you are recovering a database after a crash, or after moving it from another server, you should examine the contents of the *sysattributes* table within the recovered or moved database to see what cache bindings existed for objects in the database before you recovered or moved it. If this is the case, note that for a database that is bound to a named cache, this information is only recorded in the *sysattributes* table in the *master* database. If you are moving a database from another server, you would need to check the *master* database of the source server to see if the database had been bound to a named cache. This means you should have the output of `sp_helpcache` from the source server.

Here an example of how contorted this can all become. You decide to rebuild an existing server on another server machine. You decide to set-up all but one of the user databases on the new server machine. You have the configuration file from the original server and the database dumps from the user databases. Everything goes fine, and you start the new server. You figure that since you have one less user database, you should have more server resources for the others. But you don't. What happened? After much self-loathing, you trace your steps. The configuration file you used created all the named caches of the original server, but some of those named caches were dedicated to objects from the one user database that you didn't bring over to the new machine. Hence, the named caches got created, but nothing is bound to them. These named caches still take memory away from the default data cache. You can't use the memory you thought you had until you drop these named caches. You must be aware of what each named cache is doing and the resources that it is taking up. Further, you must remember that even the combination of **sp_configure** output and the configuration file don't tell you everything about the configuration of your server.

Named caches can be modified after creation, but there are restrictions you must be aware of. The default data cache can have only a status of mixed. The status for any named cache can't be changed from mixed to log-only if there are still nonlog objects bound to the cache. The size of any named cache can't be reduced below the default size of 512K. Similarly, the size of any named cache can't be increased above the total available for any new named caches. Note that you should never get close to this problem. The default data cache is used for all objects not bound to named caches, and for all server recovery. Hence, you do not want to have a small default data cache. You should not use most of the server memory available for data cache for named caches.

This illustrates the potential complexity of named cache—if you increased the size of a named cache so that the total memory for named caches even came close to the total memory available for data cache, then the default data cache would be reduced to near zero and the server would not be able to function. You must proceed carefully when creating named caches.

Deleting a named cache also has some restrictions. You must unbind all the objects that are currently bound to the named cache before you can drop (delete) the named cache. When the named cache is deleted, the space that was assigned to the named cache is reassigned to the default data cache. Note that the memory from the deleted named cache will not actually be reassigned until the server is restarted. Even though the named cache has been dropped, the objects that were bound to it are not moved out of memory. If you don't restart the server immediately, these objects will be moved to the default data cache when they are next accessed. When the server is restarted, all of cache is flushed and rebuilt.

Default Data Cache

The default data cache has several important characteristics. It exists by default when the server is created. It is a mixed cache, supporting both data and log pages. If you don't create any named caches, all of the server memory available for cache will be assigned to the default data cache. Each named cache that you create will take some memory away from the default data cache. The default data cache cannot be dropped. Further, you can't reduce its size to zero by creating named caches that take up all the space that was assigned to the default data cache. The default data cache is the only cache that the server can use for recovery, that is, loading database and transaction log dumps. This is another reason the default data cache must not be reduced too much by creating lots of named caches. If a named cache is dropped, the objects bound to that named cache revert to the default data cache. Finally, the default data cache, is, in all other respects, the same as any other named cache. The default data cache is the same as other named caches when it comes to what database objects can be bound, the process of binding and unbinding, and so forth.

Database Objects Bound to a Named Cache

A named cache serves no purpose unless at least one database object is assigned (bound) to it. You can bind a table, an index, a transaction log, and an entire database to a named cache (see Figure 4–4). A table and its

objects not bound to any cache

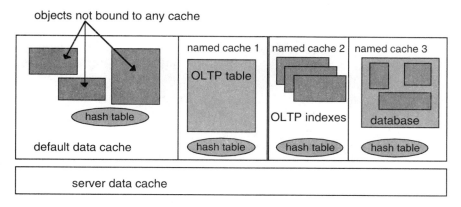

Figure 4–4. Objects Bound to Caches

associated nonclustered index(s) can be assigned to different named caches. Even a clustered index can be bound to a different named cache from that of the table's data. A database object can only be bound to one named cache at a time. Multiple objects can be bound to the same named cache. If a database is bound to a cache, the objects of that database are also bound to the same named cache. But, any of the objects within the database can be assigned to another named cache. If named caches are reconfigured, or the server is recovered and the named cache is no longer present, any database objects that were previously bound to the named cache will use the default data cache. Before binding an object to a cache, the object and the cache must already exist. If you want to assign a transaction log to a named cache, the status of that named cache must be mixed or log-only. If you want to ensure that only a transaction log is bound to that named cache, the status must be log-only. You must be in the master database to bind an entire database to a named cache.

You can't bind the *master* database to a named cache. Further, you can't bind any object within the *master* database to a named cache. However, you can bind a system table (and/or its index) of a user database to a named cache. A good example would be the table *sysindexes* and its index. This table is heavily used and is often a good candidate for binding to a named cache. Note that the database must be in single-user mode before you can bind a system table to a named cache.

Hash Tables

When the server needs to determine if a particular database page is in cache, the server looks at the hash table in the default data cache and then in the hash table in each named cache. This is much faster than having to search the chains of data pages to see which pages are in cache. With multiple server engines to take advantage of SMP hardware, the contention on a single hash table will increase as well. Having named caches allows you to reduce this contention. Multiple caches means there will be multiple hash tables as well since each named cache maintains its own separate hash table. When any server engine needs to look for a data page, it can look at the hash table in the named cache where the object is bound. Other server engines will probably be looking at a different hash table in another named (or default) cache. This reduces the contention among engines for the same hash table. This means more server engines can be used more efficiently because the bottleneck of waiting to access a single hash table has been removed.

Note that named caches have nothing to do with segments. Segments refer to storage of database objects on one or more server devices. Named caches refer to portions of memory. No matter what segments a database might have, any data page that is read or changed must be moved into memory (cache). Only when a data page is moved into memory does the concept of a named cache come into play. There is no relationship between the placement of a database object on segments (physical disk devices) and the named cache(s) used to store that data pages of the object in memory.

Syntax for Creating, Modifying, and Deleting Named Caches

Creating Named Cache

To create a named cache interactively,

```
1> sp_cacheconfig psycho_cache1, '10M'
2> go
```

Note that the units of the size of the named cache can be P (pages), K (kilobytes), M (megabytes) or G (gigabytes). Creating or changing named caches is a static server configuration change. You must restart the server for the changes to take effect.

You can also create one or more named caches by editing the configuration file and restarting the server,

```
[Named Cache: psycho_cache1]
cache size = 10M
cache status = mixed cache
```

Binding Objects to a Named Cache

Note that you can't bind objects with the configuration file. The information regarding which objects are bound to which named caches is stored in the system table *sysattributes*. This table is in each user database. To document the configuration of objects in named caches you must dump the contents of *sysattributes* for each user database, which you do by executing **sp_helpcache**.

To bind a table to the named cache just created,

```
1> sp_bindcache 'psycho_cache1', 'psycho_database', 'psycho_table1'
2> go
```

To bind the index of a table to a named cache,

```
1> sp_bindcache 'psycho_cache2', 'psycho_database', 'psycho_table1',
   'psycho_table1_index2'
2> go
```

For both of these examples, the table and the index are in the database *psycho_database*.

Unbinding these same objects would look like,

```
1> sp_unbindcache 'psycho_cache1', psycho_table1'
2> go
```

```
1> sp_unbindcache 'psycho_cache1', 'psycho_table1_index2'
2> go
```

Note that when unbinding, you don't specify the database the object belongs to.

You can also unbind all objects from a named cache with one command,

```
1> sp_unbindcache_all 'psycho_cache1'
2> go
```

Deleting named cache

You delete or drop a named cache by changing its size to zero,

```
1> sp_cacheconfig 'psycho_cache1', 0
2> go
```

This is not intuitive. Note that at first glance, this command appears to be creating a named cache. It is recommended that you first unbind all objects from the named cache before you drop it. This will remove the rows in the system table *sysattributes* that were created when the objects were bound to the named cache. You don't have to do this, but you do need to realize what the server is doing. If you delete a named cache, but don't first unbind all the objects of that named cache, the rows in *sysattributes* will remain. The server will mark each of the affected rows as "invalid." When the server is restarted, the server will ignore these rows, and the objects that were bound to the deleted named cache will be assigned to the default data cache. However, the rows are still there. Assume that, at some later time, you create a named cache with the same name as the deleted named cache. The rows in *sysattributes* that documented the objects bound in the previously deleted named cache are still there. When the server is restarted, the server will mark these rows as "valid." At that point, the object bindings that were in effect for the named cache before it was deleted have been restored. This is why it is recommended that you unbind all objects from a named cache before you delete a named cache. The commands for this would be:

```
1> sp_unbindcache_all 'psycho_cache1'
2> go
3> sp_cacheconfig 'psycho_cache1', 0
4> go
```

You can also delete a named cache by editing the configuration file to remove the lines that created the named cache and restarting the server.

Status of Named Caches

To see all the named caches and the names of the objects bound to them for the whole server,

```
1> sp_helpcache
2> go
```

Note that each named cache requires some memory to keep track of the various structures that make up the named cache. You can use **sp_help-cache** to compute what the overhead will be for any proposed named cache,

```
1> sp_helpcache '200M'
2> go

  10.38 Mb of overhead memory will be needed to manage a cache of
size 200M


(return status = 0)
```

This will compute the memory overhead required for a named cache that is 200 Mb large.

Named Caches and Server Configuration

In order to completely document the configuration of a SQL Server, you must have the output of **sp_configure**, the configuration file, and the output of **sp_helpcache**. The output of **sp_configure** documents the overall server configuration and tells you the default values and memory overhead of the configuration but does not document the configuration of the named caches or the objects bound to them. The configuration file documents the overall server configuration, and the named caches, but not which objects are bound to each named cache. The output of **sp_help-cache** tells you which objects are assigned to each named cache. Note that you can also see which objects within a database are bound to a named cache by examining the *sysattributes* table.

Named Cache Issues

Even after you comprehend all the details of how to create and modify named caches, you need to think about the issues surrounding the use of named caches in general. All the server memory that is dedicated to named caches is memory that is taken away from the default data cache. Also, recall that all database objects that are not bound to a named cache, and all server recovery operations, take place in the default data cache. You do not want to reduce the size of the default data cache too much. Each named cache also has some overhead. Overhead here means that some server memory is used just to keep track of the named cache. It is easy to create more named caches than you really need.

More server memory is always good. You must not try to compensate for insufficient server memory by constructing a complex named cache strategy. If all the parts of the database that the server needs to access are in cache, it doesn't really matter which objects are in which cache. Other than multiple hash tables that reduce contention among server engines to find data pages in cache, the benefit of named caches is reduced.

The sizing of a named cache is also important. Assume you want to create a named cache to hold a frequently accessed lookup table. Further assume that the access to the data pages within this table is random, that is that any query may access any data page. If the named cache is too small to hold all of this lookup table, then you may have more physical I/Os for queries that need to access that table than if you left it in the default data cache. If the queries require that the server read in data pages from disk, the server is constantly swapping pages into and out of the named cache. This requires physical I/O which is much more expensive (slower) than logical I/O. Assuming that the default data cache is larger than this named cache, as it should be, it would probably be better to leave the lookup table in the default data cache. However, if there are any queries that will flush all of the default data cache, they would then flush out the lookup table as well. Hence, you need to be worried about the size of the named cache and what the named cache will be used for. You then need to compare the advantages of the named cache against the need to monitor and maintain it. As the lookup table grows, will you need to resize the named cache? You then need to weigh all of this against the impact on overall server performance of reducing the default data cache by the size of the named cache.

Database objects that are bound to named caches should be accessed frequently. Each named cache is a portion of server memory that can't be used to help any queries except those that access the objects in the named cache. The benefit of named caches can only be determined by examining the balance between the queries that will always find their data in the named cache, and all the other queries that have to move data into and out of the remaining default data cache.

The more cache that is assigned to named caches, the less flexible the server configuration is. If you increase the percentage of server memory that is allocated to stored procedure cache and that reduces the data cache below that needed for all the named caches, the server won't start. Note that in previous versions of SQL Server this wouldn't have been a problem since there were no named caches. Similarly, you can create a configuration file which creates more named caches than there is overall default data cache to support them all. In this case, the server will not start with this configuration file.

When the server recovers, for whatever reason, all associated activity can use only the default data cache. For a server that supports lots of transactions, recovery will require applying many transactions in the transaction log dumps. The time needed to recover will be increased as the size of the default data cache is reduced to create named caches.

> You will often be told that named caches are beneficial in that they support a mixed workload of OLTP and DSS queries on the same server. You must see through this. Certainly, you can prevent a DSS table scan from flushing all OLTP data pages from cache by using named caches. However, there is much more to DSS work than just a named cache. To really support heavy production DSS, you should have a very different index structure than for OLTP. Hence, even though you can bind objects to separate named caches, that doesn't mean you have the indexing, and so forth, that you need for either DSS or OLTP. It is very difficult to tune a single server for both OLTP and DSS needs. Named caches do not solve this problem.

Which Objects to Bind

While the process of deciding which database objects need a named cache is lengthy and highly dependent on the environment of your individual server, there are several general recommendations that should be considered. *Tempdb* may be a good candidate for a named cache. Any lookup tables that are accessed frequently should probably be in their own named cache. The transaction log of any heavily used user database is another good candidate. The system table *sysindexes* in each user database may also benefit from a named cache. Much of the activity in any user database must access *sysindexes* no matter what the layout of the user database may be. Any table that is accessed frequently may benefit from having its indexes and table data in separate named caches. Note that this is different from assigning the table and its indexes to separate server device segments.

Examples—Named Cashes Command Syntax

Since the creation of named caches is related to buffer pools and large I/Os, one set of examples will be shown below for the integrated process, see Examples—Buffer Pools Control Syntax.

BUFFER MANAGER AND LARGE I/OS

Each named cache, including the default data cache, can be configured with multiple buffer pools. Each buffer pool is simply a linked list of data pages. Each named cache must have a 2K buffer pool and may also have some amount of its total space assigned to a 4K, 8K and a 16K buffer pool (see Figure 4–5). Previous versions of the SQL Server constrained all I/O operations to moving a single 2K page, and a buffer always meant a 2K data page. When a data page was moved into cache, it was always done one 2K page at a time. System 11 removes this constraint by allowing a single I/O to move from 2K to 16K (one to eight 2K pages). Now, a buffer can refer to a single 2K data page, or, a set of up to eight 2K data pages. Note that large I/Os are only relevant to physical I/O that moves data pages between physical disk and cache. All logical I/O that the server does when accessing data pages that are already in cache is still done one 2K data page at a time.

Buffer Pools

The way you configure this large I/O functionality that is new in System 11 is to configure the buffer pool(s) within each named cache. Each named cache, including the default cache, is made up of at least one buffer pool. A buffer is simply a pointer to a data page in memory. A buffer pool is a collection of pointers that keep track of the data pages in memory. A named cache is created by the server of the size you specify and is made up of 2K buffers. Such a named cache is said to have a 2K buffer pool. You can then break up the named cache into different portions, with each portion made up of buffers of a different size,—4K, 8K or 16K. So, if you create a named cache of 10 Mb, the named cache would initially consist of 10 Mb (5120 2K pages) all made up of 2K buffers. You could then configure

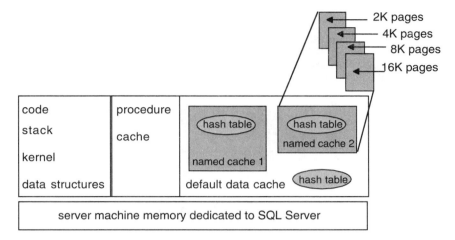

Figure 4–5. System 11 Buffer Pools

this named cache so that 2 Mb was configured to be made up of 64 16K buffers, where each buffer now points to a single 16K piece of memory. Now you will have a named cache that has an 8-Mb 2K buffer pool and 2-Mb 16K buffer pool. Note that each named cache has, at most, only one buffer pool for a particular buffer size. This means that any named cache can have, at most, only four buffer pools: one buffer pool for each of the possible buffer pool sizes of 2K, 4K, 8K and 16K. A hypothetical set of named caches and their associated buffer pools are shown in Figure 4–6.

You must be careful when discussing the "size" of a buffer pool. When you think of a "large" buffer pool, you need to be sure whether you are talking about the overall size of the buffer pool, or the size of the buffers within that buffer pool. For example, if you are told to use a larger buffer pool, does that mean increase the overall size of the pool from 2M to 10M? Or does it mean that you should increase the size of the buffers from 2K to 16K while the overall size of the buffer pool remains unchanged?

Buffer pool size is very confusing—a 2K buffer pool size means a buffer pool made up of buffers that are each 2K in size, but it sure sounds like a buffer pool of overall size 2K. A good example from the official documentation states that the "minimum buffer pool size is 512K, maximum buffer pool size is 16K." What this really means is that any buffer pool in any cache must be as big or bigger than 512K no matter what size buffers are in that pool, and, the biggest buffer allowed is 16K. Clear now?

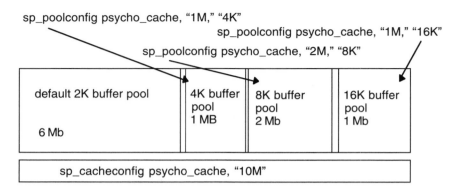

Figure 4–6. System 11 Configuring Buffer Pools

This must be from the same people who came up with the annual raise-pool concept wherein there are so many restrictions on how much of a raise any employee can get that after a while you just don't ask any more and just assume you will be getting the default 3 percent (2K?) raise.

As the server needs to move data into and out of the named cache, it will determine which size buffer is the most efficient and use that size. This only happens if the needed buffer pool exists within the named cache, and if the needed buffer pool has sufficient free buffers. If the server only needs to access a single 2K page of data then it will look for a free 2K buffer. If the server will be bringing in many pages, then it will try to use a 16K buffer for each I/O. Note that if the needed size buffer pool has not been created for the named cache, the server will not create the buffer pool on its own. Instead, the server will examine what size buffer pools have been created and if it can't find a free buffer of the desired size, it will use whatever is available. You can see which buffer pool size the server will actually use in the output of showplan. The output of showplan has been greatly improved in System 11. This is very useful because you can see what buffer pool the server will actually use. Even if you have created the needed buffer pool, the optimizer may not use it (if the number of pages returned is small for example) so it is always good to see exactly how the server will process any given query.

None of this changes the basic MRU/LRU functionality of the cache (see Figure 4–7). However, each buffer pool is set up as its own MRU/LRU page chain within the named cache. This means that buffers

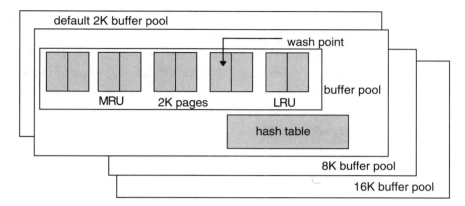

Figure 4–7.Buffer Pools and LRU/MRU Chains

(sets of data pages) may move down the MRU/LRU page chain of one buffer pool while other pages are moved independently on the MRU/LRU chain of another buffer pool. Any time the server needs to bring data into any cache, it will look for free space. If there isn't any free space, the server will move the oldest, least recently used (LRU), data back out to disk. Each named cache has its own MRU/LRU chain as well as its own hash table.

When to Use Large I/Os

Now that System 11 supports the use of large I/Os, you need to understand when you should use them. Server maintenance activities like bcp and dbcc can be greatly improved if these activities are using 16K buffer pools. Similarly, 16K buffer pools will speed up queries that update all (or almost) the rows of a table, since the server will need to scan the table. This assumes that the update isn't moving around throughout the table updating one row here and then jumping many pages to make the next update. Any query that will access most of the pages in a table, in the same order that those pages are physically arranged on disk, will benefit from large I/Os. Note that the magic here is that if you need all 16 data pages in the same sequence as they are on disk, you can read them all in with one I/O. At that point, the server doesn't need to do any physical I/O until all 8 data pages have been accessed.

Queries that involve joins among large tables, table scans of large tables and range scans may also benefit from the use of large I/Os. All access to the transaction log of a database should be improved by using a 4K buffer pool. Also, note that you can reconfigure the server for large buffer pools just for the off-hour period when you run your large batch jobs. This can speed up these batch processes and reduce the downtime required to complete such maintenance.

Creating Buffer Pools to Enable Large I/Os

No matter how beneficial buffer pools and large I/Os may be, they can't work their magic if the buffer pools are not created ahead of time. The syntax for this is

```
1> sp_poolconfig psycho_cache, '6M', '8K'
2> go
```

This will create a buffer pool that is 6 Mb large overall, made up of buffers that are 8 Kb each. This would be called an 8K buffer pool. Note the units for **sp_poolconfig**, like those of **sp_cacheconfig**, are P (2K pages), K (Kb), M (Mb), and G (Gb). When you first create a named cache, all of the cache is configured to be one buffer pool made up entirely of 2K buffers. You must then configure any additional buffer pools. Note that all the buffer pools of a named cache come out of the overall space that was originally assigned to the named cache. You can't increase the overall size of a named cache by creating buffer pools. Note that all this applies to the default data cache as well. You can also create the same buffer pool by adding to the configuration file and restarting the server.

```
[Named Cache: psycho_cache1]
cache size = 10M
cache status = mixed cache

[8K I/O Buffer Pool]
pool size = 6M
```

Unlike named caches, creating or changing buffer pools are dynamic server configuration changes and do not require a server restart to become effective. However, this is only true if the named cache that supports the buffer pools has already been created. There is a confusing subtly here. If you have a running server, and you create a named cache using **sp_cacheconfig** and then create a buffer pool, the buffer pool will not exist until the server is restarted. This is because the named cache doesn't exist until the server is restarted. While creating a buffer pool is a dynamic configuration change, if the named cache doesn't exist, the buffer pool can't either. In this case, creating the buffer pool does require the server restarting to bring the buffer pool, and the named cache, into existence.

The size of a buffer pools within a named cache can be modified. This means some amount of cache is shifted from one size buffer pool to another. For example, using the buffer pool created above,

sp_poolconfig psycho_cache, '1M', '4K', '8K'

will move 1 Mb of the overall named cache from the 8K buffer pool to the 4K buffer pool. This means that the overall size of the 8K buffer pool has been reduced from 6M to 5M. The overall size of the named cache has not changed; only the sizes of the buffer pools within the named cache. Another subtlety of this process now comes up. The server will move only whole buffers. The server will round up and only move the largest number of whole buffers that fit within the size change you requested.

Since modifying a buffer pool is a dynamic server configuration change, it can affect operations that are currently going on. Assume you were running bcp against a table that was in a named cache, and that named cache had most of its space assigned to a 16K buffer pool. If the named cache space assigned to the 16K buffer pool is then moved to a 2K buffer pool, the bcp will slow down as it begins to use the smaller 2K buffers for each physical I/O. A buffer pool can be deleted and the affected portion of cache will be returned to the default 2K buffer pool. The syntax is

sp_poolconfig psycho_cache, '0', '8K'

which will reduce the overall size of the 8K buffer pool to zero. The portion of the named cache that had been dedicated to supporting the 8K buffer pool will be reassigned to the 2K buffer pool.

There are numerous situations where you will need to reconfigure the buffer pools. You will need to modify buffer pools when the buffer pool is too small. This means the server needs larger buffers and must wait for them or use smaller buffers which reduce the benefit of large I/Os. You will also need to reconfigure the buffer pools if you need to reconfigure the server from supporting OLTP processing to periodic DSS processing.

There are also numerous restrictions that will affect your ability to reconfigure buffer pools. The overall size of all the buffer pools in a named cache cannot exceed the overall size of the named cache. Each named cache must have a 2K buffer pool whose overall size must not be less than 512K. The only allowed buffer sizes are 2K, 4K, 8K, and 16K. Any buffer pool that you create is taking space away from the 2K buffer pool.

Buffer Pool Details

A buffer pool is linked set of buffers, all of which are the same size, 2K for example. A buffer refers to a set of data pages. If the buffer pool is made up of 2K buffers, each buffer refers to only one data page. If the buffer pool is made up of 16K buffers, each buffer refers to 8 data pages. Before System 11, all the buffers were 2K, and since the server stores data in 2K pages, the term buffer wasn't seen very often, while the term data page was. With the ability to configure a separate buffer pool for 2K, 4K, 8K, and 16K buffers, the term buffer becomes important. The server still looks at all data as 2K pages, but it will move the data pages around in sets when buffer pools of buffers larger than the default 2K size are available. Each buffer pool implements the MRU/LRU strategy. This means the buffer that was most recently brought into memory (cache) will be at the MRU (most recently used) end of the buffer pool, and the oldest buffer in the pool will be at the opposite end of the buffer pool, the least recently used or LRU end. Initially, when the server starts up, the buffer pool is empty. As data pages are needed from disk, they are read into cache where they are stored in the buffers. The number of data pages moved from disk depends on the size of each buffer. When the server needs to access a data page, the server will take the buffer at the LRU end of the buffer pool, fill it with the data from disk, and move the buffer to the MRU end of the buffer pool. All the buffers in the buffer pool shift over as the newest buffer moves to the MRU end of the pool. As more data pages are needed from disk, the buffer pool starts to fill with the oldest buffers moving toward the LRU end of the buffer pool.

Once the buffer pool is full and the server needs to move more data into cache using this buffer pool, the server will go to the LRU end of the buffer pool and look for a free buffer. If all the buffers are already being used, the server must write the LRU buffer out to disk to preserve the data in the buffer that may be different from the same data page or pages out on disk. Then it can use the LRU buffer to move more data into cache. Recall that the server does not move changed data pages out of cache until a checkpoint occurs or, as in this case, the server needs to free up some pages in cache.

With System 11 you can also configure the wash point for a named cache. The wash point specifies how far along the MRU/LRU chain a given buffer can move before the server will check the buffer for any changes in its data pages (dirty pages). If any of the pages have changed, the server will write the buffer to disk. This means that all the buffers between the wash point and the LRU end of the buffer pool should be clean. A clean buffer does not need to be written to disk when the server needs the buffer to move new data from disk into cache. The server will run faster if it can find free or clean buffers most of the time. There is a trade off on setting the wash point. If it is set too far to the MRU end of the buffer pool, then the server will spend more time writing changed (dirty) buffers out to disk. If the wash point is too far towards the LRU end of the buffer pool, the server will not be able to find a free buffer as often as it needs to, and this means the server has to write the buffer out to disk before it can use it.

Large I/O issues

There are many details you must watch for when dealing with named caches. If you have a large amount of default data cache, and only a few named caches which take up a small fraction of the overall cache, you will avoid many problems. If you create a more complex named cache or buffer pool scheme, be aware of the many potential problems you may run into.

When you create a named cache, the space used comes from the 2K buffer pool within the default data cache. If you were to configure the default data cache so that it had most of its overall space assigned to buffer pools other than 2K, you could find that you couldn't create any more named caches (see Figure 4–8).

A stored procedure won't be able to make use of a larger buffer pool unless that buffer pool exists at the time the stored procedure is compiled. If you change the named caches, or the buffer pool sizes within a named cache, you may need to recompile any stored procedure that would bene-fit from having the different buffer pools.

The server will not create the necessary named caches, object bindings, or buffer pools for you. While the optimizer may detect a benefit from using a specific size buffer pool, if all the infrastructure isn't already in place, the server will use only what is available. If you don't configure any buffer pools in any named caches, the server will have to use the default 2K buffers that are the only buffer pools available.

Many of the situations where buffer pool changes appear to be the best answer may be solved better by adding more memory to the server machine. Similarly, if you have a mixed workload of OLTP and DSS

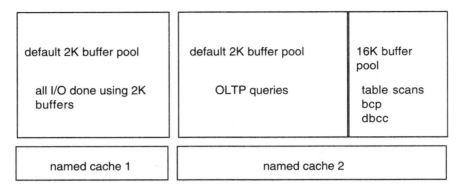

Figure 4–8. Named Caches Take Space from Default Data Cache

queries, moving some of the workload to another server machine may well be a better solution. Doing this effectively adds more memory to the overall server system. Rather than trying to dynamically modify which server tasks get how much of what size buffer pool, try to set up enough buffers of all the needed sizes to satisfy the server's workload. This means enough memory or moving portions of the workload to another server machine.

 You should consider the DBA resources you will need to keep track of these dynamic buffer pool configurations, documentation, training, trouble shooting, and so forth. Some of this effort may also backfire when there is any change to the operational schedule. If you need to recover from a failure and the server is configured for lots of named caches when what you need it lots of default cache, will you, or the DBA who gets paged, remember all of this detail and know what to do about it?

Examples—Buffer Pools Command Syntax

Before any named caches are created only the default data cache is present and no objects have been bound. Note: Config Size = 0.00 for default data cache is normal.

```
1> sp_helpcache
2> go
   Cache Name        Config Size     Run Size      Overhead
default data cache    0.00 Mb       28.58 Mb       1.18 Mb
```

132

```
Memory Available For          Memory Configured
   Named Caches               To Named Caches
     22.58 Mb                      0.00 Mb
```

There is 22.58 Mb of memory left over that will be allocated to the default cache

Cache Binding Information:

```
Cache Name       Entity Name       Type       Index Name       Status
```

(return status = 0)

Create a named cache

```
1> sp_cacheconfig psycho_cache1, '10M'
go

    0
```

The change is completed. The SQL Server must be rebooted for the change to take effect.

(return status = 0)

Error Log Message as Named Cache is Created

```
00:96/06/05 19:17:04.13—Server   configuration file
'/home/sybase/11.0.1/PSYCHO11.cfg' has been written and the previous
version has been renamed to '/home/sybase/11.0.1/PSYCHO11.002'.
```

Check Existing Caches

Note that run size = 0.00 means cache hasn't been created yet.

```
1> sp_helpcache
2> go
Cache Name              Config Size      Run Size      Overhead
default data cache         0.00 Mb       22.58 Mb      1.18 Mb
psycho_cache1             10.00 Mb        0.00 Mb      0.00 Mb

Memory AvailableFor           Memory Configured
   Named Caches               To Named Caches
     22.58 Mb                     10.00 Mb
```

There is 12.58 Mb of memory left over that will be allocated to the default cache

```
───────────────────── Cache Binding Information: ─__ ─────────

Cache Name        Entity Name           Type        Index Name        Status
(return status = 0)
```

Check Existing Caches

Note: Status of Pend/Act means cache hasn't been created yet. sp_cacheconfig gives more details about each named cache and buffer pools. sp_helpcache gives more details about memory available and overhead

```
1> sp_cacheconfig
2> go
    Cache Name          Status          Type        Config Value     Run Value
default data cache     Active          Default         0.00 Mb       22.58 Mb
  psycho_cache1         Pend/Act        Mixed          10.00 Mb        0.00 Mb
                                        Total          10.00 Mb       22.58 Mb

Cache: default data cache,   Status: Active,   Type: Default
        Config Size: 0.00 Mb,   Run Size: 22.58 Mb
```

IO Size	Wash Size	Config Size	Run Size
2 Kb	512 Kb	0.00 Mb	22.58 Mb

```
(return status = 0)
```

Check Individual Named Cache

```
1> sp_helpcache psycho_cache1
2> go
    Cache Name          Config Size     Run Size      Overhead
  psycho_cache1          10.00 Mb        0.00 Mb       0.00 Mb

───────────────────── Cache Binding Information: ─__ ─────────

Cache Name        Entity Name      Type        Index Name        Status

(return status = 0)
```

Named cache won't really exist until server restart, but the configuration file has been changed.

```
[Named Cache:psycho_cache1]
     cache size = 10M
     cache status = mixed cache
```

Attempt Creating Buffer Pool in Named Cache. You can't create a buffer pool in named cache until named cache is really created.

```
1> sp_poolconfig psycho_cache1, '6M', '8K'
2> go
The source pool (1p buffers, total size 0) is not large enough to
satisfy the request to move 6144Kb of memory

(return status = 1)
```

Restart Server—Config Size = Run Size. Named cache has been created.

```
1> sp_helpcache
2> go
   Cache Name          Config Size      Run Size       Overhead
default data cache        0.00 Mb       12.56 Mb        0.65 Mb
  psycho_cache1          10.00 Mb       10.00 Mb        0.53 Mb


Memory AvailableFor              Memory Configured
   Named Caches                  To Named Caches
     22.58 Mb                        10.00 Mb


There is 12.58 Mb of memory left over that will be allocated to the
default cache
```

```
——————————————— Cache Binding Information: ——————————————

Cache Name        Entity Name        Type        Index Name      Status
(return status = 0)
```

Create Buffer Pool in Named Cache With 6 Mb overall size, made up of 8K buffers

```
1> sp_poolconfig psycho_cache1, '6M', '8K'
2> go
 (return status = 0)
```

Server Error Log Documents Changed Configuration File

```
00:96/06/05 19:24:53.30—Server  configuration file
'/home/sybase/11.0.1/PSYCHO11.cfg' has been written and the previous
version has been renamed to '/home/sybase/11.0.1/PSYCHO11.003'.
```

Check Configuration of Buffer Pools for Specific Named Cache

```
1> sp_poolconfig psycho_cache1
2> go
```

Cache Name	Status	Type	Config Value	Run Value
psycho_cache1	Active	Mixed	10.00 Mb	10.00 Mb
		Total	10.00 Mb	10.00 Mb

```
Cache: psycho_cache1,   Status: Active,   Type: Mixed
       Config Size: 10.00 Mb,  Run Size: 10.00 Mb
```

IO Size	Wash Size	Config Size	Run Size
2 Kb	512 Kb	0.00 Mb	4.00 Mb
8 Kb	2048 Kb	6.00 Mb	6.00 Mb

```
(return status = 0)
```

Named Cache Portion of Configuration File Now Looks Like

```
[Named Cache:default data cache]
     cache size = DEFAULT
     cache status = default data cache

[Named Cache:psycho_cache1]
     cache size = 10M
     cache status = mixed cache

[8K I/O Buffer Pool]
     pool size = 6.0000M
     wash size = DEFAULT
```

Bind Table to Named Cache

```
1> sp_bindcache psycho_cache1, admindb, def_actions
2> go
(return status = 0)
```

Check Named Cache to See Object Bindings.
Note Status = V for a valid object binding.

```
1> sp_helpcache psycho_cache1
2> go
```

Cache Name	Config Size	Run Size	Overhead
psycho_cache1	10.00 Mb	10.00 Mb	0.53 Mb

──────────────── **Cache Binding Information:** ─ __ ──────────

Cache Name	Entity Name	Type	Index Name	Status
psycho_cache1	admindb.dbo.def_actions	table		V

```
(return status = 0)
```

Object Binding Recorded in Sysattributes of User Database.
Note: class = 3 for such entries.

```
1> select * from sysattributes
2> go
```

class	attribute	object_type	object_cinfo	object
3	0	T	NULL	1280007591

object_info1	object_info2	object_info3	int_value
NULL	NULL	NULL	1

char_value	text_value	image_value	comments
psycho_cache1	NULL	NULL	NULL

```
...
...
...
```

```
(17 rows affected)
```

Confirm Object That Is Bound

```
1> select object_name(1280007591)
2> go
_____

 def_actions

(1 row affected)
```

Create Second Named Cache

```
1> sp_cacheconfig psycho_cache2, '1M'
2> go
_____-
     0
The change is completed. The SQL Server must be rebooted for the
change to take effect

(return status = 0)
```

Server Error log Documents Change to Configuration File

```
00:96/06/05 19:39:41.36—Server  configuration file
'/home/sybase/11.0.1/PSYCHO11.cfg' has been written and the previous
version has been renamed to '/home/sybase/11.0.1/PSYCHO11.004'.
```

Check Named Cache Configuration. Status is Pend/Act for new named cache. New named cache only has default 2K buffer pool.

```
1> sp_cacheconfig
2> go
```

Cache Name	Status	Type	Config Value	Run Value
default data cache	Active	Default	0.00 Mb	12.56 Mb
psycho_cache1	Active	Mixed	10.00 Mb	10.00 Mb
psycho_cache2	Pend/Act	Mixed	1.00 Mb	0.00 Mb
		Total	11.00 Mb	22.56 Mb

```
Cache: default data cache,  Status: Active,  Type: Default
       Config Size: 0.00 Mb,  Run Size: 12.56 Mb
```

IO Size	Wash Size	Config Size	Run Size
2 Kb	512 Kb	0.00 Mb	12.56 Mb

```
Cache: psycho_cache1,    Status: Active,    Type: Mixed
        Config Size: 10.00 Mb,    Run Size: 10.00 Mb

        IO Size            Wash Size            Config Size         Run Size
         2 Kb               512 Kb              0.00 Mb            4.00 Mb
         8 Kb              2048 Kb              6.00 Mb            6.00 Mb

(return status = 0)
```

Named Cache Portion of Configuration File Now Looks Like

```
[Named Cache:default data cache]
     cache size = DEFAULT
     cache status = default data cache

[Named Cache:psycho_cache1]
     cache size = 10M
     cache status = mixed cache

[8K I/O Buffer Pool]
     pool size = 6.0000M
     wash size = DEFAULT

[Named Cache:psycho_cache2]
     cache size = 1M
     cache status = mixed cache
```

Restart Server—Error log shows size and buffer pools for named caches.

```
00:96/06/05 19:49:44.84 kernel
    Network and device connection limit is 1014.
00:96/06/05 19:49:44.86 server
    Number of proc buffers allocated: 3039.
00:96/06/05 19:49:44.94 server
    Number of blocks left for proc headers: 3086.
00:96/06/05 19:49:44.94 server
    Memory allocated for the default data cache cache: 11768 Kb
00:96/06/05 19:49:44.96 server
    Size of the 2K memory pool: 11768 Kb
00:96/06/05 19:49:44.96 server
    Memory allocated for the psycho_cache1 cache: 10240 Kb
00:96/06/05 19:49:44.96 server
    Size of the 2K memory pool: 4096 Kb
```

```
00:96/06/05 19:49:44.97 server
    Size of the 8K memory pool: 6144 Kb
00:96/06/05 19:49:44.97 server
    Memory allocated for the psycho_cache2 cache: 1024 Kb
00:96/06/05 19:49:44.97 server
    Size of the 2K memory pool: 1024 Kb
00:96/06/05 19:49:44.98 kernel  Initializing virtual device 0,
```

Check Named Caches After Server Restart

```
1> sp_helpcache
2> go
```

Cache Name	Config Size	Run Size	Overhead
default data cache	0.00 Mb	11.49 Mb	0.60 Mb
psycho_cache1	10.00 Mb	10.00 Mb	0.53 Mb
psycho_cache2	1.00 Mb	1.00 Mb	0.11 Mb

Memory AvailableFor Named Caches	Memory Configured To Named Caches
22.52 Mb	11.00 Mb

There is 11.52 Mb of memory left over that will be allocated to the default cache

─────────────────── Cache Binding Information: ─ __ ───────────

Cache Name	Entity Name	Type	Index Name	Status
psycho_cache1	admindb.dbo.def_actions	table		V

```
(return status = 0)
```

Check Named Caches with sp_cacheconfig—
Status is active for new named cache.

```
1> sp_cacheconfig
2> go
```

Cache Name	Status	Type	Config Value	Run Value
default data cache	Active	Default	0.00 Mb	11.49 Mb
psycho_cache1	Active	Mixed	10.00 Mb	10.00 Mb
psycho_cache2	Active	Mixed	1.00 Mb	1.00 Mb
		Total	11.00 Mb	22.49 Mb

```
Cache: default data cache,    Status: Active,    Type: Default
       Config Size: 0.00 Mb,    Run Size: 11.49 Mb
```

IO Size	Wash Size	Config Size	Run Size
2 Kb	512 Kb	0.00 Mb	11.49 Mb

```
Cache: psycho_cache1,    Status: Active,    Type: Mixed
       Config Size: 10.00 Mb,    Run Size: 10.00 Mb
```

IO Size	Wash Size	Config Size	Run Size
2 Kb	512 Kb	0.00 Mb	4.00 Mb
8 Kb	2048 Kb	6.00 Mb	6.00 Mb

```
Cache: psycho_cache2,    Status: Active,    Type: Mixed
       Config Size: 1.00 Mb,    Run Size: 1.00 Mb
```

IO Size	Wash Size	Config Size	Run Size
2 Kb	204 Kb	0.00 Mb	1.00 Mb

```
(return status = 0)
```

Delete or Drop Named Cache—Change size of named cache to zero.

Named Cache Has no Objects Bound

```
1> sp_cacheconfig psycho_cache2, '0'
2> go
The change is completed. The SQL Server must be rebooted for the
change to take effect.
(return status = 0)
```

Server Error log Documents Change to Configuration File

```
00:96/06/05 19:51:49.62—Server  configuration file
'/home/sybase/11.0.1/PSYCHO11.cfg' has been written and the previous
version has been renamed to '/home/sybase/11.0.1/PSYCHO11.007'.
```

Check Named Caches—Config Size = 0.00 means named cache will be deleted after server restart.

```
1> sp_helpcache
2> go
```

Cache Name	Config Size	Run Size	Overhead
default data cache	0.00 Mb	11.49 Mb	0.60 Mb
psycho_cache1	10.00 Mb	10.00 Mb	0.53 Mb
psycho_cache2	0.00 Mb	1.00 Mb	0.11 Mb

Memory AvailableFor Named Caches	Memory Configured To Named Caches
22.52 Mb	10.00 Mb

There is 12.52 Mb of memory left over that will be allocated to the default cache

Cache Binding Information:

Cache Name	Entity Name	Type	Index Name	Status
psycho_cache1	admindb.dbo.def_actions	table		V

(return status = 0)

Check Named Caches With sp_cacheconfig

Status = Act/Del means named cache will be deleted after server restart.

```
1> sp_cacheconfig
2> go
```

Cache Name	Status	Type	Config Value	Run Value
default data cache	Active	Default	0.00 Mb	11.49 Mb
psycho_cache1	Active	Mixed	10.00 Mb	10.00 Mb
psycho_cache2	Act/Del	Mixed	0.00 Mb	1.00 Mb
		Total	10.00 Mb	22.49 Mb

Cache: default data cache, Status: Active, Type: Default
Config Size: 0.00 Mb, Run Size: 11.49 Mb

IO Size	Wash Size	Config Size	Run Size
2 Kb	512 Kb	0.00 Mb	11.49 Mb

```
Cache: psycho_cache1,    Status: Active,    Type: Mixed
      Config Size: 10.00 Mb,    Run Size: 10.00 Mb
```

IO Size	Wash Size	Config Size	Run Size
2 Kb	512 Kb	0.00 Mb	4.00 Mb
8 KB	2048 Kb	6.00Mb	6.00MB

```
Cache: psycho_cache2,    Status: Act/Del,    Type: Mixed
      Config Size: 0.00 Mb,    Run Size: 1.00 Mb
```

IO Size	Wash Size	Config Size	Run Size
2 Kb	204 Kb	0.00 Mb	1.00 Mb

```
(return status = 0)
```

Named Cache Portion of Configuration File Now Looks Like

```
[Named Cache:default data cache]

      cache size = DEFAULT
      cache status = default data cache

[Named Cache:psycho_cache1]
      cache size = 10M
      cache status = mixed cache

[8K I/O Buffer Pool]
      pool size = 6.0000M
      wash size = DEFAULT
```

Drop Named Cache That Has Object Binding

```
1> sp_cacheconfig psycho_cache1, '0'
2> go
The change is completed. The SQL Server must be rebooted for the
change to take effect.
(return status = 0)
```

Server Error log Documents Change to Configuration File

```
00:96/06/05 19:56:03.67—Server  configuration file
'/home/sybase/11.0.1/PSYCHO11.cfg' has been written and the previous
version has been renamed to '/home/sybase/11.0.1/PSYCHO11.008'.
```

Named Cache Portion of Configuration File Now Looks Like

```
[Named Cache:default data cache]
     cache size = DEFAULT
     cache status = default data cache
```

Check Named Caches

Config Size = 0.00 means named cache will be deleted at server restart.

Object Binding for Deleted Named Cache Still Valid

```
1> sp_helpcache
2> go
```

Cache Name	Config Size	Run Size	Overhead
default data cache	0.00 Mb	11.49 Mb	0.60 Mb
psycho_cache1	0.00 Mb	10.00 Mb	0.53 Mb
psycho_cache2	0.00 Mb	1.00 Mb	0.11 Mb

Memory AvailableFor Named Caches	Memory Configured To Named Caches
22.52 Mb	0.00 Mb

There is 22.52 Mb of memory left over that will be allocated to the default cache

```
——————————————— Cache Binding Information: —__——————————
```

Cache Name	Entity Name	Type	Index Name	Status
psycho_cache1	admindb.dbo.def_actions	table		V

```
(return status = 0)
```

Check Named Caches

Status = Act/Del means named cache will be deleted at server restart.

```
1> sp_cacheconfig
2> go
```

Cache Name	Status	Type	Config Value	Run Value
default data cache	Active	Default	0.00 Mb	11.49 Mb
psycho_cache1	Active	Mixed	0.00 Mb	10.00 Mb
psycho_cache2	Act/Del	Mixed	0.00 Mb	1.00 Mb
		Total	0.00 Mb	22.49 Mb

```
Cache: default data cache,    Status: Active,    Type: Default
       Config Size: 0.00 Mb,    Run Size: 11.49 Mb
```

IO Size	Wash Size	Config Size	Run Size
2 Kb	512 Kb	0.00 Mb	11.49 Mb

```
Cache: psycho_cache1,    Status: Active,    Type: Mixed
       Config Size: 10.00 Mb,    Run Size: 10.00 Mb
```

IO Size	Wash Size	Config Size	Run Size
2 Kb	512 Kb	0.00 Mb	4.00 Mb
8 KB	2048 Kb	6.00Mb	6.00MB

```
Cache: psycho_cache2,    Status: Act/Del,    Type: Mixed
       Config Size: 0.00 Mb,    Run Size: 1.00 Mb
```

IO Size	Wash Size	Config Size	Run Size
2 Kb	204 Kb	0.00 Mb	1.00 Mb

```
(return status = 0)
```

Check Specific Named Cache

Buffer pools still exist for deleted named cache.

```
1> sp_poolconfig psycho_cache1
2> go
```

Cache Name	Status	Type	Config Value	Run Value
psycho_cache1	Act/Del	Mixed	0.00 Mb	10.00 Mb
		Total	0.00 Mb	10.00 Mb

```
Cache: psycho_cache2,    Status: Act/Del,    Type: Mixed
       Config Size: 0.00 Mb,    Run Size: 10.00 Mb
```

IO Size	Wash Size	Config Size	Run Size
2 Kb	204 Kb	0.00 Mb	1.00 Mb
8 Kb	2048 Kb	6.00 Mb	6.00 Mb

```
(return status = 0)
```

System Table sysattributes Still Has Entry for Object Binding

```
3            0 T         NULL                1280007591
             NULL        NULL      NULL          1
psycho_cache1
NULL
NULL
NULL
```

Restart Server—Error log shows only default data cache remains.

```
00:96/06/05 20:00:32.05 server
    Number of proc buffers allocated: 3042.
00:96/06/05 20:00:32.16 server
    Number of blocks left for proc headers: 3091.
00:96/06/05 20:00:32.16 server
    Memory allocated for the default data cache cache: 23120 Kb
00:96/06/05 20:00:32.21 server
    Size of the 2K memory pool: 23120 Kb
00:96/06/05 20:00:32.21 kernel  Initializing virtual device 0,
...
...
...
```

Server Error Log Shows Object Binding for Deleted Cache Marked Invalid

```
...
...
...
00:96/06/05 20:00:37.60 server   Recovering database 'admindb'.
00:96/06/05 20:00:37.61 server
    Recovery dbid 4 ckpt (31286,32)
00:96/06/05 20:00:37.61 server
    Recovery no active transactions before ckpt.
00:96/06/05 20:00:38.90 server  Cache binding for database '4',
object '1280007591', index '0' is being marked invalid in
Sysattributes.
00:96/06/05 20:00:38.92 server
    The transaction log in the database 'admindb' will use I/O
size of 2 Kb.
00:96/06/05 20:00:38.97 server
    Database 'admindb' is now online.
```

Entry for Bound Object in Remains in sysattributes

but with Ninth column = 0

```
3              0 T        NULL              1280007591
               NULL    NULL       NULL          0
    psycho_cache1
    NULL
    NULL
    NULL
```

Check Named Caches

```
1> sp_helpcache
2> go
   Cache Name          Config Size      Run Size      Overhead
default data cache       0.00 Mb        22.58 Mb       1.18 Mb


Memory AvailableFor              Memory Configured
  Named Caches                   To Named Caches
   22.58 Mb                         0.00 Mb
There is    22.58 Mb of memory left over that will be allocated to
the default cache
```

```
─────────────────── Cache Binding Information: ─ ──────────────
Cache Name        Entity Name        Type       Index Name    Status

(return status = 0)
1> sp_cacheconfig
2> go
   Cache Name       Status        Type      Config Value    Run Value
default data cache  Active       Default       0.00 Mb       22.58 Mb
                                 Total         0.00 Mb       22.58 Mb
─────────────────────────────────────────────────────────────────────
Cache: default data cache,   Status: Acttve,   Type: default
       Config Size: 0.00 Mb,   Run Size: 22.58 Mb

   IO Size          Wash Size         Config Size      Run Size
    2 Kb            512 Kb             0.00 Mb         22.58 Mb

(return status = 0)
```

Create Same Named Cache Again

```
1> sp_cacheconfig psycho_cache1, '10M'
go
------
   0
The change is completed. The SQL Server must be rebooted for the
change to take effect.

(return status = 0)
```

Check Named Caches Before Restarting Server

Note: Status = I for the invalid object binding.

```
1> sp_helpcache
2> go
   Cache Name        Config Size      Run Size      Overhead
default data cache    0.00 Mb        22.58 Mb       1.18 Mb
  psycho_cache1      10.00 Mb         0.00 Mb       0.00 Mb


Memory AvailableFor               Memory Configured
  Named Caches                     To Named Caches
    22.58 Mb                          10.00 Mb

There is 12.58 Mb of memory left over that will be allocated to the
default cache
```

```
------------------------ Cache Binding Information: -__----------------

Cache Name            Entity Name           Type   Index Name    Status
  psycho_cache1    admindb.dbo.def_actions   table                  1

(return status = 0)
```

Restart Server—Error log shows named cache sizes and buffer pools.

```
00:96/06/06 08:16:02.02 serveïr
    Memory allocated for the default data cache cache: 12866 Kb
00:96/06/06 08:16:02.04 server
    Size of the 2K memory pool: 12866 Kb
00:96/06/06 08:16:02.04 server
    Memory allocated for the psycho_cache1 cache: 10240 Kb
00:96/06/06 08:16:02.06 server  Size of the 2K memory pool: 10240 Kb
00:96/06/06 08:16:02.06 kernel  Initializing virtual device 0,
```

Check Named Caches

Note: object binding for named cache that was dropped and re-created is now valid. This is why you should unbind objects from a cache before dropping. Bindings could be re-created unintentionally later on.

```
1> sp_helpcache
2> go
```

Cache Name	Config Size	Run Size	Overhead
default data cache	0.00 Mb	12.56 Mb	0.65 Mb
psycho_cache1	10.00 Mb	10.00 Mb	0.53 Mb

Memory AvailableFor Named Caches	Memory Configured To Named Caches
22.58 Mb	10.00 Mb

```
There is   12.58 Mb of memory left over that will be allocated to
the default cache
```

Cache Binding Information:

Cache Name	Entity Name	Type	Index Name	Status
psycho_cache1	admindb.dbo.def_actions	table		V

```
(return status = 0)
```

Server Error Log Documents Object Binding Being Marked as Valid

```
00:96/06/06 08:16:07.49 server   Recovering database 'admindb'.
00:96/06/06 08:16:07.50 server   Recovery dbid 4 ckpt (31287,2)
00:96/06/06 08:16:07.50 server
    Recovery no active transactions before ckpt.
00:96/06/06 08:16:08.80 server   Cache binding for database '4',
object '1280007591', index '0' is being marked valid in
Sysattributes.
00:96/06/06 08:16:08.82 server
    The transaction log in the database 'admindb' will use I/O
size of 2 Kb.
00:96/06/06 08:16:08.87 server
    Database 'admindb' is now online.
```

Check sp_help Output of Table Bound to Named Cache

```
1> select db_name()
2> go
 _____

 admindb

(1 row affected)
1> sp_help def_actions
2> go
```

Name	Owner	Type
def_actions	dbo	user table

Data_located_on_segment	When_created
default	Jun 29 1994 8:13PM

Column_name	Type	Length	Prec	Scale
Nulls	Default_name	Rule_name	Identity	
path_key	varchar	20	NULL	NULL
0 NULL	NULL	0		
...				
...				
...				
partner_code	varchar	15	NULL	NULL
1 NULL	NULL	0		

attribute_class	attribute	int_value	char_value	comments
buffer manager	cache binding	1	psycho_cache1	NULL

```
           index_name                      index_description
        def_actions_idx       clustered,unique located on default
           index_keys              index_max_rows_per_page
        path_key,seqnum                         0
No defined keys for this object.
Object is not partitioned.

(1 row affected, return status = 0)
```

QUERY OPTIMIZATION AND THE SYSTEM 11 BUFFER MANAGER

Introduction

The System 11 query optimizer has been improved so it is aware of the buffer manager and will consider large I/Os as part of the optimization process. The optimizer can also be told to use a prefetch strategy or a fetch-and-discard (MRU) strategy. Most of the time, the server will perform best when the defaults are used for all these features. Note that while you can request either of these strategies, that doesn't mean the optimizer is required to do so. The optimizer will determine if either of these strategies is beneficial before using them.

Prefetch Cache Strategy

Since the System 11 server supports large I/Os, the optimizer can "prefetch" data, that is, bring into cache more data than is requested (see Figure 4–9). This can improve server performance since most of the time the next data page needed for a query will be very close to the previous data page on disk. Large I/Os can bring such collocated data pages into cache at once reducing the need to read from disk multiple times. The prefetch cache strategy is effective only if the data is relatively clustered. For some queries, prefetch may make table scanning more efficient than using indexes since so much more data is brought in for each single physical I/O. The default is for server to use prefetch (large I/Os). Recall that any needed large buffer pools must exist before the server can make use of this prefetch strategy.

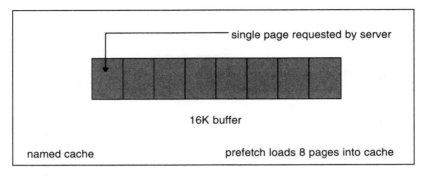

Figure 4–9. Pre-fetch Strategy

Fetch-and-Discard Cache Strategy

The server can also use the fetch-and-discard strategy (see Figure 4–10). This brings data pages into cache at the LRU end of the buffer pool so that these data pages are immediately ready for reuse by the server. Normally, the data pages that have most recently been brought into the buffer pool are placed at the MRU end of the pool. This means they would have to move down the chain to the LRU end before they would be moved out of cache. This also means they would force all other pages out of cache as they moved along the chain from MRU to LRU. Using the fetch-and-discard strategy prevents flushing other data pages out of cache. This can be useful for queries that simply need to select from a large number of data pages. The fetch-and-discard strategy can be used to keep DSS-related cache activity from flushing OLTP-related data pages out of cache.

Figure 4–10 Fetch-and-Discard Strategy

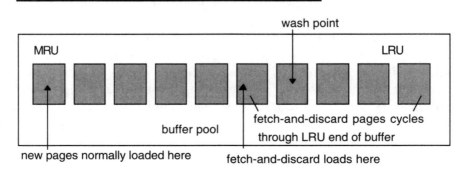

Query Optimization and Cache Strategy

To determine the most efficient (least physical I/O) way to process a query, the optimizer will examine two approaches. First, the query optimizer can use 'hints' specified by the user. Second, the optimizer will analyze the cost, in terms of physical and logical I/O, of the various possible cache strategies. The optimizer will then use the optimal strategy, the one with the lowest cost in terms of overall I/O. You can specify hints for large I/Os, fetch-and-discard and large tables joins. Various hints can be specified at the object, session, or query levels. A hint at the object level will override a hint at the session level, and so forth. See the manuals for more details on the syntax and hierarchy of setting the cache strategy.

For example, if the application is OLTP, you can disable large I/O strategy at the object level to ensure that all data brought into cache is moved in using small buffers. The syntax of the select statement has changed to support specification of prefetch size (size of large I/O to use) for an individual query. You can also specify the prefetch and fetch-and-discard strategies using sp_cachestrategy. Note that the output of showplan also shows exactly what the optimizer chose to do with the user hints, and so forth.

While the user can affect the cache strategy used by way of hints, note that any time you change the cache strategy that will be used for a table or index, any stored procedure that uses that table will be automatically recompiled to make use of the new strategy.

The query optimizer looks at many things to minimize logical and physical I/Os. Note that physical I/Os are much more costly than logical I/Os. When the optimizer is going through this process, it looks at the tables the query is accessing and looks at the named cache the table is bound to. The optimizer considers the benefits of using large I/Os and examines the buffer pools available in the relevant named caches. All this analysis is done for each single query. For the case of large table joins, the server would prefer to have the smaller of two tables be the inner table stored in a named cache. The larger outer table that will be accessed less often will then be brought into cache using the fetch-and-discard strategy.

The query optimizer will examine a query and determine how many rows will be returned. If a large number of rows will be returned, the optimizer will prefer using large I/Os. However, the larger buffer pool must exist in the named cache where the table is bound for this to be of any benefit. If the number of rows returned will be small, the optimizer will use the default 2K buffer pool to minimize physical and logical I/Os. Note that even though the query optimizer may determine that large I/Os are the preferred cache strategy, that doesn't mean that the server creates any buffer pools for you. You must create the buffer pools (except for the default 2K buffer pool) yourself before the query runs in order for the optimizer to make use of them.

With System 11, the query optimizer can handle joins of up to eight tables which are more often encountered in DSS applications. Previous server versions had been designed to deal with joins of four tables.

There are several new trace flags that should be used to see details of the query optimization process. Use of these trace flags during application development will allow you to see the process the optimizer goes through which will help you see what changes are really worth doing. You should consult the server documentation regarding trace flags 302 and 310.

Cache Strategy Issues

The ability to generate a very complex server configuration and an equally complex cache strategy is the danger of all this flexibility. You can configure the named caches, object bindings, buffer pools, and cache strategies so that no one can figure out what you were doing. You need to be sure that all this complexity is really worth it. The best approach is to move slowly and keep it simple. The desire to mix OLTP and DSS workloads can be counterproductive. You should consider separating workloads that require vastly different cache access methods. All this detail may just mask the real problem.

 All this complexity may be great for benchmarking, but will it help you with a real-world server and the applications that depend on it?

Despite the availability of all the new features, most servers will be better off with the defaults. The plethora of performance and tuning options does not mean you should rush in and use them all. Rather, the use of any of these features should be carefully planned. For example, you should obtain the showplan output for your critical queries before and after making any changes to ensure that you know what the server is doing. You need to do this to make sure that any such changes have really improved the situation.

QUERY OPTIMIZATION IMPROVEMENTS

Many changes have been made to the way the server optimizes queries, especially in the area of subqueries. The details of all these changes can be found in the Sybase document "What's New in SQL Server 11?" A thorough discussion of all these changes could fill an entire book. You need to examine all the changes that have been made and then consider the queries that are running against your server.

The changes to subquery processing affect you when you upgrade to System 11. In order to get the new processing of subqueries, you must drop and re create all stored procedures, views, and triggers that contain subqueries. See Chapter 13 for more details.

5

Configuring SQL Server System 11

The System 11 version of the SQL Server allows many more configuration options than previous versions. System 11 supports over 120 configuration parameters compared with 30 for previous versions. This increased flexibility means you can fine-tune the server configuration for your specific needs. It also means you have more possible configurations to investigate, monitor, and document. To make all this practical, the server now supports a configuration file which tracks the values of all the server configuration parameters. The System 11 Server also retains the **sp_configure** functionality of previous releases. The stored procedure **sp_configure** is used to change the values of individual configuration parameters while a configuration file is used to change and document the values of multiple configuration values.

The *Sybase SQL Server System Administration Guide*, Chapter 11, "Setting Configuration Parameters", has an excellent figure that shows the names of all the configuration parameters in System 11 as well as what the equivalent parameters were for the previous server versions.

CONFIGURATION FILE

The configuration file contains an entry for each of the server configuration parameters. The configuration parameters are organized to group logically related parameters. This means that some configuration parameters may appear in more than one group within the configuration file. You can change the server configuration by making one or more changes to the values in a configuration file and then restarting the SQL Server using the modified configuration file.

The configuration of the server is still stored in the system tables *sysconfigures* and *syscurconfigs* in the master database. The server configuration is still stored in the config block of the master device.

The server uses the configuration file to allocate server machine resources as the server starts up. You can specify a configuration file to be used at server start up using the new -c flag for the dataserver command. The dataserver command is used to execute the SQL Server binary. If you don't specify a configuration file, the server will look in the $SYBASE directory for a file called <servername>.cfg. Note that if the $SYBASE environment variable is not set correctly, the server will not find the <servername>.cfg file. If $SYBASE points to some other directory that does contain a <servername>.cfg file, from a previous version of System 11 (System 11.0 versus 11.0.1) the server may use a configuration file you did not intend. You can always check the errorlog to see what configuration file the server actually used at start up. If no such file is found, the server will still start up, but with default values used for all configuration parameters. Previous versions of the SQL Server required the use of buildmaster.-r to clear the configuration. This was often needed if you attempted a configuration change that the server machine (usually a lack of memory) could not support. At that point the server would not start and you had to clear the server configuration using buildmaster -r. With system 11 you can clear the server configuration by simply renaming the <servername>.cfg file and restarting the server without specifying a configuration file.

By creating multiple configuration files, you can quickly change the server configuration to suit differing business needs. For example, you may need to switch from OLTP configuration during the day to batch configuration at night. Similarly you may need to reconfigure the server on the weekends for maintenance tasks. The different values for the server configuration parameters for each of these situations can be stored in configuration files. Reconfiguring the server from one configuration to the next only requires applying the appropriate configuration file to the server.

Consistent with the previous versions of the SQL Server, System 11 has both static and dynamic configuration parameters. Static configuration parameters can be changed in the configuration file, but will not take affect until the configuration file is applied as the server restarts. Dynamic configuration parameters can be changed while the server is running. If you need to change the configuration of a server, there are several options. First, you can use `sp_configure` to change any single configuration parameter. If a static configuration parameter is changed, the server must be restarted for the change to take affect. Second, you can make one or more changes to the configuration file and restart the server with the modified configuration file. Third, you can use `sp_configure` to read in a configuration file to change one or more dynamic configuration parameters. You can not read a configuration file into a running server that attempts to change any static configuration parameters.

Configuration files are simple ASCII text files that are stored in the operating system file system. This means these files are not part of the SQL Server and will not be backed up as part of any database dump. You must perform operating system level backups to capture the configuration file(s). The server stores its current configuration in the *master* database. However, if you need multiple configuration files to reconfigure the server to support your business, you need to have backups of all the needed configuration files. Otherwise, you might be able to recover the server but you won't be able to re-create the multiple server configurations needed to support your business.

Each time the server successfully starts up, the current configuration of the server is written to a file called *<servername>*.bak. This backup configuration file is there in case all other configuration files are lost. The backup configuration file also protects you when you manually modify the configuration file. If your changes to the configuration file cause the server start up to fail, you can't restart the server with the *<servername>*.cfg file. You can restart the server with an older configuration file, but you probably want to get the server back to the current configuration. However, you can restart the server with the <*servername*>.bak file. The server will start up and have the configuration it had at the previous successful startup. You must realize a subtlety in this process. After each server start up, the <*servername*>.bak file is overwritten, but any subsequent configuration changes using **sp_configure** will not be written to the backup file. The backup configuration file is only updated when the server is restarted. If you need to restart a server with the backup configuration file, you must understand that it will not reflect any configuration changes made since the previous successful server start up.

The way the server starts up, writes the <*servername*>.bak file, and then reads in the configuration file needs to be followed closely. When the server starts up, it will use the configuration parameter values that were the config values when the server was last running. As the server starts up, the server uses the config values for the run values. After the server has successfully started, the server will then write the <*servername*>.bak file which represents the server configuration when it was last running (see Figure 5–3). Then, the server will read the configuration file that was specified, or the <*servername*>.cfg if there is one in the $SYBASE directory. The server then applies the configuration parameter values to the config and run values of the server.

Each time you use **sp_configure** to change a server configuration parameter, the server will write out a new version of the configuration file. This way you always have a file called <*servername*>.cfg that reflects the current server configuration. Each time the configuration file is updated, the previous version is renamed to <*servername*>.XXX where XXX is the next greater sequence number (see Figure 5–1). The first such file will be <*servername*>.001 and the sequence will continue up through 999 before overwriting the first such file. This means you now need to monitor your configuration files. You need to watch that the file system containing the configuration files does not overflow. You also have to be sure you have backups of the configuration files needed to run your business. While it is unlikely you will need 1000 configuration files, you need to be aware that after 999, the process does start over and will overwrite an existing <servername>.001 configuration file.

There is a complication to this process that you must be aware of. While the server will write out a new configuration file each time you use **sp_configure** to change the configuration, this does not happen if you edit an existing configuration file and restart the server with this new file. The server doesn't write a new configuration file since the configuration

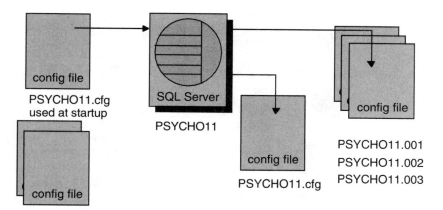

Figure 5–1. System 11 Configuration Files

file specified already exists. If you then make further changes to the configuration file, you no longer have the configuration file that was used the last time the server was restarted. This is why the *<servername>*.bak file is provided.

When the server starts up, and you do not specify a specific configuration file, it will look for and use a configuration file named *<server-name>*.cfg. This file must be located in the directory specified by $SYBASE to be found by the server. If such a file is not found, the server will start up but will use the default value for each server configuration parameter (see Figure 5–2). Note that if the defaults are applied, the server does not write out a *<servername>*.bak file. Once the server has started up, you can use **sp_configure** to write out a new configuration file which will have all the configuration parameters of the previous (nondefault) configuration. You must be careful, however. If you start up the server and no configuration file is specified or found by the server, the server starts up with the default configuration. If you then make any change to the server configuration using **sp_configure**, the server will write out a new configuration file. This new configuration file will be used (by default) for all subsequent server restarts. This new configuration file will represent the default configuration with the one change made. This will also wipe out all the configuration information that was stored in the master database which represented the previous nondefault server configuration. If all configuration files are lost, you can write out a new configuration file, but you must do so before making any other configuration changes.

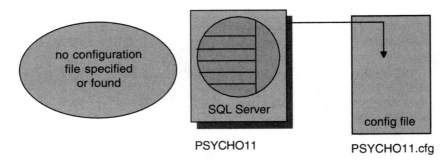

Figure 5–2. Server Startup without Configuration File

You get a call. "All I did was restart the server and it's lost its configuration." You can smell the panic. Think. Think. Think. "Did you change anything?" "NO!! We just restarted the server with a different name. How can that matter!!?" Well, it does matter. The server had been called PSYCHO_KNOWS and everything was fine. When the server was restarted with a name of NEW_NAME (using the -s option on the `startserver` command), the server went looking for the file NEW_NAME.cfg which doesn't exist, of course. The server then applied the defaults for all configuration parameters. Think about what you are doing. Configuration files are very useful, but they do have their own way of doing things. When you change the name of a server, or move a server to another server machine and give it a different name, you need to copy the configuration file you want to use to a file called NEW_NAME.cfg, or, specify a configuration file at start up time for the new server.

Advantages of Configuration Files

Multiple configuration files allow you to reconfigure the server for different processing needs quickly and efficiently. Instead of having to write and maintain script that changes multiple configuration parameters you only need to create multiple configuration files and apply them to the server at the appropriate times.

You may need to change the server configuration to support different and competing user work requirements. Your business needs to run OLTP all week long, but needs operational reports built on the previous week's

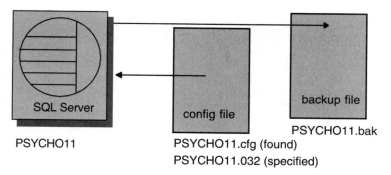

Figure 5–3. Backup Configuration File

OLTP data. Using one configuration file for weekdays and another for weekends you can quickly and automatically switch server configurations in very little time.

Running server maintenance tasks, such as dbcc runs, can often be completed in much less time if the server is reconfigured for these tasks. This is especially true for System 11 with named caches, and so forth. By reconfiguring the server, you can assign more server memory to a named cache that has a 16K buffer pool. This allows dbcc runs to operate much more quickly. This is a good example of how the increased complexity of System 11 configuration options is offset by the ability to package multiple changes into a single configuration file.

Creating a "standard" configuration file for the servers in your database system can simplify the setup and configuration of multiple servers. By distributing the standard configuration file to all sites you provide a documented configuration for all other servers to use. This is also handy when you need to audit a server to verify that it is indeed configured properly and to determine what, if any, local configuration has been done.

Configuration files also provide a more efficient way to recover from configuration errors. In previous server versions, you had to use **sp_configure** to change each configuration parameter one at a time. If you changed a parameter to a value the server machine couldn't support, by allocating too much memory to the server for example, the server would not start. Your only option was to clear the config block using the `buildmaster -r` command. This reset all the configuration parameters to their default values. Then, you had to reapply all of the configuration parameter changes, one at a time, using **sp_configure**. Using configuration files you can recover the server to the last successful configuration simply by starting the server with the most recent configuration file.

Recovery and Configuration Files

Configuration files need to be part of your recovery process. While the server will maintain the configuration file with each configuration change you make, you need to be sure the configuration files are being backed up. With previous versions of the server, recovering the *master* database was all that could, or had to be, done to restore the server configuration. Now that System 11 supports multiple configuration files, you need to be able to recover these files as well. Without all the configuration files that you set up and use to tailor the server to your business needs, you can't completely recover the server and its various configurations. See Chapter 9 for more details.

You should also consider your configuration files when moving a server from one server machine to another. You will need to transfer the configuration files along with the database dumps to completely rebuild the server on the new machine.

Configuration File Issues

Because the configuration files are simply operating system ASCII text files, anyone who has access to the files can examine and change them. You must ensure that the configuration files are properly protected at the operating system level. The server has no control over the security of these files.

You also need to remember that a configuration file that works for one server on one server machine may not work anywhere else. In order for a configuration file to work for all servers, you assume that all servers have the same server machine resources. If a server machine has less memory than the standard configuration file requires, the server will not start. In order to use a standard configuration file across multiple servers, you must ensure that all the server machines have the resources to support that standard configuration.

Consider the server configuration parameter "total memory." If any other server to which the configuration file is sent doesn't have sufficient memory to handle the configuration, that server won't boot. Have you really saved yourself any administrative effort?

The series of configuration files for a single server document all the configuration changes made to that server. Each configuration file that the server creates should represent a valid configuration for the server. However, this assumes that the server machine hardware does not change so that a previously valid configuration is no longer valid. If the memory on a server machine were reduced, or the number of other operating system processes were increased, a previously valid configuration file might result in a server that won't start. You need to realize the assumptions you make when you think you have a "good" configuration file. You need to remember these implications when you have a server that won't start even though the configuration file hasn't changed.

Configuration Files and Named Caches

When you create or change named caches, you are changing the server configuration. The structure of the named caches is recorded in the configuration file. This means that as you create named caches, and their associated buffer pools, the configuration file will grow.

Configuration File Structure

The configuration file will show DEFAULT for the value of all parameters that have not been changed from the default value. To see what the actual default value is, you must run sp_configure. Note that when the server is first installed, each and every parameter in the configuration file will have a value = DEFAULT. This will also occur if you start the server so that the default values are applied and you then write the configuration file. This occurs if you don't specify a configuration file at server start up and there is no <servername>.cfg in the $SYBASE directory. A typical configuration file is shown below. Note that at the time this configuration file was created, only the number of user connections had been changed from the default value.

```
#
#       Configuration File for the Sybase SQL Server
#
#       Please read the System Administration Guide (SAG)
#       before changing any of the values in this file.
#
```

[Configuration Options]

[General Information]

[Backup/Recovery]
        recovery interval in minutes = DEFAULT
        print recovery information = DEFAULT
        tape retention in days = DEFAULT

[Cache Manager]
        number of oam trips = DEFAULT
        number of index trips = DEFAULT
        procedure cache percent = DEFAULT
        memory alignment boundary = DEFAULT

[Named Cache:default data cache]
        cache size = DEFAULT
        cache status = default data cache

[Disk I/O]
        allow sql server async i/o = DEFAULT
        disk i/o structures = DEFAULT
        page utilization percent = DEFAULT
        number of devices = DEFAULT

[Network Communication]
        default network packet size = DEFAULT
        max network packet size = DEFAULT
        remote server pre-read packets = DEFAULT
        number of remote connections = DEFAULT
        allow remote access = DEFAULT
        number of remote logins = DEFAULT
        number of remote sites = DEFAULT
        max number network listeners = DEFAULT
        tcp no delay = DEFAULT

```
[O/S Resources]
      max async i/os per engine = DEFAULT
      max async i/os per server = DEFAULT

[Physical Resources]

[Physical Memory]
      total memory = DEFAULT
      additional network memory = DEFAULT
      lock shared memory = DEFAULT
      shared memory starting address = DEFAULT

[Processors]
      max online engines = DEFAULT
      min online engines = DEFAULT

[SQL Server Administration]
      number of open objects = DEFAULT
      number of open databases = DEFAULT
      audit queue size = DEFAULT
      default database size = DEFAULT
      identity burning set factor = DEFAULT
      allow nested triggers = DEFAULT
      allow updates to system tables = DEFAULT
      print deadlock information = DEFAULT
      default fill factor percent = DEFAULT
      number of mailboxes = DEFAULT
      number of messages = DEFAULT
      number of alarms = DEFAULT
      number of pre-allocated extents = DEFAULT
      event buffers per engine = DEFAULT
      cpu accounting flush interval = DEFAULT
      i/o accounting flush interval = DEFAULT
      sql server clock tick length = DEFAULT
      runnable process search count = DEFAULT
      i/o polling process count = DEFAULT
      time slice = DEFAULT
      deadlock retries = DEFAULT
      cpu grace time = DEFAULT
      number of sort buffers = DEFAULT
      sort page count = DEFAULT
      number of extent i/o buffers = DEFAULT
      size of auto identity column = DEFAULT
      identity grab size = DEFAULT
      lock promotion HWM = DEFAULT
```

```
      lock promotion LWM = DEFAULT
      lock promotion PCT = DEFAULT
      housekeeper free write percent = DEFAULT
      partition groups = DEFAULT
      partition spinlock ratio = DEFAULT

[User Environment]
      number of user connections = 200
      stack size = DEFAULT
      stack guard size = DEFAULT
      systemwide password expiration = DEFAULT
      permission cache entries = DEFAULT
      user log cache size = DEFAULT
      user log cache spinlock ratio = DEFAULT

[Lock Manager]
      number of locks = DEFAULT
      deadlock checking period = DEFAULT
      freelock transfer block size = DEFAULT
      max engine freelocks = DEFAULT
      address lock spinlock ratio = DEFAULT
      page lock spinlock ratio = DEFAULT
      table lock spinlock ratio = DEFAULT
```

The server configuration file has some rather stringent format requirements. The best advice here is to simply use the format of the configuration file as it is given to you. When the server is installed, several *<servername>*.cfg files will be produced, with all but the most current one having a *<servername>*.XXX file name. Use one of these as a template for any configuration file you create on your own. If you edit a configuration file and the server complains about the format, examine one of the configuration files that the server created. If you do want to edit the configuration file, be aware of the following format requirements.

The first line of the configuration file must be a comment line. The sections of the configuration file begin with a [group name] followed by the parameters of that group. Some groups do not have any configuration parameters. Note that each group must be separated by one blank line. Also, the configuration file must contain the group which defines the default data cache. There are other restrictions. For example, when you do edit a configuration file to add a new named cache, you must include not only the line that specifies the new named cache size, but also the wash size. The minimal configuration file that can be successfully read into the server is shown below. While this configuration file doesn't make any changes to the current server configuration it is an example of the minimum requirements of any configuration file.

```
#
[Named Cache:default data cache]
        cache size = DEFAULT
        cache status = default data cache
```

Here is an example of a configuration file that can be specified at start up to create a new named cache with a nondefault buffer pool. Recall that creating or modifying named caches are static configuration changes which is not allowed in a configuration file that is read by a running server.

```
#
[Named Cache:default data cache]
        cache size = DEFAULT
        cache status = default data cache

[Named Cache:psycho1_cache]
        cache size = 2M
        cache status = mixed cache

[16K I/O Buffer Pool]
        pool size = 1M
        wash size = DEFAULT
```

Server Startup Configuration File Errors

When you decide to change the server configuration by editing a configuration file and then applying it to the server by restarting and specifying the new file, make sure the configuration file you start with represents the configuration you really want. This file may contain many configuration changes, other than the ones that you changed by editing, and you need to be sure you want all the server configuration values that that file specifies.

If you want to have several server configurations that you use regularly, set up these files and give them specific names other than *<servername>*.cfg. Along with the server errorlog this will give you a record of what the server configuration was each time it was restarted. You should avoid relying on the standard *<servername>*.cfg configuration files since it will be hard to be exactly certain what was contained in that file at any given time. Recall that this file is modified each time any server configuration change is made interactively, that is using **sp_configure** or creating/changing named caches on a running server.

There is further problem with specifying a specific configuration file. By default, the server will create a new version of <*servername*>.cfg each time the configuration is changed by **sp_configure** or creating a named cache. Each time a configuration change is made, the server writes out a new version of the .cfg file and renames the previous .cfg file to <*servername*>.XXX where XXX is the next higher number than all existing files. However, when you specify a configuration file at server start up, say WEEKDAY_config.cfg, things change. Now, if you make any server configuration changes, the server will still write out a new configuration file, but it will still be WEEKDAY_config.cfg and the previous configuration file will be renamed to WEEKDAY_config.XXX. You will then have multiple sets of configuration files. If you never specify a configuration file at server start up, then each and every server configuration will be recorded in an ongoing series of <*servername*>.cfg files. If you always start the server and specify the configuration file <*servername*>.cfg, you will have the same effect. Any time you start the server with any other configuration file, you will start a separate sequence of configuration files.

The server will not start up if the configuration file specifies a configuration that the server or the server machine can't support. The causes of these problems has not changed with System 11. Attempting to apply a value that is outside the minimum or maximum allowable values or values that the server machine memory can't support are typical reasons for a server configuration to fail.

The server will also refuse to start up if the configuration file has any formatting errors. The format requirements for the configuration file have been described above, and some typical problems, along with the server error messages they cause, are shown here. The sequence begins with a partial configuration file that contains multiple errors. One of the errors is corrected in each step until a working configuration file is produced.

1a. Configuration file does not have entries for default cache parameters. Note the comment line which must be the first line of any configuration file.

```
#
[Named Cache:psycho1_cache]
```

```
        cache size = 2M
        cache status = mixed cache
[16K I/O Buffer Pool]
        pool size = 2M
```

1b. Corresponding server errorlog message.

```
00:96/05/22 10:20:29.35 kernel   configuration error: A named cache
with 'cache status=default data cache' does not exist in the config-
uration file.
```

2a. Lack of a blank line after 'cache status = mixed cache' line causes error.

```
#
[Named Cache:default data cache]
        cache size = DEFAULT
        cache status = default data cache

[Named Cache:psycho1_cache]
        cache size = 2M
        cache status = mixed cache
[16K I/O Buffer Pool]
        pool size = 2M
```

2b. Corresponding server errorlog message.

```
00:96/05/22 10:02:18.09 server   Number of proc buffers
        allocated: 1869.
00:96/05/22 10:02:18.14 kernel   Configuration Error:
Configuration file
'/home/sybase/11.0.1/THEBIRDS11_test2' has an unknown format
on line 38.
(lack of a blank line)
```

3a. Configuration file entry must include both pool size and wash size.

```
#
[Named Cache:default data cache]
        cache size = DEFAULT
        cache status = default data cache

[Named Cache:psycho1_cache]
        cache size = 2M
        cache status = mixed cache
```

```
[16K I/O Buffer Pool]
        pool size = 2M
```

3b. Corresponding server errorlog message.

```
00:96/05/22 10:00:44.18 kernel   Network and device connection
limit is 1014.
00:96/05/22 10:00:44.20 server   Number of proc buffers
       allocated: 1869.
00:96/05/22 10:00:44.25 kernel   Configuration Error:
Configuration file
'/home/sybase/11.0.1/THEBIRDS11_test2' has an unknown format
on line 37.
```

4a. new named cache fills default data cache
16K buffer pool completely filled named cache. Each cache must have at least 512K of 2K buffer pool (see Named Caches for more details.)

```
#
[Named Cache:default data cache]
        cache size = DEFAULT
        cache status = default data cache

[Named Cache:psycho1_cache]
        cache size = 2M
        cache status = mixed cache

[16K I/O Buffer Pool]
        pool size = 2M
        wash size = DEFAULT
```

4b. Corresponding server errorlog message.

```
00:96/05/22 10:03:22.48 kernel   Network and device connection
limit is 1014.
00:96/05/22 10:03:22.49 server   Number of proc buffers
       allocated: 1869.
00:96/05/22 10:03:22.55 kernel   Invalid pool size of 0k (0
buffers) encountered for the 2k pool in cache psycho1_cache. Buffer
pools must have a minimum total size of 512k or 25 buffers, whichever
is greater.
```

5. Finally, this configuration file was valid and the server started.

```
#
[Named Cache:default data cache]
        cache size = DEFAULT
        cache status = default data cache

[Named Cache:psycho1_cache]
        cache size = 2M
        cache status = mixed cache

[16K I/O Buffer Pool]
        pool size = 2M
        wash size = DEFAULT
```

SP_CONFIGURE

The system stored procedure **sp_configure** is used to review, document, change, and restore the configuration of the server. You can use **sp_configure** to view or change a single configuration parameter. You can use **sp_configure** in conjunction with a configuration file to change multiple configuration parameters, or to document the current server configuration.

Overview of Pre-System 11 Usage

In previous versions of SQL Server, **sp_configure** was used to change a single configuration parameter. In those versions, there were 30 configuration parameters. Some other parameters were configurable using build-master or **dbcc** tune commands. The need to use different commands to change different sets of configuration parameters made it difficult to change server configurations quickly and reliably. You would use **sp_configure** without any parameters to display the current values of the configuration parameters. You would also use buildmaster -yall to display the other, less-often-used configuration parameters. You would then use **sp_configure** to change the value of any one parameter.

SQL Server version 4.9.2 sp_configure Output

```
1> sp_configure
2> go
```

name	minimum	maximum	config_value	run_value
recovery interval	1	32767	1	1
allow updates	0	1	1	1
user connections	5	2147483647	100	100
memory	3850	2147483647	8192	8192
open databases	5	2147483647	0	10
locks	5000	2147483647	0	5000
open objects	100	2147483647	0	500
procedure cache	1	99	0	20
fill factor	0	100	0	0
time slice	50	1000	0	100
database size	2	10000	0	2
tape retention	0	365	0	0
recovery flags	0	1	0	0
serial number	1	999999	999999	999999
nested triggers	0	1	1	1
devices	4	256	0	10
remote access	0	1	1	1
remote logins	0	2147483647	0	20
remote sites	0	2147483647	0	10
remote connections	0	2147483647	0	20
pre-read packets	0	2147483647	0	3
upgrade version	0	2147483647	492	492
default sortorder id	0	255	50	50
default language	0	2147483647	0	0
language in cache	3	100	3	3
max online engines	1	32	1	1
min online engines	1	32	1	1
engine adjust interval	1	32	0	0
default character set id	0	255	1	1
stack size	20480	2147483647	0	28672

```
(30 rows affected, return status = 0)
```

SQL Server System 10 sp_configure Output

```
1> sp_configure
2> go
```

name	minimum	maximum	config_ value	run_value
recovery interval	1	32767	0	5
allow updates	0	1	0	0
user connections	5	2147483647	0	25
memory 3850	2147483647	20000	20000	
open databases	5	2147483647	0	12
locks 5000	2147483647	0	5000	
open objects	100	2147483647	0	500
procedure cache	1	99	0	20
fill factor	0	100	0	0
time slice	50	1000	0	100
database size	2	10000	0	2
tape retention	0	365	0	0
recovery flags	0	1	0	0
nested triggers	0	1	1	1
devices	4	256	0	10
remote access	0	1	1	1
remote logins	0	2147483647	0	20
remote sites	0	2147483647	0	10
remote connections	0	2147483647	0	20
pre-read packets	0	2147483647	0	3
upgrade version	0	2147483647	1002	1002
default sortorder id	0	255	50	50
default language	0	2147483647	0	0
language in cache	3	100	3	3
max online engines	1	32	1	1
min online engines	1	32	1	1
engine adjust interval	1	32	0	0
cpu flush	1	2147483647	200	200
i/o flush	1	2147483647	1000	1000
default character set id	0	255	1	1
stack size	20480	2147483647	0	28672
password expiration interval	0	32767	0	0
audit queue size	1	65535	100	100
additional netmem	0	2147483647	0	0
default network packet size	512	524288	0	512
maximum network packet size	512	524288	0	512
extent i/o buffers	0	2147483647	0	0
identity burning set factor	1	9999999	5000	5000

```
(38 rows affected, return status = 0)
```

175

Each configuration parameter displayed by **sp_configure** is either dynamic or static. When you make a change to a dynamic parameter, that change takes effect immediately while the server is still running. A change to a static parameter does not take effect until the server is restarted. The parameters "memory" and "user connections" are examples of static configuration parameters for SQL Server Version 4.9.2 and System 10.

The output of **sp_configure** consisted of the columns which represented, for each configuration parameter, the minimum and maximum values allowed, the config value, and the run value. Whenever you used **sp_configure** to change a configuration parameter, the config value would change to the new value you specified. If the configuration parameter were a dynamic configuration parameter, the run value would also change to match the config value. For static configuration parameters, the run value would not change to match the config value until the server was restarted. For all configuration parameters, the run value represents the actual value that the running server is using.

Permissions

In Version 4.9.2 of the server, only the server user sa had permission to change configuration parameters. In System 10 any server user with **sa_role** had the needed permissions. In System 11, any server user with **sa_role** can change almost all of the configuration parameters. The few remaining ones can only be changed by a server users with sso_role.

Syntax

With System 11, the stored procedure **sp_configure** takes on several new syntax options to deal with configuration files.

```
sp_configure
go
```

displays all configuration parameters for the running server. You can also look at the current configuration file, $SYBASE/<servername>.cfg, to see what the current server configuration is (if the server is running) or will be after the next restart (if the server is not running).

sp_configure <parameter.name> will display the various columns of data for one specific configuration parameter, such as

```
sp_configure 'total memory'
go
```

You can also specify one of the configuration parameter group names as discussed below. This will out put the same information but for all the configuration parameters of that group.

To use a configuration file, you use

```
sp_configure 'configuration file', 0, 'sub_command', 'actual_config-
uration_file_name_you_want'
```

Note that the first parameter, 'configuration file', is not something you replace with the name of a configuration file. You need to use it just the way it appears here, namely "configuration file." This tells **sp_configure** that you want to use a configuration file. The second parameter is always 0 when dealing with configuration files. This is required for backward compatibility. Note that when you use **sp_configure** to change the value of a specific configuration parameter, the second parameter is the value you want for that parameter. Therefore, the second parameter is just a placeholder when using **sp_configure** with a configuration file. The third parameter is the subcommand which can take one of four values: write, restore, read, and verify. Each of these will be explained below. The fourth parameter is the name of the configuration file that you are using (read or verify) or writing to (write or restore).

If you need to determine the configuration file that the server is currently using, you can execute

sp_configure 'configuration file'

but this returns only the first eight characters of the path/file name. In order to see the entire file/path, you need to execute an arcane command to select from the system table syscurconfigs:

select value2 from syscurconfigs where config=114

The write subcommand is used to create a new configuration file that will contain the actual run values of the currently running server.

```
1> sp_configure 'configuration file', 0, 'write', 'actual_name_
   of_the_config_file_you_want_created'
2> go
```

You don't have to specify the complete path of the file you want created. The server will assume you want it created in the $SYBASE directory.

To create a new configuration file that will contain the config values of the currently running server, use

```
1> sp_configure 'configuration file', 0, 'restore',
   'actual_name_of_the_config_file_you_want_restored'
2> go
```

You need to be aware of the subtle difference between the "write" and the "restore" subcommands. The "write" option will output the current run values, while the "restore" option will output the config values. The reason to have both options is a little hard to understand at first. If you have a server running just the way you want it, you already have the configuration file you could copy with all the current run values. If you were to edit the configuration file and realized you wanted the unedited configuration file back, you could use the "write" option to re-create the file.

Now for the "restore" option. There are two situations where you need the "restore" option. First, if you have lost all configuration files and the server is not running, you must restart the server to get any configuration information out of it. However, recall that when the server starts up and no configuration file is specified and no $SYBASE/<servername>.cfg file is found, the server will use the default values for all configuration parameters. In this case, the server will use the default values for the run values of each configuration parameter but does not change the config values. If you were to use the "write" option, you would simply get a new configuration file that would have the current run values which in this case are simply the default configuration values. The restore option will write out the config configuration values which in this case represent the nondefault server configuration that was in place before all the configuration files were lost. This way you can restart the server and still restore the configuration file of the server.

Second, if you want to create a number of configuration files, each of which contains different values for one or more static configuration parameters, the restore option is useful. As you change each static configuration value the server changes only the config value and will not change the run value until the server is restarted. If you were to use the write option, you would be writing out the configuration run values which would not reflect the change in static parameter values. Unless you are willing to restart the server for each static parameter change, you need to use the restore option to record each such configuration into a separate configuration file.

The verify option is used to examine a configuration file. The verify option will determine if the configuration specified in the file will allow the server to start up. This is useful for checking that a configuration file will still be valid after making changes manually, or when moving configuration files from one server or server machine to another.

```
1> sp_configure 'configuration file', 0, 'verify',
   'actual_name_of_the_config_file_you_want_verified'
2> go
```

To read in a configuration file to a running server,

```
1> sp_configure 'configuration file', 0, 'read',
   'actual_name_of_the_config_file_you_want_read'
2> go
```

As with the write or restore options, if you don't specify the path of the configuration file, the server will look for the file in the $SYBASE directory. The read subcommand allows you to read in a configuration file to change the configuration of a running server. However, when doing this, the configuration file being read must not change any static configuration parameters. If the server reads in a configuration file and encounters a change to a static parameter, the read fail. In this situation, none of the configuration changes in the file are applied. Note that this means the server does not require a complete configuration file. Hence, a partial configuration file can be specified at server start up or read in while the server is operating. The server will use the current value for any parameters not specified in such a file when starting up and when reading in such a file while the server is running.

Configuration File Read Errors

Reading a configuration file allows you to change multiple configuration parameters at once. This feature supports quickly changing between multiple server configurations to better support your business. However, reading a configuration file doesn't always work.

You specify a configuration file at server start up, either with the -c option on the dataserver command or by letting the server use the <servername>.cfg file in the $SYBASE directory. In this case, the configuration file can contain changes to any and all configuration parameters, including creating and/or changing named caches and their associated buffer pools. You need to watch for two ways this process can go wrong. If $SYBASE is not set correctly, the server may not find any .cfg file, or it may find one that you didn't want loaded. Also, if you change the name of the server, then the file <*servername*>.cfg will not get loaded since it refers to a different server name. You should check the server error-log when you restart to see that the server is indeed using the configuration file from the directory that you intended.

When you read in a configuration file to a server that is already running, using the "read" option of the **sp_configure** command, your options are limited. In this case, you can't read in a configuration file that contains any changes to any static configuration parameters. If you attempt this, the server will reject all the configuration changes in the file and return an error message. This also means the configuration file can't create any named caches or their associated buffer pools. Another ironic restriction is that the configuration file that you read in must contain the default data cache parameters. The reason that this makes sense, in a way, is that the default data cache must always exist. You can't change any static parameters and that means you must include the default data cache parameters, or, by their omission, you would be changing (deleting) the default data cache, which is not allowed.

Note again, that while you can't change any static parameters while reading the configuration file into a running server, including named caches, the configuration file can contain static parameter values, as long as they are the same values as the server is currently using for those static parameters. This means that if you start the server with a configuration file, say config.one, and then change one or more static configuration parameters, you will not be able to read in the configuration file config.one because it now has at least one change to a static configuration parameter.

Previous to System 11, **sp_configure** was the only way to change the server configuration. However, with System 11 and named caches, this has changed. When you create or change named caches, you are changing the server configuration. These kinds of configuration changes are static changes that require a server restart to take effect. This means that if you start the server with a configuration file, say config.two, and then create a named cache and restart the server, you can't read in the configuration file config.two, even though you didn't execute **sp_configure**. You need to realize that the commands that create and change named caches do affect the server configuration.

Staying Out of Trouble with the "read" Subcommmand

Given all the restrictions on reading a configuration file into a running server, you would be well advised not to use this technique very often. If you have a set of dynamic configuration parameters that you change frequently, reading in a configuration file is worthwhile. In this case, you should take one of two approaches. First, edit a configuration file to delete everything except the dynamic parameters that you need to change. Then, when you read this file into the running server, the server will apply the current run values for all the other parameters. This ensures that you aren't changing anything you don't intend to. Second, use a copy of the configuration file that the server is currently using and then edit only the dynamic parameters you want to change. This ensures that you will be able to read the configuration file into the running server. Note that this may or may not be the *<servername>*.cfg file. If the server was most recently started with a specific configuration file, that is the file you need to copy and edit. The *<servername>*.cfg is the configuration of the server the last time the configuration was changed by **sp_configure** or creating/changing named caches. This file may not have any relation to the current server configuration if the server was last started with a specific configuration file.

Output Hierarchy

Within the output of **sp_configure**, the configuration parameters are grouped into the following groups. Note that you can execute **sp_configure <group_name>** to see only the configuration parameters of that group. At the current time, there are two groups that contain no configuration parameters. Further, some configuration parameters are members of more than one group. For example, the configuration parameter "number of devices" appears in both the Disk I/O and Memory Use groups.

- Configuration Options (no parameters)
- Backup/recovery
- Cache manager

- Disk I/O
- General information
- Languages
- Lock manager
- Memory use
- Network communication
- O/S resources
- Physical resources (no parameters)
- Physical memory
- Processors
- SQL Server Administration
- User environment

sp_configure Output

Output Display Levels

Each server login can be configured to display one of three different levels of output from sp_configure. Each server user can change their own sp_configure display level, or the system security officer (any server user with sso_role) can change the display level for any user. The three levels of sp_configure output are basic, intermediate and comprehensive (default). Only users with sa_role can use sp_configure to change the server configuration. This feature can be confusing. A server login that has sa_role can be limited by the SSO to only see basic output of sp_configure. This means that such a user would be able to change configuration parameters that they couldn't see in the output of sp_configure.

Comprehensive Level of sp_configure Output

The output of **sp_configure** with various options is shown below. The default level of **sp_configure** output is the comprehensive level.

```
1> sp_configure
2> go
```

Group: Configuration Options

Group: Backup/Recovery

Parameter Name	Default	Memory Used	Config Value	Run Value
allow remote access	1	0	1	1
print recovery information	0	0	0	0
recovery interval in minutes	5	0	5	5
tape retention in days	0	0	0	0

Group: Cache Manager

Parameter Name	Default	Memory Used	Config Value	Run Value
memory alignment boundary	2048	0	2048	2048
number of index trips	0	0	0	0
number of oam trips	0	0	0	0
procedure cache percent	20	990	20	20
total data cache size	0	3812	0	3812
total memory	7500	15000	7500	7500

Group: Disk I/O

Parameter Name	Default	Memory Used	Config Value	Run Value
allow sql server async i/o	1	0	1	1
disk i/o structures	256	19	256	256
number of devices	10	4	10	10
page utilization percent	95	0	95	95

Group: General Information

Parameter Name	Default	Memory Used	Config Value	Run Value
configuration file	0	0	0	/home/sybas

Group: Languages

Parameter Name	Default	Memory Used	Config Value	Run Value
default character set id	1	0	1	1
default language id	0	0	0	0
default sortorder id	50	0	50	50
number of languages in cache	3	4	3	3

Group: Lock Manager

Parameter Name	Default	Memory Used	Config Value	Run Value
address lock spinlock ratio	100	0	100	100
deadlock checking period	500	0	500	500
freelock transfer block size	30	0	30	30
max engine freelocks	10	0	10	10
number of locks	5000	469	5000	5000
page lock spinlock ratio	100	0	100	100
table lock spinlock ratio	20	0	20	20

Group: Memory Use

Parameter Name	Default	Memory Used	Config Value	Run Value
additional network memory	0	0	0	0
audit queue size	100	42	100	100
default network packet size	512	#135	512	512
disk i/o structures	256	19	256	256
event buffers per engine	100	#10	100	100
executable codesize + overhead	0	4941	0	4941
max number network listeners	15	1124	15	15
max online engines	1	147	1	1
number of alarms	40	1	40	40
number of devices	10	#4	10	10
number of extent i/o buffers	0	0	0	0
number of languages in cache	3	4	3	3
number of locks	5000	469	5000	5000
number of mailboxes	30	1	30	30
number of messages	64	1	64	64
number of open databases	12	396	12	12
number of open objects	500	489	500	500
number of remote connections	20	33	20	20
number of remote logins	20	22	20	20
number of remote sites	10	749	10	10
number of user connections	25	1868	25	25
partition groups	1024	21	1024	1024
permission cache entries	15	#28	15	15
procedure cache percent	20	990	20	20
remote server pre-read packets	3	#32	3	3
stack guard size	4096	#240	4096	4096
stack size	34816	#2041	34816	34816
total data cache size	0	3812	0	3812
total memory	7500	15000	7500	7500

Group: Network Communication

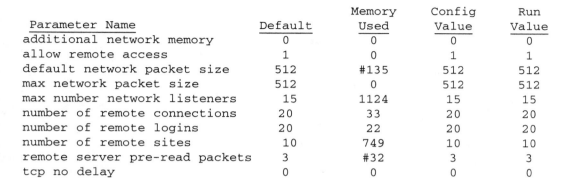

Parameter Name	Default	Memory Used	Config Value	Run Value
additional network memory	0	0	0	0
allow remote access	1	0	1	1
default network packet size	512	#135	512	512
max network packet size	512	0	512	512
max number network listeners	15	1124	15	15
number of remote connections	20	33	20	20
number of remote logins	20	22	20	20
number of remote sites	10	749	10	10
remote server pre-read packets	3	#32	3	3
tcp no delay	0	0	0	0

Group: O/S Resources

Parameter Name	Default	Memory Used	Config Value	Run Value
max async i/os per engine	2147483647	0	2147483647	2147483647
max async i/os per server	2147483647	0	2147483647	2147483647
o/s asynch i/o enabled	0	0	0	0
o/s file descriptors	0	0	0	1024
tcp no delay	0	0	0	0

Group: Physical Resources

Group: Physical Memory

Parameter Name	Default	Memory Used	Config Value	Run Value
additional network memory	0	0	0	0
lock shared memory	0	0	0	0
shared memory starting address	0	0	0	0
total memory	7500	15000	7500	7500

Group: Processors

Parameter Name	Default	Memory Used	Config Value	Run Value
max online engines	1	147	1	1
min online engines	1	0	1	1

Group: SQL Server Administration

Sybase DBA Companion

Parameter Name	Default	Memory Used	Config Value	Run Value
allow nested triggers	1	0	1	1
allow updates to system tables	0	0	0	0
audit queue size	100	42	100	100
cpu accounting flush interval	200	0	200	200
cpu grace time	500	0	500	500
deadlock retries	5	0	5	5
default database size	2	0	2	2
default fill factor percent	0	0	0	0
event buffers per engine	100	#10	100	100
housekeeper free write percent	1	0	1	1
i/o accounting flush interval	1000	0	1000	1000
i/o polling process count	10	0	10	10
identity burning set factor	5000	0	5000	5000
identity grab size	1	0	1	1
lock promotion HWM	200	0	200	200
lock promotion LWM	200	0	200	200
lock promotion PCT	100	0	100	100
number of alarms	40	1	40	40
number of extent i/o buffers	0	0	0	0
number of mailboxes	30	1	30	30
number of messages	64	1	64	64
number of open databases	12	396	12	12
number of open objects	500	489	500	500
number of pre-allocated extent	2	0	2	2
number of sort buffers	0	0	0	0
partition groups	1024	21	1024	1024
partition spinlock ratio	10	0	10	10
print deadlock information	0	0	0	0
runnable process search count	2000	0	2000	2000
size of auto identity column	10	0	10	10
sort page count	0	0	0	0
sql server clock tick length	100000	0	100000	100000
time slice	100	0	100	100
upgrade version	1100	0	1100	1100

Group: User Environment

Parameter Name	Default	Memory Used	Config Value	Run Value
default network packet size	512	#135	512	512
number of pre-allocated extent	2	0	2	2
number of user connections	25	1868	25	25
permission cache entries	15	#28	15	15
stack guard size	4096	#240	4096	4096
stack size	34816	#2041	34816	34816
systemwide password expiration	0	0	0	0
user log cache size	2048	0	2048	2048
user log cache spinlock ratio	20	0	20	20

```
(return status = 0)
```

Basic Output from sp_configure

The other **sp_configure** output levels are basic and intermediate. Each server user (login) can configure their own **sp_configure** output level. Any server user with **sso_role** can restrict a user's output level by setting the highest level for the user. In either case, the command **sp_displaylevel** command is used.

```
1> sp_displaylevel
2> go
The current display level for login 'sa' is 'comprehensive'.
(return status = 0)
1> sp_displaylevel sa, basic
2> go
The display level for login 'sa' has been changed to 'basic'.
(return status = 0)
1> sp_configure
2> go

Group: Configuration Options


Group: Backup/Recovery
```

Parameter Name	Default	Memory Used	Config Value	Run Value
recovery interval in minutes	5	0	5	5

```
Group: Cache Manager
```

Parameter Name	Default	Memory Used	Config Value	Run Value
total data cache size	0	3812	0	3812

Group: Disk I/O

Parameter Name	Default	Memory Used	Config Value	Run Value
number of devices	10	#4	10	10

Group: General Information

Group: Languages

Group: Lock Manager

Parameter Name	Default	Memory Used	Config Value	Run Value
number of locks	5000	469	5000	5000

Group: Memory Use

Parameter Name	Default	Memory Used	Config Value	Run Value
executable codesize + overhead	0	4941	0	4941
number of devices	10	#4	10	10
number of locks	5000	469	5000	5000
number of open databases	12	396	12	12
number of open objects	500	489	500	500
number of user connections	25	1868	25	25
stack size	34816	#2041	34816	34816
total data cache size	0	3812	0	3812

Group: Network Communication

Group: O/S Resources

Group: Physical Resources

Group: Physical Memory

Group: Processors

Group: SQL Server Administration

Parameter Name	Default	Memory Used	Config Value	Run Value
number of open databases	12	396	12	12
number of open objects	500	489	500	500

Group: User Environment

Parameter Name	Default	Memory Used	Config Value	Run Value
number of user connections	25	1868	25	25
stack size	34816	#2041	34816	34816

(return status = 0)

Intermediate Output from sp_configure

```
1> sp_displaylevel
2> go
The current display level for login 'sa' is 'basic'.
(return status = 0)
1> sp_displaylevel sa, intermediate
2> go
The display level for login 'sa' has been changed to 'intermediate'.
(return status = 0)
1> sp_displaylevel
2> go
The current display level for login 'sa' is 'intermediate'.
(return status = 0)
1> sp_configure
2> go
```

Group: Configuration Options

Group: Backup/Recovery

Parameter Name	Default	Memory Used	Config Value	Run Value
allow remote access	1	0	1	1
print recovery information	0	0	0	0
recovery interval in minutes	5	0	5	5
tape retention in days	0	0	0	0

Group: Cache Manager

Parameter Name	Default	Memory Used	Config Value	Run Value
total data cache size	0	3812	0	3812
total memory	7500	15000	7500	7500

Group: Disk I/O

Parameter Name	Default	Memory Used	Config Value	Run Value
number of devices	10	#4	10	10

Group: General Information

Group: Languages

Parameter Name	Default	Memory Used	Config Value	Run Value
default character set id	1	0	1	1
default language id	0	0	0	0
number of languages in cache	3	4	3	3

Group: Lock Manager

Parameter Name	Default	Memory Used	Config Value	Run Value
number of locks	5000	469	5000	5000

Group: Memory Use

Parameter Name	Default	Memory Used	Config Value	Run Value
additional network memory	0	0	0	0
audit queue size	100	42	100	100
default network packet size	512	#135	512	512
executable codesize + overhead	0	4941	0	4941
max online engines	1	147	1	1
number of devices	10	#4	10	10
number of languages in cache	3	4	3	3
number of locks	5000	469	5000	5000
number of open databases	12	396	12	12
number of open objects	500	489	500	500
number of remote connections	20	33	20	20
number of remote logins	20	22	20	20
number of remote sites	10	749	10	10
number of user connections	25	1868	25	25
remote server pre-read packets	3	#32	3	3
stack size	34816	#2041	34816	34816
total data cache size	0	3812	0	3812
total memory	7500	15000	7500	7500

Group: Network Communication

Parameter Name	Default	Memory Used	Config Value	Run Value
additional network memory	0	0	0	0
allow remote access	1	0	1	1
default network packet size	512	#135	512	512
max network packet size	512	0	512	512
number of remote connections	20	33	20	20
number of remote logins	20	22	20	20
number of remote sites	10	749	10	10
remote server pre-read packets	3	#32	3	3

Group: O/S Resources

Group: Physical Resources

Group: Physical Memory

Parameter Name	Default	Memory Used	Config Value	Run Value
additional network memory	0	0	0	0
total memory	7500	15000	7500	7500

Group: Processors

Parameter Name	Default	Memory Used	Config Value	Run Value
max online engines	1	147	1	1
min online engines	1	0	1	1

Group: SQL Server Administration

Parameter Name	Default	Memory Used	Config Value	Run Value
allow nested triggers	1	0	1	1
audit queue size	100	42	100	100
deadlock retries	5	0	5	5
default database size	2	0	2	2
default fill factor percent		0	0	0
housekeeper free write percent	1	0	1	1
identity burning set factor	5000	0	5000	5000
identity grab size	1	0	1	1
lock promotion HWM	200	0	200	200
lock promotion LWM	200	0	200	200
lock promotion PCT	100	0	100	100
number of open databases	12	396	12	12
number of open objects	500	489	500	500
print deadlock information	0	0	0	0
size of auto identity column	10	0	10	10

Group: User Environment

Parameter Name	Default	Memory Used	Config Value	Run Value
default network packet size	512	#135	512	512
number of user connections	25	1868	25	25
stack size	34816	#2041	34816	34816
systemwide password expiration	0	0	0	0
user log cache size	2048	0	2048	2048
user log cache spinlock ratio	20	0	20	20

(return status = 0)

Configuration Group Output from sp_configure

```
1> sp_configure 'Physical Memory'
2> go
```

Group: Physical Memory

Parameter Name	Default	Memory Used	Config Value	Run Value
additional network memory	0	0	0	0
lock shared memory	0	0	0	0
shared memory starting address	0	0	0	0
total memory	7500	15000	7500	7500

(return status = 0)

The Current Configuration File from sp_configure

```
1> sp_configure 'configuration file'
2> go
```

Parameter Name	Default	Memory Used	Config Value	Run Value
configuration file	0	0	0	/home/sybas

(return status = 0)

The Current Configuration File from the System Tables

```
1> select db_name()
2> go

   _____

 master

(1 row affected)

1> select value2 from syscurconfigs where config=114
2> go

      value2
      /home/sybase/11.0.1/THEBIRDS11.cfg

(1 row affected)
```

sp_configure and the "read" and "verify" Subcommands

Configuration File-Static Parameter Change

```
1> sp_configure 'configuration file', 0, 'verify', '/home/sybase/11.0/con-
fig_test.001'

2> go
Msg 5852, Level 16, State 1:
Server 'THEBIRDS11', Procedure 'sp_configure', Line 199:
Changing the value of 'total memory' is not allowed since it is a static
option.

(return status = 1)
```

Configuration File-Changes to Named Caches

```
1> sp_configure 'configuration file', 0, 'read', '/home/sybase/11.0/con-
fig_test.001'
2> go
WARNING: Dynamic loading of caches and pools through loading a new file
are not supported. However, the loadfile
'/home/sybase/11.0/config_test.001' will be inspected for consistency.
Refer to 'sp_cacheconfig' and 'sp_poolconfig' to create or alter pools and
caches.
Msg 5852, Level 16, State 1:
Server 'THEBIRDS11', Procedure 'sp_configure', Line 199:
Changing the value of 'total memory' is not allowed since it is a static
option.
(return status = 1)
```

Configuration File Currently in Use by Server—verify Is Successful

```
1> sp_configure 'configuration file', 0, 'verify', '/home/sybase/11.0/THE-
BIRDS11.cfg'
2> go

(return status = 0)
```

Output Value

The System 11 output from **sp_configure** has different columns than previous versions. Now the output columns display, for each configuration parameter, the default value and the memory used by the server to support the run value, followed by the config value and run value. The config values represent the configuration stored in *sysconfigures*. The config values are the same as the run values for dynamic values. For static values, the run value will become the config value after the server is restarted. The run values represent the configuration of the running server and are stored in *syscurconfigs*. The output that is displayed by **sp_configure** can be confusing because the units of measure are not consistent. The units for the default value of a configuration parameter vary depending on the parameter. For total memory, the unit of measure is 2K pages. For the number of user connections, it is an integer. Further, the memory used column is always measured in units of Kb. So, for example, you could have for total memory the default value of 7500 2K pages while the memory used shows 15,000 Kb. Even more puzzling is the # symbol which precedes some of the values for the memory-used values. This symbol indicates that the memory used by the server to support the particular parameter is affected by other parameters. For example, consider the configuration parameter event buffers per engine. Even if you don't change this parameter, the total memory used to support it will change as you change the number of engines. Also, the default value for some parameters is 0. This does not mean what it says; rather, it means the server computes the default value based on other parameters.

Compatibility

While you can use **sp_configure** to change an individual configuration parameter in all versions of SQL Server, you must note that a few of the configuration parameter names have changed in System 11. One of these is the "total memory" configuration parameter which was previously just the "memory" parameter. If you or any of your scripts executes **sp_configure "memory"**, the server will return an error. If you have any scripts or cron jobs that reconfigure the server, you must check them to be sure they will work with System 11. For example, any script that starts the server may need to be modified to specify a configuration file. This would only apply if you routinely change the server configuration by restarting the server with one in a series of configuration files. Before System 11, any server configuration change made by **sp_configure** had to be followed by the command **reconfigure**. In System 11, the **reconfigure** command is no longer needed. While the **reconfigure** command will not cause an error, Sybase is not committed to supporting this command into the future. You should remove the **reconfigure** command from all scripts that currently use it.

This adds to the work involved in upgrading and can be a problem since you can "complete" the upgrade without performing this sort of work. While the Sybase upgrade may complete quickly, you haven't upgraded your server until all these changes have been tracked down, implemented and tested.

SQL Server Errorlog Messages—sp_configure

When you use **sp_configure** to change a configuration option, the server records messages in the errorlog.

Changing a Single Configuration Parameter with sp_configure—dynamic

```
00:96/05/15 10:58:04.06 server—The configuration option 'number of user
connections' has been changed by 'sa' from '25' to '30'.

00:96/05/15 10:58:04.17 server—Configuration file '/home/sybase/11.0/THE-
BIRDS11.cfg' has been written and the previous version has been renamed
to '/home/sybase/11.0/THEBIRDS11.019'.
```

SQL Server Errorlog Messages—sp_configure with Configuration File

When you use **sp_configure** with a configuration file you will see a message in the server errorlog documenting what the server is using for configuration information.

No Configuration File Specified, $SYBASE Directory Contains <servername>.cfg file

```
thebirds:sybase 16: more RUN_THEBIRDS11
#!/bin/sh
#
# SQL Server Information:
#   name:                   THEBIRDS11
#   master device:          /dev/rdsk/c0t2d0s7
#   master device size:     45056
#   errorlog:               /home/sybase/11.0/install/errorlog
#   interfaces:             /home/sybase/11.0
#
/home/sybase/11.0/bin/dataserver -d/dev/rdsk/c0t2d0s7 -sTHEBIRDS11 \
-e/home/sybase/11.0/install/errorlog_THEBIRDS11 -i/home/sybase/11.0
```

```
thebirds:sybase 14: 00:96/05/15 11:02:09.68 kernel  Using config area from
primary master device.
00:96/05/15 11:02:09.72 kernel  Warning: Using default file
'/home/sybase/11.0/THEBIRDS11.cfg' since a configuration file was not
specified. Specify a configuration file name in the RUNSERVER file to
avoid this message.
00:96/05/15 11:02:10.10 kernel  Using 1024 file descriptors.
00:96/05/15 11:02:10.10 kernel  SQL Server/11.0/P/Sun_svr4/OS
5.4/1/OPT/Thu Dec  7 23:58:01 PST 1995
00:96/05/15 11:02:10.10 kernel  Confidential property of Sybase, Inc.
00:96/05/15 11:02:10.12 kernel  (c) Copyright Sybase Inc., 1987, 1995.
00:96/05/15 11:02:10.12 kernel  All rights reserved.
00:96/05/15 11:02:10.12 kernel
00:96/05/15 11:02:10.12 kernel  Use, duplication, or disclosure by the
United States Government
00:96/05/15 11:02:10.13 kernel  is subject to restrictions as set forth
in FAR subparagraphs
00:96/05/15 11:02:10.13 kernel  52.227-19(a)-(d) for civilian agency con-
tracts and DFARS
00:96/05/15 11:02:10.13 kernel  252.227-7013(c) (1) (ii) for Department of
Defense contracts.
00:96/05/15 11:02:10.13 kernel  Sybase reserves all unpublished rights
under the copyright
00:96/05/15 11:02:10.13 kernel  laws of the United States.
00:96/05/15 11:02:10.13 kernel  Sybase, Inc. 6475 Christie Avenue,
Emeryville, CA 94608 USA.
00:96/05/15 11:02:10.13 kernel  Using '/home/sybase/11.0/THEBIRDS11.cfg'
for configuration information.
```

Configuration File Specified at Server Startup

```
thebirds:sybase 17: more RUN_THEBIRDS11_config
#!/bin/sh
#
# SQL Server Information:
#   name:                        THEBIRDS11
#   master device:               /dev/rdsk/c0t2d0s7
#   master device size:          45056
#   errorlog:                    /home/sybase/11.0/install/errorlog
#   interfaces:                  /home/sybase/11.0
#
/home/sybase/11.0/bin/dataserver -d/dev/rdsk/c0t2d0s7 -sTHEBIRDS11 \
-e/home/sybase/11.0/install/errorlog_THEBIRDS11 -i/home/sybase/11.0 \
-c/home/sybase/11.0/THEBIRDS11.cfg_moved
```

```
thebirds:sybase 20: 00:96/05/15 11:04:35.79 kernel  Using config area from
primary master device.
00:96/05/15 11:04:38.90 kernel  Using 1024 file descriptors.
00:96/05/15 11:04:38.94 kernel  SQL Server/11.0/P/Sun_svr4/OS
5.4/1/OPT/Thu Dec  7 23:58:01 PST 1995
00:96/05/15 11:04:39.15 kernel  Confidential property of Sybase, Inc.
00:96/05/15 11:04:39.16 kernel  (c) Copyright Sybase Inc., 1987, 1995.
00:96/05/15 11:04:39.16 kernel  All rights reserved.
00:96/05/15 11:04:39.16 kernel
00:96/05/15 11:04:39.16 kernel  Use, duplication, or disclosure by the
United States Government
00:96/05/15 11:04:39.16 kernel  is subject to restrictions as      et
forth in FAR subparagraphs
00:96/05/15 11:04:39.16 kernel  52.227-19(a)-(d) for civilian agency con-
tracts and DFARS
00:96/05/15 11:04:39.16 kernel  252.227-7013(c) (1) (ii) for Department of
Defense contracts.
00:96/05/15 11:04:39.16 kernel  Sybase reserves all unpublished rights
under the copyright
00:96/05/15 11:04:39.16 kernel  laws of the United States.
00:96/05/15 11:04:39.16 kernel  Sybase, Inc. 6475 Christie Avenue,
Emeryville, CA 94608 USA.
00:96/05/15 11:04:39.16 kernel  Using
'/home/sybase/11.0/THEBIRDS11.cfg_moved' for configuration information.
```

No Configuration file Specified, no <servername>.cfg file in $SYBASE

Note that the default configuration is being applied, and that the file
THEBIRDS11.cfg is created.

```
thebirds:sybase 27: 00:96/05/15 11:11:34.44 kernel  Using config area from
primary master device.
00:96/05/15 11:11:34.46 kernel  Configuration Error: Configuration file,
'/home/sybase/11.0/THEBIRDS11.cfg', does not exist.
00:96/05/15 11:11:34.53 kernel  Warning: A configuration file was not
specified and the default file '/home/sybase/11.0/THEBIRDS11.cfg' does not
exist. SQL Server creates the default file with the default configuration.
00:96/05/15 11:11:34.90 kernel  Using 1024 file descriptors.
00:96/05/15 11:11:34.90 kernel  SQL Server/11.0/P/Sun_svr4/OS
5.4/1/OPT/Thu Dec  7 23:58:01 PST 1995
00:96/05/15 11:11:34.90 kernel  Confidential property of Sybase, Inc.
00:96/05/15 11:11:34.90 kernel  (c) Copyright Sybase Inc., 1987, 1995.
00:96/05/15 11:11:34.90 kernel  All rights reserved.
00:96/05/15 11:11:34.90 kernel
```

```
00:96/05/15 11:11:34.90 kernel    Use, duplication, or disclosure by the
United States Government
00:96/05/15 11:11:34.90 kernel    is subject to restrictions as set forth
in FAR subparagraphs
00:96/05/15 11:11:34.90 kernel    52.227-19(a)-(d) for civilian agency con-
tracts and DFARS
00:96/05/15 11:11:34.90 kernel    252.227-7013(c)(1)(ii) for Department of
Defense contracts.
00:96/05/15 11:11:34.90 kernel    Sybase reserves all unpublished rights
under the copyright
00:96/05/15 11:11:34.90 kernel    laws of the United States.
00:96/05/15 11:11:34.90 kernel    Sybase, Inc. 6475 Christie Avenue,
Emeryville, CA 94608 USA.
00:96/05/15 11:11:34.90 kernel    Using '/home/sybase/11.0/THEBIRDS11.cfg'
for configuration information.
```

OVERALL SERVER CONFIGURATION

System 11 also supports named caches, which are discussed in Chapter 4. You must change the way you think about server configuration with System 11. Previously, you could dump the output of **sp_configure** and you had a complete set of data that told you the server's current configuration. With System 11, the configuration of the named caches is a very important part of the server configuration. However, the output of **sp_configure** doesn't mention the named caches. You might think that dumping the configuration file would be the answer. But, then, you have a file that lists the value for any parameter that you haven't change as DEFAULT. In order to know what the default values are, you need to output of **sp_configure**. You need to keep a copy of both the **sp_configure** output and the configuration file to really know what the server configuration was. If you have multiple configuration files, you need to have copies of each of them as well.

System 11 DBA Features

DATABASE DUMPS

System 11 provides two new features that will affect your current database dump and load procedures. First, you can load System 10 database and transaction log dumps into a System 11 server. Second, when a database dump is loaded into a System 11 database, the database is taken "off-line" and no user access is allowed until the database is placed "on-line."

Loading System 10 Database Dumps

Loading System 10 dumps means you can dump a user database within a System 10 SQL Server and load that dump into a user database in a System 11 SQL Server. Note that you can only do this with user databases, not the *master* database. When you do this, the System 11 SQL Server will load the System 10 database dump and after the load is complete, the database that was loaded will then be upgraded to System 11. Note that there is no difference between an individual database upgraded by this method and a database that is upgraded as part of an entire System 10 Server upgrade. This is useful for two reasons.

One, when you are upgrading from System 10 to System 11. You don't have to stop supporting your business to upgrade the entire System 10 Server at once. You can leave your production System 10 SQL Server running, supporting your business, and install System 11 on a separate server machine. You then create the same databases (size and structure) on the System 11 Server. Then, dump each of the user databases and load them into the System 11 Server. This way you know that the upgrade will work and when you are ready, you only need to stop your business long enough to make a final dump of the System 10 user databases and load those dumps into the new System 11 server. This way, you don't have to upgrade the entire System 10 Server at once. Note that upgrading by loading System 10 database dumps into a System 11 Server does not relieve you of the burden of other upgrade details. Tasks such as dropping and recreating some database objects and checking that last chance thresholds have been activated still must be done. See Chapter 13.

Two, when you need to load old (System 10) database dumps into your System 11 Server. When you upgraded from 4.9.2 to System 10, all the dumps you had ever made at 4.9.2 were useless. If you wanted to load 4.9.2 database dump, you would have to install a 4.9.2 SQL Server, create the database, load the old database dump, go through the entire server upgrade process, dump the database at System 10, and then load into your System 10Server. With System 11, you can load any of your old System 10 database dumps at any time. This is very useful for accessing archived data from any System 10 SQL Server.

There are several issues with this new functionality. You must clearly understand that this only works one way, that is, that you can load System 10 dumps into a System 11 Server. You still cannot load 4.9.2 dumps into either System 10 or System 11 Servers, and you can not load any dump into the previous version of the server. This means you still cannot load a

System 11 dump into System 10 or 4.9.2 and you cannot load a System 10 dump into a 4.9.2 Server. Finally, this only works if the System 10 and System 11 servers are both running on the same hardware and operating system platforms. It is easy to think that because you can load System 10 dump into System 11 Server that you can dump from System 10 on any platform and load to System 11 on any platform. This is not true. For example, you cannot dump a System 10 database on an HP platform and then load that dump into a System 11 Server running on a Solaris platform.

 SunOS to Solaris works, but is not officially supported—same old story. Try it and if it works well, so much for the official story, but don't get into a position where you are dependent on this technique. Unsupported processes tend to bite you when you are in the middle of a major disaster.

Database Off-line/On-line

In previous versions of SQL Server, the database recovery process could be interrupted by any server user (see Figure 6–1). This could prevent the recovery process from completing. Assume, for example, that you needed to recover a database by loading a database dump and applying one or more transaction logs. After the database load completed and you were about to apply the first transaction log dump, any server use could access the database and could make a change (**insert, update, delete**) to the database. This could also occur in between transaction log loads. In

Figure 6–1. Pre-System 11 Database Load Process

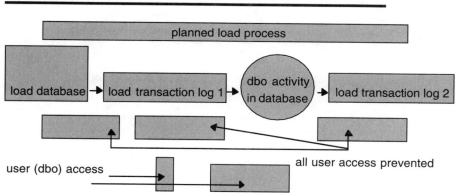

either case, any change to the database would stop the recovery process. The server must complete the sequence of database load and all required transaction log loads without any changes being made to the database. Any change made during this load sequence and the server will refuse to load any further transaction log dumps. If this occurs, your only recourse is to load the database dump again and repeat the load sequence. You can prevent this by putting the database into "dbo user only" mode using **sp_dboption**, but then, that only keeps out database users who are not aliased to dbo. The dbo user and any user aliased to dbo can still access the database between steps of the load sequence and can, potentially, prevent the process from completing.

With System 11, the load process is modified to make it more difficult for any user to interfere with the load process. As soon as the database load begins, the System 11 SQL Server automatically takes the database off-line (see Figure 6–2). This status will appear in **sp_helpdb** output and in the *sysdatabases* system table in the *master* database. Note that there is no server command to take a database off-line. The only time a database is taken off-line is when a database dump is loaded. Hence, the only command that takes a database off-line is the **load database** command. Once the database is off-line, it will remain that way until the **online database** command is executed. You should then complete the load sequence before you issue the **online database** command. This process prevents any user from accessing the database while the load sequence is in progress, while the database is off-line.

Figure 6–2. System 11 Database Load Process

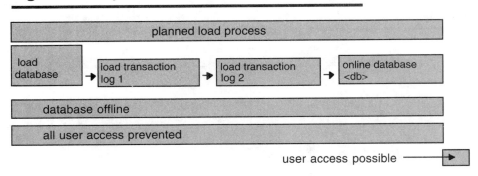

Only database users aliased to dbo and any server user with the **oper_role** have the permission to execute the **online database** command. While any of these users could issue the **online database** command, at least they must do so explicitly. Before System 11, any dbo user could access the database and might not be aware of the load sequence that was underway. Further, you had to remember to set the "dbo use only" option for the database. With System 11, while the database is off-line, these users might access the database, but they would initially be refused. They would have to issue the on-line database command and then change the database to stop the load sequence.

You can still load further transaction log dumps after a database is on-line, but if any user access occurs that changes the database, the server will not allow any further transaction log dumps to be loaded. Further, loading a transaction log will not affect the off-line/on-line status of a database. The server takes a database off-line only when the load sequence starts with the loading of a database. Once you bring the database on-line, the server assumes you are completely finished with the loading of any transaction logs. If you choose to apply (load) more transaction log dumps after the database is on-line, the server will not take the database off-line. Similarly, if you have a database that is on-line and you are loading transaction logs, there is no need to bring the database on-line after the log or logs have been loaded. Loading a transaction log does not take the database off-line.

You must understand that the System 11 ability to take a database off-line/on-line is one of the few new features that absolutely requires you to make changes to your server environment. Any scripts that you use to load a database must be changed to execute the on-line database command when the load sequence is complete. If you do not make such changes, your scripts will continue to run, but no one will be able to access the database after it is loaded. You also need to examine any such scripts because the **on-line database** command must be issued from the *master* database. This may require further changes to existing scripts.

The database off-line/on-line has another impact. When you load a System 10 database dump into a System 11 Server, the database will be off-line (see Figure 6–3). Further, the database will not be upgraded until the **on-line   database** command is executed. Part of the process of bringing a database on-line checks the database version. If the server

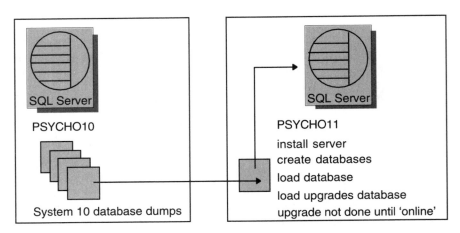

Figure 6–3. Loading System 10 Database Dump to Upgrade

detects a System 10 database was loaded, the server will upgrade the database before bringing it on-line. In this case, the server will generate lots of messages after you issue the on-line database command while it performs the upgrade. You need to understand a subtlety here. You can load a System 10 database dump into a System 11 database, and you can then apply System 10 transaction logs as well. But, once you issue **on-line database** and the server upgrades the database to System 11, you can not apply any more System 10 transaction logs to the database. You can not use **on-line database** to apply and upgrade System 10 transaction logs to a database. This process must start with loading a System 10 database dump.

If you are using database and transaction log dumps to maintain a backup or standby server, you must decide how to handle the use of the on-line database command. See Chapter 9, "SQL Server Recovery", for more details. You can keep the databases of the standby server off-line at all times and only bring them on-line when you need to fail over to the standby server. Or, you can assume that no one will have any access to the standby server. Then you can bring the standby databases on-line after the initial database load and keep applying transaction logs as they become available. Either way, you must change the process for maintaining and failing over to a standby server.

Examples—Database On-line/Off-line Command Syntax

Database Off-line—before Database Load Begins

```
1> sp_helpdb devdb
2> go
```

name	db_size	owner	dbid	created	status
devdb	30.0 MB	sa	7	Apr 04, 1996	no options set

device_fragments	size	usage	free kbytes
c0t2d0s4	20.0 MB	data only	19344
c0t2d0s6	10.0 MB	log only	8720

```
(return status = 0)
1> select * from sysdatabases where name='devdb'
2> go
```

name	dbid	suid	status	version	logptr
devdb	7	1	0	1	10278

crdate	dumptrdate	status2
Apr 4 1996 10:58AM	May 21 1996 12:47PM	0

audflags	deftabaud	defvwaud	defpraud
0	0	0	0

```
(1 row affected)
```

Bringing a Database Off-line (by Loading a Database Dump)

```
1> load database devdb from '/home/dbdump/devdb_52896.dmp'
2> go
Backup Server session id is:  16.  Use this value when executing the
'sp_volchanged' system stored procedure after fulfilling any volume change
request from the Backup Server.
Backup Server: 6.28.1.1: Dumpfile name 'devdb9614909246  ' section number
0001 mounted on disk file '/home/dbdump/devdb_52896.dmp'
Backup Server: 4.58.1.1: Database devdb: 14342 kilobytes LOADed.
Backup Server: 4.58.1.1: Database devdb: 30726 kilobytes LOADed.
Backup Server: 4.58.1.1: Database devdb: 30734 kilobytes LOADed.
Backup Server: 3.42.1.1: LOAD is complete (database devdb).
Remirroring the affected portions of the usage map that are on mirrored
devices.
Use the ON-LINE DATABASE command to bring this database on-line; SQL
Server will not bring it on-line automatically.
```

Server Error Log during this process

There are no error log messages for this process.

Sp_helpdb Output and *sysdatabases* Contents

Note the 'off-line' status of the database.

```
1> sp_helpdb devdb
2> go
```

name	db_size	owner	dbid	created	status
devdb	30.0 MB	sa	7	Apr 04, 1996	off-line

device_fragments	size	usage	free kbytes
c0t2d0s4	20.0 MB	data only	19344
c0t2d0s6	10.0 MB	log only	8720

```
(return status = 0)
1> select * from sysdatabases where name='devdb'
2> go
```

name	dbid	suid	status	version	logptr
devdb	7	1	0	1	10278

crdate	dumptrdate	status2
Apr 4 1996 10:58AM	May 21 1996 12:47PM	16

audflags	deftabaud	defvwaud	defpraud
0	0	0	0

```
(1 row affected)
```

Load Sequence and Bringing Database On-line

```
1> load tran devdb from '/home/dbdump/devdb_52896.trandmp_1'
2> go
Backup Server session id is:  19.  Use this value when executing the
'sp_volchanged' system stored procedure after fulfilling any volume change
request from the Backup Server.
Backup Server: 6.28.1.1: Dumpfile name 'devdb9614909272  ' section number
0001 mounted on disk file '/home/dbdump/devdb_52896.trandmp_1'
Backup Server: 4.58.1.1: Database devdb: 1490 kilobytes LOADed.
Backup Server: 4.58.1.1: Database devdb: 1498 kilobytes LOADed.
Backup Server: 3.42.1.1: LOAD is complete (database devdb).
Use the ON-LINE DATABASE command to bring this database on-line; SQL
Server will not bring it on-line automatically.
1> load tran devdb from '/home/dbdump/devdb_52896.trandmp_2'
2> go
Backup Server session id is:  21.  Use this value when executing the
'sp_volchanged' system stored procedure after fulfilling any volume change
request from the Backup Server.
Backup Server: 6.28.1.1: Dumpfile name 'devdb961490927C  ' section number
0001 mounted on disk file '/home/dbdump/devdb_52896.trandmp_2'
Backup Server: 4.58.1.1: Database devdb: 10 kilobytes LOADed.
Backup Server: 3.42.1.1: LOAD is complete (database devdb).
1 transactions rolled forward.
1 transactions rolled back.
Use the ON-LINE DATABASE command to bring this database on-line; SQL
Server will not bring it on-line automatically.
1> on-line database devdb
2> go
Database 'devdb' is now on-line.
```

Server Error Log

There are no error log messages for this process.

Sp_helpdb and sysdatabases Contents

Note that 'off-line' status is gone.

```
1> sp_helpdb devdb
2> go
```

name	db_size	owner	dbid	created	status
devdb	30.0 MB	sa	7	Apr 04, 1996	no options set

device_fragments	size	usage	free kbytes
c0t2d0s4	20.0 MB	data only	19344
c0t2d0s6	10.0 MB	log only	10224

```
(return status = 0)
1> select * from sysdatabases where name='devdb'
2> go
```

name	dbid	suid	status	version	logptr
devdb	7	1	0	1	11024

crdate	dumptrdate	status2
Apr 4 1996 10:58AM	May 28 1996 10:25AM	0

audflags	deftabaud	defvwaud	defpraud
0	0	0	0

```
(1 row affected)
```

Bringing a Database On-line to Upgrade the Database (System 10 Dump to System 11 Server)

```
1> on-line database cmsdb
2> go
```

Server Error Log During Database Upgrade

Database 'cmsdb' appears to be at an older revision than the present
installation; SQL Server will assess it, and upgrade it as required.
Database 'cmsdb': beginning upgrade step: creating table (table
sysattributes)
[ID 80]
Database 'cmsdb': beginning upgrade step: dropping index (table
sysreferences, index csysreferences) [ID 1003]
Database 'cmsdb': beginning upgrade step: dropping index (table
sysreferences, index ncsysreferences) [ID 1004]
Database 'cmsdb': beginning upgrade step: dropping index (table
sysreferences, index nc2sysreferences) [ID 1005]
Database 'cmsdb': beginning upgrade step: checking database references in
sysreferences [ID 1006]
(0 rows affected)
(0 rows affected)
(0 rows affected)
Database 'cmsdb': beginning upgrade step: creating index (table
sysreferences, index csysreferences) [ID 1007]
Database 'cmsdb': beginning upgrade step: creating index (table
sysreferences, index ncsysreferences) [ID 1008]
Database 'cmsdb': beginning upgrade step: creating index (table
sysreferences, index nc2sysreferences) [ID 1009]
Database 'cmsdb': beginning upgrade step: changing column name (table
sysindexes, column rowpage:maxrowsperpage) [ID 1011]
(1 row affected)
Database 'cmsdb': beginning upgrade step: creating table (table
syspartitions)
[ID 1013]
Database 'cmsdb': beginning upgrade step: noting the present database
upgrade level [ID 1015]
Database 'cmsdb' is now on-line.

SP_SYSMON

Introduction

With System 11, Sybase supplies **sp_sysmon**, a system stored procedure, that monitors and reports on the performance of the SQL Server. By using **sp_sysmon**, you can see the effects of using the new features of System 11. **Sp_sysmon** is actually a set of stored procedures that provide much better information on the performance of the SQL Server than **sp_monitor** did. **Sp_monitor** was all that was available before System 11 for this purpose. Note that **sp_sysmon** is part of the SQL Server as of Version 11.0.1. The stored procedure **sp_sysmon** should already be installed in the *sybsystemprocs* database after the System 11 Server installation or upgrade.

Overview of Use

The details of using and interpreting the output of **sp_sysmon** are covered in Chapter 10. The full outputs of **sp_sysmon** as used to monitor and tune a SQL Server are included on the CD-ROM. Note that **sp_sysmon** uses the same internal counters that SQL Monitor uses (see Figure 6–4). If you are using both products, be aware that starting either one of them will

Figure 6–4. System 11 sp_sysmon and SQL Monitor

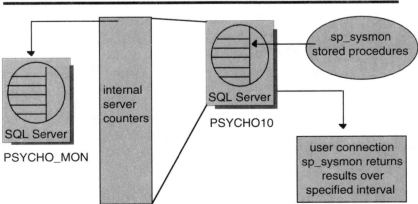

reset the counters. If the other product is running at the same time, the counters are reset and the results of the process that was running will be inaccurate.

SYSTEM TABLES

Along with the new features of System 11 come three new system tables. You need to be aware of the information contained in each of these system tables. You may need to change any existing scripts that query the system tables if you need information that is affected by these new system tables. The name and basic function of each of the new system tables is described below.

sysattributes

- Contains data specifying object configuration
- Exists in master and all user databases
- Example: named caches

syspartitions

- Each partitioned table has a row for each partition
- Exists in all databases

syslogshold

- Specifies oldest active transaction
- Can store Replication Server truncation point (if any)
- In *master* database only

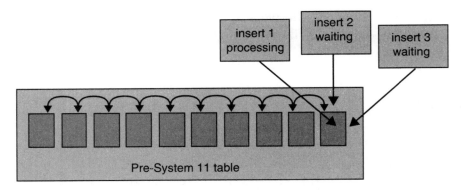

Figure 6–5. Pre-System 11 Heap Table Inserts

TABLE PARTITIONING

Normally, when you create a table in a SQL Server database, the server creates a single set of linked data pages to store the table data. This means that all inserts are done by simply adding each new row to the end of the last data page of the table. This is called a heap table. This assumes that the table does not have a clustered index. Unless the server can update a row in place, the server will also end up doing a delete followed by an insert for each update to a row in the table. This means that there is a great deal of activity on the last page of the table. This creates a "hot spot" on the last page. This leads to contention as multiple user queries need to wait for exclusive access to the last data page (see Figure 6–5). Each query that needs to insert a row will need to obtain an exclusive lock on the last page before it can insert a row. This exclusive lock prevents other queries from either changing or reading the page while it is being changed. Without this locking scheme, concurrent users could get incorrect or transient results from their queries.

Table Partitioning

Before System 11, each table had only one partition. With System 11 you can create tables with multiple partitions. This means that the server creates multiple chains of linked pages. These page chains allow the server to add new rows to the end of each page chain (see Figure 6–6). This will improve performance because multiple concurrent inserts can be done at

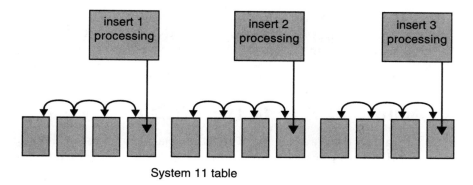

System 11 table

Figure 6–6. System 11 Table Partitioning

the same time. Table partitioning also allows placement of pieces of a table on multiple devices. This can improve performance by spreading the need for disk I/O across multiple disks. Tables can be partitioned on a single server device or across multiple devices. Once a table is partitioned, the server decides which partition to use for the next insert operation. The server randomly selects partitions to spread the new rows among the partitions. Any single transaction will have all of its inserts done on a single partition.

When to Use

Table partitioning is good for a table that is used to record some sort of history or series of events. Such a table is continually having new data appended to the existing rows. Ideally, such a table would only have rows inserted with little or no update activity. Partitioning is very good for doing fast, bulk loading of a table from a data file. Such loads are handled in SQL Server by the bcp utility. A bulk load entails moving a series of blocks of data into the table. Multiple partitions can be used to move the portions of the data file into the table in parallel. You have to break up the original data into the multiple files before you can start loading the data.

Very few tables in a typical application will need to be partitioned. Partitioning is most beneficial when used on tables that have heavy insert or update-in-place activity. Unless an update is an update in place, the update will be handled by the server as a delete followed by an insert. Unless the update is an update in place, table partitioning may not be beneficial for the update. Partitioning helps when there is significant contention among multiple processes that need to insert into the table at the same time. Partitioning is useful when you have a table with heavy insert activity on the last page which otherwise would create a "hot spot".

Creating a Partitioned Table

You must first create the table, and then partition it using the alter table command. Further, the table must not have a clustered index. For an existing table on one server device,

```
alter table psycho_data partition 6
```

You can partition a table that already contains rows of data. All the existing data will be placed into the first partition. The server will make the first partition large enough to hold all the existing data. **Sp_helpartition** will report on the partitions of a table.

Creating a partitioned table across multiple devices is more complicated. You must first create a segment that spans multiple server devices. Use **sp_addsegment** and **sp_extendsegment** to do this. You can extend an existing segment to span multiple server devices. You then create the table on this segment and then partition the table. The number of table partitions and the number of devices do not have to be the same. To change the partitioning of a table you must un-partition and repartition the table.

Restrictions

You can"t partition system tables, temporary tables, or tables that have already been partitioned. A partitioned table cannot have a clustered index. You can't truncate or drop a partitioned table. You have to unpartition the table first. For a normal table, you can use **sp_placeobject** to move the table from one segment to another. You can't do this for a partitioned table. This can affect existing applications or scripts. If you partition a table that is routinely truncated, you will need to make changes. You will need to modify the process so the table is unpartitioned, truncated, and then repartitioned.

```
alter table psycho_data unpartition
```

Unfortunately, while table partitioning holds great promise, the practical implementation of table partitioning in System 11 leaves much to be desired.

Issues

You can use a random key for the clustered index on a table and spread the inserts and updates around. This technique will reduce the contention since concurrent users will (probably) be accessing different data pages even if they are accessing rows of data that are sequential as far as the application is concerned. An example would be purchase orders. A new purchase order is given the next highest purchase order number. But, due to the clustered index key being a random number, the row for the purchase order is not added to the last page of the table but is inserted in the table at a random location.

This technique does not have the restrictions that table partitioning has and will continue to function over time as data pages fill up, and so forth. On the other hand, this technique requires the server to find where the new row belongs among the existing rows. The server may also have to rearrange lots of other rows to make room for the new row.

The benefits of table partitioning must be demonstrated on a development system and measured. Table partitioning can help performance but can only be used in certain, limited situations. Many of your most critical tables will need to have a clustered index and will be used for more than just inserts.

7

The System
Databases

Table of Topics

- Master Device and disk init
- Master Device and Default Server Disk Devices
- Loading a Database Dump of the *master* Database
- Moving Master Device to Larger Partition
- Clearing Server Configuration in *master* Database
- System Databases and Server Devices
- Mirroring of System Databases

SYSTEM DATABASES

The system databases are those databases that make up the core of the SQL Server. Clearly, the master database is one such database. However, with the release of SQL Server 10, two new system databases were introduced; *sybsystemprocs* and *sybsecurity*. Together with the *master* database, these three databases make up the system databases for SQL Server System 10 and System 11.

SYBSYSTEMPROCS DATABASE

In SQL Server Version 4.9.2, all the system stored procedures were stored in the *master* database. The system stored procedures are the stored procedures that Sybase supplies to help you manage the server. Examples include **sp_who, sp_helpdb, sp_configure** and **sp_helpuser**. With System 10 came a number of new stored procedures. This meant more space would be taken up in the *master* database storing these system stored procedures. However, the *master* database can't be extended to another device. The *master* database must always remain within the limits of the size of the master device. If the *master* device fills up, you have no choice but to move the *master* database to a larger master device. This is not a trivial task.

Many sites that had been running SQL Server 4.9.2 had not dedicated much disk space to future growth of the master device. Any increase in the size of the *master* database could force such installations to go through the effort of moving to a larger *master* device. Or, they might not upgrade to

System 10. Sybase did not want to risk the latter so they decided to move all the system stored procedures to a separate database, *sybsystemprocs*.

The *sybsystemprocs* database should not be placed on the *master* device. The master device should only have the *master* database. You don't have to put the *sybsystemprocs* database on its own device. It can share a server device with other user databases. You should make database dumps for the *sybsystemprocs* database. This is especially true if you add any stored procedures of your own to this database. You can restore the *sybsystemprocs* database by using the installation scripts. But this will only restore all the system stored procedures supplied with the server. This won't recreate your own stored procedures that you may have installed there. You can maintain scripts to recreate all your system stored procedures, but it is easier, and more complete, to simply make regular database dumps of the *sybsystemprocs* database.

You do need to choose where to put your own system stored procedures. You can install them in the *master* database, as you would have with SQL Server 4.9.2. However, it is better to not install anything of your own in the *master* database. You should install all of your own system stored procedures in the *sybsystemprocs* database. This way you can backup and restore all your procedures with a single database dump. If you create a stored procedure and name it **sp_<procedurename>**, the stored procedure can be executed from any database. With any other name, the stored procedure can be executed only from within the *sybsystemprocs* database.

Sybsecurity Database

With System 10 and System 11, the SQL Server supports various auditing functions. This allows you to track server logins and database use. In order to use these server auditing functions, you must install the *sybsecurity* database. The auditing process is supported by various tables in the *sybsecurity* database. You can install the *sybsecurity* database as part of the System 10 or 11 upgrade or installation. You can also create the *sybsecurity* database later on. However, it is easier to simply create the *sybsecurity* database as part of the initial installation or upgrade. The fact that you have installed the database doesn't have any impact on the SQL Server until you start using it. It is often easier to install the *sybsecurity* database ahead of time rather than having to find space for it later on.

You should note that the *sybsecurity* database and the auditing features that it supports are part of the normal SQL Server for Systems 10 and 11. This is separate from the Secure SQL Server which supports many advanced security features and is not covered in this book. The many auditing functions available in SQL Server Systems 10 and 11 are covered in great detail in the SQL Server manuals.

Like the *sybsystemprocs* database, the *sybsecurity* database should not be placed on the master device. Similarly, you don't have to put the *sybsecurity* database on its own device. It can share a server device with other user databases. You should make database dumps for the *sybsecurity* database. Unlike the *sybsystemprocs* database, you can't restore the contents of the *sybsecurity* database by rerunning an installation script. As you use the *sybsecurity* database, it will be filled with data specific to your server and to which server operations you are auditing. Re-creating the *sybsecurity* database would only re-create the table structure of the database. You must make database dumps of the *sybsecurity* database to ensure recoverability of this data.

MASTER DATABASE

You need to know about some issues that are specific to the *master* database. The *master* database and the master device are unique. We discuss various aspects of the *master* database and the master device as well since the *master* database and the master device are so intimately related. we discuss the master device as well. The following *master* database and device topics are provided in the next sections.

THE *MASTER* DATABASE AND MASTER DEVICE

The *master* database is the database that stores all the information relating to the SQL Server such as the names and structures of all the databases in the server, all the server user logins, and so forth. The *master* database is where the system tables for the server level are stored. There is only one *master* database per server. The *master* database is the heart and soul of the server and you must not mess with it. If you scramble the *master* database, or the master device, you scramble the whole server. Your recovery plans must make recovery of the *master* database (and *master* device) the number one priority since losing the *master* database or *master* device destroys the entire server.

The *master* database always exists on the server device called the master device. The master device is a server device that is created only through installation using sybinit. You should not be creating master devices without a very good reason and you must be very careful. The master device is never created using **disk init** the way other server devices are. Further, the *master* database can't be extended beyond the master device. This means that if the *master* database fills the master device, you can't execute the **alter database** command to extend the *master* database to another server device. This means that if the master device fills up, you must reinstall the contents of the master device on another larger device. This means a complete reinstallation of the server. You don't want to face this unpleasant duty. You must not let the master device fill up. Note that you could mirror the master device to a larger partition, drop the primary side of the mirrored server device pair, and then manually update the size of the master device in the system table *sysdevices* as detailed below (see Moving Master Device to Larger Partition).

Hence, you must realize two things. First, the *master* database can't grow beyond the size of the master device. When you create the master device through sybinit at installation, you determine the maximum size of the *master* database when you specify the size of the master device. Second, you must not cause the *master* database to grow unnecessarily. This is why you don't want any user objects in the *master* database or any user databases on the master device. Note that you must make sure the master device is not in the pool of "default" server disk devices, see below. Only the *master* database, the model database, and the first 2 Mb of tempdb should be allowed to exist on the master device.

SIZING THE MASTER DEVICE

Now that you understand the relationship between the *master* database and the master device, how big should the master device be? You shouldn't need more then 50 Mb for the master device. For a standard installation where the master device supports 2 Mb of the model database and 2 Mb of tempdb you still have 46 Mb of space for the *master* database. Note that some applications may require installing stored procedures in the *master* database. If there are lots of these stored procedures, you may need a larger than normal *master* database. This situation usually comes up when dealing with a third-party application that you are installing. You should ask the vendor how much room is required by these stored procedures and use that in planning the size of the *master* database and the master device. Similarly, for the *model* database, you may need to create a number of users or lots of database objects that you need to have in all the user databases created after this point. In that case the model database may be larger than normal. Unless you have some special need to have a large model database or have a need to fill the *master* database with lots of data 50-Mb should be more than you will ever need.

You may not see the other side of the relationship between the master device and the *master* database. Since the *master* database doesn't need much more than 50 Mb and since you can have only one server device assigned to one disk partition there is no purpose in placing the *master* database on a master device that is any larger than 50 Mb. This means you should create a 50-Mb partition on a physical disk and use that partition for the master device. From this you see the need for another 50-Mb partition to support the mirror of the *master* database. Recall that the recommended standard for partitioning all the physical disks on your server machine that will be assigned to server devices and their mirrors includes a 50-Mb partition (see Chapter 8 for more details). All too often a server will be set up wherein all the physical disks are partitioned into several equal partitions. This seems logical until the master device is set-up. These equal partitions are often several hundred megabytes each and using one of these for the master device ends up wasting several hundred megabytes that are controlled but not used by the master device as well as even more waste by the large partition used for the *master* mirror.

You check your server to see how much free space you have. You see there are several hundred megabytes free. You think all is well and you put off purchasing more disks. You don't notice that most of that free space is on the *master* device. You shouldn't be using this space for anything other than the *master* database (and *model* and part of *tempdb*). When you actually need to use the space you thought you had, you realize what has been going on. Suddenly you don't have much, if any, free space at all.

THE *LOGSEGMENT* OF THE *MASTER* DATABASE

Another unique quality of the *master* database is that the *logsegment* can't be separated from the rest of the database. This means you can't place the *logsegment* on a separate server device as you can and should with almost all other databases in the server. You won't think this is a big deal, but it is. Recall that if the *logsegment* is not on a separate server device, a server device that is dedicated to supporting only the log segment of that database, you can't dump the transaction log separately. Dumping the database is the only form of dump you can make for such a database. But recall also that while dumping the database does make a copy of the transaction log, as well as the rest of the database, it doesn't truncate the transaction log. This means that even though you dump the *master* database regularly, as you must, the size of the transaction log for the *master* database continues to grow. Certainly you should not be performing any heavy processing in the *master* database and therefore the transaction log should grow slowly. Still, the fact that the transaction log is growing at all means it will fill up eventually and it always fills up at the most inappropriate time. The only way for you to reduce the size of the transaction log of the *master* database is to dump the transaction log with the **truncate_only** option. So, you need to realize that along with a regular dump of the *master* database you must dump the transaction log with **truncate_only** after each database dump. Note that while dumping the transaction log with **truncate_only** may seem contradictory to the fact that you can't dump the transaction log separately, it isn't. The **truncate_only** option means that the size of the transaction log is reduced, but a copy of the transaction log is not made.

MASTER DEVICE NAME AND MIRRORING

Another odd characteristic of the master device comes up regarding mirroring. Once you have set-up the master device and before you have created the mirror of the master device the output of **sp_helpdevice** for the *master* device will look very odd. The output will tell you that the device_name is "master" as you would expect but the *physical device* is "d_master" which is not the case at all, as you would expect the physical device name to be the name of the disk partition that supports the master device. Further, as soon as you create the mirror of the master device, this oddity disappears and the physical name becomes the actual device name as it should have been all along. If you don't mirror the master device, you can't tell which server device is the *master* device from the information in *sysdevices* or the output of **sp_helpdevice**. You can find out the server device that is the master device using two different methods. First, you can examine the error log (see Chapter 12 for details of examining the server errorlog). Second, you can examine the RUN_<servername> file that is used to start the SQL Server. Note that this peculiar behavior of the unmirrored master device comes up during the upgrade process (see Chapter 13). During the upgrade process you may need to change the physical name of the master device entry in *sysdevices* to reflect the actual physical name of the server device. Shown below is the output of the **sp_helpdevice** command for the master device before mirroring, the output of the **disk mirror** command and the output of **sp_helpdevice** for the master device after the mirroring is complete.

```
1> sp_helpdevice master
go
2>     device_name           physical_name              description
          master                d_master          special, default disk,
                                                  physical disk, 32.00 MB

    status         cntrltype          device_number        low       high
       3               0                    0                0       16383

(1 row affected, return status = 0)
1> disk mirror
2> name="master",
3> mirror = '/dev/rdsk/c0t0d0s7',
4> writes=serial
5> go
Creating the physical file for the mirror
Starting Dynamic Mirroring of 16384 pages for logical device
'master'.
         512 pages mirrored...
        1024 pages mirrored...
        1536 pages mirrored...
        2048 pages mirrored...
        2560 pages mirrored...
```

```
            3072 pages mirrored...
            3584 pages mirrored...
            4096 pages mirrored...
            4608 pages mirrored...
            5120 pages mirrored...
            5632 pages mirrored...
            6144 pages mirrored...
            6656 pages mirrored...
            7168 pages mirrored...
The remaining 9216 pages are currently unallocated and will be mir-
rored as they are allocated.
1> sp_helpdevice master
go
```

device_name	physical_name	description
master	d_master	special, MIRROR ENABLED, mirror = '/dev/rdsk/c0t0d0s7', serial writes., reads mirrored, default disk,32.00 MB

status	cntrltype	device_number	low	high
739	0	0	0	16383

```
(1 row affected, return status = 0)
```

MASTER DEVICE AND DISK INIT

Another special situation you must watch out for relates to the physical name of the *master* device as described in the previous section. If the *master* device is not mirrored, the output of **sp_helpdevice** will show that the *device_name* is "master" as you expect, but the *physical_device* is 'd_master' and not the actual path of the disk partition that supports the master device. Now, this odd behavior of the SQL Server allows another problem to come up. When you install the SQL Server using sybinit the master device is created as part of the installation. As part of setting up the server you will need to execute **disk init** against each physical disk partition that will be used to support a server device. You must be careful, however, that you do not execute a **disk init** against the physical disk partition that supports the master device. You would expect that the server would prevent this error from occurring, and normally you would

227

be right. For any other server device, if you execute **disk init** and specify a partition that is already supporting a server device for that server, the server will generate an error. But, this process is based on the server looking in *sysdevices* and seeing that the partition is already in use.

For the master device, the server thinks the partition supporting the *master* device is "d_master" and therefore, if you execute a **disk init** and specify the path of the partition that really does support the *master* device the server will allow it to happen. Worse still, the server will continue to function. This sort of error is deadly and very embarrassing. When you dump the *master* database as part of the installation process, you will get errors and if you do **dbcc** checks on the *master* database you will get 605 errors. At this point the *master* database is dead and the only recourse is to load a dump of *master* or reinstall the server.

You must be very careful whenever you execute **disk init**. Make very sure that you have checked the server error log and verified that you know what disk partition is supporting the master device and verify that you are not trying to **disk init** that partition. Also check any script that you set up to perform multiple **disk init** commands as well. You can manually update the sysdevices table to reflect the path of the partition supporting the master device, but the real solution is to mirror the *master* device so the server will catch and prevent this error. You should be mirroring the master device anyway so it doesn't hurt to mirror it right away.

MASTER DEVICE AND DEFAULT SERVER DISK DEVICES

When you first install the SQL Server using sybinit, the master device is installed and assigned to the "default" pool of server disk space. Note that the term "default" here is different from the *default* segment. When any server disk device is assigned to the pool of default server disk devices, in other words, when any database is created or altered without specifying a specific server disk device, the additional database space will be created on a server disk device in the pool of default server disk devices. The disk devices are chosen from the default pool in alphabetical order as each disk fills up. This means that any segmentation you have set up for data integrity or performance reasons could be jeopardized by this default pool. You must make sure that any server devices that are assigned to the default pool of disk space are not involved in supporting segments of the important databases on the server. Better yet, you should not assign any disk devices to the default pool at all. This requires that any creating or altering of databases be done to specific server disk devices. This is how it should be done anyway as it forces the DBA to review the performance impacts of creating or altering the database.

Note that the master device is the only device that is automatically assigned to the default pool of disk space. You must manually assign any other server disk devices to the default pool by using the **sp_disk-default** server command. Further, you must not allow the master device to remain assigned to the default pool. You must use the **sp_disk-default** command to remove the master device from the pool. You can see if any device is assigned to the default pool by executing the **sp_helpdevice** server command. Shown below is the output of the **sp_helpdevice** and the **sp_diskdefault** command to remove the master device from the default pool of disk space.

```
1> sp_helpdevice master
2> go
```

device_name	physical_name	description
master	d_master	special, default disk, physical disk, 32.00 MB

status	cntrltype	device_number	low	high
3	0	0	0	16383

```
1> sp_diskdefault master, defaultoff
2> go
(return status = 0)
1> sp_helpdevice master
2> go
```

device_name	physical_name	description
master	d_master	special,physical disk, 32.00 MB

status	cntrltype	device_number	low	high
2	0	0	0	16383

```
(1 row affected, return status = 0)
```

LOADING A DATABASE DUMP OF THE *MASTER* DATABASE

Loading the *master* database is part of the recovery process (see Chapter 9). When you need to load a database dump of the *master* database, you will need to put the server into single-user mode. Note that you can't change the database options for the *master* database and that means you can"t put the *master* database into single-user mode the way you can for any other database. To put the server into single-user mode you have to add the −m option to the execution of the server binary in the RUN_<*servername*> script in the $SYBASE/install directory. Then you must restart the server to put it into single-user mode. Now you can load the *master* database from the dump. Note that when the server has finished loading the dump of the *master* database it will shut down the server. Also, you need to realize that the server loads the database dump of *master* which overwrites anything that was in the *master* database but that is all that the server does. The server does not try to recover any of the other databases or even open the other server devices. Normal server recovery doesn't happen until you start the server again.

MOVING MASTER DEVICE TO LARGER PARTITION

If you must move the master device to a larger partition, you will need to be aware of some details that will confuse you. This need can come up because you have filled the master device (don't let this happen) or you plan ahead for a larger master device when you upgrade your server hardware or migrate to a new machine. You should have 50 Mb for your master device, so anytime you can make the move to give the master device this much room, you should be ready to do so. See Chapter 8 for details of standard disk partitioning.

The problem comes in the actual move of the *master* database. Assuming that you have either added the new disks to the existing machine or you are moving to new disks on a whole new machine, you will want to move the current *master* database with all the information it contains about the current server into the *master* database you have created on the new larger master device.

If you are simply adding new disks to the existing server machine, you can mirror the existing master device (on the old smaller partition) to the new master device (on the new larger partition) and then drop the primary side of the mirror of the master device. This gives you the *master* database on the new larger master device. If you are installing the server from scratch the installation process will create the master device for you and you will then want to load a dump of the *master* database. This also gives you the *master* database on the new larger master device.

However, in both cases you don't get what you expect. You wanted to get the current *master* database onto a new larger master device so you would have room to increase the size of the *master* database as needed. Whether through mirroring the master device or loading a dump of the *master* database, the new *master* database (on the new larger master device) carries along with it the old (current) information in the *sysdevices* system table. This information will reflect the old (current) smaller size of the master device and the server will believe the size of the master device to still be the smaller size. You must update the information for the size of the master device manually before the server can use the extra space actually available on the new *master* device.

Warning

1. Updating system tables in not supported by Sybase. There is no guarantee that the system table schema will be maintained between releases which means manual updates that work for one version may not work on another version.

2. Do not perform such updates without consulting with Sybase Technical Support first.

3. Make sure you have dumps of everything you might need to rebuild the server in case the manual updates destroy something.

4. After updating system tables, you should restart the server to copy the changes into memory.

Note that this procedure must be done with caution and you must review the specifics of your server situation with Sybase Technical Support before proceeding. The output of the actual process is shown below. As with any other updates made to a system table this change must be done within a transaction to prevent updating other devices. See Chapter 12 for more details about updating system tables manually.

You should dump the *master* database to a disk file and drop the mirror of the master device before starting this procedure. Note that you must be certain that the partition that the master device is on is indeed the larger size you think it is.

In this example, the new master device is 25,600 2K pages which is 50 Mb which means the low database will be 0 and the high datapage will be 25,600 - 1 = 25,599; data page 0 through data page 25,599 is 25,600 pages.

```
1> sp_configure "allow", 1
2> go
Configuration option changed. Run the RECONFIGURE command to
install.
(return status = 0)
1> reconfigure with override
2> go
1> select * from sysdevices where name='master'
2> go
```

low	high	status	cntrltype	name	phyname	mirrorname
0	7904	2	0	master	/dev/rdsk/c0t0d0s7	NULL

```
(1 row affected)

1> begin tran psycho
2> go
1> update sysdevices set high=25599 where name='master'
2> go
(1 row affected)
1> select * from sysdevices where name='master'
2> go
```

low	high	status	cntrltype	name	phyname	mirrorname
0	25599	2	0	master	/dev/rdsk/c0t0d0s7	NULL

```
(1 row affected)

1> commit tran psycho
2> go
1> sp_helpdevice master
2> go
```

2> device_name	physical_name	description
master	/dev/rdsk/c0t0d0s7	special,physical disk, 50.00 MB

status	cntrltype	device_number	low	high
2	0	0	0	25599

```
(1 row affected, return status = 0)
1> sp_configure "allow", 0
2> go
Configuration option changed. Run the RECONFIGURE command to
install.
(return status = 0)
1> reconfigure
2> go
```

You must remirror the master device to a partition that is the same size as the new, larger master device.

CLEARING SERVER CONFIGURATION IN *MASTER* DATABASE

This section applies only to SQL Server System 11.

With System 11, the SQL Server uses configuration files to document the server configuration. If you need to clear the server configuration, you simply restart the server without specifying a configuration file, and you make sure there is not a <*servername*>.cfg file in the $SYBASE directory. You can simply rename the <*servername*>.cfg file to make this happen. As the server starts up, it will use the default values for all the server configuration parameters. Note that this will set all the configuration parameters to their default values. You could simply restart the server with an older configuration file, or the <*servername*>.bak file, in order to restore the server configuration to a previous version. See Chapter 5 for more details of the use of configuration files.

This section applies only to SQL Server versions 4.9.2 and System 10.

The entire configuration of the server is stored in system tables in the *master* database. When you make changes to the server configuration using the sp_configure, command you may increase a configuration parameter so much that the server can't start up with the memory available on the server machine. One example of this would be increasing the number of user connections, each of which takes a certain amount of server machine memory. Once you have increased a configuration parameter too far and you shutdown and try to restart the server, the restart will fail. At this point you can't get into the server to fix the problem since the server isn't running. You must reset the server configuration to the default values using buildmaster with the -r option. Note that you must be very careful about using the buildmaster command. If you don't get it right, it may overwrite the existing *master* database wiping out all information regarding the existing server. You should work with Sybase Technical Support before attempting to use the buildmaster command.

Warning

1. Do not use buildmaster without consulting with Sybase Technical Support first.

2. Make sure you have dumps of everything you might need to rebuild the server in case the manual updates destroy something.

You also need to realize that running buildmaster -r will reset all the server configuration parameters to the default values, not just the one (or more) configuration parameter you increased too far. This means that all the other server configuration information is lost. This is why it is vital that you dump the system tables of the server to disk files on a regular basis (see Chapter 14, for a script that should be run as a cron job to accomplish this). After you run buildmaster -r, you will need the rest of the server configuration information stored in the disk file(s) to restore the server configuration.

SYSTEM DATABASES AND SERVER DEVICES

The *master* database must always be on the master device. The other system databases, *sybsystemprocs* and *sybsecurity* should not be on the master device. Both *sybsystemprocs* and *sybsecurity* can be on a server device that supports user databases and both can be on the same device. See Chapter 8 for details and examples of placing the system databases among different disk configurations.

MIRRORING OF SYSTEM DATABASES

You should understand that all of the system databases are critical to the operation of the SQL Server. If the *master* database is lost, the server is completely useless. If the *sybsystemprocs* database is lost, the server is still technically alive. However, no system stored procedure is available which makes server operation very difficult. If the *sybsecurity* database is installed and being used for auditing, the server will stop processing if the *sybsecurity* database is lost.

This means that all three of these databases should be on server devices that are mirrored. The *master* database should always be on its own server device. Mirroring the master device requires another disk partition (or slice) for a dedicated mirror. *Sybsystemprocs* and *sybsecurity* can be placed on any server device along with other user databases. The devices that support these databases should be mirrored to prevent server downtime.

Physical Server Design

Table of Topics

❀ **Disk Controllers**

❀ **Database Location on Disks and Controllers**

❀ **Initializing Server Devices**

❀ **Database Segments**

❀ **Transaction Log Issues**

❀ **Mirroring Server Devices**

❀ **How to Layout the Devices and Segments of a Server**

❀ **Why You Should be Hesitant to Add Database Space**

INTRODUCTION

You must understand the way the SQL server is installed on the UNIX server machine. This process impacts how you add space to databases and create new databases in the future. While various aspects of the relationships between server, disks, disk controllers, and so forth, have been mentioned elsewhere, we cover them in an orderly fashion here.

You may think that as a DBA you don't need to understand the details of physical disks and partitions as seen by the operating system and how they relate to the SQL Server devices you work with. As your database system grows, you will be supporting servers that take over entire server machines and use almost all the disk space on the machine. You will need to understand these issues in order to keep up with the accelerating space demands of these large databases. You will also need to see the relationship between physical disks and segments to improve and maintain the server performance relative to the largest databases on each server. We discuss the following physical server design topics in the chapter.

SQL SERVER VERSIONS

The issues discussed here are relevant to all versions of SQL Server. However, there are two things you need to be aware of relative to the version of SQL Server you are using. The first is that of mirroring of system databases. For SQL Server System 10 and System 11, the system databases include the master database, the *sybsystemprocs* and *sybsecurity* databases. The *sybsystemprocs* database is required to store the system stored procedures in System 10 and 11. The *sybsecurity* database is only needed if you wish to utilize the auditing functions introduced in System 10 and available in System 11 as well. The second change has to do with System 11 and the Operating System software (OS) for Sun platforms.

See Chapter 7 for more details regarding the system databases. See Chapter 8 for details of placing the system databases on server devices and on different numbers of physical disks.

SQL Server 4.9.2

For SQL Server 4.9.2, there is only the one system database, the *master* database, to be concerned with. You should always mirror the *master* device. The master database should be the only database on the master device.

SQL Server System 10

All the material presented here applies to System 10. The system databases *sybsystemprocs* and *sybsecurity* were introduced with System 10. The master device should always be mirrored. You should also mirror the server device that supports the *sybsystemprocs* database and the *sybsecurity* database, if it has been installed.

System 10 introduced an addition to the options for the **create database** and **alter database** commands. The new option is "with override" which simply allows you to create a database with the log segment on the same server device as other segments, but still be able to dump the transaction log separately. This option may be useful in specific situations, but in general the rule of placing the transaction log on its own server device should still be followed. You can look up the "with override" option and you'll see that use of this option is not recommended. This option was introduced only to assist you when you have very limited disk space. This may be necessary during certain disaster recovery situations.

SQL Server System 11

System 11 includes the features noted above that were introduced with System 10. However, there is a vital change regarding the operating system. For both System 10 and 4.9.2, Sybase supported the SQL Server on both the SunOS and Solaris operating systems. With System 11, however, Sybase supports SQL Server only on the Solaris operating system.

While this is specific to the Sun hardware and software platform, it points out the general need, when upgrading, to check that the upgraded server will run on your existing hardware and operating system platform. Upgrading both the OS and the SQL Server is a much bigger project than just upgrading the SQL Server. You must verify that your upgrade plan is adequate. You must not find out, at the last minute, that you have to upgrade the OS as well as the SQL Server. This is also another reason that you should first install or upgrade to a new version of SQL Server on a system that is not being used for production. This way you can run into all these dependencies before it really counts.

OVERALL SERVER SETUP

You should simplify the configuration of each SQL Server whenever possible. You should establish simple standards for both port numbers and device names that you will use for each SQL Server. By setting up simple, memorable standards, you make it easier for yourself and any other DBA that who to deal with the server.

Port Numbers

You should set up a set of port numbers that the SQL Server and any associated products will use on each of your server machines. These are the port numbers that are specified in the interfaces file for each server (see Chapter 12 for details of how the interfaces file works). A standard set of port numbers saves you time and confusion. When building a new server you don't have to think what port numbers to use. You can check a server errorlog and tell immediately if it is running on the standard port or not. This tells you if someone (another DBA, we assume) has restarted the server on another port to isolate the server from the user community. You can detect errors in a user version of the interfaces file when you use a standard set of port numbers. Depending on the operating system you are using, a standard set of port numbers may save you a considerable amount of work when setting up or maintaining the interfaces file. You can tell the server machine SA that this standard set of port numbers will be needed on all server machines so they can ensure that no other processes are assigned to those ports.

A standard set of port numbers is shown in Table 8–1.

Table 8–1. Standard Server Machine Port Numbers

Server or related product	port number
SQL Server master and query	5001
SQL Server console (4.9.2 only)	5002
Backup Server (not part of 4.9.2)	5005
SQL Monitor	5010
DataTools SQL BackTrack license manager	5050
Replication Server	5070
Replication Server Log Transfer Manager(s)	5071, 5072, 5073, ...
Open Server(s)	5100, 5101, 5102, ...

Device Names

You must have a simple and consistent server logical device naming convention. This will cover disk devices and tape devices.

For disk devices you should name the logical device after the physical disk and partition where the logical disk device is located. This makes it much easier for you to determine which physical disk is having problems when errors occur since the server machine name for each disk is how the hardware errors are logged in the machine's errorlog. You are assured that you won't specify duplicate device names if you follow the names the machine uses for the disks. When you need to determine the physical size of a disk partition you will need to use the machine name for the disk so you should use this name for the logical devices as well.

Your approach to naming the server logical disk devices should be as simple as this. For server machine disk /dev/rdsk/c0t0d0 and partition 7 the server logical disk device would be c0t0d0s7.

PHYSICAL DISKS

The disks of the server machine are where all the parts of the SQL server are located, from the binaries that make up the server to the data within the databases. The term "disk" refers to the physical hard disk drive (also called a spindle) that is attached to a controller that is part of the server machine (see Figure 8–1). These physical disks are known to the server machine operating system by names like c0t0d0 and c0t0d4. The server machine breaks each physical disk into partitions (see Figure 8–2). The number of partitions that are allowed varies among operating systems, for Solaris the number of partitions is 8, and the partitions (also called slices) are labeled 0 through 7. The server machine accesses each partition of each physical disk through files that are located in the server machine file system /dev/rdsk with a typical example being /dev/rdsk/c0t0d0s3 for the 3 partition (slice 3) of the physical disk known to the server machine as

Figure 8–1. Server Machine Disk Controllers and Disks

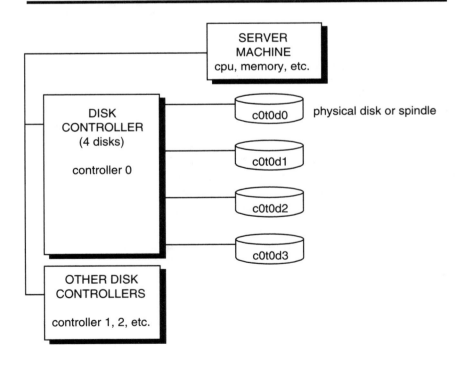

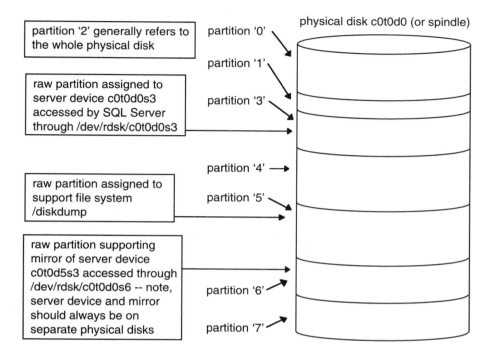

Figure 8–2. Physical Disk Partitions (for Solaris)

c0t0d0. The "r" in rdsk indicates that the partition is to be accessed in character mode as a raw partition. The character mode of accessing a partition means that the data is written to disk immediately with no buffering which is what you want for all SQL Server devices. For each partition there is a companion file, in this case, /dev/dsk/c0t0d0s3 which is for accessing the partition in block mode which you must not use for a server device. The block mode of accessing a partition means that the data is buffered before being written to disk. If the server machine or the disk had a problem before the buffer were flushed to disk, you could lose data. The files /dev/rdsk/c0t0d0s3 and /dev/dsk/c0t0d0s3 are known as "special" files that control the access mode to the 3 partition of the physical disk c0t0d0. Note that these special files are in /dev/rdsk for all 8 possible partitions for each physical disk on the server machine. You don't have to use all the partitions possible for any disk, and the size of each partition on a disk is configurable.

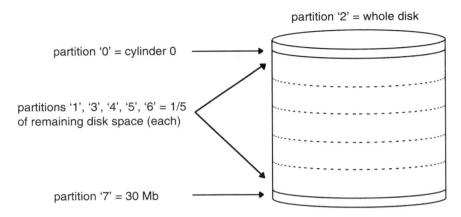

partition '2' = whole disk

partition '0' = cylinder 0

partitions '1', '3', '4', '5', '6' = 1/5 of remaining disk space (each)

partition '7' = 30 Mb

Figure 8–3. Standard Disk Partitions for Server Devices and Their Mirrors

STANDARD DISK PARTITIONING

You should have a standard for partitioning each disk on your server machines. Your server machine SA person must be consulted before trying to establish this standard. While you can argue for different partitioning schemes for different server machines, it is much easier if you can simply specify a simple set of partitioning information for all disks. You should start with a basic scheme such as this one. First, the file system disks are partitioned as needed to support the file systems specified by your standard server machine configuration. Second, for all the disks allocated to the SQL server, you want a very simple partitioning scheme as shown in Table 8–2 (also see Figure 8–3).

Table 8–2. Standard Disk Partitioning

Partition 0
Partition 2
Partition 7
Partitions 1, 3, 4, 5, 6

Partition 0

Partition 0 is never to be used by a server. It simply serves to hold the disk label which is cylinder 0 of each disk. By putting cylinder 0 in partition 0 and specifying that DBA never use it for supporting a server, you will save yourself a great deal of trauma.

Partition 2

Partition 2 refers to the entire disk and should not be used since you need to have more than one partition per disk for performance and data security reasons.

Partition 7

Partition 7 should be a relatively small size such as 50 Mb. Each server you install will need several small databases. These 50-Mb partitions provide a very convenient location for the server logical devices that will support these small databases and their mirrors. You will need more such partitions to support the *master*, *sybsystemprocs*, and *sybsecurity* databases. While you may not need a 50-Mb partition on every disk, it is much easier for you to specify one partitioning scheme for all disks.

Partitions 1, 3, 4, 5, 6

Partitions 1, 3, 4, 5, and 6 are all the same size and each these partitions is one-fifth of the remaining disk space.

Your server machine SA person will find it takes much less time to set up and verify a partitioning scheme like this than worrying about different partitioning for each disk on each server machine. In times of crisis you will want to simply ask the server machine SA person to verify the standard partitioning of a disk rather then trying to recall what the partitioning for a given disk was or should be. Further, you will greatly reduce your already onerous documentation chores with a standard partitioning scheme. You will not have to worry about keeping track of the partitions of all disks with a standard like this. And you will spend a great deal less time explaining such a standard partitioning scheme to the other DBAs you work with or train.

Disk Partitioning and Sun Operating System Issues

If you are running SQL Server on Sun platforms, you need to be aware of the Sun operating systems that are supported for the various versions of SQL Server. SQL Server 4.9.2 and System 10 run on both SunOS and Solaris operating systems. However, for System 11 SQL Server, Sun Solaris is the only supported operating system.

In SunOS, the disk partitions are referred to as partitions a through h. In Sun Solaris, the disk partitions are referred to as slices 0 through 7. The files that control access to the slices are different as well. An example for Solaris would be `/dev/rdsk/c0t1d0s2` for slice 2 of the physical disk. This is the equivalent of the file `/dev/rsdb` for the c partition in the SunOS world. There is a one-to-one correlation between the letter names of the SunOS disk partitions and the Sun Solaris disk slices as shown in Table 8–3. For all of the discussion of disk partitions (slices) presented in this chapter you can substitute the corresponding partitions if you are operating SQL Server on the SunOS platform.

Table 8–3. SunOS Disk Partitions versus Sun Solaris Slices

SunOS disk partitions	Sun Solaris disk slices
a	slice 0
b	slice 1
c	slice 2
d	slice 3
e	slice 4
f	slice 5
g	slice 6
h	slice 7

DISK PARTITIONING VERSUS PHYSICAL DISK SIZE

The standard disk partitioning discussed in this chapter is relevant to physical disks with a total capacity of 4.2-Gb. For a 4.2 Gb drive, you end up with 800 Mb for partitions 1 and 3 through 7 and 88 Mb for 7. For a 2.1- Gb drive, you could specify the 7 partition to be 30 Mb and then have roughly 400 Mb for each of the remaining five partitions, 1 and 3 through 7. For the 4.2-Gb drive, choosing to make the five equal sized partitions 800 Mb and then assigning the remaining space to the 7 partition results in a good standard partitioning scheme for these larger disks. For both the 2.1- Gb and the 4.2-Gb drives, you need to have a single small partition to support the master device or its mirror. This is why you need to create a small partition on each disk. The small partitions of each disk should be used first for the master device and its mirror. After that, the small partitions should be used to support small databases, or file systems if needed. For SQL Server Systems 10 and 11, the small partition on additional disks should be used for server devices for the *sybsystemprocs* and *sybsecurity* databases, and the mirrors of these devices.

RAW PARTITIONS VERSUS FILE SYSTEMS

Each partition of each physical disk on the server machine can contain file systems or can be used as a raw partition. SQL server uses disks to store the databases and their data and can use either file system files or raw partitions for storage. File systems are controlled by the operating system and are where all the files needed for the operating system are stored. Since they are controlled by the operating system, file systems are buffered to improve speed. The operating system will buffer the writes to a file system on disk and make a group of writes all at once. You need to understand the implications of this to the integrity of your data. If you use an operating system file system as a server logical disk device, you may improve performance, however, since the writes to disk are buffered you are risking the integrity of the data within your server. The SQL server relies on *committing* transactions in order to maintain data integrity. See Chapter 9 for a detailed discussion of how the server assumes that a committed transaction has been written to disk and the problems it would cause if the writes to disk were actually in an operating system buffer.

When the server issues a disk write, it assumes that the disk write is executed immediately without any buffering, which is the case when you use a raw partition of the physical disk for a server logical disk device. If you are using an operating system file system and the disk writes are buffered, the server will believe it has written a transaction to disk, which means the transaction is committed, even though the write is only sent to memory. If a failure occurs between the time the server believes the disk write was completed and the time the operating system buffer is flushed out to disk, the parts of any transaction that were in the buffer are lost. When the server recovers (if it can recover with pieces of transactions lost), it will believe the transaction was indeed written to disk when in fact it wasn"t and the affected databases on the server will be inconsistent.

For this reason you should not use operating system file systems for server logical disk devices. There is an exception to this rule: If you don't care about a particular database and you just want improved performance you can then try a file system logical device. This technique is often used for *tempdb* where the data is never recovered by the server so losing it is not a concern (see Chapter 9).

Note that raw partitions are ignored by the operating system other than to check user permissions on the partition(s) as processes access them.

SQL SERVER LOGICAL DISK DEVICES

You need to clearly understand the terms. The term "disk" can be confusing. A physical disk is also called a spindle. A physical disk can contain several SQL Server logical disk devices (subsequently referred to simply as server devices, or just devices), or operating system file systems, and either of these (but not both) can occupy a single partition on the physical disk. The SQL Server will refer to a physical disk partition as a logical device. We use the phrase "server logical disk" device to make it clear that

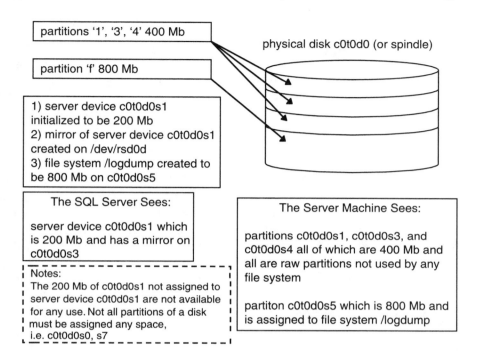

partitions '1', '3', '4' 400 Mb

partition 'f' 800 Mb

physical disk c0t0d0 (or spindle)

1) server device c0t0d0s1 initialized to be 200 Mb
2) mirror of server device c0t0d0s1 created on /dev/rsd0d
3) file system /logdump created to be 800 Mb on c0t0d0s5

The SQL Server Sees:

server device c0t0d0s1 which is 200 Mb and has a mirror on c0t0d0s3

Notes:
The 200 Mb of c0t0d0s1 not assigned to server device c0t0d0s1 are not available for any use. Not all partitions of a disk must be assigned any space, i.e. c0t0d0s0, s7

The Server Machine Sees:

partitions c0t0d0s1, c0t0d0s3, and c0t0d0s4 all of which are 400 Mb and all are raw partitions not used by any file system

partiton c0t0d0s5 which is 800 Mb and is assigned to file system /logdump

Figure 8–4. Server Devices

we are referring to the device known to the SQL Server, and that such a device is indeed a logical device in that it refers only to whatever you have assigned it to. This is in contrast to a physical disk, or device which refers to the actual disk drive, or a partition of such a physical disk. Note that in general, the term "server device" refers to a server device that is assigned to a portion of a physical disk. Tape drives and operating system files used for dumping databases and transaction log dumps are referred to as "server dump devices".

Physical disks are not known to SQL Server. Instead, a section of a partition of a physical disk is defined to the SQL Server as a logical disk device (see Figure 8–4). Once this is done, that section of the partition of the physical disk can be used by the server for creating databases, and so forth. Note that the server does not have any knowledge of the size of the partition on the physical disk—only the size of the logical disk device that you defined to the server. Note that the size of the server logical disk device that you define to the server is defined as a number of 2K pages (a data page contains 2048 bytes and is called a "2K page"; this number is platform specific), and you can assign any number of 2K pages to the server logical disk device that will fit within the partition you have selected. However, you can only have one SQL Server logical disk device for a given partition of a physical disk. So, you must do one of two things. Either define the server logical disk device to be as large as possible on the partition you are working with, or, after deciding how big a server logical disk device you need, change the sizes of the partition of the physical disk to such a size that will just allow the size of the server logical disk device you want. You can define the server logical disk device to be smaller than partition will allow, but this is a waste of space since you can't assign another server logical disk device to a partition once it has been assigned to a server logical disk device. Further, you can't assign an operating system file system to a partition that is assigned to a server logical disk device.

DISK PARTITIONING

You also need to understand the partitions that are allowed for the operating systems that are running on the server machines in your database system. For this discussion we review the specifics of the Solaris 2.x disk partitioning. You must review this information with the server machine SA for you server machines to make sure you have accurate information for your system. You may think that the partitioning of disks is up to the server machine SA, but they may not have any insight into what SQL Server needs. You must ensure that the partitioning that is done, regardless of whom is responsible, is optimal for the SQL Server. The discussion in the next sections is relevant to UNIX operating systems supplied by many vendors.

Solaris Disk Partitions

The Solaris operating system allows a physical disk to have up to 8 partitions, named 0 through 7. Each of these partitions, except for partition 2, can be assigned some portion of the space on the physical disk (spindle). The operating system will allow you to set up overlapping partitions but you should not do this. Overlapping partitions can cause disaster when one of the partitions is used for a server logical disk device. As data is written to one of the partitions and fills the partition to the point that data is now written to the disk where the partitions overlap, data that was on in the second partition is overwritten. If the second device is a server logical disk device, it will be destroyed as the data spills over from the first partition.

Partition Sizes

You can assign almost any size portion of the physical disk to any of the partitions. You can even assign the entire physical disk to one partition although you generally shouldn't do this since you want multiple partitions to support multiple-server logical disk devices or their mirrors. When you install the physical disk, the operating system will assign all the space on the disk to partition 2. You should leave this the way it is as this gives you a good way to verify the size of the whole physical disk. You see this by running the UNIX command prtvtoc which outputs the size of each partition. By leaving the 2 partition as it is, you have documentation of the size of the physical disk. There are situations when you do need to assign the entire physical disk to one partition for use as a file system. For example, your server will need a file system to use as a location for database dumps made to disk. Since these database dumps will be large, you may need to assign the entire physical disk to the one file system to be used for the database dumps.

Assigning Disk Space to Partitions

The assignment of a portion or all of the physical disk to a partition is done using the format command. You should work with your server machine SA person to accomplish this task. Unless you are expert in the use of the format command, and unless your group (i.e., DBA) is assigned to do this work, you should leave it to the SA. The improper use of the format command can very quickly destroy your server. Note that while you can assign almost any part of the disk to a partition, that doesn't mean you should. The format command will allow you to create overlapping partitions which you must not do as the data written to one partition can overwrite the adjacent partition. Further, you can assign cylinder 0 to a partition but again you must be very careful about doing this. Make sure you do not assign cylinder 0 of any disk to a partition that will support server devices or their mirrors. The standard disk partitioning scheme discussed later will prevent you from making this mistake.

Here is an example of how *not* to partition a disk.

```
*                    First      Sector    Last
*  Partition   Tag    Flags     Sector    Count       Sector
      1         3      01          0      1639440    1639439 (1)
      2         5      01          0      8380800    8380799
      3         0      00       1639440   1639440    3278879 (2)
      4         0      00       3278880   1639440    4918319
      5         0      00       4918320   1639440    6557759
      6         4      00       6557760   1639440    8197199
      7         0      00       8197200    183600    8380799 (3)
```

Mount Directory

(1) -> includes cylinder 0 — don't use for raw!

(2) -> 800.51 Mb 800 Mb = 409600 2K pages

(3) -> 89.65 Mb 89 Mb = 45568 2K pages

Note that partition 1 (or slice 1) starts with cylinder 0. If partition 1 is used to support a SQL Server device, the disk will be lost the next time the server machine is rebooted. You must verify that this situation has not occurred on your server machine. If you discover that it has, do not shut down the server machine until you can mirror or back up the data that is on the affected server device.

Cylinder 0

The physical disk has vital information regarding the size, rotation speed, and so forth, of the disk stored on the first or 0 cylinder of the disk. Cylinder 0 can be part of a partition that supports an operating system file system. You must never allow cylinder 0 to be part of any raw partition that is assigned to a server logical disk device. If you do, as soon as the server performs the **disk init** and starts writing to the raw partition the data in cylinder 0 will be overwritten and lost. The worst part of this error is that there are no symptoms until it is too late. The data contained in cylinder 0 is not accessed by the operating system until the server machine is booted. Until the next server machine reboot, the server will operate normally and you will be able to write critical business data to the device. When you next reboot the server machine, the operating system will look for the data that was in cylinder 0 to identify the disk. When it is not found, the operating system will not recognize the entire disk at all. The server device that was using cylinder 0 is lost and any other server devices on the disk are unavailable until the disk is available again. The only way to recover the disk is to get the proper data for the disk and write it back to cylinder 0, but that process destroys the data that was stored in the server device assigned to that partition. Note that this data is not readily available unless you have an identical disk somewhere in your database system. If this is the case, it is relatively easy for the server machine SA person to retrieve this data from identical disk and write it out to the disk that had cylinder 0 overwritten. If this data is not available on your system, you must obtain it from the manufacturer of the disk. While this can be done, it means the disk, and the server that relies on that disk, may be lost for a significant amount of time.

If the server device that included cylinder 0 contained user databases, those databases can be rebuilt on the same server device (after repartitioning to avoid cylinder 0 and doing **disk init** on the new, smaller partition) if you have room and loaded from tape, although you loose all data since the last database dump and any subsequent transaction log dumps that you have. If the disk contained the server master device, the entire server is lost. You must repartition so that cylinder 0 is no longer part of the server device and you must then reinstall the master device (i.e., the server itself) and load a dump of the *master* database, assuming that the new master device, which now does not include cylinder 0, is big enough for the dump of *master*. If the dump of *master* is current enough to include all changes made to the system tables (i.e., to include all databases and server devices), you should be able to recover all the databases that were on the server. If the *master* dump is not current, you will have to make any needed changes manually, but how will you remember what those changes were? This again is an argument for dumping the system tables regular (see Chapter 14 for details of the dump_systables script).

Of course, a functioning mirror of the master device would prevent this problem. Note that overwriting the data in cylinder 0 is only a problem if cylinder 0 is part of a partition that is assigned to a server device. Cylinder 0 may be part of a file system and that will not cause any problems.

Standard Disk Partitioning

Now that you understand why cylinder 0 is so important, you should set up a simple disk partitioning standard to avoid the whole problem (see Figure 8–5). You should assign cylinder 0 to partition 0 for all physical

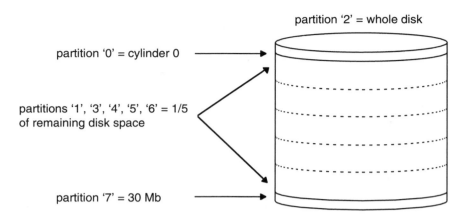

Figure 8–5. Standard Partitioning for Physical Disks Supporting Server Devices or Mirrors

disks that will have partitions assigned to server logical disk devices and make it a rule that you and the other DBAs never assign anything to partition 0. This does reduce the number of partitions by one, but you still have plenty of them left. This standard is very easy to communicate to the server machine SA person since it is the same partitioning for all the physical disks that support server logical disk devices throughout your database system. You will find it much easier to check that cylinder 0 is not being used by any server device if it is consistently assigned to partition 0 and your servers never use partition 0. Again, you can set up file systems on partitions that contain cylinder 0.

As discussed above, partition 2 should be left alone to document the overall size of the disk.

This leaves partitions 1, 3, 4, 5, 6, 7 to be assigned to the remaining space of each physical disk as you desire. However, you should further simplify the process by having a standard partitioning for these partitions as well. You will need to have a small partition somewhere in the server for the master device and another device of the same small size to support the mirror of the master device. While the master device rarely needs to be larger than 20 Mb, it is good to allow plenty or room for expansion since it is impossible to increase the size of the master device later and it is also impossible to alter the *master* database from the master device to another device. See Chapter 7 for details of how you can move a master device to a larger partition to increase the size of the master device. You should create a 50-Mb partition on every whole physical disk to support the master device, its mirror and other small databases that you may have. You may think this wastes the partition on disks other then those supporting the master device. However, you will need these small devices to support other small databases that are part of System 11 (see Chapter 13). You should keep the partitioning scheme simple by making the 7 partition of all the disks that support server logical disk devices 50 Mb.

This leaves partitions 1, 3, 4, 5, 6 and you should again keep the scheme simple by taking the remaining space on the disk, after you have assigned cylinder 0 to partition 0 and 50 Mb to partition 7, and assigning one-fifth of the space to each of the remaining partitions. This leaves you with a simple partitioning scheme that you can apply to all the server disks in your database systems. Your SA person(s) will appreciate a scheme that is this simple to remember and set up. Your standard partitioning scheme will reduce errors and make installing disks a quicker process.

Assign Whole Physical Disks to One Use

Once you have set up the previously described partitioning convention, you should also adhere to the following rule: Assign whole physical disks to support either server logical disk devices or file systems, but not both. The partitions of a physical disk should be assigned to either server devices or file systems (see Figure 8–6). This convention makes it much easier for you to direct the server machine SA person. You agree with the SA person which physical disks of the server machine are for server devices and direct them to apply your standard partitioning to all those disks. You then direct the SA person to use the remaining physical disks for the needs of the operating system and the file systems that you specify for holding the files needed for the server. This allows the SA person to partition the file system disks with complete freedom while not worrying about the server devices. You know that you can check the partitions on the physical disks for the server and not worry about any file system partitions. You can use any partitions on the disks specified for the server without fear of overwriting a file system partition. All of this reduces the

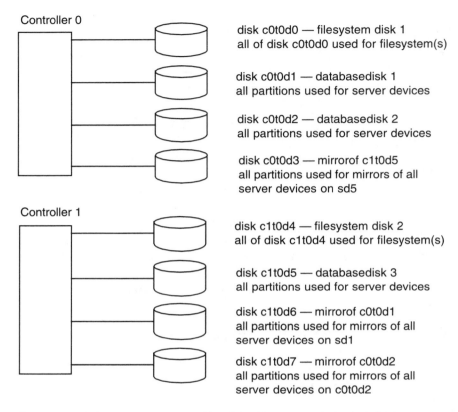

Controller 0

disk c0t0d0 — filesystem disk 1
all of disk c0t0d0 used for filesystem(s)

disk c0t0d1 — databasedisk 1
all partitions used for server devices

disk c0t0d2 — databasedisk 2
all partitions used for server devices

disk c0t0d3 — mirrorof c1t0d5
all partitions used for mirrors of all
server devices on sd5

Controller 1

disk c1t0d4 — filesystem disk 2
all of disk c1t0d4 used for filesystem(s)

disk c1t0d5 — databasedisk 3
all partitions used for server devices

disk c1t0d6 — mirrorof c0t0d1
all partitions used for mirrors of all
server devices on sd1

disk c1t0d7 — mirrorof c0t0d2
all partitions used for mirrors of all
server devices on c0t0d2

This example is for a server machine with 8 disks. Note that each physical disk is used only for one purpose, file system(s), server devices or mirrors of server devices. This ensures that all devices and their mirrors are on different controllers.

Figure 8–6. Using Whole Physical Disks for Server Devices, Mirrors, or File Systems

need for you, as DBA and the SA person to wait for each other before doing routine server device tasks. You can also simplify the mirroring process by using whole physical disks for server logical disk devices and their mirrors. You will find it much easier to simply mirror all the partitions used for server devices to the same partitions on another whole physical disk used to support the server. It is also easier to assess the impact of a disk failure if the entire disk is assigned to the server (as either server devices or their mirrors) or to file systems.

DISK CONTROLLERS

Now that you have the disks of the server machine broken into two groups, one for supporting server logical disk devices (or their mirrors) and the other for supporting operating system file systems, you need to understand the issues surrounding disk controllers. Disk controllers are the devices in the server machine that interface the physical disks to the server machine itself.

Disks and Controllers

You can attach many physical disks to a single disk controller, but you will find that throughput performance goes down after a certain number of disks are attached. You must review this with your server machine SA person to get the maximum number of disks that you can attach to a single controller before performance drops off. For Solaris the maximum number of physical disks that can be attached to one controller without adversely affecting performance is four. This number may vary with operating systems and hardware platforms. Note that this number is important when adding disk space to a server since you will need to get another controller for each set of disks you add. Further, you must be aware that there are different types of disk controllers, such as fast SCSI and slow SCSI. You need to know what kind of disks and disk controllers you have on each system and be aware of these distinctions when trying to add more disks to the server. For example, you may be able to add slow SCSI disks to a fast SCSI disk controller but not the other way around, although you are probably wasting the performance of the fast SCSI controller. You can see which disks are attached to which controller by executing the operating system command `format`. You must be logged into the server machine is UNIX user "root" to execute this command. The output of the `format` command will list each physical disk on the server machine along with the controller name and number. You must be careful with the `format` command. Don't use it if you don't know how since mistakes can erase an entire physical disk.

Tape Drives and Controllers

You also need to realize that the tape drives on each server machine are attached to a disk controller also. You can attach tape drives to the same

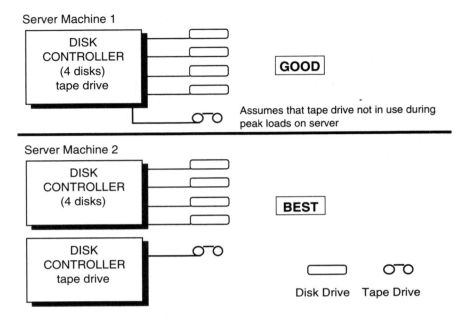

Figure 8–7. Tape Drives and Disk Controllers

controller that is supporting the maximum number of disks, but you should have a separate controller for the tape drives (see Figure 8–7). This prevents the controllers that support disks from being slowed down whenever you need to use the tape drive(s).

Spreading Disks across Controllers

You need to realize that which disks are attached to which controllers is also an important issue. You want to have the physical disks that support server logical disk devices spread over as many controllers as possible. This means that you don't attach all the server disks to one set of controllers and all the file system disk to another set (see Figure 8–8). You want to balance the number of server disks and file system disks on all the controllers. You need to do this for two reasons, both of which involve only the disks that support server devices. You will need to spread the file system disks over the controllers simply to make room to spread the server disks.

First, you need to do this for database integrity. You need to have mirrors set up for the databases on your server (we discuss mirroring

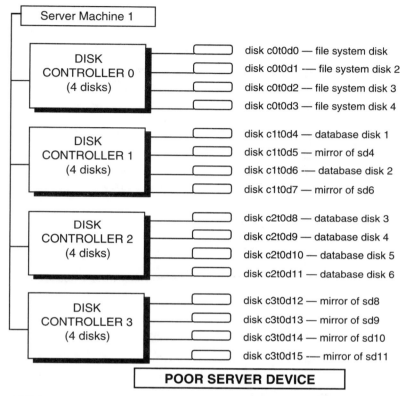

Figure 8–8. Poor Server Device Spreading Over Controllers

below). When the server writes to disks it needs to write to the primary disk and also to the disk that is the mirror. If the primary and mirror disk are attached to the same controller and the controller fails, both disks may be corrupted. You must locate these two disks on separate controllers so that a controller failure will not affect both disks.

Second, you need to do this for performance reasons. As your databases grow, you will need to spread the objects within the database over several disks by using segments which we discuss below. A good example of this is locating the indexes for the most heavily accessed tables on a separate

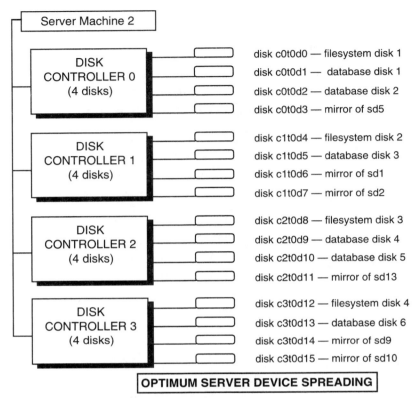

Note: Total of 16 disks, one-quarter assigned to filesystems, the remaining 12 disks split evenly between supporting database server devices and their mirrors.

Figure 8-9 Optimum Server Device Spreading Over Controllers

segment from the tables themselves. This means the server can retrieve information about an index from one server device while a request for information from the table itself is being retrieved from another server device. You need to have these two server devices attached to separate controllers or you won't see the very performance benefits you wanted in the first place (see Figure 8–9).

Standard for Assigning Disks to Controllers

You can simplify the process of deciding which disks get attached to which controller by deciding what fraction of the total number of physical disks on the server machine will support file systems and then spread those disks evenly over the number of controllers on the server machine. Then all the other disks are attached to the controllers, within the maximum number of physical disks per controller, and you are all set. Further, you should assign the file system and server device disks in the same order on each controller. If you have one-quarter of all the disks dedicated to file systems, you should have the first disk on each controller supporting file systems. This simple convention makes it very simple to determine which disks do what. This information is vital for both the DBA and SA when a disk error occurs. You need to know as quickly as possible what parts of the server or server machine are affected by failures. Also, you need to know what is on a disk when you need to find more file system space. You will be able to do this much faster if the first disk on each controller is a file system disk, instead of having to look at each physical disk to determine what is out there. Note also that you will need to be aware of the balance of file system and server device disks when you need to add disks to the server machine. You should get a new controller and a set of disks at one time. You will find that as you need more disks for either file systems or server devices, you will need disks for the other kind as well.

DATABASE LOCATION ON DISKS AND CONTROLLERS

Once you have the basic physical design decisions settled for a database that will exist in the server, you need to consider how to place the various segments of the database on the available server devices. We have already covered most of this elsewhere but we summarize the problems and the solutions here.

Transaction Log

You should place the transaction log (*logsegment*) on a server device that is separate from the server devices that support any other segments of the database. This server device should be dedicated to the logsegment which means only the *logsegment* of the database is on that server device. You should place the *logsegment* on a server device that is supported by a physical disk that is attached to a different controller from those that support the other segments of the database. You should examine the objects in the database. If there are any large objects such as a large table or the index on a large table separate segments should be created for these objects and these segments should be placed on separate server devices, preferably on physical disks attached to controllers different than the other server devices supporting the database. You want to spread these user-defined segments evenly over several server devices to maximize the I/O throughput for the most heavily accessed objects (see Chapter 10).

You may now understand the issues regarding the size of the transaction log, but you also need to realize what matters as far as placing the database transaction log on server devices,that is, disks. You will learn that for many other portions of a database you want to use multiple server devices on different disk controllers. This isn't the case for the transaction log. Since all activity in the transaction log occurs at the very end of the transaction log, and since you have no control over this behavior, it doesn't help to have the transaction log spread over multiple server devices or controllers. Hence, once you have settled on the size of the transaction log, you should place it on one server device. Recall that you do want to place the transaction log on a server device that is not supporting any other segment(s) of the database. Further, you should mirror the transaction log to further ensure recovery and to reduce downtime for your database.

Locating Multiple Databases

Now you need to consider the problems of placing several databases over the available server devices and controllers. To satisfy the needs of each database you need to spread the various segments over several server devices on physical disks attached to different controllers. However, you must integrate the needs of several if not many databases on one server. While you would prefer to have a whole set of server devices and controllers for each database that isn't practical. You have to place all the databases you have on the limited set of server devices you have, attached to a limited set of controllers.

The first database(s) you will place are *master*, *model,* and the first portion of *tempdb* which you put on the master device when you installed the server. Next, look at your databases and decide which one will be under the heaviest I/O load. Note that this may not be the largest database. Note also that we use the term decide because you really can't figure out what the I/O problems will be until the entire server with all the databases and all the users is up and running. You can make an educated guess, but any determination will need to be done after the server is in full service. For the database that you decide needs the most I/O throughput you should look at the objects that are planned for the database. Tables that are large and/or frequently accessed may need to be placed on a user-defined data segment separate from the rest of the database. Similarly, you may need a separate user-defined segment to contain the largest and/or most frequently accessed indexes for these tables. Segments created for either large tables or indexes may be better off if placed or spread over server devices different attached to controllers from those for the other segments of the database.

With the first user database placed on the server you need to fit all the other databases into the space available. This is an iterative process. You need to fit the largest databases in early, but you must give those databases that need the most I/O throughput high priority also since they will need to most flexibility as far as the number of server devices and controllers. You also need to consider the future. It may be tempting to simply place the databases so that you fill each physical disk in turn leaving as many disks free for the future as possible. This is not a good move. When you place the database(s) that need the most I/O performance you should have a good reason for creating each user defined segment and a good reason for its location. Now, as each of these segments expands you want to allow them to grow so that they don't have to span server devices in a way that upsets your initial plans. If a database needs a user-defined segment that must be isolated from the other segments of the database to avoid an I/O bottleneck then you don't want to add space to that segment on a server device on another controller supporting another segment of the same database. You need to look at each segment of your most important databases and make sure they have room to grow on the same physical disk(s) attached to the same controller they are already on. This means you do not fill every server device on every physical disk. Rather you should spread your databases and their segments over the server devices and controllers as much as possible, and leave room for each segment to grow on the disks on each controller.

You also make it easier to add space later if you leave an obvious place for such space to be added. Whether a given database segment is spread over server devices on one or several physical disks you should leave some room on at least one of the server devices on each physical disk so it will be easy to add space to the segment without upsetting the way the segment is spread over the physical disks and controllers. If you don't plan for adding space from the beginning the first time you need more space, you may be forced to add that space on a server device that conflicts with your performance objectives. You also need to make it as easy as possible to add the space properly since you will be relying on other members of your DBA team to add space as needed and they will not all be as aware of the impacts of a hasty addition of space as you are. Finally, adding space to the segment on the same physical disk that already supports the segment makes it easier to maintain the mirrors of the segment, and as discussed earlier, as part of your standard environment you should allocate entire physical disks to support server devices and other entire physical disks to support the mirrors of those server devices.

You will run into conflicts as you place each database among the steadily decreasing supply of server devices and controllers. The conflict will come when you have a very heavily used segment of one database placed on a physical disk and you need to place a heavily used segment of another database on the same physical disk or on a physical disk attached to the same controller. There will not be a "right" answer and the optimal solution will change over time as the database segments grow and spread from disk to disk. When you have performance problems you should reexamine the layout of your server and make changes as needed.

Locating the System Databases

The system databases, *master*, *sybsystemprocs* and *sybsecurity* should be mirrored. Ideally, you would place each of these databases, and their mirror, on a separate server device. This means you need a separate disk slice for each of the databases and the mirror of each slice. Depending on the standard partitioning you use, and the number of physical disks attached to the server machine, this can be problematic. We consider two examples. For both examples, we assume you are using the standard disk partitioning described previously. For a 2.1-Gb physical disk, partition it so you have five 400-Mb slices and one 50-Mb slice. For a 4.2-Gb physical disk, partition such it so you have five 800-Mb slices and an 80-Mb slice.

Minimum Configuration—Two Physical Disks

With only two physical disks, both of which are partitioned with the same standard partitioning, you should place the master device on the small slice of one disk and the mirror of the master device on the small slice of the other disk. Then, place the *sybsystemprocs* and *sybsecurity*

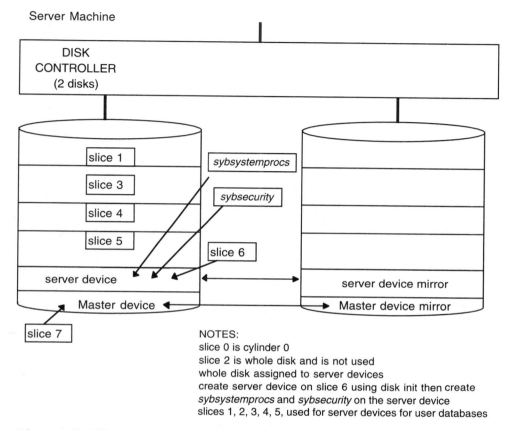

Server Machine

NOTES:
slice 0 is cylinder 0
slice 2 is whole disk and is not used
whole disk assigned to server devices
create server device on slice 6 using disk init then create
sybsystemprocs and *sybsecurity* on the server device
slices 1, 2, 3, 4, 5, used for server devices for user databases

Figure 8–10. System Database Location on Two Disks

databases on a server device created on one of the large slices and mirror this device to one of the large slices on the other disk (see Figure 8–10). As always, recall that in Solaris, the terms partition and slice are synonymous and both refer to a chunk of space on a physical disk.

Optimal Configuration—Six or More Physical Disks

With six physical disks you should place the master device on the small slice of one disk and the mirror of the master device on the small slice of a second disk. Then, place the *sybsystemprocs* database on a server device

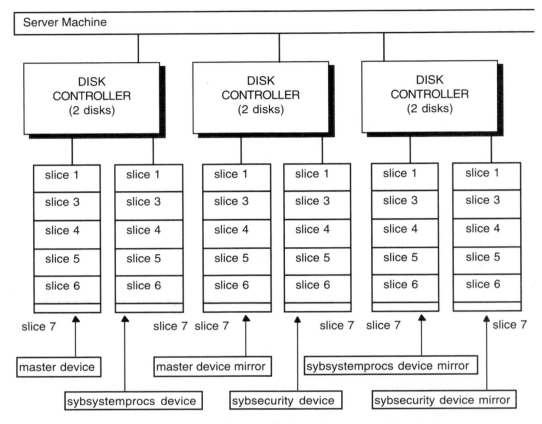

Figure 8–11. System Database Location on Six disks

created on the small slice of the third disk and the mirror of this server device on the small slice of the fourth disk. The *sybsecurity* database would then go on a server device created on the small slice of the fifth disk and its mirror on the small slice of the sixth disk (see Figure 8–11).

You should place the mirror of any server device so that the mirror is attached to a different controller than that of the primary server device. You can use any number of disk, but remember that the goal is to keep the master device on a small slice with only the *master*, model and first portion of tempdb on the device. The other system databases, *sybsystemprocs* and *sybsecurity*, should not be on the master device. Ideally, these two system databases would also be on their own server devices and be mirrored.

INITIALIZING SERVER DEVICES

Now that you have arranged the partitions of the physical disks and spread the server disks over the available controllers, you need to be aware of a some details in the process of initializing a portion of a physical disk so that it is available to the SQL Server.

The disk init Server Command

You need to understand the process by which a disk partition or an operating system file becomes a server device. This process will initialize the server device and this must be done before the server device is even known to the server. This process uses the **disk init** server command. Note that you need to do this for either type of server device, that is a server device that is assigned to a raw partition or to a file in the operating system file system. You perform this using the **disk init** command (the syntax is shown below) and we then discuss each of the parameters you must supply to the command (see Figure 8–12).

```
disk init
name = "device_name",
physname = "physicalname",
vdevno = virtual_device_number,
size = number_of_blocks
```

device_name

First we need to clarify the terms you see in the syntax of the **disk init** command. The **device_name** is what the server logical disk device will be called. The **physicalname** is the name of the raw partition or the operating system file system file that the server device will be assigned to. Note that the **physicalname** is what the operating system recognizes. The **disk init** command is simply establishing a connection between a device that the server knows about and a piece of a physical disk that the operating system knows about. The **virtual_device_number** is a number that is unique to each server device. The **number_of_blocks** refers to the size, in 2K pages, that the server device will be. As discussed earlier, the size of the server device can be as large as the raw partition it is being assigned to.

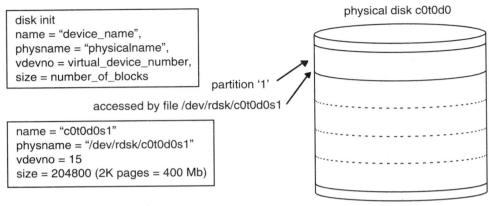

```
disk init
name = "device_name",
physname = "physicalname",
vdevno = virtual_device_number,
size = number_of_blocks
```

physical disk c0t0d0

partition '1'

accessed by file /dev/rdsk/c0t0d0s1

```
name = "c0t0d0s1"
physname = "/dev/rdsk/c0t0d0s1"
vdevno = 15
size = 204800 (2K pages = 400 Mb)
```

Name consists of physical disk name and partition name
physname is the full path to the file that controls block access to the physical disk raw partition
UNIX user 'sybase' must own the file specified by physname
vdevno must be less than configuration value 'devices' in output of **sp_configure**
vdevno must not already be in use
Size is largest whole number of Mb that fit in partition size
Partition size determined from output of prtvtoc /dev/rdsk/c0t0d0s1 for partition '1'

Figure 8–12. Initializing Server Logical Disk Devices

The **device_name** is what the server device will be called within the server. This is the name that you will use in the server commands **create database, alter database**, and so forth. You must establish and follow a server device naming convention. The simplest convention is the best. Use the operating system command format to display all of the physical disks attached to the server machine. You must be logged into the server machine as UNIX user "root" to run the format command. The output of the format command will show you what the operating system calls each of the physical disks. These are the names that you must use, along with the partition name, when creating server logical disk devices. A typical output of the format command will tell you that the physical disks have names like c0t0d0 and c0t0sd1 through c0t0d6, for example. When you decide to use the raw partition 3 of physical disk c0t0d1, you must use for the **device_name** c0t0d1s3. This convention must be applied to all the server devices in your database system. Note that you use the name of the disk as specified by the output of the format command even though the "special file" that the server will use to access the raw partition is called /dev/rdsk/c0t0d1s3.

If you are using operating system files as server devices, you don't need a server device naming convention that includes the partition name. In fact, you won't have the problems described above at all because the server will report errors for the device by the file name of that device, and the file name includes the full path of the file so it will be clear which physical disk the file (server device) is on.

> Your server crashes, the errorlog shows write errors to server device baddog1, but you don't remember which physical disk contains the raw partition (or the file in the file system) that is assigned to baddog1. Since the server has crashed you can't run **sp_helpdevice** to see what the physical disk partition is. Your stuck. You shouldn't attempt a restart of the server until you can diagnose the disk problems or you risk further server corruption. You're only choice is to run hardware diagnostics on all the disks on the server machine, which is a big waste of time. You must have a simple server device naming convention so you know immediately which physical disk is supporting which server device.

physical_name

The **physical_name** refers to a portion of a physical disk known to the operating system. For a raw partition the **physical_name** is the full path of the file that is accessed in order to access the raw partition. Recall that a partition of a physical disk can be accessed in two ways: block or character. A SQL Server device that accesses a raw partition uses only one (the character access version) of the two operating system files available to control the disk device. This means that the file used is c0t0d0s1 for the 1 partition of the server machine physical disk called c0t0d0, and this file is located in the /dev/rdsk file system. Note that the "r" in rdsk tells you this is the character version. Note also that you must check with the server machine SA to be sure what these files are called for your specific hardware platform. You would then specify /dev/rdsk/c0t0d0s1 for the **physical_name**. If you are using a file for a server device, you would specify the complete path of the file, *<path>/<device_name>* for the **physical_name**. You should indicate what file system the server device file is in as part of the **physical_name**.

Virtual Device Number (vdevno)

The **virtual_device_number** is somewhat arcane, but you must understand why it exists and how it can block your attempts to create devices. Each server device consists of some number of 2K pages. These pages are numbered sequentially from 0 to N -1 where N is the total number of pages in the device. However, there must be some way to give the pages in multiple server devices a unique page number. This is where *vdevno* comes in. It is used in combination with the page number in each server device to create a unique page number within the entire server. This means that vdevno is very important. Clearly the server will require that each time you execute **disk init** you supply a *vdevno* that is not currently in use. You can see which *vdevno* values are already in use by executing the server command **sp_helpdevice**. Note that you will have trouble with *vdevno* in the following circumstances:

> *vdevno* is already being used
>
> Earlier **disk init** failed
>
> Server device dropped
>
> **devices** value in **sp_configure**

vdevno Already Being Used

Sometimes you will find that the simplest solutions are indeed the best. Check that the *vdevno* you used in the **disk init** command isn't already being used by an existing server device. Check the output of the **sp_helpdevice** server command (without any arguments) to see the *vdevnos* already being used. Note that selecting all the rows from the system table sysdevices will not show you the *vdevnos* in use. The *vdevno* values are not stored in sysdevices rather they are computed for the output of **sp_helpdevice.**

Earlier disk init Failed

If an earlier attempt to execute **disk init** with a particular *vdevno* value failed for any reason (size specified was larger than the raw partition for example), you can't use that same *vdevno* value again until the server is rebooted.

Server Device Dropped

If you have dropped a server device from the server (using the stored procedure **sp_dropdevice**, note that a server command creates server devices but a stored procedure drops them) since the last server restart, you can't use that *vdevno* of the server device that was dropped until the server is rebooted.

devices Value in sp_configure

The maximum number of server devices allowed is part of the server configuration. You can see what the maximum number is by executing the server command **sp_configure** and looking for the value of **devices**. This value is 10 by default when the server is installed. Note that a value of 10 for **devices** means you can only create server devices with *vdevno* values of 0 through 9. When you try to execute **disk init** with a *vdevno* of 10, it will fail. Note that this a very common reason that **disk init** fails. Note further that the error you will see when **disk init** fails does not tell you it is due to a lack of allowable *vdevno* values. Instead, you will get an error that the specified physical device doesn't have room to create the server device. When you see such an error, check the *vdevno* values in use and the maximum allowable value of **devices**. If you need to increase the number of **devices**, you do that using **sp_configure**, and you must reboot the server to have this configuration change take effect. You need to be aware that increasing the maximum allowed number of server devices does use some of the server machine's available memory so you don't want to set **devices** to a number higher than you really need. Also, remember that **devices** set to 10 means the maximum *vdevno* allowed is 10 -1 = 9, and that the master device always uses *vdevno* = 0. Also, when you have a **disk init** fail, remember that you can't use that *vdevno* again until you reboot the server. Note that the maximum number of devices as specified by **devices** does not include server dump devices. You do not need to worry about **devices** or *vdevno* when adding server dump devices.

 You need to be careful with this process. You can easily become very confused. Your first **disk init** fails because you specified a size that was too large for the disk partition, but now you try again with that problem fixed and you fail again, this time because you tried to reuse the same *vdevno*. You try to use *vdevno* + 1 but that fails because you happened to exceed the maximum allowable *vdevno*, which is confusing since it is *N* -1 where *N* = the value of **devices** in the output of **sp_configure**. You now become befuddled trying to see if the size you specified is too large (still) since the error messages you get tell you there isn't enough room on the physical disk, or if the *vdevno* is in use (which is isn't) or why you can't use *vdevno* = 10 when **devices** = 10. Relax, and figure it out. Don't just keep trying **disk init** over and over.

Another *vdevno* mess. By being a little too clever, the DBA can really mess things up. For performance reasons, all of tempdb, including the 2 Mb that are created on the master device at installation time, was moved to a separate logical server device on a separate physical disk. (Don't do this—please!) This may have been great for performance, but when the DBA then fiddled with some other **sp_configure** server parameters, the server would not start, probably due to increasing one of the server configuration param eters so that it required more memory than was physically available. To cure this the DBA ran buildmaster -r which resets all the server configuration parameters to their default values. The server would start, but the DBA couldn't do anything. Why? For reasons that were never fully explained, when tempdb was moved, the new server logical device was defined using **disk init** with a value of *vdevno* = 20. This, like so many DBA maneuvers, doesn't appear to be a blunder until much later. Since buildmaster -r had been run, the maximum number of devices was reset to 10, which means the highest allowable *vdevno* = 9. So, the server would start but it would not recognize the server logical device that contained tempdb. This situation isn't deadly, but for the DBA on pager duty when it all comes unraveled, it can be a very tiring experience. The cure was to use isql and simply use **sp_configure** to change the maximum number of devices and restart the server. Note that you couldn't do anything in this case that required tempdb until you got the maximum number of devices increased. Commands like **sp_helpdevice** use tempdb and won't run if tempdb is unavailable. This is yet another example of how DBA actions ripple through your entire database system.

number_of_blocks

The **number_of_blocks** refers to the size of the server device specified in 2K pages. You need to be careful of the various terms—blocks, 2K pages, allocation—units which refer to the amount of disk space the server acquires at one time (equal to 8 2K pages), and so forth. For **disk init**, a block is a 2K page. You are assigning a server device to a raw partition on a physical disk. The size of the partition in question can be seen by executing the operating system command `ptrvtoc /dev/rdsk/<diskname>`. Note that you supply the name of the physical disk as it is known to the operating system, such as `prtvtoc /dev/rdsk/c0t0d0s1`. Note that you need to supply the name of the file that controls a slice that you have permission to access. In this example, you as UNIX user sybase, must have permission to access the file `/dev/rdsk/c0t0d0s1` and prtvtoc will then report on the formatting of the entire disk. The output will show the number of sectors and cylinders for all the partitions of the physical disk (see Chapter 13 for an example of the output of the `prtvtoc` command).

The number of sectors for a partition is what you care about. The size of the partition in bytes is computed by multiplying the number of sectors by 512 bytes/sector. You then compute the number of megabytes in the partition by dividing the number of bytes by 1024 * 1024 (which = 1 Mb). The size of the partition will probably not be a whole number of megabytes. Now, you need to round this number down to the nearest whole number of megabytes and convert that number of megabytes into the number of 2K pages to use for the **disk init** command. You need to understand how the server goes out and gets disk space when it is executing a **create database** or **alter database** command.

When the server goes out to a server device to create or alter a database, it looks for space on the disk in 0.5-Mb chunks called allocation units which are 256 2K pages which is 0-5 Mb. You normally don't care about this because the **create database** and **alter database** server commands only allow you to specify a whole number of megabytes for the size of the database or the amount you are adding to the database. You will care, how-ever, in the following scenario. One of your fellow DBAs decides to create or add to a database, but they didn't check that the space they requested was available on the server device(s) specified. The server goes to each server device to allocate the space requested. For any server device that doesn't have the full amount of space requested, the server allocates as much as it can, in 0-5 Mb chunks. If the server device was created with a **disk init** command whose size parameter specified something other than a whole number of Mb, specifically xx.yy Mb where xx is some number of megabytes and yy is greater than 0.5 Mb, the server will allocate as many whole megabytes as it can and an additional 0.5 Mb. This may never be a problem for you. When you need to re-create this database, either as a rebuild after disaster or on another server as part of a migration, you may not be able to load the dump of this database without creating corruption. The new database that you create using the create database and alter database server commands must be done using sizes in whole megabytes. Since the load of a database is just a physical copy of the data pages in the order they appear in the database, when they are loaded they must appear in the same order in the new database after loading. Since you can't recreate the 0.5 Mb on the new database, you can't be sure that the load won't create corruption. For this reason, always **disk init** server devices with a size that is the largest whole number of megabytes that will fit in the space that is actually available.

If you are assigning a server device to an operating system file, you need to examine the overall size of the file system where the file will be and determine what if any space in that file system will be needed by other files, and then determine the size available for the server device and convert that into the number of 2K pages available for the **disk init** command. The size of the file system can be obtained from the output of the operating system command df -k. Determining the amount of space available for your server device versus any other files that need to be in the file system is more complex. You may need to have a file system dedicated to each server device that will be supported by a disk file, and then your **disk init** should assign all of the file system space (the largest whole number of megabytes) to the server device.

Some disk trivia. The reason a 2K page keeps appearing as a basic unit of server storage space is that this is the unit of data that is moved in a single I/O action. Hence, you move a 2K chunk of data each time you read from or write to disk. Since this is the size of the chunk that is moved for each I/O it might as well be the basic size of all operations within the server.

Final Notes on disk init

Here are a few additional notes on the **disk init** command that you should know.

You do not use **disk init** for creating the master device that will support the *master* database. The master device is created when you run buildmaster that is supplied with the SQL Server, or, more normally, when you run sybinit that is the normal way to install a SQL Server.

Further, you must not execute **disk init** specifying a partition that is already being used for the master device. If you do, this you will destroy the server. Worse still, the server will continue to run until you need to do something with it. You must check very carefully any time you are doing a **disk init** to verify where the master device is to be sure you are not affecting it. Similarly, you must not execute **disk init** on a partition that is already being used for any server device. In theory, the server will not allow you to do this, but you should not depend on the server. You should verify that you are using the correct partition. Also, you must not **disk init** to any partition that will be used for the mirror of a server device. A mirror of a server device is always created on a raw partition using the **disk mirror** command.

You are new on the job. You are asked to install SQL Server. What could be easier? You take the specifications for the server devices and away you go. You don't check the server device naming convention in use at the site. Actually they don't enforce a server device naming convention and that is the problem. You go ahead and **disk init** the list of devices you were told to. All is well until you dump the *master* database to disk as you always should after installing the server. You get errors. You run **dbcc** and get errors. You panic. You look bad. After the panic fades, you decide to check things. You find the master device was on one of the partitions that you did a **disk init** on. The list of server devices included a device on the partition that had the master device. This is confusing but you should have checked. The only solution now is to reinstall. Not a good first impression. Always check where the master device is for the server you are working on and for any and all servers that may be on the same server machine. Don't assume anything, especially about a new environment

When you execute the **disk init** command the server device created is not automatically assigned to the pool of default disk space. Default disk space is where database objects are created when no server device is specified. Normally you don't want to have any of your server devices be default devices since you must place all databases (at least) on specific server devices to control server performance and data integrity. If you do want a server device to be a default disk, remember that you must do this as a separate step using the stored procedure **sp_diskdefault**.

In order to execute the **disk init** command successfully you must have the permissions to access the special files that control the raw partitions of the physical disks. For example, if you are creating server devices as UNIX user "sybase" then UNIX user "sybase" must own the device files `/dev/rdsk/c0t0d0s1` in order to create a server device that is assigned to the 1 raw partition of the physical disk c0t0d0.

DATABASE SEGMENTS

Once you have the server devices spread over the controllers and the file system disks filling out the maximum number of disks attached to one controller, you need to understand segments. The topic of segments is very misunderstood. They can be confusing and complicated, but they do serve a purpose that makes them worthwhile. You may think that segments means nothing more than putting the transaction log for a database on a separate server device. You are wrong. Segments are the way in which a DBA can control toplacement of database objects including the transaction log. The DBA needs to control the placement to improve server performance. You must understand what segments can do to help you, and also how they can hurt you. Once you have set up segments for your databases, you must maintain them. You will find that the advantages of segments can easily be lost by one DBA on your team who doesn't understand them and alters a database adding space on a new device and assigns multiple segments to the new device.

Why Segments Exist

You can best appreciate why segments exist by considering a server that doesn't have any. You create a database and fill it with data. The transaction log records are on disk along with the database tables and other objects, all mixed up together. As the database fills up the space available on the server device, you create another server device on another disk partition and alter the database to put further growth on the new server device. Whenever you recover the server, which is every time you restart the server, you cause the server to look at the contents of the transaction log. Since it is spread out all over the server device(s), this is a long process. If the transaction log records were all in one place, it would save time on recovery. You want to tell the server to put all the transaction log records and only such records in one place. Hence the need for segments.

The Transaction Log Segment

The most common use for segments is placing the transaction log (the log segment) on a separate server device from the rest of the database. This is required by SQL server before you can dump the transaction log and keep a copy of it (see Chapter 9 for discussion of why you want to dump a copy of the transaction log).

Large Object on a Separate Segment

Now you should imagine a large table on your hypothetical server. This table is heavily accessed and has several indexes on it. You could improve server performance if you could place this table on a separate server device. You could do more by placing the table on a partition of a disk that was on a different controller from other databases. This way your server could send requests regarding the table to a whole separate I/O chain while handling all other requests through some other controller and disk(s). You also would benefit as the space allocated for the table would be controlled. When all objects vie for the same disk space, you never know how much space is free as other objects become bigger or smaller. By placing the table on its own segment, you have guaranteed that only pieces of the table will be in that segment and no other database objects can use that space. Here you need a nother segment for a given table. You would want to do the same thing for an index for a large table. This is especially good if many queries to the table use an index that "covers" the query, which means the index entries contain the data the query needs. You only need to access the index, not the actual table, to answer these queries. If you place such an index on a segment that is on a partition that is separate from those used for the table and the rest of the database, the server can get better I/O throughput since some requests go to the controller and disk that hold the table while others go to the controller and disk that hold the index.

Note that if you want to place a table (or an index) on a specific segment, you simply include the **on   <segmentname>** clause in the **create table** server command. The same syntax applies to the **create index** command.

This discussion of your hypothetical server makes it clear why you want to have segments at your disposal. Segments are the only way you can control what is placed where on the disks. This control allows you to get better throughput and controls which objects can compete for which parts of the server's disk space.

Segments and the create database Server Command

You need to understand how segments are created and how to manage them. Whenever you execute the **create database** or **alter database** server commands, you are creating segments. When you execute

create database <dbname>

on <server_device_name> = <size_in_Mb>

the server allocates the space to the database and assigns the segments called *system*, *default* and *logsegment* to the server device. The *system* segment means that system tables, and so forth, are placed here while the *logsegment* means all the transaction log records will be stored here and the *default* segment means all other objects will be placed on this device. Note that we have three segments of the database on the same device and this means you have objects that belong to the *system*, *default* and *logsegment* segments all stored together on the same server device (see Figure 8-13). You can see this by executing **sp_helpdb <dbname>** which outputs information about the database including a list of all the server devices that contain portions of the database and the segments assigned to each device. In order to see the segments and the server devices you must first be in the database by executing the **use <dbname>** command. Note that this means objects created in any of these three segments can completely fill the disk space of the server device. Note also that segments are assigned to a device. This means for any database, all the portions of a server device that are assigned to that database will have the same segment assignments. You need to understand this and it is confusing. A single server device can support multiple databases, but the segments of any database are assigned on a device basis. Another implication of this you need to realize is that if you want to put objects in a separate segment, you will need to use a server device that does not already support any parts of the database (see Chapter 11 for discussion of the implications this has for capacity planning).

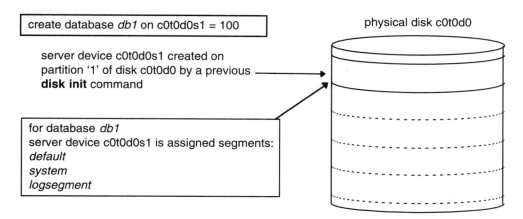

Figure 8–13. Segments Assigned Automatically (by 'default')

For your production databases, except *master*, you need to place the *logsegment* on a separate server device. Note that the *master* database can't be extended beyond the master device and therefore the *master* database can't have its transaction log (*logsegment*) separated to another device. The *master* database always has the segments system, *default* and *logsegment* assigned to all the disk space assigned to the *master* database. Normally you will do this when you first create the database using the syntax

create database <dbname>

on <server_device_1> = <size1> ,

log on <server_device_2> = <size2>

This will automatically set up server_device_2 with the *logsegment* assignment only (see Figure 8-14). Note that server_device_1 still gets the segment assignments of *system* and *default*. If you don't create the transaction log on a separate device as shown here, the transaction log will be mixed in with the *system* and *default* segments. You can move the transaction log later to a separate device using **sp_logdevice** as described in the *System Administration Guide*. For the remainder of the discussion we assume you have created the database with the transaction log on a separate device.

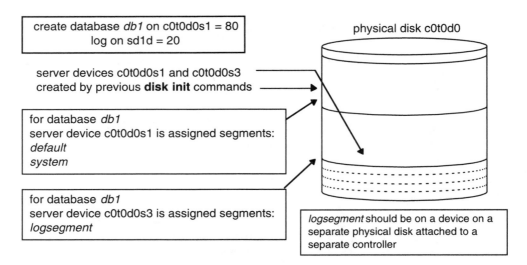

Figure 8–14. Log Segment on Separate Server Device

Segments and the alter database Server Command

Now that you have created the database on server_device_1 with the transaction log (*logsegment*) on server_device_2, server_device_1 has the segments system and *default* and server_device_2 has only the *logsegment*. You need to understand what happens when you alter the database. When you alter a database to add space on a server device that already supports part of the database, the new space will be given the same segment assignments that already exist on that server device. We have two possible situations for the database you have set up so far. If you alter the database on server_device_1, the new space will get the same segment assignments that already exist for this database on server_device_1, namely *default* and *system*. If you alter the database on server_device_2, the new space will get the segment assignment of *logsegment* only.

When you alter a database to a server device that is not currently supporting the database the new device will get the segment assignments *default* and *system*. Note that the new device would also get the segment assignment *logsegment* if the *logsegment* was not already assigned to be the lone segment on a separate server device. You alter the database to server_device_3 and it gets the segment assignments *default* and *system*.

Creating a User-Defined Segment

You have segments under control up to this point. Now you need to set up a segment that is not *default* or *system* or *logsegment* and we call these segments user-defined segments. In order to set up a user-defined segment, you must first decide if your user-defined segment needs to be on its own device separate from the others. While it probably doesn't make much sense to add another segment without putting it on its own device, we cover the process here so you'll know how. In your database, you could add a segment called *myseg0* to server_device_1 using the server command

sp_addsegment <segment_name>, <server_device>

which for this case would be

sp_addsegment myseg0, server_device_1

The output of **sp_helpdb <dbname>** will show that device server_device_1 now has the segment assignments of *system*, *default* and *myseg0*.

You now want to do the more interesting case of adding a new user-defined segment that will have its own device. You don't want to have any other segments assigned to this server device. First, you must alter the database to this device:

alter database <dbname>

on <server_device_3> size = <size3>

You recall that since server_device_3 has not been supporting any part of database *dbname* before this point, the segment assignments will be the standard set of *system* and *default* (see Figure 8–15). Again, this standard set of segment assignments would include *logsegment* if you have not already made server_device_2 the log device, that is, only the *logsegment* is assigned to that device. Now you will add your segment to this device using **sp_addsegment myseg1, server_device_3.** You can run **sp_helpdb <dbname>** and see that server_device_3 now has three segments assigned to it: *system*, *default* and *myseg1*. You need to realize that you are not finish at this point. If you don't finish the job, the whole reason you created *myseg1* is in jeopardy. Your new segment, *myseg1* is on a separate device, but the segment assignments of *system* and *default* are still there as well. As you create objects within the database *dbname* that are

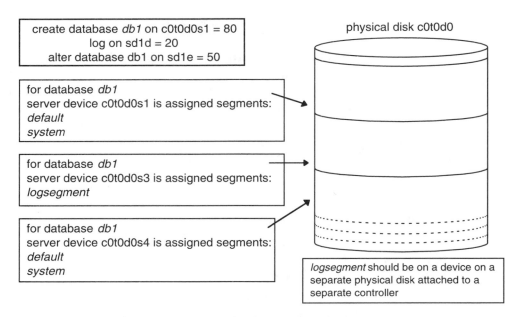

Figure 8–15. Altering Database to New Server Device

stored in the segment *default* or *system* you can place them on any of the server devices that support the *system* or *default* segments. This means that such objects could be placed on server_device_3.

You don't want this to happen for two reasons. First, you wanted segment *myseg1* on a separate server device, preferably on a controller that does not support the server devices for the other segments of database *dbname* to improve performance. You wanted to separate the I/O for *myseg1* from the I/O for the other segments of the database. By allowing objects of the *system* and *default* segments to live on server_device_3, you have lost control. Any requests that access objects of the *system* and/or *default* segments that live on server_device_3 will conflict with the I/O for the objects in *myseg1*. You probably wanted *myseg1* separated from the other segments because the objects you put in *myseg1* are accessed often. You don't want anything to interfere with that process.

Second, you assigned some amount of disk space to *myseg1*. By allowing objects of other segments to use the disk space you thought you were assigning to *myseg1* you don't know how much space is being used for *myseg1* or the other segments. You could find that *myseg1* runs out of space as objects in *system* and *default* segments are really filling the disk space.

In order to prevent this problem, you need to drop the *default* and *system* segments from the server device named server_device_3 using the **sp_dropsegment** server command. For this case, they would look like this:

sp_dropsegment system, server_device_3

sp_dropsegment "default", server_device_3

You will have to put " " around *default* because it is a reserved word within SQL server. Note that in the rare case that server_device_3 is the only server device that supports *system* or *default* segments for the database, you can't drop these segments from the device. You shouldn't run into this since server_device_3 should be a server device that will support a segment that is separate from the server devices that already support *system* and *default* segments. The order in which you add (or extend) and drop segments is important. You need to understand that when you create a table or other database object, you specify a segment in the create statement, or you don't. However, when you don't specify a segment, the server assumes the segment is *default*. You need to realize that any time you create a database object, you are specifying a segment where the object will be located. That is why you can't drop all segments from a server device which means you must first add a user-defined segment to the desired device and then drop the segments you don't want.

Segments and Capacity Planning

You have now seen how to set up a user-defined segment. You are finished for the moment, but the next problem is how to add space to the segment *myseg1*. This is where you can lose control again. You must realize that you may have done everything correctly but one of your fellow DBAs can add space to the database so that your carefully constructed segments are made useless. You can alter the database *dbname* on server_device_3 and all will be fine. You may recall that if you alter a database on a server device that already supports the database, the added space will carry the same segment assignments that the server device had for this database before the **alter database** command was executed. This makes sense since segment assignments apply to all portions of the database on any one server device. However, if you need to add space to any segment other than *system* and *default* and you need to add this space on a server device that does not already support the database, you must be careful. You can execute

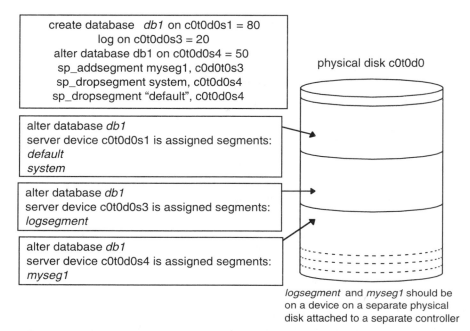

create database *db1* on c0t0d0s1 = 80
log on c0t0d0s3 = 20
alter database db1 on c0t0d0s4 = 50
sp_addsegment myseg1, c0d0t0s3
sp_dropsegment system, c0t0d0s4
sp_dropsegment "default", c0t0d0s4

physical disk c0t0d0

alter database *db1*
server device c0t0d0s1 is assigned segments:
default
system

alter database *db1*
server device c0t0d0s3 is assigned segments:
logsegment

alter database *db1*
server device c0t0d0s4 is assigned segments:
myseg1

logsegment and *myseg1* should be
on a device on a separate physical
disk attached to a separate controller

Figure 8–16. Creating User-Defined Segment

alter database <dbname> on server_device_4

but the server automatically assigns segments *system* and *default* (and *logsegment* if the *logsegment* for database dbname is not assigned as the only segment on one or more of the server devices supporting the database) to the disk space that belongs to database *dbname* on server_device_4. If you are trying to add space to the *system* or *default* segments of database *dbname*, you are finished. However, if you are adding space to the segment *logsegment*, you must use the **sp_extendsegment** server command to add this new space to the existing server devices that support the segment *logsegment*. Note that for the *logsegment* segment only, when you execute **sp_extendsegment logsegment, <server_device>** the server automatically adds the *logsegment* segment to the new server device and drops the other segments that were assigned to the new server device (i.e. the *system* and *default* segments). You will see that **sp_extendsegment** is copying the segment assignments that already exist for the other server devices that support the *logsegment* segment, namely that the *logsegment* segment is the only segment that those devices support for the database *dbname*. If you are adding space to any user-defined segment you must follow the process detailed previously. You must first **alter database** to server_device_4, then add the user-defined segment to the new server device and drop the segments *system* and *default* from the new server device.

During one of your few off-hours one of your colleagues needs to add space to the largest production database in the entire system. Later, when you stumble on this fact (nobody documented the event), you notice that the new space was put on a server device that had not been supporting the database before. More interesting still is the fact that the space on this new (to this database anyway) server device has been assigned the segments *system* (OK), *default* (OK) and *data* (huh?). You know that this database has had a user-defined segment called *data* for some time, but that segment was created specifically to isolate the biggest tables of the database onto a server device that was separate from the rest of the database and even on a separate physical disk and controller. This was done to improve performance, but now that part of the space that belongs to the *data* segment is on this new server device which is not on the same controller or physical disk as the rest of the *data* segment. The fact that the *data* segment is now co-mingled with the *default* and *system* segments means the whole point of separating the *data* segment is a risk for two reasons. First, objects on the data segment may or may not be on the separate (from the rest of the database) disk as you intended. As the server needs to access this segment, it may need to go to this new server device where it will have to compete for disk access with everything else on the new server device. Second, since the segments are co-mingled, objects that are created in the *system* of *default* segments may get placed on this new server device along with parts of objects from the *data* segment. Again, as the server needs to access objects in this part of the *system* or *default* segments, it will be competing with access to the objects that are in the part of the *data* segment that is on the same device. Finally, there isn't a good way to fix this problem once it happens. You would have to identify each object in the segment *data* that uses the new server device and move that object to space on the correct devices for the *data* segment. This could be done by dropping tables, and so forth, after using bcp to bulk copy out the data to a file. After clearing the *data* segment on the new server device, you would then drop the *data* segment from the new device. This process is tedious and error-prone. It shouldn't be necessary. You must realize the administrative headaches you are taking on when you set up user-defined segments. They are useful, but they come at a price.

Addition of Space to a User-Defined Segment

From all of this you should also notice the impact segments have on capacity planning (see Chapter 11), and on your ability to add space to a database as needed. For each segment of a database that needs to be separated from the other segments of the database you need a separate device (see Figure 8-27). In the example here we needed a device for the *default* and *system* segments (both are assigned to the same server device), a device for the *logsegment* segment and a device for the user-defined segment *myseg1*. Further, if any of these devices runs out of space, you must add space on yet another server device since segments for any one database apply to all of a server device. So, when you run out of space on any of the three server devices mentioned you would need to have space on another device ready to use. As all three devices fill up you would need three more for a total of six server devices for one database. Couple this with mirroring which mirrors a whole device and you are suddenly looking at a lot of disks to support, and allow expansion of, user-defined segments.

Final Notes on Segments

Keep the following in mind as you work with segments:

Multiple segments for multiple databases on a server device

system and *default* ssegments on same device

Many meanings of "default"

Data and log devices

Restrictions on log device

Log segment not on separate device

Must ddd device to server before adding segments

Can't drop all segments

Segments part of a single database

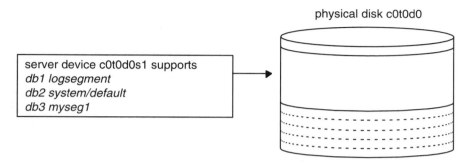

physical disk c0t0d0

server device c0t0d0s1 supports
db1 logsegment
db2 system/default
db3 myseg1

Figure 8–17. Segments of Multiple Databases on Same Device

Multiple Segments for Multiple Databases on a Server Device

You must understand the subtlety of segments. We have repeatedly discussed the need for a given segment to be on a separate server device from the other segments (note that the *system* and *default* segments are often assigned to the same device). This implies that each segment must be completely alone on the server device. This is correct, but only for each database. A server device can have the *logsegment* segment of *database1* and the *default* and/or *system* segments of *database2* and the user-defined segment *myseg1* of *database3*. All of these can be set up on a single server device as long as each one belongs to a separate database (see Figure 8–17).

system and default Segments on Same Device

Note that the *default* and *system* segments are often collocated on the same server device(s). You can separate these segments if you wish, but you will be better off putting the individual objects (tables and indexes most commonly) on their own dedicated segments as needed and leave the *system* and *default* segments alone.

Many Meanings of "default"

Don't confuse the *default* segment with a server device that is part of the pool of *default* disk space. Further, realize that when you execute **create database**, the devices you specify will be assigned the segments *system* and *default* by *default*, that is, these segment assignments are made automatically and if you don't want the segments assigned that way you must manually add new segments and drop those that you don't want. Be careful when you see or think about the term "default" and make sure you know what you mean by the term.

Data and Log Devices

The SQL Server documentation often refers to server devices as "data" devices or as "log" devices. Here the "data" device(s) are those server devices that support all the segments of a database other than the *logsegment* segment.

Restrictions on Log Device

Once you have placed the *logsegment* segment on a server device that supports only the *logsegment* segment, you can't add any other segments to that server device for that database. Once a server device is a *logsegment* device, it will remain that way unless you move the *logsegment* segment to another server device using **sp_logdevice**. Further, once the *logsegment* segment is on its own server device, you can't add or extend the *logsegment* to all the server devices supporting the database. Recall that when you add or extend the *logsegment* segment to a server device the *logsegment* segment becomes the only segment for that server device for that database. You can't extend the *logsegment* segment to all the server devices supporting the database because that would make all the server devices exclusively *logsegment* devices and there would be no room for database objects that normally go in the *system*, *default* and user-defined segments.

Log Segment Not on Separate Device

You can set up a database so that the *logsegment* segment is co-mingled with the *system* and *default* segments. This is done only when you do not need to dump (and recover) the transaction log. You can't dump the transaction log for a database that doesn't place the *logsegment* segment on a separate server device.

Must Add Device to Server Before Adding Segments

You can't add or extend segments for a database to a server device that isn't already assigned to the database. You must alter the database to include space on the new device (which will assign a set of segments to the new device, that is, *system* and *default*) before you can do anything with the segment assignments.

Can't Drop All Segments

You can't drop the *system*, *default* or *logsegment* segments from all of the server devices supporting a database. At least one server device must support each of these segments. The database must have room for each of these segments. Similarly, you can't drop a server device that is the only device supporting any of these segments of the database. For a user-defined segment, you must first drop the segment from the database before you can drop the last server device supporting that segment. For server devices that are not the only ones supporting any of the segments of the database, you can drop all the segments from the server device. This makes the server device completely unusable by the server.

Segments Part of a Single Database

Always remember that segments only apply within a single database. Always remember that any segment assigned to a server device applies to all the space on that device that is assigned the database.

TRANSACTION LOG ISSUES

The transaction log of each database is used by the SQL Server to record all changes made to the database. In order to ensure that the server can recover the database, the server provides various mechanisms to protect the contents of the transaction log. There are many issues surrounding the transaction log and how the transaction log relates to the greater issue of database segments.

Transaction Log on Separate Server Device

You must pay attention to the transaction log of each database on the server. The transaction log is one of the vital elements of the Sybase SQL Server that ensures data integrity and recovery from database or server or server machine failures. You need to understand the following issues to provide your users with the optimum balance of data security, recoverability and speed. You don't have to place the transaction log (also known as the log segment or just the log) on a server device separate from those server devices that support the other segments of a database, but you almost always want to. We discuss why this is the general rule and why you will sometimes break this rule.

The most important reason to place the transaction log or *logsegment* on a separate server device is to be able to dump the transaction log independently of the database (see Chapter 9 for more discussion of the process of recovering databases). If you don't place the transaction log on a separate server device you can't dump the log without dumping the entire database. Dumping the database takes much longer and for larger databases often requires dumping to tape since your server may not have enough file *system* disk space to allow dumping databases to disk. Dumping to tape is also slower than dumping to disk. Longer dump times slow the *system* down for longer periods of time which reduce the time the *system* is available for business use. The fact that dumping the complete database is slower will prevent you from dumping as often as you should. Further, if you dump the database, which also dumps the transaction log along with the rest of the database, the transaction log is not truncated. When you dump the transaction log separately all the committed transactions in the transaction log are automatically dropped, which is called truncating the transaction log.

You must be able to dump the transaction log in order to recover the database as completely as possible. There are two levels to this recovery. The first assumes you must rebuild the database from dumps already completed and the second assumes the server itself is still functioning and can access the sysdatabases *system* table in the *master* database.

All of this means you should, in almost all cases, place the transaction log (*logsegment*) of each database on a separate server device. As explained previously you should place the transaction log (same as *logsegment*) on a separate server device that is part of a separate physical disk and the physical disk should be one that is attached to a different disk controller than those that control the other physical disks of the database.

Transaction Log Not on Separate Device

Now that you have this general rule about placing the transaction log on a separate server device for every database, you need to know about the exception to the rule. For certain databases you do not want the transaction log separated from the data segments, that is, from the rest of the database. Such a database could not be recovered to a state more current than the last full database dump. A database that is used to archive some portion of a production database would fit this description. You will set up such a database for an application that will do a great deal of processing on a very infrequent basis, perhaps at the end of each month to reduce all the orders for your business to summary statistics of interest to decision support users. This type of database requires a very large transaction log for a very brief time while it process large quantities of data. After the periodic processing is complete the database can easily be dumped. The processing is usually started by either the individual responsible for the periodic processing or is scheduled to run automatically via a `cron` job at the UNIX level. This means it is easy for the database to be dumped completely immediately after the processing is complete and in fact the dumping should be part of the same script or scripts that perform the processing. Such a database would not be impacted by recovery based on database dumps only and therefore does not require that the transaction log be on a separate server device to support dumping the transaction log separately from the database. Between these periods of intense processing the database may be virtually static as it is used mostly on a read-only basis to support report generation. During these periods there is no need for a large transaction log. This type of database is an example of a database that does not need or want a separate transaction log segment. During the periods of intense processing the user(s) of the database will require a very large transaction log. If a separate transaction log of sufficient space were created, it would be empty most of the time and unavailable to the database for any other use. Therefore, you should consider creating such a database with the segment *logsegment* applied to each and every server device that supports the database. You accomplish this by executing the **create database** command without the **log on** clause. This set of circumstances may not come up often but you should be aware of this option.

Sizing the Transaction Log

You will often wonder what the appropriate transaction log size is for any given database. Note that the discussion that follows covers the impact of the transaction log filling and therefore you should see Chapter 12 for discussion of thresholds which can prevent the transaction log from filling up.

Impact of Large Transaction Log

In fact, the proper size will vary from day to day and perhaps even more frequently than that. You don't want the transaction log to fill since the server must be able to make entries in the transaction log for all the activity in the database to ensure recoverability. If the log fills up, the database becomes useless until at least some space in the log is freed up by dumping the transaction log. However, once the transaction log has filled completely you can't reduce its size (truncate) by dumping the log because even the dumping of the log requires making an entry in the transaction log. This is how the server keeps track of the order in which transaction logs were made. So if the log fills completely you must dump the transaction log with the **no_log** option, but you must not use the **no_log** option unless you have verified that the transaction log is really full (see Chapter 12 for a procedure to do this). This means that the transaction log has been truncated, but a copy of the deleted transaction log records was not made. This means you can't recover the database using transaction logs beyond the point of the previous transaction log dump since the server can't log the transaction log dump and therefore the server doesn't have a complete record of all activity in the database. Since there is a gap in the set of transaction log dumps, the server won't allow you to dump the transaction log again until you do a complete database dump. This means you can't recover the database to a state more current than the most recent full database dump. You need to understand the implications this has for your ability to recover the database. When the log fills completely the database is effectively lost to your users. You must dump the transaction log with the **no_log** option which takes time and creates more downtime for the database. Note that the larger the transaction log is, the longer it takes to perform the dump (with **no_log** option) before you can have the database available again. Now, since you can't continue to make transaction log dumps you should make a complete database dump or you risk losing the database changes made from the time of the failure onward. So, you should make a full database dump which creates further downtime. Overall, you don't want to let the transaction log fill for any database that is accessed by applications that are critical to your business. Your first inclination will be to make the transaction log so big that it can never fill up. You would be making a big mistake.

Default Transaction Log Sizing

You need to think about why users may need more log space one day and why they don't need as much the next. As with all database space, you can't retrieve it once it has been assigned to the database without a complete logical rebuild of the database (see Chapter 9 for more details). You are certainly aware of the general rule that the transaction log should be 20 percent of the overall database space and that rule is fine for many databases. Still, as your databases become large, do you really need 2 Gb of transaction log for a 10-Gb database? You can only answer that by knowing what goes on in the database. For small databases the 20 percent rule may be fine, but beyond that you may be wasting a lot of server disk space. You need to determine what the transaction volume for the database is and how large the typical transaction is and compare this with how often you are going to dump the transaction log. Based on these numbers you can figure out how big your transaction log must be to support all the transactions that would be in the transaction log at any one time. Note that such a scientific analysis is not something you have the time or the tools to carry out. After all this is one database in one server among many in your database system. A more practical approach is to size the transaction log when you initially create the database with the help of the application designers, if possible. Then let the application go into production and see what happens. You don't want to increase the transaction log in the futile effort of preventing the transaction log from ever filling up. See below for a description of how any one transaction in the log can cause the log to fill no matter how big it is. You probably don't want any transaction log to exceed 200 Mb without a very good reason. If you need more space than that for the transaction log of a single database, you must be able to explain what the database is doing with that much space day after day. You also need to explain what is going on with the size of the transaction log dumps as well (see Chapter 9 for more details of the implications of large transaction log dumps).

How Transaction Log Is Truncated

You need to understand the way the transaction log works and how it relates to the issue of the log filling up. Before database changes are made, the server records those changes for each database in the transaction log for that database. The records in the transaction log represent each step in each transaction that is being applied to the database. Each transaction has a beginning, intermediate steps, and either a commit or a roll back. Whether the transaction commits or rolls back, the transaction is complete as far as the database is concerned. Since all changes to the database are recorded in the log, the log will continue to grow. You can reduce the size of the transaction log only by truncating the log which occurs when you dump the transaction log. Dumping the transaction log makes a copy of the transaction log records for committed transactions on the dump device you specify and then deletes the records of all the committed transactions. This usually reduces the size of the log each time you dump it. However, there is a catch that is not immediately obvious—a catch that can be deadly and confusing. When you dump the transaction log, the server then starts looking at the transactions in the log to determine which transactions can be deleted to reduce the size of the log. The server scans through the log looking for the beginning of the first transaction that has not completed. When it finds the beginning of the first transaction that has not (at the time of the **dump transaction**) yet completed with either a commit or a roll-back, the server stops deleting records from the transaction log. This means the server will delete only the completed transactions from the transaction log up to the beginning of the first incomplete transaction.

Can't Dump a Full Transaction Log

You may encounter the following situation. Once the transaction for a particular database is full, you can't make any more entries in the transaction log for that database. Since you can't turn off transaction logging for a database this means the database is no longer available for inserts or updates; selects will still operate since a select is not logged. When the transaction log fills and the SQL Server attempts to write to the transaction log the write fails generating an 1105 error (thresholds can prevent this—see Chapter 12). Note that the 1105 error in the server errorlog indicates a database segment is full, not necessarily the log segment. See Chapter 12 for details of how to verify which segment caused an 1105 and what to do about it. For this discussion we assume the 1105 error was caused by the transaction log being full and dumping the transaction log did not free up any space. Once the transaction log is full and dumping with the no_log option does not reduce its size the server will not be able to make any further transaction log dumps. This may not seem logical but consider the way the server will use the transaction log(s) and database dump when recovering the database. To recover a database you will first load the most recent database dump and then apply the subsequent transaction log dumps in the order they were made. The server looks at the timestamp on each transaction log to make sure the correct order of the transaction logs is preserved as they are applied to the database. In order to mark the time of each transaction log dump the server makes an entry in the transaction log itself indicating when the transaction log dump was started. So if the transaction log is full, the server can't write into the transaction log to record the time of the dump.

Dumping a Full Transaction Log

You have only one option at this point and that is to dump the transaction log with the **no_log** option. This option has implications for your ability to recover the database so use it only when you have to and only after you understand the implications (see Chapter 9). When you use the **no_log** option, the server does not attempt to make any entries in the transaction log, and since it can't record the time of the transaction log dump, there isn't any point in making an actual dump of the log entries either, since the server would not allow you to apply it to the database anyway. With the **no_log** option the server simply deletes all the completed transactions up to the beginning of the first transaction it finds that is still open.

Dumping Transaction Log Doesn't Free Up Space

Now we can continue the discussion of the 1105 error. Once you have the 1105 error and you have verified that the transaction log is indeed full (see Chapter 12, for a procedure to verify this), you must use

dump transaction <databasename> with no_log

However, you will see situations where even this does not reduce the size of the transaction log. How can this be? You need to recall that the server deletes only the transaction log entries for completed transactions up to the point of the beginning of the first transaction that has not completed. But, what if the very first entry in the transaction log is the beginning of an open transaction? This means even the **no_log** option will not reduce the size of the transaction log. The only way to cure this situation is to kill the server process that owns the open transaction. If you can identify the offending server process id (*spid*) you can kill the *spid* from within the server and that should remove the transaction log entries for that transaction. However, there is no direct way for you to identify which server process is responsible. You can make reasonable deductions to determine which *spids* might be the cause and kill all of them, but if this doesn't work pretty quickly you might just as well shut down and restart the server. Restarting the server will allow you to dump the transaction log after the database has recovered.

Transaction Log Size

Finally, with all this background, you can see why transaction log size is relevant to database physical design. We need to discuss the appropriate size of the transaction log for the database. You will be tempted to make the transaction log huge, thinking you can somehow prevent the transaction log from ever filling up. You would be making a reasonable assumption, but you would be wrong. As the preceding discussion explained, you can make the transaction log bigger and bigger, but one open transaction can still force the log to fill completely, no matter how large the transaction log is. Certainly, the larger the transaction log, the longer it will take to fill up, but you must realize an important impact of this. When the transaction log does finally fill and you must use the

dump transaction <databasename> with no_log

option, the larger the transaction log, the longer it will take to dump the transaction log. You must understand that since a full transaction log basically shuts down the database which can shut down your business (again, selects will operate, but any updates will fail), a larger transaction log which will delay the crisis of a full transaction log will actually make the crisis worse because the **dump transaction** will take that much longer. You can't completely avoid filling the transaction log just by making it bigger.

Initial Transaction Log Sizing

With all that said, you need to make a reasonable guess as to the initial size of the transaction log, say 20 percent of the database size and then see how it goes. If this transaction log fills up repeatedly and you can explain why the applications that run against the database have a good reason for creating enough transactions at one time to fill the transaction log, then you should expand it using the **alter database** command. You need to be careful though. This 20 percent rule of thumb can get you into trouble. Take a real-world example. A production database is 5 Gb and the transaction log is 200 Mb, which is only 4 percent of the overall database size. If the transaction log ever fills up, it takes about 30 minutes to dump the transaction log to disk. Can your business afford to be without this database (for updates and inserts) for more than 30 minutes? Further, can you provide any reasonable explanation as to why your users have a need to fill more than 200 Mb of the transaction log while running the applications that depend on this database? Probably, most of the data in this database is not new but old and getting older all the time. Hence, your users are probably working only with a small percentage of this database at any one time, and if you look at this much smaller subset of the database as the actual database size, the size of the transaction log at 200 Mb seems much more reasonable. The 20 percent rule of thumb is probably useful until the size of the transaction log goes beyond 100 Mb. For a transaction log larger than 100 Mb, you need to make sure you and your users understand how long it will take to dump the transaction log if it ever gets full. Note that while we have discussed the impacts of dumping a full transaction log, you can still have very long dump times for a large transaction log that is not completely full. If you normally dump the transaction log periodically and for some reason you miss several of those transaction log dumps, the next transaction log dump will take much longer as the transaction log continues to fill up as the normal dump times go by without a successful dump of the transaction log.

Transaction Log Never Big Enough

You must educate your users and your management that the transaction log can't be turned off for any database, that no matter how large it is it can still fill up if only one user opens a transaction and never executes a commit or rollback and that it takes longer to dump the transaction log the larger it becomes. Your users will always want a larger transaction log to prevent database downtime due to a full transaction log, but those same users will not want to suffer the greater database downtime that occurs when you need to dump a larger transaction log.

MIRRORING SERVER DEVICES

Now that you have all your database segments under control, you need to worry about mirroring which simply assigns another raw partition or file system to a server device and writes any writes to the server device to the mirror. In case of a failure of the server device, the server can continue by using the mirror. Note that we are not discussing the area of hardware or operating system mirroring; only the mirroring of SQL Server server devices within the server itself.

Mirroring Defined

SQL Server mirroring maintains a copy of the server device on another server device. The original server device is called the primary and the mirror is called the secondary or mirror device (see Figure 8–18). SQL Server will then write any changes to the database to both the primary

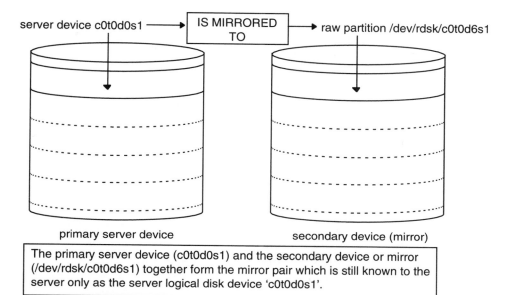

server device c0t0d0s1 ⟶ IS MIRRORED TO ⟶ raw partition /dev/rdsk/c0t0d6s1

primary server device   secondary device (mirror)

The primary server device (c0t0d0s1) and the secondary device or mirror (/dev/rdsk/c0t0d6s1) together form the mirror pair which is still known to the server only as the server logical disk device 'c0t0d0s1'.

Figure 8-18 Mirroring of a Server Disk Device

server device and the mirror device. When the SQL Server detects an error on the primary server device it will fail over to the secondary server device and processing will continue without interruption. If the server detects errors on the mirror device it will simply drop the mirror and continue processing using just the primary device. You may want to use RAID devices to provide this same capability for your most critical databases. The subject of RAID, the various levels, how to determine the needs of your system, how to decide between a vendor's disk and generic disks for the RAID array, and so on are not covered here.

Why Mirroring is Needed

The reasons to mirror your server devices and thereby your databases are several. First, the most obvious one is to prevent downtime. More accurately, mirroring allows you to control, not eliminate, downtime caused by physical disk problems. If a server device is not mirrored and the underlying physical disk crashes, those databases that rely on the server device(s) on that physical disk will fail. Depending on which databases are involved the SQL Server may not be able to continue (master device,

device that contains the transaction log for a critical database, etc.). In both cases the databases in question are immediately out of service. With mirroring, the SQL Server detects the errors with the server device and stops using it. The server device is dropped by the SQL Server and the server automatically switches over to the mirror device. You must still shut down the server and the server machine to replace the drive, but you get to choose when the downtime occurs.

Mirroring the Master Device

You should mirror the master device which will provide a mirror of the *master* database, the first 2 Mb of *tempdb* and the *model* database. Having a mirror of the master device is critical for two reasons. First, if anything goes wrong with the master device, you lose the *master* database which means the entire server and all the databases are completely shut down. By mirroring the master device, your server can move through these problems and continue processing. Second, if you lose the master device, your server is dead and recovery is much more complicated. When you lose the master device, if you don't have a mirror, you may need to recover the server by first rebuilding the *master* database, reapply any server configuration changes necessary to fully recover the server (for a 4.9.2 Server you need to add the dump device before you can load dumps), load a dump of *master,* and then fix any other problems to recover the server fully. With a mirror of the master device, the most tedious part of recovering the server is already at hand, namely recovering the *master* database. You must mirror the master device. Since the master device is typically the smallest device on the server, you have no excuse not toprovide a mirror.

Mirroring Transaction Log(s) of User Databases

You should mirror the device(s) that support the transaction log for each and every user database that is critical. Here we mean critical in the sense that you need ensure that in the event of problems you can recover the database as completely as possible. Depending on the nature of your business, you must decide how much data you can afford to lose. Note that if you have a problem and you must drop back to your last database dump and the subsequent series of transaction log dumps to recover, you are still losing the database changes that have occurred since the last transaction log dump. By setting up a mirror of the transaction log for this database, you provide insurance that you can get a copy of the transaction log that is current even if the transaction log on the primary device is lost. Without the mirror, if you lose the transaction log, you have no way to recover the database to a state more recent than the last transaction log dump (see Chapter 9 for details of this process). Note that in order to mirror the transaction log for any database, you must mirror the primary server device where the transaction log is located.

Mirroring and Replacing a Failed Disk Drive

Mirroring is also very useful when you do need to replace a physical disk drive. Even if you choose not to mirror all the server devices, you should be prepared to mirror any disk drive that supports the server. This means you need to be ready to mirror all the server devices that are on any given physical disk. When you have a disk failure it is much easier for you, and a lot faster, if you simply mirror all the server devices on the disk to another physical disk on the server (see Figure 8-19). For some disk drive problems the drive is still accessible even though it is beginning to fail. In this case mirroring allows you to save all the data in all the server devices on the disk drive before a hard failure occurs. Sometimes the disk failure that forces you to replace the disk will have damaged some portion of the disk and one or more of the server devices that are assigned to the disk. However, for all the other server devices, you can mirror off to another disk, drop the server devices that are on the damaged disk, and replace the drive. Then you simply mirror back from your spare drive to the replacement drive. This is much faster and less error-prone than rebuilding databases from dumps. Further, if done properly, you will not loose any data from the databases that you mirror off the damaged drive. In order to do this you need to have a disk drive or drives on the server machine that can handle the overall storage and number of partitions needed to mirror all of the server devices on any given disk that is supporting the server.

Note that if you mirror all the server devices on your server, you don't need to do even this much to replace a bad drive. You simply drop the devices on the failed disk from their respective mirror pairs, shut down the server machine and replace the drive. After you have the server machine back on-line, you remirror the affected server drives.

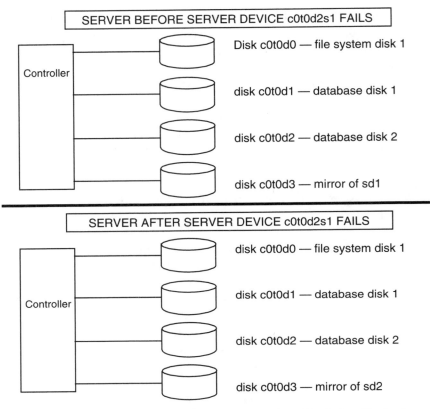

This example assumes disks c0t0d1, c0t0d2, and c0t0d3 have identical partitioning to allow mirroring of all server devices on c0t0d1 to c0t0d3 and c0t0d2 to c0t0d3. After failure of server device c0t0d2s1, drop mirrors on c0t0d3 and mirror from all but failed server device on c0t0d2 to c0t0d3. Drop primary devices of these mirror pairs (i.e. drop the server devices on c0t0d2). Shut down server machine, replace disk c0t0d2, remirror from devices on c0t0d3 to c0t0d2. Only need to recreate and load databases that were supported by the failed device on c0c0d2.

Figure 8-19 Mirroring to Simplify Replacing a Failed Disk

It is December 25. You are home. Your son is opening his Brio set. You have been looking forward to this probably more than he has. You reviewed the server errorlogs earlier in the morning since you are on call through the holiday. You noticed that one of your many production servers had a device write error and it failed over to the mirror. You notify your management and they agree that since the production system is processing normally, there is no need to replace the disk drive immediately. You don't get paged, and you don't need to page the server machine SA person who is home with their family. The users worldwide that depend on the production server throughout the holidays don't even know anything happened. You replace the drive the next week after mirroring off any other server devices that were on the physical drive that failed. Note that if you had assigned whole physical disks to server devices and whole physical disks to be mirrors of those devices, you wouldn't even need this step. You could simply drop the mirrors on the failed or failing disk and replace it. At times like these the disk space needed to support mirrors seems very cheap. After you son goes to bed, you get your Brio layout whipped into shape. Er, your son's layout.

Mirroring During Server Upgrade

Mirroring is also very useful during a major upgrade. By mirroring all the server devices, including the master device, and then dropping (using the **disk unmirror** command) but not removing the mirrors prior to starting the upgrade process, the previous version of the server is available (see Figure 8-20). If the upgrade runs into problems, you can fail back to the previous version of the server with all the data in all the user databases intact. Basically you start the upgrade and if you need to, revoke the UNIX level permissions to the operating system files that control access to the physical disk partitions that support the server and reestablish the mirrors for these devices. Doing this for the server devices that were being upgraded and restarting the server force the server to fail over to the mirrors which are really the previous version of the server. Note that this implies you have enough disk space and enough partitions to mirror every server device at once (see Chapter 13 for more details of upgrading using this mirroring technique).

Mirroring During Server Machine Hardware Upgrade

Another time that mirroring is very useful is during a server machine hardware upgrade. While your server may be operating normally, you may need to either add a large amount of disk space to accommodate database growth or replace some or all of the existing disk drive with larger faster drives. In either case, you can add some of the new disk drives, mirror the existing server devices to the new drives, drop the old server

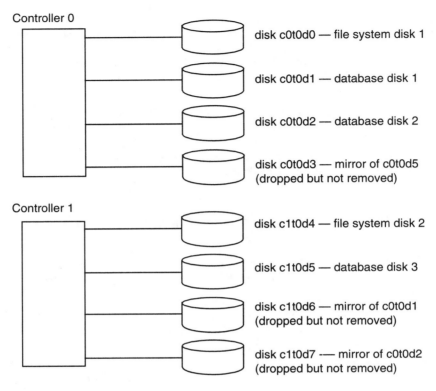

Stop all database changes, drop all mirrors with **mode=retain** option, then perform upgrade. Test applications against new server version. If necessary, fail back to the mirrors which had been dropped just before the upgrade began. These mirrors contain the previous version of the server the way it was just before the upgrade. Don't allow any changes to production data until convinced upgrade was successful.

Figure 8–20. Mirroring to Simplify a Server Version Upgrade

devices and remove the old drives. Then you can add the rest of the new drives and by mirroring spread the server devices around on the new drives as you wish (see Figure 8–21). Note that this approach, as with the others mentioned above, saves a lot of time and hassle for you, the DBA, is less error-prone, and results in a server that is completely up to date (i.e., no data loss due to rebuilding from dumps that may not be completely up to date).

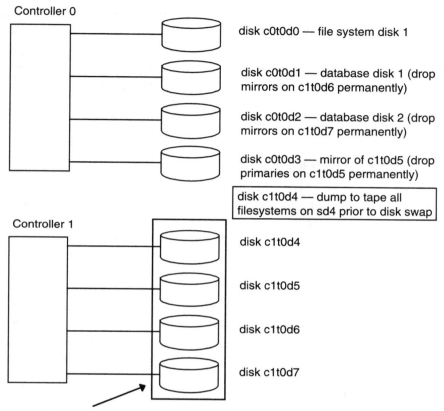

Controller 0

disk c0t0d0 — file system disk 1

disk c0t0d1 — database disk 1 (drop mirrors on c1t0d6 permanently)

disk c0t0d2 — database disk 2 (drop mirrors on c1t0d7 permanently)

disk c0t0d3 — mirror of c1t0d5 (drop primaries on c1t0d5 permanently)

disk c1t0d4 — dump to tape all filesystems on sd4 prior to disk swap

Controller 1

disk c1t0d4

disk c1t0d5

disk c1t0d6

disk c1t0d7

After dropping mirrors and making tape dump of file systems on c1t0d4, remove disks c1t0d4, c1t0d5, c1t0d6 and c1t0d7 and replace with new drives. Remirror c0t0d1 to c1t0d6, c0t0d2 to c1t0d7 and c0t0d3 to c1t0d5. Load dump of filesystems to the new c1t0d4. To get devices on c1t0d5 to be primaries again, drop primaries on c0t0d3 permanently, then remirror from c1t0d5 to c0t0d3.

Then repeat the process to replace the four other old drives, c0t0d1, c0t0d2, c0t0d3, and c1t0d4

Figure 8–21. Mirroring to Simplify Major Server Machine Disk Upgrade

Mirroring All Server Devices

Choosing what you will mirror and what you won't is very important. As you will see later, you will save yourself a lot of time and disk management mistakes if you simply mirror all the devices in the server. However, you need to understand the issues involved so you can decide on the mirroring plan that is best for your server.

You will note that in these examples of the benefits of mirroring there is a theme, namely that you should mirror all your server devices. This may seem extravagant in terms of disk space and disk controllers, but you need to weigh such costs against the cost to your business of lost data, downtime while you manually fix the problems that mirroring can automatically take care of and the additional hassles you must deal with keeping track of which server devices are mirrored and which aren't.

Mirroring Priorities

If you have the disks (and if you don't, you should get them), you should be using all of each physical disk to either support only server devices (using the standard disk partitioning described earlier) or mirrors of server devices. It is easier to maintain the mirrors of server devices if all the physical disks that support the server are partitioned identically and then you simply mirror all the server devices (partitions) of one whole disk to another whole disk.

If you don't choose to go this way, you need to mirror some things more than others. First you must always mirror the *master* database which, of course means you must mirror the master device. Since the server mirrors a server device to a raw partition this means you must mirror the master device. A mirror of the master device will allow the server to operate continuously if the master device (*master* database) fails. Since the *master* database is the heart and soul of your server any problems with the *master* database bring down the whole server. You should always mirror the *master* device of each of your servers.

After the *master* database, you should mirror the transaction log of the most critical database(s) on the server. The database dumps that you have along with the transaction log dumps allow you to recover the database to the point in time of the most recent transaction log dump. If you can still get at the transaction log on disk, you can recover the database to the state it was in at the moment of the failure. If there is any problem with the disk that supports the transaction log, you can still recover the transaction log from the mirror device. Mirroring the transaction log ensures you can recover the database and all the transactions that have been committed against it even though a disk failure has occurred. Note that it is more important to mirror the transaction log than the database itself. If any of the disks that support the database fail and the database is not mirrored, you can reload the database from database dumps and transaction logs, and since you can recover the up-to-date transaction log from disk, you can recover the database completely. If you mirror the database itself but not the transaction log and the disk supporting the transaction log fails, you have no way to recover the database beyond the most recent transaction log dump.

You will need to spend your time checking that the mirrors of the transaction logs are working. This can become tedious when you need to add space to one of the databases and the new space needs to be on a server device that was not previously mirrored. This is why, from a management perspective, it is a whole lot easier to simply mirror all the server devices (partitions) in the server, and to mirror all server devices on one physical disk to another whole physical disk. This ensures that no matter where you add space, the data is mirrored.

One exception to this is *tempdb*. Since *tempdb* is never recovered there isn't the need to mirror *tempdb* or the transaction log of *tempdb*. Still, if *tempdb* is not mirrored and the disk that supports *tempdb*, or its log, fails *tempdb* fails and the entire server is effectively shut down. For *tempdb* you want to mirror both the database and the transaction log to ensure that your server will not be brought down by a single disk failure. You need to trade this off against the overhead involved with mirroring since mirroring means writing the same data to two different disks all the time. If *tempdb* for your server is very heavily loaded, you may want to drop mirroring for *tempdb*. You need to understand that you are trading performance against system availability.

Creating Mirrors

Now that you are aware of the reasons to mirror server devices and which server devices are the most important to mirror, we cover the mechanics of mirroring a server device. You should have noticed a recurring theme throughout this section, namely that your mirror devices not databases. You must understand this concept. You create a logical server device that associates a server device with a raw partition of a physical disk or a file in a file system using the **disk init** server command. You then create a mirror of the server device. Note that you can't create a mirror of a server device on a partition that is already supporting a server device. This also means you must not use **disk init** on the partition that you want to use as the mirror of a server device. Finally, if you do want to mirror to a partition that is already supporting a server device, you must first drop that server device. It doesn't matter how many databases have space on the server device. They all get mirrored. Further, it doesn't matter how a given database is segmented or spread across multiple server devices. A mirror mirrors only a single server device; a mirror does not mirror a database or a segment. You must ensure that you are mirroring all the server devices you need to be mirroring to protect the databases or database segments you need to. You set up mirroring of a server logical disk device using the server command

```
disk mirror
name = "device_name",
mirror = "physicalname",
writes = { serial | noserial }
```

First we need to discuss the following components of the **disk mirror** command:

device_name

physicalname

writes

Primary and secondary sevices on same controller

Primary and secondary devices on separate controllers

disk mirror example

device_name

The **device_name** is the name of the server disk device that you wish to mirror. Again, this **device_name** is the name of the device that is known to the SQL Server, not the name of the device known to the UNIX operating system. The server device that you use as the **device_name** becomes the primary server device.

physicalname

The **mirror** is the device that will mirror the primary device and the **physicalname** is the full path of the operating system file that controls the access to the raw partition that will be the mirror.

Note that you must not create the mirror device using **disk init**. Further, if you need to mirror to a raw partition that is currently in use as a server device, you must clean off anything on the server device and drop the server device before using it as a mirror device. The mirror device is the secondary device relative to the primary server device.

writes

The **writes** parameter specifies how you want the mirror to function. The default is **writes = serial** which means the server writes database changes to the primary server device, waits for that write to complete, and then writes to the secondary or mirror device. The **writes = serial** option is the most secure.

Primary and Secondary Devices on Same Controller

If both the primary and secondary devices are assigned to partitions on physical disks that are attached to the same controller, it is possible for a controller error to corrupt the write to both devices, and this is why you should have a device and its mirror on separate physical disks attached to separate controllers. You also want the device and its mirror on disks on separate controllers to allow the server to function if any one controller were to fail all together.

Primary and Secondary Devices on Separate Controllers

If your primary and secondary devices are on separate controllers, you don't need to use **writes = serial** and can use the faster **writes = noserial** option. You must note that the default is **writes = serial** so you must specify the **noserial** option to get the faster mirroring. For the examples that follow we assume you are using the standard server device naming conventions discussed previously in this chapter.

disk mirror Example

For example, if you already have created a server device (using **disk init**) called c0t0d1s1 and you want to mirror this server device to a raw partition 1 which is part of the physical disk called c1t0d6, and this raw partition is controlled by the UNIX operating system file /dev/rdsk/c1t0d6s1 and the physical disks c0t0d1 and c1t0d6 are attached to separate disk controllers (if not you should consider the **writes = serial** option), you would specify the mirror as follows:

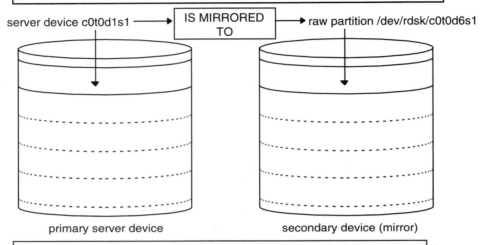

Note that UNIX user 'sybase' must own the files that control access to both the primary server device (/dev/rdsk/c0t0d1s1) and the secondary mirror device (/dev/rdsk/c1t0d6s1).

server device c0t0d1s1 ⟶ IS MIRRORED TO ⟶ raw partition /dev/rdsk/c0t0d6s1

primary server device   secondary device (mirror)

The primary server device (c0t0d1s1) and the secondary device or mirror (/dev/rdsk/c0t0d6s1) together form the mirror pair which is still known to the server only as the server logical disk device 'c0t0d1s1'.

Figure 8–22. The Mirror Pair

```
disk mirror
name = "c0t0d1s1",
mirror = "/dev/rdsk/c0t0d6s1",
writes = noserial
```

Primary Device, Mirror Device, and Logical Server Device

The primary server device taken together with the mirror device (also called the secondary device) form one logical server device which we also call the mirror pair (see Figure 8–22). It is important that you understand this relationship. While the primary device is a server device that you created with **disk init** and is therefore known to the server, the mirror device is not a server device by itself and you don't create the mirror with the **disk init** command. In fact, you never identify the mirror device to the server other than through the use of the **disk mirror** command.

Notice that when you need to drop a mirror, you use the **disk unmirror** command that references only the server logical device. You must notice that you can drop either "side" of the mirror relationship, either the primary (the server device) or the secondary (the mirror which is really a raw partition), but, whichever side of the mirror relationship you drop, you specify the same server logical device. This can confuse you, especially when a crisis hits. If you need to drop either side of the mirror pair, you use the server command

```
disk unmirror
name = "device_name",
side = { primary | secondary },
mode = { retain | remove }
```

Here again you must be clear on the terms. First we need to discuss the following components of the **disk unmirror** command:

device_name

side

mode

device_name

The **device_name** is identical to what you used to define the mirror.

side

The **side** parameter specifies which side of the mirror pair you want to drop. You can drop either the primary or secondary side of the mirror. If you need to replace a disk drive, for example, the choice of which side of the mirror pair needs to be dropped is clear. The side of the mirror pair that is on the disk to be removed from the server machine is the side of the mirror pair that you need to drop.

mode

The **mode** parameter allows for another level of complexity and confusion regarding mirroring. If you unmirror or drop one side of a mirror pair, you can specify **mode = retain** or **mode = remove**. The **retain** option tells SQL Server not to read from or write to the device specified by the

side = <*device*>, but the server does not free the device for other uses. The device is still there and can be brought back on-line using the server command **disk remirror** (see below). Note that if you use the **mode = remove** option, the specified side of the mirrored device is dropped permanently and you can not use the **disk remirror** command to restore the mirror of the server device. Of course, you can use the **disk mirror** command to create a new mirror of the server device. You must realize what it takes to mirror or remirror a server device since the server must make a complete copy of the server device data even if no changes have occurred between the primary and mirror.

Dropping One Side of a Mirrored Device

When you need to drop either side of a mirrored device, you need to be very careful that you understand what all the terms mean. Here you need to be very clear on what the **device_name** refers to. The **device_name** is the logical device name by which the SQL Server knows about the mirror pair. If you drop either side of the mirror pair with either **mode = retain** or **mode = remove**, the server still refers to the remaining device as **device_name**. Consider the example of defining a mirror pair discussed earlier. The syntax to drop the primary side of the mirror pair, which is the actual server device that the mirror pair was originally named for, would look like this:

```
disk unmirror
name = "c0t0d1s1",
side = primary,
mode = retain
```

And if you wanted to drop the secondary side of the mirror pair, which is actually a raw partition that the server has no prior knowledge of, the syntax would look like this:

```
disk unmirror
name = "c0t0d1s1",
side = secondary,
mode = retain
```

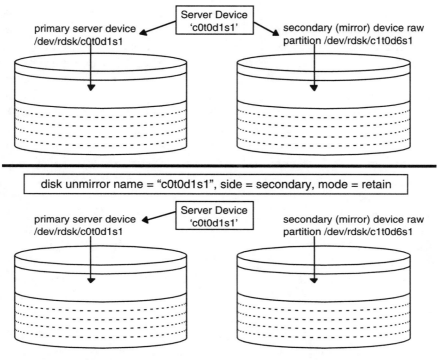

The secondary device will continue to have a copy of data on /dev/rdsk/c0d0d1s1 but will only reflect the data as of the time the **disk unmirror** command was executed. If the **mode = remove** option was used, the data in /dev/rdsk/c1t0d6s1 would be lost permanently.

Figure 8–23. Dropping Secondary (Mirror) Device of a Mirror Pair

Dropping Secondary Device

In both examples we choose to retain the side of the mirror that was dropped. Now you need to realize what has happened in each case. First, consider the second case where you dropped the secondary side of the mirror pair. In that case, before you dropped anything, you had a mirror pair called c0t0d1s1 that consisted of a primary side which was the server device called c0t0d1s1 and the secondary device which is the raw partition controlled by the operating system file /dev/rdsk/c1d0d6s1 (see Figure 8–23). By dropping the secondary side of the mirror pair, and specifying **mode = retain**, you still have the server device called c0d0d1s1 and you still have the raw partition /dev/rdsk/c1d0d6s1 that contains a copy of the server device c0t0d1s1—a copy that was up to date until the time the **disk unmirror** command was executed, but which will not be updated any further. If you specified the **mode = remove** option, you would simply be back where you started with the server device called c0t0d1s1 referring to raw partition /dev/rdsk/c0t0d1s1 and nothing else. Whichever mode you specify, you are left with the server device called sd1b which is a server device of the size you specified when you created the server device using the **disk init** command, and this server device c0t0d1s1 is associated with the 1 partition of the physical disk c0t0d1 controlled by the UNIX operating system file /dev/rdsk/c0t0d1s1. Note that this is precisely the process the server goes through when it detects an error on the secondary side of the mirror pair and drops the mirror or secondary device with the **mode = retain option.** You will not be impressed by this lengthy explanation at this point.

You must note that if you were to now execute the server command

disk remirror name = "c0t0d1s1"

the situation would be returned to exactly the way it was before the **disk unmirror** command was executed, that is, the primary server device would be /dev/rdsk/c0t0d1s1 and the secondary or mirror device would be /dev/rdsk/c1t0d6s1.

Dropping Primary Device

Now you must consider the first case where you dropped the primary side of the mirror pair. In that case, before you dropped anything, you had the same mirror pair as before, but note that the primary side of the mirror pair, the server device called c0t0d1s1 really points to the raw partition 1 on the physical disk called c0t0d1 and controlled by the UNIX operating system file /dev/rdsk/c0t0d1s1, and the secondary device which is the raw partition controlled by the operating system file /dev/rdsk/c1d0d6s1 (see Figure 8–24). By dropping the primary side of the mirror pair, and specifying **mode = retain**, you still have the server device called c0t0d1s1, but it now is assigned to only the secondary side of the mirror pair, a raw partition on another physical disk. Note that the 1 partition of the physical disk called c1t0d6 has never been identified to the server through **disk init**. You need to be clear on what is happening

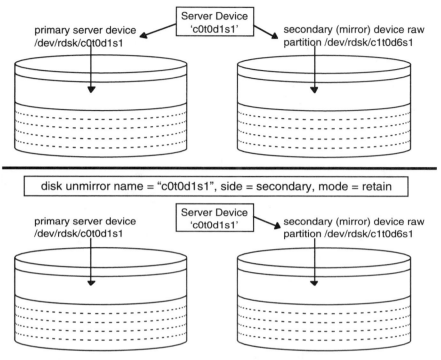

The primary device will continue to have a copy of data on /dev/rdsk/c1d0d6s1 but will only reflect the data as of the time the **disk unmirror** command was executed. If the **mode = remove** option was used, the data in /dev/rdsk/c0t0d1s1 would be lost permanently.

Figure 8–24. Dropping Primary Server Device of a Mirror Pair

when you drop the primary side of the mirror pair. When you execute the **disk unmirror** command, the SQL Server automatically converts the secondary side of the mirror pair into a normal server device just as if you had created that server device with **disk init**. The server simply takes the actual size of the primary device and uses that to size the secondary device which is now the only active server device in the mirror pair. This can be confusing. Note that this is precisely the process the server goes through when it detects an error on the primary side of the mirror pair and fails over to the secondary device making it the primary and making it a normal server device.

You must note that if you were to now execute the server command

```
disk remirror
name = "c0t0d1s1"
```

the situation would be returned to exactly the way it was before the **disk unmirror** command was executed, that is, the primary server device would be /dev/rdsk/c0t0d1s1 and the secondary or mirror device would be /dev/rdsk/c1t0d6s1.

Remirroring

When you need to restore the device of the mirrored device pair you have previously dropped, you need to use the **disk remirror** command which looks like this:

```
disk remirror
name = "device_name"
```

And as before **device_name** is identical to what you used to define the mirror. You must notice that the remirror command doesn't care whether you dropped the primary or secondary side of the mirror pair. It simply brings whichever device was dropped back on line and will bring the device back up to date relative to the device of the mirror pair that was not dropped. Note that the **disk remirror** command will not work if you used the **mode = remove** option of the **drop mirror** command.

You should notice here that if you drop the primary device from a mirror pair (/dev/rdsk/c0t0d1s1), that causes the secondary device (/dev/rdsk/c1t0d6s1) to become the primary. If you dropped the primary device with the **mode = remove** option and you now execute

```
disk mirror
name = "c1t0d6s1",
mirror = "/dev/rdsk/c0t0d1s1",
write = serial
```

you will have the same raw partitions in a mirrored pair as before but now which raw partition is primary and which is secondary has been reversed, that is, the primary device will be /dev/rdsk/c1t0d6s1 and the secondary or mirror device will be /dev/rdsk/c0t0d1s1, and the mirrored pair will be known to the server as server device c1t0d6s1.

Following our example, you started out with server device c0t0d1s1 which was assigned to `/dev/rdsk/c0t0d1s1` and mirrored to `/dev/rdsk/c1t0d6s1`, then dropped the primary side of the mirror pair, which leaves server device c0t0d1s1 assigned to `/dev/rdsk/c1t0d6s1` with the size that was used originally in the **disk init** command that created c0t0d1s1. Now, since you executed the **disk unmirror** command with the **mode = retain** option, you can reinstate the mirror relationship at a later time. If you had one side of the mirror device fail and the server dropped that side of the mirror pair and you later find the failure was not serious enough to warrant replacing the disk you would then want to remirror. Using the **disk remirror** command is only slightly easier than performing the original **disk mirror** since the server still has to completely copy from the primary device (which ever the primary device is after, one side of the mirror pair is dropped) to the mirror device, but it is easier in that you don't have to remember what the mirror device is.

Primary and Secondary Devices of Different Sizes

There is an implication in all this that you need to remember. If you have a small device, say 100 Mb (c0t0d1s1), and you mirror this small device to a larger device, say 200 Mb (`/dev/rdsk/c1t0d6s1`), and then for whatever reason you drop the primary side of the mirror pair, you will have a server device of 100 Mb on the secondary device of the mirror pair (see Figure 8–25). Note that mirroring uses the entire secondary device, usually the whole raw partition assigned, but after dropping the primary, the secondary device becomes a server device with the size of the former primary server device. In this case, it would appear that you had executed **disk init** on `/dev/rdsk/c1t0d6s1` with a size of 100 Mb, even though the partition could support 200 Mb. Hence, you have wasted a lot of space. This is the reason you need to have a standard disk partitioning scheme that ensures your disks have partitions that are very similar. All the physical disks on the server machine that you are using to support the SQL Server may not be the same size. To make mirroring as easy as possible you should segregate the SQL Server disks into groups that are the same size and after applying the standard partitioning to all the SQL Server disks, you can use the disks of the same size in the mirror pairs that you need. Further, you should assign whole physical disks to primary server devices and whole physical disks to be

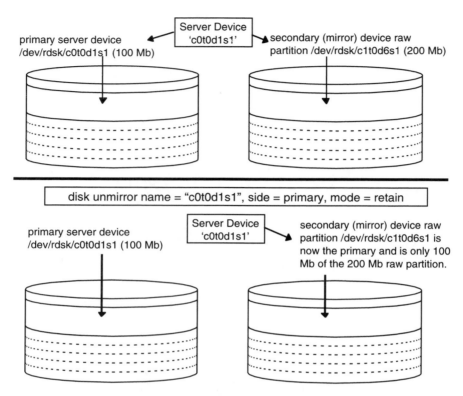

Figure 8–25. Mirroring from Small to Large Partitions

used for the mirrors of these primary server devices. Since the physical disks involved in the mirror pairs are the same size, the standard disk partitioning scheme will result in the partitions of the disks being identical. This means you can mirror, drop either side, and remirror without wasting any disk space at all.

You need to notice that this means you can mirror from a smaller partition to a larger partition, drop the primary (server device on the smaller partition) which causes the secondary to become a server device on the larger partition, and then remirror to the smaller partition. The ability to mirror from a larger partition to a smaller partition is based solely on the actual size of the server device, not on the size of the partition that supports the device.

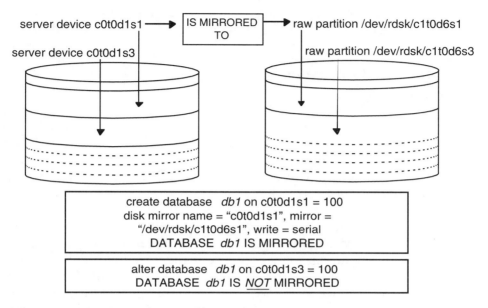

Figure 8–26. Devices are Mirrored — Databases May Not Be

Adding Database Space and Mirrored Devices

Finally, once you have set up the mirrors of your server devices, note that adding space to a database becomes more complex (see Figure 8–26). As long as you are adding space on a server device that is already supporting the database that needs more space, which implies the mirroring is already set up correctly, then adding space proceeds without any concern for the mirror, since again, the mirror copies the entire primary server device. When you need to add space to a database, or more accurately a segment of the database, and all the server devices supporting that database segment are already full, you must alter the database onto a new device, a device that has not been supporting the database or the database segment previously. Clearly, you can alter the database to the new device, but if you don't check the mirroring, you may be extending the database to a device that is no longer mirrored. This is a hidden danger in mirroring. Again, mirroring is done on a server device basis, not on a database or database segment basis. It is easy for one of your fellow DBAs, either through haste or laziness, to alter the database to a new device and not go the extra distance to check that the new device is mirrored also.

Mirroring Devices versus Databases

Recall that you canít mirror a database directly, since a database will, in general, span several server devices and you can mirror only server devices. You should consider another approach that when applied as a standard makes managing the mirrors of your database server devices much easier. Once you have determined which disks of the server machine will support the SQL Server, then decide which whole physical disks will be primary server devices, create the server devices for all the databases on your server, and then create mirrors for all the server devices on the remaining whole physical devices assigned to support the secondary side of the mirror pairs. You will note that you are mirroring every server device in the whole server. This may seem extravagant, but it is much easier to maintain than having some server devices mirrored and others not.

It is the end of your business cycle, be it the end of year or end of month, and the load on your server(s) is heavier than ever. One of your fellow DBAs had to add space to one of the production databases. No problem, what could be simpler? You didn't check, and they didn't check and it turns out that the new device they used for the new database space isn't mirrored. Your users report their applications crashing after getting errors that indicate corruption in the database. No problem—the database is mirrored. Just check the mirrors, see which one failed over to the secondary device, and processing should continue. You start checking and find that the corruption occurred on the one portion of the entire database that wasn't mirrored. You are lost. You must restore the entire database to recover this one portion, because there is no way to recover just a segment or an individual object from the database dumps. You spend hours rebuilding the database all because you didn't have all of it mirrored. You could have prevented this by mirroring all the server devices on the entire server. That way no matter where you (or anyone else) added space, the server device would already be mirrored. With this sort of setup, to cause such a disaster, your fellow DBA would have to drop the mirror of the device before they altered the database, or they would have to perform a **disk init** of a whole new server device on a disk partition not normally part of the SQL Server. This is a lot more work for them and is therefore unlikely. It is very easy for them to simply alter a database to an existing server device that isn't mirrored and cause disaster.

Administration of Mirrored Devices

You must understand that once you have set up the mirroring for your server you are not finished, and not just because you need to add space in the future. You must monitor the mirrors to make sure they are functioning. The server will print error messages to the server errorlog when a failure of either side of a mirror pair occurs. You must monitor the errorlog for these failures. Whenever you restart the server, you must go through the errorlog that shows the server starting up. This is where you would see the master device being opened and the mirror of the master device being accessed as well. You must also check the *status* of any other mirrors that you have set up. The procedure **p_mirror** is useful for this and you should check it regularly, along with dumping the server system tables (see Chapter 14 for details). The output you get from **p_mirror** or from **sp_helpdevice** or from simply selecting from the *sysdevices* table in the *master* database will show you the *status* of each server device. Note that a failed mirror will have a *status* value that is different from the *status* values for the other server devices. This makes it easy for you to spot any problems with mirrors.

It is the Friday before you have a week off for training. You are called at home. One of your fellow DBAs tells you one of the production servers won't restart, and it is your problem. You had asked the server machine SA to repartition one of the file systems so that it filled the entire physical disk to allow storage of more transaction log dumps. You had checked all the server devices that the server was using by running **p_devspace** and had checked all the existing file systems by running df -k at the UNIX command line. What happened? The DBA who set up the server had decided, for reasons that are not clear, to place the master device on a partition on a physical disk that was used for file systems. The master device was the only server device on that disk and when you checked **p_devspace** you failed to check what physical disk the master device was on. You assumed that all the server devices were on physical disks separate from the physical disks used for file systems, but you didn't check. The server machine SA had then extended the file system so that it took over the entire physical disk which erased the master device. You think, well, you screwed up, but that's why we have a mirror of the master device, and you'll just restart the server with the *master* mirror. You start looking at the old errorlogs and notice that for the last month whenever the server was restarted, the master device mirror had failed, but no one was checking this. So, you have no mirror of the master device. You find a dump of the *master* database on disk and have to re-create the partition for the master device, load the dump of *master*, and then recover the server. Note that your initial screwup would have been a minor and forgettable event if the mirror had been functioning. You must mirror *master*, and you must check the mirror every time the server starts, and check it periodically between restarts. Further, you must regularly dump the *master* database and you must dump the server system tables frequently so you have all the information you need in the event you need to rebuild the server.

Better living through mirroring. Mirroring saves personal lives. It's all done with mirrors.

HOW TO LAY OUT THE DEVICES AND SEGMENTS OF A SERVER

The process of sizing the server for the database(s) needed to support your applications is detailed in Chapter 11. The process centers around how many independent segments (i.e., segments that are the only segments assigned to a server device) are required for the largest database of the server. Once this number of segments is determined, you know that you need the same number of server devices (and a few more for master device, etc.) at a minimum. Ideally each of these segments would be on a physical disk attached to a separate controller. This tells you the number of controllers you need (you may need more, of course). From here you need to allocate the number of disks on each controller to support the size of each segment. Knowing how many physical disks can be attached to each controller before impacting I/O performance allows you to populate the controllers with disks. Now you need to allocate disks to support mirrors of server devices and see if you have enough room left over to support the other database(s) and file systems required.

An example of this process is shown in Figure 8–27. In this example you have a database *db1* that requires the standard segments of *system*, *default*,

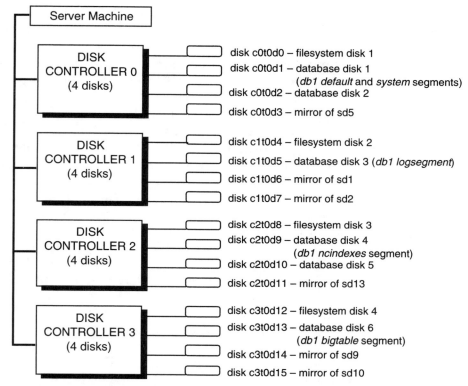

Database *db1* has system/default, logsegment and 2 user-defined segments 'ncindexes' and 'bigtable'.

Note: Total of 16 disks, one-quarter assigned to filesystems, the remaining 12 disks split evenly between supporting database server devices and their mirrors.

Figure 8-27. Example Server Device, Mirror and Segmentation Layout

logsegment, and two user-defined segments *ncindexes* for the nonclustered indexes and *bigtable* to support one huge table that is heavily accessed. For maximum performance the user-defined segments *ncindexes* and *bigtable* must be supported by physical disks that are attached to separate controllers from those controlling the disks for *system/default* segments or the *logsegment*. This means the server machine must have four controllers at a minimum. This requirement for segments on separate controllers dictates the basic configuration of the server machine. At this point you populate the controllers with the maximum number of disks allowed without impacting I/O performance (four for Sun machines). After allocating one-quarter of the total number of physical disks for file system (4 disks) and splitting the remaining 12 disks in half for server devices and their mirrors, you have the basic server layout. Note that this layout assumes you have enough disk space on the physical disks for each controller to support the segments of *db1*. You must realize that if one of the segments of *db1* grows beyond the disk space available on the current controller, you would need to add another controller to support more disk space for that segment. If you simply add space to the segment on another controller then the I/O for that segment would contend with the I/O for the other segment of *db1* that is already supported by the controller.

For example, if segment *ncindexes* needed more disk space, and the disks c2t0d9 and c2t0d10 (the only database disks on controller 2) were already full with *ncindexes* and other databases, you need to add space to *ncindexes* on disks on another controller. However, if you add the needed space on disks on controller 0 or 1 or 3, you will have I/O for objects in the *ncindexes* segment contending with I/O for objects in the existing segment of *db1*. If you added space to *ncindexes* on *sd2* (controller 0), then I/O for ncindexes segment would contend with I/O for *default/system* segments. This means capacity planning is more complex for databases that require multiple user-defined segments to improve performance. You can't simply look at total free disk space. You must be aware that you really need free space on the correct controller to be able to add space to a given segment. This also means you need to justify having many user-defined segments very carefully since you will need to spend more time managing them.

WHY YOU SHOULD BE HESITANT TO ADD DATABASE SPACE

Now that you are aware of the many complexities regarding database placement on server devices, you need to be aware of the reasons you, as DBA, don't want to add space to any database on the server without careful consideration. The actual act of adding database space is so easy it is difficult to appreciate the negative impact that a hasty addition can have. If you need to add database or transaction log space on server devices that are currently supporting the database or transaction log in question, you are probably fine. Recall that you may not want to add space to the transaction log for the reasons discussed earlier, that is, that one open transaction can fill a very large transaction log and the larger the transaction log the longer it takes to dump once it is full. If the transaction log fills completely and must be dumped with the **no_log** option, the database is not available for changes while the transaction log is dumped, and the larger the transaction log the longer the database will be unavailable.

Whenever you add space to any database on your server you must check that all the server devices that should be mirrored are mirrored. Make sure the space you are adding is on a device that is mirrored already, or set up the mirror or be sure you don't need that device mirrored. Again, it is best to simply mirror everything because that way you don't have to wonder if your fellow DBAs will understand which server devices need mirrors and which server devices don't.

Finally, you need to understand that while a server device may have lots of free space there may not be any free space, that you can use. When you need to add space to a database or its transaction log, you need to add space to that segment, not just to the database. If you need to add space to the transaction log you can't add that space on any server device that is already supporting any other segment(s) for that database since the transaction log must be on a server device that doesn't support any other database segments. If you need to add space to a user-defined segment, the same logic applies. Unlike the transaction log, you can have a server device supporting a user-defined segment and some other segment. You probably set up the user-defined segment to isolate certain database objects (large tables and their nonclustered indexes) from the rest of the database for performance reasons. You should not add any other segment of the database to the server devices that support the user-defined segment. If you do mix the segments on such a server device, you may lose all the performance gain you had as users contend for the two types of database objects on the server device. You need to understand that just because a server device has free space, it may not have any free space that you can use. Further you don't want any user objects on the master device and that means any free space on the master device is not really available for use. If you created the master device to be much larger than the *master* database ,it will have lots of free space. Be aware of this when you look at how much free space you have in the whole server. You should not count any free space on the master device in your total of free space on the server. You should be careful to examine the total free space on the server to make sure it is on the right server devices to support the growth of the various segments of the databases that are growing the fastest.

For all these reasons you need to treat the simple act of adding database space very carefully. Adding database space has many long-ranging impacts.

SUMMARY

The process of installing and maintaining a server requires that you as the DBA, have a good understanding of what many DBAs think of as server machine SA functions. You can ignore these SA functions, but you will not be able to control your server's environment very well. As your servers grow in size and complexity the need to be able to understand and manage segments on server devices becomes critical. In order to provide your users with the best uptime possible, you must take the time to understand the issues behind the process of partitioning physical disks, segments, and mirroring. Understanding these issues also provides motivation for establishing and enforcing various standards for your server environment such as disk partitioning, using whole physical disks for server devices (or their mirrors) or file systems (but not both), mirroring the master device and mirroring all of the database segments if possible.

SQL Server Recovery

Table of Topics

- ❀ Archiving
- ❀ More Server Devices is Better
- ❀ Recovery Notes
- ❀ Backup Server
- ❀ Database Dumps
- ❀ Transaction Log Dumps
- ❀ Logical Dumps and Datatools' SQL BackTrack
- ❀ Recovery Matrix

INTRODUCTION

The process of recovery for the SQL Server is another topic that is largely ignored. It isn't exciting to most and it usually comes up only when things have gone bad in a big way. You need to understand more about the recovery process and what the implications are for the way you operate your database system.

Note that you can do yourself a great deal of good simply by making use of the references that are available to you. With the advent of on-line documentation for Sybase products you now have an incredible way to search through thousands of pages of documentation looking for what you need, and more often, finding related information that will help you understand the products better. Specifically SyBooks is available on CD-ROM for the System 11 document set for SQL Server, Open Server, and the Troubleshooting Guide. While these are the System 11 versions of these documents the vast majority of the information is relevant to the 4.9.2 Version of SQL Server. Similarly there is another CD available called AnswerBase which is a compilation of many technical notes and installation guides that cover many of the technical issues you are likely to encounter. You must obtain and use these references. Further, Sybase offers classed covering DBA topics and the class Advanced DBA for System 11 is especially worthwhile.

You should consider another benefit of the SyBooks and AnswerBase CD-ROMs. You will frequently need to work off-hours to support your business and their databases that seem to be popping up all over the world. When this occurs, working at home or any remote location with a

PC and a CD-ROM drive can be a welcome option. With the advent of these CDs, you can have the complete library of Sybase manuals with you anywhere. This is actually better than having a set of manuals since AnswerBase contains a great deal of information that is not officially published anywhere else.

 You must read the *SQL Server Troubleshooting Guide*. It isn't thrilling, but it will remove most of the "thrills" of the real disasters that are waiting for you and your users. Learn how to recover from these disasters now.

SQL SERVER VERSIONS

The issues discussed here are relevant to all versions of SQL Server. However, there are several things you need to be aware of relative to the version of SQL Server you are using. First, only System 11 has configuration files and named caches which add some details to the process of recovery. Next are the system databases. For SQL Server System 10 and System 11, the system databases include the *master* database, and the *sybsystemprocs* and *sybsecurity* databases. The *sybsystemprocs* database is required to store the system stored procedures in Systems 10 and 11. The *sybsecurity* database is needed only if you wish to utilize the auditing functions introduced in System 10 and available in System 11 as well. You need to realize that these new system databases need to be part of your recovery process. Also, System 11 SQL Server on the Sun platform is supported only on the Solaris operating system.

See Chapter 7 for more details regarding the system databases. See Chapter 8 for details of the placing the system databases on server devices and on different numbers of physical disks.

SQL Server 4.9.2

With SQL Server 4.9.2, there are no configuration files or named caches to worry about. For the system databases, there is only the one system database, the *master* database, to be concerned with. You should always mirror the master device. The *master* database should be the only database on the master device. SQL Server 4.9.2 doesn't support multiple database dumps to a tape device.

SQL Server System 10

As with SQL Server 4.9.2, System 10 does not have configuration files or named caches to worry about. The system databases *sybsystemprocs* and *sybsecurity* were introduced with System 10. The master device should always be mirrored. You should also mirror the server device that supports the *sybsystemprocs* database and the *sybsecurity* database, if it has been installed. Only System 11 supports named caches and large I/O buffer pools which can be used to speed up **dbcc** runs. Previous versions of SQL Server don't support these large I/O buffer pools.

System 10 introduced an addition to the options for the **create database** and **alter database** commands. The new option is "with override" which simply allows you to create a database with the log segment on the same server device as other segments but still be able to dump the transaction log separately. This option may be useful in specific situations, but in general, the rule of placing the transaction log on its own server device should still be followed. You can look up the "with override" option and you'll see that use of this option is not recommended. For example, if you need to recover a database that has been created or altered by using this option, you can't dump the current contents of the transaction log. Normally, when you need to recover a database, you would **execute dump transaction <dbname> with no_truncate**. This accesses the log device for the database and copies out the current contents of the transaction log. This can be done even if the other devices of the database are not available. Along with full database dumps and all the normal transaction log dumps, you could recover the database to the exact moment in time where the failure occurred. This option was introduced only to assist you when you have very limited disk space. This may be necessary during certain disaster recovery situations.

SQL Server System 11

System 11 introduces configuration files and named caches, both of which have an impact on the recovery process. You must be prepared to reconstruct all the aspects of the SQL Server configuration as part of the recovery process (see Recovery Notes in this chapter). System 11 includes the features noted above that were introduced with System 10. However, there is a vital change regarding the operating system. For both Systems 10 and 4.9.2, Sybase supported the SQL Server on both the SunOS and Solaris operating systems. With System 11, however, Sybase supports only SQL Server on the Solaris operating system.

While this is specific to the Sun hardware and software platform, it points out the general need, when upgrading, to check that the upgraded server will run on your existing hardware and operating system platform. Upgrading both the OS and the SQL Server is a much bigger project than just upgrading the SQL Server. You must verify that your upgrade plan is adequate. You must not find out, at the last minute, that you have to upgrade the OS as well as the SQL Server. This is also another reason that you should first install or upgrade to a new version of SQL Server on a system that is not being used for production. This way you can run into all these dependencies before it really counts.

As with SQL Server 4.9.2 and System 10, the master device should always be mirrored and you should also mirror the server device that supports the *sybsystemprocs* database, and the *sybsecurity* database, if it has been installed.

RECOVERY PLANNING REVOLVES AROUND THE COST OF DOWNTIME

No matter how much you understand about database dumps, **dbcc** runs, or mirroring, the real point behind recovery is minimizing downtime for your business. Also, you need to decide how much effort you need to put into preparing for recovery of your database system. If your business needs to access the databases 24 hours a day every day, you must well ahead and you can justify the resources it will take to be as ready as possible when the inevitable disaster hits.

Everything that follows revolves around this concept of the cost of downtime. If you can have exclusive access to the server(s) every weekend, then you have time to do maintenance on the server and the server machine such as running **dbcc** checks, and so forth. This allows you to set up a very different recovery plan from a DBA whose system can't ever be down. In that case you may be required to set up and maintain a standby server that is a complete duplicate with the primary system. This represents a great deal of time and money all tied up in a server and server machine that simply sit and wait. But, compare the cost of this duplicate hardware to the cost of downtime. You must determine how long you think it would take to rebuild the primary server and server machine, and what the cost to your business would be from that much downtime. Perhaps the duplicate server isn't so expensive after all.

THE DATABASE IS NOTHING WITH-OUT THE TRANSACTION LOG

It is important that you understand the basic process of recovery that the SQL Server goes through. With an understanding of this process, you can plan your recovery better and understand some of the background behind the procedures that the manuals tell you to perform. This explanation will cover the basic recovery process which links the database and its transaction log. From this you will see why the transaction log is absolutely vital and why you must protect it carefully. Note that the following discussion is about one database and its transaction log, the recovery process, and what the checkpoint process has to do with it all. However, you should remember that this same process applies, and is constantly underway, for each and every database in your system. The entire process of recovering a SQL Server database is very complex and involves many subtleties. Here you need only understand why the transaction log is the most important piece of the database.

From reading the manuals and using the SQL Server, you would think that the database (here we mean everything but the transaction log) and the transaction log are completely separate entities. You would think that if the disk that supports the transaction log fails, well, that's OK because you still have the actual database out on other disks so you have one set of the business data that the database represents (see Figure 9–1). Conversely, you would think that if the disks that support the database fail, well, that's OK too because from the database dump and the set of transaction logs (including the current transaction log that has not been dumped), you can re-create the database and again have a set of business data that the database represents. This view is not unreasonable, and various things contribute to it, such as the fact that a committed transaction is immediately written to disk, which makes it sound as is the database is being kept up to date with all committed transactions. Also, it seems that if you have a problem with the transaction log, the database itself is OK. After all, it seems that the database itself is updated only when a transaction is

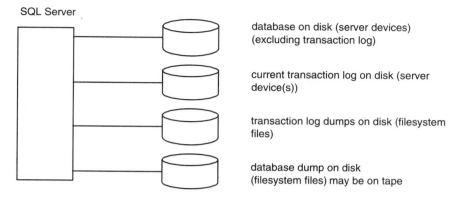

SQL Server

database on disk (server devices)
(excluding transaction log)

current transaction log on disk (server
device(s))

transaction log dumps on disk (filesystem
files)

database dump on disk
(filesystem files) may be on tape

Figure 9–1. The Database on Disk and the Dumps

committed and you would be asking what sense it would make to write a partial transaction to the database. This is one reasonable view, but it is wrong on several subtle, but vital points. We review the process that the server goes through and see how the database and the transaction log are affected as well as reviewing what the checkpoint process really does.

We start with the observation that any access of the database or the transaction log takes place in data cache, that is, server machine memory. Any read or write to a data page of the database actually takes place in memory after the page has been loaded from disk if necessary. As a transaction begins and reads from or writes to data pages of the database, the needed pages are loaded from disk if they are not in cache. Once a page is in cache, it is not automatically written back out to disk even if changes are made to the page. The server writes only pages out of cache if it needs to load a page that is not currently in cache and there is no more room in cache. At that point the server looks for the page in cache that has gone the longest without any changes. The "oldest" page is then written to disk and the required page is loaded into cache in place of the page that was just written out. The algorithm for determining which page in cache should be written out to disk is called LRU or the Least Recently Used algorithm.

This is great, but you must notice what this implies. Suppose the server has room in cache for only 10 data pages at one time (the DBA should add memory!!) and the database consists of 20 data pages as in Figure 9–2. We are ignoring indexes and the transaction log pages at the moment, both of which also must be in cache to be changed. Assume the transaction that we are following is an update of all rows in the database. As the transaction

Figure 9–2. Server Loading Database Data Pages into Data Cache

	SQL SERVER DATA CACHE (RAM)		
DATABASE ON DISK	**DATA PAGES IN CACHE**	**TRANSACTION LOG IN CACHE**	**TRANSACTION LOG ON DISK**
data page 1 ⟶	data page 1 **	updates to data page 1	
data page 2	data page 2 **	updates to data page 2	
data page 3	data page 3 **	updates to data page 3	
data page 4	data page 4 **	updates to data page 4	
data page 5	data page 5 **	updates to data page 5	
data page 6	data page 6 **	updates to data page 6	
data page 7	data page 7 **	updates to data page 7	
data page 8	data page 8 **	updates to data page 8	
data page 9	data page 9 **	updates to data page 9	
data page 10 ⟶	data page 10 **	updates to data page 10	
data page 11			
data page 12			
data page 13			
data page 14			
data page 15			
data page 16			
data page 17			
data page 18			
data page 19			
data page 20			
Data pages loaded into cache until cache is full.	** Data pages modified in cache but not written to disk.	Changes to data pages recorded in transaction log.	Nothing recorded in transaction log on disk until transaction is committed.

moves along it will load a page of the database into cache, update the rows in that page, and then load the next data page. Note that as each row of a page in cache is modified, the data in the row before and after the modification is written to the log which is also in cache (see Figure 9–2). This works fine until the eleventh page of the database is needed, at which time the first page (the oldest page) will be written back to disk to make room for the eleventh page to be loaded in to cache (see Figure 9–3). At the instant that the first page is written back to disk, the database itself (again, the database here excludes the transaction log) is not in a consistent state. The update transaction has not committed, but the changes due to a part of the transaction have been written back to the database on disk (note that when this happens, the portion of the transaction log that contains the changes to this page are also written to disk). If the transaction log were lost, the changes made in the first page would still be part of the database, and without the transaction log, there would be no way to tell which changes in the database on disk are parts of committed transactions or parts of transactions that were underway.

Further, as each update to a database page is made in cache, the update is recorded in the transaction log but only in cache. Until the transaction commits, the portion of the transaction log that describes all the changes made by the transaction is not written to disk. If the transaction log is lost, there will be no record of what the transaction did. You must recall that at the same time, there is no guarantee that any of the database pages that were changed in cache have been written out to disk to make room for other pages. You can wind up with pieces of the transaction out on disk in the database and no way to decode which changes on disk should be there and which should be changed back. And, without the transaction log, which stores the data in a row before and after the change, there is no way to tell how to change a database page on disk back to the way it was before the transaction started. This means that after all 20 data pages of the database have been loaded and updated, but before the transaction commits, all the changes recorded in the transaction log for these updates are only in cache, while some (half in this case) of the modified database data pages are already out on disk (see Figure 9–4).

The fact that the transaction log records for a particular transaction are not flushed to disk until the transaction is committed should clarify for you why the transaction log should be stored on a server device that is supported by a raw partition. When the server commits the transaction, it writes out the relevant portion of the transaction log to disk and the server believes it has been written to disk immediately. If you use a UNIX

Figure 9–3. Oldest Cached Data Page Written to Disk

SQL SERVER DATA CACHE (RAM)			
DATABASE ON DISK	**DATA PAGES IN CACHE**	**TRANSACTION LOG IN CACHE**	**TRANSACTION LOG ON DISK**
data page 1** ◄	── data page 11 **	updates to data page 1	updates to data page 1
data page 2	data page 2 **	updates to data page 2	
data page 3	data page 3 **	updates to data page 3	
data page 4	data page 4 **	updates to data page 4	
data page 5	data page 5 **	updates to data page 5	
data page 6	data page 6 **	updates to data page 6	
data page 7	data page 7 **	updates to data page 7	
data page 8	data page 8 **	updates to data page 8	
data page 9	data page 9 **	updates to data page 9	
data page 10	data page 10 **	updates to data page 10	
data page 11		updates to data page 11	
data page 12			
data page 13			
data page 14			
data page 15			
data page 16			
data page 17			
data page 18			
data page 19			
data page 20			
Cache is full; oldest data page is written to disk.** Data page contains changes, but transaction has not been committed.	Data page 1 in cashe is written to disk and data page 11 loaded into cashe.	Changes to data pages recorded in transaction log.	Nothing recorded in transaction log on disk until transaction is committed—assume cached tran log pages remain in cache.

Figure 9–4. All Database Changes Made to Satisfy Query

SQL SERVER DATA CACHE (RAM)			
DATABASE ON DISK	**DATA PAGES IN CACHE**	**TRANSACTION LOG IN CACHE**	**TRANSACTION LOG ON DISK**
data page 1**	data page 11 **	updates to data page 1	updates to data page 1
data page 2**	data page 12 **	updates to data page 2	updates to data page 2
data page 3**	data page 13 **	updates to data page 3	updates to data page 3
data page 4**	data page 14 **	updates to data page 4	updates to data page 4
data page 5**	data page 15 **	updates to data page 5	updates to data page 5
data page 6**	data page 16 **	updates to data page 6	updates to data page 6
data page 7**	data page 17 **	updates to data page 7	updates to data page 7
data page 8**	data page 18 **	updates to data page 8	updates to data page 8
data page 9**	data page 19 **	updates to data page 9	updates to data page 9
data page 10**	data page 20 **	updates to data page 10	updates to data page 10
data page 11		updates to data page 11	
data page 12		updates to data page 12	
data page 13		updates to data page 13	
data page 14		updates to data page 14	
data page 15		updates to data page 15	
data page 16		updates to data page 16	
data page 17		updates to data page 17	
data page 18		updates to data page 18	
data page 19		updates to data page 19	
data page 20		updates to data page 20	
Cache is full; oldest data page is written to disk.** Data page contains changes, but transaction has not been committed.	Data page 11 through 20 loaded into cached.	Changes to data pages recorded in transaction log.	Nothing recorded in transaction log on disk until transaction is committed.

file, system then the writes to disk are buffered and the server has no idea if the write has actually been made or not. Since the server assumes the write of the transaction log records occurs immediately, you can really mess up the recovery of a database if the server machine were to crash (all data in any buffers would be lost) before the buffered writes made it to disk.

Note that this behavior of writing database pages out to disk before transaction commits can't be avoided unless the server were to require that enough memory always be available to store all the pages of the database, including data and index pages. Hence, the server can't require that all needed pages be in cache. If this were possible, the server could load all the pages affected by the update transaction, make all the updates to the rows of all the pages, and then, as part of committing the transaction, write all the changed pages to disk for both the database and the transaction log. This would result in both the database and the transaction log containing all the changes made by the transaction. Until the transaction committed, the database would not be changed. However, this is not the way it works, for two reasons. First, as mentioned already, this would require that all the pages affected by any transaction be loaded into cache which would prevent many real-world transactions. Second, waiting for the transaction to commit before writing any of the transaction's changes is bad for performance since all the pages would need to be written at once. It is faster for the server to simply leave the changed pages in cache until they become old and are moved out to make room for new pages.

Note that while the transaction is running the pages that are being updated are locked by the server so that no other user can access them. From the point of view of the other users, the changes to the database caused by the transaction are not made available to them until the entire transaction commits.

Now that you understand what the server is doing when a transaction is running you need to understand what the **checkpoint** process and the server command checkpoint do and how they affect the pages in cache and on disk. You now know that there are changes to database pages that remain in cache and may not be written to disk for some time. You can also see that if the server were to fail and need to recover the database it would have to read the transaction log to see which database pages had been changed as part of a transaction. The server would also have to determine from the transaction log whether the transaction committed, rolled back, or simply failed to commit and then either let the database page changes stand or change them back to the way they were before the transaction started respectively. Depending on how many changes have been made through multiple transactions there may be many database pages that would need to be changed to bring the database on disk into line with what was happening at the time of the server failure. Note that bringing the database on disk into line means you make the database on disk reflect the changes due to the committed transactions and you make sure that any changes that made it to disk for transactions that didn't commit are changed back. This is why the transaction log contains both the row data before and after each change to each row of a database page.

Since there may be many such changes to check and possibly reverse it might take the server a long time to perform all these changes. This time period is called the recovery interval. You can reduce the time the server takes to recover a database by reducing the number of changes that the server must check which is done by a process called checkpoint. When checkpoint runs, it flushes all the database pages in cache that have been changed since the last checkpoint out to disk. After the checkpoint process runs, the database on disk is in agreement with all the database pages in cache (see Figure 9–5). Note that the checkpoint process writes a record in the transaction log to record that fact that, at this instant, the database on disk and the data pages in the data cache are in sync. This means that from this point back, the changes recorded in the transaction log have already been written to the database on disk. The server must check only the transaction log from the most recent checkpoint forward when recovering the database. Of course, if the server needs to roll back a transaction that began before the last checkpoint, then the server will need to read the transaction log farther back than the last checkpoint to reverse all the database changes made by that transaction.

There are two ways that checkpoints are done and you need to be clear on both. The server itself will automatically check the transaction log for each database approximately once per minute to see how much has been recorded in the transaction log for committed transactions. The server then figures out how long it would take to recover all these changes. This means how long it would take to repeat all the changes recorded in the transaction log since the last checkpoint in order to recreate all the changes due to committed transactions. If the server computes a recovery time greater than the recovery interval that is specified for the server (**recovery_interval** is part of **sp_configure** output and is configurable), then the server will execute a **checkpoint** to flush all the changed database pages (only those changes made since the last **checkpoint**) from cache to disk. Note that again this flushes all the changed

Figure 9–5. Checkpoint—All Data Pages with Changes Written to Disk

	SQL SERVER DATA CACHE (RAM)		
DATABASE ON DISK	DATA PAGES IN CACHE	TRANSACTION LOG IN CACHE	TRANSACTION LOG ON DISK
data page 1**	data page 11 **	updates to data page 1	updates to data page 1
data page 2**	data page 12 **	updates to data page 2	updates to data page 2
data page 3**	data page 13 **	updates to data page 3	updates to data page 3
data page 4**	data page 14 **	updates to data page 4	updates to data page 4
data page 5**	data page 15 **	updates to data page 5	updates to data page 5
data page 6**	data page 6 **	updates to data page 6	updates to data page 6
data page 7**	data page 7 **	updates to data page 7	updates to data page 7
data page 8**	data page 8 **	updates to data page 8	updates to data page 8
data page 9**	data page 9 **	updates to data page 9	updates to data page 9
data page 10**	data page 10 **	updates to data page 10	updates to data page 10
data page 11**		updates to data page 11	updates to data page 11
data page 12**		updates to data page 12	updates to data page 12
data page 13**		updates to data page 13	updates to data page 13
data page 14**		updates to data page 14	updates to data page 14
data page 15**		updates to data page 15	updates to data page 15
data page 16			
data page 17			
data page 18			
data page 19			
data page 20			
Cache is full; oldest data page is written to disk. ** Data page contains changes, but transaction has not been committed.	Data pages 11 through 15 loaded into cache.	Changes to data pages recorded in transaction log.	Checkpoint flushes all changed ("dirty") data pages to disk whether committed or not.

database pages, not just the changed pages due to committed transactions. The other way the **checkpoint** process is executed is manually by you. It is a good idea for you to issue a checkpoint just before you shut down the server with the nowait option to reduce the recovery time as much as possible. Note that the **shutdown** command without the **nowait** option does a **checkpoint** in every database automatically. Also, the **dump database** command performs a **checkpoint** in the database so that the dump represents all the changes that had been made to the database at the instant the dump was made. Again, note that the dump of a database also contains database page changes that may or may not be due to committed transactions, and when the database is loaded, the only way the server can figure out which changes should stay and which should be reversed is to read the transaction log. This is why the **dump database** command also dumps the transaction log along with the database.

Now that you have been convinced that the database really isn't an accurate representation of the state of your business data without the transaction log, you need to consider what happens when the transaction log is not available. If something goes wrong with the server device that supports the transaction log, the server can't recover the database the next time the server is started. As the server tries to recover the database it will be unable to read all of the transaction log and will mark the database as "suspect" and you won't be able to execute **use <dbname>** or otherwise access the database. The term suspect is very appropriate. As you may now appreciate, the database may be completely accessible with no corruption that any **dbcc** check could find, but without the transaction log the server can't tell you which pieces of the database reflect a change to your business data or just a possible change that was part of an incomplete transaction. Hence, the database is indeed suspect. Now, you can manually update the system table *sysdatabases* and tell the server that the database is no longer suspect. The server may have no problem running after you do this, but you must realize what you are doing. If you tell the server that a database that was marked suspect is no longer suspect, you are telling the server that any database page changes that are out on disk are now valid business data. You must confer with your users before taking such a drastic step. You should consult Sybase Technical Support as well. Just because you can convince the server that the database is suddenly OK doesn't mean it is. Again, this is further evidence of the need to keep the transaction log on a separate server device, on a separate physical disk, attached to a different controller, than the server devices that support the rest of the database. It is also further evidence of why the transaction log of the database should be mirrored. While you should mirror all the server devices, if you can't, you should mirror the transaction logs as a second priority after mirroring the master device.

Since the transaction log is so vital, you must be aware of another recovery situation involving the transaction log. Note that all recovery situations involve the transaction log. If one or more of the server devices supporting the database fails and you aren't mirroring that server device, you will need to drop and re-create the database and reload from database and transaction log dumps. However, to re-create (recover) the database including all the transactions that were in the transaction log at the time of the failure, you need to dump the current contents of the transaction log. If you can't do this through the normal means of **dump transaction** due to the database not being accessible you need to try dumping the transaction log with the **dump transaction <dbname> with no_truncate**. This will use data stored in the *master* database to directly access the current transaction log out on disk and dump it to a file that can later be applied to the database after the full sequence of normal transaction log dumps have been applied. Note that you must have the server running and the *master* database must still be usable for this approach to work (see Figure 9–6).

Figure 9–6. Dumping Current Contents of Transaction Log

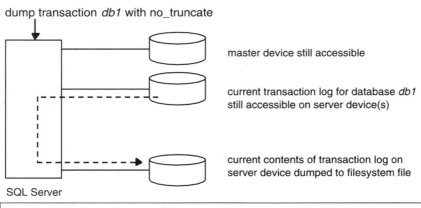

dump transaction *db1* with no_truncate

master device still accessible

current transaction log for database *db1* still accessible on server device(s)

current contents of transaction log on server device dumped to filesystem file

SQL Server

SQL Server has some problem and you need to drop and recreate database *db1*. In order to recover *db1* to the state it was in at the time of the problem you need the current contents of the transaction log. Server must still be running, master device and server device(s) that support *db1* transaction log not damaged.

Once the current contents of the transaction log have been dumped you can drop the database and begin re-creating it. You must note that since the server has had a failure you may not be able to restart the server. You must make your attempt at dumping the current contents of the transaction log before you shut down the server, assuming the failure didn't bring the server down.

You can prevent this situation my mirroring the transaction log server devices. That way you won't need to dump the current contents of the transaction log because the server will simply fail over to the secondary server device (the mirror) for the transaction log and the server should move along normally from there. However, consider the situation where even though the transaction log is mirrored, one of the server devices for the database itself fails. You must still drop and re-create the database and load it. Dropping the database will get rid of both server devices (the primary and its mirror) of the mirrored transaction log. So, you must remember that even though the transaction log is mirrored, when server devices other than those supporting the transaction log fail, you must still dump the current contents of the transaction log before you start trying to repair the server.

Given that you need to dump the current contents of the transaction log when you have a server device failure for the database and that you need to have the *master* database to perform such a transaction log dump, this is why you mirror the master device (recall you mirror server devices not databases) and why you should mirror the transaction logs next. You should, if possible, mirror all of your server devices (see Chapter 8).

Finally, we started with the premise that it would be reasonable to think that the database (excluding the transaction log) formed one set of consistent data that represents your business. And that the current transaction log along with all the transaction logs since the last database dump along with the last database dump form a second set of consistent data that represents your business. You can now see that as it turns out, only the second half of this theory is correct. You will be better able to deal with the various recovery situations you will encounter when you understand what is going on. You should now understand that the database is nothing without the current transaction log. Without the current transaction log, the only way to bring the database back to a consistent state is to go back to the last database dump, load it, and apply all the transaction log dumps that you have. You now realize that this won't bring the database back to the state it was in when the failure occurred. Further, you should realize that when you don't have the current contents of the transaction log that

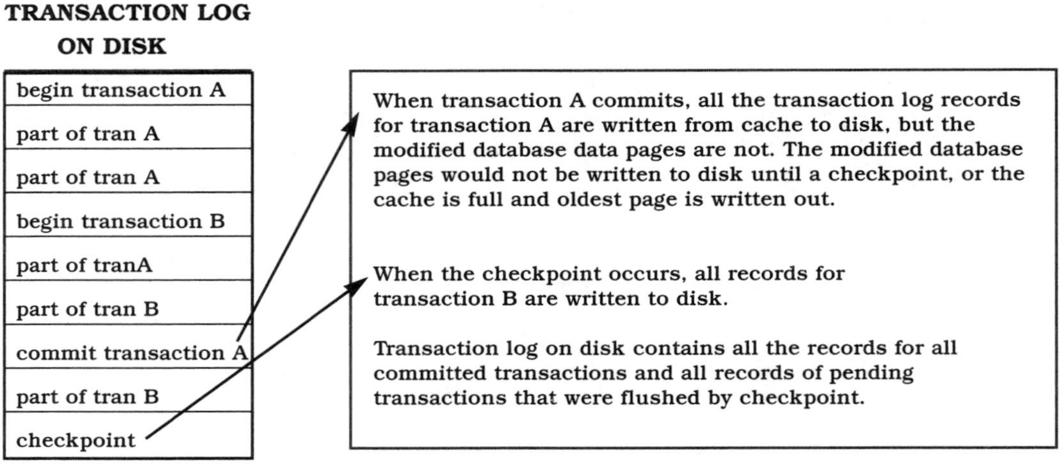

TRANSACTION LOG
ON DISK

begin transaction A	When transaction A commits, all the transaction log records for transaction A are written from cache to disk, but the modified database data pages are not. The modified database pages would not be written to disk until a checkpoint, or the cache is full and oldest page is written out.
part of tran A	
part of tran A	
begin transaction B	
part of tranA	When the checkpoint occurs, all records for transaction B are written to disk.
part of tran B	
commit transaction A	Transaction log on disk contains all the records for all committed transactions and all records of pending transactions that were flushed by checkpoint.
part of tran B	
checkpoint	

Figure 9–7. Transaction Log Records on Disk

is out on disk, you have lost not only the transactions that were in progress at the time of the failure, but also the committed transactions for which the database changes had not yet been flushed out to disk (see Figure 9–7).

All of this explains why you must protect the master device and the transaction log of each database. Even though you have database and transaction log dumps, you can only rebuild from these up to the point of the last transaction log dump. Depending on the nature of your business and the applications you are supporting, the loss of the transactions that are in the current transaction log may represent a very large cost to your business.

RECOVERY IS TRANSACTION BASED

As a DBA, you think of recovery in terms of the server and what error messages you see during the recovery process. You must realize that the server recovers in terms of transactions, not in terms of business data. If the applications that run on the server do not package their transactions in line with the business, then even though you recover all the committed transactions you may not have saved the business. You can't check all the applications to see what they are doing in any given transactions, but you must keep this in mind when users ask you if the server has recovered. It may have, but that doesn't mean the database is guaranteed to be in a state that represents a valid business condition. If an accounting application updated the deposits and account balances in separate transactions even though you recover the server completely, you can't tell which accounts had deposits or balance updates pending against them. The server simply rolls back all pending transactions that didn't commit. The server does not tell you if the associated balance update for each deposit was completed.

This is clearly an application design and logical database design problem but you must know about it to lobby for care during application design and modification. This sort of problem is why you want to prevent downtime all together because these sorts of transaction problems would never happen if the server never went down. The application going down might still cause them. Further they are an argument for tight security on the primary OLTP server. Any user that can get into the server can potentially, without malice, update the database in a way that is not consistent with the business, and again, the server will recover without complaint.

STANDBY SERVER STRATEGIES

While you normally think of recovery in terms of database and transaction log dumps, it really means everything involved in reestablishing a working and consistent set of data that users can access to support your business. One way to minimize the downtime caused by a server failure is to set up a standby server. A standby server can be used to support the business while the primary is repaired. There are many issues involved with setting up such a server and we discuss them below. We assume that a standby server will be running on its own dedicated server machine and that the primary server in question is the OLTP server.

First, you need to go back to determining the cost to your business of server downtime. Until you have that set of information, you can't really address the issues surrounding the creation of a standby server. You also need to determine whether the standby server needs to be a long-term or a short-term replacement for the primary server. In order to provide a standby server that is a long-term replacement for the primary server, the standby server should be as close to a complete duplicate of both the server and the server machine as possible. This includes the server machine hardware type, operating system version, number of processors, number of physical disks and controllers, amount of memory and network connections, mirroring of server devices, dump devices for backups, **cron** jobs, logins, and so forth. You also need to determine which of the primary databases will be supported by the standby server. For a long-term replacement the standby must duplicate all the databases on the primary server.

For a short-term standby server you can build up a smaller or less powerful server and server machine which would support only those databases that would be needed to get the business through a short period of time while the primary server is repaired. If you do not provide a standby server that is a duplicate of the primary, you need to be aware that server performance will probably be inferior and your ability to provide complete recoverability may be limited as well if you don't have enough disk space to dump databases quickly to disk for example. Note that a standby server is expensive in terms of purchase and also in terms of personnel. You must have sufficient staff to install and maintain the standby system. Note that in order for a standby server to do you any good it must be ready when needed. This means some of your personnel will need to work on the standby server regularly, even though it doesn't provide any service most of the time.

You need to decide if it is worth it to your business to have a standby server that is a complete duplicate. Note that no matter what standby server scheme you go with, there will be some amount of downtime while you fail over from the primary to the standby server. You need to weigh the cost of this downtime against the cost of the various possible standby server configurations. You may find that for the cost of a long-term standby server you could keep enough spare parts on hand to virtually rebuild the primary server machine. In that case you need to determine how long a complete rebuild of the primary server would take and compare that with the time it would take to fail over.

Once you are ready to build a standby server you need to determine how you will keep it in sync with the primary server. The point of having a standby server is to reduce overall server downtime by coming back up on the standby faster than you could if you waited for the primary to be repaired. To realize this benefit you must maintain the standby server in a state that is as close to that of the primary as possible.

You can take the regular database dumps from the primary and load them into the same databases on the standby. This is typically what is done to refresh a decision support server. This means the standby is behind the primary by the database dump interval in the worst case. If you dump the databases on the primary once each day then the standby will be about one day behind the primary before the standby loads the next set of primary database dumps. When the time comes to fail over to the standby you would need to apply, in the worst case, a whole day's worth (a whole database dump interval) of transaction logs to the standby server databases after copying all these transaction log dumps between the server machines. This will take time and may be too long a time. Note also that this assumes the primary server machine is still available to supply the transaction log dumps. This may not be the case and that means you should be copying the transaction logs from the primary server machine to the standby server machine as soon as they are dumped on the primary.

If the time to apply all the transaction logs is unacceptable then you need to use an approach that keeps the standby more in sync all the time. This means that as you copy the transaction log dumps from the primary server machine, you apply them to the databases on the standby server (i.e. **load transaction <dbname>**). This way you are maintaining the standby databases so they are only behind the primary by the transaction log dump interval (see Figure 9–8). This assumes that you apply the transaction logs to the standby server databases as soon as they are copied between the machines. Depending on how much you need to minimize the time needed to fail over, you may decide to load the transaction logs to the standby server databases less frequently, perhaps every few hours. Again, you need to determine what the cost and benefit is of each stage of

Figure 9–8. Keeping Standby Server in Sync Using Transaction Logs

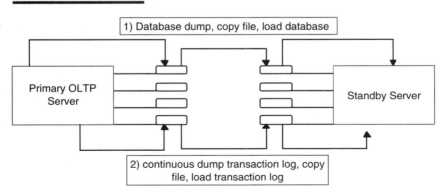

1) Database dump, copy file, load database

Primary OLTP Server

Standby Server

2) continuous dump transaction log, copy file, load transaction log

the failover process to decide the optimal approach for your business. Note that this process can be labor intensive. If there is any problem loading a transaction log to one of the standby server databases that can't be cured by recopying the transaction log dump from the primary, you have no choice but to wait for the next primary database dump and load that into the standby database, apply whatever transaction log dumps have occurred since the database dump on the primary, and then resume applying the transaction log dumps from the primary as they occur. Once you have had a failure of the process of loading a transaction log, it is unlikely that you can cure it by simply retrying the transaction log load. Hence you must wait for the next primary database dump to begin the process of bringing the standby database into sync closer to the primary than the point the standby database was in when the loading of the transaction log failed. No matter how often you load the transaction logs into the standby server databases, you must copy them from the primary server machine to the standby server machine as soon as each transaction log dump on the primary server machine completes. When the primary server machine fails is too late to remember that you need the transaction log dumps to bring up the standby server.

When you do need to fail over with this approach, you still need to dump the current transaction log of the primary database and apply it to the standby database so that the standby is completely up to date with all the committed transactions that the primary database had. You may think the standby server is at a disadvantage since it is, at worst, one transaction log dump interval behind the primary. But consider this. If there were no standby server at all, and the primary suffered a failure, you would still need to dump the current transaction log on the primary to apply to the database after dropping, re-creating, and reloading. Hence, the standby server is no further behind than the primary would be, since the primary could not be recovered beyond the last transaction log dump without dumping the current contents of the transaction log. And, the standby has an advantage in that it doesn't need to drop, create, and reload the database. The standby database only needs to copy and apply the dump of the current contents of the transaction log that was made on the primary server and then it is ready for use. Note that if the dump of the current contents of the transaction log on the primary database fails, the standby can't get completely up to date, but then, the primary database can't either after dropping, re-creating, and reloading since it won't have that dump either.

There are some details that are required for this process to work. The standby server must not be accessible to the users for two reasons. First, any changes in the standby databases will prevent the loading of transaction logs and even the presence of any users will prevent the loading of transaction logs even if no changes have been made in the database.

Second, the database option "no chkpt on recovery" must be activated for each of the databases you will be updating with transaction logs. The reason for this is that anytime the SQL Server is restarted, it recovers the databases within the server. When the server recovers a database, it normally executes a checkpoint to synchronize any dirty pages (pages in memory that contain changes that haven't yet been written out to disk) with the associated data pages on disk. However, even executing a checkpoint will change the database and that will prevent the next transaction log load from proceeding. If you don't activate this database option, you won't have any problems with the transaction log loads until the server is restarted.

In order to make all this happen, you need to be copying the transaction logs from the primary server machine to the standby server machine continuously. Further, if the process fails on the standby server, you will probably need to get the next primary database dump as well. All of this is faster and much easier for you to maintain if it can be done with dumps on disk. This means the primary and the standby both need to have enough disk space to support database and transaction log dumps. Note that you may need to support transaction log dumps that span several database dump intervals in case one of the database dumps is bad. This and the need to keep the current primary database dump on disk for all the databases on the primary can add up to a lot of disk space (see Chapter 11). Also, while you want to dump the database and transaction log to disk on the primary primarily because it is faster, you want the same disk space capacity for the standby to support copying the dumps from the primary to the standby. After failing over to the standby you will need the disk space for the same reasons as the primary does now, that is, to speed up the dumps. Note that for System 10 this is even better since you can speed up the dumps by dumping to multiple disk files (striping).

In order to fail over to the standby server and be ready to support the users as quickly and as smoothly as possible, you must maintain the standby so that it is a duplicate of the primary in all respects. Since the databases on the standby are first loaded with a database dump from the primary and then updated with transaction log dumps from the primary, the standby databases will have all the same changes made to the primary databases. But, this doesn't cover any changes made to the primary *master* database. For System 10 Servers this is also a problem for the *sybsystemprocs* and *sybsecurity* databases. This means that the standby server will not have any server logins that were added to the primary. You must sync the server logins manually when you first create the standby server by using the bcp utility to dump the data from the *syslogins* table of the *master* database on the primary server. Note that you must use the -c option of bcp to get a readable output file. This is needed because you must manually edit out the first row of the bcp output file which represents the "sa" login. You must edit this line of data out of the bcp output because the standby server has an entry for the "sa" login already and the standby server will not allow you to bcp in a file that tries to insert a duplicate entry in syslogins. Note that if your system uses the two-phase commit process, you also need to have the server user "probe" in syslogins. As with the "sa" login you need to edit the data for the "probe" user out of the bcp output file if the "probe" user is already in the *syslogins* table on the standby server.

You need to understand that when the time comes to fail over, you will need to again sync the *syslogins* table between the standby and primary servers. You will need to delete all the rows of the standby server's *syslogins* table, except for the "sa" login (and the "probe" login if needed) to make room for loading the bcp file from the primary server. You must not truncate the *syslogins* table on the primary. If you did, that there would be no logins at all and you couldn't access the server again to load the bcp file or do much of anything else.

There are many details of the failover process that you need to work out in advance. If you don't have a detailed plan of how to fail over, you will waste time figuring it out during the crisis. The whole point of having a standby server is to reduce server downtime and any delays caused by a lack of planning simply reduce the value of having a standby server. You will need to plan how to get all the users accessing the standby server once it is ready to go. This will require that a new interfaces file be distributed or the users will need to change their local DSQUERY environment variable to point to the standby server instead of the primary server. If you plan on doing the latter, that is, having the users change their local DSQUERY, you must be sure that the interfaces file they currently have already has an entry for the standby server.

Once again you can see the benefit of smaller databases. Here smaller databases means less disk space is required to store database dumps which allows for more transaction logs to be kept for a longer time. Smaller databases also mean the dumps and loads will happen faster. Further, smaller databases will allow **dbcc** runs to be done more quickly and, hence, more often which improves the chances that all the database dumps and all the transaction log dumps are clean, which improves the chances that this whole process will run smoothly providing your users with an up-to-date standby server and minimizing the time it would take you to fail over to the standby. All of this leads you back to archiving to keep the databases as small as possible.

You need to also plan ahead for some very basic standby server maintenance tasks. Up to this point we have been keeping the primary and standby server in sync as far as the data in the databases is concerned. You also need to consider how you will keep the databases in sync when you add space to a database on the primary. You must add the same amount of space on the standby database as well or the next load may not work. While the transaction log loads to the standby database may keep working, they will fail as soon as they need to access space that is beyond the boundaries of the standby database. Also, the next time you need to load a database dump into the standby database, that will certainly fail. While you can get away with adding more space to the standby database than was added to the primary database, you must not do this for three reasons.

First, the next time you need to add database space on the standby server you may need to add space to a different segment (see Chapter 8) to match the database segment that was extended on the primary. However, since you added more space on the standby than the primary last time, now the segmentation of the standby is different from the primary. While a transaction log or database load may still succeed with different segmentation, you will have big problems later if database objects from one segment on the primary database get loaded into a different segment on the standby. Second, when the time comes to fail over to the standby, you want the standby to be the same as the primary. The segmentation of the primary was set up for a reason (a good reason) and you must duplicate this segmentation on the standby databases, or the performance of the standby server may not match the primary. Third, it is much easier for you to add space to the standby database if you can simply use the exact same command that you used on the primary database. You should, as part of creating the standby server, set up the exact same controllers, physical disk, and partitions as on the primary. Then, as part of creating the databases on the standby server, you should simply use the exact same scripts

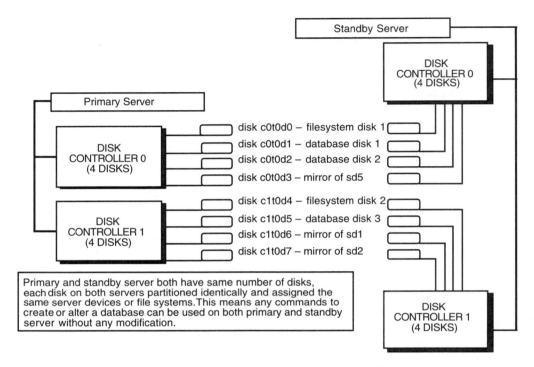

Figure 9-9. Primary and Standby Server Disk Layout

that were used to create the databases on the primary server. If you don't have such scripts use the **p_dbcreate** script described in Chapter 14, to generate the script from the existing primary databases. As long as you follow this procedure, then each time you add space on the primary database, you can simply execute the very same command on the standby database and both the databases will continue to have the same segmentation (see Figure 9-9).

Finally, if you determine you donít need a dedicated standby server, you can set up a server that is normally a decision support server or a server dedicated to running **dbcc** checks. Then, when needed, you could load the databases of such a server with the latest primary database dumps if needed and apply whatever transaction log dumps are necessary to bring the standby databases into sync with the primary databases. As with a dedicated standby server, you should maintain the same segmentation and disk layout as on the primary so that this server can function as the primary if needed.

Replication Server can be used to replicate transactions from the primary to the standby. However, applying transaction logs replicates all the transactions at once and may be a simpler solution for maintaining a standby server.

MASTER Database Not for Users

You must not allow any user-created database objects in the *master* database. You must not put anything into the *master* database either. Recovering the *master* database is faster and simpler when there is less in the *master* database. Further, if you need to restore the *master* database or even just clear the server configuration due to a poor choice of **sp_config figure** options, you will end up running `buildmaster` with some options and that will wipe out any user created objects in the *master* database. If you have created any objects in *master* they will be lost and you will have to maintain a script to re-create them. You could load a dump of *master,* but that is a fair amount of work and depending on why you ran `buildmaster` you may not want to load a dump of *master* as it contains system table information about devices, and so forth, that you may not want to load.

If you need stored procedures or other database objects for DBA use, you should create a dedicated database for this purpose and create all the objects in that database (*dbadb*). That way you can make a database dump of the *dbadb* and restore all your database objects quickly and completely. This also provides a quick and safe way to transfer the contents of *dbadb* to another server through a simply database dump and load. If you had created these same database objects in *master* you would have to manually extract their definition and re-create each one in the *master* database of the new server.

For System 10 and System 11, you could put your own procedures and database objects into the *sysbsystemprocs* database, but as with the *master* database, when rebuilding after a failure the *sybsystemprocs* database will be rebuilt and all of your own database objects will be wiped out. It is simpler to keep all such objects in a database of your own creation and make database dumps of that.

The Use of DBCC

You are certainly aware of the need to run **dbcc** checks on all the databases in the server on a regular basis. However, there is more to it than that. We will review many points that you should be aware of, even if you are religious about running **dbcc** checks. Note that the syntax of the various **dbcc** commands and the details of what they do documented very well in the *Sybase SQL Server System Administration Guide* and the *SQL Server Troubleshooting Guide* and therefore we do not cover this material here.

Running **dbcc** checks represents a form of server downtime since you have to put a database into single-user mode to get accurate results. If you don't put the database into single-user mode, you may get spurious **dbcc** errors that are caused by the other users in the server running transactions that are making changes in the database while the **dbcc** is in progress. Further, the *master* database should be included in your **dbcc** runs, but since you can't set any database options for the *master* database (see Chapter 7) you can't put the *master* database into single-user mode. The only way to get accurate results for **dbcc** runs on the *master* database is to put the whole server into single-user mode which is done using the −m option in the dataserver command, and this requires restarting the server. All this takes time away from the users and therefore is server downtime.

Since the time taken to run **dbcc** checks on the databases on your production OLTP server represents server downtime it competes with your users and the needs of your business. As the business demands the server be available more and more hours of each day, week, and month, and as the sizes of the databases grow, as they inevitably do, you quickly find yourself not having the time, or not being permitted to take the time away from the users, to run the complete set of **dbcc** runs as you should. Soon you are aren't running all the recommended **dbcc** checks on all the databases, and then you start running **dbcc** only against certain tables. Eventually you aren't even running all the **dbcc** checks against all the databases and this is a bad way to go.

You can use a large buffer pool to speed up your **dbcc** runs. Just before the **dbcc** runs start, reconfigure the SQL Server so that the default cache is almost entirely made up of 16K buffers. To do this, you will need to use **sp_poolconfig** to assign almost all the default data cache to a 16K buffer pool. Recall that any named cache, including the default data cache, must have at least 512K of 2K buffer pool at all times. By creating the 16K buffer pool, the server can perform **dbcc** checks much faster. You must reset the configuration of the default data cache when the **dbcc** runs are done. Having all of the default data cache assigned to a 16K buffer pool would not be optimal for general server processing. This is a good example of a situation where configuration files are ideal. You would have one configuration file for general server processing and one for **dbcc** runs. Just before the **dbcc** runs start, you restart the SQL Server and specify the configuration file that creates the 16K buffer pool in the default data cache. Then, when the **dbcc** runs are complete, you restart the server specifying the configuration file for general server processing.

At some point you can't afford to take the risk of not finding database corruptions and it is time to consider your options. You must return to running **dbcc** checks on all the databases on a regular basis. You should go back and consider the cost to your business of server downtime, and the cost to your career when you have to explain why you weren't running all the recommended **dbcc** checks. You have two options.

The first, and this just keeps coming up, is to reduce the size of the databases by archiving as much of the data out of the on-line production server databases and into archive databases. This is covered in detail as part of Chapter 10. Second is to simply move the entire **dbcc** process off the on-line servers and onto a dedicated DBCC server on a dedicated server machine. This way you are free to run any and all **dbcc** or other processes without interfering with the production server. You then need to re-create the production databases on the DBCC server and load a recent database dump into each (see Figure 9–10). Then you can start running the whole set of **dbcc** runs. When the **dbcc** runs are done you should check for errors as you normally would. Unlike a normal **dbcc** situation though, you need to plan how to fix any corruptions that **dbcc** finds because you still have to fix these errors on the production database on the production server machine. At least you have narrowed the location of any corruption

Figure 9–10. Loading DBCC Server from Primary Server

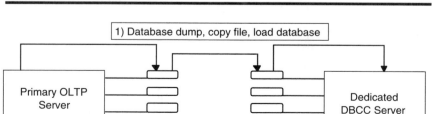

to a specific table and that means you can minimize the server downtime needed to fix the problem.

Still, you must not forget that you must run **dbcc** checks for all the databases in the primary server and this includes the *master* and *model* databases (and *sybsystemprocs* and *sybsecurity* for System 10). You can't load a dump of the primary *master* database into the DBCC server since the controllers, physical disks, and partitions aren't going to be the same since a DBCC server can't really justify being a complete duplicate of the production server. Hence you can't run **dbcc** checks for *master* and *model* databases anywhere other than the primary SQL Server. You can run without the single-user mode and see if you get any **dbcc** errors for *master* and *model*. If you don't, than that's it. If you do, then you need to restart the primary server in single-user mode and rerun the **dbcc** checks. Note that while all this is server downtime, the time needed to run **dbcc** checks against the *master* and *model* databases is very short. Still, you must not neglect the **dbcc** runs against the *master* and *model* databases. Any problems with the *master* database must be detected as soon as possible.

Using a dedicated DBCC server is fine, but that means a corruption may go undetected for a longer period of time. Suppose **dbcc** of *db1* (8 Gb) takes 30 hours to run after requiring 7 hours to load on the DBCC server. You may not find an error for 37 hours during which you have made another database dump. The latest dump now contains the corruption as do all previous dumps made since the last clean **dbcc** run. This means you may have multiple database dumps and many transaction log dumps that contain the corruption. You could go all the way back to the latest database dump made before the last clean **dbcc** run and you can load transaction log dumps all the way up to the present time. Note that a database dump doesn't affect the sequence of transaction log dumps. You can load a sequence of transaction log dumps that move right through the time of a database dump. Of course, depending on the **dbcc** errors found, you may not be able to bring the database back since there may be corruption in the transaction log dumps as well. If any failures occur during the process of loading transaction logs, that's it, and you can't recover the database any further than the point of the transaction load failure. If you have another server with the data (a standby or DBCC server), you can check the database there and if it doesn't have the corruption you can dump from that server and use that dump if needed for recovery. If you have a copy of the database object where the corruption has occurred on another server and it doesn't contain the corruption, you can drop the corrupted database object and re-create it from the other server, which can be much faster than dealing with the whole database.

The DBCC server should have same segmentation as the primary server. Since you are going to load database dumps and run **dbcc** checks, any differences in the way the DBCC server database is set up regarding the size or ordering of the chunks of disk space and the segments assigned to each chunk will result in **dbcc** errors. This really boils down to reproducing the right parts of *sysusages* between the primary and DBCC servers (see Chapter 12, for details of what *sysusages* means). Further, as with the decision support server and the standby server, you will need to add space to the database on the DBCC server whenever you add space to the database on the primary server. While the DBCC server probably will not have the exact same disks and controllers as the primary server, you do need to have the same segmentation as the primary. This means you will need to have the same number of server devices and they need to be the same size or larger than those of the primary. This means the DBCC server will need the same number of partitions of the same or larger size as the primary. You should ensure that the DBCC server have the same server devices grouped together on the same physical disks as the primary. This is because you will add space to the primary databases on the available server devices until they fill up, at which time you will need to add space

Figure 9–11. Primary and DBCC Server Disk Layout

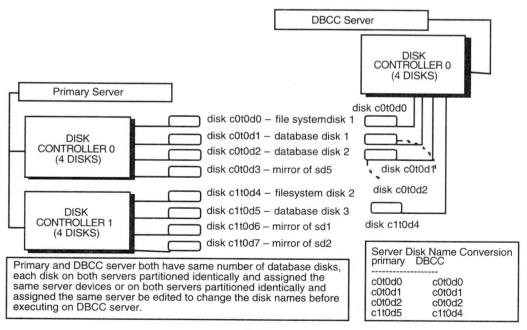

on a new server device (new to the database anyway). It will be much easier for you to add the same space on the DBCC server if the same number of disks are partitioned the same way as the primary server (see Figure 9–11). Then, when you run out of space on a server device on the primary server, you will also run out of space on the DBCC server as well. This makes it easier to remember to add the space on the DBCC server in the correct way (extending segments to new server devices, etc.) since you will do the same things as you did on the primary server.

Once you have the same number of same size server devices on the DBCC server as on the primary server you can run the **p_dbcreate** script described in Chapter 14, on the primary. The script will out put the commands needed to completely re-create the databases on the primary server which means the output commands reflect the names of the server devices on the primary server. You need to edit this output to reflect the names of the appropriate names of the server devices on the DBCC server. Since you have set up the same size and quantity of server devices as are on the primary server, you only need to edit the server device names, not the amount of database space created on each, and you will have a set of commands that will recreate the databases on the DBCC server.

Recall that as you add databases to the primary server, you must also add them to the DBCC server and update any procedures or scripts that move the primary database dumps to the DBCC server machine, load the databases on the DBCC server, and run the **dbcc** checks to include the new databases as well.

Similar to the reporting and standby servers is the need for enough disk space to hold the database dumps from the primary databases. This allows you to automate the process of loading the databases on the DBCC server and running the **dbcc** checks since you don't have to rely on a tape operator to move dump tapes between server machines. As soon as the dumps complete, you can copy the latest set of database dumps from the primary server machine and load into the DBCC server databases and begin the **dbcc** checks again.

By not archiving and running with larger and larger databases, you are exposing yourself to more and more risk simply because of the time delay you encounter when trying to detect corruptions in a large database.

Here is a good example of the insidious kind of corruption that would only be caught by **dbcc** checks. Everything seems fine on the primary server. You load a recent dump onto the DBCC server and begin the **dbcc** checks. Suddenly you are looking at 605 errors in the **dbcc** output. Note that a 605 error means data on disk doesn't match data in cache (see the *SQL Server Troubleshooting Guide* for more details). You panic because it has been a very long time since you last ran a complete set of **dbcc** checks because it takes 30 hours to run all the checks on the largest database and nobody is really concerned. Now you wonder how long this corruption has existed and how many of your database dumps are corrupt as well. If you had to rebuild from a database dump, how far back would you have to go and how far forward could you go with transaction log dumps before encountering the same corruption? You jump to conclusions and shut down the primary server to user access while you run **dbcc** checks on the database object that had the 605 errors on the DBCC server. The **dbcc** checks on the primary server report only minor corruptions and not a single 605 error. The users are relieved, but angry that they lost lots of server time for a nonexistent problem. What happened?

It turns out the corruption was a data page in the primary server that was full of data but was not linked properly to the other data pages for the database object in question. An interesting detail about the way the **dump database** command works is that is dumps only the pages of the database that are linked properly, so the database dumps had been running without any errors but were not dumping this one page. So, until the dump was loaded into the DBCC server, there did not appear to be any problem. The **dbcc** runs on the DBCC server, however, went looking for the page that was (still) on the primary server database but was not on the DBCC server database that was loaded from the dump and that caused the 605 error. This also explains why the same **dbcc** runs report only minor errors when run against the primary server database.

The point is that you need to run the **dbcc** checks regularly so that you can tell yourself and your users how long you might need to go back to get a clean dump. This also points out the need to periodically verify the database and transaction log dumps that may appear to be dumping without problems but may be useless when the time comes to really rebuild the database. The proper way to have handled this situation would have been to detect the 605 error much sooner after the corruption in the primary database happened. Then you would have known when the last clean dump had been made so you could describe the worst case damage to your users. Then you would have scheduled the downtime necessary to check the primary database, which would reveal the true and minor corruption. Then you would schedule the downtime needed to run **dbcc** checks that would fix the page linkage problem. Panic was not required and was not productive. The sudden downtime on the production server could have been completely avoided.

Once again the theme of archiving comes up. If the databases are kept smaller then **dbcc** checks can be run more often which reduces the period of time when a corruption can appear and yet go undetected. This in turn reduces the worst-case loss of data resulting from being forced to revert to the last clean database dump. You should look at the cost to your business of server downtime and of losing some period of business data and compare that with the costs of archiving and running **dbcc** checks more often. You will find the cost of any amount of lost data to be quite staggering and probably beyond measure. If nothing else, you must make your users aware of the situation so that all involved can share the risk.

If possible, you should have a service-level agreement with the users that defines what risks they are willing to take and when. You should include things lsuch as how to handle a transaction log problem during the business hours, i.e. does the DBA dump the database or not? Other examples would include when to run **dbcc** checks and how quickly the DBA should move to correct any corruption found.

Get any agreement to share risk in writing. Specify the worst-case length of time that the server might be unavailable and the worst-case loss of data that might result from not archiving and not running **dbcc** checks more often. Keep a copy away from your work site. Perhaps have the text printed on T-shirts to be worn to the regular meetings you have with the users and your management. Don't get mad; just be prepared to get even.

There are third-party products that can help you with the **dbcc** process. For example, you can use Image Analyzer from Platinum Technologies. This product allows you to examine your database dumps without loading them into a SQL Server. This means you could take the database dumps you are normally making and run them through Image Analyzer while the SQL Server is back on-line. Image Analyzer can run on any machine in your system . This means you could move the database dumps to another machine and run Image Analyzer there to further reduce the workload on the server machine. Note that Image Analyzer runs at the UNIX level. That means it is independent of the SQL Server. You do not need to have a SQL Server on the machine where you run Image Analyzer.

The advantage of this, of course, is that you can, in theory, eliminate the server downtime normally dedicated to running **dbcc** checks. You would make your normal database dumps and return the SQL Server to normal operation. You then run Image Analyzer on the database dump and it will check for consistency problems. If there are problems, Image Analyzer will identify the database object where the problem exists. You then must run **dbcc** within the SQL Server to fix the problem. However, the time needed to run **dbcc** on a single database object is generally much smaller than regularly running the complete **dbcc** suite against all the databases in your server. Further, you only need to run **dbcc** against a database object within the SQL Server when Image Analyzer actually finds a problem.

Note that this approach does not completely remove the need to run **dbcc** checks. When Image Analyzer finds a problem, it does not report the problem in terms of the error numbers that SQL Server uses. Image Analyzer will tell you that it found a problem with page linkages in a table, for example. At that point, you don't know what the problem is and you would have to run **dbcc** checks on that table to determine the details of the problem. Then you could use the Sybase error messages from **dbcc** to fix the problem. Further, Image Analyzer does not perform all of the **dbcc** checks that the SQL Server **dbcc** does. For instance, Image Analyzer does not check any indexes. If you were to depend on Image Analyzer as a complete replacement for all the normal SQL Server **dbcc** runs, you could have corruption in an index that would go undetected for some time. The corruption would only be detected when the production system ran into the corruption during business processing. You should consider running a complete SQL Server **dbcc** suite on your databases at some regular interval to catch such corruptions. Note that using Image Analyzer would still save you most of the time you now spend on **dbcc** runs. You could run Image Analyzer on each and every database dump you make, and run SQL Server **dbcc** checks only on a weekly or monthly basis. You could also run the SQL Server **dbcc** checks on another server machine after loading the database dumps.

You must also realize that this approach also adds some very useful functionality that is not available from SQL Server. In the normal process of database dumps, and so forth, you have no way of knowing if the database dumps are any good. This means that you have no way of knowing if the database dump will really do you any good when you need it. If the database dump contains corruption for any reason, you won't know about it until you try to load the dump into SQL Server. While the normal SQL Server **dbcc** checks will assure you that the database is clean of corruptions, that doesn't mean the database dump is any good. The tape drive may have various problems or the tape can be bad. Either way, the SQL Server **dbcc** runs won't detect these problems. SQL Server can only detect these problems when it tries to load the database dump. This means, even if you run all the recommended SQL Server **dbcc** runs, you may not have a database dump at all. Using Image Analyzer allows you to perform checks that verify that the database dump is usable. This functionality is not available within SQL Server other then actually trying to load the database dump into SQL Server.

Image Analyzer can also examine database dumps that are on tape. This is useful, especially for database dumps that are larger than 2 Gb and therefore won't fit on disk in a UNIX file system. You can examine such dumps on tape which also verifies that the tape can be read.

This all takes on greater importance as the size of your databases grows. For many businesses, there simply isn't time to shut down the applications that depend on the database long enough to make full dbcc checks on any regular basis. Even the time to make database dumps is hard to find. With Image Analyzer you can reduce the downtime needed to just that for the database dumps themselves. This is very beneficial for large databases where the SQL Server dbcc runs can take many hours to complete.

MIRRORING

The benefits of mirroring server devices has been discussed already. We repeat some of the discussion here for emphasis. You don't have to mirror all the server devices, but you should. You should mirror all the server devices so that database space added to any server device will still be mirrored.

Through the detailed discussion of the way the database and its transaction log interact it should be clear that if you don't mirror all the server devices you should mirror server devices in the following priority. First, the master device must be mirrored. Any problems with the master device will bring the whole server to a halt, and therefore the master device must be mirrored. Further, any time you have a problem for any of the other databases on the server you will need information stored in the *master* database to recover the user database, another reason the master device should be mirrored. Note that for System 10 you should also mirror the server devices that support the *sybsystemprocs* and *sybsecurity* databases.

Second, you should mirror the server device or devices that support the transaction log of the most critical database. As described above, you need the transaction log to make sense out of the database itself. You should prioritize the databases on the server and mirror the transaction log server devices in that order until you run out of devices to use as mirrors. Again, you really should mirror all of the server devices.

Third, after the master device and the transaction logs of all the user databases you should mirror the server devices that support the most critical database. This will simply prevent server downtime. Even though the transaction log is already mirrored if there is a failure of one of the server devices supporting the database itself the database will no longer be available and you will have server downtime. You should mirror the user databases in the same order that you established for mirroring transaction log server devices.

Finally, you may think *tempdb* is exempt from all this, but you would be wrong. You certainly don't need to mirror *tempdb* for recovery purposes since no one ever tries to recover the contents of *tempdb*. However, since preventing server downtime is really what the recovery process is all about, you should mirror *tempdb* as well. Unless your applications never use *tempdb*, which is unlikely, the whole server will come down if *tempdb* has a problem. Therefore you should mirror *tempdb*.

Even if you don't mirror everything during normal operations you should be prepared to mirror the server devices on any one physical disk to another set of partitions somewhere on the server. This is why all your physical disks that are supporting server devices should be partitioned the same way so you can mirror from any partition on one physical disk to the same size partition on another disk (see Chapter 8). When you have a disk failure, it is usually localized to one specific place on the disk which means only one server device will be lost. Using mirroring, and being properly prepared to do so, you can simply mirror all the unaffected server devices on the disk that failed to other physical disk partitions on the server machine and then replace the bad disk. This means you only have to drop, re-create, reload, and apply transaction log dumps for the databases that used the server device that failed. All the other databases are unaffected and can be mirrored back to the server devices that will be created on the replacement disk. This saves a great deal of time, all for the cost of reasonable partitioning and perhaps a little extra disk capacity.

Mirroring can save you a great deal of server downtime because it allows you to chose when the downtime occurs for a failed server device. But, in order to gain this benefit you must ensure that the mirrors are all working. If a mirror fails and you don't notice you are in worse shape then if you don't have a mirror at all. Once the mirror fails and you don't notice you are running as if there was never a mirror at all but you think the server device is mirrored. You must check that all the mirrors are functioning properly (see Chapter 14, for the script **p_mirror** that will help you check all the mirrors on the server).

ARCHIVING

The topic of archiving to move older data out of the on-line production databases is discussed in detail in Chapter 10. There it is discussed as a performance and tuning tool, while here the emphasis is on recovery. Archiving simply means reducing and then controlling the size of the databases on your production servers. This technique is very powerful since it means all your recovery procedures will run faster and recover quicker. The time to run **dbcc** checks is greatly reduced as is the time to dump or load a database. This allows you to run **dbcc** checks more often on the current production data which will detect corruptions sooner which means in the worst case you won't have to go back so far to find a clean database dump to rebuild from.

With archiving, you create archive databases and on a regular basis you move the older production data into the archive databases (see Figure 9–12). At the end of each archiving interval, you can take the completed

Figure 9–12. Archive Databases on Primary and Decision Support Server

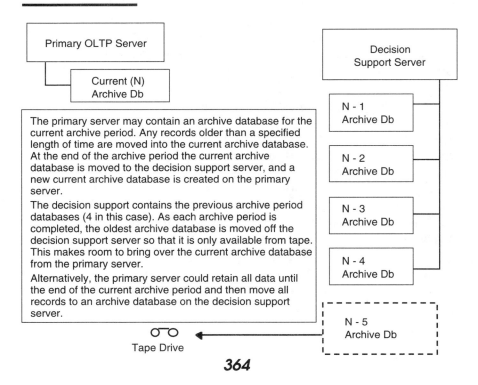

Primary OLTP Server

Current (N) Archive Db

Decision Support Server

N - 1 Archive Db

N - 2 Archive Db

N - 3 Archive Db

N - 4 Archive Db

N - 5 Archive Db

The primary server may contain an archive database for the current archive period. Any records older than a specified length of time are moved into the current archive database. At the end of the archive period the current archive database is moved to the decision support server, and a new current archive database is created on the primary server.

The decision support contains the previous archive period databases (4 in this case). As each archive period is completed, the oldest archive database is moved off the decision support server so that it is only available from tape. This makes room to bring over the current archive database from the primary server.

Alternatively, the primary server could retain all data until the end of the current archive period and then move all records to an archive database on the decision support server.

Tape Drive

archive databases and load them into a decision support server or a DBCC server and run the complete **dbcc** set on them without interrupting the production server. You can correct any corruptions found and then make a clean dump of the archive database. Now you know that you have a clean dump of all this data up to the time the latest archive interval starts. Further, the current databases are smaller and the **dbcc** checks for them run much faster because they are not worried about checking the same old data over and over.

MORE SERVER DEVICES IS BETTER

Many times the question comes up of why it is better or worse to have more or fewer server devices supported by any one physical disk. See Chapter 11 for more details. This translates into a question of how best to partition the physical disk. There are three reasons you want to use more partitions not fewer, one of which will benefit you from a recovery point of view.

A. This relates more to preventing server downtime and enhancing server recovery but that too is a form of improved server performance. When a physical disk goes bad, usually only a piece of it does. The rest of the disk may be fine. The fewer partitions and server devices you have on a single physical disk, the more of your database that is lost for any single disk problem. If you have six server devices on six physical disk partitions and the disk develops a bad block in one partition, only the one server device is lost. With only one server device for the whole physical disk, all of the database(s) on that server device are lost even if only one block of the disk goes bad.

B. More partitions of a physical disk, with a server device assigned to each partition makes it more meaningful and therefore more useful to identify which server device is being used the most. This assists you in tracking down server performance problems.

C. Internally the SQL Server maintains a queue of access requests for each server device. The fewer the number of server devices for a given number of server device access requests, the more that pile up waiting for each server device. More server devices help minimize any waiting that would go on due to these internal queues.

RECOVERY NOTES

Here we discuss various tips that will help you plan your recovery process.

When you bulkcopy (using bcp) out the contents of the system table *syslogins* you must use the -c option. You must be able to edit out the sa and probe login information if present. Note that the probe login is needed to support two-phase commit . When you are dumping the *syslogins* information and you are going to load it into another server's *master* database you must not have any entries in the bcp file that are duplicates of what is already in *syslogins* otherwise you will be attempting to insert duplicate rows and the bcp load will fail. You must check the *syslogins* table that you are loading to see which server logins are there already. The sa login must be there but the probe user may or may not be present. Whichever combination is there you must edit them out of the bcp file before you try to load the *syslogins* table. Note that you must not truncate the syslogins table. If you do the server user sa login will not be there, nor will there be any other server logins and you won't be able to bcp in the data or do anything else with the server.

When recovering from problems, you must have a current dump of various system tables and you must have this data before the server goes down. See Chapter 14 for a script which should be used as a cron job to make dumps of these system tables on a regular basis. You should also make sure the file system dump is running right after the cron job that dumps the system tables to ensure that the most recent dump of the system tables is captured to tape as soon as possible.

You should make sure the RUN_<*servername*> script that is created by the sybinit is backed up as part of the file system dump of the server machine and is current since it and the server errorlog are the only places to find actual device path name for the master device when it isn't mirrored. You will need this information for various recovery procedures.

Planning for recovery must begin early. You should dump *master* right after installing sybinit and perform **dbcc** checks on *master* as well. You must make sure the **dbcc** checks are clean before dumping *master*. Repeat this several times during the installation or upgrading.

When you need to re-create a database either on the same server or on another server and you plan to load a dump of the database, you need to re-create the segmentation of the database exactly to ensure that the database dump will load the correct database objects and data into the proper database segments. See Chapter 12 for a full discussion of the sysusages system table and the **p_dbcreate** stored procedure that will create the commands needed to recreate the database.

Also, since the configuration of SQL Server is controlled by configuration files, you must ensure that you have copies of all the configuration files you may need to reconstruct the operation of the SQL Server. If you have only a single configuration that you use all the time, then all you need is a copy of the current configuration file. This file would normally be in the directory specified by $SYBASE and would normally be called <servername>.cfg. However, if you have multiple configuration files that you use in normal operations, say one file for daily operations and one for **dbcc** runs, you need to have copies of all the needed configuration files. Recall that the SQL Server maintains only the current configuration of the server as part of the master device. Hence, if you need to recover the *master* device as part of some recovery situation, the server will recover only the server configuration at the time of the disaster. You must recover all other configuration files from UNIX level backups.

Further, you must realize that while you can recover the server configuration from the master device (use the write option of the **sp_confgure** command), you must realize a limitation of this approach. The master device will have only the server configuration that was in place at the time that the master device has been recovered to. If you are recovering from dumps of the *master* database, the server configuration in the dump of the *master* database will reflect the server configuration at the time that *master* database dump was made.

Similarly, you must not rely on the output of **sp_configure** to reconfigure a SQL Server. For previous versions of the Server (4.9.2 and System 10), a UNIX-level file containing the output of **sp_configure** would have allowed you to reconstruct the server configuration as of the time that output was generated. With System 11, **sp_configure** does not document the configuration of the server's named caches. As part of dumping the server system tables (see script for this purpose in Chapter 14), you also need to dump the output of **sp_helpcache**, **sp_cacheconfig** and **sp_poolconfig <cachename>** for each named cache to really have all the information needed to re-create the server named cache configuration.

You must also remember that since not all the configuration information relevant to the server is in the configuration file or the **sp_configure** output, you are more dependent on information inside the server. While the configuration file will tell you all the named caches and their configuration, that will not tell you the database objects bound to each named cache. The details of which database object are bound to which cache are stored in the system table *sysattributes* in each database. If you have **sp_helpcache** output that is up to date, then you have the information needed to reconstruct the database object bindings. However, without this information, you may think you can reconstruct the bindings simply be recovering the database from dumps. This is true, but realize that the bindings that are in a database dump are only those that were in effect when the database dump was made. If you recover a database up to the very moment of a failure, then you have re-created the database, including the *sysattributes* data, up to the moment as well. If you do not recover the database to the very moment of a failure, you must remember that you may not have the database object bindings that you think you have.

BACKUP SERVER

Backup Server is used by SQL Server to make all database dumps and loads. Backup Server is a separate process that runs on the server machine. Note that this means you have another process to check on to make sure it is running and another errorlog to check as well. It also means you need to have a separate startup script for the Backup Server. The Backup Server is an open server application and as such requires that the SQL Server be configured to allow remote access during any dump or load. The Backup Server is installed using sybinit just as the SQL Server is and sybinit will configure the SQL Server to allow remote access as part of the installation.

You must have the Backup Server running before you can make any dump or load from or to the SQL Server. However, you don't need to restart the Backup Server when you restart the SQL Server. Anytime you do restart the SQL Server or the Backup Server, you should verify that the two servers are communicating by executing

SYB_BACKUP...sp_who

from within the SQL Server. If this command returns, then you don't need to restart the Backup Server. If the command does not, return then you should kill the Backup Server if it is running and restart it. You must then check again for communication between the SQL Server and the Backup Server. You should make starting the Backup Server part of the RUN_<*servername*> script that starts the SQL Server. This will ensure that any restart of the SQL Server will look for a running Backup Server and if it doesn't see one, will restart the Backup Server automatically.

Backup Server must be running or any scripts or `cron` jobs that perform dumps or loads in the server will fail.

Backup Server is always called SYB_BACKUP from within the SQL Server. Note that if you go into the system table *sysservers* and change the value of *srvname* for the Backup Server from SYB_BACKUP to anything else, you can't make any dump or load from or to the SQL Server. When you install the Backup Server using `sybinit`, you are asked for the name of the Backup Server. If you accept the default, then the value of the *srvnetname* in *sysservers* will also be SYB_BACKUP. You should not do this because the *srvnetname* is what a client calls when it wants to communicate with another server. If more than one SQL Server in your database system were set up with a Backup Server that had a *srvnetname* of SYB_BACKUP, then any time any SQL Server tried to make a dump, it would call SYB_BACKUP and it would not be clear which Backup Server actually got the call (see Chapter 12 for details of how sysservers works. You must have a unique name for each Backup Server).

Backup Server allows you to dump to a server logical device just like 4.9.2 (4.9.2 requires dump devices), but it also allows you to dump to a specific tape or disk device without having the device already defined as a dump device to SQL Server. This is a very big improvement for the DBA since you can specify any tape drive on the server machine you want without maintaining server dump devices for each one. More importantly, for dumps made to disk files, you can specify the specific disk file name directly so you don't have to dump to a server disk dump device and then copy the disk file to another file name. This was required under 4.9.2 when using dump devices to prevent the next dump from overwriting the dump file.

You can install Backup Server on a remote server machine and dump from a SQL Server on another server machine, but the process is very slow. If you want to do this, you must test it out in your particular environment. This ability is still useful for installation or disaster recovery when you may need to dump or load between server machines.

Backup Server allows you to dump to multiple devices at once (striping). This means you can dump a database to four disk devices at once and the dump completes in roughly one-fourth the time. This applies to striping to tape devices as well. One example is a 5-Gb database that takes 2.5 hours to dump to a single tape but takes only 20 minutes to dump to five disk devices.

Backup Server supports multiple dumps to a single tape. Since the Backup Server allows multiple dumps to a single tape it assigns a file name to each dump, or you can specify a file name as part of the **dump database** syntax. Note that if you don't specify a dump file name the Backup Server generates on for you that is very difficult to comprehend. The **load database** command now has the **with listonly** option that will list all the file names of all the dumps on a tape for you. You then must use the file name when loading from the dump tape, unless there is only one dump on the tape. Note that if you make repeated runs of existing scripts that dump to tape and you don't change tapes between runs, you may wind up with multiple dumps on one tape.

You must change any scripts that you run that make dumps (or loads) to reflect the new syntax of the **dump database** and **dump transaction** server commands. For dumps to tape you must specify the **capacity** of the tape device and for the first dump to a tape you must include **with init** to start writing to the tape.

Backup Server does away with the need for the console process. You don't need an entry in the interfaces file for the console port number either.

Under 4.9.2 you could see a **dump database** or **dump transaction** command executing simply by looking at the output of **sp_who**, and by looking at the I/O count for the process you could determine how far along it was, but with Backup Server this doesn't work anymore. Once the Backup Server is working on the request to dump or load the only way to see if there is a dump or load in progress is to look for a process running on the server machine supporting the Backup Server called sybmultbuf. This process is running while the dump or load is in progress.

DATABASE DUMPS

Database and transaction log dumps are the heart of any of your recovery plans. You will need to consider the points discussed below in deciding how to make the dumps you need to recover the databases in the server. Several of the items discussed below apply to both database and transaction log dumps. Note that while SQL Server doesn't require the server to be off-line while making database dumps, the server performance is reduced while dumps are running. You should measure the performance of your critical applications while dumping the database(s) during peak business load and determine whether you can dump the database(s) while the business is operating. In most cases you will find that the application performance is reduced enough that your users will not want database dumps done while they are using their application(s). Therefore, you need to consider the time the server spends making database dumps as server downtime, which should lead you to consider archiving.

You need to decide whether to make a given database dump or transaction log dump to a disk file or to tape. Then you need to determine if you wish to place multiple dumps on a single tape. Note that SQL Server 4.9.2 doesn't support multiple dumps to one tape while SQL Server System 10 with the Backup Server does. See Chapter 14 for a UNIX shell script that will support placing multiple dumps on a single tape. Transaction log dumps should be made frequently to allow recovery as close to up to the minute as possible and that means running the dumps during the time the server is on-line. You should dump these transaction logs to disk files since that is faster than dumping to tape and will interfere less with server performance. Database dumps can be made to either tape or disk depending on your needs. If you have the disk space on the server machine it is better to dump to disk since that is faster and therefore minimizes the time when server performance is slowed by the **dump database** running.

However, you can't make database dumps to disk if the size of the database dump is greater than 2 Gb. In this case, database dumps to tape is your only option. This is a limitation of UNIX and 32-bit addressing. As 64-bit addressing becomes commonplace, this restriction should no longer apply.

Clearly a database dump to tape is captured permanently while any dump to disk is at risk if the server machine or the disk supporting the file system has a failure. Once you start dumping anything to disk, you must ensure that all the file systems that contain transaction log or database dumps are captured by a UNIX-level file system dump to tape. Ideally this file system dump to tape would begin soon after the database dumps to disk are complete to minimize the window during which the database dumps are only on disk. It is best to simply dump all the file systems on the server machine to tape regularly to ensure that all dumps to disk are captured no matter where they are located.

Note that you will now have to perform a two-step process to restore any dump that is on a file system dump tape. You will first have to restore the file itself to a file system and then load the dump into the database. This will take more time than if you loaded a dump made directly to tape.

You should have some process to verify that the dumps you are making are good. Again, for dumps made to disk and then to tape, the process of verifying the dumps will take longer. A good way to verify the dumps is to regularly load the most recent database dump into another server and apply some of the transaction logs as well. Note that if you are maintaining a decision support server (see Chapter 10) or using a dedicated DBCC server (discussed previously), you are already loading database dumps and applying transaction logs routinely to keep these servers in sync with the primary production server. This process will automatically verify all the dumps that are loaded.

As discussed in great detail above, you must protect the current transaction log, but that doesn't do any good if the database dump and all other transaction log dumps aren't available and don't contain any corruption. This of course ties in with running **dbcc** checks frequently and correcting the corruptions that are found as soon as possible. You need to remember that unless you have a whole set of transaction logs that are clean and a good clean database dump you can't recover the database (see Chapter 8 for discussion of the transaction log).

Along with dumping all the databases on a regular basis and you must always dump the *master* database as well. Because the *master* database can't have its transaction log on a separate server device, you can't dump the transaction log separately. This means you can't truncate the transaction log for the *master* database the way you can for other databases. You must use the command

dump transaction master with truncate_only

to truncate the transaction log of the *master* database and you must execute this command immediately after the dump of *master* is complete (see Chapter 7 for details).

You should also dump the *model* database. If you need to re-create the *model* database, you do that using sybinit to recreate the *master* database which automatically creates the *model* database. Then you can load a dump of *model* to restore any and all database objects you have created in *model*. See the *Sybase SQL Server Troubleshooting Guide* for the various procedures you need to use depending on the circumstances of the loss of the *model* database.

If one of the segments of a database fills up, you will get an 1105 error. If the database segment that fills up is the transaction log (see Chapter 12 for details of dealing with the situation). However, from a recovery point of view you have a greater problem. Once the transaction log has filled to the point of generating the 1105 error, there isn't even enough room left in the transaction log to log the **dump transaction** command. The only choice is to use dump transaction <databasename> with no_log

which will not make a transaction log entry that a dump was done. This means you don't get a copy of the current contents of the transaction log which means you can't recover beyond the last successful transaction log dump. Further, once the problem is cleared and the database can be used again, you still can't recover beyond the last good transaction log dump. Since the **dump transaction with no_log** doesn't get logged into the transaction log, the server has no idea that the dump ever occurred. This breaks the chain of transaction logs since the last full database dump. The server won't even let you dump transactions any more because of the non-logged dump you had to do to clear the transaction log. At this point you have a troublesome decision to make. You can continue processing waiting for the next regularly scheduled full database dump knowing that while you wait any database changes can't be recovered in the event of a server failure. Or, you can stop the business while you make a full database dump immediately. This is not a technical decision, but a business decision. You must communicate the risks to the users and decide with them what to do.

Note that you can prevent this 1105 dilemma in System 10 and System 11 by using thresholds (see Chapter 12). A threshold on the transaction log prevents it from filling up to the point that a **dump transaction with no_log** is required. Instead the threshold will suspend or abort (configurable) all the user transactions as the transaction log runs out of room, but before it is completely filled up. This way you are given a chance to clear the log or even add more space to the log before the user transactions are allowed to continue. This should prevent the situation described above.

As with most of life, these failures generally occur during times of peak server load which usually also represent times of peak business activity. It is during such times that the business needs access to the server the most, and can least afford to lose any of the data the business is so desperate to put into the server.

Finally, a note about loading database dumps. Since the whole point of dumping the database is to be able to load the dump when you need to recover the database, you need to realize that the process of loading the database dump involves checking each and every data page of the database. Even if there is only 10 Mb of data in the database dump, but the database is 100 Mb overall, when that dump is loaded into the database, the server will examine and initialize all of the 90 Mb of data pages that are empty after it loads the 10 Mb of actual data. You need to be aware of this since it will mean that the time to recover a database from a database dump is based on the overall size of the database, not on the size of the database dump. Of course, when making the database dump, the less data in the database, the less time the dump will take.

TRANSACTION LOG DUMPS

Note that several points in the Database Dumps section apply to transaction logs as well. You should review the previous section as well as the material below.

The most important reason to place the transaction log or log segment on a separate server device is to be able to dump the transaction log independently of the database. If you don't place the transaction log on a separate server device you can't dump the log without dumping the entire database. Dumping the database takes much longer and for larger databases often requires dumping to tape since your server machine may not have enough file system disk space to allow dumping databases to disk since the maximum file system size is 2 Gb. Backup Server can dump (stripe) to multiple disk files which supports database dumps to disk larger than 2 Gb. Dumping to tape is also slower than dumping to disk. Longer dump times slow the system down for longer periods of time which reduce the time the system is available for business use. The fact that dumping the complete database is slower will prevent you from dumping as often as you should. Further, if you dump the database, which also dumps the transaction log along with the rest of the database, the transaction log is not truncated. When you dump the transaction log separately, all the committed transactions in the transaction log are automatically dropped, which truncates the transaction log.

You must be able to dump the transaction log in order to recover the database as completely as possible. There are two levels to this recovery the first assumes you must rebuild the database from dumps already completed and the second assumes the server itself is still functioning and can access the *sysdatabases* system table in the *master* database.

In the event of a server failure that prevents you from accessing the *master* database, you must rebuild the server and databases from dumps. You will load the most recent database dump for each database, but the database can be recovered only to the state it was in at the time of the most recent full database dump. To recover the database to a state more recent than the last database dump, you must have the transaction log dumps that were made between the last database dump and the server failure.

In the event you can still access the *sysdatabases* table in the *master* database, which usually means the server suffered a disk failure on a disk that supported one or more databases but did not support the *master* database, you can use the **dump transaction** command with the **no_truncate** option to dump the entire contents of the transaction log. By applying this transaction log dump, you can bring the database back to the state it was in right up to the time of the failure. Both of these situations rely on the transaction log dumps being made which is only possible if the transaction log is on a server device that does not support any other segment of the database.

Dumping the transaction log is an incremental process. This means each transaction log dump makes a copy of the transaction log as it was at the time of the dump and then deletes the inactive portion of the log which means the completed transactions are dropped. This means that a transaction log dump, unlike a database dump, does not have to dump the same information over and over. This and the fact that a transaction log dump does not dump the actual database makes a transaction log dump much faster and smaller. Because the transaction log dump is smaller, you can dump transaction logs to disk which makes them faster still. This means you can (and must) dump the transaction log while users are running on the system and you will be minimizing the performance slowdown caused by dumping. You can (and must) dump the transaction log often so that you can recover the database to a more current state than database dumps alone would provide.

Since we are discussing transaction log dumps, recall that in order to make a transaction log dump in the first place, not only does the transaction log need to be on a separate server device, but also the database options **select into/bulkcopy** and **truncate log on checkpoint** must not be enabled. If **select into/bulkcopy** is enabled, as soon as any nonlogged activity takes place (such as a "fast" bcp in), the server will refuse to dump the transaction log since the continuity of the transaction log has been broken. Similarly, if the **truncate log on checkpoint** option is enabled, each time the checkpoint process executes it will simply delete the committed transactions from the transaction log without making a copy of them, which again breaks the continuity of the transaction log. The server will not dump the transaction log unless the log represents a complete picture of all the activity in the database since the last full database dump.

Note that the *master* database can't be extended beyond the *master* device and therefore the *master* database can't have its transaction log separated to another device. The *master* database always has the segments system, default and logsegment assigned to all the disk space assigned to the *master* database. This means you can't recover the *master* database to a state that is any more current than the last database dump. This is why you must dump the *master* database anytime you make changes to it (see Chapter 7 for details).

You can simplify the recovery process by using thresholds on your databases. The normal process is to dump the transaction log for a critical database on a regular basis, say every 15 minutes. This will result in a large number of transaction logs to apply during the process of recovering the database. You can use thresholds, specifically the last-chance threshold, to monitor the free space in the transaction log. This way you are only making transaction log dumps when needed. This will reduce the number of transaction log dumps you need to apply to fully recover the database. (See Chapter 12 for more details on thresholds).

LOGICAL DUMPS AND DATATOOLS' SQL BACKTRACK

Up to this point we have been discussing database, transaction log, and file system dumps. All of these are physical dumps. This means the data out on disk is copied to another disk file or to tape directly. Physical dumps are faster but can't necessarily be loaded to other hardware platforms or other SQL Server versions.

A logical dump refers to a dump of the server database objects in such a way that you get a dump of the server commands necessary to re-create the database objects as well as dumping the data associated with the objects. This means a logical dump can be read by humans to see what the commands are to re-create an object and you can edit the commands in the logical dump as well. A logical dump of your server can be taken to another SQL Server version or to another hardware and operating system platform. Since a logical dump contains the commands to create each server object, you can extract just the data or command associated with one or more objects that you need to re-create on an existing or new server.

Recall from Chapter 11 that if you don't make logical dumps, you should be prepared to load any of your databases at any time to a server that isn't supporting a production application so you can extract a database object, its definition or its data to re-create that object on the production system where it was lost.

Note that you are always admonished to create and maintain scripts to re-create all the objects in the servers in your database system. You are further chided to also bulkcopy (using `bcp`) out the table data for each and every table in your system. For a database system of any size, this advice is useless. The concept of the DBA having time to regularly bulkcopy out all the data in all the tables, manually edit scripts to re-create each new object, capture all changes to existing objects as well as having the disk space to store all this is far removed from reality. Even one mistake in such a set of scripts would result in a rebuilt server that might not even run, let alone have all the objects in the right places with all the right data.

As your database system grows, the concept of anyone manually managing a set of scripts to re-create the servers, the databases, the stored procedures, the triggers, the segmentation, and so forth, is absurd. You need an automated way to capture all of this information quickly and reliably. You, as the DBA, should have far better things to do than worry about scripts like this and a logical database dump of all the database on your system is just what you need.

You need to have a logical dump of your servers for several reasons. First, you will need to have the commands needed to rebuild a server, a database, or any of the objects in a database to recover from various disaster situations. If you have a logical dump of your system, you can extract the needed commands and data for the object that was corrupted. This is also very useful when you want to change the segmentation of a database to improve server performance. While you will need to drop and re-create the database, it is very useful to have all the commands for all the objects at hand so you can edit them to place each on the appropriate new segment. Second, having the commands is the only way to create selected database objects on another server. Otherwise you must examine the existing object and write your own commands to re-create the object in the other server. Third, when you need to migrate from one server machine to a new server machine from a different vendor, your physical dumps made through SQL Server are worthless since they are hardware dependent. Fourth, you will need a logical dump to migrate database objects between SQL Server versions, that is, you can't move a physical database dump from a 4.9.2 Server to a System 10 or System 11 Server.

Fifth, your users will frequently delete a piece of a database object such as 10 rows of a million-row table and then want them restored. Without a logical dump the only way to do this is to find space somewhere to re-create the whole database, load from physical database dump, and then extract the 10 rows they need. And, finally, the sixth reason is that a logical dump gives you the complete set of scripts to re-create everything from the server, the **disk inits**, the configuration of the server, the databases, their segmentation across server devices, and all the database objects to the data in those objects. Once you have an automated way to produce logical dumps for all your servers, you don't have to worry about maintaining scripts to re-create your servers anymore. A logical dump also serves to document the server which can be very useful when the time comes to make changes.

You can make logical dumps of your servers and databases manually by writing scripts that will select all the information needed from each of the system and user tables. You then need to bcp out the data for each table, and you will need to keep track of all the relationships needed to rebuild any object, such as in what order you create the rules and the datatypes, and so forth. Assuming you could keep all this straight, how would anyone else find all this and extract what they need from it? Consider also that when you go to re-create something, you must worry about the order in which you recreate all the dependent objects. For example, if you try to re-create a database manually, you must worry about the order in which you create *everything* because each object may require that other objects be in place before the current object can be created. All of this requires a great deal of manual intervention and is very error-prone.

Unless your databases are very small, you should automate the process of making logical dumps and integrate this into the rest of your normal dump procedure. The product SQL BackTrack from DataTools will do this and a lot more. SQL BackTrack works with the SQL Server to provide logical dumps of any part of your server from the whole thing down to an individual database object. SQL BackTrack also dumps the data for tables as well as making the logical dump of the table's definition. Further, SQL BackTrack can make physical dumps of a database as well and allows you to extract the logical definition of a database object from the physical dump. The product is very flexible. For example, you can retrieve the logical dump of a table from either the logical or physical dump of the database and then specify at the command line that you want the table re-created on a different segment of the database. SQL BackTrack also allows you to make incremental physical backups of a database similar to the file system dumps made at the UNIX level. This can reduce server downtime by reducing the time it takes to do your regular database dumps.

SQL BackTrack also simplifies the whole process. Compare making a logical dump of a database manually, which would require dumping the system tables using bcp, then selecting all the information needed to reproduce all the tables, rules, user-defined datatypes, stored procedures, and triggers, and then you must still bulkcopy out all the data for all the tables to a single command line for SQL BackTrack which will handle the whole thing. When it comes time to load all or a portion of the logical dump, the same comparison holds, namely, done manually you would have to remember the order in which to create everything and where all the bcp files were, compared to the single command line for SQL BackTrack.

The database is 5.6 Gb spread across many server devices. The users approach. Like frightened gazelles thundering across the Serengeti, you can see the clouds of dust on the horizon that signal yet another user-induced panic in the jungle. Breathlessly they explain how no one did anything, but 10 rows of a table just disappeared, and they gotta have that data right now. The users start to mill around your cubicle stomping their hooves. Turns out that the table has only 10 rows, but you have to load the entire database dump to get the data. You just don't have the time or the disk space to store, update, and catalog a bcp dump of all 800 tables in the server. So, you stop running **dbcc** checks on the dedicated DBCC server so you can load last night's database dump, but first you have to clear enough space on the DBCC server by dropping databases. Then you have to create the 5.6-Gb database and wait while it loads. The users are getting ugly—much baring of teeth and meaningless threats.

Finally you can bcp out the 10 rows of data and give them to the users. It only took most of your day and you will have to do it all over again the next time someone (officially no one) deletes data from your production system. The user herd thunders off. You begin sweeping up the gazelle droppings and pull out that purchase request for that third-party product that makes logical dumps of entire servers automatically. Time to go see the king of the jungle for some approvals. Sure hope The Great One is awake in the corner office.

SQL BackTrack Version 3.0 can be executed from within a stored procedure. This means that you can call SQL BackTrack from within a stored procedure. This is very important because the SQL Server thresholds execute a stored procedure when the free space remaining drops below the execute a stored procedure when the free space remaining drops below the threshold level. Before Version 3.0, SQL BackTrack could only be executed from the operating system level, for example, by a cron job. This was a problem with Systems 10 and 11 since they support thresholds. Thresholds are a very important part of your recovery process because they tell the SQL Server when the free space is running low in a segment. Thresholds are most useful when used to detect low free space in the transaction log (*logsegment*). When a *logsegment* threshold is crossed, the server executes the default sp_thresholdaction stored procedure or a stored procedure of your own name. Either way, the logical thing for the stored procedure to do is to dump the transaction log to try to free up space in the log. If you were using SQL BackTrack previous to Version 3.0, you couldn't call it from within any stored procedure. Hence, you need to be using Version 3.0 (see Chapter 12 for more details on SQL Server thresholds).

RECOVERY MATRIX

Each of the events listed in this matrix will occur sometime. You must be prepared to deal with them. You should think about how you will recover in each of these instances. For each type of failure we address the recovery process needed to restore the server. Note that there are many solutions to each problem. If a standby server is available, you can fail over to the standby server and extract data needed to rebuild the primary. The same applies if you have a decision support or DBCC server that can fill in as a standby server while the primary server is repaired. We also assume you have the normal set of database dump and transaction log dumps that are known to be clean.

Don't you just love the phrase—"known clean dumps." It's sorta like "guaranteed for life" or "I'll always love you." Just exactly how do you ever know for sure? More to the point, who has time to really verify each and every dump let alone do what the manuals require of running all **dbcc** checks and fixing any corruption found before each and every database or transaction log dump? Sure, your users will understand why their system will be down 30 hours to run full **dbcc** checks on all 8 Gb of database before dumping the transaction log, and you have to dump the transaction log every 15 minutes to provide recovery that is close to the current state of the database.

For each failure, we discuss what you need to do to recover. Unless you are sure you understand the failure and how to recover, you should contact Sybase Technical Support before proceeding.

Server Restart

As the server restarts, it goes through the recovery process for each database on the server. The server must have access to the current transaction log to fully recover a database.

1105 Error

If the 1105 error is due to a database segment other than the transaction log being full, then you need to add space to the segment that is full. If the 1105 error is due to the transaction log being full see Chapter 12 for discussion of dealing with a full transaction log.

With the proper use of thresholds, you can argue that you will never see an 1105 again. If all goes perfectly, you may never see an 1105 again for a transaction log filling up. However, you will still get 1105 errors when any other segment of a database fills up. Also, the *master* database can't have its *logsegment* on a separate device so 1105 errors can still occur for the transaction log on this database. You would have to create thresholds on all segments of all databases to prevent all possible 1105 errors. Further, even if you do have thresholds in place on all transaction logs, all the associated stored procedure can do is try to dump the transaction log. If dumping the log doesn't free up any space in the log (usually due to an open transaction), you still have to deal with the situation as if an 1105 had occurred on the transaction log. You still have to determine why the log can't be truncated and then decide what to do about it. Also, you must realize that any time you add a database to a server, or recover on from an old database dump, there is no guarantee that the transaction log has a threshold, or that it is active, or that is has an associated stored procedure that works. See Chapter 12 for more details on thresholds.

If the 1105 error occurs in *tempdb* because the transaction log is full, simply execute

dump transaction tempdb with no_log

Normally you would be worried that this would break the sequence of transaction log dumps and affect recovery, but you never try to recover *tempdb* so it doesn't matter. If the transaction log dump doesn't work, restart the server which clears *tempdb* completely.

Transaction Log Dumps Fail

You should be dumping the transaction logs of the production databases on the server regularly. This allows you to recover the database closer to its state when a failure occurred and truncates the transaction log more often which prevents it from filling up. If this process of regularly dumping the transaction log fails, the transaction log starts to fill. If you lose the transaction log, you won't be able to recover the database as close to its state at the time of the failure since the last transaction log dump was longer and longer ago as this problem persists.

Loss of One or More Transaction Log Dumps

If you are regularly using the transaction log dumps to keep another server in sync with the primary server, you will know immediately that you have a problem because the load of the transaction log will fail. Either the transaction log you were loading has a corruption of some kind or the next transaction log in the sequence is missing. If the load of the transaction log fails with an error message indicating the dump is "out of sequence" then you need to find that missing transaction log dump. If you can't, then you are indeed missing one of the transaction log dumps and you can't recover the primary server database beyond the last available transaction log dump in the sequence. You have to make a full database dump before you can resume dumping the transaction log. Any changes made to the database before the next full database dump can't be recovered in the event of a server problem.

Normal dbcc Finds Corruption

You will need to run the appropriate **dbcc** command or commands to fix the corruption, which will require putting the database (or the whole server to run **dbcc** checks in *master*) into single-user mode and this will require forcing all the users out of the database or the server for the *master* database.

If your attempts to fix the corruption fail, you may have to reload the database from dumps. If that fails then you have lost the database (see below).

Loss of User Database

If you can still get at the *master* database and if the server device that supports the transaction log for the database is still accessible, you must use the **dump transaction** command with the **no_truncate** option to dump the current contents of the transaction log to disk. Next you will need to drop and re-create the database. You can use the information you have in the dumps of the system tables that you have been making regularly to see how the database was segmented, that is, how much database space is on which server devices and in what order. After re-creating the database you load the most recent database dump and apply the transaction log dumps since the last database dump, including the dump made of the current contents of the transaction log.

Loss of Server Device

If the other server devices on the same physical disk are still accessible, you should mirror them off to other partitions on other physical disks. Then drop the primary side of the server devices that you just mirrored (see Chapter 8). Now you can replace the physical disk. Once the new disk is installed you need to drop, re-create, load from the most recent database dump, and apply all the transaction logs since the last database dump for the database on the server device affected.

If you do have to replace the physical disk, see below.

Loss of Mirror of Server Device

You don't have any immediate problem. You should try to determine why the mirror failed and whether it was the primary or secondary side of the mirrored server device. You may try to remirror the server device and if that works, you are all set. Check with the server machine SA person to make sure there aren't any errors in the server machine hardware errorlog before you remirror.

If you need to replace a physical disk follow the steps below. Note that having the server device mirrored means you choose when the server downtime occurs to fix a failed server device.

Loss of Physical Disk

If you aren't mirroring all the server devices on the physical disk that is lost you will have lost the server devices on that physical disk. You need to determine which server devices are affected from looking at the dumps you have on disk of the system tables. If the server has not crashed and if you can still get to the *master* database, you should dump the current contents of the transaction log to disk using the **dump transaction** command with the **no_truncate** option. You should do this for all databases that are affected by the disk loss. Then the server and the server machine can be shut down and the physical disk replaced. Once the server machine is back up and the server is running you can use the information in the dumps you have of the system tables in the *master* database to re-create the server devices that were on the disk that failed. Once that is done, you will need to drop all the databases that used a server device on the failed disk, re-create each database with the same segmentation that it had before the failure, and load the most recent database dumps. Then you will need to apply the transaction logs since the last full database dump for each database including the dump of the contents of the transaction log just before you brought down the server to replace the disk.

If you are mirroring all the server devices, you don't have an immediate problem. When you are ready to replace the bad disk, simply unmirror each server device that has either its primary or mirror on the physical disk that failed. Depending on whether the primary or mirror of the server device were on the physical disk that failed, you would unmirror the primary or secondary respectively and use the **mode = remove** option (see Chapter 8). Once the proper **disk unmirror** commands have been completed, you can shut down the server, the server machine, replace the disk, and restart the server machine and server. Then you should re-create the partitions as they were on the failed disk and mirror the server devices affected by the disk failure back to the appropriate partitions on the new disk.

Note that this is the whole point of mirroring. It allows you to decide when to take the server downtime.

If the master device was on the physical disk that went bad and you don't have a mirror on another physical disk then you have lost the master device (and the *master* database) and that is the same as losing the whole server (see below).

Loss of Server Machine

The server recovery needed for this disaster is highly dependent on what exactly happened to cause the server machine to fail. If the server machine is restored and there is no known damage to the disks that support the server, you can restart and see if the server recovers. Depending on the errors you see as the server recovers, you may need to rebuild the master device, one or more user databases, or the whole server.

If the server has been wiped out you will need to reinstall the server from scratch (see Chapter 13). Once the server is installed, you can use the scripts you have for **disk init**, and so forth, to create the server devices and the databases that were on the server before the crash. Since you have recent dumps of the system tables for the server, you can examine them as soon as the server machine is repaired (or restore them from file system dumps) and verify that you have created the same server devices on the same partitions, and so forth. Then you can use a recent dump of the *master* database to restore the *syslogins* table. Now you can load the database dumps to restore the database of the server. Note that you do need to have access to the information in the *master* database system tables and that is why you must be dumping this data regularly.

If you have a logical dump of the server, you can use that to re-create all the server devices, and so forth. This again is a reason to make regular logical dumps of your server (see description of SQL BackTrack above).

Loss of master or Master Device

This is the same as losing the whole server.

If only the master device is damaged you can re-create it by running buildmaster. Make sure the server is not running when you do this. You will also need to specify the size of the master device to the buildmaster command. You should recall that you can obtain the size of the master device from the RUN_<*servername*> script created by sybinit or the server errorlog. Be careful that you specify the size of the master device in the proper units for buildmaster. You must review all the possible options in the *Sybase SQL Server Troubleshooting Guide* to see what you need to do for each of the possible failure scenarios.

Once the master device or the *master* database are rebuilt, you can load a database dump of *master*. This should restore all the information about the server that was in the *master* database previously which should allow the server to recognize all the server devices and databases that were on the server before the failure. If any changes were made to the server that would have changed system tables in the *master* database since the last dump of *master*, you must re-create those changes exactly or you may have problems. This is why you must dump *master* regularly.

If other parts of the server are damaged as well, you will need to repair those next.

Loss of Database Object and/or Data from Database Object

If you have any other server that has a copy of the database, you can retrieve the database object from that server. Examples of such a server would include a standby server, a decision support server, or a DBCC server. If the database object is not available this way, you must load a database dump that does contain the object somewhere on your system and retrieve the object from there. Note that the need to have enough disk space on a server machine somewhere in your database system to support re-creating and loading old database dumps to retrieve old database objects is discussed in Chapter 11.

This situation can be greatly simplified if you are making regular logical database dumps. Since the SQL Server does not directly support making logical dumps, you should investigate a third-party product such as SQL BackTrack from DataTools. With a logical dump that contains the object you need, you can simply retrieve the data or the commands needed to re-create the database object directly. The SQL BackTrack product was discussed earlier.

Loss of Data or Database Object from Previous Server Version

Assume that you upgraded the server from 4.9.2 to System 11 and now someone needs to retrieve data that was on the 4.9.2 Server but was updated or otherwise deleted from the server before the upgrade. This means you must somehow determine which 4.9.2 dump has the data the user needs and then re-create the database on a 4.9.2 SQL Server and load the database. Once you have the 4.9.2 database loaded, you can retrieve what the user needs. If the user now needs the data or database object loaded into the System 11 Server, you need to recall that there are changes between the server that may complicate this recreation.

If you realize that you haven't made the dumps that you should have and you haven't verified the dumps as you know you should and you never checked to see if all the segments of the biggest production server in your company are really mirrored and the server is lying in pieces in a pool of blood and you can hear the footsteps of management coming down the hall followed by the herds of neglected users you can always resort to the following:

Step 1. Update resume (with nowait).

Step 2. Go (to next job).

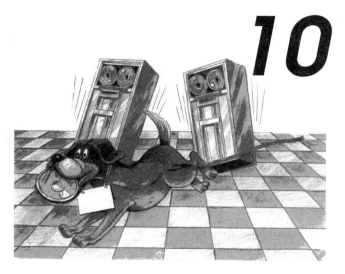

Performance
and Tuning

Table of Topics

❧ **Indexes and Queries**
❧ **Spreading Segments Over Server Devices**
❧ **Spreading Individual Tables**
❧ **Archiving**
❧ **Decision Support Server**
❧ **Standard Set of Application Transactions**
❧ **SQL Monitor**
❧ **Other Built-in SQL Server Performance Tools**
❧ **Application Transparent Server Tuning**
❧ **Preventing Downtime**

INTRODUCTION

There has been a lot written about the performance and tuning, and, like the weather, you wonder if anyone is really doing anything about it. While there are many theories, and they look good on paper, many of them simply don't apply to the real world production systems that you deal with every day. We discuss many real-world issues that can affect your server performance. Further, the class on SQL Server Performance and Tuning offered by Sybase is excellent. If you have had experience with System 10 you should consider the Sybase SKILS CD-ROM-based training course called Performance and Tuning Migration System 10 to System 11. You should attend such a class before you make any serious attempt at determining or improving your server's performance. Here we discuss issues that are specific to the SQL Server that will help you do what you can.

SQL SERVER VERSIONS

The material presented here applies to all versions of the SQL Server, with the exception of the section discussing the use of **sp_sysmon** which is supported only in System 11.

SQL Server 4.9.2

The 4.9.2 Version of the server does not support Backup Server, or the many new configuration features of System 11, or **sp_sysmon**.

SQL Server System 10

System 10 introduced Backup Server which improved database dump and load times which have an impact on the overall performance of the server. However, since System 10 did not have the support needed to take advantage of the SMP hardware and software platforms, the performance improvement over 4.9.2 was not universal. System 10 also does not support the server configuration options or **sp_sysmon** found in System 11.

SQL Server System 11

System 11 introduces many new configuration parameters, named caches and much improved scalability. All these new features make the tuning of the SQL Server more flexible and more complex. System 11 also has configuration files and other new features to track the server configuration. The stored procedure **sp_sysmon**, which was not available until System 11, provides performance and tuning data that is needed to make use of all the new performance features. The housekeeper function within SQL Server System 11 is also new and is used to assist in writing dirty pages in cache out to disk. This reduces the activities that must be done when a checkpoint is executed.

USING SP_SYSMON

The stored procedure **sp_sysmon** is a very important part of the Sybase SQL Server System 11 product. This stored procedure is part of the SQL Server software as of Version 11.0.1. This stored procedure provides you with a lot (perhaps too much) of server performance data. Sybase SQL Monitor is also useful but is a separate product that you must purchase and install. You can, and should, use both **sp_sysmon** and SQL Monitor, but if you don't have both, by all means make use of **sp_sysmon**.

Note that SQL Monitor and **sp_sysmon** do not provide the same information. While they overlap a great deal there are vital differences. SQL Monitor can report on the server access to a specific database object while **sp_sysmon** can't. Similarly, **sp_sysmon** reports many details, and summaries, of the more obscure aspects of server performance that SQL Monitor does not. You should use both if you can. You must note that both **sp_sysmon** and SQL Monitor access the same counters in the SQL Server. Therefore, if you are running **sp_sysmon** and you start SQL Monitor, SQL Monitor will clear the counters which will distort the output of **sp_sysmon** for that interval. You can benefit from using both **sp_sysmon** and SQL Monitor, but you must be aware of how they operate and keep them from interfering with each other.

You must be aware of the performance impact of executing **sp_sysmon**. The official Sybase comment on this is that **sp_sysmon** consumes 5–7 percent of server performance for a single processor system. The performance impact for multiprocessor systems may be higher. What this means is subject to much debate. The real point is that you know that running **sp_sysmon** will slow down your server, but you need to determine the impact for your server. Try running **sp_sysmon** once each hour for a week and see if any of your applications are noticeably slower.

All that is needed to run **sp_sysmon** is to execute the stored procedure and supply a time interval, typically 1 to 10 minutes. The stored procedure will run for the time interval you specify and will then out put the results. During the time interval, various counters internal to the SQL Server are sample the server performance. At the end of the interval, these counters are sampling to populate the report generated by **sp_sysmon**. Note that you need to ensure that the application that access the server should be running in a steady state mode before you sample server performance with **sp_sysmon**. The output from **sp_sysmon** will not be meaningful if the named caches are just being filled, for example.

In order to make use of **sp_sysmon**, you need to have a baseline measurement of server performance. You need to run **sp_sysmon** during periods of peak server use and during periods of relative calm. The **sp_sysmon** outputs from these periods give you a view of the baseline (or existing) server performance. Only then can you begin looking for performance problems that can be solved through server configuration changes. A good approach is to use **sp_sysmon** along with a cron job to regularly sample server performance for some period of time. This period of time should span a business cycle of the application the server is supporting. For example, if the server is supporting order entry for your business, you should gather server performance data throughout the quarter. Certainly, the time closest to the end of the quarter will see the most stress placed on the server. However, you also need performance data for the rest of the business cycle to determine the best balance of server resources and overall demand. You may well find that there are spikes in server load at the end of each month. Without performance data from the entire business cycle, you can't really determine what the best server configuration is for your business.

You must not fall into the mindset that because **sp_sysmon** monitors many aspects of server performance that you must start changing lots of server configuration parameters. You must use **sp_sysmon** responsibly. You may find that nothing needs to be changed, or, that server performance is not the real cause of overall application performance problems.

STEP-BY-STEP USE OF SP_SYSMON

Since **sp_sysmon** tells you so much about the server, you can easily be overwhelmed. You need to look at the output in a systematic way. We cover the most important aspects of **sp_sysmon** output below. The order in which we examine the **sp_sysmon** output is very deliberate. It corresponds to the importance to each output relative to server performance. It is easy to randomly pick one area of server performance, try various server configuration changes, and actually make other aspects of server performance worse. You need to continually check the same outputs over time, before and after any configuration changes, to see if you are really making things better.

The output of **sp_sysmon** is broken into various performance groups. The same measurement of server performance may appear in more than one group. The groups are listed below, in the order they appear in the output of **sp_sysmon**:

Kernel Utilization

Task Management

Transaction Profile

Transaction Management

Index Management

Lock Management

Data Cache Management

Procedure Cache Management

Memory Management

Recovery Management

Disk I/O Management

Network I/O Management

SP_SYSMON

You should refer to the *Sybase SQL Server Performance and Tuning Guide* for detailed discussions of all the sections of the output of **sp_sysmon**. We discuss some of the most important sections here. The intent here is to give you a relatively short list of things you should check in search of performance problems. No such list can ever be complete nor will it be relevant to the specifics of your server and applications. However, this list can help you deal with the overwhelming amount of detail that the output of **sp_sysmon** provides.

We discuss recommendations for changing the server configuration in order to cure problems. With any such changes you must have **sp_sysmon** output before and after the change(s). You must verify that the changes you make actually make things better.

The output of a **sp_sysmon** execution is presented below. The output that corresponds to the sections discussed below carries the same number as the section.

We will discuss the following topics in the output of **sp_sysmon**:

1. Kernal utilization—Engine busy utilization

2. Task management—Task context switches due to voluntary yields

3. Task management—Task context switches due to group commit sleeps

4. Task management—Task context switches due to last log page writes

5. Task management—Task context switches due to other causes

6. Transaction management—ULC flushes to Xact log by full ULC

7. Transaction management—ULC flushes to Xact log by end transaction

8. Transaction management—ULC flushes to Xact log by change of database

9. Transaction management—ULC flushes to Xact log by other

10. Transaction management—ULC semaphore requests waited

11. Transaction management—avg # writes per log page

12. Lock management—lock detail—<Lock Type>—waited/total requests

13. Data cache management—cache statistics summary (all caches), cache search summary, total cache hits

14. Data cache management—cache statistics summary (all caches), cache turnover, buffers grabbed dirty

15. Data cache management—cache statistics summary (all caches), large I/O effectiveness, pages by lrg I/O used

16. Data cache management—default cache utilization

17. Data cache management—default cache, cache searches,found in wash

18. Data cache management—default cache, cache searches, cache misses

19. Data cache management—default cache, pool turnover, grabbed dirty

20. Large I/O usage—large I/Os denied

21. Large I/O usage—large I/O detail—pages used/pages cached

22. Procedure cache management—procedure removals

23. Recovery management—checkpoints, # of free checkpoints/# of normal checkpoints

24. Disk I/O management—I/Os delayed by

25. Disk I/O management—total requested disk I/Os

26. Disk I/O management—completed disk I/Os

27. Disk I/O management—total completed disk I/Os

28. Disk I/O management device activity detail reads

29. Disk I/O management device activity detail writes

30. Disk I/O management device activity detail device semaphore waited

Kernal Utilization

Engine Busy Utilization

This number is the percentage of the time each server engine was busy executing tasks. Note that this number is measured relative to the amount of time the operating system gives to the server engine. If this number is 100 percent, that means the server engine was always busy, but only for the amount of time the operating system gave to the server engine. A value > 80 percent means you should try adding another server engine. You must monitor the effects of adding a server engine to verify that the change has improved engine utilization. You should never have more server engines than physical processors. It is better to have fewer server engines that are heavily loaded rather than more engines that are less loaded.

Note that you must use operating system level commands to see the percentage of processor time the server engines are getting. If the server engines are getting less than 100 percent of the processor time, that means some other process is running on that processor. You should understand what other processes are being supported by the processors.

Task Management

Task Context Switches Due To:

If any of the items (other than "Other Causes") shows a high number (>10 percent) you should know why. A high number for any of these items tells you that the server engines are task switching, which reduces performance. You should look into any cause of a high number in this section.

Voluntary Yields

If this is a high number, you can increase the time slice that the operating system gives to each server process. You can increase the configuration parameter time slice to allocate more time to the process.

Group Commit Sleeps

A high value for this parameter indicates that transaction logging is a performance bottleneck.

Last Log Page Writes

A high value for this parameter indicates that transaction logging is a performance bottleneck.

Other Causes

This number should be high, and as you fix any performance problems, it should get higher. The point here is that "other causes" means task switches due to things you can't fix.

Transaction Management

ULC Flushes to Xact Log

by Full ULC

If this value is >20 percent, you need a larger ULC. You configure the ULC for the entire server using the user log cache size configuration parameter for the **sp_configure** command, or by modifying the server configuration file.

by End Transaction

This value should be high and should be much higher than the value for "by Full ULC" or "by Change of Database"

by Change of Database

This value should not be large. If it is, you have many queries that are accessing multiple databases. You should verify that this is normal and required. This sort of access is not as efficient as access to a single database.

by Other

If this value is >20 percent you should reduce the size of the ULC.

ULC Semaphore Requests

Waited

This value should be < 5 percent. If not, you can try a larger ULC, reducing the multidatabase queries and reducing log activity by redesigning the transactions.

Average Number of Writes per Log Page

This value should be close to 1. If this number is greater than 1, it means the same log page is being written to disk multiple times. You should consider why your server needs to write the same log page multiple times.

Lock Management

Lock Detail

<Lock Type>

Waited

You should review the values for each type of lock type. Once you have identified the lock types that have the highest waited values, you should examine the Total Requests for the same lock types.

Total Requests

You should review the values for the percent of total column for the lock types that have the highest values of waited. If the percent are total values are low, then the fact that these lock types were not always granted does not have a great impact on overall server performance. You need to identify the lock types where the lock was not granted and the lock type was a large portion of all locks requested. You then need to identify the cause of this locking and of the lock contention.

Data Cache Management

Cache Statistics Summary (All Caches)

Cache Search Summary

Total Cache Hits

This value should be >80 percent. You should review the same parameter for each cache. You may need larger caches or different database object bindings to the caches you have to increase this number.

Cache Turnover

Buffers Grabbed Dirty

This value should be very small, ideally zero. For a nonzero value, you should review the same parameter for each of the caches to determine which cache has the problem. This value can be reduced by increasing the buffer wash size for the buffer pools within the cache.

Large I/O Effectiveness

Pages by Lrg I/O Used

The value for percent of total tells you how effective the use of large I/Os has been for all caches. If this value is < 50 percent you are wasting cache. A low effectiveness may be caused be defragmentation of the data in the tables. The cure for this is to bcp out and in table data or drop and recreate clustered indexes. Note that dumping and loading a database will not affect the defragmentation of the data.

Default Cache

Utilization

Note that this refers to the "utilization" of this named cache relative to all the other named caches. You should compare this value for all the named caches to see if any of the caches are over or underutilized.

Cache Searches
Found in Wash
If this number is large, then the wash section for this named cache is too big. You change the size of the wash section by setting the size of the wash section of an individual buffer pool within the named cache. The wash size is an option of the **sp_poolconfig** command.

Cache Misses
Clearly this number should be small, ideally zero. You should examine this number for each of the named caches. Cache misses generally means the cache is not large enough for the database objects that have been bound to the cache. If this number is >20 percent you should consider a larger cache. This means that a value of Cache Hits of <80 percent is similarly bad.

Pool Turnover
Grabbed Dirty
This number should be zero. Any nonzero value indicates that the wash size (wash section) is too small. You change the size of the wash section by setting the size of the wash section of an individual buffer pool within the named cache. The wash size is an option of the **sp_poolconfig** command.

Named Cache1

At this point, the output of sp_sysmon will show statistics for each named cache in the server.

...
...
...

Named Cache2

...
...
...

Large I/O Usage

Large I/Os Denied

A large number for this value indicates that large I/Os are not effective. You should investigate why large I/Os are being used and determine what the best arrangement of cache and buffer pool should be.

Large I/O Detail

There is a section for each size of buffer pool (2K, 4K, 8K and 16K) currently configured within the named cache.

Pages Cached

Pages Used

You should examine the ratio of pages used to pages cached. If this ratio is > 50 percent that is fine. If the ratio is < 50 percent then you are wasting cache to get the needed page(s) into memory.

Procedure Cache Management

Procedure Removals

If either of these numbers are > 10 percent the procedure cache is too small. You need to add more memory to the procedure cache by increasing the server configuration parameter "procedure cache" which will increase the percentage of server memory allocated to the procedure cache. Unless

401

you allocate more server machine memory to the SQL Server, increasing the percentage of server memory allocated to the procedure cache will take memory away from the data cache(s).

Recovery Management

Checkpoints

of Normal Checkpoints

of Free Checkpoints

You should see that most of the checkpoints are free checkpoints. If not, you can increase the server configuration parameter housekeeper free- write percent. You must monitor the effects of changing this percentage.

Disk I/O Management

I/Os Delayed by

The values for each of the four different outputs should be zero. If they are not, you should change the appropriate server configuration parameter to eliminate the problem.

Total Requested Disk I/Os

This value should be very close to the total completed I/Os value. If not, there is some disk I/O bottleneck at the operating system level.

Completed Disk I/Os

This value is reported for each server engine. You should check this to see the disk I/O load balancing across the server engines.

Total Completed I/Os

This value should be very close to the total requested Disk I/Os value. If not, there is some disk I/O bottleneck at the operating system level.

Device Activity Detail

Reads

Compare this value across all server devices. You should be able to explain why some devices are more heavily accessed than others. Check the load balancing between server devices. You may need to redistribute database objects across disks to balance the disk I/O load.

Writes

Same story as for reads above.

Device Semaphore Waited

This value is reported for each server device. Any nonzero value indicates that the server device can't handle the I/O requests made to it.

OUTPUT OF SP_SYSMON

```
DBCC execution completed. If DBCC printed error messages, contact a
user with

System Administrator (SA) role.
```

Sybase SQL Server System Performance Report	
Run Date	Jul 29, 1996
Statistics Cleared at	16:41:36
Statistics Sampled at	16:42:36
Sample Interval	1 min.

Kernel Utilization

1) Engine Busy Utilization:
       Engine 0   95.5 %

CPU Yields by Engine	per sec	per xact	count	% of total
	0.0	0.0	0	n/a
Network Checks				
Non-Blocking	12831.2	29572.5	768886	100.0 %
Blocking	0.9	2.0	53	0.0 %
Total Network I/O Checks:	12832.1	29574.6	768939	
Avg Net I/Os per Check	n/a	n/a	0.00010	n/a
Disk I/O Checks				
Total Disk I/O Checks	12832.1	29574.6	768939	n/a
Checks Returning I/O	12797.9	29495.7	766887	99.7 %
Avg Disk I/Os Returned	n/a	n/a	0.01121	n/a

Task Management	per sec	per xact	count	% of total
Connections Opened	0.0	0.0	0	n/a
Task Context Switches by Engine				
Engine 0	43.8	100.8	2622	100.0 %

Task Context Switches Due To:

		per sec	per xact	count	% of total
2)	Voluntary Yields	0.5	1.1	29	1.1 %
	Cache Search Misses	17.2	39.7	1033	39.4 %
	System Disk Writes	0.2	0.5	12	0.5 %
	I/O Pacing	15.9	36.6	952	36.3 %
	Logical Lock Contention	0.0	0.0	1	0.0 %
	Address Lock Contention	0.0	0.0	0	0.0 %
	Log Semaphore Contention	0.0	0.0	0	0.0 %
3)	Group Commit Sleeps	0.9	2.0	53	2.0 %
4)	Last Log Page Writes	0.5	1.1	29	1.1 %
	Modify Conflicts	0.0	0.1	2	0.1 %
	I/O Device Contention	0.0	0.0	0	0.0 %
	Network Packet Received	0.2	0.4	11	0.4 %
	Network Packet Sent	1.1	2.5	64	2.4 %
	SYSINDEXES Lookup	0.0	0.0	0	0.0 %
5)	Other Causes	7.3	16.8	436	16.6 %

Transaction Profile

Transaction Summary	per sec	per xact	count	% of total
Committed Xacts	0.4	n/a	26	n/a

Transaction Detail	per sec	per xact	count	% of total
Inserts				
Heap Table	1.9	4.4	114	75.5 %
Clustered Table	0.6	1.4	37	24.5 %
Total Rows Inserted	2.5	5.8	151	1.9 %
Updates				
Deferred	0.3	0.6	15	0.2 %
Direct In-place	0.0	0.0	0	0.0 %
Direct Cheap	127.4	293.6	7634	99.8 %
Direct Expensive	0.0	0.0	0	0.0 %
Total Rows Updated	127.6	294.2	7649	97.7 %
Deletes				
Deferred	0.5	1.2	30	90.9 %
Direct	0.1	0.1	3	9.1 %
Total Rows Deleted	0.6	1.3	33	0.4 %

Transaction Management

ULC Flushes to Xact Log	per sec	per xact	count	% of total
6) by Full ULC	108.4	249.8	6494	97.1 %
7) by End Transaction	0.5	1.0	27	0.4 %
8) by Change of Database	0.0	0.0	1	0.0 %
by System Log Record	2.7	6.3	164	2.5 %
9) by Other	0.1	0.1	3	0.0 %
Total ULC Flushes	111.6	257.3	6689	
ULC Log Records	513.2	1182.7	30751	n/a
Max ULC Size	n/a	n/a	2048	n/a
ULC Semaphore Requests				
Granted	899.9	2074.0	53924	100.0 %

10) Waited	0.0	0.0	0	0.0 %
Total ULC Semaphore Req	899.9	2074.0	53924	
Log Semaphore Requests				
Granted	149.4	344.3	8952	100.0 %
Waited	0.0	0.0	0	0.0 %
Total Log Semaphore Req	149.4	344.3	8952	
Transaction Log Writes	96.9	223.3	5807	n/a
Transaction Log Alloc	122.6	282.5	7344	n/a
11) Avg# Writes per Log Page	n/a	n/a	0.79071	n/a

Index Management

Nonclustered Maintenance	per sec	per xact	count	% of total
Ins/Upd Requiring Maint	127.4	293.7	7637	n/a
# of NC Ndx Maint0.1	0.1	3	n/a	
Avg NC Ndx Maint / Op	n/a	n/a	0.00039	n/a
Deletes Requiring Maint	127.4	293.7	7637	n/a
# of NC Ndx Maint	127.4	293.7	7637	n/a
Avg NC Ndx Maint / Op	n/a	n/a	1.00000	n/a
RID Upd from Clust Split	0.0	0.0	0	n/a
# of NC Ndx Maint	0.0	0.0	0	n/a
Page Splits	0.0	0.0	0	n/a
Page Shrinks	0.0	0.0	0	n/a

Lock Management

Lock Summary	per sec	per xact	count	% of total
Total Lock Requests	1234.4	2844.8	73966	n/a
Avg Lock Contention	0.0	0.0	1	0.0 %
Deadlock Percentage	0.0	0.0	0	0.0 %

Lock Detail	per sec	per xact	count	% of total
Exclusive Table				
Granted	1.2	2.8	74	100.0 %
12) Waited	0.0	0.0	0	0.0 %
Total EX-Table Requests	1.2	2.8	74	0.1 %

```
Shared Table
  Granted                  0.1       0.2         4      100.0 %
  Waited                   0.0       0.0         0        0.0 %
                          ___       ___         _        _____
Total SH-Table Requests    0.1       0.2         4        0.0 %


Exclusive Intent
  Granted                  0.1       0.2         6      100.0 %
  Waited                   0.0       0.0         0        0.0 %
                          ___       ___         _        _____
Total EX-Intent Requests   0.1       0.2         6        0.0 %


Shared Intent
  Granted                 12.1      28.0       728      100.0 %
  Waited                   0.0       0.0         0        0.0 %
                          ___       ___       ___        _____
Total SH-Intent Requests  12.1      28.0       728        1.0 %


Exclusive Page
  Granted                  0.6       1.3        33      100.0 %
  Waited                   0.0       0.0         0        0.0 %
                          ___       ___        __        _____
Total EX-Page Requests     0.6       1.3        33        0.0 %


Update Page
  Granted                  0.6       1.5        38       97.4 %
  Waited                   0.0       0.0         1        2.6 %
                          ___       ___        __        _____
Total UP-Page Requests     0.7       1.5        39        0.1 %


Shared Page
  Granted                538.3    1240.7     32258      100.0 %
  Waited                   0.0       0.0         0        0.0 %
                         _____    _____     _____       _____
Total SH-Page Requests   538.3    1240.7     32258       43.6 %


Exclusive Address
  Granted                402.3     927.2     24108      100.0 %
  Waited                   0.0       0.0         0        0.0 %
                         _____     _____     _____       _____
Total EX-Address Requests 402.3    927.2     24108       32.6 %
```

Shared Address

Granted	279.0	642.9	16716	100.0 %
Waited	0.0	0.0	0	0.0 %
Total SH-Address Requests	279.0	642.9	16716	22.6 %

Last Page Locks on Heaps

Granted	1.9	4.4	114	100.0 %
Waited	0.0	0.0	0	0.0 %
Total Last Pg Locks	1.9	4.4	114	0.2 %

Deadlocks by Lock Type	per sec	per xact	count	% of total
	0.0	0.0	0	n/a
Deadlock Detection				
Deadlock Searches	0.0	0.0	0	n/a
Lock Promotions				
	0.0	0.0	0	n/a

Data Cache Management

Cache Statistics Summary (All Caches)

Cache Search Summary				
13) Total Cache Hits	1260.9	2906.0	75556	89.9 %
Total Cache Misses	142.2	327.7	8520	10.1 %
Total Cache Searches	1403.1	3233.7	84076	
Cache Turnover				
Buffers Grabbed	17.2	39.7	1033	n/a
14) Buffers Grabbed Dirty	0.0	0.0	0	0.0 %
Cache Strategy Summary				
Cached (LRU) Buffers	3464.3	7984.2	207589	100.0 %
Discarded (MRU) Buffers	0.0	0.0	0	0.0 %

Large I/O Usage
    Large I/Os Performed   1.4   3.2   83   10.3 %
    Large I/Os Denied   12.1   27.8   723   89.7 %

    Total Large I/O Requests   13.5   31.0   806

Large I/O Effectiveness
    Pages by Lrg I/O Cached   100.8   232.3   6040   n/a
15) Pages by Lrg I/O Used   59.5   137.1   3565   59.0 %

Dirty Read Behavior
    Page Requests   0.0   0.0   0   n/a

default data cache	per sec	per xact	count	% of total
	0.0	0.0	0	n/a
16) Utilization	n/a	n/a	n/a	100.0 %
Cache Searches				
Cache Hits	1260.9	2906.0	75556	89.9 %
17) Found in Wash	6.7	15.4	400	0.5 %
18) Cache Misses	142.2	327.7	8520	10.1 %
Total Cache Searches	1403.1	3233.7	84076	
Pool Turnover				
2 Kb Pool				
LRU Buffer Grab	4.6	10.7	278	26.9 %
19) Grabbed Dirty	0.0	0.0	0	0.0 %
16 Kb Pool				
LRU Buffer Grab	12.6	29.0	755	73.1 %
Grabbed Dirty	0.0	0.0	0	0.0 %
Total Cache Turnover	17.2	39.7	1033	
Buffer Wash Behavior				
Buffers Passed Clean	57.3	132.1	3434	87.9 %
Buffers Already in I/O	0.0	0.0	0	0.0 %
Buffers Washed Dirty	7.9	18.2	472	12.1 %
Cache Strategy				
Cached (LRU) Buffers	3464.3	7984.2	207589	100.0 %
Discarded (MRU) Buffers	0.0	0.0	0	0.0 %

Large I/O Usage

	per sec	per xact	count	% of total
Large I/Os Performed	1.4	3.2	83	10.3 %
20) Large I/Os Denied	12.1	27.8	723	89.7 %
Total Large I/O Requests	13.5	31.0	806	

Large I/O Detail
16 Kb Pool

	per sec	per xact	count	% of total
21) Pages Cached	100.8	232.3	6040	n/a
Pages Used	59.5	137.1	3565	59.0 %

Dirty Read Behavior

	per sec	per xact	count	% of total
Page Requests	0.0	0.0	0	n/a

psychocache_1

	per sec	per xact	count	% of total
	0.0	0.0	0	n/a
Utilization	n/a	n/a	n/a	0.0 %

Cache Searches

	per sec	per xact	count	% of total
	0.0	0.0	0	n/a
Total Cache Searches	0.0	0.0	0	

Pool Turnover

	per sec	per xact	count	% of total
	0.0	0.0	0	n/a
Total Cache Turnover	0.0	0.0	0	

Buffer Wash Behavior
  Statistics Not Available - No Buffers Entered Wash Section Yet

Cache Strategy
  Statistics Not Available - No Buffers Displaced Yet

Large I/O Usage

	per sec	per xact	count	% of total
	0.0	0.0	0	n/a

Large I/O Detail
  No Large Pool(s) In This Cache

Dirty Read Behavior

	per sec	per xact	count	% of total
Page Requests	0.0	0.0	0	n/a

Procedure Cache Management	per sec	per xact	count	% of total
Procedure Requests	0.3	0.6	15	n/a
Procedure Reads from Disk	0.0	0.0	1	6.7 %
Procedure Writes to Disk	0.0	0.0	0	0.0 %
22) Procedure Removals	0.0	0.0	1	n/a

Memory Management	per sec	per xact	count	% of total
Pages Allocated	0.0	0.0	1	n/a
Pages Released	0.0	0.0	1	n/a

Recovery Management

Checkpoints	per sec	per xact	count	% of total
23) # of Normal Checkpoints	0.0	0.1	2	100.0 %
# of Free Checkpoints	0.0	0.0	0	0.0 %
Total Checkpoints	0.0	0.1	2	n/a
Avg Time per Normal Chkpt	0.00000 seconds			

Disk I/O Management

Max Outstanding I/Os	per sec	per xact	count	% of total
Server	n/a	n/a	34	n/a
Engine 0	n/a	n/a	34	n/a
24) I/Os Delayed by				
Disk I/O Structures	n/a	n/a	0	n/a
Server Config Limit	n/a	n/a	0	n/a
Engine Config Limit	n/a	n/a	0	n/a
Operating System Limit	n/a	n/a	0	n/a
25) Total Requested Disk I/Os	129.9	299.4	7785	n/a
26) Completed Disk I/O's				
Engine 0	143.4	330.5	8593	100.0 %
27) Total Completed I/Os	143.4	330.5	8593	

        Device Activity Detail

/dev/rdsk/c0t2d0s4

c0t2d0s4	per sec	per xact	count	% of total
28)Reads	16.1	37.1	964	37.0 %
29)Writes	27.4	63.1	1641	63.0 %
Total I/Os	43.5	100.2	2605	30.3 %
Device Semaphore Granted	73.2	168.8	4388	100.0 %
30)Device Semaphore Waited	0.0	0.0	0	0.0 %

/dev/rdsk/c0t2d0s5

c0t2d0s5	per sec	per xact	count	% of total
	0.0	0.0	0	n/a
Total I/Os	0.0	0.0	0	0.0 %

/dev/rdsk/c0t2d0s6

c0t2d0s6	per sec	per xact	count	% of total
Reads	0.9	2.2	56	0.9 %
Writes	97.9	225.6	5865	99.1 %
Total I/Os	98.8	227.7	5921	68.8 %
Device Semaphore Granted	98.8	227.7	5921	100.0 %
Device Semaphore Waited	0.0	0.0	0	0.0 %

d_master

master	per sec	per xact	count	% of total
Reads	0.2	0.5	13	16.5 %
Writes	1.1	2.5	66	83.5 %
Total I/Os	1.3	3.0	79	0.9 %
Device Semaphore Granted	1.3	3.0	79	100.0 %
Device Semaphore Waited	0.0	0.0	0	0.0 %

Network I/O Management

	per sec	per xact	count	% of total
Total Network I/O Requests	1.2	2.8	73	n/a
Network I/Os Delayed	0.0	0.0	0	0.0 %

Total TDS Packets Received	per sec	per xact	count	% of total
Engine 0	0.2	0.4	11	100.0 %
Total TDS Packets Rec'd	0.2	0.4	11	

Total Bytes Received	per sec	per xact	count	% of total
Engine 0	5.4	12.4	322	100.0 %
Total Bytes Rec'd	5.4	12.4	322	
Avg Bytes Rec'd per Packet	n/a	n/a	29	n/a

Total TDS Packets Sent	per sec	per xact	count	% of total
Engine 0	1.1	2.5	64	100.0 %
Total TDS Packets Sent	1.1	2.5	64	

Total Bytes Sent	per sec	per xact	count	% of total
Engine 0	484.4	1116.4	29026	100.0 %
Total Bytes Sent	484.4	1116.4	29026	
Avg Bytes Sent per Packet	n/a	n/a	453	n/a

—————————————— **End of Report** ——————————————

(return status = 0)

CACHE CONFIGURATION SUGGESTIONS

While no set of suggestions can relate to your exact situation, the following list of suggestions should get you started. You should consider binding the following objects to named caches for you server.

1. *sysindexes* table and index—Both are accessed frequently.

2. *syslogs* table (i.e., transaction log)—Especially beneficial for multiple deferred operations or triggers. Note that deferred updates

and Replication Server read the transaction log.

3. *tempdb*—If there are lots of queries that generate lots of work or temp tables due to group by or order by clauses, you should consider binding *tempdb* to its own cache.

4. Frequently accessed tables—In multiple caches to reduce spinlock contention—this can reduce the contention for spinlocks because each cache has its own hash table and spinlocks to control access to the hash table.

5. Indexes separate from data—Index pages usually accessed more than data pages and there are usually more index entries per page. This means you can often get an index into less space than the table the index is built on. With System 11 you can also separate the clustered index from the data pages of the table.

6. Small lookup tables—If frequently accessed.

7. Text/image columns—If frequently accessed.

8. Entire database—If frequently accessed and the server has sufficient memory.

9. *sysobjects, syscolumns, sysprotects*—If your server supports lots of adhoc access, which means queries that aren't executed in stored procedures, then the optimizer reads these system tables to determine the query plan.

10. Most caches should have a small 16K pool.

11. Caches where there will be little or no physical I/O should not have any large buffer pools.

THEORY IS NICE

The theory is that you can identify a very few number of transactions that the application runs against the server and that you can then identify the indexes required. Beyond this the theory tells you to worry about joins and how to denormalize some of the tables to reduce the number of joins the server needs to do.

You will benefit from going through the process, but you need to know what you can do about the application that your business runs on every day that has been around for years. You are not going to simply step in tomorrow and denormalize the million-row tables that are the very basis of your business. You probably don't have the downtime or the disk space to create many new indexes on your largest tables either. The application is not static, and you can't completely control who is able to run exactly what queries as they try out changes to the applications.

A good example of the theory of database performance and tuning that is specific to the SQL Server is the update in place. The theory is great; namely that if you do everything just right you can perform updates in place. This saves the server a lot of work as opposed to the normal update which performs a delete followed by an insert which may require shuffling the data pages around as well.

As good as the predicted performance gain may be, look again at all the requirements you must meet before the server will perform an update in place. Some of these requirements are the update must not affect any index on the table, the update does no joins, and the table does not have an update trigger. Now you need to wonder how many mission-critical applications are going to depend on tables that meet all these restrictions. You should also wonder how a real-world application could get very far if it did rely on tables that did not have any triggers. You should wonder what about referential integrity, and so forth. You need to realize that the performance and tuning theory is fine and will get you to think about the process, but it will not provide some magic answer that will speed up the server a great deal overnight.

With that said, you should understand some very practical points about the SQL Server. With these points covered, you can proceed to the many full texts that assume you are building the application from scratch and that, you as a DBA, have complete control over the way the users and the developers will create and maintain the applications that your business depends on. Note that you will see a problem right away. Many of the applications you deal with these days are from third-party vendors. They may well be the best applications in their fields, but they are also likely to be ports from some other database system to SQL Server. This means even less of the theory of performance and tuning will apply because the application was not designed, either logically or physically, for the particular needs of the SQL Server. Therefore the options remaining for you as a DBA that will dramatically improve server performance are few.

WHAT YOU CAN DO IN THE REAL WORLD

You need to separate temporary performance degradation due to your business cycle or the day of the week or month from an ongoing downward trend. Then you need to determine if a temporary slowdown is worth the effort to investigate, let alone cure. This is a business decision. That is, does the business invest enough resources to provide a certain performance level no matter where in the business cycle you are? Or does the business prefer to have less spare capacity being maintained all the time.

In the real world you need to realize you can't make the server run faster for everyone. In fact you need to first decide which users you are going to please, and which users you are going to need to disappoint. You will probably get rid of the latter users by moving them to another server where their queries can run without slowing down everyone else.

First, you need to get as many of the transactions that the server is trying to satisfy to be as short as possible. This will reduce the blocking as various server processes don't stay connected as long and don't need to hold locks for as long. This again goes back to the design of the application. You can't simply make the transactions shorter. The design of the application has to be changed. This also means that you need to identify who is doing what in the server and limit access to the server to those who really need to have the highest throughput. Other users must be moved off the server especially those users that need to run reports or other uncontrolled queries. The remaining short queries should be executed as stored procedures by the application. You should not have multiple applications running against the same server since you can't tune the server layout for multiple conflicting priorities. Note that what you are doing here is limiting the number of kinds of queries the server has to respond to. This will require that the users not have open access to the server and can only execute queries that are part of a fixed set of queries available through the one application running against the server through stored procedures. You must also note that this implies no users are allowed to isql or use any other application to access the server directly. Depending on the corporate culture you are dealing with this can be a real shock.

Assuming you can get past the previous step, you need to prioritize the queries that you are trying to tune the server for. This implies that some queries are more important than others. While your users will not agree with this, it is more important that transactions that make money directly for the business (such as entering an order) get through the server more quickly than transactions that don't (such as looking up the last five years of orders for some executive committee). If you are going to improve the performance of the server at all you must get some control over what the server is being asked to do. Only then can you begin to apply the methods that come from the theory. You need to minimize the number of different types of queries because even if you tune the server for the most important queries, it only takes one user who is running a long and low-priority query (such as requesting the last five years of sales data) to slow down and outright block all the short and important queries.

The lower priority queries must be moved off the OLTP server to a decision support server. Depending on the needs of the user base, you may want to create more and different indexes on the tables of the report server to support more complex queries. You will need to establish a host of procedures and processes to maintain a decision support server that will supply the best performance for most of that server's users (see below).

Once you have settled on a set of queries you are worried about you can work on creating the best set of indexes that will "cover" most if not all of the important queries. This is a case where some of the theory is really useful (see below). You need to be careful in your selection of indexes as it is easy to create too many and spend all the server's time simply updating and maintaining all the various indexes.

With a good set of indexes you can improve the server's performance simply by getting all these indexes into cache. With enough server machine memory you can keep the nonclustered indexes in memory which will eliminate all of the physical I/O for the queries that are covered by these indexes. Note that you also want to get most, if not all, of the stored procedures into cache as well and the server assigns a percentage of the server machine memory that is available to the server to the procedure cache. Hence, more cache is good, which means more memory is good for server performance. All of this goes back to capacity planning see Chapter 11).

A very basic, powerful, and often ignored process that will help server performance more than all the theories put together is archiving. This simply means that you have a process that systematically identifies data in the server that is no longer needed in the OLTP server and moves that data to an archive database on another server. This keeps the databases on the OLTP server as small as possible which makes everything easier from performance to recovery (see Chapter 9).

These techniques are not glamorous and will not win you any awards for theoretical database design, but they do work. They are also unpopular if the server environment has been allowed to evolve with users doing whatever they want whenever, they want. As with so many problems in the real world, the biggest hurdles to solving them are political (and all too often they become personal) not technical. You can do little more than understand what can be done and work to make it happen within the environment you are in.

The high-price consultants arrive amid great fanfare. As the ticker-tape parade fades into the distance, you, the DBA who couldn't attend the long lunch for management and the consultants because you had to attend to the production systems, are left with the wisdom of the ages, delivered for about 4 times of what you make. You are told to drop the mirrors on all the production server devices and remirror with the `noserial` option, ithat is, with parallel mirroring. You are assured that this will improve performance by 100 percent since it will replace the `serial` mirroring that you had set up because it provides maximum data integrity (see Chapter 8). Fine. You drop the mirrors and you can't see any improvement in the application performance, but not all the users are on the system so you proceed to mirror everything again using the `noserial` option. After a week of waiting even management agrees that the application is as slow as ever, and in fact, there was no speedup when there was no mirroring at all.

You can't fool ignorant people, no matter how much they charge you in the process. The logic was flawless, but it was irrelevant. If your application is slow, it may not be as simple as turning off mirroring to get a 100 percent speedup. You need to keep this in mind as you are given "advice." Only you and your users know your system and only you and your users live and die by its performance. Try anything you like, but the odds are that you will have to look long and hard to find the real sources of the slow performance you are trying to find and fix.

And, just as a footnote, the expensive out-of-town help couldn't come back to explain your situation because they charge so much you can't afford them any more.

INDEXES AND QUERIES

You must note that this discussion does not replace the very detailed and lengthy discussions available in other sources regarding the SQL Server query optimizer and how it selects the index(s) it will use to satisfy a given query.

As mentioned previously, all the important queries for the database should be covered by an appropriate index on each table. This refers to a nonclustered index whose key is built on the field or fields of the table that the queries need to access.

A nonclustered index builds index pages that make it easy to find the individual rows of the table that contain the data in the key for the index. Eventually, the nonclustered index will point to the individual rows of the table spread throughout the table. But, for the fields (columns) of the table that form the key of the index, the nonclustered index will actually contain an ordered set of the key fields. The nonclustered index, as far as the table data in the columns that make up the key is concerned, forms a clustered index for the fields that make up the key since the index stores this subset of table data in the order of the keys. This means that, for queries that only need data from the columns that make up the key of the index, so called covered queries, the server doesn't have to go to the data page to retrieve rows of the table. Instead, the data needed to satisfy the covered query is available within the index pages. For a covered query the index pages contain many more "rows" of the table data relevant to the query on a given data page since only the data that forms the index key is stored on the index page. This means there is more data relevant to the covered query per page in the index which reduces the I/O needed to satisfy the query. For a covered query the server can satisfy the query by just accessing the values of the key that the index maintains in order. The index also has a pointer to the full row of the table for each value of the key but for a covered query the server doesn't need to access the full row.

You need to keep many things in mind whenever you start thinking about server performance. Even with the best indexes in the world, if your query is going to return more than about 20 percent of the rows of the table, the optimizer will just table scan (retrieve all the rows of the table) anyway. If you are looking at the query plans (see **set showplan** in SQL Server Performance Tools section below) and an unexpected table scan appears, you need to determine how many rows were returned relative to the size of the tables. If you are retrieving a lot of rows, you need to review why this query is even running against the OLTP machine. You should move all such transactions to the decision support server. Note that there really isn't a good index for a query that needs lots of rows returned.

You must remember that all the indexes in the world won't help much if more than one user wants to update the same data page. This usually comes up when all the data in a table is ordered by some unique number such as an order number. Assuming that the table has a clustered index on the order number and the order numbers increase linearly with time, you are guaranteed that every user who is trying to enter a new order (a very important query for your business) will be fighting over the last few data pages of the table. In order to prevent this, you must assign an artificial (i.e., doesn't have anything to do with the order or the time it was created) key to each row of the table in a random manner. Then you need to re-create the clustered index so that it is based on this artificial key column that is randomly distributed throughout the rows of the table. This means that even for new orders, the rows will be spread randomly throughout the database. Users who need access to these new rows will be trying to access pages throughout the table, not just at the very end of it. This greatly reduces the blocking users see while they wait for the data page they need. Blocking is very costly in terms of server performance since it represents time during which nothing useful is being done for the process that is being blocked (note that you can see which server users, if any, are being blocked in the output of **sp_who**). Note that you need lots of disk space to re-create a clustered index. The other way to do this is to bcp out the table data, truncate the table, drop and re-create the clustered index, and bcp the table data back in, but this approach is very slow.

There is another real-world problem that you must be aware of. The query plans for stored procedures are done once when the stored procedure is first compiled. A stored procedure is always compiled the first time it is called after the server has started up. The query plan is then retained and will be used for all subsequent executions of the stored procedure. This is what makes the use of stored procedures useful for speeding up queries, but it implies that you are always running the queries in the stored procedure against the same set of data every time. The problem is that the query plan may not be appropriate the next time the stored procedure is executed. Consider a stored procedure that takes in a parameter called "order number" and runs against a table with a million rows, each one representing an order. Assuming that the primary key is order number, a query that retrieves all the order rows where order number is greater than the order number supplied to the stored procedure at execution, will return vastly different numbers of rows based on the order number that is passed to the stored procedure. If your application passed order number = 999,990 to the stored procedure the first time it was executed (and therefore was recompiled) since the server was last started, the query plan will probably make use of any available indexes just as you expect. But, you need to remember that if the next execution of the stored procedure is past order number = 100, the query plan using the index(s) will result in much worse server performance than if the query simply did a table scan since virtually the whole table must be returned. For queries that return lots of data, the use of an index may be worse than just table scanning because of the overhead of traversing the index levels for each value of the index key. You must also note that if you manually execute the query or queries in the stored procedure to examine the query plan you may think everything is fine, but you are not executing the stored procedure's query plan and therefore are not seeing what the stored procedure is planning on doing. This can be very confusing and can lead to lots of lost time. Finally, again, you must reduce the number of queries that your application submits to the server and you should eliminate any queries that require lots of data returned. Such queries should be moved off the OLTP server to the decision support server.

You can use the `with recompile` option in the stored procedure so that it is recompiled each and every time it is executed, but you will have a hard time telling if this has improved things since you will then have the added overhead of always recompiling which may slow the query down as much as the use of an improper query plan did. This all leads to an observation that even if you identify a set of queries that the application makes and even if all of those queries are made through stored procedures, you can still get some killer queries if the application allows users to pass anything they want to the stored procedures. This gets back to fixing the application rather than the server.

You will be tempted to create every table with the clustered index the same as the primary key. This is not always a good idea and in some cases can ruin server performance. Consider a table where the primary key is order number. All the new orders will have the highest order numbers and if the clustered index is created on the primary key, then all the data records are ordered by order number. This means all your users who are entering new orders will be contending for the last pages in the table which will lead to lock contention and poor server performance. You must spread the user access out across all the data pages of the table to improve performance. On the other hand, if your users wanted to look at old order data and create reports based on ranges of order numbers, then this clustered index may be ideal, especially for a decision support server where the users are not updating but only selecting.

Finally, you must not ignore the basics while you delve into the theory of performance and tuning. All your indexes are examined by the query optimizer in the SQL Server to determine the best one (if any) to use. The way the query optimizer does this is to decide how many pages would have to be read using the index or simply by scanning the whole table. The query optimizer makes this decision based on the distribution page that exists for each index. Without getting into how the query optimizer uses the distribution page to select an index, the point here is that the statistics information on the distribution page must be current or the optimizer will be making uninformed decisions. You must run **update statistics** and **sp_recompile** on all the tables in each database. Note that **sp_recompile** is executed on a table and when executed, causes any and all stored procedures that reference the table to be recompiled. Even if a table is static, it still must have the distribution page updated at some point after the table is created and loaded. As part of your regular server maintenance you should update all the user tables in the server, as well as update the active tables more often. You can't check to see how recent the distribution page is for a given index and that is why it is better to just update them all on a regular basis rather than trying to remember which tables were updated and when. You can detect indexes that have not had any distribution page created at all, that is, **update statistics** has never been run since the table or index was created or last truncated and loaded. The query to do this is

select object_name(id) from sysindexes where distribution = 0 and indid > 0 and id > 100

which selects the rows of *sysindexes* that have *distribution* = 0, indicating no distribution page. Note that you eliminate system tables by specifying *id* > 100. Tables that don't have a clustered index will have *indid* = 0, but they don't have a distribution page so you eliminate them with *indid* > 0.

A new performance nightmare is brought to you by clever developers. The performance of your server has been slowly degrading. You decide to drop and re-create some indexes. Now the performance is absolutely terrible. The users are marching with torches. It looks as if you will have to get another job. What happened< Turns out you can "force" the server to use a specific index for a query. This was undocumented pre-System 11. In System 11 you can actually specify the name of the index you want the server to use. However, pre-System 11, the "forced" index was specified by the index "*id*" number. Hence, if you drop and re-create indexes and don't re-create them in the exact manner as they were originally created, you can have queries where the server is being forced to use an index that is completely wrong. This can be lurking anywhere in your application code. This is an excellent example of cleverness and nonstandard features causing you a lot of pain. Be aware that such murkiness exists within SQL Server.

SPREADING SEGMENTS OVER SERVER DEVICES

One of many aspects of server performance that is argued about revolves around how to place the database segments on or over the available server devices. You should consider the example below before you dive into a complex segmentation scheme.

You should imagine that you have a database *db1* that consists of three segments. The first segment is the combined *system* and *default* segments, the second is the *logsegment* for the transaction log and the third is called *ncindexes* where all the nonclustered indexes are stored. You can also assume that you are told that spreading each of these segments so that a part of each segment is on a different server device will help improve performance by speeding up the I/O for each of multiple users. The logic can be taken further be requiring that the multiple server devices of each segment be attached to separate controllers to provide multiple parallel I/O paths to portions of each segment. We take each of the segments in turn and explain why this advice is dubious at best.

You can start with the *logsegment* segment. Each transaction makes changes to the database. And all these changes are recorded in the transaction log, whether the transaction commits or is rolled back. Hence, the transaction log will always be a performance bottleneck as all users who are changing the database (i.e., causing changes to the database all of which must be recorded in the transaction log) wait in line while the server records each user's changes on the last data page of the current extent of the transaction log segment. All the user changes that need to be recorded in the transaction log will be contending for access to the end of the transaction log while waiting for their log records to be written. There is nothing you can do to change this behavior, so there is no performance gain by spreading the transaction log across multiple server devices on different controllers. All you can do is determine how large the transaction log should be and allocate that much space on server devices on the same physical disk. You shouldn't normally need a transaction log larger than a whole physical disk so the log segment should always be on one physical disk, occupying multiple partitions if necessary.

Consider the *ncindexes* segment next. This segment contains the non-clustered indexes for the largest or most heavily accessed tables in the database. As such, these indexes should be used by most, if not all, queries that are run against this database. Further, the most important queries should be "covered" by the indexes you create on the table. This means that the server doesn't have to go to the data page to retrieve rows of the table; the data needed to satisfy the query is available within the index pages. Since the index pages contain only the table data from the columns that make up the index key (versus all the columns of the table), there will be more data relevant to the query on each index page compared to the pages that store the table data. This reduces the I/O needed to satisfy the query. Further, if you have sufficient memory on the server machine and you don't have too many indexes, you should have most, if not all, of the data pages for the *ncindexes* segment in the server's cache so that no physical I/O is needed at all. While the tables themselves may well be far too large to fit in any practical amount of memory, carefully chosen indexes, based on keys that are made up of as few of the table's columns as possible that cover the most important queries (i.e., those that must run the fastest and are needed by most of your users to support the business) will often fit within the server's data cache. Getting most, if not all of the most frequently used index pages into cache makes spreading the *ncindexes* segment irrelevant.

Now for the remaining segment that supports the *system* and *default* segments. To gain any benefit from spreading this segment around, you are assuming that the tables in this segment are heavily accessed, which means they should be properly indexed (a few indexes that cover the important queries) and these indexes should all be created on the *ncindexes* segment discussed above. This means that for the important queries these tables should not be accessed much at all since the indexes will satisfy the queries and the indexes are all in cache.

Given this discussion you should conclude that rather than pursue some arcane segment and server device allocation scheme you should go back to the real cause of all the problems which is the set of queries that the application is asking the server to satisfy and buy as much memory as possible.

You should also consider the difficulties you and your fellow DBAs will have maintaining any complex segmentation scheme. If it isn't clear where to add space to a given segment, you can count on its being done wrong. Any performance gains due to a complex segmentation scheme can be wiped out by one careless addition of space for a segment on the inappropriate server device.

Spreading Individual Tables

If you can't cover all the queries with nonclustered indexes for whatever reason you can then take individual tables that are heavily accessed, create a segment for each, and spread that segment over several physical disks, preferably on separate controllers. But, this requires that the data in such a table be accessed in a random pattern, that is, the user access will occur throughout the table space, not just at the end where new data pages are added. You will probably require some form of artificial key or random number that is one column of this table (not related to any attribute of the entity, that is, not a real piece of information about the data stored in the table) and build the clustered index of this table on that randomly distributed number. This assures that the query access will be spread out across the table space minimizing hot spots where users contend for the same data pages which causes slow overall server performance.

Archiving

Of all the server performance enhancing techniques available, perhaps the most powerful is quite simple and requires more of a cultural shift for the users than anything technical to do with the server. This technique is archiving. You identify the databases that hold the data that represents your business. These databases are the ones that grow all the time as your business moves along. You set up a process that will scan these databases and identify all the data that is older than some time span. The data that is too old is moved to another database. The benefits of this process are many and varied. First, the size of the databases that are in use every day does not keep growing, which means you can establish processes to handle dumps, **dbcc** checks, and so forth, that will work for a long time. Also, all these processes run much faster on a smaller database. You only need to maintain the indexes over the current data and that means smaller indexes (due to smaller tables), and more indexes will fit in the same amount of cache, which means you get more use out of the server machine memory you have available to the server. Even a table scan, when necessary, will run faster on smaller tables.

In order to make this work you must set up a process that can be run regularly to archive the production databases. This process must be complete so you don't have to worry about it each time you run it. The process could involve a script that runs once a day to determine which rows in the database are old enough to be archived, and indicate that in a column added to the tables for that purpose. Another approach is to simply add the date and time when the row was added to the database and let the script compare that information with the current date. You could also archive data based not on how old the data is but how big the database is. Either way you will have to examine the current logical and physical design of your databases to see how best to archive the data.

Once the data to archive has been identified, you then need to move that data out of the database and into a separate archive database that is created for each archiving period. If you are archiving quarterly you would set up a database for the present quarter where you would archive data until the next quarter starts. You need to decide whether you need all the data on-line at all. If so, you will need one large database that will grow over time as more and more business history is added to it. If not, you can decide how many previous archive periods you need on-line and keep only that many archive databases in the server. This means that in each archiving period one old database would be dropped from the OLTP server (see Figure 10–1).

At the end of each archive period you will either have created a new archive database for the next archiving period or you will have increased the size of the one ongoing archive database. In either case you should run a full **dbcc** check against the archive database and fix any problems that you find, and dump the database to tape. This assures you that you have all of this data on a known clean dump. This means you only have to worry about corruption and other problems in the current data which is a smaller database. Depending on the nature of your business, the current data set may be very much smaller which will save you a great deal of time. In this way archiving also helps you by speeding and simplifying recovery (see Chapter 9).

Archiving is well worth it, but it will require some changes to existing applications. Your application will need to know that only data for the current archiving period is stored in the database(s) that the application is used to accessing. The application needs to be able to detect requests for older data and know how to access the appropriate archive database. Depending on how many archive periods you keep on-line, the application may need to know about the location of very old archive databases that should be on the decision support server. You will want to minimize the number of archive databases that are kept on the OLTP server—ideally only the archive database that is being filled for the current archive period would be there, since any access to any database takes resources that the server should be applying to current transactions. Note that the need for application changes is a theme throughout this discussion. For archiving, the time invested in making such changes is well worth it.

DECISION SUPPORT SERVER

Along with archiving, setting up a decision support server will help you improve the performance of the OLTP server more than almost anything else. As has been mentioned repeatedly, to make any progress in server

Figure 10–1. Archive Databases on Primary and Decision Support Server

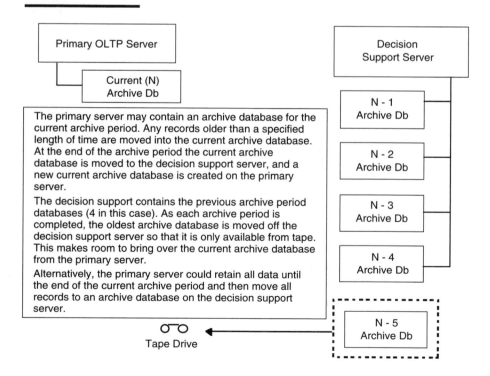

tuning you must first identify the short, important transactions that the applications on the OLTP server need to run as fast as possible and move anything else off to a decision support server. This will allow you to reduce the number and type of queries you are trying to tune for. Further, with a copy of the production data on the decision support server, you can also improve the response for the longer running, more complex queries by setting up more and different indexes on the tables than you should have on the OLTP server.

The decision support server needs to have a copy of the production database data that is on the OLTP server that is refreshed at some regular interval. Your determination of the proper refresh interval will be a taxing political question. You must identify who needs what data and how current it must be. Some of your users will say that their queries must be run against data that is absolutely up to date, but you need to filter this a great deal. There is a trade-off between how many users can get a certain level of performance running against the OLTP server. In order to improve performance for some users you may have to force the others to use data that is somewhat out of date on the decision support server.

Note that using a decision support server to offload the OLTP server is a very good approach, but as with other proposed solutions discussed here, it may well involve changing your applications. If an application is running that allows users to query all the sales orders ever entered into the system and you now archive all but the last three months of the sales order data to an archive database on the decision support server as well as dumping the OLTP sales order data and loading into the decision support server on a nightly basis, the application now needs to examine the user's request and send queries to three places depending on the data needed. Or, you modify the application to simply only access either the OLTP server or the decision support server. This will prevent users from trying to access both up-to-date data and archive data at the same time. Either you must modify the applications or your users must run the applications twice, once on the OLTP server and again for any data older than the archiving period.

This raises the question of how to keep the decision support server up-to-date with the OLTP server. You can do this by loading the database dumps you normally make on the OLTP server into the decision support server right after the dumps are complete. If you are dumping your OLTP server once a day, then your decision support server will always be one day behind, at worst. The use of database dumps is relatively simple since you already go to the trouble of making the OLTP server database dumps and by loading the dumps into the decision support server, you are also verifying that the dumps are good. Note that you must maintain the decision support server databases at the same size (or larger) as the OLTP server databases that are being dumped and loaded. This means that any time you add space to the OLTP server databases, you will need to add the same amount of space to the decision support server. Also, the process of loading the decision support server will take longer and longer as the database dumps become larger or you add more databases. You have to decide at what point the downtime of the decision support server due to database loading cuts too much into the benefit of having the decision support server at all. You can speed the process of dumping and loading if you have enough server machine disk space on the OLTP and decision support servers to dump the database to a disk file, copy that file to disk on the decision support server machine, and then load the dump. This is limited since you can only dump to a single disk file which limits the maximum dump size to around 2 Gb. [For System 10, you can use disk striping (dump to multiple disk files at once) with the Backup Server to speed the dumping process and to dump databases where the dump would be larger than a single UNIX file system.] Your users will become increasingly frustrated that the decision support server is available less and less often. You are also setting up another server that should be on a separate server machine which means more of all the software, hardware, facilities and personnel resources that are always in short supply.

When the time to load all the OLTP dumps necessary becomes too long, there is another approach you can implement. This involves loading the OLTP dumps into the decision support server once and from then on moving the transaction logs, which you should be dumping regularly on the OLTP server anyway, to the decision support server and applying them to the databases there. This process still involves some downtime but it is less time than for a complete load of the entire database. This approach does require more monitoring, and when it fails you have to load the entire database from dumps which will lock out your users for an extended period of time. You need to recall that for both a **load database** or a **load transaction** command the database in question can't have any users in the database. While you would think the method of loading transaction logs would allow you to keep the decision-support databases in sync with the OLTP databases to within the transaction log dump interval on the OLTP server, this isn't practical. Since you have to get rid of any users in

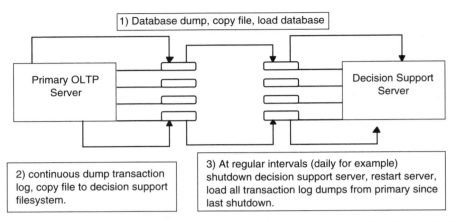

Figure 10–2. Keeping Decision Support Server in Sync Using Transaction Logs

the database to load the transaction logs you won't be able to load any transaction logs until off-hours and then you will need to load all the transaction logs that have accumulated from the OLTP databases since the last time you updated the decision support databases (see Figure 10–2).

Both of these approaches to keep the decision support server in sync suffer from another problem which may actually limit the decision support server performance even though it offloads and helps the OLTP server performance. You must move any user queries that are not short, important transactions to the decision support server. This allows you to create only the indexes needed to support the reduced set of queries that will run on the OLTP server. This should help you speed up the performance of the OLTP server. But, these indexes are just the opposite of what you want for indexes on the decision support server. The decision-support server is for longer-running, complex queries that may need to retrieve large amounts of data from various databases for reporting or data analysis purposes. The server performance for this sort of data access can be improved significantly by creating more and different indexes on the tables in the databases. These indexes may be built on more, and sometimes all, of the columns in a table. On the OLTP server you should reduce the number of indexes on each table to minimize the time the server spends maintaining indexes and to fit as many of the indexes into cache as possible. Since you are dumping and loading from the databases on the OLTP server, you are forcing the decision support server to have the same minimal set of indexes as the OLTP server. The only way around this is to keep the users off the decision support server even longer while you build the different indexes after each database load. This will further reduce the time the decision support server is available to your users.

For the transaction log approach to work, you must maintain all the databases on the decision support server as "read-only" because any activity in the database causes the next transaction log load to fail. This means you can't create new indexes and it also means the users can't run any queries that would update or write any data in the databases.

The load database approach doesn't have to have the databases in "read-only" mode, but each load will overwrite any changes made such as new indexes.

Both approaches will maintain all parts of the databases affected, but this doesn't include the *master* database. Since you can't just load the *master* database from the OLTP server to the decision support server, that means any of the system tables will not be in sync. This means the server logins, for example, will not be maintained between the two servers. Even if you were willing to load the *master* database every time, you shouldn't unless all the server devices have the same physical names, and so forth. You can't really keep the *master* database of the decision support server in sync with the OLTP server.

The dump-and-load database approach is the simplest and works well for small databases. It prevents you from maintaining any indexes different from the OLTP server, but again, for small databases which will load quickly you will have time to build indexes each time you load since the tables in the databases will also be smaller. As the databases involved get bigger, you will spend more and more time loading and creating indexes than you will letting users use the server. At some point you will need to decide if it is time to go without the indexes or move to the transaction log loading process. Note that Replication Server may provide a better way to maintain the decision support server. Replication Server can replicate the tables you need from the OLTP server into the decision-support server without any downtime on the decision support server at all while you maintain a unique set of indexes as well. It can be a major project to replicate all the tables in all the databases of your OLTP server, but the benefits can be many and you could also replicate data from multiple servers so that the decision support server can support reporting queries that are more complex than any that could ever be run on the OLTP server.

STANDARD SET OF APPLICATION TRANSACTIONS

While you can measure server performance in several ways, it is still difficult for you, the DBA, to really measure server performance from the user's perspective. From their point of view, the server is "slow" based on how long it takes for them to run their various queries. Whether or not the number of writes to disk is higher than normal doesn't really interest them; only the overall throughput shows up in their world. You can save yourself a lot of troubleshooting time if you can agree with the users what exactly the server performance is before it gets worse. The best way to do this is to establish some set of transactions that you can run through the application to see what the overall server performance is at any given time. For example, while SQL Monitor will tell you a great deal about the server, it slows the server down a little while it is running. A set of transactions allows you to measure the server performance without any other processes to affect the results. Further, it is good to have timing data for such a set of transactions before the users complain. Without a baseline of how the application's transactions were behaving in the past, you don't have much to go on when the users tell you the application is "slow."

You should see that establishing a standard set of transactions is also part of the whole tuning process. The standard set of transactions should be the same set of transactions that you identified as the most important queries for which you are trying to improve server performance.

It isn't always practical to establish such a set of transactions, but if you can you should run them when server performance is good or at least acceptable. Then you should run them at some regular interval to measure server performance over time and throughout your business cycle. When you upgrade the server, or alter any part of the logical or physical database design, you can run these same transactions in your development environment to detect any performance problems early in the development process. Then, when you do roll out the new application changes to production you should again run these transactions to get a measure of performance that you can compare with the data from the past.

SQL MONITOR

SQL Monitor is a Sybase product that works with the SQL Server to provide you with a graphical display of the server's performance. The data displayed is very useful for tracking down server performance problems. You should understand the SQL Monitor version 11.0.1 has several new and important features that are a distinct improvement over previous versions. SQL Monitor Version 11.0.1 can access any version of SQL Server from 4.9.2 through System 11. However, note that some of the most interesting monitoring outputs for database objects and network activity are available only when monitoring a System 10 or System 11 Server. Similarly, the monitored outputs regarding data caches (named caches) are only available when monitoring a System 11 Server.

SQL Monitor 11.0.1 also introduces the historical option which allows you to record server performance to files which can be recalled for later comparison and analysis. This feature is very useful but does require further installation effort.

The SQL Monitor consists of two portions: the server portion that runs on the same server machine as the SQL Server and reads the shared memory of the server, and the client portion that can run anywhere and reads the data that is in the server portion and displays it to you. Note that this means you have another process running on the server machine which can take resources away from the SQL Server.

When you start SQL Monitor, you should disable the checking of memory which uses the **dbcc memusage** command that can slow down the SQL Server substantially. You do this by using the -nomem option when you execute sqlmon which is the client portion of the product.

The default configuration of SQL Monitor can support up to five connections between the server portion and all client portions. This means five different SQL Monitor clients can be connected to one SQL Monitor Server but each client can only have one window open. Or one client that can open five windows can be connected. You can have only a total of five windows open among all clients. You can increase the maximum number of connections to 20 by using the -n20 option of the SQL Monitor Server startup script, but you must also change the shared memory start address which involves running buildmaster, and so forth. You must not do this procedure when the SQL Server is running. You must consult the *SQL Monitor Server Supplement* for the details of this process.

The SQL Monitor product does have some limitations. First, it can show only performance data for a limited number of server devices in the bar chart used for showing disk I/O rates, and so forth. This is a problem for a large server with numerous server devices. You also have no control over which server devices are shown and you can't switch between sets of server devices. The text display that comes along with the bar graphs does tell you about all the server devices, but it gives you only the total I/O data for each server device. This is especially frustrating on a larger server where you purposely create lots of server devices to support multiple user-defined database segments to improve performance, but you can't see them all with your performance monitoring tool.

SQL Monitor also doesn't provide a long enough time history for the performance data. It will display data for 60 intervals, and depending on what interval you have selected for the performance parameter in question, that may be sufficient, but that doesn't help you correlate performance from a month or a year ago with what is happening right now. You can print the windows but then you are forced to keep a file of hardcopy output for comparison. You really need to be able to call up data that spans your business cycle and be able to compare data from several previous business cycles to put the current server performance into any useful perspective.

Since the use of SQL Monitor can slow the SQL Server performance somewhat, you need to determine the performance impact for your SQL Server on your specific hardware and operating system platform. A good way to determine this is to run your standard set of transactions (described above) with and without the SQL Monitor server running on the server machine. Note that even if you have stopped all the SQL Monitor Clients, the SQL Monitor Server is still running on the server machine and should be stopped as well.

There are several windows that can be displayed by SQL Monitor. Each one provides you with data about a different aspect of server performance.

SQL Monitor (Main Window)

This window simply lists the windows that are available, and if you have not specified the -nomem option when you started, the SQL Server Client (sqlmon)—the pie chart of server machine memory usage—will also be displayed.

Cache

This window displays graphs of the data cache and procedure cache performance. By observing the physical and logical reads for the data cache, you can determine whether most of the requests for data pages are being satisfied with data pages already in the data cache. Using this and the similar graph for the procedure cache, you can tune the amount of server cache and the balance between data and procedure cache.

Data Cache (System 11 only)

This window displays the logical and physical reads for each cache configured in the server.

Device I/O

This window displays graphs and summary data for the number of disk accesses as well as the rate of disk access. This data can help you optimize the load balancing across the server devices. Note that this is another reason to name server devices after their physical disk partition names. As you watch the display of disk access rates for each server device you need to be able to tell which server devices are attached to which controller.

Network Activity (Systems 10 and 11 only)

This window displays information about packet sizes, packet traffic, and so forth.

Object Lock Status (Systems 10 and 11 only)

This window displays information about locks on tables, including a great level of detail on the types of locks held, the process holding the locks, and so forth.

Object Page I/O (Systems 10 and 11 only)

This window displays information about page I/O for a table in the server. Note that this is how SQL Monitor would be very useful for identifying the most accessed tables in the server. Also, this is a capability that sp_sysmon does not provide.

Performance Summary

This window shows you the overall performance of the entire SQL Server. Metrics include CPU use and transactions per second as well as network load, locking, and device I/O.

Performance Trends

You can look at this window for a continuous graph of the same performance measurements as the Performance Summary window.

Process Activity

Here you can isolate one or a series of server processes for monitoring, and watch the CPU usage and disk access rates for the chosen processes.

Process Detail

Here you can get more detail about a single server-process.

Process List

This window shows you the current server processes and status; it is very similar to the output of the **sp_who** server command.

Process Lock Activity

This window displays lock information for a specific server process.

Stored Procedure Activity

This window displays information about stored procedure executions and timings.

Transaction Activity

This window provides a bar chart showing a summary of all transaction rates by transaction type. You can use this to see what percentage of your transactions are being done as updates in place, for example.

OTHER BUILT-IN SQL SERVER PERFORMANCE TOOLS

There are several tools you can use to monitor and refine server performance that are built into the SQL Server.

A. **sp_monitor** is a stored procedure that will output the current status of various server performance parameters. Typical output for two successive executions is shown below. Note that for each parameter there are two numbers. The first number is the measure of the parameter since the server was last started. The second number in parentheses is the measure of the parameter since the last time **sp_monitor** was executed. By making runs of **sp_monitor** at regular intervals you can look at the change in a parameter over the interval and see the rate of change for the parameter. For example, you can take the data for total_write which measures the number of disk writes made by the server. Since the server was last started there have been 3,472,865 disk writes but we are more interested in the performance of the server recently. Looking at the second set of output we see 3,472,895(30) for total_write and note the value for seconds for the second set of output of 28 seconds. This tells you that in the last 28 seconds there have been 30 writes to disk by the server. This is very close to a server disk-write rate of 1 per second.

You can run this stored procedure as a `cron` job at some regular interval during the operating hours of the server. This data can be output to a disk file on the server machine and these files can be kept on disk for some period of time. When you run into a server performance problem you can look through these files and see what the server has been doing in the recent past. This data is also useful for simply monitoring server performance before there is any problem.

☙ Sybase DBA Companion

```
1> sp_monitor
2> go
```

last_run	current_run	seconds
Apr 1 1995 1:20PM	Apr 1 1995 1:21PM	35

cpu_busy	io_busy	idle
18489(0)-0%	74797(1)-2%	1707049(34)-97%

packets_received	packets_sent	packet_errors
740556(10)	1056871(10)	0(0)

total_read	total_write	total_errors	connections
2141401(2)	3472865(83)	0(0)	19377(1)

```
(return status = 0)
...
...
...
1> sp_monitor
2> go
```

last_run	current_run	seconds
Apr 1 1995 1:21PM	Apr 1 1995 1:22PM	28

cpu_busy	io_busy	idle
18491(2)-7%	74801(4)-14%	1707072(23)-82%

packets_received	packets_sent	packet_errors
740562(6)	1057195(324)	0(0)

total_read	total_write	total_errors	connections
2142628(1227)	3472895(30)	0(0)	19378(1)

```
(return status = 0)
```

B. You can execute **set showplan** before executing a stored procedure or SQL script or individual statement and the server will
display the query plan that it will use to satisfy the query or
queries. Note that **set showplan** doesn't display any activity
that would go on due to triggers on the table(s) that would be
activated by the queries you are executing. Further, as noted
above for indexes, examining the query plan for a stored procedure manually may not help you track down the performance
problems you are after. Recall that the query plan for a stored
procedure is created once when the stored procedure is first created and after that only when the stored procedure is recompiled.

You also need to remember that server locking can lead to blocking which will severely degrade server performance. The server
locks each page as it is accessed until the user accessing that page
is finished with it. You should know that if a query wants over
200 pages for update the server will simply escalate to a table
lock. The table lock can block lots of users on a big table. This is
yet another reason you must avoid queries that return lots of
data if you are going to be able to improve performance. Note
that for big tables 200 pages is not much, which means if you are
doing queries that do updates, you may be locking the whole
table each time they run. Queries that cause locking problems are
another performance problem you need to watch out for. You
need to keep in mind that escalating to a table lock will not be
displayed by **set showplan** so you won't detect this behavior
when you examine the query plan manually.

C. When you are trying to find a performance problem it can be
useful to examine the query plan without actually executing the
query. You can get this behavior by executing **set noexec** along
with **set showplan** before you execute the query.

D. Similarly, you can get the server to display the reads and
writes for the query, both those to cache and those to disk. You
get this behavior by executing **set statistics io on** or **set
statistics time on**. You can use both of these at the same
time.

APPLICATION TRANSPARENT SERVER TUNING

While much of the preceding discussion involved ways to identify changes that need to be made to the application and the resulting queries, there are things you can do to the SQL Server directly that can improve performance and require no changes to the application(s) at all. You must realize that these changes are not going to cure problems with the application(s), but you should be aware of them. You probably can't tell what the overall effect of any of these would be without trying them out. Only then can you tell if one of these changes would have a real impact versus the performance problems inherent in the application(s).

More Memory Is Good

Most server performance and tuning work attempts to reduce the amount of physical disk access that must go on to satisfy a query. The more parts of the database you can squeeze into cache in server machine memory, the better. For the database pages that represent these objects, whether they are data, indexes, triggers, or stored procedures, the more that are in memory, the more that simply won't require any physical disk I/O to access. You should try getting more server machine memory before trying much else.

Within the memory you have on the server machine, you will need to decide how to allocate it between data cache and procedure cache. Data cache is where the data pages are held while being read or changed. Procedure cache is where stored procedures are held. In both cases, the more times the server can find what it needs in memory (cache), the faster everything will go. The only way to really figure out the correct allocation for both kinds of cache is to use SQL Monitor and see how often the server finds what it needs in each cache (hit rate). You then alter the allocation by changing the percentage of SQL Server memory that will be allocated to procedure cache using **sp_configure** with the procedure cache option (20 percent is the default). The server will allocate all the memory needed for its own operation and then allocate 20 percent of the remaining memory to the procedure cache. This means you don't directly allocate the data cache; it gets whatever isn't allocated to the procedure cache.

All this simply means that you should get as much memory as possible and then, after the server is up and running, adjust the allocations for data and procedure cache.

Solid State Device

This simply takes the advice of having more memory to its logical conclusion. A Solid State Device (SSD) is simply a server device that is supported physically in RAM rather than on a physical disk partition. This makes all access to the database objects in the SSD very fast. Using what you learn from SQL Monitor, you can determine which server devices are most heavily accessed and move them to an SSD. Frequently you will find that *tempdb* is very heavily accessed as are the transaction logs of the most popular databases on the server. If it is pretty obvious that one or a few databases or database segments are being hit much harder than the rest, you may get a very significant increase in server performance by moving them to SSD.

File system Server Devices

As discussed in detail in Chapter 8, you don't want to assign server devices to file system files because the I/O is buffered and therefore you can't guarantee that the data is recoverable. For *tempdb* you don't ever try to recover the database so you can move it off to a file system server device and the buffered I/O will speed up access to *tempdb*. Often it is the transaction log of tempdb that benefits most from such a move. Note that you can try this and if it doesn't improve things, just revert to the way it was. Since *tempdb* is cleared out each time the server is restarted, you can move it around from one server device to another much more easily than a user database.

Mirroring

Mirroring of server devices and thereby databases, has been discussed in detail in Chapter 8, and is done primarily to prevent server downtime and enhance recoverability. From a performance and tuning point of view, if you have a situation where you are reading from a database a great deal, you may benefit from the fact that the server can read in parallel from both physical devices that make up the server device and the mirror.

More Server Devices Is Better

Many times the question comes up of why it is better or worse to have more or fewer server devices supported by any one physical disk. This translates into a question of how best to partition the physical disk. There are three reasons you want to use more partitions, not fewer. Two of them will benefit you in your performance and tuning efforts.

A. More partitions of a physical disk, with a server device assigned to each partition makes it more meaningful and therefore more useful to identify which server device is being used the most. You can determine which server device is most heavily used using SQL Monitor, but if you have only one huge server device assigned to all the space on the physical disk, that could mean any of the databases on the huge server device has a problem. Your ability to monitor, identify, and fix server performance problems is much better with more granular observations. You get more granular performance data as you have more server devices. Certainly this can be taken too far, but for Solaris you have only eight partitions maximum, with two of those unavailable for server devices (see Chapter 8). Using six partitions for six server devices is better than just one huge partition and server device.

B. Internally, the SQL Server maintains a queue of access requests for each server device. The fewer the number of server devices to handle all the server device access requests, the more that pile up waiting for each server device. More server devices helps to minimize any waiting that would go on due to these internal queues.

C. This relates more to preventing server downtime and enhancing server recovery, but that too is a form of improved server performance. When a physical disk goes bad usually only a piece of it does. The rest of the disk may be fine. The fewer partitions and server devices you have on a single physical disk, the more of your database that is lost for any single disk problem. If you have six server devices on six physical disk partitions and the disk develops a bad block in one partition, only the one server device is lost. With only one server device for the whole physical disk, all of the database(s) on that server device are lost even if only one block of the disk goes bad.

vdevno and SQL Server 4.9.2 and System 10 Performance

This is not relevant to SQL Server System 11. While the SQL Server maintains a queue for each server device, it also checks the list of server devices to see if an I/O request has been satisfied. The server checks this list in order of *vdevno*. If the server makes an I/O request of server device 10 (i.e., *vdevno* = 10) and then wants to check to see if that I/O request has been completed, the server has to first check server devices 0 through 9 first. If the server device in question were 1, this process would be faster. You can identify the server devices that support the most I/O activity and see which database segments are supported by those server devices. You could try shuffling the *vdevno* values so that the most heavily accessed server devices have the lowest possible values. But, in order to change the *vdevno* value of a server device you have to drop the server device and then do a new **disk init**. This also means dropping the server device that currently has the lower *vdevno* value as well as whatever database segments were supported on both the server devices.

You should realize that this sort of tuning is best done when first installing or rebuilding the server. The performance gains from this sort of change are not great and the work involved in shifting existing *vdevno* values around is considerable as is the risk that you won't get everything back quickly.

PREVENTING DOWNTIME

Preventing server downtime may not seem like a server performance issue to you, but it is. Your users will always want better server performance, but they say that assuming that the server is always available. You have the unpopular job of getting in the way by running **dbcc** checks, making database and transaction log dumps, mirroring server devices,

and so forth, to prevent downtime. You must remember that any downtime lowers the overall average server performance, and all the things you
do to prevent server downtime are just as important, if not more so, than
efforts that might improve performance, especially if those efforts involve
any risk of server downtime.

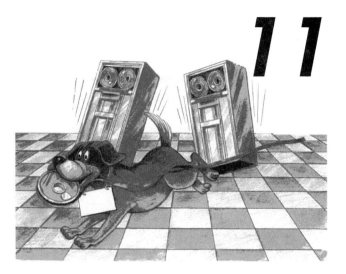

Capacity
Planning

Table of Topics

INTRODUCTION

The need for capacity planning is almost always overlooked. You guess how big a few of the databases on the server will be, get some vague comments from the application developers and order the machine. You will need more disk space before the machine hits your receiving dock. Often, if not every time, you will inherit the machine(s) and have had no input as to their initial configuration. At the same time, no matter how often you get stuck with the poor decisions of others, you invariably get a chance to change at least part of it.

It is the end of the business cycle. The server crashes. You need to replace the old worn-out disks and controllers. You need more disk space. You keep getting errors from the old disks. You know it's bad this time because the CIO has decided to watch you recover the server. He or she sits in your cubicle and pretends to take in interest in you as a human being. You get tense. The CIO, after exhausting their abilities at small talk, turns to you and says, "What do you need to prevent this in future?" That is the time to have a good answer. Be prepared to lay out the server the way it should be done (i.e., your way). You will get a chance. You just never know when that chance will come. Be prepared to tell the CIO what you need. At least be prepared to figure out what you need.

All too often the little capacity planning that is discussed is endless, detailed equations of how to figure out to the nearest Kb how big a table will be. You then order disks at 2 Gb each, and the table will probably grow exponentially anyway since you should be worrying only about the tables that support the business applications and your business should be growing or you have bigger things to worry about (i.e., where your next job will be) than any given table. You need to think about the capacity of your database system to support the business. This does not mean the size of individual tables or indexes. It means the capacity to support the applications, their backups, their development and test environments, and the ability to support maintenance of the whole system.

SQL Server Versions

All the material presented here applies to all versions of the SQL Server. Despite all the new features introduced in System 10 and System 11, the issues surrounding capacity planning have not really changed. Further, if you dwell on the specific features of any single SQL Server version, you are more likely to miss the really important parts of capacity planning. This material, although unchanged by new versions of the server, remains critical to the health of your database system. Far too much time is spent pursuing disk space after a server is in production. You can prevent this situation by planning ahead. This process is a lot less exciting than investigating the nature of multiple named caches, but it is much more important. You must have a server that can handle the databases before you can worry about performance tuning.

System 11 needs, and can make use of, more memory than previous versions of the SQL Server. You should plan on more server machine memory for a System 11 SQL Server than you did for a System 10 or 4.9.2 SQL Server.

The Overall Database System

You are used to thinking of the capacity of your server. As your server grows and other servers are added to your database system, you need to think of the capacity of the whole system. You can't support your business on one server on one machine any more. You will need to consider the ability of your database system to provide the following services to support your business. Note that you will need to move data between multiple servers all the time. You must ensure you can move files between the server machines that make up your database system. This may or may not require that all the server machines are made by the same vendor.

Primary OLTP Server

You will need a server to support the OLTP applications that support your business. This server needs to have the capacity to support all of the functions described in this chapter. This server should be configured to support a high rate of small transactions with a limited number of indexes on each table, and so forth. Access to this server should be very limited to prevent ad hoc user queries that can cause server performance to slow to a crawl.

Standby Server

Depending on the nature of your business you may need a standby server that you can fail over to in short period of time. How fast you need to fail over is dependent on the cost of downtime to your business. You also need to determine if such a standby system needs to support all the databases of the primary or just a subset of critical databases that would allow the most important business functions to continue until the primary is repaired. You may or may not need the same capacity on the standby server as on the primary OLTP server. A big factor in this is whether the standby server is required to replace the primary OLTP server for an indefinite period of time. If so, the standby server should be virtually identical to the primary OLTP server in terms of processor power, memory and disk space. Keeping the standby server in sync with the OLTP server is a labor-intensive process.

Decision-Support Server (DSS) or Report Server

One of the fundamental things you must do to improve and maintain the performance of the primary OLTP server is force all (absolutely all!) ad hoc or decision support queries to a separate server. This Decision Support Server (DSS) or reporting server must be kept in sync with the primary OLTP server. This can be done by loading database dumps from the primary server periodically. This method is fine as long as the lag time between the primary and DSS server is acceptable to the users of the DSS server. If you dump the databases on the primary every day, the DSS server will be behind the primary by a full day as it has no further updates between the daily database loads. Another method is to dump the transaction log of each of the databases on the primary and apply these transaction log dumps to the databases on the DSS server. This process will keep the DSS server up to date to within the interval between primary server database transaction log dumps. Note that either of these methods will require considerable disk space capacity on both the primary and DSS server machines. Further, these same techniques would be used to keep the standby server in sync with the primary OLTP server. The standby server will also require the same disk space capacity as the primary and DSS servers to support syncing the servers. Keeping the DSS server in sync with the OLTP server is a labor-intensive process.

Development Server

You must not allow the primary OLTP server in your database system to be used to support any form of application development or testing. You must provide a separate server dedicated to supporting the needs of application development. This server should have sufficient capacity to support copies of the databases that exist on the primary server. Certainly such a development server does not need the capacity of the primary for such things as mirroring or for storing database or transaction log dumps to ensure recoverability. Still, the development server must have sufficient disk capacity to support copies of however many of the primary server's databases are involved in the applications being developed. In general you should assume that all the databases on the primary server may need to be loaded on the development server. Also, the development server will need disk space to support moving large data sets into and out of the server, as well as any logical dumps that are very useful in the development environment since database objects change frequently as the application development process moves along.

Test Server

Depending on the nature of your database system and the complexity of the applications being developed you should consider another separate server to support application testing. This server should be of similar size to the development server. You would perform final acceptance testing of applications using copies of the primary databases on this server. Having the test server separate from the development server supports realistic performance testing of a given application without interference from development work going on for other applications. Further, application testing on a separate server will not delay development work.

DBCC Server

As the databases on the primary server grow and as your business expands across the country and around the world, you will not have time to perform much, if any, maintenance on the primary server. Your databases do not have to become very large before a complete **dbcc** run will take many hours to complete and you still should fix the errors uncovered by the **dbcc** run before making a database dump. Your business can't afford to be down long enough to allow all this activity to go on. You will need to setup yet another separate server to support **dbcc** runs. This server, the DBCC server, supports **dbcc** runs, loading old dumps, experiments like logical dump times, striping across multiple drives, and so forth.

Previous Release Server

As you upgrade the servers in your database system to the latest release you reach the point where all the servers are at the new release. You should still have a server at the previous release to retrieve data from dumps made previous to the upgrade. Depending on the nature of your business and the time between database dumps you may need a server at the previous release level for a year or more. Such a server does not have to be a large powerful machine and this server could even be installed on the DBCC server machine. Still, this server will need sufficient disk space to hold the largest database you might need to retrieve data from.

Replication Server

Replication Server will require a dedicated server machine of its own. You certainly can install the product on one of your other server machines, but the performance of the SQL server on that machine may suffer. You will also have an easier time maintaining your replication system if most or all of the components run on a dedicated server machine. Note that Replication Server requires a SQL Server database to hold information about other Replication Servers, subscriptions, and so on. Hence the machine dedicated to Replication Server will also be supporting a SQL Server to hold this database. You will need to consider the performance of this dedicated machine since Replication Server requires considerable CPU cycles to carry out its functions. Further, you will need to size the disk space for Replication Server to support storing transactions (stable queues) for whatever period of time your system requires. The longer you need to be able to operate while one of the nodes in your replication system is down, the more disk space you will need.

Support for the Database System

You will need to consider the support you will require for the database system. While this is often overlooked, it is vital. You can downsize to client-server all you want, but you will need support from various persons and/or organizations. Your database system will require support from tape operators for database and file system dumps, restores and archiving of tapes off-site. You will need sufficient SA support to install, repair and modify all the server machines in your system. You will need sufficient facilities to house, air condition, power and keep secure all of your server machines and their data. All these support considerations need to be compared against your business needs. All these support functions must have the capacity to support all the servers of your system for all the hours your business requires. This is a major capacity planning problem as your database system grows and your business grows to expect the system to be available at almost all hours.

THE INDIVIDUAL SERVER

For each of the SQL servers in your database system, you need to consider many factors that will require various amounts of capacity. Here we are primarily concerned with disk space since that is always in short supply. You are encouraged to waste your time arguing about the merits of various processor architectures (this is a joke!). You need to be more practical. There aren't that many high-end platforms that you are really going to consider for your mission-critical business applications. Further, benchmarks are well known to be virtually useless in determining the ability of any platform to support your applications in *your* environment. If you have all the other issues surrounding capacity planning for your system so completely figured out that which processor you are running is all that is left, you are way ahead of most of the world. We discuss various issues regarding disk space on a given individual SQL Server. Disk space will drive most, if not all of the practical capacity problems. If you find you are truly CPU bound, then you can consider changing platforms, but you will still need all the disk space you needed before.

The Databases

Knowing the sizes of your databases is the minimum step you should for your server. You should have a good idea of how big all the databases on your server need to be. If this is an existing server and you need to look at capacity planning for the future, you have the existing databases and some history of how fast they grow. If this is a new server installation, you need to know the most important applications the new server will support. The application developers should have some idea of how much space their products, require although their idea of a big business environment and yours may be shockingly different.

Number of Segments

This is where you probably tuned out when you did your capacity planning. You ordered enough disks to support the total size of all the databases and a little more and that was it. You need to think more about what you will be doing with the disk space (see Chapter 8, for more discussion of segments). If the applications need to have any user-defined segments, those segments need to be kept on server devices separate from the rest of the database for performance reasons. This means you need more server devices which means more disk partitions and that can mean more physical disks. You need to factor in how these database segments are going to be spread over the controllers also. For example, the server devices supporting the transaction log segment (*logsegment*) and the partitions supporting their mirrors should not be on physical disks that are connected to the same controller. You must have some idea of how large the segments of the database will be and how they need to be separated from each other over controllers. Also, you don't want to place more than one heavily accessed segment of any database on a given disk or, ideally, one controller. If you need to separate a segment for performance reasons, adding another heavily accessed segment to the same physical disk will just reduce the I/O throughput. You need to know which segments are most heavily accessed and when. At the same time you can't predict most of this very well. You need to be aware of segments as well as overall database space when laying out or expanding a server. Once you have some performance history, you can further expand your server's disk space to support segmentation refinements to further improve performance. Note that it may take considerably more disk space to support the existing and near-term growth of separated database segments than to support just the overall database size.

Mirrors

Mirroring will take a little or a lot of disk space depending on how much of the database you mirror (see Chapter 8 for details of the mechanics of mirroring). You should consider not only the recovery issues, but also your ability to maintain the mirroring of your server devices. You should consider mirroring all the database segments in your server if only to simplify the maintenance of the mirrors. If you only mirror a select set of server devices, you will constantly have to check that any space added to the databases is still mirrored, and so forth. Even if a database is static and could be recovered completely from previous database dumps, you should consider mirroring the database to ensure you server could continue operating through a disk failure.

Size of Physical Disks

Capacity planning involves the overall disk space needed for the current and future database needs. However, you must be careful when comparing the need for total disk space to the space available on the disks. In order to support segments and mirrors, you need to have separate slices of disk space. There are only a limited number of slices available on a physical disk. The maximum number of slices you can have on any one physical disk does not change with overall disk size. If you need 10 slices to support your server, you will need to get two physical disks. If you have 4.2-Gb disks, you may well have lots more overall disk space than you need in order to get the needed number of slices. This 'extra' space will then be doubled when you mirror all the server devices. You must remember this for both segments and mirroring when you do your capacity planning.

You must also educate whomever authorizes the purchase of disks. It is very logical to look at the total space needed, divide by the physical size of the disks available, and consider the matter closed. You must explain carefully that you need physical spindles and slices. You must have the needed spindles and slices to support the needed segments and mirrors.

Memory

The amount of memory you have installed in the server machine will directly impact the server performance. In general, you can't have too much memory. The amount of memory needed is equal to all the database objects you would like to have in cache (memory) at all times. You should have memory equal to the size of all the nonclustered indexes in the server. If the majority of the queries are covered (see Chapter 10) by these indexes, then all the data pages needed for the queries will be in cache which will greatly reduce the amount of physical disk I/O that must be performed. You also need memory for the procedure cache which will contain stored procedures. If at all possible, buy as much memory as the server machine will allow. Memory is one of the cheapest and fastest ways to improve server performance with no impact on existing applications or database structure.

You need to understand that System 11 needs more memory than previous versions of the SQL Server. System 11 needs more memory in general and can make use of more memory to support multiple named caches, large I/O buffer pools, and so on. For all these reasons, you should not rely on capacity planning efforts for System 10 or 4.9.2 Servers. You should plan on more memory for a System 11 Server installation.

File system Space

File system disk space is also often overlooked. You left that to the server machine SA person who assumes you need only enough file system space to support the server machine operating system and some swap space. You need to reconsider. You will need file system space to support all the SQL Server files and any other products you need on the server. The server files include all the files necessary to install the server as well as various optional files for character sets, and so on. When you upgrade from one server release to another you will need sufficient file system space to hold another set of installation files for the new release (see Chapter 13). You will need to keep all the files for the previous release until the upgrade is complete and you are convinced you don't need to regress. You will need duplicate sets of files any time you upgrade any of the related server products. Note that you must determine the actual space available on disk before you can perform any capacity planning. Depending on the specifics of your platform you may have 10 percent (depends on the platform) less disk space after formatting.

Dumping Databases to Disk

As part of your recovery plan, you will be dumping the databases in your server. You can dump them to tape, but you should consider dumping them to disk. Dumping them to disk is faster than tape which frees up the server and allows other server users to get their work done sooner. Dumping to disk allows you to capture all the database dumps to tape at once with a file system dump done at the server machine operating system level, see Chapter 9, "SQL Server Recovery". You may need to move database dumps from one server machine to another for various reasons. This means you may also need file system space for database dumps from other servers. Dumping databases to disk takes a great deal of disk space since you now need enough file system space to hold copies of all the databases you need to dump.

Transaction Log Dumps to Disk

Your server will need to dump the transaction log of various databases periodically (see Chapter 9) for details of this. Dumping the transaction log(s) to disk is a good idea since they will be done quicker than dumping to tape which means you can dump the transaction log more often and disturb the server users for briefer periods. You need to decide what your backup and recovery plan is. This plan will describe how often you dump the transaction log and how often you dump the databases to disk and to tape. You also need to know how long you need to keep the transaction log dumps on disk. You certainly need to keep all the transaction log dumps made since the last database dump, but you may also need to keep previous set in case the most recent database dump is not usable for some reason. You need to examine the size of the transaction log dumps for each of your databases throughout your business cycle (day, week, month, quarter, year) to decide how much file system space you need to hold all the transaction log dumps you need according to your recovery plan. The tape drives on your server machine are not perfect and will fail from time to time. You should plan additional file system space to hold the additional transaction log dumps that would pile up while you had a failed tape drive replaced. Also if your dumping of the transaction log is delayed for any reason you will have a very large transaction log dump when you resume dumping and your file system will need to have the free space to absorb the large dump file. Note that in the event of such a failure you could move the transaction log dumps to any other machine in your system but you still need to have such space available, even if only on a remote machine. Depending on your recovery plan and how you handle the process of making tape dumps, you may not have a tape operator on duty through weekends or holidays to change tapes. This is another case where you would need extra file system space for transaction log dumps.

Your server has been running normally for months with transaction log dumps being made to disk every hour during the business day. Suddenly the transaction log dumps grow quickly to twice and then three times their normal size. You will eventually find out that a new application was applied to the databases on your server. This new application has the interesting habit of dropping and creating any required stored procedures each and every time a user runs the application. This has resulted in a very large increase in the logged activity in the databases. The application developers didn't realize this because the part of their application that did this was an "off-the-shelf" module supplied by another division of your own company. You have been able to store a week's worth of transaction log dumps on the existing file system space but now can't keep even two days' worth before the file system is full. You have to change your recovery plan immediately. The point here is that a lack of disk space can cripple your operation very quickly, and it isn't just a lack of database space that you need to worry about.

Tuning

After the server is up and running you may, sooner or later, find you need to either add or change some of your indexes. This will need to be done as you try various experiments to tune the performance of your server. Consider that if you need to create a new clustered index on a table you will need to add disk space to the database equal to about 120 percent of the size of the table.

Your server runs a little slower all the time. An analysis reveals that for reasons best known to themselves the original database designers decided not to create a clustered index on one of the largest tables on the server. Over time the table and the other databases on the server have grown to fill almost all the space available. Now, to improve performance, you need to create the clustered index, but you don't have that kind of disk space available. You are now in the position of needing to add disks just to create the index—disks that will be empty after the new index is created since the process of creating a clustered index essentially builds a copy of all the data in the table in the new sort order and when that is complete drops the original set of data. As a side issue your server machine does not have any more room to accept more disk controllers or more disks. You start to think that capacity planning is important after all.

As part of your efforts to improve the performance of your server, you may need to build more indexes or drop and re-create others. Either way you will need to be able to add enough disk space to the database segment(s) that support these indexes before you can create new indexes. You should allow for this in your overall capacity planning because the space to perform these index creations is so large. Without this kind of capacity, you may not be able to do some fundamental performance tuning.

Moving Data Around

Your server may need to import and export data to and from other servers or systems. Frequently you will need to dump and load portions of the database to and from disk files. Whether these files originate on your server or not you need to have sufficient file System space to support whatever quantity of data you expect. If you need to import a 10-Mb file and store copies of this file for a week, you need to have 70 Mb of file system space for this data. You also need to understand the impact to your business of any failure during the process of moving this data through your database system. If the network is down for a day, do you need to store the same files for a longer period of time? If so, you would need to plan for more file system space.

Logical Dumps to Disk

You must plan on being able to retrieve objects or data from your database dumps. For various reasons you will need to do this without reloading a dump into an existing database on the server. If you need to retrieve 10 rows of a user table from a database dump made a month ago, you can't just load the dump into the existing database because that would wipe out all the database changes made in the last month. The database dumps that you make to tape or disk using SQL Server are physical dumps. They are a simple copy of everything in the database and the transaction log. When (note that we don't say "if") you need to retrieve an object from the database dump there is no way to do this directly. You must load the entire database somewhere on your server, or on another server in your system, and then retrieve the object from this database. Clearly this will require a lot of database disk space in order to be able to load a complete copy of your largest database. This process is also very slow and requires creating the database on the same or another server. The alternative to this is to make logical dumps of your databases. A logical dump means that the definition of each object is retrieved from the server and dumped to a file system file. This file can be used to rebuild the object(s) on the same or other servers. In fact, the logical dump of a database object is independent of the server version and hardware platforms since it is the Transact-SQL definition of the object. You need to plan enough file system space to support whatever logical dump plan you deem appropriate. Such a plan may call for a logical dump once a week or only when significant changes are made to the data or objects in a given database. The ability to make logical dumps is not supported by Sybase SQL Server. You need to install a third-party software product such as DataTools SQL BackTrack, (see Chapter 9 for details).

Interserver Needs

The servers in your database system may need to transfer large files between themselves. For example, you may keep a copy of a database on another server as a standby in case the primary database or server fails. One way to do this is to move the transaction log dumps of the primary database to the secondary server machine and apply the transaction log dumps to the database on the secondary server. This requires sufficient file system space on both server machines to store enough transaction log dumps to span the longest interval you expect to go between transfers between server machines. Note that for smaller databases you may perform this process by transferring a full database dump periodically rather than a set of transaction log dumps.

Server Machine Limitations

You need to think about the limitations of the server machine itself. You need to be aware of things like the CPU and memory of the server machine, but here we continue to focus on the disk space capacity of the server machine. This takes several forms. First, you need to know how many disk controllers the machine can accept. This number and the maximum number of physical disks that can be attached to each controller without causing an I/O bottleneck will tell you the maximum disk space you can ever have. Secondly, you need to consider the physical space where the server machine is installed. You will need more rack space to install more disks. If the existing rack(s) are full, you will need to add a new rack or racks to have room to install any new disks. Remember that just because the server machine will accept more disks doesn't mean you can put them in. You should consider this part of your capacity planning.

Replication Server

If you plan on installing Replication Server on your server, you need to take that into account in your capacity planning. Replication Server requires what is called a stable queue to store transactions while they are being moved from the primary database to the replicate database(s). This stable queue is assigned to one or more raw disk partitions similar to the way server disk devices are supported by physical disk raw partitions. You need to have an estimate of how large a stable queue you will need for your server. The size of stable queue you need is based on how long you estimate Replication Server needs to function while part of the replication system is unavailable (the network, for example). It is not unreasonable to need 1 Gb or more for a stable queue for production systems. Further, while the current release of Replication Server does not support mirroring of the stable queue, that feature may be available in soon to be released versions of the product. You should plan on having disk space equal to twice the size of the stable queue you require.

Server Machine Tape Drives

You need to think about the tape drives on your server machine. You may think this is a minor problem, but you may be wrong. If you are dumping multiple databases to tape, you need to think about how many of your databases will fit on one tape. If the total size of all the databases on the server that you need to dump to tape exceeds the capacity of your tape drive you will have to wait for the first tape to fill up, then eject and insert a second tape. This means considerably more time and more possible errors than a single tape dump would entail. Even if you plan on dumping your databases to disk and capture them all with a file system dump to tape done at the operating system level you should consider how much will fit on one tape. You pay a lot for somebody to be available to insert that second tape. Further, in a disaster station it is much easier to be able to make a dump on the fly if you need only one tape to do it.

Another factor to consider is the overall time it takes your server to make dumps to tape or disk. If your business runs around the clock, you will have a narrow window for daily database and file system dumps. If you can't make the complete dump within that window of time you will have to change your dump plan. The speed of your tape drives as well as their capacity are factors in your capacity planning.

REAL WORLD EXAMPLE— THE OVERALL DATABASE SYSTEM

The preceding discussion may seem unreasonably complex so we will consider a real-world example. The server described below is typical of a large production system. We discuss real world needs as they follow each of the descriptions in the previous sections. We first discuss the capacity planning required for the basic database system that supports one primary OLTP server. For each server in the database system we discuss the general operational needs of the server, the disk capacity needed, and the server machine performance requirements. We then discuss the capacity planning issues surrounding the primary OLTP server in detail in the next section.

Primary OLTP Server

The primary OLTP server supports the mission-critical applications that support your business. The OLTP server is where the majority of your day-to-day on-line processing occurs. It is the primary site of the data that represents your business. Your users are attached to this server to perform their business tasks. You must not allow users to perform anything but the OLTP that your business runs on. You must optimize the indexes on this server to support OLTP, that is, short, fast transactions that are quickly committed to minimize blocking and maximize throughput.

Your primary OLTP server is supporting 17 databases. The details of the disk space for this machine are discussed below. The total size of all the server devices set up for the server is 12 Gb, with 8 Gb actually assigned to databases at the moment. This leaves 4 Gb for growth of the existing databases. You may think that 4 Gb is a lot of free space. When you consider the number of segments of the largest databases and that each needs to grow on a server device connected to a separate controller the space free for each of those segments is only a portion of the total free space. Also, when the largest production database is 5 Gb and you are adding space to that database as needed in 100-Mb chunks, 4 Gb doesn't seem like very much at all. Further, all of the database segments are mirrored and one-quarter of the available physical disks are assigned to the operating system and to supporting file systems. The primary OLTP server has 16 2.4-Gb physical disks with 4 of these disks attached to one controller. Of the 4 disks attached to each controller, 1 disk is assigned to supporting file systems. This provides more controllers to spread the server devices over than a configuration where all the disks for file systems were assigned to one controller. Overall, after formatting, and so forth, the server machine has 32 Gb of disk space. Of that 32 Gb, 8 Gb (one-quarter) supports file systems, the largest being the directories that store transaction log dumps and database dumps. This leaves 24 Gb for the server itself with 12 Gb assigned to server devices and the other 12 Gb used for mirrors of all the server devices. Recall that you want to use a whole physical disk for server devices and a whole physical disk for the mirrors of those same physical devices.

The OLTP server machine needs the CPU, memory, network interfaces, and so forth, necessary to support the response time and number of concurrent users that your business applications require. Note that we focus on capacity planning of disk space in the following discussion. You need to assess the capacity of the server machine in other ways as well. You must estimate how many users will need to use the server at one time and use that to plan for sufficient memory to support that many user connections as well as the data and procedure cache needed to support the databases. Overall you need to know what kind of transaction rate is needed and if your server machine can supply the processing power needed to keep up.

Standby Server

The standby server and its server machine should have CPUs and memory identical to the primary machine. Note that the term "hot standby" is abused a lot. To really be a "hot standby," the server would have to be capable of detecting a failure on the primary and immediately switching over to the "hot standby" with virtually no interruption in service. This is hard to achieve. A standby machine will have to be capable of supporting the full business load for some period of time. If you require that the standby server support all your production applications for an indefinite period of time, you need to make this server machine as powerful as the primary. In any case the standby machine, however warm you think it is, will need the same amount of disk space as the primary since it will have a complete copy of all the production databases and should be mirrored just like the primary. The standby machine will be expected to support all production functions that the primary does and therefore should have the same file system space, and so forth, as the primary. You can reduce this to some extent, but the savings in hardware will be small compared to the complexity of switching over to the standby if it isn't set up similarly to the primary. Further, when you need to fail over to the standby, you really can't control how long you will need to stay on the standby. You must consider the trade-off between hardware for the standby now versus the cost to your business of depending on a slower standby machine for some period of time.

To support the business in the same way as the primary does the standby machine needs the same amount of disk space, that is, 32 Gb and it should be assigned to controllers in the same way as for the primary. The layout of the disks and controllers should be identical to that of the primary. You can then use the same scripts for creating server devices (**disk init**) and databases (**p_dbcreate**) on both machines which is a significant savings of time for you.

The standby server machine processing capacity needs will depend on how you intend to recover from a failure of the primary. If you plan on running on the standby only long enough to complete repairs on the primary, then the standby may not need to have the processing capacity of the primary. If you choose to have a less powerful standby machine then you need to make sure your users understand this. You will also need to be ready to repair the primary OLTP server quickly since your business will suffer as long as you are running on the standby. You should plan on having the same server machine performance capacity on the standby as you have on the primary. This means you can fail over to the standby and your business can function normally for the indefinite future while the primary is repaired.

Decision Support Server (DSS) or Report Server

The Decision Support Server (DSS) or report server should be able to support a full copy of all the production databases that are on the primary OLTP server. The DSS server should be used for all user queries that are not strictly OLTP. If you allow users to do anything but OLTP on your primary server you will suffer intolerable performance degradation. Worse, you won't have any way of curing the performance problems because you won't have any idea what is running on the server at any given time. Any one user could log in and start scanning all the tables on the server. The DSS server should have a very different set of indexes optimized for decision support queries. These indexes will be very different and there should be more of them than for the primary OLTP machine.

Since the DSS machine is not used to directly support the business transactions, you don't need to mirror every database segment. Further, if you have a failure on this server, you can re-create the database and reload from dumps from the primary OLTP server. Therefore you need only half the server disk space of the OLTP server, but you should still have the same file system capacity. You will need this capacity to support database and transaction log dumps to disk that you will need to apply to the DSS server to keep its databases in sync with the primary OLTP server. For this example, that means you need 20 Gb of disk space, with 8 Gb supporting file systems and 12 Gb assigned to server devices. Note that you always need to mirror the master device. The DSS server may not need the same layout of disks per controller as the OLTP or production standby servers do. You will save a great deal of time creating databases on the DSS server if you have the same number of physical disks supporting databases on both the DSS and OLTP servers. If you partition these disks on the DSS server, the same way as on the OLTP server you can simply dump the definition of a database on the OLTP server (using **p_dbcreate**), edit in the different server device names, and create the database on the DSS server (see Chapter 14 for a full discussion of this process).

The DSS server machine performance capacity you need is debatable. If your users require fast turnaround on their decision support queries you may need the same level of CPU capacity, and so forth, as you need for the primary server. Usually this is not the case as decision support users can wait longer for a response. Generally a longer response time is expected for these sorts of queries since you can't optimize server performance for queries you can't see ahead of time. You will probably be fine using a server machine with significantly less processing power than the primary OLTP server.

Development Server

The development server is for application development work. It needs to have sufficient disk capacity to support whatever development work your organization is supporting. Assuming that this development server is supporting development of applications that will eventually run on the OLTP server, you need the disk capacity to hold a complete copy of the databases currently on the OLTP server, allow for the growth of the existing databases on the OLTP, disk space for any and all versions of the software under development, and space for large data sets that are frequently needed from other sources to populate tables during development. If you have a separate test server as described in the next section, you should make sure that all final testing of applications is done on the test server. This will allow development work to move ahead while final testing is done in a separate controlled environment independent of the sometimes wild and uncontrollable environment that is necessary for application development to proceed.

Given all this, the development server should have 20 Gb of disk space, 8 Gb for file system space and 12 Gb for the databases. Note that you need to determine if you can support applications development for servers other than the OLTP server on this single development server machine. You are better off to have a single machine dedicated to the development server for each large OLTP server in your system. You don't want developers working on too many applications on the same server since they may block each other and can slow the server down substantially. Also, developers have a habit of crashing the server and often the server machine itself. You must keep all development work off the OLTP server and the OLTP server machine. The development server machine does not require the same number of disk controllers as the OLTP server. Again, you will save a great deal of time creating databases on the development server if you have the same number of physical disks supporting databases on both the development and OLTP servers. If you partition these disks on the development server the same way as on the OLTP server, you can simply dump the definition of a database on the OLTP server (using

p_dbcreate), edit in the different server device names, and create the database on the development server.

The required performance of the development server machine is again debatable. You need to run the applications at a reasonable rate to assess performance of the queries that make up the application, but supplying too much server machine performance can actually fool the developers into thinking the application doesn't need tuning. Generally the development server machine will be a machine that is not the latest technology; rather it will be a machine that was new a few years ago and becomes a development server machine after being replaced by the latest OLTP server machine.

Test Server

The test server is similar to the development server but even less controlled. Your database system may not require a separate test server. You need to assess the development process that you are supporting. Frequently there is a need to quickly prototype an application or modify an existing application and such efforts need to go on as quickly as possible. This work should be done on the development server. Once the application is ready to roll out to the production system, it should move to the test server where it can be run against a current copy of the data on the OLTP server. This provides a final test environment that is isolated from other development activities. With a separate test server, you can test one application while development continues on other applications on the development server.

The disk space requirements of the test server are the same as for the development server since you will need to support a copy of all the databases on the OLTP server and have room for database and transaction log dumps from the OLTP server to keep the data on the test server up to date. For our example database system, the test server would need 20 Gb of disk space, 8 Gb for file system space and 12 Gb for database space. As with the development server, you will save a great deal of time creating databases on the test server if you have the same number of physical disks supporting databases on both the test and OLTP servers. If you partition these disks on the test server the same way as on the OLTP server, you can simply dump the definition of a database on the OLTP server (using **p_dbcreate**), edit in the different server device names and create the database on the test server.

As with the development server machine, the performance required for the test server machine does not have to be incredible.

DBCC Server

For a database system that supports even one large database, you will need a dedicated DBCC server. In an ideal world you would have sufficient downtime whenever you needed it to run a full set of database consistency checks (**dbcc**) on each database before you make each database dump. As database size grows, the time it takes to make a **dbcc** run and the database dump grows as well. Soon your business can't afford to have the system off-line for the hours that it would take to run **dbcc**s before each dump, let alone to run **dbcc**s again to fix any corruptions found in the database (see Chapter 9 for more discussion of these factors). At that point you need a server where you can load the database dumps of your production databases and run the full **dbcc** set without interfering with your business. A DBCC server is also a good place to load older database dumps when you need to retrieve data or database object information that has been lost from the production system. Note that Sybase SQL Server does not support dumping or recovering anything smaller than the entire database. For a large database this can be a real problem and a DBCC server is a good place to retrieve such information. Further, the very act of loading a database into the DBCC server can serve another function within your recovery plan. If you load the database from a database dump made to tape, you are verifying that the dump tape is good.

The DBCC server will need enough disk space to support all of the databases on the OLTP server and any other databases that are large enough to require **dbcc** runs on a separate machine. For our example, the DBCC server needs 20 Gb of disk space with 8 Gb for file system space and 12 Gb for database space. As mentioned previously, you will save a great deal of time creating databases on the DBCC server if you have the same number of physical disks supporting databases on both the maintenance and OLTP servers. If you partition these disks on the DBCC server the same way as on the OLTP server, you can simply dump the definition of a database on the OLTP server (using **p_dbcreate**), edit in the different server device names, and create the database on the DBCC server.

The performance of the DBCC server machine can be significantly less than the other server machines discussed so far. Simply running **dbcc** runs over and over does not require large amounts of processing power.

You need to have a dedicated server machine for this server so the **dbcc** runs don't interfere with other server work. You don't need a very fast server machine for this work.

Previous Release Server

As your database system moves along, you will upgrade the servers from one release to the next. While most releases are backward compatible, you need to be aware of the fact that not all of them are. Clearly the relevant example is that of upgrading from Sybase SQL Server 4.9.2 to System 11. All of your database dumps made while running 4.9.2 are no longer usable with System 11. You can't recover any data from the 4.9.2 dumps without maintaining a server at the 4.9.2 level. You should be ready to maintain a server at the previous release level whenever you consider upgrading the servers in your database system. Always verify that the upgrade will work with the pre-upgrade dumps that you have (see Chapter 13).

A previous release server would need only enough disk capacity to support the largest database dump you think you might need to recover from before the System 10 upgrade. For our example the largest database is 5 Gb so the previous release server should have 10 Gb of disk space to support this database and the file systems needed to support a 4.9.2 SQL Server. Note that you may be able to run this server on one of the other server machines in your system, specifically the maintenance server.

The performance of the server machine to support a previous release version of the server is not an issue. This server is only for loading database dumps and retrieving data.

Replication Server

If your database system is going to include the use of Replication Server you need to consider the capacity planning issues regarding the product. You aren't going to find any accurate performance information about Replication Server because it depends too much on your individual servers, the transaction load on those servers, how much of that load is being replicated, and network load as well as the performance of each server machine involved in the Replication Server system. You should consider a dedicated server machine to support Replication Server and the associated SQL Server that it requires.

The disk space needed for the Replication Server machine depends entirely on the number and size of the stable devices you need to store all the transactions that Replication Server needs to store during the replication process. There are many factors that go into determining the size of the stable devices required, but for our example you can assume that the Replication Server machine needs 10 Gb of disk space with 4 Gb for file system space and 6 Gb for the stable devices. Note also that if you are using Replication Server in your database system, you should plan on supporting at least one and perhaps two development Replication Servers. You need a development Replication Server environment to test the process of creating subscriptions, the time it takes for subscriptions to materialize for large tables and how to recover from the crash of any of the components of Replication Server. You would have to add more disk space to support the Replication Server development environment on the development server machines involved.

The performance required for the Replication Server machine will depend on the amount of data that is being replicated and how fast your users need to see each transaction replicated. There are many variables in predicting the performance of Replication Server and the only true measure is to install it on a machine and let it run your applications.

REAL WORLD EXAMPLE— THE INDIVIDUAL SERVER

We now discuss the various factors that you must consider when estimating the disk space capacity required by the primary OLTP server in your database system. Since the disk capacity required for each of the other server machines depends on the capacity required of the OLTP server this detailed estimation for the OLTP server is required.

The Databases

You must determine the size of each database that your OLTP server will support, or for an existing server is supporting. In either case you need to estimate how much each database will grow in the future. You may think that some historical data will be helpful but often your databases are growing exponentially so looking at past growth may hurt more than it helps. You need to decide how long you want your current configuration to be adequate, say a year for example. You must determine what disk capacity will be required to support each database for the next year. In our example we have a total of 8-Gb database space presently and we have 12 Gb of overall database space. This allows for 50 percent growth, although, as we have discussed, placing segments on separate devices, and so forth, will reduce the effective capacity. Note that if we look at the history of the largest database over the last year, we observe that it was around 2.5 Gb a year ago while the current size is 5 Gb. It has doubled in size and the business has been growing at an even faster rate this year compared to last. You will have a hard time predicting what the size of this database will be in a year.

Number of Segments

You need to consider how many segments your most important database requires. For our example the most important databases are the three largest ones. Consider the largest first. It needs *default system* segments as well as a *logsegment*, a nonclustered index (*ncindexes*) and a *data* segment for several of the largest tables. These separate segments were created to improve performance. Therefore you need to place each of them on a different controller. This means you need four controllers. For the OLTP server machine in our example we have 16 physical disks, and as discussed in Chapter 8, we allow only 4 physical disks per controller, a value which may vary depending on the hardware platform your server is running on. The OLTP server machine has four controllers. You also need to consider the needs of the two other critical databases. Each of them has *default/system* segments, *logsegment* and a nonclustered index segment (*ncindexes*). For each database, these segments should be placed on disks attached to different controllers. Unless you are going to install a disk controller for each segment of every database on the server, you need to balance the load over the controllers you have. You need to place the segments of different databases on the controllers you have to minimize contention for the disk controller. By placing each segment of the most important database on a separate controller, you have optimized the disk I/O for that database, but be aware that you will be placing segments of other databases on those same controllers.

Note that you must be aware of two different and competing capacity requirements. First, one database needs some number of segments, each of which should be on different controllers. Second, each database requires some number of segments but your server machine has only so many controllers. At some point, segments from different databases will compete for disk I/O with segments of other databases. You need to balance the two requirements and monitor the disk I/O over time to see if the load balancing is being maintained.

Mirrors

You need to determine you mirroring plan. As we have discussed previously, the simplest plan to set up and to maintain is to mirror all segments of every database and to assign whole physical disks to either server devices or their mirrors. You need to assess the needs of your business and the time it will take you to maintain the mirrors. If you decide to mirror only selected devices of selected databases you must be prepared to check frequently to prevent database space being added to a segment in such a way that the segment is no longer fully mirrored. Note that we said "mirror only selected devices" because you can only mirror a server device; you can't mirror a segment without mirroring all the devices that support that segment. For our example we need to mirror all the segments of all the databases so we need to same amount of disk space for mirroring that we need for the database space itself namely 12 Gb (see Chapter 8).

Memory

As described earlier, the more memory the better. At a minimum you should determine the maximum amount the server machine can accommodate and trade that cost against the cost to the business of slower server performance. Install no less than 128 Mb and preferably 500 Mb. Memory only looks expensive until compared with the cost of server performance and the personnel resources to perform server tuning.

Within the memory you have on the server machine, you will need to decide how to allocate it between data cache and procedure cache. Data cache is where the data pages are held while being read or changed. Procedure cache is where stored procedures are held. In both cases the more times the server can find what it needs in memory (cache) the faster everything will go. The only way to really figure out the correct allocation for both kinds of cache is to use SQL Monitor and see how often the server finds what it needs in each cache (hit rate). You then alter the allocation by changing the percentage of SQL Server memory that will be allocated to procedure cache using `sp_configure` with the procedure cache option (20 percent is the default). The server will allocate all the memory needed for its own operation and then allocate 20 percent of the remaining memory to the procedure cache. This means you don't directly allocate the data cache; it gets whatever isn't allocated to the procedure cache.

File System Space

While the database space allowed for previously may be sufficient for the current size of the databases, you may need additional space for tuning the server. When you need to improve server performance, one of the factors to consider is the indexes on tables in each database. In order to create new indexes, or any index if none was created initially, you need more database space. Creating a clustered index is very costly in terms of space. You will need about 150 percent of the table size for creating a clustered index. For our example server the largest table is roughly 800 Mb so you would need to plan sufficient disk space capacity for the index segment of the database to allow for 1.2 Gb of additional database space. You need to recognize that this disk space needs to be available to the index segment of the database which means it has to be located on the devices supporting the index segment of the database. The additional space for building the new index needs to be on the index segment of the database or else the completed index won't be on the index segment. The index segment was created to isolate the indexes to one controller for improved performance. Note that while the database space used to create a clustered index is free after the index is built, you can't shrink the database back down without the considerable effort of rebuilding the database. Further you may well need to build a different clustered index at some later time so the space may be needed again in future.

A third-party application is installed in a great hurry. No one bothers you with it because that would take time. It turns out the application was written a long time ago for another platform and was ported-again in a great hurry. Things run for a while and then performance drops through the floor. Suddenly they have time to hunt you down. You look at the tables and discover there isn't a single index on the tables the application is using. Clearly it is time to create some indexes, but that will take a lot of space, space the server doesn't have. You now need to add disks just to have room to create new indexes, with the clustered indexes taking the most space.

Dumping Databases to Disk

The amount of file system disk space you will need is larger than you like to think. Here we consider the file system space that is not called out in the following sections. This includes disk space for the operating system software, swap space (discuss this with your server machine SA to determine required space), all the files needed to install and maintain the SQL Server, and all other products that you may need to run on the server machine and all the files needed to upgrade the server, server machine, or any of the other products running on the machine. A good rule of thumb is to assign one-quarter of all the physical disks on the server machine to file system space. You will need this much file system space for various uses. You need to increase the amount of file system space to allow for the following specific items that require large amounts of space.

Transaction Log Dumps to Disk

You need to plan ahead if you are going to dump the large databases on your server to disk. You can dump the smaller ones to the file system space you examined above, but for the largest databases you need to specifically plan for enough file system capacity. For our example the largest three databases on the server are 5 Gb, 2 Gb, and 1 Gb in size for a total of 8 Gb. In order to dump each of these to disk, you will need 8 Gb of file system space. Note that these 8 Gb need to be dedicated to database dumps and should not be used for anything else. If you allow other files to occupy any of this space, the database dumps may not succeed.

For System 10, database dumps are made through the Backup Server. This allows you to dump to multiple disk files or tape drives. This can reduce the time it takes to dump a database dramatically. For tape drives or disk files that are in file systems on physical disks that are attached to separate controllers, you can reduce the dump time by the number of disk files or tape drives you are using. Hence you can dump a database to four tape drives or disk files in one-fourth the time of the same dump made to a single tape drive or disk file. Note that this means you need to plan the number of disk file systems or tape drives and their location over the available controllers.

Tuning

You need to allow for dumping the transaction log of your most important databases throughout your database dump cycle. If you dump the databases once per day, you should be dumping the transaction log throughout each day. You need to determine how long you need to retain the transaction logs on disk and make an educated guess as to the average size of the transaction log dump files. Using all this, you can come up with the file system capacity needed. You should take into account the business cycle your business goes through. Make sure you are allowing for the periods of peak activity. For our example server an entire physical disk is dedicated to storing the transaction log dumps for just the largest database. During periods of low business activity this is plenty of room. However, at the end of the business cycle there is only room for three days of transaction log dumps. For our example server we would prefer to be able to store a full week's worth of transaction log dumps.

Moving Data Around

You will need more file system space for storing data that is going to or being received from the outside world. Frequently the databases on your server will need to import or export data to other systems. For example, you may be receiving customer data from an outside vendor each night. You must know about this activity on your server and supply sufficient capacity to store any such data for the required duration. Depending on the nature of your business, data files like this can be very large or may need to be retained for a long period of time. Both factors can lead to a need for large amounts of file system space.

Logical Dumps to Disk

Along with your normal database dumps, you must consider the need to make logical dumps. A logical dump of a database allows you to retrieve individual data or objects (see Chapter 9, for more discussion of logical dumps). If you are planning to make logical dumps of your database, you should plan on sufficient file system space to store the latest logical dump of each database. You will need to determine which databases justify a logical dump being stored on disk and for how long. Typically a logical dump will occupy significantly less disk space than the actual database because a logical dump does not capture any of the index structure of the database, only the index definitions. For our example server we only need to store the latest logical dump and we need to have logical dumps of all the databases on the server. Using a factor of 50 percent to estimate the space required for a logical dump of the databases on our example server, we need to plan on having 6 Gb of file system space for the logical database dumps of all our databases (12 Gb total database space × 50%).

Interserver Needs

You need to consider additional file system space to allow for interserver file transfers. You may need to dump a database on one server and move it to another server in your system or outside. Any server in your system that needs to move dumps or other files to another server will need space to store the files. Note that this is different from the need for storing data that is being imported or exported. Here we refer to dump or data files that are being moved between servers. You need to examine the way your database system functions to determine if you need file system space to support such transfers. For example, the DBCC server will need file system space to allow database dumps from other servers (principally the primary OLTP server) to be copied to the DBCC server where they are stored until needed for **dbcc** runs. In the discussion of the DBCC server we allowed 20 Gb of disk space, 12 Gb for databases and 8 Gb for file system space. This is sufficient if we are going to load the database dumps into the DBCC server from tapes. If you need to automate the process, you need to be able to copy the database dumps you need from their home server to the DBCC server. For our example server, the largest database is 5 Gb so the DBCC server would need to have 5 Gb of file system space to store a copy of the dump. You need to determine if the existing file system capacity of 8 Gb is sufficient to support a 5-Gb database dump file and all the other needs of the DBCC server.

Server Machine Limitations

We have been discussing server machine disk space as if we can add disks without limit. You must determine how many controllers can be physically installed in each server machine in your database system. With the maximum number of disks per controller, you have the upper limit on how much disk space you can install on each machine. As you reach the upper limit on disk space, you will have to decide whether to replace the server machine or offload some of its disk space to another server. Further, this applies not only to the physical limitations of any one server machine but the area where the machines are installed as well. You must have sufficient rack space to install more disks, as well as the power and air conditioning to support all these devices.

Replication Server

For our example server, Replication Server would be running on a dedicated machine and would not impact the disk space capacity planning of the primary OLTP server machine.

Server Machine Tape Drives

You need to examine your database system to ensure you can move data tapes between server machines. You may need to move database dump tapes to load a database on the reporting server or on the DBCC server. In either case you must be sure the tape dump made on one server machine is readable by the tape drive on the other server machine. Note that this doesn't just mean the tape drives are from the same vendor or have the same capacity. The device file used to dump to a tape drive will affect the amount of compression used during the dump. If the other tape drive does not support that level of compression using the same compression techniques the tape may not be readable. You must experiment to be sure you can move tapes between server machines.

You also need to look at the capacity of the tape drives on each server machine relative to the databases you will need to dump to tape. As the databases grow you will approach the capacity of the tape drive. You can put each database dump on a separate tape but this takes lots of operator time and lots of tapes. If you are dumping multiple database dumps to a single tape [this is not supported for 4.9.2 SQL Server, but can be done (see Chapter 14)] or if you are dumping databases to file system disk files and then dumping the file system to tape you will eventually fill the entire tape. Now the operators need to load a second tape, and so forth. You need to be planning for tape operator capacity as well if you are going to be able to support multitape dumps.

Summary

In summary, we have a primary OLTP server that supports databases that occupy a total of 8 Gb of disk space. However, to support the OLTP users, the DSS users, the need for a standby server, a DBCC server, and a development and test environment you now need to have six servers running on six separate server machines (assuming the previous release server runs on one of these six machines as well) and you will need a seventh server machine to support Replication Server. Overall, you are now in need of 164 gigabytes of disk space. You need to plan for this kind of growth and get used to the idea that you need hundreds of Gb of disk space. Keep in mind that you now have many things growing in parallel. If one of the databases grows by 1 Gb, the file system space for the database dump on this server machine has to grow by the same amount as does the room on the dump tape. The size of the transaction log dumps may grow as well. Any server machines where the database disk dump file will be copied have to grow also. And so on.

Also you should think about the number of people who will be required to install, support, and upgrade all this equipment. You alone can't handle all these tasks. Even if you do support all these functions for your current database system, consider what is coming as your business grows.

Note that the example OLTP server discussed would need to have 48 Gb of disk space to accommodate all the possible needs. However the server machine has only a maximum of 32 Gb of disk space physically available. This example is taken from real-world systems and points out how you have to change your outlook to be ready for the demands of your overall database system. The OLTP server machine was considered huge when it was installed only a few years ago and it was purchased with all the disks it could handle. Now the machine can't physically accept any more disk drives. The machine will have to be replaced just to add the disk capacity that the server already needs. Note that until the server machine is replaced, it simply can't support all the activities that are desired. Dumping databases to disk, for example simply can't be done. This means you as DBA, must continue physically moving database dump tapes between machines until the server machine is replaced.

CAPACITY PLANNING FOR THE DATABASE SYSTEM

We have been discussing the capacity planning process for each of the servers in the system. You also need to plan for adding servers. As the needs of your business grow so will the databases on your servers. At some point you will need to move some of the data off of one server and set up another server. Frequently you will set up a server for each major application group as each one becomes large enough to require a separate server and machine. Often you will want to move the databases to be located nearer the users of that data, and politics will play a big role in deciding which database lives on which server and where the server is located geographically. You need to be aware of this process and be planning how you will handle the movement of these databases to other locations. Note that each location will then need all the capacity that we have discussed here as far as server, machines, disk space, physical environment and support personnel.

Operational Details of SQL Server

> ❧ **Reading the Errorlog**
> ❧ **Impacts of Creating New Database**
> ❧ **Modifying System Tables Manually**
> ❧ bcp **Command**
> ❧ **Free Space in a Database**
> ❧ **Full Transaction Log or Other Segment (1105 Error)**

INTRODUCTION

There are many aspects of the operation and use of SQL Server that you need to understand. We discuss several of them because they come up often while you are performing your DBA duties.

SQL SERVER VERSIONS

SQL Server 4.9.2

SQL Server 4.9.2 does not report the free space in each segment as part of the output of **sp_helpdb** or **sp_helpsegment**, nor does it support thresholds. Since the 4.9.2 version of the server runs on both SunOS and Solaris, both forms of interfaces file are supported. The 4.9.2 version does not report the free space in each segment in the output of **sp_helpdb** or **sp_helpsegment**.

SQL Server System 10

The System 10 Version of SQL Server runs on both SunOS and Solaris, so both forms of the interfaces file are supported. The System 10 Version does not report the free space in each segment in the output of **sp_helpdb** or **sp_helpsegment**. When upgrading from 4.9.2, you must manually activate the last-chance threshold in each database. The Sybase SQL Server *System Administration Guide* for System 10 documents this process the threshold chapter.

SQL Server System 11

Since System 11 runs only on Solaris, the interfaces file must be in the Solaris format. When upgrading from 4.9.2 (or from System 10 if that was upgraded from 4.9.2), you must manually activate the last-chance threshold in each database. The *Sybase SQL Server System Administration Guide* for System 11does not document this process under the threshold chapter.

THRESHOLDS

Thresholds monitor the free space in each segment of each database and when the free space falls below the specified number of pages, the threshold will execute the associated threshold stored procedure. You must create and assign the stored procedure that will be fired when each threshold is crossed. Note that there is no "default" or supplied threshold procedure. While you will immediately think of using this new feature on the transaction log (*logsegment*), you should consider using them for the other segments of your databases as well. When a threshold is crossed, the associated stored procedure is executed and any **print** or **raiserror** statement(s) will send messages to the SQL Server errorlog.

There are two types of thresholds. The first is the type that you create by specifying what database and segment the threshold applies to, the threshold itself as the number of remaining free pages, and the name of the stored procedure to be executed when the threshold is crossed. The second type is called the "last-chance" threshold and refers to only the transaction log (*logsegment*) of each database. This threshold will ensure that there is always enough free space left in the transaction log to allow a **dump transaction** command to be executed. This last-chance threshold is automatically set up when you create a database, and the *logsegment* is on a separate server device from the rest of the database. Further, the point at which this threshold is activated (i.e., the number of free pages remaining in the transaction log) is automatically adjusted each time you add space to the transaction log. When the free space in the transaction log falls below the level of the last-chance threshold, it executes the stored procedure **sp_thresholdaction**. Note that by default every last-chance threshold fires the stored procedure called **sp_thresholdaction** unless you modify this behavior for a database using **sp_modifythreshold** to specify a different stored procedure. Note also that this stored procedure is not supplied and if you don't create **sp_thresholdaction** in the database, nothing will happen when the last-chance threshold is crossed. Typically you create a stored procedure (call it **sp_thresholdaction**, create it in the *sybsystemprocs* database and then all the last-chance thresholds in the server will use it) that contains a **dump transaction** or other commands and a **print** or **raiserror** statement and that will cause the associated message(s) to be printed to the server errorlog.

You must realize that there is a vital part of the threshold story that can easily go unnoticed. While the last-chance threshold is automatically created for any database that is created under System 10 or System 11, this does not apply to any databases that were upgraded to System 10 or System 11. This means that after the upgrade from 4.9.2 to System 10 or System 11 (see Chapter 13), the databases in the server will not have a last-chance threshold. You have to execute the following command in each such database to create the last-chance threshold:

```
select lct_admin ("lastchance", db_id())
```

You need to check each of your databases to see if the last-chance threshold is active. In the example below, we examine a database in a System 11 SQL Server.

```
1> use psychodb
2> go
1> sp_helpthreshold
2> go
segment name        free pages      last chance?        threshold procedure
 logsegment            744               1                 sp_thresholdaction

(1 row affected, return status = 0)
```

We see that there is a threshold for this database and that the threshold is a last-chance threshold. Now, we examine another database in the same server.

```
1> use psychodb2
2> go
1> sp_helpthreshold
2> go
segment name        free pages      last chance?        threshold procedure

(0 rows affected, return status = 0)
```

482

This tells us that the second database doesn't have any thresholds at all. How can this be? It turns out that this System 11 Server was installed and all the databases were loaded from a System 10 SQL Server. System 10 supported thresholds so there should have been thresholds in these databases before they were dumped and loaded. But, it also turns out that the System 10 SQL Server was a 4.9.2 SQL Server that was upgraded. The thresholds were never added to the database and nothing in the upgrade process flags this condition. You have to check for yourself.

Now we need to create or enable the last-chance threshold for this database. The server command to do this is

select lct_admin("lastchance", db_id)

where *db_id* is the database **id** number of the database where you are activating the last-chance threshold. Note that you can use the dbid of a database other than the one you intended and you may still get a nonzero result. You must check before and after you execute this command to be sure you activated the last-chance threshold in the database you intended. In this case, the database db_id = 9, and the result of the command is the value 1232 which is number of free pages at which the last-chance threshold will fire. You need to understand that this value will vary with the size of the database.

```
1> select lct_admin("lastchance", 9)
2> go
_____

      1232

(1 row affected)
1> sp_helpthreshold
2> go
segment name        free pages        last chance?        threshold procedure
  logsegment            1232                1                 sp_thresholdaction

(1 row affected, return status = 0)
```

This shows that the *logsegment* of the database now has a threshold and that this is a last-chance threshold. You can also check to see if there are any thresholds on a particular segment using the server command

```
sp_helpthreshold <segmentname>

1> sp_helpthreshold logsegment
2> go
```

483

segment name	free pages	last chance?	threshold procedure
logsegment	1232	1	sp_thresholdaction

```
(1 row affected, return status = 0)
```

You must also watch for a result of 0, as in the following example:

```
1> select lct_admin("lastchance", 13)
2> go
--------
      0
```

```
(1 row affected)
```

This means something is wrong. You need to see if the database with db_id=13 was really the database you had in mind. This result can happen when you execute this command for a database that does not have the transaction log on a separate server device. Recall that you can't have a last-chance threshold if the transaction log is not on a separate server device. You need to understand an implication of this fact. If you have a database that does not have the log on a separate server device and you then move the log to a separate device, you need to check that the database does indeed have a last-chance threshold, and activate it if there isn't one.

All of this should convince you that while thresholds are very useful, there are several situations where they may not get set up for you. You must not assume that because thresholds are supported in System 11 that all databases have a last-chance threshold. You must check for yourself before you depend on the last-chance threshold. You can still experience 1105 errors even though you think your databases have a last-chance threshold.

When a last-chance threshold is triggered, the server will, by default, suspend all the user activity in the server for that database that needs to write to the log. This means users can still access data, but they can't insert, update or delete anything. Note that this suspension is only for the database where the transaction log has nearly filled up. Users that are affected by this will be shown in the output of **sp_who** with a status of suspended. If a user tries to change anything, that user process is suspended. The server is waiting for more space to become available in the transaction log. If the associated threshold stored procedure executes normally and dumps the transaction log, then there should be more free space and the server will resume all user activity. If the threshold stored procedure does not fire or the transaction dump does not free up any space, the users will remain suspended. At this point, you have to clear the transaction log and that should unsuspend the users.

If, for whatever reason, you can't get the server to unsuspend the suspended users, you can do it manually. You do this with the server command

```
select lct_admin("unsuspend",db_id )
```

You shouldn't be using this command often, if at all. You also need to realize what the use of this command will do. User processes were suspended because at least one user process had almost filled the transaction log. When you unsuspend the user processes for the database, those processes will resume processing. At least one of these processes will now continue to fill the log. The last-chance threshold doesn't fire until there is very little free space left in the transaction log. This means you will have very little time before at least one user process does completely fill the transaction log. At this point, you will be dealing with 1105 errors for the database.

You can modify this default behavior so that the server will abort all user processes in the database when the last-chance threshold is reached. You do this with the server command

```
sp_dboption <databasename>, "abort tran log on log full", true
```

You should consider use of this carefully. Your business may not want critical transactions aborted for lack of transaction log space. If one user is causing the transaction log to fill, you may be able to kill that user and let other suspended processes complete. If you use the "abort tran log on log full" option, then, as soon as the transaction log is filled by any user, all users are aborted.

You can use thresholds to reduce the number of transaction log dumps that you make for a production database. If you are currently dumping the transaction log every 15 minutes for example, you can change this process to use thresholds. If, for example, you set up the last-chance threshold to dump the transaction log only when it is nearly full, you may reduce the number of transaction log dumps that are generated during a business day. If you ever need to recover the database, the recovery process will be simpler if there are fewer transaction logs to find and load.

The *Sybase SQL Server System Administration Guide* has two example threshold stored procedures. Both of these dump the transaction log. Either one would be appropriate for use as the sp_thresholdaction stored procedure. This is the stored procedure the server will use, by default, when the last-chance threshold is crossed. There are more details regarding the operation and use of thresholds that you can find in the *Sybase SQL Server System Administration Guide*.

INTERFACES FILE

The interfaces file is very important to the operation of the SQL Server and related products. Basically the interfaces file is a list of all the SQL Servers, Open Servers and related products such as the components of Replication Server and Backup Server. This list documents the names of all these servers and the server machine name and port number where they run.

For the purposes of this discussion, we examine the interfaces file in the SunOS format. This format is much easier to follow since the machine name and port number are shown explicitly for each entry. Sybase SQL Server System 11 is not supported on the SunOS operating system and therefore would have interfaces files in the Solaris format. (See Converting SunOS Interfaces File to Solaris in the next section for examples of both formats and how to convert between them).

For each server in the interfaces file, you will find one or more lines that begin with "master" or "query" or "console" (there are a few other possibilities, but they are rare). The interfaces file is used in three different ways. Each is discussed next.

First, the interfaces file is read by the SQL Server when the server is started. As the server starts, it reads the interfaces file to find the server name specified in the startup script. The server name is either specified by the value of the DSLISTEN environment variable or is specified as a command line option (-s) to the execution of the `dataserver` binary itself (see Chapter 14). When the server finds the server name it uses the server machine name and port number information specified for the master entry to determine where it is supposed to start up. The SQL Server will also use the information in the console entry to determine where the console process is to be started. Note that the server should be using the server version of the interfaces file as shown in Figure 12–1, which contains all of the information for the master, query and console entries for SQL Servers. Other servers, like the SQL Monitor Server (*<servername>*_MSV in the interfaces file) need only master and query entries. [For System 10 and

```
...
...
...
#
DDSDBA1
      query tcp sun-ether machine1 1025
      master tcp sun-ether machine1 1025
      console tcp sun-ether machine1 1026
#
DDSDBA2
      query tcp sun-ether machine2 1025
      master tcp sun-ether machine2 1025
...
```
server version of interfaces file

```
...
...
...
#
DDSDBA1
      query tcp sun-ether machine1 1025
#
DDSDBA2
      query tcp sun-ether machine2 1025
...
...
```
client version of interfaces file

Figure 12–1. Examples of Interfaces Files (Normal— SunOS Format Shown for Clarity)

11, the console program does not exist, so this entry in the interfaces file is no longer needed (see Chapter 12)]. Note that the SQL Server doesn't have to be started as the same server name as is stored in *sysservers* for the local server. The SQL Server really doesn't have a name and will start up as whatever name is in the startup script. This can cause confusion. When you start the server you tell it a server name that the server uses to locate a machine name and port number in the interfaces file. This does not affect the name of the server which is simply an entry in *sysservers* and is returned by

`select @@servername`

Second, the interfaces file is read by an operating SQL Server whenever it needs to communicate with any of the other servers on the network. Note that which servers appear to be on the network is limited by those

487

servers that appear in the interfaces file that the SQL Server looks at. The SQL Server can only communicate with the servers that appear in the interfaces file that you specify in the startup script or are specified by the environment variable SYBASE. Note that the environment variable SYBASE only specifies the directory where the file called "interfaces" is located, not the actual interfaces file itself. If you don't specify the location of the interfaces file, the server assumes it is located in the directory that is specified in the environment variable SYBASE. When the SQL Server needs to communicate with a remote server it looks for the remote server, in the interfaces file and when it finds the remote server name, it uses the associated server machine name and port number for the "query" entry to know where to communicate with the remote server.

Third, any client that needs to communicate (log in) to a SQL Server must look through the interfaces file to find the desired server name and use the information it finds in the query entry to determine where to look for the SQL Server. Note that all clients should be using the client version of the interfaces file as shown in Figure 12–1. You need to understand that the environment variable DSQUERY simply specifies the server name. If you run isql or some other application and you don't specify which server you wish to access the server name is taken to be the value of DSQUERY. At that point the interfaces file that the client has access to will be scanned looking for the information about the server name = DSQUERY. If you have problems with an application that can't log in to a server check the way that the DSQUERY or the server name is being set up and the interfaces file that is being used.

Since the interfaces file is so intrinsic to the startup and operation of the SQL Server and since it must contain the information (server machine name and port number) for all the servers and related products that need to talk to each other, you should maintain a master copy of both the server and client versions of the interfaces file in one location on your database system. The master copy of the server version should then be copied to all the server machines in your database system, while the master copy of the client version should be copied to all the clients or the file servers that support clients. In this way each server machine has a local copy of the server version of the interfaces file that has information for all the other servers in the database system. The clients all have a copy of the client version of the interfaces file which contains only the query entry for those servers that you, as DBA, want the clients to know about.

You may think that having two versions of the interfaces file is unnecessary but an example of their use will show the value of this approach.

```
...
...
...
#
DDSDBA1_TESTING
    query tcp sun-ether machine1 1925
    master tcp sun-ether machine1 1925
    console tcp sun-ether machine1 1926
#
DDSDBA2
    query tcp sun-ether machine2 1025
    master tcp sun-ether machine2 1025
...
```

server version of interfaces file
(modified)

```
...
...
...
#
DDSDBA1
    query tcp sun-ether machine1 1025
#
DDSDBA2
    query tcp sun-ether machine2 1025
...
...
```

client version of interfaces file

Figure 12–2. Examples of Interfaces Files (DDSDBA1 Isolated from Users—SunOS Format Shown for Clarity)

When you need to isolate a server from the users it is much better to isolate it via changes to the server version of the interfaces file. You can isolate the server by restarting the server in single-user mode but that doesn't guarantee that you, as DBA, will be the single user and you can find yourself locked out of your own server. You can also put all the databases into dbo use only, but that prevents you from doing any real-world testing where you need to log in to the server as individual server users to test permissions etc. It is easier for you to simply edit the server version of the interfaces file and change the server name and the port number for the server you wish to isolate. An example of such changes is shown in Figure 12–2. Now you edit your server startup script to start the server as DDSD-BA1_TESTING and the server finds that this server should be started on machine1 port 1925. The server will start up and be available to those persons whom you have informed about the new server name and port number. Users who need to assist you in the testing will need to be granted access to the server machine where they can use the local modified copy of the server version of the interfaces file or they will need to create their own temporary interfaces file on their client machine. Users trying to log in through the client version of the interfaces file will try in vain as there is no server called DDSDBA1 operating on machine 1 port 1025. This allows you to test the server in its normal operating state while you control who gains access to the server.

Note that it is safer for you to change both the server name and the port number in the server version of the interfaces file. Suppose you change only the port number and then some other person or process were to redistribute the master copy of the server version of the interfaces file that would overwrite your change to the port number while the server name remained the same? Suddenly the server would be available to all the users without your knowledge. To prevent this, you should change both the server name and the port number in the local copy of the server version of the interfaces file on the server machine that supports the server you are isolating. If the master copy of the interfaces file gets distributed now, it will change both the server name and the port number to their original values. The users still can't get in because the server will still be (in our example) DDSDBA1_TESTING while they are trying to access DDSDBA1. Of course you won't be able to access the isolated server either. You will try to access DDSDBA1_TESTING and get a "server not found in interfaces file" error. At that point, being a DBA, you should figure out pretty quickly that the entry in the interfaces file has been overwritten. You can change the local copy of the server version of the interfaces file again and again access the isolated server which will be just as you left it, without any changes made by users.

You must be sure that you do not use spaces before the text of the lines for the master, query, or console entries in the interfaces file. These lines must be preceded by a single tab character. If you use spaces the server will not read the entry and it will appear that the server is not in the interfaces file. This error is especially frustrating since there is no way to see it as you examine the interfaces file on the screen. Further, note that this can crop up in some unintended ways. For example, if you use `ftp` to move the interfaces file from one server machine to another, you must use the binary mode. If you don't, the interfaces file will be moved, but the tabs will be replaced by spaces. If you are having problems with a server and it appears to be related to the interfaces file, you must check for spaces before the entries for the server that is having problems.

CONVERTING SunOS INTERFACES FILE TO SOLARIS

The interfaces file is very different for SunOS versus Sun Solaris. While the information contained in both versions is identical, the way it is encoded in the Solaris interfaces file is very hard to understand. You need to be able to convert from one version of the interfaces file to the other and back. You can use the sybtli utility (in $SYBASE/bin) to create Solaris interfaces file entries. You can also use sybinit (sybconfig for 4.9.2 SQL Server) to create either SunOS or Solaris interfaces file entries depending on which version of sybinit you are running. If you have installed a Solaris SQL Server, sybinit will create only Solaris interfaces file entries. Recall that System 11 runs only on Solaris. You need to understand how to manually perform the conversion for those instances when you don't have all the needed utilities available.

You have Sybase SQL Server running on an old SunOS machine. New client machines are being installed that run Solaris. The clients need interface file entries for your SunOS SQL Server. You don't have the Solaris version of the Sybase utilities to use on the client machines. What to do? Now you wish you have learned how to manually convert interfaces file entries from SunOS to Solaris formats. Don't laugh, this happens all the time.

Solaris Interfaces File

Here is a typical interfaces file for the Solaris operating system. The interfaces file contains entries for a System 11 SQL Server, its associated Backup Server, and a 4.9.2 SQL Server.

```
## THEBIRDS11 on thebirds
##      Services:
##          query tcp    (5001)
##          master tcp   (5001)

THEBIRDS11
        query tli tcp /dev/tcp \x000213898196c4510000000000000000
        master tli tcp /dev/tcp \x000213898196c4510000000000000000
```

```
## THEBIRDS11_BCK on thebirds
##      Services:
##          query tcp    (5002)
##          master tcp   (5002)


THEBIRDS11_BCK
       query tli tcp /dev/tcp \x0002138a8196c4510000000000000000
       master tli tcp /dev/tcp \x0002138a8196c4510000000000000000
#
# THEBIRDS492 on thebirds (129.150.196.81) using tcp
#     services: query (1025) master (1025) console (1026)
#
THEBIRDS492
       query tli tcp /dev/tcp \x000204018196c4510000000000000000
       master tli tcp /dev/tcp \x000204018196c4510000000000000000
       console tli tcp /dev/tcp \x000204028196c4510000000000000000
```

Converting From Solaris Interfaces File Entry to SunOS

Taking one of the Solaris format entries above, you would convert the entry to SunOS format as follows:

```
THEBIRDS492
       master tli tcp /dev/tcp \x000204018196c4510000000000000000
```

Hexidecimal		Decimal	
x0002	header	N/A	
0401	port number	1025	(0401 Hex = 4*16*16 + 1*1)
81	IP address 1	129	(81 Hex = 8*16 + 1*1)
96	IP address 2	150	(96 Hex = 9*16 + 6*1)
c4	IP address 3	196	(c4 Hex = 12*16 + 4*1)
51	IP address 4	81	(51 Hex = 5*16 + 1*1)

SunOS interfaces file entry would be

```
THEBIRDS492
       master tcp sun-ether thebirds 1025
```

where thebirds is the host name at IP address 129.150.196.81.

Converting from SunOS Interfaces File Entry to Solaris

In order to go the other way, you would convert a Solaris format entry to SunOS format as follows. Since we are converting an interfaces file entry for a Backup Server which is part of the System 11 SQL Server, and since System 11 is supported only on Solaris, you can assume that this example is for a System 10 Backup Server.

```
THEBIRDS_BCK
        master tcp sun-ether thebirds 1026
```

The machine with host name of thebirds has IP address of 129.150.196.81.

```
Decimal       Hexidecimal

1026          0402 (1026/16*16 = 4, 1026 - (4*16*16) = 2)
 129            81 (129/16 = 8, 129 - 8*16 = 1)
 150            96 (150/16 = 9, 150 - 9*16 = 6)
 196            c4 (196/16 = 12, 196 - 12*16 = 4)
  81            51 (81/16 = 5, 81 - 5*16 = 1)
```

Note that port number is converted into four digits hexadecimal (1026 —> 0402).

SunOS Interfaces File

Finally, here is the same interfaces file as shown at the beginning of this section, only now it is in the SunOS format. You should again note that SQL Server System 11 is supported only on Solaris, but the following interfaces file could be for a System 10 SQL Server and its associated Backup Server.

```
#
THEBIRDS11
        query tcp sun-ether thebirds 5001
        master tcp sun-ether thebirds 5001
#
THEBIRDS11_BCK
        query tcp sun-ether thebirds 5002
        master tcp sun-ether thebirds 5002
```

```
#
THEBIRDS492
        query tcp sun-ether thebirds 1025
        master tcp sun-ether thebirds 1025
        console tcp sun-ether thebirds 1026
```

COMMUNICATION BETWEEN SERVERS

In order for two SQL Servers to communicate with each other using Remote Procedure Calls (RPC)(one server executes an RPC to the other), several things must be set up. You need to understand what these steps are and how to check the status of this communication process.

First, the remote server must be configured to allow remote connections (i.e., **sp_configure "remote access", 1**), as shown in Figure 12–3.

Second, both servers must have entries in their interfaces file for the other server. This is another reason to maintain one master copy of the server version of the interfaces file and distribute a copy to each server machine. The client version of the interfaces file doesn't need all the information about all the servers. A client only needs to have an interfaces file that contains information about the servers the users need to access. If a user is accessing a server and needs to execute an RPC to another server, that request is handled by the server itself, which will use the server version of the interfaces file to find out about the other server.

Third, each server must have an entry for the other server in the system table *sysservers* as shown in Figure 12–3. The system table *sysservers* contains the information the server uses to determine what the remote server is called. The server then uses this information to find the remote server in the interfaces file. This allows each server to have two names; one that the server uses internally to call a remote server, and the other the name that appears in the interfaces file for the remote server. Thus you could have an application running on several servers that is hardcoded to call "servername1" and in *sysservers* for each server you have an alias that assigns a unique server name to "servername1" so that for each server the same application that calls "servername1" would then be calling the individual server on that server machine.

A good example of this rather confusing process is the Backup Server. The only way to make dumps (or loads) is through the Backup Server. The

```
1> sp_configure                                    configuration of ServerB
2> go
  name            minimum    maximum  config_value run_value
  ----------------  -------------  --------------  ------------------  -------------

  ...
  ...
  ...
  devices              4          256       30           30
  remote access        0            1        1            1
  remote logins        0  2147483647       64           64
  remote sites         0  2147483647       10           10
  remote connections   0  2147483647      128          128
  pre-read packets     0  2147483647        0            3
  upgrade version      0  2147483647      491          491
  ...
```

```
1> select * from sysservers                sysservers on ServerB
2> go
  srvid srvstatus srvname  srvnetname
  ------ ---------- ----------- --------------
     0     0      serverB  SERVERB
     1     1      serverA  SERVERA
     2     1      serverC  SERVERC
```

```
1> select * from sysremotelogins            sysremotelogins on ServerB
2> go
  remoteserverid  remoteusername   suid   status

  ------------------   ----------------------   ------   --------
       1              NULL         -1      0
       2              NULL         -1      0
```

Figure 12–3. Remote Server Logins from ServerA to ServerB

Backup Server is an open server application and therefore is a remote server to the SQL Server. However, you must understand that the SQL Server is hardcoded to call SYB_BACKUP whenever the SQL Server needs to dump or load. As soon as you have more than one SQL Server in your database system, you have a problem. All the SQL Servers will be calling SYB_BACKUP when they need to dump and load. By default, when you install the SQL Server and Backup Server [(using `sybinit`) (see Chapter 13)], the entry in *sysservers* for the Backup Server is SYB_BACKUP for both *srvname* and *srvnetname*. If you don't change this, all the servers will be calling SYB_BACKUP (*srvname*) and the servers will all look at the associated SYB_BACKUP (*srvnetname*) and then go out to their interfaces file (server version) and all call for the Backup Server that is running at the machine and port number specified in the interfaces file for the server (Backup Server) named SYB_BACKUP. If all the servers have a Backup Server running on the server machine and if the interfaces file on each server machine points to the Backup Server running on that server machine for the entry SYB_BACKUP, then all is well. As soon as you have a common interfaces file however, things get confused. Multiple servers will be calling SYB_BACKUP, which in the common interfaces file points to one server machine and port number. To cure this problem you must change the *srvnetname* in *sysservers* for each server to reflect a unique name for each Backup Server. The easiest way to do this is to change *srvnetname* to *<servername>*_BCK. Now, each SQL Server will call SYB_BACKUP (the *srvname* in *sysservers* for the Backup Server) which will be associated with *<servername>*_BCK (*srvnetname* in sysservers) and will appear in the interfaces file as a unique server machine and port number since all the different *<servername>*_BCKs will be in the common interfaces file. Note that you must not change the *srvname* (SYB_BACKUP) for the Backup Server. If you do, the SQL Server will not be able to communicate with any Backup Server at all.

Fourth, each server must have an entry in the system table *sysremotelogins* that tells the server how to treat remote logins from the other (remote) servers as shown in Figure 12–3. In the example shown, the value of *suid* = −1 and *status* = 0. This means that for any of the server logins on server A which execute an RPC to server B, the server login from server A will be compared with the same server login on server B and the passwords must match. If they don't, or if the server login from server A doesn't exist on server B, then the execution of the RPC fails. This is the most secure way to handle remote logins but it does require that you maintain the server logins and their passwords on both servers. Further, you can set up other configurations where some server logins on server A are mapped into different server logins on server B. Also you can set up the trusted mode using **sp_remotelogin** which will drop the requirement that the server login passwords agree between the two servers. You must be aware of these options and how each of your servers is configured. You must know what level of security you have on your servers.

Note that each remote server in *sysservers* has a *srvid* that is joined with *remoteserverid* in *sysremotelogins* to get the permissions for remote logins from each remote server. For our example, as far as server B is concerned, server A has *srvid* = 1 in *sysservers* and this corresponds with *sysremotelogins* column *remoteserverid* = 1 which has *suid* = −1 and *status* = 0 as discussed above.

Fifth, the server executing the RPC (i.e., the local SQL Server) must be "named" which means there is an entry in *sysservers* for the local server (*sysservers* srvid = 0) and **select @@servername** will return the "name" of the local server (non-NULL).

With this configuration it is required that the server login on server A that executes the RPC to server B must also exist as a server login on server B and the server login must have the same password on both server A and server B. If the options were set differently there might not be such a requirement.

To test such a link, isql into server A and **execute server B...sp_who** and see what happens. If you get reasonable results back (i.e., you believe the returned results to be from server B) then the link is working from server A to server B. If you need to have the link working both ways you should also isql into server B and **execute server A...sp_who** and see if you get reasonable results. Note that the server-name you use with **...sp_who** will depend on the entries in *sysservers* for each server. For server A, the entry in *sysservers* for the remote server should be server B for the syntax **server B...sp_who** to function correctly. Note that in *sysservers* server B would be the value of *srvname* while the associated value of *srvnetname* could be anything. It is the value of *srvnetname* that the server uses to scan the interfaces file to find the remote server.

CREATING STORED PROCEDURES FROM SQL SCRIPT OR DEFNCOPY OUTPUT

You will often need to write a script and then move it into a database where it will be a stored procedure. Once you have the SQL script working the way you want, you need to add to the top of the script the statement

```
create procedure <stored_procedure_name> as
```

and you need to add the statement go at the end of the script. Additionally, if you are making changes to an existing stored procedure you should add the statement

```
drop procedure <stored_procedure_name>
```

and `go` before the create procedure statement.

Note that when you use the utility `defncopy` to copy out the SQL that defines a database object and then need to use the resulting output file to create a stored procedure or trigger you also need to edit the file and make sure the **drop procedure**, **create procedure** (or **create trigger**, **drop trigger**), and the necessary **go** statements are in the correct places before you try to create the database object.

WHAT *SYSUSAGES* MEANS

The system table *sysusages* (in the *master* database) is very important and very misunderstood. This table stores the information about where all the pieces of each database are stored on disk. More specifically, each row of *sysusages* represents the assignment of some chunk of disk space to a database in the server. When you execute the **create database** or **alter database** commands, you are adding rows to *sysusages*. Further, each row of *sysusages* tells you exactly where the chunk of database space is located out on the server devices (i.e., physical disks), and each row of *sysusages* has a *segmap* value which tells you which segments have been assigned to the chunk of database space.

The way all this information is stored in *sysusages* is very confusing, and we discuss various aspects of each row of *sysusages*. See Figure 12–4 for an example of the data in *sysusages* and related system tables.

Which Database Affected

The *dbid* column in sysusages joins with the *dbid* column in *sysdatabases* to relate the *dbid* of each chunk of disk space (space fragment) to a database *name*. You can see which rows of *sysusages* support which database based on the *dbid* value. Using *db1* as an example in the data from system tables shown in Figure 12–4, the last three lines of the *sysusages* table belong to *db1* which has a *dbid* of 4. You need to keep in mind that the order of the rows in *sysusages* for a given *dbid* reflect the exact order in which the database space was created. So, for *db1* the three rows of *sysusages* represent a complete record of the size and order of each chunk of database space assigned to *db1*.

```
1> select * from sysusages
2> go
dbid   segmap   lstart   size    vstart
------ -------- -------- ------- ------------------

  1       7       0      1536    4
  1       7      1536    1024    3588
  2       1       0      1024    2564
  2       3      1024    51200   251658240
  2       4      52224   51200   268435456
  3       7       0      1024    1540
  4       3       0      5120    201326592
```
sysusages table

```
dbid  database name
----- ------------------

  1     master
  2     tempdb
  3     model
```
data found in *sysdatabases*

low	high	status	cntrltype	name	phyname
184549376	184733445	738	0	sd4e	/dev/rsd4e
201326592	201510661	738	0	sd4f	/dev/rsd4f
218103808	218287877	738	0	sd4g	/dev/rsd4g
234881024	235132235	738	0	sd4h	/dev/rsd4h

data found in *sysdevices*

device_fragments	size	usage
sd4f	10 MB	data only
sd4f	10 MB	data only
sd4g	5 MB	log only

device	segment
sd4f	default
sd4f	system

data found in **sp_helpdb** *db1*

Figure 12–4. Example of sysusages and Related Tables

Amount of Database Space

Each row of *sysusages* identifies a chunk of disk space. The size of each chunk is stored in each row of *sysusages* in the *size* column. For *db1* the three rows of *sysusages* that represent the disk space of the database have sizes of 5120, 2560, and 5120, respectively, and these are all in 2K pages. The total disk space for *db1* is then 12,800 2K pages which is 25 Mb.

499

Location of Database Space

You can tell where each piece of the database is located from the value of the *vstart* column of *sysusages*. This is where the virtual device number (*vdevno*) comes into play. Recall that *vdevno* came up during the **disk init** command. Now you can see why. Each data page (2K page) in the entire server needs to have a unique page number. Each data page also has a unique page number within the database. So, for each row in *sysusages* we have the unique page number within the database which is the value of *lstart* (logical starting page). Note that for each database, *lstart* simply jumps from row to row by the size of each row's chunk of database space. For the example of *db1* you can see that *lstart* starts out at 0 for the first chunk of disk space which is 5120 datapages big, and the next row of *sysusages* for *db1* has *lstart* of 5120. You need to realize that the first data page for *db1* is *lstart* = 0, so 5120 pages starting from page 0 is 5119 and the next chunk of disk space for *db1* starts at page 5120 and has size 2560 which bring us to 7679, and so on. You will see that while the *lstart* values for *db1* are marching along sequentially, the *vstart* values are not. For each row of *sysusages* that represents disk space for *db1* we have the unique page number within the whole server which is the value of *vstart*. The *vstart* value is a combination of the *vdevno* and the *lstart* value for each chunk of disk space. This explains why *vedvno* can't be reused among **disk init** commands. The value of *vedvno* must be unique among all server devices because the *vstart* values are based on *vdevno* and the *vstart* values must be unique within the server.

You are finally ready to determine where each chunk of disk space is located. To do this you must look at the data in *sysdevices*. For each server device, which is a physical disk partition (or a disk file), *sysdevices* has a *low* and a *high* value. This tells you the starting (*low*) data page number and the ending (*high*) data page number for the server device. By comparing these ranges of data pages to the *vstart* page number in *sysusages* you can determine which server device is associated with each chunk of database space. Note that a row in *sysusages* will never overlap a server device. Each row in *sysusages* represents a piece of disk space from a **create database** or an **alter database** command and these commands require that you add space to one or more server devices, but you are required to define how much space goes on each device. The server will make an entry in *sysusages* for the space assigned to each server device and if one of the server devices fills up the server fills all the server device but does not try to assign space on another server device. All this means is that you don't need to worry about the size of the disk space in a row of *sysusages*. You only need to locate the *vstart* value between the *low* and *high* values in *sysdevices* and you have located the server device that has the chunk of database space.

For the example of *db1*, we see that the first row of *sysusages* for *db1* has a *vstart* of 201,326,592 and looking at the data from *sysdevices* in Figure 12–4, we see that this value for *vstart* is between the *low* (201,326,592) and the *high* (201,510,661) data page values for the server device sd4f. In fact, this chunk of database space is the first chunk of database space on the server device sd4f.

Segments Assigned to Database Space

Segments have been discussed fully in Chapter 8. Each chunk of database space, or each row of *sysusages*, supports a set of segments for the database. The value of *segmap* for each row of *sysusages* tells you what segments are assigned to each chunk of database space. The way in which multiple-segment assignments are encoded into the *segmap* value is not very intuitive. The encoding involves the logical OR of the bitmaps of the numbers of all the segments that are assigned to the chunk of disk space. The numbers for segment assignments are shown in Table 12–2.

Table 12-2 Segment Assignment Numbers

Segment Type	Segment Number	Segment Number Bitmap
system	1	000001
default	2	000010
logsegment	4	000100
first user-defined	8	001000
second user-defined	16	010000
third user-defined etc.	32 etc.	100000

Note that the segment numbers jump from 2 to 4 and from 4 to 8 because they are the decimal version of the binary bitmap of the segment number. Now, you need to understand that when you combine segment assignments, you add the segment numbers together. For a piece of database disk space that has the segment assignments of *system*, *default*, and *logsegment*, which are the assignments you get when you simply create a database, the *segmap* value is 7. For pieces of the database that are supporting the *logsegment* only, the *segmap* value is 4. Note that the segment number for user-defined segments increases rapidly from 8 to 16 to 32 and then 64 and 128. If you have a lot of user-defined segments, you will have very large segment numbers and *segmap* values. You must realize that just because you might have a *segmap* value of 128 does not mean there are 128 segments, and the *segmap* value cannot range continuously from 1 to 128. It steps between 1 and 128 jumping from the various combinations of 1 and 2 and 4 and 8 and so on.

Can't Remove Database Space (except for tempdb)

Now that you have some idea what each row in *sysusages* tells you, you need to remember that you can't just delete rows from *sysusages* to reduce the size of a database. The one exception to this is *tempdb*. If you need to reduce the size of *tempdb* you can delete some or all of the rows of sysusages that represent the chunks of disk space assigned to *tempdb*, except for the first 2 Mb on the master device which should never be removed. You then restart the server and *tempdb* will have been reduced. Consult the *Sybase SQL Server Troubleshooting Guide* for the details of this process.

Updating sysusages Manually

Note that anytime you are manually updating system tables, you must observe various warnings about such a procedure (see Modifying System Tables Manually below).

Warning

1. Updating system tables in not supported by Sybase—there is no guarantee that the system table schema will be maintained between releases which means manual updates that work for one version may not work on another version.

2. Do not perform such updates without consulting with Sybase Technical Support first.

3. Make sure you have dumps of everything you might need to rebuild the server in case the manual updates destroy something.

4. After updating system tables, you should restart the server to copy the changes into memory.

When you execute **sp_addsegment, sp_extendsegment** or **sp_dropsegment** you are running stored procedures that look at *sysusages* and determine all the rows that belong to the server device specified in the execution of the stored procedure and the database in which the stored procedure was executed. Then the *segmap* value is altered for all the appropriate rows. This is how a server device is assigned to the logsegment and only the logsegment, that is, the *segmap* value, is set to 4. This also explains why you must set up such a device before any data for any other segment is written to the server device. When the database space on the server device was originally assigned through the **create database** or **alter database** commands the *segmap* value was set up to be 7 or 3 respectively (i.e., *default*, *system* and *logsegment* segments, or *system* and *default*). If any objects are created on this device on the *default* or *system* segments, the data pages of those objects will be marked as belonging to the *default* or *system* segments. If you then tried to assign all future allocations of space on the server device to the *logsegment* alone by manually changing *segmap* to 4 for the relevant rows of *sysusages*, the server will now allow only data pages that belong to the *logsegment* to be written to the server device, but there will still be those data pages that already existed for the objects that belong to the *default* and *system* segments. This means the server will still refuse to perform a **dump transaction** command because the server device must contain only *logsegment* data pages for the command to work. Until all the pages can be assigned to the *logsegment* you can't simply change the *segmap* value to 4 and get the effect of having only *logsegment* data pages on the server device.

Now we reach a contradiction. If you use the stored procedures you can't assign the *segmap* value to 4 until all the datapages are free to be assigned to *logsegment*. You can however go into sysusages manually and update anything you like. You must not do this without a good reason and a good plan and a good backup. You must realize that while you can manually update the *segmap* values in sysusages, that won't necessarily get you the effect you want. The stored procedures are there for a reason and you should use them.

There are situations when you will want to alter the *segmap* values in sysusages manually. You must understand that this process is not supported by Sybase, but you should understand that it exists and when you might use it.

If you need to re-create a database quickly you use the **for load** option of the **create database** command. However, after that command completes, you are left with all the correct chunks of space in the correct order in *sysusages* for loading the database dump, but the *segmap* values for all the rows for the database are set to 3, except for one, assuming that one line of the **create database** statement contains the **log on** clause, which means the *segmap* value would be 4 for that row. Now you are supposed to wait for the **create database** (with the **for load** option) to complete, load the database dump and then manually use the **sp_addsegment, sp_extendsegment** and **sp_dropsegment** to correctly recreate the same *segmap* values for the rows of *sysusages* as existed previously for the database. Manually performing all these stored procedure executions, in the correct order with no mistakes, can be very tedious for large databases that have data spread out over many server devices. You can update the *sysusages* tables manually by using the *lstart* values of the rows for the database. Note that the *vstart* values are based on the *vdevnos* of the server devices and as such could change if you were rebuilding the server and didn't do all the **disk inits** in the same order, and so forth. However, the *lstart* values will be the same as long as all the chunks of space for the database are created in the same order and sizes as existed in the original database. So, you can update the *segmap* values based on the *lstart* values by specifying that for *lstart* greater than x and less than or equal to y the *segmap* value should be z.

Taking *db1* again as an example and assuming you are recreating *db1* on the server you could **create database** using the **for load** option to create the three rows in *sysusages* of the same size as the original. Any manual update to *sysusages*, or any system table, must be done within a transaction (i.e., **begin tran <name>**). That way you can examine the impact of your changes and if they are wrong, you can roll the transaction back leaving *sysusages* as it was. Now you would update the rows of *sysusages* where *dbid* = 4 such that for *lstart* greater than or equal to 0 and less than 5120 *segmap* = 3. Then for *lstart* > or = 5120 and < 7680 (the value of *lstart* for the next row of *sysusages* for *db1*, note that the data page numbers for the current row of *sysusages* run from *lstart* = 5120 to 7679) *segmap* = 4 and finally for *lstart* > or equal to 7680 *segmap* = 3. This will re-create the exact same rows in *sysusages* as existed in the original. You must use > or = and < because you can't control how the server will create the chunk of database space. If you request 10 Mb of space on a server device, the server may create it in one shot and only one row will appear in *sysusages*, but sometimes the server will create two rows in *sysusages* for say 7 Mb and 3 Mb. By using the approach shown above, you avoid any problems caused by this server behavior.

Of course, you need to have the data from *sysusages* before you can use this approach, but then, manually rebuilding the database using the **sp_createsegment**, and so forth, commands would require the same data to know what size chunks of the database to create in which order. Note that this process is done for you using the script **p_dbcreate** described in Chapter 14. This script will generate the commands for a database to create the database with the **for load** option and to update the *sysusages* rows for the database to re-create the exact same segmentation. This is very useful and fast when you need to rebuild a database on the same server. It is also useful when you need to re-create the database on another server since you still need to re-create the same size chunks of space in the same order only on the new server. If the new server has the same server devices with the same names (and sufficient free space) you can execute the output of **p_dbcreate** directly. The more likely event is that you have different server devices. In that case, you need to determine a conversion map between the original server devices and the new server devices and edit the new server device names into the output of **p_dbcreate** before executing. This is a very good approach for creating the databases on a reporting or standby server, for example.

load database and sysusages

There is another reason you need to understand what the rows in *sysusages* mean. As mentioned previously the order of the rows in *sysusages* for a given database tells you the exact order in which the chunks of space were allocated for that database. This is also the order in which the database will be dumped. When you load the database from dump, this is also the order in which the pages of the database will be brought into the database. All this is means that when you re-create the database, either on the same server or on another server; you must re-create the database so the same chunks of space are created in the same order and in the same size. For the example of *db1* this means that you must re-create the database such that there are rows in sysusages that show a 10-Mb chunk assigned to *system* and *default* segments (*segmap* = 3) followed by a 5-Mb chunk assigned to *logsegment* (*segmap* = 4) and finally a row or *sysusages* that shows a 10-Mb chunk of database space with a *segmap* = 3. Note that it doesn't matter how many rows of *sysusages* there are for the newly created database as long as the overall size and order of the chunks are the same. Note the dump of *db1* will bring in 10 Mb of *segmap* = 3 data followed by 5 Mb of *segmap* = 4 data, and so forth. This means that *sysusages* can show two rows of *segmap* = 3 database space as long as the size of these two chunks adds up to 10 Mb, and the next bunch of rows in *sysusages* for *db1* adds up to 5 Mb all of which have *segmap* = 4, followed by any number of rows in *sysusages* that are all *segmap* = 3 and add up to 10 Mb of space overall.

If you don't re-create the database so that the overall size and order of the chunks of database space re-create the size and order of the original, the load from dump will place data pages from the transaction log on server devices that the server thinks are for *system* and *default* segment objects (and vice versa). This is fine until you try to write something to one of these segments and the server becomes confused since it will try to write a change to an object of the *default* segment that is on a server device that is marked as *logsegment* only (*segmap* = 4) in *sysusages*. This is a form of corruption that may not be recoverable. You must be careful when re-creating database that will be loaded from a dump.

OBJECTS ON A SEGMENT

You need to know how to check the segments in each database to see which database objects are on each segment. You can do this with the **sp_helpsegment** command. If you execute **sp_helpsegment** within a database, you will see all of the segments in that database. Then you can execute **sp_helpsegment <segmentname>** and the server will show you all the database objects on that segment. The server will also show you the total free space available on the segment in 2K pages. An example of this is shown next.

```
machine1: isql -Usa -STHEBIRDS11
Password:
1> use psychodb
2> go
1> sp_helpsegment
2> go
```

segment name	status
0 system	0
1 default	1
2 logsegment	0

```
(return status = 0)
1> sp_helpsegment system
2> go
```

segment name	status
0 system	0

device	size	free_pages
c0t2d0s4	350.0MB	21400

table_name	index_name	indid
sysalternates	sysalternates	1

```
...
...
...
(return status = 0)
1> sp_helpsegment "default"
2> go
```

segment name	status
1 default	1

device	size	free_pages
c0t2d0s4	350.0MB	21400

table_name	index_name	indid
psycho_actions	spray_idx	1

```
...
...
...
(return status = 0)
1> sp_helpsegment logsegment
2> go
```

segment name	status
2 logsegment	0

device	size	free_pages
c0t2d0s6	50.0MB	25504

table_name	index_name	indid
syslogs	syslogs	0

(return status = 0)

READING THE ERRORLOG

The SQL Server errorlog contains a wealth of information that you will need during times of crisis. Since the server may not be available due to a crash, you may need to extract information from the errorlog. We discuss the following items that can be found in the errorlog, and we flag each of these same items in the example errorlogs for a 4.9.2, System 10, and System 11 Server.

1. SQL Server version
2. Location of errorlog
3. Maximum user connections
4. Master device
5. Master device is mirrored
6. Interfaces file information
7. Server name
8. Server devices and mirrors
9. Asynchronous I/O in use for server devices
10. Recovery of databases
11. Default sort order and character set

SQL Server Version

The first line of the errorlog displays the SQL Server version and EBF level that is being executed.

Location of Errorlog

The errorlog shows where the errorlog is being kept. If you are looking at an old errorlog, then you already know where it is kept, but this is useful when you start a server and you should check that the errorlog is being sent where you think it is.

Maximum User Connections

The errorlog displays the maximum possible number of file descriptors which tells you the maximum number of user connections that the server can support. Note that this doesn't mean the server is configured for this many user connections. Further, if you see a small number of file descriptors and you know you will need more user connections, you will need more file descriptors (see the *Sybase SQL Server Installation Guide* and *System Administration Guide Supplement* for your server machine platform).

Master Device

The errorlog shows you the physical disk partition that supports the master device. This information is vital if you need to run `build-master` or other procedures to fix the master device and the server itself is down. This is also the only way to determine what the disk partition is for the master device if you have never mirrored the master device. As discussed in Chapter 7, until the master device is mirrored *sysdevices* doesn't reflect the actual physical device. Note that the errorlog shows you the physical disk partition that is supporting the master device as "virtual device 0," which means *vdevno* = 0 and that is the master device.

Master Device is Mirrored

If the master device is mirrored (you should always mirror the master device), that will be reported in the errorlog. You must check this each time the server starts to make sure the mirror of the master device is functioning properly.

Interfaces File Information

The errorlog will tell you the server machine name and port number where the server is running.

Server name

The errorlog will tell you the name of the server which means the entry in *sysservers* for the local server. Recall that this is the only way a server can be named, that is, by making an entry in *sysservers* using **sp_addserver** with the **local** option. If the server (the local server) has not been named by using **sp_addserver** with the **local** option, the errorlog will simply say "server is unnamed." Even though you specified the name of the server during installation to sybinit, that name was only used for the creation of the RUN_<*servername*> script to start the server.

Server Devices and Mirrors

The errorlog will display each of the server devices along with its *vdevno*. Note that the errorlog will refer to each server device as a virtual device. If the server device is mirrored there will be an additional line "mirror: <*physical_name_of_mirror*>".

Asynchronous I/O in Use for Server Devices

As each server device is displayed, so is the fact that asynchronous I/O is being used for the device. You should check that all the server devices are using asynchronous I/O. If you create a server device on a file system the errorlog will display that fact for the server device. Make sure you see the correct I/O method being used for each server device.

Recovery of Databases

As the server recovers each database, the errorlog will contain messages about how many transactions were rolled forward or back. This is also where you should look for any error messages regarding recovering a database.

Default Sort Order and Character Set

After the server has recovered, the errorlog shows the ID number for the default sort order and the default character set. These are important since you should compare all the servers in your database system that need to share database dumps and verify that they all use the same default sort order and character set.

Example of 4.9.2 SQL Server Errorlog

Items 1 through 11 are shown in the errorlog below. Each item is marked with a comment line /* <item> */ above the relevant portion of the errorlog.

```
/home/DDSDBA1/errorlog 57 % more errorlog
/* 1) SQL Server Version */
00: 95/04/01 14:53:42.20 kernel: SQL Server/4.9.2/EBF 2825
Rollup/Sun4/OS 4.1.2/1/OPT/Sat Apr  9 10:25:53 PDT 1994
/* 2) Location of Errorlog */
00: 95/04/01 14:53:42.27 kernel: Logging SQL Server messages in file
'/home/DDSDBA1/bin/errorlog'.
00: 95/04/01 14:53:42.27 kernel: Using config area of disk for boot
    information
00: 95/04/01 14:53:42.39 kernel: kdconfig: opening secondary master
    device
00: 95/04/01 14:53:42.43 kernel: Using config area from primary
    master device.
/* 3) Maximum User Connections */
00: 95/04/01 14:53:42.69 kernel: Using 2048 file descriptors.
00: 95/04/01 14:53:42.69 kernel: Network and device connection limit
    is 2043.
00: 95/04/01 14:53:42.71 kernel: Dump/Load buffers configured with 8
    pages.
/* 4) Master Device */
00: 95/04/01 14:53:42.99 kernel: Initializing virtual device 0,
    "/dev/rsd4b"
/* 5) Master Device is Mirrored */
00: 95/04/01 14:53:43.00 kernel: mirror: /dev/rsd5b
00: 95/04/01 14:53:43.00 kernel: Virtual device 0 started using
    asynchronous i/o.
```

```
00: 95/04/01 14:53:43.10 kernel: network name ddsdba1, type
      sun-ether, port 1025
00: 95/04/01 14:53:43.23 server: Number of buffers in buffer cache:
      5393.
00: 95/04/01 14:53:43.23 server: Number of proc buffers allocated:
      1797.
00: 95/04/01 14:53:43.23 server: Number of blocks left for proc
      headers: 1943.
00: 95/04/01 14:53:43.81 server: Opening Master Database ...
00: 95/04/01 14:53:44.17 server: Loading SQL Server's default sort
      order and character set
/* 6) Interfaces File Information */
00: 95/04/01 14:53:44.19 kernel: network name machine1, type
      sun-ether, port 1025
00: 95/04/01 14:53:44.26 server: Recovering database 'master'
00: 95/04/01 14:53:44.33 server: Recovery dbid 1 ckpt (2391,23)
00: 95/04/01 14:53:44.33 server: Recovery no active transactions
      before ckpt.
/* 7) Servername */
00: 95/04/01 14:53:44.59 server: server name is 'ddsdba1'
00: 95/04/01 14:53:44.65 server: Activating disk 'sd1d'.
/* 8) Server Devices and Mirrors */
00: 95/04/01 14:53:44.65 kernel: Initializing virtual device 18,
      "/dev/rsd1d"
00: 95/04/01 14:53:44.65 kernel: mirror: /dev/rsd10e
/* 9) Asynchronous I/O in use for Server Devices */
00: 95/04/01 14:53:44.66 kernel: Virtual device 18 started using
      asynchronous i/o.
00: 95/04/01 14:53:44.66 server: Activating disk 'sd1e'.
00: 95/04/01 14:53:44.66 kernel: Initializing virtual device 19,
      "/dev/rsd1e"
00: 95/04/01 14:53:44.67 kernel: Virtual device 19 started using
      asynchronous i/o.
...
...
...
/* 10) Recovery of Databases */
00: 95/04/01 14:53:44.84 server: Recovering database 'model'.
00: 95/04/01 14:53:44.86 server: Recovery dbid 3 ckpt (266,25)
00: 95/04/01 14:53:44.86 server: Recovery no active transactions
      before ckpt.
00: 95/04/01 14:53:45.01 server: Clearing temp db
00: 95/04/01 14:53:57.38 server: Recovering database 'db1'.
00: 95/04/01 14:53:57.43 server: Recovery dbid 4 ckpt (6401,1)
      oldest tran=(6401 ,0)
00: 95/04/01 14:53:57.50 server: 1 transactions rolled forward.
```

```
00: 95/04/01 14:53:57.84 server: Recovering database 'db2'.
00: 95/04/01 14:53:57.90 server: Recovery dbid 5 ckpt (51206,23)
      oldest tran=(51206 ,22)
00: 95/04/01 14:53:57.91 server: 1 transactions rolled forward.
...
...
...
00: 95/04/01 14:53:57.84 server: Recovering database 'dbn'.
00: 95/04/01 14:53:57.90 server: Recovery dbid 5 ckpt (51206,23)
      oldest tran=(51206 ,22)
00: 95/04/01 14:53:57.91 server: 1 transactions rolled forward.
00: 95/04/01 14:59:42.38 server: Recovery complete.
/* 11) Default Sort Order and Character Set */
00: 95/04/01 14:59:42.38 server: SQL Server's default sort order is:
00: 95/04/01 14:59:42.38 server:          'bin_iso_1' (ID = 50)
00: 95/04/01 14:59:42.38 server: on top of default character set:
00: 95/04/01 14:59:42.39 server:          'iso_1' (ID = 1).
```

Example of System 10 SQL Server Errorlog

Items 1 through 11 are shown in the errorlog below. Each item is marked with a comment line /* <item> */ above the relevant portion of the errorlog.

```
/home/DDSDBA1/errorlog 53 % more errorlog
00:95/04/01 14:26:02.69 kernel  Using config area of disk for boot
      information
00:95/04/01 14:26:02.89 kernel  Using config area from primary
      master device.
/* 1) SQL Server Version */
00:95/04/01 14:26:03.05 kernel  SQL Server/10.0.2/P/Sun4/OS
4.1.x/1/OPT/Fri Oct 28 10:22:26 PDT 1994
/* 2) Location of Errorlog */
00:95/04/01 14:26:03.07 kernel  Logging SQL Server messages in file
'/home/DDSDBA1/errorlog/errorlog'.
/* 3) Maximum User Connections */
00:95/04/01 14:26:03.07 kernel  Using 2048 file descriptors.
00:95/04/01 14:26:03.08 kernel  Network and device connection limit
      is 2045.
/* 4) Master Device */
00:95/04/01 14:26:03.45 kernel  Initializing virtual device 0,
      '/dev/rsd4h'
```

```
/* 5) Master Device is Mirrored —> note that the master device is
      NOT mirrored in this example */
00:95/04/01 14:26:03.46 kernel   Virtual device 0 started using
      asynchronous i/o.
00:95/04/01 14:26:03.46 server   Disk I/O affinitied to engine: 0
00:95/04/01 14:26:03.60 server   Number of buffers in buffer cache:
      4978.
00:95/04/01 14:26:03.60 server   Number of proc buffers allocated:
      1659.
00:95/04/01 14:26:03.61 server   Number of blocks left for proc
      headers: 1518.
00:95/04/01 14:26:04.83 server   Opening Master Database ...
00:95/04/01 14:26:05.08 server   Loading SQL Server's default sort
      order and character set
/* 6) Interfaces File Information */
00:95/04/01 14:26:05.15 kernel   network name machine1, type
      sun-ether, port 1025
00:95/04/01 14:26:05.18 server   Recovering database 'master'
00:95/04/01 14:26:05.21 server   Recovery dbid 1 ckpt (1385,19)
00:95/04/01 14:26:05.24 server   Recovery no active transactions
      before ckpt.
/* 7) Servername */
00:95/04/01 14:26:05.67 server   server name is 'ddsdba1'
00:95/04/01 14:26:05.73 server   Activating disk 'sd4b'.
/* 8) Server Devices and Mirrors — devices are NOT mirrored */
00:95/04/01 14:26:05.73 kernel   Initializing virtual device 36,
      '/rsd4b'
/* 9) Asynchronous I/O in use for Server Devices */
00:95/04/01 14:26:05.74 kernel   Virtual device 36 started using
      asynchronous i/o.
00:95/04/01 14:26:05.74 server   Activating disk 'sd4d'.
00:95/04/01 14:26:05.74 kernel   Initializing virtual device 10,
      '/dev/rsd4d'
00:95/04/01 14:26:05.75 kernel   Virtual device 10 started using
      asynchronous i/o.
...
...
...
00:95/04/01 14:26:06.04 server   Activating disk 'sybsecurity'.
00:95/04/01 14:26:06.04 kernel   Initializing virtual device 2,
      '/dev/rsd6h'
00:95/04/01 14:26:06.05 kernel   Virtual device 2 started using
asynchronous i/o.
00:95/04/01 14:26:06.05 server   Activating disk 'sysprocsdev'.
```

```
00:95/04/01 14:26:06.05 kernel  Initializing virtual device 1,
        '/dev/rsd5h'
00:95/04/01 14:26:06.06 kernel  Virtual device 1 started using
        asynchronous i/o.
/* 10) Recovery of Databases */
00:95/04/01 14:26:06.18 server  Recovering database 'sybsecurity'.
00:95/04/01 14:26:06.21 server  Recovery dbid 5 ckpt (365,2) oldest
        tran=(365,1)
00:95/04/01 14:26:06.23 server  1 transactions rolled forward.
00:95/04/01 14:26:06.64 server  audproc: Loading global audit
        options from sysauditoptions.
00:95/04/01 14:26:06.66 server  audproc: Global audit options
        successfully loaded.
00:95/04/01 14:26:06.69 server  Recovering database 'model'.
00:95/04/01 14:26:06.70 server  Recovery dbid 3 ckpt (323,7)
00:95/04/01 14:26:06.70 server  Recovery no active transactions
        before ckpt.
00:95/04/01 14:26:06.82 server  Clearing temp db
00:95/04/01 14:26:09.94 server  Recovering database
        'sybsystemprocs'.
00:95/04/01 14:26:09.95 server  Recovery dbid 4 ckpt (4122,27)
00:95/04/01 14:26:09.95 server  Recovery no active transactions
        before ckpt.
00:95/04/01 14:26:10.40 server  Recovering database 'db1'.
00:95/04/01 14:26:10.41 server  Recovery dbid 6 ckpt (5299,6)
00:95/04/01 14:26:10.41 server  Recovery no active transactions
        before ckpt.
00:95/04/01 14:26:12.46 server  Recovering database 'db2'.
00:95/04/01 14:26:12.48 server  Recovery dbid 7 ckpt (2381666,9)
00:95/04/01 14:26:12.48 server  Recovery no active transactions
        before ckpt.
...
...
...
00:95/04/01 14:26:36.72 server  Recovering database 'dbn'.
00:95/04/01 14:26:36.75 server  Recovery dbid 8 ckpt (42729,5)
00:95/04/01 14:26:36.75 server  Recovery no active transactions
        before ckpt.
00:95/04/01 14:26:57.56 server  Recovery complete.
/* 11) Default Sort Order and Character Set */
00:95/04/01 14:26:57.56 server  SQL Server's default sort order is:
00:95/04/01 14:26:57.58 server          'bin_iso_1' (ID = 50)
00:95/04/01 14:26:57.58 server  on top of default character set:
00:95/04/01 14:26:57.58 server          'iso_1' (ID = 1).
```

Example of System 11 SQL Server Errorlog

Items 1 through 11 are shown in the errorlog below. Each item is marked with a comment line /* <item> */ above the relevant portion of the errorlog

```
machine1: more errorlog_PSYCHO11
00:96/07/15 12:14:54.07 kernel  Using config area from primary
    master device.
00:96/07/15 12:14:54.20 kernel  Warning: Using default file
    '/home/sybase/PSYCHO11.cfg' since a configuration file was not
    specified. Specify a configuration file name in the RUNSERVER
    file to avoid this message.
00:96/07/15 12:14:56.22 kernel  Using 1024 file descriptors.
/* 1) SQl Server Version */
00:96/07/15 12:14:56.31 kernel  SQL Server/11.0.1/P/Sun_svr4/OS
    5.4/EBF6158/OPT/Fri Apr  5 20:30:14 PST 1996
00:96/07/15 12:14:56.31 kernel  Confidential property of Sybase,
    Inc.
00:96/07/15 12:14:56.31 kernel  (c) Copyright Sybase Inc., 1987,
    1996.
00:96/07/15 12:14:56.31 kernel  All rights reserved.
00:96/07/15 12:14:56.31 kernel
00:96/07/15 12:14:56.31 kernel  Use, duplication, or disclosure by
    the United States Government
00:96/07/15 12:14:56.31 kernel  is subject to restrictions as set
    forth in FAR subparagraphs
00:96/07/15 12:14:56.31 kernel  52.227-19(a)-(d) for civilian agency
    contracts and DFARS
00:96/07/15 12:14:56.31 kernel  252.227-7013(c)(1)(ii) for
    Department of Defense contracts.
00:96/07/15 12:14:56.31 kernel  Sybase reserves all unpublished
    rights under the copyright
00:96/07/15 12:14:56.31 kernel  laws of the United States.
00:96/07/15 12:14:56.31 kernel  Sybase, Inc. 6475 Christie Avenue,
    Emeryville, CA 94608 USA.
00:96/07/15 12:14:56.31 kernel  Using '/home/sybase/11.0.1/PSY
    CHO11.cfg' for configuration information.
/* 2) Location of Errorlog */
00:96/07/15 12:14:56.33 kernel  Logging SQL Server messages in file
    '/home/sybase/install/errorlog_PSYCHO11'.
/* 3) Maximum User Connections */
00:96/07/15 12:14:56.38 kernel  Network and device connection limit
    is 1014.
```

```
00:96/07/15 12:14:56.41 server   Number of proc buffers allocated:
      3041.
00:96/07/15 12:14:56.56 server   Number of blocks left for proc
      headers: 3091.
00:96/07/15 12:14:56.57 server   Memory allocated for the default
      data cache e: 12866 Kb
00:96/07/15 12:14:56.60 server   Size of the 2K memory pool: 12866 Kb
00:96/07/15 12:14:56.60 server   Memory allocated for the
      psycho_cache1 cache: 10240 Kb
00:96/07/15 12:14:56.61 server   Size of the 2K memory pool: 9216 Kb
00:96/07/15 12:14:56.62 server   Size of the 8K memory pool: 1024 Kb
/* 4) Master Device */
00:96/07/15 12:14:56.64 kernel   Initializing virtual device 0,
      '/dev/rdsk/c0t2d0s7'
00:96/07/15 12:14:56.65 kernel   Virtual device 0 started using
      asynchronous i/o.00:96/07/15 12:14:56.84 server   Opening
      Master Database ...
/* 5) Master Device is NOT Mirrored */
00:96/07/15 12:14:57.65 server   Loading SQL Server's default sort
      order and character set
00:96/07/15 12:14:57.69 kernel   ninit:0: listener type: master
00:96/07/15 12:14:57.69 kernel   ninit:0: listener endpoint: /dev/tcp
/* 6) Interfaces File Information */
00:96/07/15 12:14:57.69 kernel   ninit:0: listener raw address:
      \x000204018196c4500000000000000000
00:96/07/15 12:14:57.69 kernel   ninit:0: transport provider:
      T_COTS_ORD
00:96/07/15 12:14:57.84 server   Recovering database 'master'
00:96/07/15 12:14:57.91 server   Recovery dbid 1 ckpt (1955,28)
00:96/07/15 12:14:57.91 server   Recovery no active transactions
      before ckpt.
00:96/07/15 12:14:58.02 server   3 transactions rolled forward.
00:96/07/15 12:14:58.39 server   Database 'master' is now online.
00:96/07/15 12:14:58.41 server   The transaction log in the database
      'master' will use I/O size of 2 Kb.
/* 7) Servername */
00:96/07/15 12:14:58.52 server   server name is 'PSYCHO11'
/* 8) Server Devices and Mirrors (none are mirrored) */
00:96/07/15 12:14:58.55 server   Activating disk 'c0t2d0s4'.
00:96/07/15 12:14:58.55 kernel   Initializing virtual device 1,
      '/dev/rdsk/c0t2d0s4'
/* 9) Asynchronous I/O in use for Server Devices */
00:96/07/15 12:14:58.58 kernel   Virtual device 1 started using
      asynchronous i/o.
00:96/07/15 12:14:58.58 server   Activating disk 'c0t2d0s5'.
00:96/07/15 12:14:58.58 kernel   Initializing virtual device 2,
      '/dev/rdsk/c0t2d0s5'
```

```
00:96/07/15 12:14:58.59 kernel  Virtual device 2 started using
     asynchronous
00:96/07/15 12:14:58.59 server  Activating disk 'c0t2d0s6'.
00:96/07/15 12:14:58.59 kernel  Initializing virtual device 3,
     '/dev/rdsk/c0t2d0s6'
00:96/07/15 12:14:58.60 kernel  Virtual device 3 started using
     asynchronous i/o.
/* 10) Recovery of Databases */
00:96/07/15 12:14:59.00 server  Recovering database 'model'.
00:96/07/15 12:14:59.01 server  Recovery dbid 3 ckpt (442,15)
00:96/07/15 12:14:59.01 server  Recovery no active transactions
     before ckpt.
00:96/07/15 12:14:59.16 server  The transaction log in the database
     'model' will use I/O size of 2 Kb.
00:96/07/15 12:14:59.19 server  Database 'model' is now online.
00:96/07/15 12:14:59.21 server  Clearing temp db
00:96/07/15 12:15:02.51 server  Recovering database
     'sybsystemprocs'.
00:96/07/15 12:15:02.53 server  Recovery dbid 10 ckpt (8075,20)
00:96/07/15 12:15:02.53 server  Recovery no active transactions
     before ckpt.
00:96/07/15 12:15:03.21 server  The transaction log in the database
     'sybsystemprocs' will use I/O size of 2 Kb.
00:96/07/15 12:15:03.25 server  Database 'sybsystemprocs' is now
     online.
00:96/07/15 12:15:03.51 server  Recovering database 'admindb'.
00:96/07/15 12:15:03.53 server  Recovery dbid 4 ckpt (31287,19)
     oldest tran=(31287,17)
00:96/07/15 12:15:03.58 server  1 transactions rolled forward.
00:96/07/15 12:15:04.95 server  The transaction log in the database
     'admindb' will use I/O size of 2 Kb.
00:96/07/15 12:15:04.99 server  Database 'admindb' is now online.
00:96/07/15 12:15:05.08 server  Recovering database 'cmsdb'.
00:96/07/15 12:15:05.10 server  Recovery dbid 5 ckpt (84917,6)
00:96/07/15 12:15:05.10 server  Recovery no active transactions
     before ckpt.
00:96/07/15 12:15:05.29 server  2 transactions rolled forward.
00:96/07/15 12:15:07.50 server  The transaction log in the database
     'cmsdb' will use I/O size of 2 Kb.
00:96/07/15 12:15:07.54 server  Database 'cmsdb' is now online.
00:96/07/15 12:15:07.62 server  Recovering database 'curqtr_db'.
00:96/07/15 12:15:07.64 server  Recovery dbid 6 ckpt (102487,27)
00:96/07/15 12:15:07.64 server  Recovery no active transactions
     before ckpt.
00:96/07/15 12:15:09.47 server  The transaction log in the database
     'curqtr_db' will use I/O size of 2 Kb.
```

```
00:96/07/15 12:15:09.51 server  Database 'curqtr_db' is now online.
00:96/07/15 12:15:09.59 server  Recovering database 'pagedb'.
00:96/07/15 12:15:09.60 server  Recovery dbid 7 ckpt (12720,15)
00:96/07/15 12:15:09.60 server  Recovery no active transactions
     before ckpt.
00:96/07/15 12:15:10.01 server  The transaction log in the database
     'pagedb' will use I/O size of 2 Kb.
00:96/07/15 12:15:10.05 server  Database 'pagedb' is now online.
00:96/07/15 12:15:10.13 server  Recovering database 'quedb'.
00:96/07/15 12:15:10.14 server  Recovery dbid 8 ckpt (13081,15)
00:96/07/15 12:15:10.15 server  Recovery no active transactions
     before ckpt.
00:96/07/15 12:15:11.25 server  The transaction log in the database
     'quedb' will use I/O size of 2 Kb.
00:96/07/15 12:15:11.29 server  Database 'quedb' is now online.
00:96/07/15 12:15:11.37 server  Recovering database 'cms_map'.
00:96/07/15 12:15:11.38 server  Recovery dbid 9 ckpt (4127,12)
00:96/07/15 12:15:11.38 server  Recovery no active transactions
     before ckpt.
00:96/07/15 12:15:11.67 server  The transaction log in the database
     'cms_map' will use I/O size of 2 Kb.
00:96/07/15 12:15:11.70 server  Database 'cms_map' is now online.
00:96/07/15 12:15:11.76 server  Recovering database 'PSYCHORS_RSSD'.
00:96/07/15 12:15:11.78 server  Recovery dbid 11 ckpt (12000,4)
00:96/07/15 12:15:11.78 server  Recovery no active transactions
     before ckpt.
00:96/07/15 12:15:12.39 server  The transaction log in the database
     'PSYCHORS_RSSD' will use I/O size of 2 Kb.
00:96/07/15 12:15:12.44 server  Database 'PSYCHORS_RSSD' is now
     online.
00:96/07/15 12:15:12.49 server  Recovering database 'corruptable'.
00:96/07/15 12:15:12.51 server  Recovery dbid 12 ckpt (13733,10)
00:96/07/15 12:15:12.51 server  Recovery no active transactions
     before ckpt.
00:96/07/15 12:15:13.23 server  The transaction log in the database
     'corruptable' will use I/O size of 2 Kb.
00:96/07/15 12:15:13.27 server  Database 'corruptable' is now
     online.
00:96/07/15 12:15:13.28 server  Recovery complete.
/* 11) default Sort Order and Character Set */
00:96/07/15 12:15:13.28 server  SQL Server's default sort order is:
00:96/07/15 12:15:13.28 server      'bin_iso_1' (ID = 50)
00:96/07/15 12:15:13.28 server  on top of default character set:
00:96/07/15 12:15:13.28 server      'iso_1' (ID = 1).
00:96/07/19 10:50:36.10 server  DBCC TRACEON 8399, SPID 1
```

IMPACTS OF CREATING NEW DATABASES

You certainly know how to create a new database, and Chapter 8, discussed details of the process and how to plan where to put a database. You need to complete the task by remembering all the impacts of a new database and how to deal with them.

If appropriate, you must add the new database to the cron script that dumps databases, updates statistics, performs **dbcc** checks, and so forth. Further, you must check that the server machine has sufficient disk space or tape capacity to handle the additional database dump.

MODIFYING SYSTEM TABLES MANUALLY

From time to time you will need to update data in the system tables manually. You should review your plan for doing this with Sybase Technical Support before you begin. Also make sure you have a good dump of the *master* database before you make changes.

Warning

1. Updating system tables in not supported by Sybase. There is no guarantee that the system table schema will be maintained between releases which means manual updates that work for one version may not work on another version.

2. Do not perform such updates without consulting with Sybase Technical Support first.

3. Make sure you have dumps of everything you might need to rebuild the server in case the manual updates destroy something.

4. After updating system tables, you should restart the server to copy the changes into memory.

You must use **sp_reconfigure** to enable the **allow updates** option for the server. Without doing this you can't make updates to a system table.

You should select all the data from the system table before making any changes. This provides a record of what was there before you changed anything. You then begin a transaction and perform your updates. Before you commit the transaction, you should select all the data from the system table again to be sure you made the change you intended and only that change. Then you commit the transaction and you should now select all the data again to document the changes.

You must remember to reset the **allow updates** option, that is, turn it off so nobody else can update any of the system tables. This process is demonstrated in Chapter 7.

BCP COMMAND

The bcp command is very important for various operations. The command has many options and the format files, in particular, require a great deal of explanation. We do not cover the many aspects of the bcp command syntax here. The *Sybase SQL Server Utility Programs for UNIX* manual covers this subject very well.

FREE SPACE IN A DATABASE

You will need to know the free space available in each database. Often you really need to know the free space in a particular database segment. Just because there is free space in the database overall does not mean there is free space where you need it. If you need to add data to a table that is on its own user-defined segment, free space in the system segment may not help you.

The followingdatabase has been created with 400 Mb for data and 50 Mb for log. The actual server commands and outputs are shown after the computations below.

from **sp_spaceused** (this output shows space used by the whole database)

521

reserved	data	index_size	unused
314544 KB	113282 KB	167800 KB	33462 KB

```
113282 data
167800 index
 33462 unused, but already assigned to database objects
_____

314544 matches reserved
```

Now, database is 450 Mb overall, 50 Mb of log

```
450 Mb = 460800 Kb
 50 Mb  = 51200 Kb

 460800 Kb total database
- 51200 Kb log
_____

 409600 Kb
-314544 Kb reserved
_____

  95056 Kb = 92.8 Mb free space
```

compare with free kbytes shown in sp_helpdb <dbname> output

```
42800 Kb
51008 Kb
_____

93808 Kb free space = 91.6 Mb free space (within 2% of 92.8 Mb)
```

A related question comes up all too often; Do we have enough free space to create (or re-create) a clustered index on a specific table?

```
from sp_spaceused <tablename>
```

name	rowtotal	reserved	data	index_size	unused
service_orders	20599	116654 KB	17028 KB	84602 KB	15024 KB

For 17028 Kb of actual table data, we need roughly 120 percent of table space to create a clustered index, 1.2 * 17028 Kb = 20434 Kb (20 Mb) and we have 93,808 Kb (91.6 Mb) of free space in the database. We have plenty of room to build the new clustered index.

Here is the actual SQL Server output that was used to perform these free space computations.

```
1> sp_helpdb cmsdb
2> go
```

name	db_size	owner	dbid	created	status
cmsdb	400.0 MB	sa	9	Apr 25, 1996	no options set

device_fragments	size	usage	free kbytes
c0t2d0s4	150.0 MB	data only	0
c0t2d0s4	200.0 MB	data only	42800
c0t2d0s6	50.0 MB	log only	51008

device	segment
c0t2d0s4	default
c0t2d0s4	system
c0t2d0s6	logsegment

```
(return status = 0)
1> sp_spaceused
2> go
```

database_name	database_size
cmsdb	400.0 MB

reserved	data	index_size	unused
314544 KB	113282 KB	167800 KB	33462 KB

```
(return status = 0)
```

```
1> sp_spaceused service_orders
2> go
```

name	rowtotal	reserved	data	index_size	unused
service_orders	20599	116654 KB	17028 KB	84602 KB	15024 KB

```
(return status = 0)
```

FULL TRANSACTION LOG OR OTHER SEGMENT (1105 ERROR)

This procedure may not seem important since thresholds should be able to stop all user processes before the transaction log actually fills up. However, this procedure is still relevant for three reasons. First, it provides you with a process to determine exactly which segment within your database actually caused the 1105 error. Thresholds can and should be used to prevent the transaction log from filling up, but there are other segments in your database and any of them can fill up. Second, thresholds are not always present and may not always work. If you have upgraded a database from 4.9.2 to either System 10 or System 11, you have to manually activate the last-chance threshold for the database. If this has not been done, there is not a last-chance threshold on the transaction log and you can get 1105 errors. Third, the last-chance threshold that will prevent the transaction log from filling up can exist only in databases where the transaction log is on a separate server device. If this is not the case, the database can still experience 1105 errors on the transaction log.

The effects of a full transaction log have been discussed in Chapters 11 and 9. When you encounter an 1105 error, you need a step-by-step process that you can follow to verify exactly what the problem is before you can fix it. We discuss such a procedure below.

The procedure boils down to verifying that you indeed have a repeatable 1105 error, verifying which segment of which database is full, and resolving the problem. Note that it is entirely possible that the transaction that encountered the 1105 error may have been rolled back as a result of the 1105 error itself. When you try to verify the segment being full, you may find that there is some space available. At that point you must decide whether or not to try to free up more space in the segment or wait for the user to encounter the 1105 error again at which time you would repeat the process here. Also, while the 1105 error itself will report which segment in which database is full, you must verify this for yourself.

Verify Which Database Is Involved

You must first verify which database encountered the 1105 error. You should be able to determine this from the user reports and from the server errorlog. If you are unable to determine which database had the 1105 error, you need to proceed to the next step 2) and repeat the process described for each and every database on the server.

Determine Which Database Segment Is Full

If you know which database had the 1105 error you proceed as described next. If you are not sure which database had the 1105 error you must repeat the process described here for each and every database on the server.

check free space in database segments

checkpoint to verify transaction log is full

create table to verify *system* and *default* segments full

create table to verify user-defined segment full

Check Free Space in Database Segments

You can do this with the **sp_helpdb** and **sp_helpsegment** commands respectively. If you execute **sp_helpdb <databasename>**, the server will show you the free space (in Kb) available in each segment of the database. Note that this column is only presented in SQL Server Systems 10 and 11. This is very useful when checking the free space in the server and when looking for segments that are filling up. This information can help you determine where an 1105 error has occurred. You can also get this information from **sp_helpsegment <segmentname>**, but the free space is then reported in 2K pages (see Objects on a Segment in this chapter). An example of this is shown below.

```
machine1: isql -Usa -STHEBIRDS11
Password:
1> use psychodb
2> go
1> sp_helpdb psychodb
2> go
    name        db_size owner      dbid       created         status
  psychodb      400.0 MB sa          9      Apr 25, 1996   no options set

device_fragments        size           usage       free kbytes
  c0t2d0s4            150.0 MB       data only          0
  c0t2d0s4            200.0 MB       data only        42800
  c0t2d0s6             50.0 MB       log only         51008
```

```
   device                 segment
 c0t2d0s4                 default
 c0t2d0s4                 system
 c0t2d0s6               logsegment
```

(return status = 0)

Checkpoint to Verify Transaction Log Is Full

First, get into the database and execute **checkpoint**. If the **check-point** command returns normally, the transaction log is not completely full. This means you must not use the **dump transaction** command with the **no_log** option. Using **dump transaction** with **no_log** when the transaction log is not completely full can cause corruption and other problems. The fact that the transaction log is not full tells you one of three things:

1. Wrong Database. If indeed it is a transaction log (*logsegment*) that filled and caused the 1105, you are not looking at that transaction log. You need to determine the database that encountered the 1105 error.

2. Transient 1105 Error. It is entirely possible that the transaction that encountered the 1105 error may have been rolled back as a result of the 1105 error itself. Now you need to decide if you need to free up more transaction log space or simply wait for the 1105 problem to reoccur.

3. 1105 on Some Other Segment. You may be in the database that encountered the 1105 error, but it wasn't the transaction log that filled.

If the **checkpoint** command does not return normally and produces an 1105 error, that means the transaction log is completely full; there isn't even enough room to write the checkpoint record. You need to move to "Dealing with a Full Transaction" to deal with the full transaction log.

Create Table to verify *system* and *default* Segments Full

Next attempt to create a table in the database. Note that you should create a small table with a table name that is very unusual, perhaps something like

```
create table psycho1(a int)
```

This makes it easy to remove the table later on since the table name will stand out among the names in *sysobjects* in case you forget to remove it immediately after this experiment. If the **create table** completes normally, than you have verified that there is space to create objects in the database. Note that for a simple database, one that does not have any user-defined segments, this verifies that the *default* and *system* segments are not full.

If the **create table** command fails and you get the 1105 error again this means the segment in which you were trying to create the table is full. You must add space to the segment, see "Dealing with a Full Segment".

Once you have finished with this segment, you should drop the table you just created. Be very careful to ensure that you are dropping the correct table, that is, the table you just created while verifying which segment was full.

Create Table to Verify User-Defined Segment Full

Now attempt to create a table in the user-defined segment that you suspect is full. If the database does have user-defined segments and you suspect that a user-defined segment is full, you must attempt to create a table in each user-defined segment to verify exactly which segment is full. The syntax would be

```
create table psycho1 (a int) on <segment_name>
```

If the **create table** command fails and you get the 1105 error again, this means the segment in which you were trying to create the table is full. You must add space to the segment, see "Dealing with a Full Database Segment.".

Once you have finished with this segment, you should drop the table you just created. Be very careful to ensure that you are dropping the correct table, that is, the table you just created while verifying which segment was full.

Dealing with a Full Transaction Log

At this point you should attempt a **dump transaction** without any options, that is, a normal transaction log dump. This will make a copy of the transaction log and truncate any transaction log pages that contain completed (committed or rolled back) transactions). After the **dump transaction** command completes, you should try **checkpoint** again. If it works normally, then the transaction log is not completely full. You should check how full the transaction log is using

```
sp_spaceused syslogs
```

or

```
sp_helpdb <databasename>
```

or

```
sp_helpsegment logsegment
```

and compare the results with the size of the transaction log for the database. If this tells you that the transaction log is close to full you need to decide whether to wait for further 1105 errors or try to free up more transaction log space. Since you have already dumped the transaction log, any completed transactions should have been truncated. This means you have an ongoing transaction that needs to be completed (committed or rolled back) so that more of the transaction log can be truncated

If the second attempt at **checkpoint** still fails and gives the same 1105 error you have no choice. You must free up space in the transaction log before the database can accept any more changes. You can **dump transaction** with the **no_log** option which will truncate the log without trying to write the checkpoint record in the transaction log. After this command completes you should try **checkpoint** yet again.

If this **checkpoint** completes normally, you should use **sp_spaceused** to check how much space in the transaction log was freed up. If the transaction log is now close to empty you are finished. Note that you have broken the sequence of transaction logs and that affects your ability to recover the database (see Chapter 9).

If this **checkpoint** command does not succeed and you still get an 1105 error, that means the transaction log is still completely full and it can't be truncated at all because there is an ongoing transaction (one that has not committed or been rolled back) at the very beginning of the transaction log. Recall that even one ongoing transaction in the transaction log prevents the truncation of any of the following pages of the transaction log whether or not they contain completed or ongoing transactions.

At this point you need to kill the server process that generated the ongoing transaction or get the associated user to log out of the server which would kill and roll back the ongoing transaction. The problem here is how to identify which user is responsible for the ongoing transaction. Unless you have some way of telling which user(s) might be responsible, perhaps through the way your application(s) interact with the user, you have little choice other than to kill user processes and hope that clears things up or to simply shut down and restart the server which will effectively kill all the server users and roll back any ongoing transactions.

Note that you can always add space to the transaction log (*logsegment*) to clear up the 1105 error, but this usually doesn't help, and you don't want to have the size of the transaction log constantly increasing (see Chapter 8). Unless you have a good reason to increase the size of the transaction log, you should clear up the 1105 error by freeing space within the current transaction log.

Dealing with a Full Database Segment

Once you have verified that a specific database segment is full, you must add space to the segment before any further changes can be made to objects in that segment. Note that we are assuming the full segment is not the transaction log (*logsegment*). You must be careful any time you add space to the database. If you are adding space to a segment, on a server device that is already supporting that database segment you can proceed without too much concern. If this is not the case, or if you need to add space to a user-defined segment, you must be very cautious. User-defined segments are generally created to isolate specific database objects (tables or indexes) to specific server devices for performance reasons. If you start adding space to such a segment on the wrong server device(s), you may be setting up a situation where a given server device is supporting multiple segments and any performance benefits of isolating the objects on the user-defined segment (i.e., the whole reason for bothering with the user-defined segment in the first place) may be lost. See Chapter 8 for discussion of the problems with adding space to database segments and Chapter 11 for discussion of the need to plan ahead to provide server devices to support adding space to database segments.

Multiple Segments on a Server Device

As a final note, you should be aware that if a server device supports multiple database segments (this is very normal), it is possible that the segment reported to be full in the 1105 is only one of the segments that is full. For example, it is very normal for a database to be created with the transaction log (*logsegment*) on a separate device. This means the two other segments that are always created for any database, the *default* and *system* segments, are both supported by the other server devices assigned to the database. Hence, you may get an 1105 error that tells you the *system* segment is full, but if you try to create a table in the database, which would try to create the table in the *default* segment, you would get an 1105 error also. This simply means you may get 1105 errors reporting multiple segments being full. If those segments are supported by the same server devices, then, indeed, all those segments are full and adding space on any of the server devices that support these multiple segments will add space to all the segments of that server device at the same time.

Installing and Upgrading SQL Server

Table of Topics

INTRODUCTION

Upgrading the SQL Server is a routine part of your job as the DBA. Upgrading comes in many forms. The simplest is applying an EBF (Emergency Bug Fix—note that "emergency" is overstated since EBFs come out on a regular basis), followed by a 'rollup' that is an update of the server containing many bug fixes that have been developed over some period of time and finally a "version" upgrade which generally involves modifying portions of the databases in a manner that prevents you from going back to the previous version of the server. We discuss the following topics:

SQL SERVER VERSIONS

There are differences in the process of installation and upgrading for each of the SQL Server versions. Since these differences are fairly involved, we cover the installation and upgrade of each version in a separate section. We list only the highlights here.

SQL Server 4.9.2

Installation uses sybconfig. 4.9.2 can run on either SunOS or Solaris.

For Upgrading, you will need to consult with Sybase Tech Support if you aren't at 4.9.2.

SQL Server System 10

Installation uses sybinit and involves creating the *sybsystemprocs* database. Creating the *sybsecurity* database is optional, but it is required if you want to use the auditing features of the server. System 10 can be installed on both SunOS and Solaris.

Upgrading from 4.9.2 involves several issues, such as checking for reserved word conflicts, setting up the raw disk partitions needed for the new system databases *sybsystemprocs* and *sybsecurity*, and so forth.

SQL Server System 11

Installation requires Solaris 2.4 or higher for the Sun platform. Installation uses `sybinit` and involves creating the *sybsystemprocs* database. Creating the *sybsecurity* database is optional but is required if you want to use the auditing features of the server.

Upgrading may require that you first upgrade the server machine OS to Solaris. You can upgrade from either System 10 or 4.9.2. Upgrading from System 10, you can go one of two ways. First, you can simply upgrade the entire existing System 10 Server. Second, you can install the System 11 Server, create the databases, and load dumps of the System 10 Server directly into the System 11 Server. The System 11 Server will upgrade these databases as the last step of the load process. Upgrading from 4.9.2 involves all the steps of upgrading from 4.9.2 to System 10, that is, reserved word issues, new databases *sybsystemprocs* and *sybsecurity*, and so forth.

INSTALLING SQL SERVER

The process of installing a SQL server is very simple if done properly. Part of the mystery of installing a server is that for a normal site, you don't install the server very often. When you need to, it has often been a long time since you last installed a server. Note that the documentation that is supplied with the product is very good, but it assumes you have the disks installed and partitioned before you start. You also need to realize that the documentation stops after the very basic installation is done. We will cover the more detailed and complex real-world process of installing a server and configuring it for use. We cover the preparatory work that must be done before installation begins and the actual output of a `sybinit` (`sybconfig` for 4.9.2) session for installation of each version of the server is included on the CD-ROM. The differences are not great but it is good to see what the process looks like before you begin.

You need to understand that `sybinit` can be rerun if you make a mistake or change your mind. However, you also need to realize that `sybinit` completely wipes out any and all data regarding any server that was previously installed on the raw partitions where `sybinit` is creating the master device and, the sysprocsdev and sybsecurity devices. You can rerun as often as needed to get it right, but once you are settled on the basic installation of the server you need to be very careful about running `sybinit` again. Note that you may need to run `sybinit` again to change the configuration of the server, but you must realize that by choosing the wrong options in the program you can wipe out the existing server.

Preparing for Installation

Before you can begin the actual installation of a Sybase SQL Server you must prepare the server machine. This involves several steps and we will discuss each of the following server installation preparation checklist items:

Obtain and read the Installation guide, release notes and administration supplement

Verify sybase technical support arrangements

Verify server machine SA support

Inform users and management

`su` privileges

Server machine installation

`setenv` SYBASE `/home/sybase`

Product files in installation directory

Run `sybinit`

Obtain and Read the Installation Guide, Release Notes, and Administration Supplement

Before you do anything else, you absolutely must order, obtain, and read the *Sybase SQL Server Installation Guide*, *Release Notes* and the *System Administration Guide Supplement* that should have been included when you ordered the product. These documents contain important information that is specific to the hardware and operating system platform you will be using to support SQL Server. These documents are not shipped with every update to the SQL Server so make sure you keep these documents available at all times. Note that if you are supporting servers on multiple platforms, you need to build up a small library of installation guides for each SQL Server version on each platform and operating system.

If you are a real DBA, you'll actually find reading these documents interesting and entertaining. The information they contain is what makes you marketable and the lack thereof is what causes your fellow DBAs to take a sick day whenever a server needs to be installed. You will also find that these documents are as valuable as gold-pressed latinum, that is, seemingly worthless now, but trust me they will be very valuable in the future. You should lock them up somewhere since they are specific to the platform and you will need them in the event of a disaster that requires a complete server installation. Do not skip this step. You will be sorry. The tips in these documents will make you a guru without really trying.

Verify Sybase Technical Support Arrangements

Verify what level of support you have with Sybase Technical Support. You must not wait until your installation has gone sour to find out the bean counters didn't pay for Technical Support. If you don't have 24-hour, 7-day a week support, you should consider the wisdom of installing during off-hours unless you can wait until the next day to get support. Before beginning the installation you should call Sybase Technical Support and verify that they know about your support arrangements as well. You should verify that all the proper persons in your organization are known to Sybase Technical Support as persons authorized to call in cases and verify that your current phone and fax numbers are accurate as known to Sybase.

Verify Server Machine SA Support

You must verify that you have the server machine SA support you need. Verify that there is an SA assigned to support your server machine and that the person is aware of the impending server installation. Be nice to this person. Discuss your needs with them well ahead of time. From reading the installation guides you should be able to point out what specific UNIX kernel parameters should be set up and verified to support SQL Server. Ask the SA person about operating system patches, which are needed. Are they readily available and is all the hardware installed and configured? Make sure you give the SA person sufficient lead time to fix any problems before you begin installation. Note that you may be both the DBA and the SA person for this server machine. That is fine but make sure you understand everything you will need for this server installation. Perhaps you know some other SA persons who are more experienced with the hardware and especially with installing SQL Server on the platform. If so, you should query them now before you are stuck. Further, you must verify what sort of arrangements have been made for technical support from the hardware/software vendors supplying the platform you are installing on. This should include any third-party hardware and/or software that needs to be operational to support the SQL Server. Examples of this would include SQL BackTrack, a third-party software product that supplies logical and physical backup and recovery of database objects. If you need to have such a product installed and operational as part of the server installation, you must clarify the technical support arrangements for the product.

Be nice to the server machine SA person(s) and all the people you deal with in Technical Support. Making cookies works well. Visit them if at all possible and distribute the cookies. Call it a "Goodwill Tour." It works. They are so accustomed to being ignored and/or treated like dirt that they will be stunned by your kindness. They will remember and they will help you when your ass is out over the edge and the CIO is perched in your cubicle cawing, "'When will the server be up? When will the server be up?"

For reasons best known to themselves, the managers of your department, without involving any technical person, decide that moving to a new hardware platform will improve the throughput of your businesses applications by 1000 percent (10x). They make this decision with no benchmarks or other testing of any kind. The hardware arrives and you are told to install the SQL Server on all machines. There are only two SA persons in your organization who are experienced with this new hardware platform. One of them is going to Tokyo next week to install machines for your company. The other will be on vacation for two weeks a week from now. You have been given a deadline two weeks from now to have all four new machines installed and configured with SQL Servers installed and all user databases created and loaded. Don't you wish you had a window office so you could make decisions like this? Make sure you have the SA support you need.

Inform Users and Management

Make sure your users and your management know how long the server installation will take and what the possible problems may be. If you are installing a new server on the same hardware and operating system ofother servers you have installed before you can make promises. Don't underestimate the time needed for installing and testing a new server on either a new hardware or operating system platform. In either case you should identify or have someone else identify a test plan that will provide some objective way of determining that the newly installed server is doing what it was installed to do. This may involve running business applications against the new server for some period of time before the business switches to the new server. Note that if the new server will be supporting an existing application, you need to support both the old and new servers through the installation and testing of the new server.

su Privileges

Make sure you have su privilege on the server machine or that someone who does will be available to you throughout the server installation process. You will need to become root to run the format command. You will need to run the format command to verify all the disks that are attached to the server machine. Each of the DBAs who will support the server must have access to these privileges. Many organizations do not allow the DBA to have root access to the server machine, reserving this for the server machine SA. This is fine, but, as the DBA, you must ensure that someone with root access is available to you during the installation.

Server Machine Installation

Before you can begin the installation of a server you need to complete the tasks of installing the server machine, connecting the server machine to the network, installing the physical disks, and partitioning the physical disks that will support server devices.

Install Server Machine

The first step is, of course, to install the server machine. You need to have the server machine installed and checked out by the server machine SA. You also need to ensure that the server machine is on the network and that it can communicate with the other server machines in your database system. Finally, the physical disks must be installed. As a part of your capacity planning effort, you should have a very clear idea of how many physical disks are required for the server devices and file systems needed to support the server you will be installing.

Check What Disks Are Installed

You need to check that all the disks you think are installed are known to the server machine. You need to su to root and execute the format command. This is one of the reasons that each DBA must have su privilege on all the server machines. Note that you must not be creative with the format command. Further, you should inform the server machine SA that you need the output of the format command (and others, as we shall see) and that you intend to execute these commands as you need to. If the server machine SA objects, then they will have to supply these outputs whenever you need them. After executing the format command exit from it by typing control-D (^D) and don't try anything else with the format command.

The output of the format command tells you three things. First, the names of all the physical disks that the server machine is aware of. Second, which physical disks are attached to which controllers. This information is vital to spreading database segments over controllers properly. Third, how many physical disks are attached to any one controller. As discussed previously, you must determine the maximum number of physical disks that can be attached to one controller on your particular hardware platform before I/O bottlenecks are created. For the Sun box used here, the maximum number of physical disks that should be attached to one controller is four. In the output shown below the server machine is machine 1. After becoming the "root" user using the su command the format command displays each of the physical disks and which controller it is attached to. Looking at the output for one physical disk;

```
0.  c0t3d0 <SUN2.1G cyl 2733 alt 2 hd 19 sec 80>
/iommu@f,e0000000/sbus@f,e0001000/espdma@f,400000/esp@f,800000/sd@3,0
```

This shows you that the first physical disk is t3d0 and it is attached to controller c0. The second line is information about the physical disk sd0. From looking at the entire output of the format command we see that there are six physical disks and two controllers (c0, c1) and there are four or less physical disks attached to each controller.

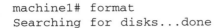
```
machine1# format
Searching for disks...done


AVAILABLE DISK SELECTIONS:
    0. c0t3d0 <SUN2.1G cyl 2733 alt 2 hd 19 sec 80>
       /iommu@f,e0000000/sbus@f,e0001000/espdma@f,400000/esp@f,
       800000/sd@3,0
    1. c0t5d0 <SUN4.2G cyl 3880 alt 2 hd 16 sec 135>
       /iommu@f,e0000000/sbus@f,e0001000/espdma@f,400000/esp@f,
       800000/sd@5,0
    2. c1t0d0 <SUN4.2G cyl 3880 alt 2 hd 16 sec 135>
       /iommu@f,e0000000/sbus@f,e0001000/QLGC,isp@0,10000/sd@0,0
    3. c1t1d0 <SUN4.2G cyl 3880 alt 2 hd 16 sec 135>
       /iommu@f,e0000000/sbus@f,e0001000/QLGC,isp@0,10000/sd@1,0
    4. c1t2d0 <SUN4.2G cyl 3880 alt 2 hd 16 sec 135>
       /iommu@f,e0000000/sbus@f,e0001000/QLGC,isp@0,10000/sd@2,0
    5. c1t3d0 <SUN4.2G cyl 3880 alt 2 hd 16 sec 135>
       /iommu@f,e0000000/sbus@f,e0001000/QLGC,isp@0,10000/sd@3,0
Specify disk (enter its number):
```

Partition Disks

Once you have verified the physical disks and controllers on the server machine, you must decide which physical disks will be used for server devices, mirrors of server devices and file systems You should apply your standard disk partitioning to all the physical disks that will support server devices and the mirrors of server devices. The physical disks that will support file systems are partitioned as needed for the individual file systems. You must work with the server machine SA to work out the partitioning for file system disks.

The standard disk partitioning for physical disks that support server devices or their mirrors has been presented previously. In summary it is as follows:

1. Assign cylinder 0 of the physical disk to partition 0, and never use partition 0, have the server machine SA change the ownership on the files that control partition 0 access (/dev/dsk/<disk_name>a and /dev/r<disk_name>a) to root so that UNIX user sybase can't access them.

2. Assign enough cylinders to partition 7 to provide 50 Mb of space. You won't be able to assign exactly 50 Mb but get as close as you can.

3. Assign one-fifth or the remaining disk space to each of the partitions 1, 3, 4, 5, 6—the space given to each partition should be identical. If needed to create five equal partitions add any left-over space to partition 7.

4. Don't use partition 2 at all. Have the server machine SA change the ownership on the files that control the 2 partition so UNIX user sybase can"t access the 2 partition.

5. Have the server machine SA change the ownership of all files that control the raw partitions of physical disks that will support server devices to UNIX user sybase—except for partition 0 and 2.

Compute Size of Partitions for Server Devices

Once you have the disks partitioned, you must check each partition to determine the exact size of each partition you will be using to support server devices. You need to execute the `prtvtoc` command for each physical disk that will support server devices. The output of the `prtvtoc` command for one physical disk is shown below. For each partition that will support a server device, you must convert the number of sectors to Mb. For example, for partition (or slice) 1, there are 1,639,440 sectors. Multiply this by 512 bytes/sector and divide by 1024*1024 bytes/Mb to get 800.51 Mb. The number of megabytes is then rounded down to the nearest whole number of Mb and then converted into the equivalent number of 2K pages that you need to use when creating the server device on the partition using the **disk init** command. Note that this is another advantage of establishing and applying a standard disk partitioning scheme. Most of the partitions will be the same size, greatly reducing the number of times you need to convert the number of sectors to megabytes.

```
machine1: /usr/sbin/prtvtoc /dev/rdsk/c0t5d0s1
* /dev/rdsk/c0t5d0s1 partition map
*
* Dimensions:
*      512 bytes/sector
*      135 sectors/track
*       16 tracks/cylinder
*     2160 sectors/cylinder
*     4392 cylinders
```

```
*       3880 accessible cylinders
*
* Flags:
*    1: unmountable
*   10: read-only
*
*                          First      Sector     Last
Partition   Tag   Flags   Sector      Count      Sector   Mount Directory
    0        0     00        0         2160       2159
    1        3     01       2160       1639440    1641599  -> cylinder 0
    2        5     01        0         8380800    8380799
    3        0     00       1641600    1639440    3281039 -
                                                  > 800.51 Mb 800 Mb =
                                                  409600 2K pages
    4        0     00       3281040    1639440    4920479
    5        0     00       4920480    1639440    6559919
    6        4     00       6559920    1639440    8199359
    7        0     00       8199360    181440     8380799 -
                                                  > 88.59 Mb 88 Mb =
                                                  45056 2K pages
```

Note that you are only concerned with determining the size of partitions that will support server devices. As discussed previously (see Chapter 8), you can greatly simplify your life by assigning whole physical disks to server devices and other whole physical disks to support the mirrors or server devices. Still, you only need to determine the exact size of a partition that will support a server device.

For this example, using the whole physical disk , the partitions that will be used to support server devices are partitions 3, 4, 5, and 6, all of which have 1,639,440 sectors, and partition 7 which has 181,440 sectors. You convert the number of sectors to the size of the partition in bytes by multiplying the number of sectors by 512 bytes per sector (this value is for the Sun Solaris environment and you must verify the correct value for your environment). Once you have the partition size in bytes you use that value for two things. First, convert the partition size in bytes to megabytes by dividing the partition size in bytes by 1024 * 1024 which is 1 Mb. You don't want to divide by one million. Second, convert the partition size in bytes to the equivalent number of 2K pages. One data page for SQL Server running in the Sun Solaris environment is 2048 bytes or 2K. Again, you must verify the size of a data page in bytes for the server running on your specific environment.

For the one specific partition sizes of our example, the numbers work out like this.

sectors	# of bytes	Mb	2K pages
1639440	839393280	800.51	409860
	# of bytes = sectors * 512 (bytes/sector for Solaris)	MB = # of bytes / 1024 *1024 (bytes per MB)	2K pages = # of bytes / 2048 (bytes/datapage for SQL Server for Sun Solaris)

Not you need to recall that as discussed previously (see Chapter 8), there are several things about physical disk partitions and server devices that come up now. You can have only one server device assigned to a one physical disk partition. If you assign a 30-Mb server device to a 500-Mb partition, you are wasting 470 Mb of disk space. That is why you need to have a small physical partition for the master device of 50 Mb.

Note that for a System 11 SQL Server you should have the *master* database, the *sybsystemprocv* database, and the *sybsecurity* database on separate server devices and all three of these devices should be around 50 Mb. You will need to provide small partitions for all three of these devices, preferably on different physical disks.

Once you have computed the actual size of each partition, you should round this size down to the nearest whole number of megabytes. You don't want to execute **disk init** with a size that is anything other than a whole number of megabytes. Note that you will need to execute **disk init** later on for each server device you need to support the server and the databases, except for the master device. The master device is created for you when you run `sybinit` or `buildmaster`, which you should not use unless you know what you are doing, or are instructed to do so by Sybase Technical Support.

Note that for a System 10 SQL Server `sybinit` will also create the *sysprocsdev* and *sybsecurity* devices for you while you are running `sybinit`.

You must not **disk init** the master device. You must know the size of the partition that will support the master device and be prepared to tell `sybinit` how big the master device should be. You should tell `sybinit` that the master device size is the largest whole number of megabytes that will fit on the partition. Note that for System 10 you also must not **disk init** the *sysprocsdev* or the *sybsecurity* devices.

File Systems Available

You need to verify the file systems that are available on the server machine. You get this information from the command df -k. Sample output for the df -k command is shown below. Note that the file systems should be set up by the server machine SA. Hence, you don't need to check the partitions of the disks that support the file systems. You should avoid mixing file systems and server devices on the same physical disk.

```
machine1: df -k
Filesystem          kbytes      used      avail    capacity   Mounted on
/dev/dsk/c0t3d0s0    674471    262434    344597      44%          /
/proc                    0         0         0        0%        /proc
fd                       0         0         0        0%       /dev/fd
swap                501984         8    501976        1%        /tmp
/dev/dsk/c0t3d0s7  1032142    217464    711468       24%      xport/home
/dev/dsk/c1t0d0s1   806647     35190    690797        5%    /export/disk1
```

You need to check that the directory where you will install the server and its associated products has sufficient space. For this example, the SYBASE home directory (also called the installation directory) will be machine1:/home/sybase. The SYBASE home directory is the directory where you load all the server files from the product tape, or where you copy such files from another machine. Whenever possible it is better to load the product tape. That way you have all the optional files that may be needed for configuring the server. You need to check the Sybase installation guide for your platform and operating system to verify the disk space needed for loading all the server files. Note that you must also ensure that all the file systems you need to install and support the SQL Server must be owned by UNIX user sybase, the UNIX user who will be starting and shutting down the server and making dumps to tape and to file systems.

Permissions on Devices and /home/sybase Directory

You must verify that you and any other DBA's that will support this server can access the server machine as the UNIX user sybase, which is required in order to run the sybinit program to install SQL Server. Since you will install the server as UNIX user "sybase" you need to change the ownership of various files to "sybase" before you run `sybinit`.

Note that you should not run `sybinit`, or start the SQL Server as UNIX user root. You can do this, and certainly root has the permissions needed to execute these programs. However, you run the risk of wiping out anything and everything on the system. You should not run as root unless you have a specific need to. You do not need to be root to run `sybinit` or to start the SQL Server.

You must verify that you have changed the ownership of the installation directory which means changing the ownership of all the files in `/home/sybase` and all the subdirectories to UNIX user sybase. Since `sybinit` will create the master device you also need to change the ownership of the file that controls the raw partition that will support the master device to UNIX user sybase also. Note that `sybinit` will create the sysprocsdev and sybsecurity devices in addition to the master device so you need to change the ownership of the files that control the raw partitions that will support these devices as well.

First, check all the partitions (or slices) that are available on the system.

```
machine1: cd /dev/rdsk
machine1: ls
c0t3d0s0     c0t3d0s7     c0t5d0s6     c0t6d0s5     c1t0d0s4     c1t1d0s3
c1t2d0s2     c1t3d0s1
c0t3d0s1     c0t5d0s0     c0t5d0s7     c0t6d0s6     c1t0d0s5     c1t1d0s4
c1t2d0s3     c1t3d0s2
c0t3d0s2     c0t5d0s1     c0t6d0s0     c0t6d0s7     c1t0d0s6     c1t1d0s5
c1t2d0s4     c1t3d0s3
c0t3d0s3     c0t5d0s2     c0t6d0s1     c1t0d0s0     c1t0d0s7     c1t1d0s6
c1t2d0s5     c1t3d0s4
c0t3d0s4     c0t5d0s3     c0t6d0s2     c1t0d0s1     c1t1d0s0     c1t1d0s7
c1t2d0s6     c1t3d0s5
c0t3d0s5     c0t5d0s4     c0t6d0s3     c1t0d0s2     c1t1d0s1     c1t2d0s0
c1t2d0s7     c1t3d0s6
c0t3d0s6     c0t5d0s5     c0t6d0s4     c1t0d0s3     c1t1d0s2     c1t2d0s1
c1t3d0s0     c1t3d0s7
```

Now, check the ownership of one of the files that controls access to a raw partition.

```
machine1: ls -l c0t5d0s3
lrwxrwxrwx   1 root        other          88 Jul 22 16:49 c0t5d0s3 ->
../../devices/iommu@f,e0000000/sbus@f,e0001000/espdma@f,400000/esp@f,
800000/sd@5,0:d,raw
```

Note that this is not correct in that the raw partition appears to be owned by root. You must use the L option of the ls command to see what is really happening in the Solaris environment.

```
machine1: ls -Ll c0t5d0s3
crw-r----   1 sybase    sys        32, 43 Jul 22 16:49 c0t5d0s3
```

setenv SYBASE /home/sybase

You must verify that the environment variable SYBASE is set to point to the SYBASE installation directory which is /home/sybase. You can check this by executing echo $SYBASE and, if needed, you can set this environment variable by executing setenv SYBASE /home/sybase. If you don't have this set correctly sybinit won't be able to complete the server installation, or it won't run at all.

Product Files in Installation Directory

You must have all the SQL Server product set files in the installation directory /home/sybase. If you have multiple versions of SQL Server or other Sybase products, you should install each version of each product in a separate directory. For example, the files for System 10 Version of SQL Server should be loaded into /home/sybase/10.0.2 while the files for System 11 are in /home/sybase/11.0.1. You can load these files from the product tape or, if you are installing a version of the SQL Server that is already running on a server machine in your database system you can copy the files over the network. You are better off loading the files from the original product tapes since that will ensure that you have all the files needed to support all the installation and configuration options. On an existing server you may find that someone deleted various files to make space for other needs.

 It's late. Your manager says you can't take a lunch hour, you can't take a sick day (you've been sick for two weeks), your previously approved vacation has been revoked (in violation of all company policy), and you have to stay until the server is installed on the new platform. You think you are in good shape. Since no one bothered to inform you of the project plan (there isn't one), you don't have time to order the latest product tape for the server. Not to worry. You just copy the installation directory from another server in your database system. You begin `sybinit` and things start to fail. You investigate and find some of the subdirectories of the installation directory (`/home/sybase`) don't contain files—only links to other directories. Of course, those other directories don't exist on your new server machine so you don't have the files. You don't know why anyone would have moved parts of the product set to other directories on the other server machine, and you don't know exactly which machine does in fact have these linked subdirectories. The fun begins. You should have all the files of the product set on the server machine before you start installing.

run sybinit

Now you are ready to run the `sybinit` program. This is included with the server product(s) and will install the SQL Server. When you run `sybinit` you are creating the master device, the *master*, *model*, *tempdb* and *sybsystemprocs* databases (*sybsecurity* is optional), and installing the system stored procedures, such as **sp_who**, creating an entry in the interfaces file for the server, creating a file you can use to start the server (a `RUN_<servername>` file), installing the default character set and sort order as well as any additional character sets you need, and installing the default language and any additional languages you need.

After the `sybinit` program has successfully completed, you will have installed the basic server. From there you will need to configure the server and create the server devices. After that you will be ready to create user databases.

Installing SQL Server System 11

Note that SYBASE SQL Server System 11 on Sun platforms is supported only for the Solaris operating system. Hence, you may need to upgrade the operating system to Solaris before you can install SQL Server System 11. Previous versions of the SQL Server, 4.9.2 and System 10, were supported for both the SunOS and Solaris operating systems.

You will use the `sybinit` program to install a System 11 SQL Server You will need a number of pieces of data to answer the questions posed by `sybinit` for System 11 SQL Server. Note that the output of `sybinit` shown on the CD-ROM may not match the output you will see when you run the `sybinit` program on your specific platform, but the output shown shows you what to expect as `sybinit` moves through the installation process.

There are several differences between SQL Server 4.9.2 and System 11 that you need to understand before installing the System 11 Version. Note that this discussion assumes you are installing from scratch, not upgrading a 4.9.2 Server to System 11. The big difference as far as installing goes is the presence of three server devices that are created during the process of installing the System 11 Server versus only one—the master device for a 4.9.2 installation. For System 11 the `sybinit` program will create the master device and a device called sysprocsdev to support the *sybsystemprocs* database. The *sybsystemprocs* database stores most of the system stored procedures that were stored in the *master* database in the 4.9.2 Server. With the growth in the number of such stored procedures in System 11, the need to move most of them out of the *master* database came up. The alternative would have been to require anyone upgrading from 4.9.2 to System 11 to enlarge the master device. However, many installations don't have much, if any, more room on their master device and enlarging the master device can require reinstalling the whole server. This would not be popular with the installed base so the *sybsystemprocs* database was born.

The third server device that is created by the `sybinit` program for System 11 is the sybsecurity server device which supports the *sybsecurity* database. This database is needed to activate the server auditing functions, which are a new set of features for System 11. The auditing features allow the server to record various information regarding whom is doing what and when to the server and the data in the server. Note that creating the sybsecurity server device and database are not required to install the server. However, the sybsecurity server device, like the sysprocsdev and the master devices, should be on their own server device and should be mirrored, and as always, preferably all on separate controllers. This means that if you don't create a small (30-Mb minimum) partition early in the installation of the server, you would have to put the *sybsecurity* database on some server device that is already supporting other databases if you ever decide you need the auditing features activated. Since you should create the small server device and its mirror now as part of the installation, you should go ahead and install the auditing capabilities at the same time. This will make it much less painful for you when you do decide you need the auditing capabilities of System 11. Note that once you have installed the sybsecurity server device and database you don't have to acti-vate them so they won't affect the server performance, and so forth.

Note that `sybinit` will boot the newly installed SQL Server as part of the installation process. This is fine. You just need to remember that you already have a server running when you are finished with `sybinit`.

Recall that System 11 SQL Server uses a separate product, the Backup Server to make database and transaction log dumps. The `sybinit` program is used to install the Backup Server as well. You can either install the Backup Server as part of the same `sybinit` session (as shown in the actual `sybinit` output below) or run a completely new `sybinit` session.

Note that for System 11 you don't need a customer authorization string or a serial number to install the server. The customer authorization string is required when you load the server files from the Sybase product tape. The process of loading these files is covered in the installation guide and is platform specific.

Release Directory

You need to specify the actual release directory which should be the same as the SYBASE installation directory which would be `/home/sybase`.

Server Name

You must specify the server name. Note that there are times when you don't want to give a new server its final production name. This would occur when you are installing a new server that will eventually replace an existing server. Since the existing server must continue in production until you can cut over to the new server, the new server should not be given the same name as the existing production server.

Configure Server Interfaces File Entry

You need to specify the information needed for `sybinit` to create an interfaces file entry for the server. Note that this interfaces file entry will be made in a file in the installation directory and you will need to add the server to your production interfaces file later on after the server installation is complete. You will need to specify the port number of the server which you should specify in accordance with the standards you have established for all the servers and server machines in your database system (see Chapter 8). Note that the server machine name is assumed to be the same as the machine you are running `sybinit` from, and if not you will need to change that entry within `sybinit`. You will be able to specify a Retry Count and a Retry Delay parameter as well as the basic machine name and port number. These affect what happens when a client connection to the server fails. You need to decide whether you need to change the default of 0 for one or both of these. In general, if your clients are failing to connect there is a real problem and simply waiting a short time to reconnect doesn't help. These parameters are discussed more fully in the Installation Guide.

File for Master Device Raw Partition

You will need to provide the complete path and file name of the file that controls the raw partition that will support the master device.

Size of Master Device in Megabytes

Note that the size of the master device is specified in megabytes, not sectors as it was with `sybconfig` for the 4.9.2 SQL Server. Recall that you want to specify the largest whole number of megabytes that will fit on the raw partition (see Chapter 8).

File for Sysprocsdev Device Raw Partition

You will need to provide the complete path and file names of the file that controls the raw partition that will support the sysprocsdev device. This device will support the *sybsystemprocs* database which contains the system stored procedures. This device should be separate from the master device, preferably on a separate physical disk that is attached to a separate disk controller.

Size of Sysprocsdev Device in Megabytes

You specify the size of the sysprocsdev device in megabytes. Recall that you want to specify the largest whole number of megabytes that will fit on the raw partition (see Chapter 8).

Errorlog Location

You are asked to specify the errorlog location. You should accept the default which will put the errorlog in the install subdirectory of the sybase installation directory. This means the errorlog will be `/home/sybase/install/errorlog`. You need to realize that the `sybinit` process is going to start the newly installed SQL Server. The server must be started to install stored procedures and make several configuration changes. The errorlog that results from booting the server should be preserved along with all the installation files. Hence, accept the default, allow `sybinit` to generate errorlogs as it boots the new server and when you have finished with the server installation, then move the errorlog to its final production location. Note that you need to periodically delete old server errorlogs from the production errorlog directory (`/home/<servername>/errorlog`) to prevent the file system from filling up which would kill the server. If you place the `sybinit` errorlog(s) in the production errorlog directory you will soon delete them. These errorlogs are part of your documentation of the installation process and you should preserve them.

Backup Server Name

You must specify the name for the Backup Server. Note that you are not installing the Backup Server at this point. Here `sybinit` is simply changing the name of the Backup Server in the system table sysservers from the default of SYB_BACKUP to the name you specify. You must install the Backup Server using `sybinit` after you have finished installing the server. You should be following your server naming conventions and the Backup Server name would be *<servername>*_BCK.

Languages Installed and Default

The default language you specify should be the same as the other servers in your database system. Be very careful before specifying a default language different from the other servers in your database system. Make sure you know the impacts this may have as you move data between servers and into and out of the system. Note that you can specify any additional languages to be installed at the same time.

Character Sets Installed and Default

The default character set should be the same as the other servers in your database system. Make sure you know the impacts of having different character sets installed on different servers. Note that the selection of the default character set will have an impact on the default sort order that can be installed. This is the sort of information that you will get from reading the installation guide and related documentation. Note that you can specify any additional character sets to be installed at the same time.

Sort Order Installed

The sort order is linked with the default character set as described above. Note that the sort order is critical. Once the sort order has been set up and you load any data into the server you can't change the sort order without doing a logical dump and load of all the data in the entire server. You must realize that if you change the sort order later you can't load any of the database dumps you have made previously using SQL Server. Hence, you must choose the sort order with care. The sort order tells the server how to order the actual data out on disk. When you change the sort order, you must physically reorder the data on disk which will take lot of time for a large database. If you need to change sort order later on, you must review the situation with Sybase Technical Support and have a complete plan for recovering your databases before you make the change. The best advice is to check all the other servers in your database system. They should all have the same sort order and default character set. Your new server should match the others in your database system. The best way to determine exactly what character set and sort order are installed on a given server is to look at the server errorlog. Just after the server recovers after it is started, the errorlog shows the ID number for the default character set and the sort order. Make sure your new server displays the same ID values as the other servers in your database system. Note that this is another reason you need to be prepared to support a logical dump and load of the databases on your server (see Chapter 9).

File for Sybsecurity Device Raw Partition

You will need to provide the complete path and file name of the file that controls the raw partition that will support the sybsecurity device. This device will support the *sybsecurity* database which allows you to use the auditing features of the System 11 SQL Server. Note that installing this device is optional. You can install the server without this feature. However, if you ever decide to install the auditing features later you will then need to come up with a small (30-Mb) disk raw partition and mirror. After you have the server set up and running, it may not be easy to find or create such a partition. Hence it is simply easier for you to install the auditing features even if you don't activate them. This device should be separate from the master and sysprocsdev devices, preferably on a separate physical disk that is attached to a separate disk controller.

Size of Sybsecurity Device in Megabytes

You specify the size of the *sybsecurity* device in megabytes. Recall that you want to specify the largest whole number of megabytes that will fit on the raw partition (see Chapter 8).

The following sections discuss information you must supply to sybinit to install the Backup Server for System 11. Note that this can be done as part of the same sybinit session you have completed to install the server or you can start a completely independent sybinit session. You must install the Backup Server before you can make any database or transaction log dumps of any database in the server.

Backup Server Release Directory

You need to specify the actual release directory, which should be the same as the SYBASE installation directory which would be /home/sybase.

Backup Server Name

You must specify the Backup Server name and you should follow a simple server naming convention, which would be *<servername>*_BCK. Note that there are times when you don't want to give a new server its final production name. This would occur when you are installing a new server that will eventually replace an existing server. Since the existing server must continue in production until you can cut over to the new server, the new server should not be given the same name as the existing production server.

Backup Server Errorlog

You will be asked to supply the location of the Backup Server errorlog, and you should accept the default. See the errorlog Location section above..

Backup Server Interfaces File Information

You need to specify the information needed for sybinit to create an interfaces file entry for the Backup Server. Note that this interfaces file entry will be made in a file in the installation directory and you will need to add the server to your production interfaces file later on after the server installation is complete. You will need to specify the port number of the Backup Server which you should specify in accordance with the standards you have established for all the servers and server machines in your database system (see Chapter 8). Note that the server machine name is assumed to be the same as the machine you are running sybinit from, and if not, you will need to change that entry within sybinit.

Backup Server Language and Character Set

The Backup Server language and character set should be the same as those you chose for the server itself.

Installing SQL Server System 10

The installation process for System 10 is virtually identical to that for System 11. The only real difference for the Sun platform is that System 11 SQL Server is only supported on Solaris.

The inputs you need to give to sybinit are identical, with one exception. At the very end of the installation of the Backup Server, you will be asked for the name of the Backup Server tape configuration file. With System 11, the Backup Server is able to determine the characteristics of tape drives it doesn't already know about. The Backup Server will use the file specified for this purpose. You should simply take the default as it is presented.

You should refer to the Installing SQL Server System 11 section to review the inputs needed for sybinit.

Installing SQL Server 4.9.2

You will use the sybconfig program to install a 4.9.2 SQL Server. You will need a number of pieces of data to answer the questions posed by sybconfig for 4.9.2 SQL Server. They are listed below. We discuss many of these items individually before we review the output from the sybconfig program. Note that the output of sybconfig shown here may not match the output you will see when you run the sybconfig program on your specific platform, but the output shown shows you what to expect as sybconfig moves through the installation process.

Note that you must have the environment variable SYBASE set to point to the SYBASE installation directory /home/sybase. The sybconfig program uses the SYBASE variable to find the files needed to install the server, but it doesn't ask you what the path is to the SYBASE installation (or home) directory. You can check this by executing the UNIX command echo $SYBASE.

You need to remember that sybconfig starts the newly installed server so it can install stored procedures and make several configuration changes. When you have finished installing the server and move to the production directory structure and server startup scripts, you will need to stop and restart the server. You must remember to stop the currently running server before you attempt to start the server from the production directory.

Type of Master Device (Raw Partition or File system)

You always want to use a raw partition for the master device (see Chapter 8, for discussion of raw partitions versus file systems).

Path Name for Master Device (Assuming Raw Partition)

You will need to provide the complete path and file names of the file that controls the raw partition that will support the master device.

Size of Partition in Sectors (Assuming Raw Partition)

Note that the size of the master device raw partition is specified in sectors which you can get from the output of the `prtvtoc` command as discussed previously. You need to remember that you want to specify a whole number of megabytes. Make sure the number of sectors you specify is a whole number of megabytes. Recall that #sectors * 512 bytes/sector gives total number of bytes. Note that 512 bytes/sector is platform specific and you must check this parameter for your specific platform.

Server Name

You should select a server name. You can use the server machine name and/or the version of the SQL Server. For example, for a server machine with the host name of psycho with a 4.9.2 Server installed, you could use PSYCHO_492 for the SQL Server name.

Server Query Port Number (5001)

The query port number for the server should be in line with the standard port numbers you have set up for your system (see Chapter 8).

Default Language

The default language you specify should be the same as the other servers in your database system. Be very careful before specifying a default language different from the other servers in your database system. Make sure you know the impacts this may have as you move data between servers and into and out of the system.

Default Character Set

The default character set should be the same as the other servers in your database system. Make sure you know the impacts of having different character sets installed on different servers. Note that the selection of the default character set will have an impact on the default sort order that can be installed. This is the sort of information that you will get from reading the installation guide and related documentation.

Sort Order

The sort order is linked with the default character set as described above. Note that the sort order is critical. Once the sort order has been set up and you load any data into the server, you can't change the sort order without doing a logical dump and load of all the data in the entire server. You must realize that if you change the sort order later you can't load any of the database dumps you have made using SQL Server. Hence, you must choose the sort order with care. The sort order tells the server how to order the actual data out on disk. When you change the sort order, you must physically reorder the data on disk which will take lot of time for a large database. If you need to change sort order later on, you must review the situation with Sybase Technical Support and have a complete plan for recovering your databases before you make the change. The best advice is to check all the other servers in your database system. They should all have the same sort order and default character set. Your new server should match the others in your database system. The best way to determine exactly what character set and sort order are installed on a given server is to look at the server errorlog. Just after the server recovers after it is started, the errorlog shows the ID number for the default character set and the sort order. Make sure your new server displays the same ID values as the other servers in your database system.

Additional Languages

You can install additional languages later if needed.

Additional Character Sets

You can install additional character sets later if needed.

Serial Number

You will need the serial number of the SQL Server to run the `sybconfig` program. This serial number is not meaningful and you can use any number—for example, 99999. Note that the serial number appears in the output of `sp_configure`.

Output from sybconfig

The actual output from a `sybconfig` session is on the CD-ROM.

Post-Installation Tasks

When you have successfully completed the `sybinit` process you have the basic server installed. You need to perform numerous steps before the server is ready to perform any useful work for your business. The steps listed in the following checklist are needed for all versions of the SQL Server with only one exception. You need to review these steps and add or delete any steps as appropriate for your server.

Dump *master* database

Change sa password

Configure server memory

Configure number of devices

Configure dump devices (4.9.2 only)

Create and execute **disk init** script

Create and execute **disk mirror** script

Create server configuration script

Create and execute addservers script

Create or update interfaces file

Bring in *syslogins* data

Add dump users to *model* database (4.9.2 only)

Create user databases

Dump *master* database

Start dumps of file systems to yape

Setup scripts for production environment

Dump master Database

You must make a database dump of the *master* database immediately after completing the basic installation process. If you screw up any of the following steps, you may need to recover the *master* database. Note that depending on the version of the server you may need to install a server dump device before you can dump the *master* database. You may also need to change the ownership of files controlling the tape drive or the disk file system where you need to make the dump so that the required file(s) are owned by the UNIX user who is making the dump of the *master* database. You should still be operating as UNIX user sybase at this point.

When sybinit runs it, creates several default dump devices. You can use these to make a dump of *master*, but check them first using **sp_helpdevice** to make sure they will dump the database to a disk file or tape device that actually exists on the server machine and has room to support the dump file. For a 4.9.2 SQL Server, you will have to add a dump device to the server before you can dump the *master* database. Also, you should dump the *master* database at several points during the full installation process.

Change sa Password

You must change the server user sa password. If you want the new server to communicate with other servers in your database system the sa password should be the same on all servers. You need to review the specifics of your security and interserver communication needs to determine if this is absolutely required. In general, the server user sa password should be the same on all servers.

Configure Server Memory

You need to configure the server to use as much of the server machine's available memory as possible. A good first cut is to assign 80 percent of the server machine's memory to the server. Note that you must leave 10 to 20 Mb (verify this with the server machine SA for your specific hardware and operating system platform) for the operating system. The server must have sufficient memory assigned to it before you can make other configuration changes such as increasing the number of devices and user connections. Both of these configuration changes require assigning more memory to support the increased number of devices and users connections.

Configure Number of Devices

The server will be installed with the maximum number of devices (logical disk devices) set to 10 by default. You can see this and the other configuration parameters by executing **sp_configure** without any other arguments. You will need to increase this number to support the number of devices you will need for all the user databases you will create on the server.

Configure Dump Devices (4.9.2 Only)

If you are installing a 4.9.2 Server you will need to add dump devices for tape drives and any disk files that you intend to dump to. Note that you may need to install at least one dump device before you can make a dump of the *master* database as described above.

Create and Execute disk init Script

Now you need to create and execute a script that will create the server logical disk devices needed to support creation of the user databases. This script will simply be a set of **disk init** commands with the server device names and sizes taken from your server map. Remember to round down to the nearest whole number of megabytes before computing the size in 2K pages for each **disk init** command (see Chapter 8), for more discussion of the **disk init** command. Note that once you have this script set up ,you shouldn't just run it all at once. The script is a vital piece of documentation in case you need to rebuild the server, but the **disk init** process is very important and even one typo can screw up all the other **disk init** that follow. You should create the script, then cut and paste each **disk init** command and execute them one at a time on the server. This way you can catch any errors as they occur. Recall that any **disk init** error will lock up the *vdevno*. It is much easier to catch such errors if you are doing one **disk init** at a time. You can then edit your script with the corrections and move on, restarting the server if needed to reuse the *vdevno*.

As discussed in Chapter 8), you must not execute a **disk init** for the master device, and you must remove the master device from the default pool of disk space.

Create and Execute disk mirror Script

Now you should create and execute a script to create all the disk mirrors you need. As with the **disk inits**, you should create this script, and then execute each **disk mirror** command one at a time.

Create Server Configuration Script

As you make changes to the server configuration you should be recording these changes in a configuration script. This script would contain the server commands needed to assign server machine memory to the server and to increase the maximum number of devices allowed for example. This script makes it very easy to rebuild the server if needed. You should also dump the server configuration frequently during installation and configuration by executing the **sp_configure** command. The output will allow you to build the configuration script if you don't do so as you go along.

Create and Execute addservers Script

You need to create and execute an addservers script. This script will contain all the server commands to add the local and remote servers to the new server. This script will probably be very similar to a script that should be on your other server machines. The remote servers for the new server are probably all the same servers that existing servers need to talk to. Note that all existing servers that need to communicate with the new server will also need to have the new server added to their *sysservers* table as well as to their own addservers script.

Create or Update Interfaces File

You need to review the entire database system and determine which users and which other servers need to have information about the new server added to their interfaces file(s). Note that you probably need to set up (if you haven't already) an interfaces file that contains the information about all the other servers in your system on the new server machine. Depending on the nature of the new server you may or may not want to add the new server to the interfaces file that all your users have access to. Note that an easy way to handle this is to make sure a copy of your current server version of the interfaces file for your database system is copied to the installation directory (/home/sybase) before you install the new server. This way the new server is appended to the existing interfaces file which already contains the information about all the other servers.

Bring in syslogins Data

Now that the new server is up and running, you should add any and all users to the new server. Depending on the intended use of the new server, you may want to add only a subset of the users of your overall database system. You can generate a script to find each entry in the *syslogins* table in the *master* database of one of your existing servers and generate a script to execute **sp_addlogin** for each such user. You can also simply use the bcp utility to dump all the entries in the *syslogins* table to a disk file and then copy the file to the new server machine and bcp the file into the *syslogins* table of the new server. This is much faster if you need to move all the users from one server to another. Note that you must edit the file before you load it into the new server. The new and existing servers will both have an entry for *suid* = 1 which is the server user sa. The *syslogins* table has a unique index on *suid* and will abort the bcp in if it contains a row for *suid* = 1. You could work around this by deleting all the entries from *syslogins* of the new server but you must not do this. You should never leave a server without the sa login. You should examine *syslogins* of the new server and eliminate any entries other than the sa entry. You then edit the disk file and delete the row for *suid* = 1 for the sa login. Now you can load the disk file without problem. Note that this is only appropriate when you want to have all the users from an existing server added to the new server. Note also that it is better to add all these users to the new server now so that the *suid* for each user will be the same for the new server as on the existing server. This is very important if you are intending to load a database dump from the existing server to the new server since the dump will contain user information for the database and object permissions within the database that are all based on the *suid* values.

If you need to add some users to the new server who are not on the existing server, add them after loading all existing users. This will minimize *suid* problems later. If you have been setting up your database systems carefully, all the users should have the same *suid* on all servers. This will save you a lot of time chasing down permissions problems later.

Add Dump Users to model Database (4.9.2 only)

Any user that needs to be able to dump a database must be added to the database and granted permission to dump the database. In general you will have a group of users who handle making the database dumps for your database system. For a 4.9.2 Server, you will save lots of time if you add each of these users to the *model* database so they will appear as users in every user database that is created later on in the server. Don't forget to add these same users to the *master* database as well. First, you create a group in the *model* database for users who need to be able to dump a database, add each such user to the model database and to the new group and then grant permission to dump databases to the new group. You should document this process as a script in case you need to rebuild the server later.

Create User Databases

Now that you have the server running, the server configured for memory and number of devices, the server disk devices created (initialized and made known to the server by executing **disk init**) and the users who need to dump databases added to the *model* database, you can create the user databases. You should prepare a script that creates all the user databases that you know about at this time. This script, as with the others discussed above, will allow you to rebuild the server quickly when needed. This script also saves time whenever you need to set up any of the user databases on another server.

Dump master Database

You must dump the *master* database again after creating the user databases. You may well need to create more databases later on, but for now, dump the *master* database after you have created the initial set of user databases. You should be dumping the *master* database regularly from this point on anyway.

Start Dumps of File systems to Tape

You must now start dumps to tape of file systems, capturing files and any log dumps and database dumps that are being made to disk files. If you are copying dump scripts from existing systems you must check them and make any changes needed to reflect the disk or tape devices on the new server machine that are different from those on the machine where the existing script was running.

Setup Scripts for Production Environment

You now set up any and all scripts needed to regularly dump databases, transaction logs, perform **dbcc** runs, **update statistics**, and so forth. (see Chapter 14).

Installation Errors

You will find that many things can go wrong with the `sybinit` (or `sybconfig` for 4.9.2) process. You need to realize that for many of the common problems you can go to another window or UNIX session, correct the problem that `sybinit` is complaining about and then proceed with the installation process. We discuss some of the most common problems and how to fix them in the following troubleshooting guide:

File permissions

$SYBASE not set correctly

Device file permissions

Server won't boot

Installation errorlog files

File Permissions

The most common problem is simply file permissions. The `sybinit` process needs to read and create many files in several different directories as well as access the devices needed to create server devices (master device, and so forth.). If any of these files have incorrect permissions for the UNIX user sybase the installation will fail. Note that you will see these errors in the `sybinit` process itself, in the log file for the installation (which is listed at the beginning and end of the `sybinit` session) and in the errorlog of the server that is booted as part of the installation for problems with device access.

You must ensure that the UNIX user sybase has all the access needed. This is why you are better off to simply change the ownership of all the files in and below the installation directory, that is, `/home/sybase` and all subdirectories to UNIX user sybase. And, you must change the ownership of the files that control the raw partitions that will support the master device (and sysprocsdev and sybsecurity) to UNIX user sybase.

$SYBASE Not Set Correctly

If the environment variable SYBASE is not set correctly, the installation process will not get very far. You need to make sure the variable SYBASE is set to the installation directory, /home/sybase. Note that sybinit specifically asks you to specify the release directory (same as installation or home directory) for the sybinit process.

Device File Permissions

We have discussed device file permissions repeatedly, but we will cover it again because it comes up so often. You must change the ownership of the files that control the raw partitions that will support the master device (and sysprocsdev and sybsecurity) to UNIX user sybase.

You should not be fooled by some of the errors you will see that are really caused by device file permission problems. Note that the server errorlog may say something like "insufficient space on device" when in reality the problem is file permissions. Whenever you get an error during the installation process, you should check exactly what device(s) you are asking sybinit to use and check the ownership on the files that control those devices.

Server Won't Boot

The server may not boot during or after the installation process. The problem is often related to file ownership and permission problems. However, the server may not boot for all the same reasons any server may not boot. These include memory problems, disk failures, network problems, and so on. You must check the errorlog for the server to determine what is going wrong. Note that you may not get much help from sybinit, as they may simply say "waiting for server to boot" and hang up at this point. You need to find the errorlog for the server and figure out what is going on. If you don't see the problem and its solution right away, you can kill the installation process and find the RUN_<servername> file that the installation process has created. You then kill the start server process, try to fix the problem, and then try starting the server manually using the start server file created by the installation process. This saves you from having to run through the whole installation process each time you try to fix the problem. When the server finally boots, kill it and return to the installation process.

You must understand what the server errorlog is telling you (see Chapter 12). Whether you are in the midst of the installation or well past that point, if the server won't boot, examine the server errorlog very carefully.

After installation is complete you must check the errorlog to make sure the server that you are running is indeed the version you think you are running. The installation process runs the server binary that came off the product tape so you are pretty likely to be running the correct version of the server during installation. But once you get past installation, you may have several versions (EBFs, and so forth.) of the server in the same directory (`/home/sybase/bin`) and you need to check the errorlog to make sure you are booting the correct version. Sometimes problems that prevent the server from booting are caused by trying to boot an older version of the server.

Installation Errorlog Files

You need to understand that there are several log files for `sybinit` that you may need to examine to diagnose problems. First, there is the `sybinit` process itself that will display various messages on the screen as the installation process moves along. Second the `sybinit` session generates a log file itself, and the file name is displayed at the beginning and end of each `sybinit` session. Third is the server errorlog. During the installation process the server errorlog will be in one of the subdirectories of the installation directory (`$SYBASE/install`). Finally you should check the hardware errorlog for the server machine where you will find errors relating to the server machine and operating system hardware. Any and all of these errorlogs will help you find and fix problems during and after installation.

UPGRADING SQL SERVER
OVERVIEW

Introduction

Upgrading the SQL Server is a routine part of your job as the DBA. Upgrading comes in many forms. The simplest is applying an EBF (Emergency Bug Fix—note that "emergency" is overstated since EBFs come out on a regular basis), followed by a "rollup" that is an update of the server containing many bug fixes that have been developed over some period of time and finally a "version" upgrade which generally involves modifying portions of the databases in a manner that prevents you from going back to the previous version of the server.

SQL Server Versions

SQL Server 4.9.2

All the upgrades discussed here assume you are already at the SQL Server 4.9.2 Version level. If your server is not at this level, contact Sybase Technical Support for assistance. There is no upgrade path for SQL Server from a version lower than 4.9.2 to either System 10 or System 11.

SQL SERVER SYSTEM 10

System 10 runs on both SunOS and Solaris. You will need to consider issues such as reserved word conflicts and new server devices to support new databases *sybsystemprocs* and *sybsecurity*. System 10 introduces Backup Server which will change the way you make database and transaction log dumps.

SQL SERVER SYSTEM 11

Upgrading to System 11 from 4.9.2 involves all the same issues as upgrading to System 10. Further, System 11 requires and can make use of more server machine memory. You may need to add more memory to the server machine. System 11 is only supported on Solaris. If you are running SunOS, you will need to upgrade to Solaris before you begin upgrading the SQL Server to System 11.

Installation Guide, Release Notes, and EBF Cover Letter

Whenever you install an EBF for the SQL Server, you must have available the various documents related to installing and configuring the server. The *Sybase SQL Server Installation Guide* and the *Release Notes* for the version of the server that you are applying the EBF to are very useful. The EBF cover letter tells you what bugs are fixed in the EBF and other information relevant to the upgrade process. These documents will also alert you to operating system patches required to support the upgrade.

If you are going to perform a version upgrade (examples include 4.9.2 to System 11), there will be a whole separate installation guide (or a release bulletin) for the upgrade. You must obtain, read, and retain this material. Version upgrades can be deadly and the information contained in these documents can save you and your users from untold disaster.

Sybase Technical Support

Before you actually install any EBF or other upgrade, you must establish what version of the server you are currently running. The best way to do this is to isql into the server and execute

select @@version

Note that you must establish not only the server version (such as 4.9.2) but also the EBF level.

Once you know what the server version and EBF level are you need to contact Sybase Technical Support and ask them to review what bug fixes (features?) are in the EBF you are running and tell them which EBF you are planning to apply to your server. You must verify that the new EBF and the current EBF are indeed compatible.

This becomes very important if you have a "one-off" EBF. A one-off EBF means an EBF that was created for your site to fix a special set of bugs that you are encountering. This also implies that the bug fixes you have in your current EBF may not be compatible with the new EBF, especially if the new EBF is a "rollup" EBF, which means it contains many bug fixes that may or may not include the special bug fixes you need at your site. Reviewing the current and new EBF in this much detail is the only way to prevent problems.

You need to ask if the current EBF you have is part of the code line (i.e., the set of SQL Server source code that most of the customer base is running). If you have any special bug fixes that are not part of the code line, you may be affected in two ways. First, you can still upgrade (apply the new EBF), but you may loose the special bug fixes you need (called regression), and second, you can still upgrade, but some of the new bug fixes may not have been tested against the one-off bug fixes in your current EBF and you may find the new EBF will actually make things worse, that is, you may end up with new bugs.

Risks of the Upgrade Process

Before you attempt any form of server upgrade, you should understand why you are applying the upgrade and what you will do if it fails. For most EBF upgrades you can regress (go back to a previous EBF) simply by re-installing the previous EBF. For version upgrades this is often not possible. You must be prepared to deal with the possibility that the upgrade may fail and you must have a plan to get back to a functioning and stable server. Note that even if the upgrade succeeds, it is possible that due to conflicts between bug fixes in EBF levels, and so forth, that the data currently in your server will become corrupted. Even though you can go back to the previous EBF level, you will still have to fix the data corruption.

These concerns are all the more acute when dealing with a version-level upgrade such as 4.9.2 to System 10 or 11. In the event that the upgrade fails, you can find yourself in a state where the data in the databases has been irreversibly modified to be compatible with System 10, but the upgrade didn't complete so you don't have a functioning server. You can't just reinstall the 4.9.2 Server because the data itself was modified. You need to discuss these possibilities with Sybase Technical Support before you upgrade and you must have a plan for recovery in the event of a failed upgrade before you begin.

EBF Upgrades

The process of upgrading the SQL Server from one EBF level to another is not complicated. However, since it comes up often, you should standardize the process so that any of the DBAs can do it as needed. Further, by standardizing the process, you can easily, quickly, and safely move back to a previous EBF if needed. You should set up the same process on all your servers, both production and development, so that any of the DBAs can be trained once and will be able to install a new EBF or regress to an old EBF on any machine in your database system.

Documents

As discussed previously you must obtain and read the release notes or bulletin or cover letter that explain the new EBF fixes and any details of the installation process. It is always a good idea to review the installation guide for the server version you are currently running to ensure that all the server machine operating system patches are in place and any other parameters of the hardware have been set up before applying the new EBF.

Loading the New EBF

You need to load the new EBF from tape or copy it from another server machine in your database system into the standard directory for storing server binaries. Note that you need to get the new EBF executable file into `/home/sybase/bin`. Note also that the server executable file name should be standardized to make locating any EBF easy and error free. Such a standard would be `<servername-lowercase>.<version> datasvr.<EBFlevel>` and an example would be `ddsdba1.1101datasvr.6158`.

Verify Current Server Version and EBF Level

You must verify the current server version and EBF level that you are running. You need to `isql` into the server and

select @@version

An example of the output of this command is shown below.

```
machine1: isql -Usa -SREARWINDOW11
Password:
1> select @@version
2> go
```

```
SQL Server/11.0.1/P/Sun_svr4/OS 5.4/EBF6158/OPT/Fri Apr  5 20:30:14
PST 1996

(1 row affected)
```

This output tells you that you are running the System 11.0.1 Version of the server and that you are using the EBF 6158. Note that if this isn't the EBF level (or the server version) you thought you were running, you need to stop and reassess what has been going on. You should not proceed with the upgrade until you are sure the new EBF will not cause problems when applied to the current server. Or, you need to get the server running at the EBF (and version) level it should be before you can plan the EBF upgrade.

Archive the Current Server Binary

Now that you know the current server version and EBF level you should archive the currently executing server binary by copying the file that is actually executed when you start the server into a file that reflects the EBF level. Recall that in the standard environment you start the server by executing /home/sybase/install/RUN_<servername> which actually executes the server binary file which is the file dataserver. This means that each time RUN_<servername> is executed, the file dataserver is executed to actually start the SQL Server. This also means that the file dataserver contains the binary for the currently executing server version and EBF level. This file should be copied to a file name of <servername-lowercase>.<version>datasvr.<EBFlevel> and an example would be ddsdba1.1101datasvr.3434. This preserves the currently executing server in case you need it later. Note that if you have followed the standard procedure, the currently executing server should already exist in such a file and if so, you don't need to copy it again.

Shut down the Server

Now you need to shut down the currently executing server. As with any normal (nonemergency) shut down of the server, you should follow the steps described in Chapter 9, to ensure that the server and its databases are stable before shutting down the server.

Copy New EBF into Server Binary File

With the server shut down, you now copy the new EBF server executable into a file that will archive this new EBF version of the server such as <servername lowercase>.<version>datasvr and an example would be ddsdba1.1001p2datasvr. Applying the new EBF really boils down to copying the new EBF server executable (binary) file to this file (i.e., s_ddsdba1.1001p2datasvr) and then copying the new EBF server executable (binary) file to the file dataserver as well. The next time RUN_<*servername*> is executed, the new EBF will be executed as the server.

This approach makes it very easy to install a new EBF or regress to an older EBF level. Note that no editing of files is involved. This means the whole EBF upgrade process can be accomplished by simple UNIX commands. This approach is very valuable when you need to perform EBF upgrades during off-hours from a remote terminal.

Restart Server

Restart the server watching the errorlog to verify that the new server EBF is really executing (see Chapter 12, for more discussion of watching the errorlog during server startup).

Verify Server Is Executing New EBF

Once the server has fully recovered you should isql into the new server and **select @@version** to verify that the new EBF level is being executed as you expect.

Document the EBF Installation

Finally you must document what you did so the other DBAs will know that this server was upgraded to this new EBF level.

VERSION UPGRADES

A version upgrade is an upgrade that involves more than simply restarting the server with a new binary. This may also mean an upgrade from which you can't regress to the previous version in any easy way. Examples of a version upgrade would be 4.2 to 4.8 and 4.9 to System 10. In these cases the actual data in the databases is reworked and this means dumps of the previous version can't be loaded into the upgraded server. A version upgrade is more involved than an EBF upgrade for these reasons. A version upgrade may also require changes to your applications. Changes such as SQL syntax or feature changes to be compliant with one of the ANSI standards can wreak havoc with an existing application. Only through application testing against the new version of the server will you determine what the impact of the new version is on your application(s).

You must be aware of the risks to your database system if the upgrade goes poorly. You must think of how to recover to the previous version if needed. Further you need to think of the impacts on other servers. You may need to upgrade other servers in the system immediately to support a reporting server, for example, that takes its data from the primary OLTP server. Once you upgrade the primary server, you must upgrade the report server as well or you can't keep the report server up to date. Further, you may need to have a separate dedicated server at the older version level somewhere in your system to support loading dumps made at the previous version. You must be prepared to recover data from objects in the database at the previous version.

Version upgrades involve much more planning and testing prior to the actual upgrade. We discuss the process of upgrading from SQL Server 4.9.2 to System 11 (or System 10) next.

Preparing to Upgrade 4.9.2 to System 11 (or System 10)

The following steps are taken with the server at the 4.9.2 level. Some of these steps are simply to prevent trouble during the upgrade. These steps should be done well before the actual upgrade begins. For that reason the set of steps include restoring the databases to their original options so that normal processing can resume while the results of the pre-upgrade checks are reviewed. Note however that the steps for dropping mirrors, and so forth, should not be performed until you are ready to proceed with the complete upgrade.

You will notice the discussion of mirrors throughout the upgrade process. The use of mirrors allows you to regress to the 4.9.2 Server quickly in case the upgrade to System 11 fails. This regression method requires that any database you wish to regress be mirrored quickly. Databases that are not mirrored would have to be dropped, re-created, and loaded from dumps if they are not mirrored before the upgrade begins. Note that you should mirror all the databases on your server for many reasons, but here the reason is to provide a quick regression path for all the databases of the server.

Reset All Database Options

You need to set all the databases on the server to have no options set. Note that you do not want to remove the **select into/bulkcopy** option on *tempdb*. Other than that, all databases should show no options set in the output of **sp_helpdb**.

Use sybinit for Pre-Upgrade Database Check

In order to run the pre-upgrade checks of the 4.9.2 Server, you must run sybinit. Note that you are not running sybconfig. When you start sybinit, you must be UNIX user sybase. When you start sybinit, you select the "upgrade an existing SQL Server" option and then select the pre-upgrade check "Test SQL Server upgrade eligibility now." The actual output from the sybinit session will look like this:

```
SQL SERVER UPGRADE

1.   Test SQL Server upgrade eligibility now
2.   Check for reserved word conflicts
3.   sybsystemprocs database configuration

4.   Upgrade SQL Server now
```

```
Ctrl-a Accept and Continue, Ctrl-x Exit Screen, ? Help.

Enter the number of your choice and press return: 1
Testing SQL Server 'THEBIRDS492' for eligibility to upgrade to
release '11.0  '.

........................Done

Server 'THEBIRDS492' passed preupgrade eligibility test.
```

Log of sybinit during Pre-Upgrade Database Check

The following output is from the sybinit session during which the upgrade eligibility test is run. Note that the directory /home/sybase/11.0 is the location of the new System 11 files while the current 4.9.2 Server files are located in the normal installation (or home) directory of /home/sybase.

Use sybinit for Pre-Upgrade Reserved Word Check

In order to run the reserved word check of the 4.9.2 Server you must run sybinit. Note that you are not running sybconfig. When you start sybinit you must be UNIX user sybase. When you start sybinit, you select the "upgrade an existing SQL Server" option and then select the Pre-upgrade "Check for reserved word conflicts" (see the sections below for the actual output from the sybinit session).

Output of sybinit Reserved Word Check

The following output is from the sybinit session during which the reserved word conflict check is run. The output shown below starts from the SQL SERVER UPGRADE menu.

SQL SERVER UPGRADE

1. Test SQL Server upgrade eligibility now
2. Check for reserved word conflicts
3. *sybsystemprocs* database configuration

4. Upgrade SQL Server now

Ctrl-a Accept and Continue, Ctrl-x Exit Screen, ? Help.

Enter the number of your choice and press return: 2
...Done
The log file for sp_checkreswords output is
'/home/sybase/11.0/init/logs/checkres.dmp'.

Warning: 2 conflicts with 11.0 reserved words were found. Sybase suggests that you resolve these conflicts before upgrading the SQL Server. Run 'sp_checkreswords' on each database for more information. Press <return> to continue.

—> reserved word conflicts are...

machine1: more checkres.dmp
Reserved Words Used as Database Objects for Database 'admindb'
Database-wide Objects

Reserved Words Used as Database Objects for Database 'cms_map'
Database-wide Objects

Reserved Words Used as Database Objects for Database 'cmsdb'
Owner
dbo

```
Object Type                        Reserved Word Object Names
user table                         references
Database-wide Objects
```

```
Reserved Words Used as Database Objects for Database 'curqtr_db'
Owner
dbo
Object Type                        Reserved Word Object Names
user table                         references
Database-wide Objects
```

```
Reserved Words Used as Database Objects for Database 'master'
Database-wide Objects
```

```
Reserved Words Used as Database Objects for Database 'model'
Database-wide Objects
```

```
Reserved Words Used as Database Objects for Database 'pagedb'
Database-wide Objects
```

```
Reserved Words Used as Database Objects for Database 'quedb'
Database-wide Objects
```

```
Reserved Words Used as Database Objects for Database 'suneds_sunu'
Database-wide Objects
```

```
Reserved Words Used as Database Objects for Database 'tempdb'
Database-wide Objects
```

You need to be aware of several things in the output of the reserved word conflict check. The file of reserved words simply tells you of objects in databases in the server that are reserved words in System 11 SQL Server. These words can't be used in Transact-SQL statements, and so forth, once the server is upgraded to System 11. However, you must understand that each and every database in your 4.9.2 Server will have a column of the system table *sysobjects* called *schema*. The column named *schema* is fine in the 4.9.2 SQL Server but *schema* becomes a reserved word in the System 11 server. But, you don't need to do anything about this conflict since the upgrade process itself will automatically change the column name to *schema2*. You can look at the server documents for the system table *sysobjects* for both the 4.9.2 and System 11 Servers and you will see that the column *schema* in 4.9.2 becomes *schema2* in System 11.

Now for the other reserved word conflicts. Note that the reserved word conflicts will not prevent you from upgrading to System 11. You can complete the upgrade without changing the object names (table, column, etc.) that are causing the conflict. However, once you try to access the object (table, column, etc.), the server will complain and generate an error. Note that you can also turn on an option within the server (see **set quoted identifier on**) to allow reserved words that are enclosed in double quotes. The point you must retain is that the reserved word conflicts don't prevent you from upgrading, but they may prevent you from executing all the queries of your business after the upgrade.

For the other reserved word conflicts, you need to determine how many other objects depend on the objects that use reserved words. If possible, you should change the objects as soon as possible. If the objects that have reserved word conflicts are vital to your business, you may need to delay the upgrade until these conflicts can be worked out or until you are confident you can operate using the reserved words in double quotes. This is another reason you must perform these Pre-upgrade checks well in advance of the actual upgrade.

For the output shown above for the reserved word conflict check, we see that the table bugs has a column named *user* and the table syb_breaks has a column named *level*. Both *user* and *level* are reserved words in System 11. You need to determine the impact to your applications if queries can't access these columns of these tables, and the work needed to change the object and all objects that depend on it.

You will also find that the reserved word conflict check may flush out objects that are not owned by server user sa. If this is the case, you should simply notify the user who does own the object and simply inform them that their object(s) will not be usable after the upgrade. That will motivate them. If they never reply, just delete the objects.

Reset All Database Options

Since you are performing these pre-upgrade checks well ahead of the actual upgrade, you will need to reset all the database options to what they were before you performed the pre-upgrade checks. Note that, as always, this is another time when you will appreciate the fact that you are dumping the system tables of your server regularly. You may need the output of this process to check what the database options were.

Drop Mirrors and Devices for New System 11 Devices

The System 11 SQL Server requires a separate server disk device called sysprocsdev to support the sybsystemprocs database which houses all the system stored procedures for the System 11 SQL Server. If you are installing the auditing capabilities available under System 11, you will also need a separate server disk device called sybsecurity to support the *sybsecurity* database. While you can place both the *sybsystemprocs* and *sybsecurity* databases on any available server device, it is best if you place each of them on a separate server device created just for this purpose. Specifically, it is best to not place these databases on the master device. The master device should be supporting as little as possible to simplify recovery. Both of these devices need to be 30 Mb minimum and need to be separate from other server devices and should be mirrored as well (see Chapter 8, for details of disk partitioning to support the System 11 Server). You need to set up the disk partitions to support these devices before you begin the upgrade process. Since these devices (and their databases) get created by the sybinit process, you must drop the devices (and their mirrors if they are mirrored) that currently occupy the disk partitions that will support these new devices and databases. If you don't have any 30-Mb partitions available, you need to decide where to locate the new server devices needed and then drop the devices and mirrors if there are any on those partitions.

If you don't have the 30-Mb partitions you need, then you haven't been doing the capacity planning for disk space that you should have. Note that capacity planning is not just about total disk space. In this case it is about having the appropriate disk partitions for the needed System 11 devices and their mirrors on physical disks that are separate from the disk housing the master device, and so forth. Note that the standard disk partitioning scheme discussed in Chapter 8, would make it very easy to accommodate the devices needed by the System 11 SQL Server.

Check Remaining Server Device Mirrors

Now that you have dropped the mirrors and devices on the partitions needed to support the new System 11 devices, you should check that all the other devices in your server are currently mirrored. As discussed in

Chapter 8, it is simply easier for you to administer a server where each and every server disk device is mirrored. As we shall see later these mirrors provide a good regression path in case you need to move back from System 11 to the 4.9.2 Server.

Check Partitions For New System 11 Devices

You need to ensure that the partitions you have selected for the new System 11 devices to be created during the sybinit process (sysprocs-dev and sybsecurity) are the size you think they are (to be passed along to sybinit) and that they are owned by UNIX user sybase during sybinit.

dbcc Checks on All Databases

You must ensure that all the databases are free from corruption before upgrading.

Check Free Space in All Databases

The upgrade will remap database objects that are compiled such as stored procedures and triggers. The remapped objects will take up more space in each database so you need to check the free space in each database. If the free space in a given database is less than 10 percent of the total size of the database you should add space to increase the free space to 10 percent of the total database space. Run **sp_spaceused** in each database to determine how much free space is available. Note that you should perform this step even though the pre-upgrade check of the database (performed using sybinit) told you there was sufficient space in each database.

Check for Objects Related to Indexes

Here you need to perform two queries in each and every database in the server. If either query returns more than 0 rows you have an object that doesn't have a corresponding entry in sysindexes or an index that doesn't have a corresponding entry in sysobjects. Note that **dbcc** may not catch such problems and the upgrade can fail when it hits such an object or index. If you find any problems like this you should contact Sybase Technical Support for the procedure to properly delete the offending object or sysindexes entry. The queries are shown below;

select id from sysobjects

where (type = 'U' or type = 'S')

and id not in (select id from sysindexes)

select id from sysindexes

where id not in (select id from sysobjects)

Dump Transaction Logs and Checkpoint All Databases

You must dump the transaction log for each and every database and run **checkpoint** in each database. This will provide a copy of the transaction log in case you must recover and it frees up space in the transaction log to support the upgrade. If there is a standby server of the server being upgraded, you should apply these transaction log dumps to the standby server. This will keep the standby server as up to date as possible in the event of a problem with the upgrade.

Upgrading 4.9.2 to System 11 (or System 10)

Now you are ready to perform the actual upgrade of your server from 4.9.2 to System 11. There are many steps you need to perform, many of which will seem unnecessary to you. These steps are to protect you, your users and the data from becoming partially upgraded with no way to return to the 4.9.2 Version of the server. You should review all the steps listed below before you start upgrading.

The actual output of a sybinit session during the upgrade from 4.9.2 to System 11 is included on the CD-ROM.

The detailed steps below assume you are upgrading a SQL Server from the 4.9.2 level to System 11. Note that as with all specific procedures, you should contact Sybase Technical Support for a review of your server's specific hardware, software, EBF level, and configuration before starting the upgrade.

Isolate Server from Users

Before you start the actual upgrade, you need to isolate the server from the users. The best way to do this is to shut down the server (after notifying the users, etc.) and then restart the server but on a different port number (see Chapter 12 for details of how the interfaces file works and how to change port numbers). This will prevent any user from logging into the server while the upgrade is underway. The basic idea here is to bring the server up on a server machine port that is different from the port number the users have in their copy of the interfaces file. This assumes that the server machine has its own version of the interfaces file separate from the interfaces file(s) used by the users. You should note the time it takes for the server to recover on the new port number.

Dump Transaction Log Again

You must dump the transaction log for each and every database and run **checkpoint** in each database again. This will flush out any transactions that were completed by users after the previous transaction log dump and before the server was shutdown. If there is a standby server of the server being upgraded, you should apply these transaction log dumps to the standby server. This will keep the standby server as up-to-date as possible in the event of a problem with the upgrade.

Verify Transaction Log is Empty

For each database, execute **sp_spaceused syslogs** to determine the used and free space in the transaction log. Since the server has been restarted and the users isolated, there shouldn't be any open transactions that could hold the transaction log full.

Dump All Databases to Tape

Once you have the server isolated from the users, you should not be making any changes to the user data. Now you must dump all the databases including *master* and *model* to tape. If you prefer to dump to disk, make sure a dump to tape of the disk dump files is made before you proceed with the upgrade. To be really safe, you should try to load these dumps on another server. You will think this is paranoid and you will be correct. You need to decide what the cost to the business would be if the last dump of the databases at the 4.9.2 level were bad and the upgrade failed. If that occurs, you can only recover the server to the point of the previous database dump(s).

Dump Server Configuration to Disk Files

You must dump the system tables that are dumped by the script `dump_systables` to disk files (see Chapter 14). The easiest way to do this is to simply execute the `cron` job script manually. You must check that the output file is created and that it is from the latest execution of the script. In addition you must dump the output of executing **sp_helpdb** within each and every database on the server. This means you must `isql` into the server, **use db1**, **sp_helpdb db1**, repeat this for every database in the server, and dump the output to a disk file.

Dump Contents of syslogins System Table

You should use the `bcp` utility to dump the contents of the `syslogins` table to a disk file. This dump will be needed if there are any problems later with user accounts. This disk file will tell you what the user's *suid*, login *name*, *password* and default database were on the 4.9.2 Server. This information should be available in case you need to rebuild the server. Note that you must use `bcp` with the `-c` option so you can edit the output. You will need to edit out the information for the sa and probe server logins before you can `bcp` the file into the syslogins.

Dump master With Devices Mirrored

You must now dump the *master* database to disk. Since you are running a 4.9.2 Server at this point, you must dump *master* to a disk dump device and then rename the file so the dump is not overwritten by subsequent dumps. You should name this dump of the *master* database `dump_<servername>_master_4.9.2_withmirrors_date_time.out` to make it easy to rebuild the server if needed. Note that this dump of the *master* database contains data from the system table *sysdevices* reflecting the primary and secondary (mirror) server disk devices that contain 4.9.2 data.

Check Mirrors

You should check the mirrors of all the server devices to make sure none of them had failed before you made the dump of the *master* database in the previous step. You should document the mirrors [save the output of **p_mirror** (see Chapter 14)] of the server devices for later use.

Drop Secondary Side of Mirrored Devices

For each of the server devices that has a mirror (see Chapter 8), for reasons why you should mirror all the server disk devices), you should perform the following command:

```
disk unmirror name = '<devicename>',
side = secondary,
mode = remove
```

This will permanently drop the secondary side (the mirror) of the device pair. Note that both the primary server device and the secondary server device of the pair contain server data at the 4.9.2 Version level. You should put the commands to drop the mirror of each server device in a script to make dropping all the mirrors more efficient.

Check That All Mirrors Dropped

You run **p_mirror** again to verify that all the server disk devices do not have mirrors.

Turn Off All Database Options

Make sure that all database options are turned off, except for the **select into/bulk** copy option for *tempdb* which must always be turned on.

Set sa Password NULL

You need to reset the server user sa password to NULL.

Test sa Password

You must verify that the server user sa password is indeed NULL by using `isql` and logging into the server as sa.

Verify master as Default Database for sa

You must verify that the default database for the server user sa is *master*.

Dump master without Mirrors

You must now dump the *master* database to disk again. Since you are running a 4.9.2 Server at this point, you must dump *master* to a disk dump device and then rename the file so the dump is not overwritten by subsequent dumps. You should name this dump of the *master* database `dump_<servername>_master_4.9.2_nomirrors_date_time.out` to make it easy to rebuild the server if needed. Note that this dump of the *master* database contains data from the system table *sysdevices* reflecting the primary server devices only which still contain 4.9.2 data (see Figure 13–1(b)).

Increase TIMEOUTCOUNT in Upgrade Script

If your server takes a long time to recover even with no user access, you may need to increase the parameter TIMEOUTCOUNT in the upgrade script. Consult Sybase Technical Support for the details of making this change. A long time is defined to be more than 10 minutes to recover.

Reconfigure Server for Upgrade

The upgrade process takes a significant portion of the server machine memory available to the server. To make room for this, you should reconfigure the server to reduce the user connections to 10 and the stack size to 286,720. You will have to restart the server to make these configuration changes take effect.

Add Entry to Interfaces File for <servername>_SYS11

Now that you are about to begin the actual upgrade process, you should rename the server to make it clear that you are no longer accessing a 4.9.2 Server. Make a new entry in the interfaces file on the server machine for this new server and modify your RUN_<servername> script as well.

Restart Server

You need to restart the server as *<servername>*_SYS11.

Dump master for New Configuration

You must now dump the *master* database to disk again. Since you are running a 4.9.2 Server at this point you must dump *master* to a disk dump device and then rename the file so that the dump is not overwritten by subsequent dumps. You should name this dump of the *master* database dump_<servername>_master_4.9.2_nomirrors_newconfig_-date_time.out to make it easy to rebuild the server if needed. Note that this dump of the *master* database contains data from the system table sysdevices reflecting the primary server devices which still contain 4.9.2 data.

Use sybinit to Start Server Upgrade

You start sybinit just as you did for the pre-upgrade checks done previously.

Perform sybinit Pre-upgrade Database Check

You repeat the pre-upgrade database check to verify that nothing has changed since the previous check.

Perform sybinit Reserved Word Check

You repeat this check just in case there have been changes in any of the objects since the last reserved word check. You must compare the output from this run of the reserved word check with the previous output. If there are new reserved word conflicts, you must determine whether or not the upgrade can proceed.

Perform sybsystemprocs Database Configuration

Now that you are really upgrading the server you need to provide `sybinit` with parameters defining which disk partition will support the sysprocsdev and how big it will be as well as size of the *sybsystemprocs* database.

Upgrade Server

Now you select "Upgrade SQL Server now" from the SQL SERVER UPGRADE menu in `sybinit`. You are now performing the actual upgrade of your server.

Install Backup Server and Auditing

With the upgrade complete, you must install the Backup Server and should install the auditing capabilities of the System 11 SQL Server as well. You can restart `sybinit` or simply stay within the same `sybinit` session and go back to the NEW OR EXISTING SQL SERVER menu.

Post Upgrade 4.9.2 to System 11 (or System 10)

Once you have successfully completed the upgrade of your server to System 11 you have several tasks remaining before you can go home. These tasks are listed in the following checklist:

Dump *master* database after upgrade

Set sa password

Reset all database options

Reset server configuration

Reset server name

Install thresholds

Install roles for all DBA and operator users

Dump *master* database again

Dump all databases

Check all production scripts

Mirror primary devices

Update table statistics

Allow user access

Drop and re-create database objects

Dump master Database after Upgrade

You must now dump the *master* database to disk again. Since you are running a System 11 Server at this point you must use the Backup Server for dumping *master* to disk. Note that with System 11 and the Backup Server you can now dump a database or transaction log directly to a file on disk. You don't have to (although you still can) use a server dump device. You should name this dump of the *master* database, dump_<*servername*>_master_11x_date_time.out to make it easy to rebuild the server if needed. Note that this dump of the *master* database contains data from the system table *sysdevices* reflecting the primary server devices only which now contain System 11 data.

Set sa Password

You must reset the server user sa password immediately. Recall that you set the sa password to NULL before the upgrade began. Note that System 11 encrypts passwords so the entries for passwords in the system table *syslogins* will no longer be human readable by humans. Hence you can't even check to see if the sa password is NULL and you will have to remember what the sa password was before the upgrade to reset it, or look it up on one of the other servers in your database system that is still at the 4.9.2 Version level.

Reset All Database Options

You must check each database on the server to reestablish any and all database options that were in effect before the upgrade took place. This is another time when you need to have a dumped the server system tables to disk (see Chapter 14).

Reset Server Configuration

Now you must reset the stack size and the number of user connections to their pre-upgrade values. Recall that before the upgrade process began you changed the configuration of the server to have only 10 user connections and a stack size of 286,720. Note that you may not be able to reconfigure both of these parameters at once. Using the configuration of the server that was upgraded above as an example, you would be increasing the number of user connections from 10 to 800 while reducing the stack size from 286,720 to 40,960. If you try to change both of these at once the server may not start if there is not enough memory to support 800 user connections and the stack size of 286,720 while the server reduces the stack size. You may need to reduce the stack size, restart the server, verify the server configuration, and then repeat the process for the user connections.

Reset Server Name

During the upgrade you changed the server name to
<*servername*>_SYS11 to make sure you couldn't run scripts that called for
<*servername*> and to make sure you were aware that you were no longer
running a 4.9.2 Server. Now that you are preparing the server for on-line
use, you need to reset the server name in the startup scripts and in the
interfaces file to the pre-upgrade server name, or a new server name if
appropriate for your applications. Note that this does not involve changing the "name" of the server as it has been in the system table *sysservers*
(see Chapter 12 for more details of how a server is named permanently).

You're the only DBA who isn't a senior DBA in the group. You make a
big deal about how you must be allowed to do one of the upgrades
from 4.9.2 to System 10. You get management to agree to this and
they force one of the senior DBAs to come in on one of their (very
rare) days off. You then try to upgrade and find it isn"t working. You
panic and page the senior DBA during their lunch hour. The senior
DBA takes one look at the errorlog of the "new" server and points out
that you have started the 4.9.2 Server executable on the System 10
master device. You look like an idiot. You are shuffled off to a do-noth-
ing job on a server that no one cares about in another building. You
should not be surprised. Read the errorlog when things go wrong.

Install Thresholds

With System 11 you can have thresholds on all databases. More specifically, you can set up the last-chance threshold for each database. You must
note that the last-chance threshold is not automatically setup when you
upgrade a database to System 11. You must use the **select lct_admin
("lastchance", db_id())** command to establish the last-chance
threshold for each database that is upgraded. This threshold will prevent
the transaction log from filling up completely. You do need to review the
material in the Sybase manuals to learn about thresholds and determine if
you need any additional thresholds for your user databases. Note that the
default behavior under System 11 is to suspend all user transactions in a
database once the transaction log fills to the point of the last-chance
threshold. If you prefer to have user transactions aborted while generating
the familiar 1105 error (segment full), you can use **sp_dboption** to set the
abort tran on log full option for the database.

Install Roles for All DBA and Operator Users

You will need to learn about roles as part of System 11. You can now assign the role of operator (**oper_role**) to a set of server logins and those logins will be able to dump and load databases without your having to grant permission to execute those commands in the individual databases as you had to under 4.9.2. You also need to determine how you want to handle the whole question of the sa account. You can assign **sso_role** and **sa_role** to any of the logins that previously had the sa password. This allows you to audit the individual login that is performing sa work in the server. On the other hand you need to watch for problems stemming from not using sa to perform sa tasks. An example would be any scripts that are hardwired to run as server user sa. Such scripts will need to be changed manually and you then have to determine what server user should be used when the script logs into the server as part of the script.

Dump master Database Again

You must now dump the *master* database to disk again. Since you are running a System 11 Server at this point you must use the Backup Server for dumping *master* to disk. Note that with System 11 and the Backup Server, you can now dump a database or transaction log directly to a file on disk. You don't have to (although you still can) use a server dump device. You should name this dump of the *master* database, dump_<*servername*>_master_11x_oldconfig_date_time.out to make it easy to rebuild the server if needed.

Dump All Databases

You must now dump all the databases in the server to tape (or to disk files and then make a file system dump to tape). Note that these will be your first dumps made at the System 11 Version level and that you can't use any of the dumps made at the 4.9.2 Version level any more.

Check All Production Scripts

Now that you have upgraded to System 11 and are about to allow user access, you must ensure that any and all scripts (or cron jobs) that were operating before the upgrade are again operating. Note that you may have to modify these scripts to work with the System 11 features such as server user roles and encrypted passwords.

Mirror Primary Devices

Ever since the server was isolated from the users before the upgrade, the business data in the server has been unchanged. This is necessary in case you have to regress to mirrored 4.9.2-level data or if you have to rebuild the server using dumps made at the 4.9.2 Version level. Ever since then you have not allowed any changes to the business data since those changes could not be recovered if you regressed to the 4.9.2 Version level. Now that you are ready to allow user access and hence allow changes to the business data that you must be able to recover, you need to determine if you are committed to the System 11 Server. This means you should have tested your applications against the upgraded server to ensure that they function properly and that all the data appears to be present. Once you allow user access to the System 11 Server you must stay at System 11 or you will lose data when you regress.

As part of this, you should mirror the primary server devices that have System 11 data to the partitions that were mirrors of these server devices before the upgrade. Note that this will wipe out the 4.9.2 data that is stored on the partitions that once again become mirrors of the primary server devices.

Update Table Statistics

You should execute **update statistics** and **sp_recompile** on all tables in the server. You can use the script described in Chapter 14.

Allow User Access

You need to restart the server (the System 11 Server) on the pre-upgrade port number that is in the client's interfaces file (see Chapter 12 for details of how the interfaces file works and changing port numbers). This should allow user access just as before the upgrade, that is, same server name and port number as were in the client version of the interfaces file before the upgrade began.

Drop and Recreate Database Objects

This step applies to databases that have been upgraded to System 11 from either System 10 or 4.9.2. Due to changes in the way SQL Server System 11 processes subqueries, you must drop and recreate the database objects that contain subqueries. This is important. If you don't perform this step, you may get very severe performance problems. The problem is that database objects will continue to use the pre-System 11 processing that was in effect when the object was recompiled. In some situations, System 11 may execute these database objects much more slowly than if they were compiled under System 11. Then, when such an object is recompiled under System 11, the performance may change again. You need to drop and re-create these objects as part of the server upgrade. That way, any performance changes are known immediately, and you prevent performance problems by making sure that all such objects have been re-created under System 11.

Sybase supplies a stored procedure that is part of System 11 that will identify the database objects that need to be dropped and re-created. You need to run the stored procedure **sp_procqmode** in each database. Note that **sp_procqmode** will identify database objects that need to be dropped and recreated even if those objects don't have subqueries. You should simply drop and re-create all the objects identified by **sp_procq-mode**.

```
1> sp_procqmode
2> go
 Object Owner.Name              Object Type        Processing Mode
 dbo.actions_trigger            trigger            pre-System 11
 dbo.assignments_trigger        trigger            pre-System 11
 dbo.attachments_trigger        trigger            pre-System 11
 dbo.cover_hist_trigger         trigger            pre-System 11
 dbo.customers_trigger          trigger            pre-System 11
 dbo.labor_trigger              trigger            pre-System 11
 dbo.parts_trigger              trigger            pre-System 11
 dbo.reference_trigger          trigger            System 11 or later
 dbo.service_order_trigger      trigger            pre-System 11
 dbo.states_trigger             trigger            pre-System 11
 dbo.action_status_proc         stored procedure   pre-System 11
 dbo.cms_who                    stored procedure   pre-System 11
 dbo.sp_disks                   stored procedure   pre-System 11

(return status = 0)
```

Regressing from Failed System 11 (or System 10) Upgrade

If you fail to upgrade your server to System 11 successfully, you can fall back or regress to your 4.9.2 Server using one of the *master* database dumps you made during the upgrade process and using the mirrors you had of the 4.9.2 Server databases before you began the upgrade. The process of this regression is discussed below and illustrated in Figure 13–1. Note that this approach will recover only those databases that were fully mirrored at the 4.9.2 Version level. All other databases could be re-created and reloaded from dumps assuming you can recover the *master* database to its 4.9.2 condition. The steps of the recovery are listed below.

If you have attempted to upgrade your server to System 11 and have failed to do so, you must contact Sybase Technical Support for a review of the situation. You must make sure that the regression plan shown below is the best alternative for your system before you start regressing. It may turn out that you can easily fix the cause of the upgrade failure and complete the upgrade. You must not try to regress in haste. On the other hand, you must know about this regression process before you begin upgrading so you can take the steps necessary to make this regression process viable.

Shutdown server

Install 4.9.2 Server on same master device

Load dump of *master* (4.9.2 version)

Change permissions on primary server devices

Restart server

Recover server at 4.9.2

Shut Down Server

If the server is still running after the failed upgrade attempt, you must shut it down. The server must be shut down so you can re-install the 4.9.2 master device on the existing System 10 master device.

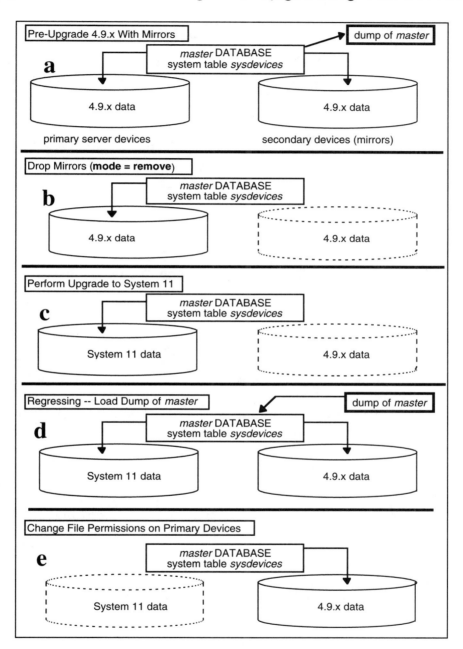

Figure 13–1. Regression to 4.9.2

Install 4.9.2 Server on Same Master Device

You need to load the dump of the *master* database you made before the upgrade when the server was at the 4.9.2 Version level. In order to do this, you must have a 4.9.2 Server running and this requires that you re-install the 4.9.2 master device by running `buildmaster`. Note that the master device at this point is at the System 11 Version level and you will be over-writing the existing master device with the 4.9.2 Version. You do this by executing `buildmaster -d /dev/rdsk/<partition_of_master_device> -s <size_of_master_device_in_2K_pages>`. Note that you must run the 4.9.2 Version of `buildmaster`, not the System 11 Version.

Load Dump of master (4.9.2 Version)

You must add the –m option to your RUN_<*servername*> script to start the server in single-user mode, and you must ensure that you are starting the 4.9.2 Server, not the System 11 Server. At this point you should still have the server isolated from the user community so that no one but you can log in to the server as the single user. You restart the server in single user mode and load the dump of the *master* database that you made during the upgrade attempt. The name of this *master* database dump should be `dump_<servername>_master_4.9.2_withmirrors_date_time.out` and you must be sure you are loading the correct *master* database dump. The *SQL Server Troubleshooting Guide* has details on the process of loading a dump of the *master* database. Loading a dump of *master* will shut down the server. See "Dump master with Devices Mirrored" in the "Upgrading 4.9.2 to System 11 (or System 10)" section.

Note that the idea here is to load the *master* database dump that was made while the server was at 4.9.2 and had the server devices mirrored. After the load of the *master* database dump is complete, the *master* database will again contain the information about the server devices and their mirrors just as it did early in the upgrade process when all the server devices had data at the 4.9.2 Version level. At this point the mirrors of the server devices are no longer dropped since the *master* database (specifically the system table *sysdevices*) has now been restored to reflect the server configuration before the mirrors were dropped.

Note further that at this point the primary side of each mirrored pair has data that is at the System 11 Version level, while the mirrors of these mirrored pairs were dropped just before the upgrade started. This means you have primary devices with data at the System 11 Version level and mirrors of those server devices with data at the 4.9.2 Version level (see Figure 13–1(d)).

Change Permissions on Primary Server Devices

You must change the ownership and/or file permissions on the files that control the access to the disk partitions that support the primary server devices of each server device mirrored pair. The point is that you make it so that the UNIX user who is starting the server (should be UNIX user sybase) canít gain access to the primary server devices.

Restart Server

When the server is started the next time, it will open the restored *master* database and look in the system table *sysdevices* and find the names of all the server devices and their mirrors which will appear to have never been dropped. But, when the server tries to access the primary server devices (which contain data at the System 11 Version level) the file ownership and/or permissions will prevent that from happening. The server will detect this and will then fail over to the mirrors of the primary server devices. At this point you have your server running on a primary master device and on secondary server devices that all contain data at the 4.9.2 Version level (see Figure 13-1(e)).

Recover Server at 4.9.2

Now you must decide what your plan is regarding the upgrade. If you plan to operate at the 4.9.2 Version level for any length of time, you should drop the primary side of each of the mirror pairs to get rid of the server devices that have System 11 data on them. You could then remirror from the former secondary (now the primary and unmirrored server devices) server devices to restore the mirrored pairs at the 4.9.2 Version level.

Note that you can use this regression process only if you have mirrors of the server devices and you made the dump of the *master* database at the right time and you dropped the mirrors of the server devices at the right time (before upgrade process started). See Figure 13–1 for illustration of the flow of the regression process.

Upgrading SQL Server 4.9.2 to System 10

The process of upgrading from 4.9.2 to System 10 is virtually identical to that of the upgrade to System 11. You should follow the steps presented for upgrading from 4.9.2 to System 11 for preparing, upgrading, and post-upgrading. The actual output of a `sybinit` session for this upgrade is on the CD-ROM.

Upgrading SQL Server System 10 to System 11—Full Upgrade

Upgrading from System 10 to System 11 is simpler than upgrading from 4.9.2. Here we discuss performing a full upgrade of a System 10 SQL Server to System 11. Many of the issues that exist between 4.9.2 and System 11 have already been dealt with since you are starting at System 10. Since you are running System 10, you already have the server devices for *sybsystemprocs* and *sybsecurity* and you should not have any reserved word conflicts, although System 11 does introduce a few new reserved words. The steps you need to follow to prepare for upgrading from System 10 to System 11 are presented in the following checklist. For each step, you should refer to the same step described in the section Preparing to Upgrade 4.9.2 to System 11. The actual output of a `sybinit` session for this upgrade is on the CD-ROM.

Reset all database options

Use `sybinit` for pre-upgrade database check

Log of `sybinit` during pre-upgrade database check

Use `sybinit` for pre-upgrade reserved word check

Output of `sybinit` reserved word check

Drop mirrors and devices for new System 11 devices

Check remaining server device mirrors

dbcc checks on all databases

Check free space in all databases

Dump transaction logs and checkpoint all databases

Upgrading SQL Server System 10 to System 11—Loading System 10 Database Dumps

Upgrading from System 10 to System 11 can also be performed in another manner. You can first install a new System 11 SQL Server, create the databases that will exist on this new System 11 SQL Server, and then load database dumps from your existing System 10 SQL Server. The process of loading a System 10 database into a System 11 SQL Server actually upgrades the database to System 11. This process has several advantages. You do not have to bring down your existing production system until you are completely ready to do so. Since you are loading the databases one at a time, you can deal with any problems that might come up in each database. Instead of risking the whole server, you are able to isolate the risk of upgrade problems to one database at a time. The output of this process is on the CD-ROM.

Dump Databases on System 10 SQL Server

You need to make a database dump of each System 10 database that you need to move to the System 11 SQL Server.

Install System 11 SQL Server

You should follow the entire process for installing the new System 11 SQL Server as discussed above. In addition, you will need to bcp the syslogins data out of the System 10 SQL Server and bcp this data into the System 11 SQL Server (see Chapter 9 for details of this process).

Create databases on System 11 SQL Server

You need to re-create each database that you are moving from the System 10 SQL Server. As with any re-creation of a database, you need to be careful to re-create the size and order of each chunk of disk space for each database. You can use the script p_dbcreate discussed in Chapter 14, to dump the structure of the System 10 databases. You can then use the output of **p_dbcreate** for each database to create the same database on the System 11 SQL Server. You should use the "for load" option of the create database command, which is part of the output of **p_dbcreate**.

Load System 10 Database Dumps into System 11 SQL Server

After bringing the System 10 database dumps to the System 11 server machine, load each database.

Bring Loaded Databases On-line

At this point, the databases that have been loaded will be off-line. You then need to execute the on-line database command for each database. This will upgrade each database from System 10 to System 11. After this has been done for each database, the upgrade from System 10 to System 11 is complete.

Drop and Recreate Database Objects

As with the full upgrade to System 11, you need to drop and re-create any objects that contain subqueries. See Drop and Recreate Database Objects in under the section on full upgrade to System 11.

Scripts

General Server Scripts

- Dump Database Transaction Log (dumplog)
- Dump Databases for SQL Server 4.9.2 (dumpdb_492)
- Load Databases for SQL Server 4.9.2 (loaddb_492)
- **update statistics** on all tables
  (update_statistics_all_tables)
- Dump Database Creation Script (dump_db_create)
- Run **dbcc** Checks (checkdb)
- Dump Data from System Tables (dump_systables)

❄ **Stored Procedure to Dump Database Creation Script (p_dbcreate)**

❄ **Stored Procedure to Check Mirrors (p_mirror)**

❄ **Stored Procedure to Output Device Space (p_devspace)**

❄ **Stored Procedure to Output All Segments on Devices (p_servermap)**

❄ **Dump Databases** (dumpdb)

❄ **Load Databases** (loaddb)

❄ **Stored Procedure to Monitor Database Load (p_dbload)**

❄ **SQL Server Startup Script**

We cover a number of scripts that can be used to dump databases, create useful stored procedures, and check your server. The scripts are described in two sections. The first section covers scripts that are applicable to dumping SQL Server 4.9.2 and System 10 databases, creating stored procedures that will help you document and monitor your servers and starting your servers. The second section describes a set of scripts specifically created to support a System 11 production server. These scripts will help you monitor and maintain a System 11 Server.

The full text of all scripts is available on the CD-ROM.

GENERAL SCRIPTS

Here we discuss the details of some scripts that will be useful to you in several ways. First, we provide a set of scripts that you should have on each of your servers. Second, each script provides the basic syntax you need to build other scripts. Note that these scripts were written for the C shell. However, they are commented profusely to enable you to convert them to your particular environment.

SYSTEM 11 PRODUCTION SCRIPTS

The following set of scripts will allow you to monitor and maintain a System 11 production SQL Server. These scripts could be used to support a System 10 or 4.9.2 SQL Server with some minor modifications. However, we discuss them assuming they will be used with a System 11 SQL Server. All these scripts have the same structure and all are written in the Bourne shell for maximum portability. These scripts are self-contained in that they don't rely on calling other scripts to get their work done. One of the scripts (dumping server configuration) does use several stored procedures that are described in the General Scripts section. These scripts use only standard UNIX and Sybase SQL commands, and do not use any sed, awk, or perl. This makes them easier to understand and modify.

All these scripts assume that the server sa password is stored in a file called .kparm. You must create this file and edit in the sa password. You must also set the permissions on this file so that only the appropriate server machine users can examine the contents. Typically, the file should be accessible only by the UNIX sybase user. The location of this file, and the path to any other files used in the scripts may need to be changed for your specific server machine. For each script, things that may need to be modified for your server machine are identified by *****.

All these scripts send e-mail with the full output of the script, and where appropriate, they also send a separate email in the event of a script failure. Whenever a script sends e-mail for a script failure, you can add the commands needed to page the DBA when a failure occurs. Each of these scripts generates output files which are overwritten each time the script is executed. This prevents file systems from filling up with output files. You can keep the e-mail from the scripts to form an archive of the script outputs. Note that you must edit each script to send the output e-mail to the appropriate e-mail address.

The following scripts assume the Sybase utility isql is in the bin subdirectory of the directory identified by the SYBASE environment parameter. If this is not the case on your server machine, you would need to change this.

Dump database (dump_listof_dbs)

Dump yransaction log (logdump_listof_dbs)

603

Truncate transaction log (`trunclog_listof_dbs`)

Remove old files (`remove_old_files`)

Update statistics (`update_listof_dbs`)

Executing dbcc (`dbcc_listof_dbs`)

Scanning server error log (`scan_errorlog`)

Dumping server configuration (`dump_server_config`)

Monitor report (`monitor_report`)

Execute sp_sysmon (`execute_sp_sysmon`)

Server auto-restart

Crontab entries for scripts

For each script the text of the script is shown with explanations for each part. Note that the comments in the script are lines that start with a #. Note also that when a command or syntax has been commented once in one script, the comment is not repeated in the following scripts.

SQL Server Versions

The scripts described here will work (with some modifications) with all versions of SQL Server.

SQL Server 4.9.2

Several of the scripts presented here are written specifically for SQL Server 4.9.2 to get around limitations of that server version. These limitations include not being able to dump multiple database dumps to tape, and so forth. SQL Server 4.9.2 does not support the *sybsystemprocs* database where system stored procedures are usually stored. The scripts presented here that create and use stored procedures assume that the stored procedures are in the *sybsystemprocs* database. If you use these scripts with a 4.9.2 Server you need to change the script to create or use a stored procedure from either the *master* database or some other database where you have placed the stored procedure.

The script `dump_systables` is written for System 11. If you are using this script with a 4.9.2 or System 10 Server you need to be aware that further server configuration information is available by using the UNIX level command

```
$SYBASE/bin/buildmaster -d<master_device_physical_name> -yall
```

You should consider executing this command to dump the details of the server configuration. However, the buildmaster command should be only used by experienced users. Review the *Sybase SQL Server Error Messages* manual for detailed instructions on the use of this command.

Scripts that depend on use of the Backup Server are not relevant to the 4.9.2 Version of SQL Server.

SQL Server System 10

For the System 10 SQL Server, stored procedures described here should be created in the *sybsystemprocs* database.

SQL Server System 11

For the System 11 SQL Server, stored procedures described here should be created in the *sybsystemprocs* database.

DUMP DATABASE TRANSACTION LOG (DUMPLOG)

This script will dump the transaction log for each of the database names given. This script would normally be executed as a `cron` job. When executed as a `cron` job the server user sa password should be placed in a file that only UNIX user db a has permission to see. Then the contents of this password file should be used in the `crontab` entry for the script. Assuming the password file is `/usr/dba/<servername>` the `crontab` entry to execute the `dumplog` script every hour from 10AM to 10PM would look like this:

```
0 10-22 * * * /dba/<servername>/scripts/dumplog `cat
/usr/dba/.<servername>` db1
```

This entry in the `crontab` would execute the `dumplog` script on the hour (0 minutes after the hour) every hour from 10AM to 10PM and each time the script is executed it would dump the transaction log for the database called *db1*.

To execute the dumplog script, use

```
dumplog <sa_password> <db1, db2, db3, ... , dbn>
```

which will dump the transaction log to a disk file for each database listed.

```csh
#!/bin/csh -f

# this first line is very important — it identifies this script as
# being a C shell script
# and yes, the first line appears to be a comment line
# now test to see if enough arguments were supplied, the 0th
# argument is the name of the script that
# is being executed, the 1st argument is the password and the 2nd
# argument is the list of database names

if ($#argv < 2 ) then

# echo sends the text to the screen and
# echo ${0} sends the 0th argument to the screen which is the name
# of the script followed by the
# rest of the text specified
# if the script isn't supplied the correct number of arguments it
# simply outputs the required parameters
# and exits

        echo ${0}: invalid  format: $#argv parameters provided, at
    least 3 required
        echo ${0}: required format: ${0} '<sa password>
    <database(s)...>'
        exit(1)

# exit(1) means the script exits and returns a status of 1
# indicating an error — this is useful when
# executing this script as part of a larger script

endif

# here we test to see if the server user is 'dba' — if not exit
# with error status

if (`whoami` != "dba") then
```

```
        echo you must be UNIX user dba to dump the transaction log
        exit(1)
endif

# umask specifies the permissions to be setup for any files created
# in the script
# note that the umask value (in this case 006) will be XORed with
# 666 to arrive at
# the file permissions
# unalias removes any alias for the rm command — often the UNIX user
# accounts have
# rm aliased so that you have to confirm each rm execution

umask 006
unalias rm

# here we setup various parameters needed later
# the SYBASE variable points to the SYBASE directory where all
# product files are installed

setenv SYBASE /home/sybase

# the SERVER variable is set to the name of the SQL server we need
# to access

setenv SERVER PDSOPS21

# the BIN variable points to the subdirectory of the SYBASE
# directory where the executables
# are stored

set BIN=${SYBASE}/bin

# the variable logdir is the directory where the transaction log
# dumps will be created
# the variable outfile is the location of the errorlog for the
# execution of the script
# the variable password is set to the first argument supplied when
# the script was executed
# shift simply shifts the arguments supplied — remaining arguments
# are all database names

set logdir=/diskdump
set outfile=${logdir}/dumplog.out
set password=$1
shift
```

```
# the variable dmptime contains the date and time

set dmptime=`date +%y%m%d%H%M%S`

# test to see if another dumplog is already executing — if so exit
# with error status and send mail
# this is useful — it prevents multiple dumplog executions — if one
# dumplog is running and gets
# hung up for any reason the following cron executions will abort
# themselves. If one dumplog is
# running there is no point in having another execution start up as
# it will simply be blocked by
# the previous execution.
# ps -ef lists all the processes running on the machine
# grep will extract only the process that are running that contain
# 'dumplog' and
# wc -l returns the wordcount, but the -l flag returns the line
# count of the grep output

ps -ef > /tmp/ps.dumplog
set cnt = `grep dumplog /tmp/ps.dumplog | wc -l`

# subtract 2, 1 for the current execution and 1 for the cron
# expr causes the expression inside the ` ` to be evaluated

set cnt1 = `expr $cnt - 2`
if ($cnt1 > 0) then

# the mail command uses -s to specify subject of mail and dba is the
# user the mail is sent to

        mail -s "${SERVER} dumplog aborted" dba < /tmp/ps.dumplog
exit 1
endif

# remove the temporary file used to hold the listing of the cron
# jobs running

rm /tmp/ps.dumplog

# setup the list of databases that will have a transaction log dump

set dbs_to_trandump=($argv)

# write the date when the looping over the databases starts to the
output # file
```

```
echo "dumplog:${SERVER}: started at `date`." > $outfile

# setup the set of databases, and for each one dump the transaction
# log to disk

foreach dbname ($dbs_to_trandump)

# create the disk file name that will contain the transaction log
# dump

set logfile=${dbname}.log_${dmptime}

# execute the utility program isql — note that you need to include
# the path to the isql executable
# since the cron execution may not have the same path you have when
# you run isql. The -e option
# echoes the input to the output file. Note that there is an output
# file created for each database that
# is dumped. Once isql is executed continue to send commands to isql
# until we reach the finish_sql
# label.

${BIN}/isql -Usa -S${SERVER} -I$SYBASE/interfaces -e >
${dbname}_logdump.out << finish_sql
$password
dump tran $dbname to '${logdir}/${logfile}'
go
exit
finish_sql

# if the execution of isql returns with status=1 then something went
# wrong, send mail to dba

        if ($status) then
                echo dumplog:${SERVER}: log dump of $dbname failed
        at `date`. > $outfile
                mail -s "${SERVER}: log dump of $dbname failed" dba
< $outfile
        endif

# if the transaction log dump completed write out the time of the
# completion

        echo dumplog:${SERVER}: completed xact log dump of $dbname
at `date` > $outfile
end
```

```
# whatever happened during the execution output the date when the
# cron job finished and send
# the entire output file to dba.

echo "dumplog:${SERVER}: exiting at `date`." > $outfile
mail -s "${SERVER}: log dump cronjob complete" dba < $outfile
exit
```

DUMP DATABASES FOR SQL SERVER 4.9.2 (DUMPDB_492)

Warning

Dumping multiple databases to a single tape is not supported as part of the Sybase SQL Server product.

This script is used to dump one or more databases to a tape device. Note that Sybase SQL Server Version 4.9.2 does not support dumping multiple databases to one tape. However, as shown in the script, you can dump multiple databases to a nonrewinding tape device. As one database dump finishes, the next dump starts up and as long as the tape device doesn't try to rewind, things will work out fine. Note again that dumping multiple databases to one tape is not supported by Sybase—use at your own risk.

Since this script is designed to dump to tape, it is assumed that a tape operator will be executing the script manually since the tape must be loaded in the drive before the script can begin. For this reason the script prompts for the server login and password of the user that is executing the script. Note that this means any user who needs to execute this script must have permission to dump the databases. This requires that all such users be granted **dump database** permission in each database. For a 4.9.2 Server, you should set up all such users in the *model* database before creating all the user databases so that these users will have **dump database** permission in all the user databases.

This script can be executed as a `cron` job if desired. You would have to change the script to assign the command line arguments for user name and

610

password to the appropriate variables since the script currently will prompt and wait for the input of both parameters.

To execute the script, after loading the tape in the correct tape drive,

```
dumpdb_492 <username> <password>
```

```
#!/bin/csh -f
umask 006
setenv SYBASE /home/sybase

# here the script prompts for the username and password
# echo - n simply writes to the screen without a new line character
# at end of text
# and the user input is assigned to the variable by set username =
# $<
# stty echo simply echoes the text to the screen
# clear simply clears the screen

echo -n Please enter your SQL Server login:
set username = $<
stty -echo
echo -n Please enter your SQL Server password:
set password = $<
stty echo
clear


# setup the output file for this script

set outfile=/diskdump/public_dumpdb.out

# write to both screen and output file the date when the dump script
# started

echo "dumpdb:PDSOPS21: started at `date`."
echo "dumpdb:PDSOPS21: started at `date`." > $outfile

# mt is the UNIX command to control the tape drive. Here we use the
# -f option to specify the
# tape device nrst8 which is a nonrewinding tape device. This means
# it doesn't rewind until we
# explicitly ask it to. We then specify that we want to rewind the
# tape. This positions the tape for
# the first database dump.

mt -f /dev/nrst8 rewind
```

```
# write a file to the tape as a tape header — since SQL Server
# 4.9.2 doesn't provide this feature we
# do it manually. This tape header will tell you the name of the
# server machine and the date the
# dump script was started. This can be very useful when you need to
# determine the date and source
# of an old dump tape.
# we echo the server machine name and the date to a temporary file
# called dumptape_header
# uname -a outputs the hostname and operating system version
# dd is the UNIX command for copying and converting data files — if
# is input file, of is output file, bs
# is the block size of both input/output files, count=n specifies
# copy only n input records

echo `/usr/bin/uname -a`" "`/usr/bin/date` >/tmp/dumptape_header
dd if=/tmp/dumptape_header of=/dev/nrst8 bs=80 count=1

# now we start dumping each of the databases. Note that the list of
# databases to dump is hardcoded
# in the script. This script is designed to be executed by a tape
# operator who should not need to determine
# which databases to dump. Further, for a production system you
# shouldn't be changing which databases
# are being dumped very often.

foreach dbname (master db1 db2 db3 db4 model)
        echo "dumpdb:PDSOPS21: dump of $dbname started    at
    `date`."
        echo "dumpdb:PDSOPS21: dump of $dbname started    at
    `date`." > $outfile

# note that the databases are being dumped to logical device ntape
# dump8 which
# refers to the server machine device nrst8 — you need to change
# this to the
# appropriate logical dump device for your server machine
# note that here we don't use $SYBASE/bin/isql because this script
# won't be executed by UNIX user
# 'dba' — the tape operator should not have access to the s setup
# for 'dba' — the tape
# operator will need to execute the isql code that is available to
# their workstation — you will have to
# change this based on your specific environment.
```

```
/usr/local/sybase/bin/isql -U$username -SPDSOPS2 -e > ${outfile}
<<finish_sql
$password
dump database $dbname to ntapedump8
go
exit
finish_sql

# if the isql execution returns with status=1 then something failed
# write to the tape operators screen and the output file

if ($status) then
        echo "dumpdb:PDSOPS21: database dump of $dbname has FAILED
      at `date`."
        cat   ${dbname}_dbdump.out
        echo "dumpdb:PDSOPS21: database dump of $dbname has FAILED
      at `date`." > $outfile
        cat   ${dbname}_dbdump.out > $outfile
else
        echo "dumpdb:PDSOPS21: database dump of $dbname completed
      at `date`."
        echo "dumpdb:PDSOPS21: database dump of $dbname completed
      at `date`." > $outfile
endif
end

# when all of the databases have been dumped to tape write the date
# to both the operators screen
# and the output file

echo "dumpdb:PDSOPS21: exiting at `date`."
echo "dumpdb:PDSOPS21: exiting at `date`." > $outfile

# send the output file to dba

mail -s "dumpdb:PDSOSP21: output" dba < $outfile

# here we use the UNIX mt command to rewind and eject the tape
# the mt command takes several options here offline will rewind and
# eject the tape

mt -f /dev/nrst8 offline                    # rewind tape
exit
```

LOAD DATABASES FOR SQL SERVER 4.9.2 (LOADDB_492)

 This script is for loading one or more of the database dumps you made using the `dumpdb` script discussed earlier. Recall that the `dumpdb` script allows you to dump more than one database to a tape which is not a supported feature of the Sybase SQL Server. Now that you have a tape with multiple database dumps on it, we discuss how to load a database from the tape. The SQL Server has no idea that the tape has multiple database dumps on it. In fact, when you issue the server command load database *db1* and specify the tape drive the server will just start reading the tape assuming that the database dump for *db1* is there. The script must take care of positioning the tape such that the database dump for *db1* is the very next file on the tape. Recall that the `dumpdb` script put a header on the tape to identify the date and server machine where the tape was created, and then the script dumped the databases requested to tape. This means we need to know where the dump of database *db1* is on the tape and position the tape to that file before we tell the server to begin loading *db1*.

Each database dump on the tape is a file and therefore if we know how many databases were dumped before *db1* was dumped, we know the number of the file we need to load *db1* from the tape. For example, let's assume you used the `dumpdb` script to dump databases *db0,db1,db2* and *db3* to tape. Recall that the `dumpdb` script puts a header file on the tape. The header file is the first file on the tape but this is the 0th file or `count = 0` for the UNIX `mt` command. Hence, the database dump of *db0* is the `count = 1` file and the database dump of *db1* is the `count = 2` file. Using this `count`, you can use the UNIX command `mt` with the `fsf` or fast-forward option to position the tape to the beginning of the third file (`count = 2`) which is the beginning of the *db1* database dump.

Since this script is for loading a database dump, it would not normally be used as a `cron` job. Usually the need to load a database from tape comes up only if there has been a major problem and therefore the script should be executed manually. To execute the `loaddb` script manually

```
loaddb_492 <servername> <sa_password> <databases_to_load>
```

The script takes the names of the databases to load and equates the name of each with a count value. The script can then position the tape for loading. This approach has some dependencies you need to be aware of. The number of databases being dumped and the order in which they are dumped must remain fixed between the `dumpdb` and `loaddb` scripts. Also, if one or more of the dumps should fail to start for any reason during the execution of the `dumpdb` script, the total number of files on the dump tape will be off by one, and you would need to edit the `loaddb` script to change the `count` value(s) for the database(s) you are trying to load. This is where the mail that is sent to UNIX user dba after the `dumpdb` script comes in. Before loading a database dump from tape examine the mail message that was generated when the dump tape was made. If there are any failures before the database dump that you need to load, you need to make changes to the `loaddb` script.

```csh
#!/bin/csh -f

umask 006                    # make our files -rw-rw—

# here we test to see if we have all the required parameters and if
# not we read the header file off
# the tape and write to the screen what all the required parameters
# are and exit with status=1 which
# indicates an error condition.

if !($#argv) then
        dd if=/dev/rst8 bs=80 count=1
        echo loaddb: format: loaddb.PDSOPS21 '<Server Name> <Server
    Password> <Database(s)>'
        exit (1)
endif
setenv SYBASE /home/sybase
setenv SERVER PDSOPS21
set BIN=${SYBASE}/bin

# here we assign the servername and password parameters. The use of
# shift just moves us along the
# string of arguments supplied when the script was executed.

set srvname = $1
shift
set password = $1
shift
set databases_to_load = ($argv)
echo "loaddb: started at `date`."

# rewind the tape to position it at the very first file on the tape.
# Note that we are specifying the
```

```
# rewinding tape device here and that you need to change rst8 to
# whatever the non-rewinding tape
# device is on your server machine.

mt -f /dev/rst8 rewind                     # rewind tape

# here we setup the databases that we need to load. For each one we
# use the database name to
# determine the count value, i.e. how many files into the tape is
# the dump of database dbx? If
# the database name requested isn't in the script's list of possible
# databases to load the script
# will exit with status=1 (error condition).

foreach dbname ($databases_to_load)
        echo loaddb: beginning load of $dbname
        switch ($dbname)
                case db0:
                        set counter = 1
                        breaksw
                case db1:
                        set counter = 2
                        breaksw
                case db2:
                        set counter = 3
                        breaksw
                case db3:
                        set counter = 4
                        breaksw
            default:
                        echo invalid database name $dbname
                        exit (1)
        endsw

# here we fast-forward the tape to the beginning of the nth file
# where n=counter+1 — recall the
# first file on the tape is the 0th file, so the 5th file on the
# tape is counter=4

        mt -f /dev/nrst8 fsf $counter

# if positioning the tape returns an error condition the script
# exits advising the user to get
# help from the dba.

        if ($status) then
```

```
                echo database load script failed during positioning
        of tape — contact DBA for help
                exit (1)
        endif

# write the date the load started to the output file

echo "loaddb: started at `date`." >
/dba/${SERVER}/diagnostics/${dbname}_loaddb.out

# execute isql for the first database to be loaded. You will need to
# change the logical tape device
# from ntapedump8 to the appropriate tape device for your server.

${BIN}/bin/isql -Usa -S${srvname} -e > /dba/${SERVER}/
  diagnostics/${dbname}_loaddb.out <<finish_sql
$password
load database $dbname from ntapedump8
go
exit
finish_sql

# if the isql execution fails write that out to the output file and
# exit with status=1

        if ($status) then
                echo load of $dbname failed at `date`.
output to output file
                exit (1)
        endif

        echo load of $dbname completed at `date`
output to output file

# rewind and eject the tape

        mt -f /dev/rst8 off                     # rewind tape
end

# write out date of end of loaddb script and send output file to dba

echo "loaddb: ended at `date`." >
/dba/${SERVER}/diagnostics/${dbname}_loaddb.out
mail -s 'load of database complete' dba < /dba/${SERVER}/
  diagnostics/${dbname}_loaddb.out
exit
```

UPDATE STATISTICS ON ALL TABLES (UPDATE_STATISTICS_ALL_TABLES)

This script will execute the server command **update statistics** and the server stored procedure **sp_recompile** for each and every user table on the entire server. This script is very useful because it is difficult to keep track of which tables on the server have been updated or should be updated. Even though you may have a list of several critical tables that must be updated frequently, you should use this script on a regular basis to make sure that all the tables in the server are updated. You need to prevent the situation where you run across tables that have never had update statistics performed. This can happen if it has never been done, but also when a table is truncated, and so forth. Until you **update statistics** for such a table it will appear to the server that it has never been done.

The `crontab` entry would look like this:

```
0 21 6 * *
/dba/<servername>/scripts/update_statistics_all_tables <server-
name> `cat /usr/dba/<servername>`
```

This entry in the `crontab` would execute the update_statis-tics_all_tables script at 21:00 (09:00 PM) on the 6th day for every month and every year. Note that `crontab` days start with 0 for Sunday and run through 6 for Saturday.

You can manually execute this script as follows,

```
update_statistics_all_tables <servername> <sa_password>
```

```
#!/bin/csh -f

# setup various parameters and the output file

unalias rm
setenv SYBASE /home/sybase
setenv BIN ${SYBASE}/bin
set SERVER = $1
set PASSWORD = $2
set outfile=/dba/$${server}/diagnostics/update_statistics.out
cp /dev/null $outfile

# first we need to generate a list of all the databases in the
# server
```

```
set TEMPFILE=/tmp/${SERVER}_databases.list
cp /dev/null $TEMPFILE
${BIN}/isql -Usa -P$PASSWORD -S$SERVER -I$SYBASE/interfaces
  << finish_sql > $TEMPFILE
use master
go
select name from sysdatabases where name != "tempdb" order by name
go
finish_sql

# append the output of all the databases to the output file
# select the servername and date/time to the output file

echo " " > $outfile
echo "all databases in server...." > $outfile
echo " " > $outfile
cat $TEMPFILE > $outfile
echo " "
${BIN}/isql -Usa -P$PASSWORD -S$SERVER -I$SYBASE/interfaces
  << finish_sql > tfile
select @@servername
go
select getdate()
go
finish_sql

# see the dump_db_create script discussion for details of the
# following part of the script

set num_lines=`wc -l $TEMPFILE | cut -c1-9`
set last_line=`expr $num_lines - 2`
set first_line=`expr $last_line - 2`
set databases_list=`tail -$last_line $TEMPFILE | head -$first_line`
rm -f $TEMPFILE

# Finally we can setup the list of databases

foreach dbname ($databases_list)

# now repeat the process but this time generate a list of all the
# user tables in each database

set TEMPFILE2=/tmp/${dbname}_tables.list
cp /dev/null $TEMPFILE2
${BIN}/isql -Usa -P$PASSWORD -S$SERVER -I$SYBASE/interfaces -e
```

```
    << finish_sql > $TEMPFILE2
use $dbname
go
select name from sysobjects where type="U" order by name
go
finish_sql

echo " " > $outfile
echo "@@@@@@@@@@@@@@@@@@@@@@@@" > $outfile
echo "all tables in database $dbname...." > $outfile
echo "@@@@@@@@@@@@@@@@@@@@@@@@" > $outfile
echo " " > $outfile
cat $TEMPFILE2 > $outfile
echo " " > $outfile

# cut out the first 4 and last 2 lines of the listing of all the
# user tables in this database

set num_lines=`wc -l $TEMPFILE2 | cut -c1-9`
set last_line=`expr $num_lines - 4`
set first_line=`expr $last_line - 2`
set tables_list=`tail -$last_line $TEMPFILE2 | head -$first_line`
rm -f $TEMPFILE2

# now we start updating statistics and executing sp_recompile for
# each user table
# in each database

echo "@@@@@@@@@@@@@@@@@@@@@@@@@@@@@@@@@@@@@@@@@@@@@" > $outfile
echo "updating statistics for tables in database $dbname" > $outfile
echo "@@@@@@@@@@@@@@@@@@@@@@@@@@@@@@@@@@@@@@@@@@@@@" > $outfile
echo " " > $outfile
foreach table_name ($tables_list)
${BIN}/isql -Usa -P$PASSWORD -S$SERVER -I$SYBASE/interfaces -e
  << finish_sql > $outfile
use $dbname
go
select getdate()
go
update statistics $table_name
go
sp_recompile $table_name
go
select getdate()
go
finish_sql
```

```
# the first end is for the loop for each user table
# the second end is for the loop for each database in the server

end
end

mail -s "$SERVER update statistics" dba < $outfile
exit(0)
```

DUMP DATABASE CREATION SCRIPT (DUMP_DB_CREATE)

This script is used to dump the Transact SQL commands needed to re-create each database on the server to a disk file. The commands that are generated can be used to re-create each database on the same server or re-create the database on another server. To re-create the server on another server you must first edit the output to change the server device names from those of the source server where the **p_dbcreate** sql script was run to the server device names of the target server. The cron tab entry to execute this script would look like this:

```
0 23 * * * /dba/<servername>/scripts/dump_db_create <server-
name> `cat /usr/dba/<servername>`
```

This entry in the cron tab would execute the dump_db_create script at 23:00 hours (11:00 PM) every day.

To execute the dump_db_create script manually

```
dump_db_create <servername> <sa_password>
```

```
#!/bin/csh -f

# setup various parameters and the output file

unalias rm
setenv SYBASE /home/sybase
setenv BIN ${SYBASE}/bin
set SERVER = $1
set PASSWORD = $2
```

```
set outfile=/dba/${SERVER}/diagnostics/dump_db_create.out
cp /dev/null $outfile

# first we need to generate a list of all the databases in the
# server — we want to generate the
# commands necessary to (re)create all of the databases on the
# server

set TEMPFILE=/tmp/${SERVER}_databases.list
cp /dev/null $TEMPFILE
${BIN}/isql -Usa -P$PASSWORD -S$SERVER -I$SYBASE/interfaces
  << finish_sql > $TEMPFILE
use master
go
select name from sysdatabases where name != "tempdb" order by name
go
finish_sql

# append the output of all the databases to the output file
# select the servername and date/time to the output file

echo " " > $outfile
echo "all databases in server...." > $outfile
echo " " > $outfile
cat $TEMPFILE > $outfile
echo " "
${BIN}/isql -Usa -P$PASSWORD -S$SERVER -I$SYBASE/interfaces
  << finish_sql > $outfile
select @@servername
go
select getdate()
go
finish_sql

# after we generate the list of databases on the server we need to
# edit out the first two lines
# and the last two lines of the output — they contain the column
# names and the number of rows
# selected, respectively. The output of the select for the databases
# goes to a temporary file. We remove
# the lines we don't want by determining the number of rows in the
# temporary file. Note that the
# output of the wc -l command gives us the number of lines (wc is
# the word count command, and the
```

```
# -l option counts lines not words) and the name of the file. We use
# the cut command with the -c option
# to cut out only columns 1 through 9 that contain the number of
# rows in the temporary file.
# With that done we can set a parameter for 2 lines less than the
# total number of lines and another
# parameter for the first parameter -2. Now we feed the temporary
# file through the tail command
# specifying that tail output the last x lines of the file where
# x = num_lines - 2 — this will give us a
# the temporary file without the first two lines, then we feed that
# into the head command telling it
# to only output the first x - 2 lines which gives us all the
# previous lines but not the last two lines.
# This gets rid of the first 2 and last 2 lines of the temporary
# file.

set num_lines=`wc -l $TEMPFILE | cut -c1-9
set last_line=`expr $num_lines - 2`
set first_line=`expr $last_line - 2`
set databases_list=`tail -$last_line $TEMPFILE | head -$first_line`
rm -f $TEMPFILE

# Finally we can setup the list of databases
# then execute the stored procedure p_dbcreate for each database

foreach dbname ($databases_list)
${BIN}/isql -Usa -P$PASSWORD -S$SERVER -I$SYBASE/interfaces
  << finish_sql > $outfile

# the following command assumes the stored procedure p_dbcreate has
# been created in the sybsystemprocs # database. You can place the
# stored procedure in another database and then change the following
# command. For a 4.9.2 SQL Server there is no sybsystemprocs and you
# would use the master database.

use sybsystemprocs
go
p_dbcreate $dbname
go
finish_sql
end
exit(0)
```

RUN DBCC CHECKS (CHECKDB)

This script is used to run the full **dbcc** set. This script would be used after loading a database from a dump tape onto the DBCC server. This assumes that the database to be loaded, database *db1* in the script below, has already been created on the DBCC server. This would be a good place for you to use the **p_dbcreate** SQL script described previously since that script will dump the database definition from the source server and after you edit the **p_dbcreate** output to reflect the actual server device names on the DBCC server, you can create the database with the **for load** option on the DBCC server and execute the checkdb script shown below.

You can execute the script manually as well:

```
checkdb <sa_password>
```

Note that this script is hardcoded for running the **dbcc** checks for a single database. You could modify the script to accept the database name as a parameter input at execution time. You need to determine how you want to run the **dbcc** checks for each database on your server. For the largest databases you may not want to run **dbcc** checks on all the databases only on selected tables, and so forth. In that case you would need a separate script set up for each database.

```
#!/bin/csh -f

# select @@servername returns the name of the server you are
# connected to
# select db_name() returns the current database
# select getdate() returns the current date/time
# dbcc traceon (3604) causes the output of the dbcc runs to be sent
# to your screen or in this
# case to the output file of the script
# the script outputs the date/time as each dbcc run completes — this
# timing information is
# very important when planning dbcc runs on your production servers
# to fix corruptions
# found after running dbcc checks on the DBCC server

isql -Usa -P$1 -SDDSMAIN1 > dbcc_db1.out << finish_sql
select @@servername
go
use db1
```

```
go
select db_name()
go
select getdate()
go
dbcc traceon (3604)
go
dbcc checkalloc (db1)
go
select getdate()
go
dbcc checkdb (db1)
go
select getdate()
go
dbcc checkcatalog (db1)
go
select getdate()
go
finish_sql
mail -s "dbcc runs for db1 completed" dba < dbcc_db1.out
exit(0)
```

DUMP DATA FROM SYSTEM TABLES (DUMP_SYSTABLES)

This script is executed as a `cron` job to dump various server system tables to a disk file. This script should be executed daily. This will record the configuration of the server each day. Note that since System 11 SQL Server can have multiple configuration files, these should be dumped as well. These configuration files are UNIX-level files and should be captured by your UNIX-level backups. The file system dump to tape that should be done each day on the server machine will capture this file each day. This gives you a daily record of the configuration of the server. This script should be run on each of the server machines in your database system that supports a SQL Server. It is crucial that you dump this information to disk regularly. When (not if) you have a crisis you will need this information to recover and once the crisis has arrived, you generally won't have any way to retrieve the information.

```
0 20 * * * /dba/<servername>/scripts/dump_systables `cat
/usr/dba/<servername>`
```

This entry in the `crontab` would execute the `dump_systables` script on the hour (0 minutes after the hour) at 8PM each day. Each time the script is executed, it would dump the selected system tables to the specified disk file. The disk file is overwritten each time the script is executed.

To execute the `dump_systables` script manually,

```
dump_systables <servername> <sa_password>
```

which will dump the system tables specified in the script to the file specified in the script.

```
#!/bin/csh -f
if ($#argv < 2) then
        echo ${0}: invalid format, $#argv parameters given, 2
required.
        echo ${0}: required format: ${0} '<svrname> <password> .'
        exit (1)
endif
umask 006                                  # make our files -rw-rw—
setenv SYBASE /home/sybase
setenv BIN   ${SYBASE}/bin
set SERVER=$1
shift
set PASSWORD=$1
shift

# set the directory where the output of the script will be placed

set dir=/dba/${SERVER}/diagnostics
cd $dir

# execute isql as server user 'sa', send output to the file
# specified
# use the master database to select all data from the system tables
# shown
# then execute the stored procedure sp_configure to document the
# server
# configuration
# next use the database sybsystemprocs
# execute the stored procedures p_mirror and p_devspace to record
# the status
# of all server device mirrors and the server device space
# respectively
```

```
# finally select all the data in the syslogins system table — this
# allows you to
# record all the users of the server — very important when
# rebuilding a server

${BIN}/isql -Usa -S${SERVER} > ${dir}/${SERVER}_dump_systables.out
  << finish_sql
$PASSWORD
use master
go
select * from sysusages
go
select * from sysdevices
go
select * from sysdatabases
go
select * from sysservers
go
select * from sysremotelogins
go
exec sp_configure
go
exec sp_helpdevice
go
exec sp_helpdb
go
select * from syslogins
go
use sybsystemprocs
go
exec p_mirror
go
exec p_devspace
go
exec p_servermap
go
exit
finish_sql

# append the date to the output file

date > ${dir}/${SERVER}_dump_systables.out
chmod 600 ${SERVER}_dump_systables.out
exit
```

STORED PROCEDURE TO DUMP DATABASE CREATION SCRIPT (P_DBCREATE)

This script will create the stored procedure **p_dbcreate** which will dump the commands needed to re-create a database on the server. This stored procedure is called by the dump_db_create script described above. The stored procedure should be created in the server database *sybsystemprocs*.

The commands that are generated use the **for load** option of the **create database** command. This is much faster than the **create database** command alone because the server assumes (in fact, requires) that you immediately load the database from a database dump after you create the database with the **for load** option. Using the **for load** option prevents the server from initializing all the data pages as it would with the normal **create database** command. This can save you a great deal of time for large databases.

This script also outputs the Transact-SQL commands necessary to update the system table *sysusages* in the *master* database to set up all the segments on the proper devices once each database has been (re)created. For a full discussion of *sysusages* and what it does see Chapter 12. You can achieve the same affects by using only the **create database** portion of the **p_dbcreate** output and then manually adding, dropping, and extending segments as necessary to make sysusages for the new database match the segmentation of *sysusages* on the source server.

This script should be loaded into *sybsystemprocs*. If you want to be able to execute this stored procedure from any database, you need to name it **sp_dbcreate**. If you want server users other than sa (or users that have been granted **sa_role** in System 10) to be able to execute the stored procedure you need to execute the following server command

grant execute on p_dbcreate to public

The script can be executed manually as follows;

isql -Usa -S<servername> -P<sa_password>

use sybsystemprocs

go

p_dbcreate <database_name>

go

628

```
use sybsystemprocs
go
create proc p_dbcreate @dbname varchar(40) as
```

```
# start by selecting or outputting the text of the create database
# command
# next, select all the rows from sysusages for the database and
# convert the
# number of logical pages in each row of sysusages to Mb — one page is
# 2 Kb for SunOS servers and 1024 squared is 1 Mb
# the way we get the name of the server device for each row in
# sysusages is
# by noting that each server device has a low and high virtual page
# number
# and each row in sysusages has a virtual page number indicating the
# starting
# virtual page number of the fragment of disk space described by the
# row
```

```
select 'create database ' + @dbname + ' on'
select
name + '=' + convert(char(4),(size*2048)/(1024*1024)) +
',' from master..sysusages u, master..sysdevices d
where u.vstart >= d.low
and u.vstart <= d.high
and d.cntrltype=0
and u.dbid=(select dbid from master..sysdatabases where
name=@dbname)
order by u.lstart
select 'for load'
```

```
# here we generate the commands necessary to update the system table
# sysusages to reflect the segments assigned to each server device
# in the original database. We do this by generating commands that
# will
# update the segmap value of the rows in sysusages on the target
# server
# to have the same values as the original server. We again use the
# virtual
# page start, low and high values to determine which rows in
# sysusages
# should get which segmap value.
```

```
select 'update sysusages set segmap=' +
convert(char(4),u.segmap) + ' where
dbid=(select dbid from master..sysdatabases where name="'
```

```
+ @dbname +
'") and lstart >= ' + convert(char(9),lstart) +
'and lstart < ' +
convert(char(9),lstart+size) from
master..sysusages u, master..sysdevices d
where u.vstart >= d.low
and u.vstart <= d.high
and d.cntrltype=0


# throughout this script we must only affect changes to those rows
# of
# sysusages that belong to the database in question — here we limit
# the
# rows of sysusages that will be affected to those that have the
# dbid of the
# database we are (re)creating — we select dbid = (select dbid ...
# name = database
# in question) because the dbid may not be the same on the target
# server as on
# the primary even though the databases will have the same name

and u.dbid=(select dbid from master..sysdatabases where name=@dbname)
go
```

STORED PROCEDURE TO CHECK MIRRORS (P_MIRROR)

This script will create the stored procedure **p_mirror** that is used to check the *status* of the mirror for all server devices. This stored procedure simply lists all of the server devices currently set up and the mirror for each server device, if any, along with the *status* of each server device. You should examine this output to see that all the server devices that should be mirrored are indeed mirrored. The *status* column is also important. Once you have all your server devices and mirrors set up, the *status* for all server devices with mirrors should be the same and all server device without mirrors should have the same *status* as well. Scanning the *status* column will show you any devices that have changed status. Note that a server device that has a mirror may have failed to the mirror and while the server device and the mirror will show up in the **p_mirror** output as if everything were normal, it is the *status* output that will tell you that the server device has failed over to the mirror device. This stored procedure is called as part of the dump_systables script.

This script should be loaded into *sybsystemprocs*. If you want to be able to execute this stored procedure from any database, you need to name it **sp_mirror**. If you want server users other than sa to be able to execute the stored procedure you need to execute the following server command

grant execute on p_mirror to public

This stored procedure can be run manually also, as follows;

isql -Usa -S<servername> -P<sa_password>

use sybsystemprocs

go

p_mirror

go

The sql to create the stored procedure **p_mirror** is shown below. Note that the stored procedure simply selects each server *device name, phyname, mirrorname,* and *status* from the system table *sysdevices* in the *master* database. This information is selected for devices only where *cntrlytpe = 0* because we only want to look for mirrors of SQL Server devices, not dump devices.

```
use sybsystemprocs
go
create procedure p_mirror as
select getdate()
select @@servername
select db_name()
select "logical"=substring(name,1,10), "physical"=substring
  (phyname,1,20), "mirror"=substring(mirrorname,1,20), status from
  master..sysdevices where cntrltype=0
go
```

STORED PROCEDURE TO OUTPUT DEVICE SPACE (P_DEVSPACE)

This script creates the stored procedure **p_devspace** which outputs the total, used and free space for all server devices. This stored procedure is called from the script dump_systables. This output is useful when you are adding database space or checking how much free space you have on the server.

This script should be loaded into *sybsystemprocs*. If you want to be able to execute this stored procedure from any database you need to name it **sp_devspace**. If you want server users other than sa to be able to execute the stored procedure, you need to execute the following server command

grant execute on p_devspace to public

You can execute the stored procedure manually

isql -Usa -S<servername> -P<sa_password>

use sybsystemprocs

go

p_devspace

go

```
use sybsystemprocs
go
create procedure p_devspace as
select device_name = sysdev.name,
total_Mb = (sysdev.high - sysdev.low + 1) / 512,
used_Mb = sum(sysuse.size)/512,
free_Mb =
(sysdev.high - sysdev.low + 1)/512 -
sum(sysuse.size)/512
into #space_on_devices
from sysdevices sysdev,
sysusages sysuse
where
sysdev.cntrltype = 0
and
sysuse.vstart
between
```

632

```
sysdev.low
and
sysdev.high
group by
sysdev.name
/* now for any devices that have been
initialized but not yet in use by any
databases... */
insert #space_on_devices
select sysdev.name,
total_Mb = (sysdev.high - sysdev.low + 1) / 512,
used_Mb = 0,
free_Mb = (sysdev.high - sysdev.low + 1) / 512
from sysdevices sysdev, sysusages sysuse
where
sysdev.cntrltype = 0
and not exists
(select * from sysusages sysuse2
where sysuse2.vstart between sysdev.low and sysdev.high)
/* now output the total results */
select distinct * from #space_on_devices
order by device_name
compute sum(total_Mb),
sum(used_Mb), sum(free_Mb)
return
go
```

STORED PROCEDURE TO OUTPUT ALL SEGMENTS ON DEVICES (P_SERVERMAP)

This script will create the stored procedure **p_servermap** which will output the various database segments that are on all of the server devices. This stored procedure is called by the script dump_systables. This output will list all the server devices that have database segments on them. The output also shows the size of each database segment and the total space each device that is taken by database segments. This output and the output of **p_mirror** and **p_devspace** would allow you to generate the entire server map. The output of **p_servermap** shows you each server device, the database segments on each device, the segment number of each segment, and the size of the segment. Note that the segment number is unique within each database. This means that you would need to execute the following server commands to see what the segment names are for each segment number in each database. Note that this script outputs only information for those server devices that have database segments—server devices that have been created but not yet assigned to any database will not appear. You need to use the output of **p_devspace** to determine the complete set of all server devices.

```
isql -Usa -S<servername> -P<sa_password>

use <dbname>

go

select * from syssegments

go
```

This script should be loaded into *sybsystemprocs*. If you want to be able to execute this stored procedure from any database, you need to name it **sp_servermap**. If you want server users other than sa to be able to execute the stored procedure, you need to execute the following server command:

```
grant execute on p_servermap to public
```

This script can be executed manually:

```
isql -Usa -S<servername> -P<sa_password>

use sybsystemprocs

go

p_servermap

go
```

```
use sybsystemprocs
go

# we first select the devices and for each device the relevant
# entries from sysusages
# we select this data into temporary table #smap
```

```
create procedure p_servermap as
select device_name =substring( sysdev.name,1,11),
database_name=substring(sysdb.name,1,20),
seg#=substring(convert(char(4),sysuse.segmap),1,4),
size_Mb = substring(convert(char(7),sysuse.size/512),1,7)
  into #smap
from sysdevices sysdev,
sysdatabases sysdb,
sysusages sysuse
where
sysdev.cntrltype = 0
and
sysuse.vstart
between
sysdev.low
and
sysdev.high
and
sysuse.dbid = sysdb.dbid
```

```
# next we select from #smap to #smap2 summing up all the entries for
# each database, segment and segment number on each device. This
# means
# that multiple entries in sysusages for one segment of one database
# will be
# summed into one entry for the segment
```

```
select device_name,database_name,
seg#,space_per_seg=sum(convert(int,size_Mb))
into #smap2
from #smap
group by device_name,database_name,seg#
```

```
# we output the meaning of the segmap numbers. The segmap numbers 1
# through 7
# are the same for all databases. For segmap values greater than 7
# you need to look
# at the data in syssegments for each database to see the segment
# name for each
# user defined segment. Note that for System10 the auditing database
# (sybsecurity)
# has a segment called auditsegment and the segmap value is 8 —
# since this segment is
# on the same server device as the system, default and logsegment the segmap
# value
# will be 15.
```

```
set nocount on
select "segmap values 1 through 7
seg# and segment name
 1 — system
 2 — default
 3 — default/system
 4 — log only
 5 — log/system
 6 — log/default
 7 — log/system/default
 8 — user defined
15 — audit/log/sys/def
16 — user defined"
set nocount off

# select the final output from #smap2 and this time compute the
# total space used by all database segments on each server device

select device_name,database_name,
seg#,space_per_seg
from #smap2
order by device_name,database_name,seg#
compute sum(space_per_seg)
by device_name
return
go
```

DUMP DATABASES (DUMPDB)

This script uses the features of the Backup Server to dump databases to tape and to disk. The reason for this is the same reason you will probably need to dump databases to both tape and disk. You want to dump all your databases to disk, but you don't have sufficient disk space because you (more likely your predecessor(s)) didn't bother with capacity planning. So, for the databases that are small enough, you dump to disk and for the large databases you still have to dump to tape. For this script we assume that database *db1* is so large it requires its own tape, then database *db2* is still too large to dump to disk and it dumped to a second tape along with the master database. The remaining databases are dumped to disk files. Note also that anytime you are dumping databases to disk files, you must ensure that a file system dump is made immediately following the completion of the database dumps to disk to ensure that the disk dumps are captured to tape.

You should also note the database dump of the master database is followed by the truncation of the *master* transaction log. The *master* database does not allow the transaction log to be on a separate server device which means you can't dump the transaction log separately from the *master* database. Dumping the transaction log is the normal way to truncate or remove the inactive portion of the transaction log. Since you can't dump the transaction log for the *master* database, the log will continue to grow until it eventually fills up and stops the server. The only way to truncate the transaction log of the *master* database is to execute the **dump transaction** with the **truncate_only** command as shown in the script. Note that this command needs to be executed after the **dump database** *master* command (see Chapter 7 for more details). You need to make sure you are truncating the *master* database transaction log periodically. You don't have to do it as part of the dump database script, but you must make sure it happens on a regular basis.

As with the dumpdb_492 script, this script is designed to be run by the tape operator and therefore is not normally executed as a cron job. The script assumes the tape operator is available to load the two tapes needed for the large database dumps. For this reason the script prompts for the server login and password of the user who is executing the script. Note that this means any user who needs to execute this script must have permission to dump the databases. This requires that all such users be granted **oper_role**.

To execute the script manually:

dumpdb <username> <password>

```
#!/bin/csh -f
umask 006
setenv SERVER PDSOPS21
setenv SYBASE /home/sybase

# here we setup a tape device number — this makes it easier to
# change the
# tape device number as you move this script to other server
# machines
# you only need to change the tape device number here
```

```
setenv TAPEDEVNO  8
setenv REWINDINGTAPE    /dev/rst${DEVNO}
setenv NONREWINDINGTAPE   /dev/nrst${DEVNO}
echo -n Enter Your Server Username:
set username = $<
stty -echo
echo -n Enter Your Server Password:
set password = $<
stty echo
clear
echo dumpdb:${SERVER}: beginning dump of ${SERVER} system 10 server
set dir=/diskdump
set outfile=${dir}/${srvname}_dumpdb.out

# the C shell command tee copies standard input to standard output
# and copies the input
# to a file specified. This means all the commands in the script are
# echoed to the user's
# screen and to the output file specified

setenv COPYINPUT '/bin/tee -a '${outfile}
mt -f ${NONREWINDINGTAPE} rewind

# set the first database to dump to the first tape — this is the
# only dump going to the first tape
# because the database dump will almost fill the tape

set dbname=db1
echo "dumpdb:${SERVER}: [${dbname}] started at `date`." > ${outfile}

# dump database db1 to the first tape
# note the System 10 dump database command requires the new options
# capacity=5000000 which tells the Backup Server that the tape drive
# has a capacity of 5 Gb
# with init which tells the Backup Server to initialize or overwrite
# this tape — this is only
# specified for the first dump to a given tape

$SYBASE/bin/isql -U${username} -S${SERVER} -e <<finish_sql_tape1 |
$COPYINPUT
${password}
dump database ${dbname} to '${NONREWINDINGTAPE}'
capacity=5000000
with init
go
exit
```

```
finish_sql_tape1

# if the database dump of the first database fails do not go on to
# the
# second tape — exit with status=1 (error condition)

if ($status) then
        echo "dumpdb:${SERVER}: database dump of ${dbname} has
     FAILED at `date`." | $COPYINPUT
        cat   ${dbname}_dbdump.out | $COPYINPUT
        exit(1)
else
        echo "dumpdb:${SERVER}: dump of ${dbname} completed at
     `date`." | $COPYINPUT
endif

# rewind and unload the first tape

mt -f ${NONREWINDINGTAPE} off

# request load of second tape before continuing

echo -n "Load 2nd PDSOPS21 server tape.  Press return when ready to
  continue. "
set waiting = $<
echo -n "Are you sure the 2nd tape is loaded<  Press return if ready
  to continue. "
set waiting = $<
mt -f ${NONREWINDINGTAPE} rewind                       # rewind tape

# set the second database and the master database to dump to the
# second tape
# note that after db2 is dumped to tape you don't use the with init
# option when
# dumping the master database

set dbname=db2
set dbname2=master
echo "dumpdb:${SERVER}: [${dbname}] started   at `date`." |
  $COPYINPUT
$SYBASE/bin/isql -U${username} -S${SERVER} -e <<finish_sql_tape2 |
  $COPYINPUT
${password}
dump database ${dbname} to '${NONREWINDINGTAPE}'
capacity=5000000
with init
```

```
go
dump database ${dbname2} to '${NONREWINDINGTAPE}'
capacity=5000000
go
dump tran master with truncate_only
go
exit
finish_sql_tape2
if ($status) then
        echo "dumpdb:${SERVER}: database dump of $dbname has FAILED
    at `date`." | $COPYINPUT
        cat  ${dbname}_dbdump.out | $COPYINPUT
else
        echo "dumpdb:${SERVER}: dump of $dbname completed at
    `date`." | $COPYINPUT
endif


# rewind and unload the second tape

mt -f ${NONREWINDINGTAPE} off                          # rewind tape

# setup the remaining databases to dump to individual disk files
# note that for a database dump to a disk file you simply specify
# the disk filename —
# you don't have to worry about server dump devices unless you
# prefer to

foreach dbname (db3 db4 db5 db6 db7)
echo "dumpdb:${srvname}: [${dbname}] started   at `date`." | $TEE
$SYBASE/bin/isql -U${username} -S${SERVER} -e <<finish_sql_diskdumpdb
  | $COPYINPUT
${password}
dump database ${dbname} to ''/diskdump/${dbname}_databasedump.out"
go
exit
finish_sql_diskdumpdb
if ($status) then
        echo "dumpdb:${SERVER}: database dump of $dbname has FAILED
    at `date`." | $COPYINPUT
        cat  ${dbname}_dbdump.out | $COPYINPUT
else
        echo "dumpdb:${SERVER}: dump of $dbname completed at
    `date`." | $COPYINPUT
endif

# here is the end of the loop for the databases dumped to disk
```

```
end

echo "dumpdb:${SERVER}: exiting at `date`." | $COPYINPUT

# mail the output file from the dump to dba

mail -s "dumpdb:${srvname}: output" dba < $outfile
clear
exit
```

LOAD DATABASES (LOADDB)

There is no script needed to load databases from a dump tape as there is for SQL Server 4.9.2. SQL Server 4.9.2 didn't think there could be more than one dump per tape so it just loaded what ever file was on the tape at the time the load database command was executed. Backup Server allows for multiple database dumps on a single tape and therefore the server demands to know what the file name is before it will load a dump. If you have only one dump file on a tape you don't have to specify the file name of the file; just load the database or transaction log dump. Also, Backup Server doesn't require that you use a server dump device to dump or load. You can use the physical device name or the actual filename for a database dump or load to or from a disk file. To load from a dump tape, execute

load database db1 with listonly

which will give you a listing of all the dumps on the tape and the file name for each dump. Note that unless you specify a file name when you create the dump the server will generate the file name itself. The file names the server creates are not good. They involve the day of the year and the number of seconds since midnight. You will end up simply listing out the filenames as described above. You can't figure out what the file name should be. You can look at the output of whatever process you used to create the dump and the file name will be there.

If you wanted to automate this process you must change the script dumpdb to use specific file names, that is, the **file='filename'** option for the **dump database** command. Then for the load script you could have a switch statement and depending on the database to load, specify the file name used for that database dump. This would require that you set up the file names and not change them unless you change both the dump and load scripts.

CREATE STORED PROCEDURE TO MONITOR DATABASE LOAD (P_DBLOAD)

This script will create the stored procedure p_dbload, which will tell you how many megabytes have been loaded for any load database command running on the server when the stored procedure is executed. This simple procedure is very useful. You can provide this to your users and they can monitor the load themselves. For database loads that take any significant amount of time, your users will appreciate being able to see how far along the load is. This script should be loaded into *sybsystemprocs*. If you want to be able to execute this stored procedure from any database, you need to name it **sp_dbload**. If you want server users other than sa to be able to execute the stored procedure you need to execute the following server command:

grant execute on p_dbload to public

This stored procedure can be run manually also, as follows;

isql -Usa -S<servername> -P<sa_password>

use sybsystemprocs

go

p_dbload

go

The sql to create the stored procedure **p_dbload** is shown below.

```
Use sybsystemprocs
go
create procedure p_dbload as

# we simply look at the sysprocesses system table and select any
```

```
# processes that are executing load database
# then we use the physical_io field to compute the number of Mb that
# have been loaded

select spid,cmd,(convert(int,physical_io))*2048/(1024*1024) "Mb
loaded" from master..sysprocesses where cmd="LOAD DATABASE"
go
```

Sample output from use of this stored procedure is shown below, show-ing the progress of the database load over time.

```
trainwreck% isql -Usa -SPSYCHO_DB
Password:
1> p_dbload
2> go
 spid           cmd           Mb loaded            Time
   1       LOAD DATABASE          60      Apr 01 1996 11:59AM

(1 row affected, return status = 0)
1> p_dbload
2> go
 spid           cmd           Mb loaded            Time
   1       LOAD DATABASE          62      Apr 01 1996 12:00PM

(1 row affected, return status = 0)
1> p_dbload
2> go
 spid           cmd           Mb loaded            Time
   1       LOAD DATABASE         103      Apr 01 1996 12:04PM

(1 row affected, return status = 0)
```

SQL SERVER STARTUP SCRIPT

This is an example of a script that you would use to restart a 11.0.1 SQL Server manually.

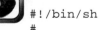

```
#!/bin/sh
 #
# SQL Server Information:
#  name:                     PSYCHO11
#  master device:            /dev/rdsk/c0t2d0s7
```

```
#   master device size:       10752
#   errorlog:                 /home/sybase/11.0.1/install/errorlog
#   interfaces:               /home/sybase/11.0.1
#
/home/sybase/11.0.1/bin/dataserver -d/dev/rdsk/c0t2d0s7 -sPSYCHO11 \
-e/home/sybase/11.0.1/install/errorlog_PSYCHO11 -i/home/sybase/11.0.1
```

This is an example of a script that you would use to manually restart a 11.0.1 Backup Server.

```
#!/bin/sh
#
# Backup Server Information:
#   name:                     PSYCHO11_BCK
#   errorlog:                 /home/sybase/11.0.1/install/backup.log
#   interfaces:               /home/sybase/11.0.1/interfaces
#   location of multibuf:     /home/sybase/11.0.1/bin/sybmultbuf
#   language:                 us_english
#   character set:            iso_1
#   tape configuration file:  /home/sybase/11.0.1/backup_tape.cfg
#
#
/home/sybase/11.0.1/bin/backupserver -SPSYCHO11_BCK \
-e/home/sybase/11.0.1/install/backup.log -I/home/sybase/11.0.1
  /interfaces \
-M/home/sybase/11.0.1/bin/sybmultbuf -Lus_english -Jiso_1 \
-c/home/sybase/11.0.1/backup_tape.cfg
```

SYSTEM 11 DUMP DATABASE (DUMP_LISTOF_DBS)

This script dumps one or more databases to disk files. Note that this script creates a stored procedure that actually does the database dump. This is done to trap any errors that may occur during the database dump. If we didn't create a stored procedure, then the script would know only the error status of the isql command. If isql succeeded, but the database dump had a problem, the script would not be aware of that. The script depends on knowing the error status of the dump database command to send additional e-mail notifying you of the dump failure.

Each database dump is sent to a separate disk file. The file name of each database dump contains the date and time of the dump as well as the database name. Note that this script sends the database dump directly to a disk file. This requires the use of Sybase Backup Server which is part of SQL Server Systems 10 and 11. If you want to use this script with a 4.9.2 SQL Server, you would have to add commands to the stored procedure that is created by this script to create a dump device before the database dump and drop the dump device after the dump is complete.

```
#!/bin/sh
#
# Bourne shell script to dump a list of databases to disk
# 8/30/96 Brian Hitchcock
#
if [ $# -lt 2 ]
then
echo $0: invalid format: $# argv parameters provided, at least 2
required
echo $0: required format: $0 '<SERVER> <database(s)...>'
exit 1
fi
#
# setup parameters
#
# ***** you must edit the path for SYBASE and PWD environment
# variables
SYBASE=/export/home/sybase
SERVER=$1
PWD=`cat /export/home/sybase/.kparm`
# ***** you must edit the path for the dumpdir directory
dumpdir=/export/home/dbdump
outfile=${dumpdir}/${SERVER}_dumpdb.out
outfile2=${dumpdir}/${SERVER}_dumpdb.out2
shift
dbs_to_dump="$*"
#
# begin dumping
#
echo "database dump:${SERVER}: started at `date`." > $outfile
echo "database dump:${SERVER}: started at `date`." > $outfile2
echo " " > $outfile
echo " " > $outfile2
#
# begin loop for each database to dump
#
```

```
for dbname in $dbs_to_dump
do
dmptime=`date +%m%d%y_%H%M%S`
dumpfile=${SERVER}_${dbname}_${dmptime}.dmp
proc_name=dump_temp_sproc_${dmptime}
# ***** you must edit the path for isql and for the interfaces file
# the following sql script will create a temporary stored procedure
# that will actually perform the dump. By doing this we can trap
# any errors that occur during the execution of the sql.
# ***** for SQL Server 4.9.2 you must edit in the name of a
# ***** valid server dump device in place of ${dumpdir}/${dumpfile}
#
# isql to the SQL Server
#
$SYBASE/bin/isql -Usa -S${SERVER} -P${PWD} -I$SYBASE/interfaces -e >
${outfile} << finish_sql
create procedure $proc_name as
        declare @status int

        dump database $dbname to `${dumpdir}/${dumpfile}'
go
declare @return_status int
execute @return_status=$proc_name
drop procedure $proc_name
if @return_status = 0
begin
print "**************************************************"
print "Stored Procedure Execution Complete — no errors"
end
else
begin
print "!!!!!!!!!!!!!!!!!!!!!!!!!!!!"
print "FAILURE of Stored Procedure"
end
go
exit
finish_sql
#
# save return status of the isql command
# isql failures indicate problems with password, interfaces file
# or server down
#
isql_status=$<
#
# save return status of sql script that creates and
# executes stored procedure
```

```
#
sproc_status=`tail -1 ${outfile}`
#
# if isql failed
#
if [ $isql_status -ne 0 ]
then
echo " " > $outfile
echo database dump:${SERVER}: isql for dump of $dbname failed at
  `date`. > $outfile
echo " " > $outfile
echo " " > $outfile2
echo database dump:${SERVER}: database dump of $dbname failed at
  `date`. > $outfile2
echo " " > $outfile2
# ***** you must edit the recipient of the email
/usr/ucb/mail -s "${SERVER}: database dump of $dbname failed"
  psychoDBA@dbahost < $outfile
#
# if isql did not fail, test the return status from the stored
# procedure
#
else
#
# if stored procedure completed successfully
#
if [ "$sproc_status" = "Stored Procedure Execution Complete — no
  errors" ]
then
echo " " > $outfile
echo database dump:${SERVER}: completed database dump of $dbname at
  `date` > $outfile
echo " " > $outfile2
echo database dump:${SERVER}: completed database dump of $dbname at
  `date` > $outfile2
fi
#
# if stored procedure failed
#
if [ "$sproc_status" = "FAILURE of Stored Procedure" ]
then
echo " " > $outfile
echo database dump:${SERVER}: sproc for database dump $dbname failed
  at `date` > $outfile
/usr/ucb/mail -s "${SERVER}: database dump of $dbname failed"
psychoDBA@dbahost < $outfile
```

```
echo " " > $outfile2
echo database dump:${SERVER}: sproc for database dump $dbname failed
  at `date` > $outfile2
fi
fi
#
# end of loop for each database to dump
#
done
#
# append full output file to summary output file
# email output
#
echo " " > $outfile
echo "database dump:${SERVER}: exiting at `date`." > $outfile
echo " " > $outfile
echo " " > $outfile2
echo " " > $outfile2
echo "database dump:${SERVER}: exiting at `date`." > $outfile2
echo " " > $outfile2
echo " " > $outfile2
echo "*******************************************************" >
  $outfile2
cat $outfile > $outfile2
# ***** you must edit the recipient of the email
/usr/ucb/mail -s "${SERVER}: database dump cronjob complete"
  psychoDBA@dbahost < $outfile2
  exit
```

DUMP TRANSACTION LOG
(LOGDUMP_LISTOF_DBS)

This script dumps the transaction log of one of more databases. Each transaction log dump is sent to a separate disk file whose name contains the date and time of the dump and the database name. Recall that in order to dump a transaction log, the log must be on a separate server device.

Note that this script sends the transaction log dump directly to a disk file. This requires the use of Sybase Backup Server which is part of SQL Server Systems 10 and 11. If you want to use this script with a 4.9.2 SQL Server, you would have to add commands to the stored procedure that is

created by this script to create a dump device before the transaction log
dump and drop the dump device after the dump is complete.

```
#!/bin/sh
#
# Bourne shell script to dump the transaction log of each of a
# list of databases to disk
# 9/6/96 Brian Hitchcock
#
if [ $# -lt 2 ]
then
echo $0: invalid format: $# argv parameters provided, at least 2
  required
echo $0: required format: $0 '<SERVER> <database(s)...>'
exit 1
fi
#
# setup parameters
#
# ***** you must edit the path for SYBASE and PWD environment
  variables
SYBASE=/export/home/sybase
SERVER=$1
PWD=`cat /export/home/sybase/.kparm`
# ***** you must edit the path for the dumpdir directory
dumpdir=/export/home/dbdump
outfile=${dumpdir}/${SERVER}_dumplog.out
outfile2=${dumpdir}/${SERVER}_dumplog.out2
shift
dbs_to_logdump="$*"
#
# begin dumping
#
echo "transaction log dump:${SERVER}: started at `date`." > $outfile
echo "transaction log dump:${SERVER}: started at `date`." >
  $outfile2
echo " " > $outfile
echo " " > $outfile2
#
# begin loop for each database transaction log to dump
#
for dbname in $dbs_to_logdump
do
dmptime=`date +%m%d%y_%H%M%S`
dumpfile=${SERVER}_${dbname}_${dmptime}_log.dmp
```

```
proc_name=dlog_temp_sproc_${dmptime}
# ***** you must edit the path for isql and for the interfaces file
# the following sql script will create a temporary stored procedure
# that will actually perform the dump. By doing this we can trap
# any errors that occur during the execution of the sql.
# ***** for SQL Server 4.9.2 you must edit in the name of a
# ***** valid server dump device in place of ${dumpdir}/${dumpfile}
#
# isql to the SQL Server
#
$SYBASE/bin/isql -Usa -S${SERVER} -P${PWD} -I$SYBASE/interfaces -e >
  ${outfile} << finish_sql
create procedure $proc_name as
        declare @status int

        dump tran $dbname to '${dumpdir}/${dumpfile}'
go
declare @return_status int
execute @return_status=$proc_name
drop procedure $proc_name
if @return_status = 0
begin
print "**************************************************"
print "Stored Procedure Execution Complete — no errors"
end
else
begin
print "!!!!!!!!!!!!!!!!!!!!!!!!!!!!"
print "FAILURE of Stored Procedure"
end
go
exit
finish_sql
#
# save return status of the isql command
# isql failures indicate problems with password, interfaces file
# or server down
#
isql_status=$<
#
# save return status of sql script that creates and
# executes stored procedure
#
sproc_status=`tail -1 ${outfile}`
#
```

```
# if isql failed
#
if [ $isql_status -ne 0 ]
then
echo " " > $outfile
echo database logdump:${SERVER}: isql for logdump of $dbname failed
  at `date`. > $outfile
echo " " > $outfile
echo " " > $outfile2
echo database logdump:${SERVER}: database logdump of $dbname failed
  at `date`. > $outfile2
echo " " > $outfile2
# ***** you must edit the recipient of the email
  /usr/ucb/mail -s "${SERVER}: database logdump of $dbname failed"
  psychoDBA@dbahost < $outfile
#
# if isql did not fail, test the return status from the stored
# procedure
#
else
#
# if stored procedure completed successfully
#
if [ "$sproc_status" = "Stored Procedure Execution Complete — no
  errors" ]
then
echo " " > $outfile
echo database logdump:${SERVER}: completed database logdump of
  $dbname at `date` > $outfile
echo " " > $outfile2
  echo database logdump:${SERVER}: completed database logdump of
$dbname at `date` > $outfile2
fi
#
# if stored procedure failed
#
if [ "$sproc_status" = "FAILURE of Stored Procedure" ]
then
echo " " > $outfile
echo database logdump:${SERVER}: sproc for database logdump $dbname
  failed at `date` > $outfile
# ***** you must edit the recipient of the email
  /usr/ucb/mail -s "${SERVER}: database logdump of $dbname failed"
  psychoDBA@dbahost < $outfile
echo " " > $outfile2
```

```
echo database logdump:${SERVER}: sproc for database logdump $dbname
  failed at `date` > $outfile2
fi
fi
#
# end of loop for each database transaction log to dump
#
done
#
# append full output file to summary output file
# email output
#
echo " " > $outfile
echo "database logdump:${SERVER}: exiting at `date`." > $outfile
echo " " > $outfile
echo " " > $outfile2
echo " " > $outfile2
echo "database logdump:${SERVER}: exiting at `date`." > $outfile2
echo " " > $outfile2
echo " " > $outfile2
echo "******************************************************" > $out-
file2
cat $outfile > $outfile2
# ***** you must edit the recipient of the email
/usr/ucb/mail -s "${SERVER}: database logdump cronjob complete"
  psychoDBA@dbahost < $outfile2
exit
```

TRUNCATE TRANSACTION LOG
(TRUNCLOG_LISTOF_DBS)

This script will truncate the transaction log of one or more databases. Recall that for any database that does not have the log on a separate server device, you must truncate the transaction log or it will fill up. Even for databases where there is little activity, if the log is not truncated (if the log is on a separate server device, dumping the transaction log will truncate it), it will gradually fill up. While you can use the database option that truncates the log on each checkpoint, if this is ever turned off, the log can start filling. You should make sure that every database in the server is being handled by either the logdump or trunclog script, with the exception of *tempdb*. For *tempdb,* the database option truncate log on checkpoint is always enabled.

```sh
!/bin/sh
#
# Bourne shell script to truncate the transaction log of each of a
# list of databases
# 9/6/96 Brian Hitchcock
#
if [ $# -lt 2 ]
then
echo $0: invalid format: $# argv parameters provided, at least 2
  required
echo $0: required format: $0 '<SERVER> <database(s)...>'
exit 1
fi
#
# setup parameters
#
# ***** you must edit the path for SYBASE and PWD environment
  variables
SYBASE=/export/home/sybase
SERVER=$1
PWD=`cat /export/home/sybase/.kparm`
# ***** you must edit the path for the dumpdir directory
dumpdir=/export/home/dbdump
outfile=${dumpdir}/${SERVER}_trunclog.out
outfile2=${dumpdir}/${SERVER}_trunclog.out2
shift
dbs_to_trunclog="$*"
#
# begin dumping
#
echo "transaction log truncate:${SERVER}: started at `date`." >
  $outfile
echo "transaction log truncate:${SERVER}: started at `date`." >
  $outfile2
echo " " > $outfile
echo " " > $outfile2
#
# begin loop for each database transaction log to truncate
#
for dbname in $dbs_to_trunclog
do
dmptime=`date +%m%d%y_%H%M%S`
```

653

```
dumpfile=${SERVER}_${dbname}_${dmptime}_log.dmp
proc_name=tlog_temp_sproc_${dmptime}
# ***** you must edit the path for isql and for the interfaces file
# the following sql script will create a temporary stored procedure
# that will actually perform the dump. By doing this we can trap
# any errors that occur during the execution of the sql.
# since we are truncating the log, we don't need a dump device or
# a dump file
#
# isql to the SQL Server
#
$SYBASE/bin/isql -Usa -S${SERVER} -P${PWD} -I$SYBASE/interfaces -e >
  ${outfile} << finish_sql
create procedure $proc_name as
        declare @status int

        dump tran $dbname with truncate_only
go
declare @return_status int
execute @return_status=$proc_name
drop procedure $proc_name
if @return_status = 0
begin
print "************************************************"
print "Stored Procedure Execution Complete — no errors"
end
else
begin
print "!!!!!!!!!!!!!!!!!!!!!!!!!!!"
print "FAILURE of Stored Procedure"
end
go
exit
finish_sql
#
# save return status of the isql command
# isql failures indicate problems with password, interfaces file
# or server down
#
isql_status=$<
#
# save return status of sql script that creates and
# executes stored procedure
#
sproc_status=`tail -1 ${outfile}`
#
```

```
# if isql failed
#
if [ $isql_status -ne 0 ]
then
echo " " > $outfile
echo transaction log truncate:${SERVER}: isql for logtrunc of
$dbname failed at `date`. > $outfile
echo " " > $outfile
echo " " > $outfile2
echo transaction log truncate:${SERVER}: database logtrunc of
  $dbname failed at `date`. > $outfile2
echo " " > $outfile2
# ***** you must edit the recipient of the email
/usr/ucb/mail -s "${SERVER}: transaction log truncate of $dbname
  failed" psychoDBA@dbahost < $outfile
#
# if isql did not fail, test the return status from the stored
# procedure
#
else
#
# if stored procedure completed successfully
#
if [ "$sproc_status" = "Stored Procedure Execution Complete — no
  errors" ]
then
echo " " > $outfile
echo transaction log truncate:${SERVER}: completed database logtrun
  of $dbname at `date` > $outfile
echo " " > $outfile2
echo transaction log truncate:${SERVER}: completed database logtrunc
  of $dbname at `date` > $outfile2
fi
#
# if stored procedure failed
#
if [ "$sproc_status" = "FAILURE of Stored Procedure" ]
then
echo " " > $outfile
echo transaction log truncate:${SERVER}: sproc for database logtrunc
  $dbname failed at `date` > $outfile
# ***** you must edit the recipient of the email
/usr/ucb/mail -s "${SERVER}: transaction log truncate of $dbname
  failed" psychoDBA@dbahost < $outfile
echo " " > $outfile2
echo database dump:${SERVER}: sproc for database logtrunc $dbname
```

```
failed at `date` > $outfile2
fi
fi
#
# end of loop for each database transaction log to truncate
#
done
#
# append full output file to summary output file
# email output
#
echo " " > $outfile
echo "transaction log truncate:${SERVER}: exiting at `date`." >
  $outfile
echo " " > $outfile
echo " " > $outfile2
echo " " > $outfile2
echo "transaction log truncate:${SERVER}: exiting at `date`." >
  $outfile2
echo " " > $outfile2
echo " " > $outfile2
echo "******************************************************" > $out-
file2
cat $outfile > $outfile2
# ***** you must edit the recipient of the email
/usr/ucb/mail -s "${SERVER}: transaction log truncate cronjob
  complete" psychoDBA@dbahost < $outfile2
exit
```

REMOVE OLD FILES
(REMOVE_OLD_FILES)

 This script will remove files that are older than the specified number of days. This script is needed to remove old database and transaction log dumps. Otherwise, the file system can fill up which will prevent any more dumps from occurring. Note that you must ensure that the UNIX-level tape backups of your dump directory have occurred before you remove the dump files. For example, you should be making a UNIX-level tape backup of your server machine every night. Then, use this script to remover all dump files that are older than two days. This means each dump file should be on two dump tapes before they are removed.

```
#!/bin/sh
#
# Bourne shell script to remove old dump files
# that are older than X days
# 9/11/96 Brian Hitchcock
#
if [ $# -lt 2 ]
then
echo $0: invalid format: $# argv parameters provided, at least 2
  required
echo $0: required format: $0 '<"/path/filename pattern to remove">
  <days old>'
exit 1
fi
#
# setup parameters
#
remove_file=$1
days_old=$2
# ***** you must edit the dumpdir path
dumpdir=/export/home/dbdump
outfile=${dumpdir}/remove_files.out
outfile2=${dumpdir}/remove_files.out2
#
# begin
#
echo "remove old files ${remove_file}: started at `date`." >
  $outfile
echo "remove old files ${remove_file}: started at `date`." >
  $outfile2
echo " " > $outfile
echo " " > $outfile2
#
# begin by listing files that are going to be removed
#
find ${remove_file} -mtime +${days_old} -a -exec ls -l {} \; >
  $outfile
#
# compute number of files affected
#
num_files=`find ${remove_file} -mtime +${days_old} -exec ls -l {}
  \; | wc -l`
```

```
#
# actually remove the files
#
find ${remove_file} -mtime +${days_old} -a -exec rm -rf {} \;
#
# if the directory of the files to be removed does not exist
#
remove_dir=`dirname "${remove_file}"`
if [ ! -d "${remove_dir}" ]
then
echo " " > $outfile
echo remove old files ${remove_file}: find failed at `date`. >
  $outfile
echo "————————————————-> directory not found!" > $outfile
echo " " > $outfile
echo " " > $outfile2
echo remove old files ${remove_file}: find failed at `date`. >
  $outfile2
echo "————————————————-> directory not found!" > $outfile2
echo " " > $outfile2
# ***** you must edit the recipient of the email
/usr/ucb/mail -s "${SERVER} remove old files ${remove_file} failed"
  psychoDBA@dbahost < $outfile
#
# if directory does exist
#
else
#
# output number of files affected
#
echo " " > $outfile
echo remove old files ${remove_file}: number of files deleted =
  ${num_files} > $outfile
echo " " > $outfile2
echo remove old files ${remove_file}: number of files deleted =
  ${num_files} > $outfile2
fi
# append full output file to summary output file
# email output
#
echo " " > $outfile
echo "remove old files ${remove_file}: exiting at `date`." >
  $outfile
echo " " > $outfile
echo " " > $outfile2
echo " " > $outfile2
```

```
echo "remove old files ${remove_file}: exiting at `date`." >
  $outfile2
echo " " > $outfile2
echo " " > $outfile2
echo "*****************************************************" > $out-
file2
cat $outfile > $outfile2
# ***** you must edit the recipient of the email
/usr/ucb/mail -s "${SERVER} remove old files ${remove_file} cronjob
  complete" psychoDBA@dbahost < $outfile2
exit
```

UPDATE STATISTICS (UPDATE_LISTOF_DBS)

This script will execute update_statistics and sp_recompile for
every table in one or more databases. The output will show you the time
it takes to update each table.

```
#!/bin/sh
#
# Bourne shell script to execute update statistics and sp_recompile
# for all tables in
# each database in a list of databases
# 10/18/96 Brian Hitchcock
#
if [ $# -lt 2 ]
then
echo $0: invalid format: $# argv parameters provided, at least 2
  required
echo $0: required format: $0 '<SERVER> <database(s)...>'
exit 1
fi
#
# setup parameters
#
# ***** you must edit the path for SYBASE and PWD environment
  variables
SYBASE=/export/home/sybase
SERVER=$1
```

```
PWD=`cat /export/home/sybase/.kparm`
# ***** you must edit the path for the dumpdir directory
dumpdir=/export/home/dbdump
outfile=${dumpdir}/${SERVER}_updatestats.out
outfile2=${dumpdir}/${SERVER}_updatestats.out2
tempfile=${dumpdir}/${SERVER}_updatestats.temp1
shift
dbs_to_update="$*"
#
# begin updating
#
echo "update statistics:${SERVER}: started at `date`." > $outfile
echo "update statistics:${SERVER}: started at `date`." > $outfile2
echo " " > $outfile
echo " " > $outfile2
#
# begin loop for each database to update stats/sp_recompile
#
for dbname in $dbs_to_update
do
#
# setup loop for each table within the current database
# determine the tables in the database
#
$SYBASE/bin/isql -Usa -S${SERVER} -P${PWD} -I$SYBASE/interfaces -e >
  ${tempfile} << finish_sql1
use $dbname
go
select name from sysobjects where type="U" order by name
go
finish_sql1
#
# output list of tables for current database
#
echo " " > $outfile
echo "@@@@@@@@@@@@@@@@@@@@@@@@" > $outfile
echo "all tables in database $dbname...." > $outfile
echo "@@@@@@@@@@@@@@@@@@@@@@@@@" > $outfile
echo " " > $outfile
cat ${tempfile} > $outfile
echo " " > $outfile
#
# cut out the first 4 and last 2 lines of the listing of all the
# user tables in this database
# see the dump_db_create script discussion for details of the
# following part of the script
```

```
#
num_lines=`wc -l ${tempfile} | cut -c1-9`
last_line=`expr $num_lines - 4`
first_line=`expr $last_line - 2`
tables_list=`tail -$last_line ${tempfile} | head -$first_line`
rm -f ${tempfile}
#
# now we start updating statistics and executing sp_recompile for
# each user table
# in each database
#
echo "@@@@@@@@@@@@@@@@@@@@@@@@@@@@@@@@@@@@@@@@@@" > $outfile
echo "updating statistics for tables in database $dbname" > $outfile
echo "@@@@@@@@@@@@@@@@@@@@@@@@@@@@@@@@@@@@@@@@@@" > $outfile
echo " " > $outfile
#
# begin loop of update stats/sp_recompile for each table in current
# database
#
for table_name in $tables_list
do
$SYBASE/bin/isql -Usa -S${SERVER} -P${PWD} -I$SYBASE/interfaces -e >
  ${outfile} << finish_sql2
use $dbname
go
select getdate()
go
update statistics $table_name
go
sp_recompile $table_name
go
select getdate()
go
finish_sql2
#
# the first done is for the loop for each user table
# the second done is for the loop for each database in the server
#
done
#
# end of loop for each database to update
#
done
#
# append full output file to summary output file
# email output
```

```
#
echo " " > $outfile
echo "update statistics:${SERVER}: exiting at `date`." > $outfile
echo " " > $outfile
echo " " > $outfile2
echo " " > $outfile2
echo "update statistics:${SERVER}: exiting at `date`." > $outfile2
echo " " > $outfile2
echo " " > $outfile2
echo "******************************************************" > $out-
file2
cat $outfile > $outfile2
# ***** you must edit the recipient of the email
/usr/ucb/mail -s "${SERVER}: update statistics cronjob complete"
  psychoDBA@dbahost < $outfile2
exit
```

EXECUTING DBCC
(DBCC_LISTOF_DBS)

This script will execute the full set of **dbcc** commands for one or more databases. The set of **dbcc** commands that is executed consists of **check-db**, **checkalloc**, and **checkcatalog**. The script keeps all the **dbcc** output in a file and then examines that file for any errors. The script then sends e-mail with a summary of the number of errors found, the lines of the **dbcc** output that contain the errors followed by the full **dbcc** output.

```
#!/bin/sh
#
# Bourne shell script to execute dbcc checks for each of a
# list of databases
# 9/9/96 Brian Hitchcock
#
if [ $# -lt 2 ]
then
echo $0: invalid format: $# argv parameters provided, at least 2
  required
echo $0: required format: $0 '<SERVER> <database(s)...>'
exit 1
```

```
fi
#
# setup parameters
#
# ***** you must edit the path for SYBASE and PWD environment
  variables
SYBASE=/export/home/sybase
SERVER=$1
PWD=`cat /export/home/sybase/.kparm`
# ***** you must edit the path for the dumpdir directory
dumpdir=/export/home/dbdump
outfile=${dumpdir}/${SERVER}_dbcclog.out
outfile2=${dumpdir}/${SERVER}_dbcclog.out2
outfile3=${dumpdir}/${SERVER}_dbcclog.out3
outfile4=${dumpdir}/${SERVER}_dbcclog.out4
shift
dbs_to_dbcc="$*"
#
# begin dumping
#
echo "dbcc log:${SERVER}: started at `date`." > $outfile
echo "dbcc log:${SERVER}: started at `date`." > $outfile2
echo " " > $outfile
echo " " > $outfile2
#
# begin loop for each database to dbcc
#
for dbname in $dbs_to_dbcc
do
dmptime=`date +%m%d%y_%H%M%S`
proc_name=dbcc_temp_sproc_${dmptime}
# ***** you must edit the path for isql and for the interfaces file
# the following sql script will create a temporary stored procedure
# that will actually perform the SQL. By doing this we can trap
# any errors that occur during the execution of the sql.
#
# isql to the SQL Server
#
$SYBASE/bin/isql -Usa -S${SERVER} -P${PWD} -I$SYBASE/interfaces -e >
  ${outfile3} << finish_sql
create procedure $proc_name as
        declare @status int
  select getdate()
  dbcc checkdb($dbname)
```

```
  select getdate()
  dbcc checkalloc($dbname)
  select getdate()
  dbcc checkcatalog($dbname)
go
declare @return_status int
execute @return_status=$proc_name
drop procedure $proc_name
if @return_status = 0
begin
print "**************************************************"
print "Stored Procedure Execution Complete — no errors"
end
else
begin
print "!!!!!!!!!!!!!!!!!!!!!!!!!!!!"
print "FAILURE of Stored Procedure"
end
go
exit
finish_sql
#
# save return status of the isql command
# isql failures indicate problems with password, interfaces file
# or server down
#
isql_status=$<
#
# scan dbcc output for the current database
# looking for any errors
#
Msg_count=`grep Msg ${outfile3} | wc -l`
grep Msg ${outfile3} > ${outfile4}
DBlib_count=`grep DB-LIBRARY ${outfile3} | wc -l`
grep DB-LIBRARY ${outfile3} > ${outfile4}
Error_count=`expr $Msg_count + $DBlib_count`
echo $Error_count
#
# save return status of sql script that creates and
# executes stored procedure
#
sproc_status=`tail -1 ${outfile3}`
#
# now that we have grep-ed for errors, dump dbcc output for
# this database to the output file
```

```
#
cat ${outfile3} > ${outfile}
#
# if isql failed
#
if [ $isql_status -ne 0 ]
then
echo " " > $outfile
echo dbcc log:${SERVER}: isql for dbcc of $dbname failed at `date`.
  > $outfile
echo " " > $outfile
echo " " > $outfile2
echo dbcc log:${SERVER}: database dbcc of $dbname failed at `date`.
  > $outfile2
echo " " > $outfile2
# ***** you must edit the recipient of the email
/usr/ucb/mail -s "${SERVER}: dbcc of $dbname failed" psychoDBA@dba
  host < $outfile
#
# if isql did not fail, test the return status from the stored
# procedure
#
else
#
# if stored procedure completed successfully
#
if [ "$sproc_status" = "Stored Procedure Execution Complete — no
  errors" ]
then
echo " " > $outfile
echo dbcc log:${SERVER}: completed database dbcc of $dbname at
  `date` > $outfile
echo "————————————————> total error count = ${Error_count}" > $outfile
echo " " > $outfile2
echo dbcc log:${SERVER}: completed database dbcc of $dbname at
  `date` > $outfile2
echo "————————————————> total error count = ${Error_count}" >
  $outfile2
#
# if isql and stored procedure completed successfully
# output any errors found
#
if [ "$Error_count" -ne "0" ]
then
cat ${outfile4} > $outfile2
```

```
/usr/ucb/mail -s "${SERVER}: dbcc of $dbname failed"
  psychoDBA@dbahost < $outfile4
#
fi
fi
#
# if stored procedure failed
#
if [ "$sproc_status" = "FAILURE of Stored Procedure" ]
then
echo " " > $outfile
echo dbcc log:${SERVER}: sproc for dbcc of $dbname failed at `date`
  > $outfile
# ***** you must edit the recipient of the email
/usr/ucb/mail -s "${SERVER}: dbcc of $dbname failed"
  psychoDBA@dbahost < $outfile
echo " " > $outfile2
echo dbcc log:${SERVER}: sproc for dbcc of $dbname failed at `date`
  > $outfile2
fi
fi
#
# end of loop for each database to dbcc
#
done
#
# append full output file to summary output file
# email output
#
echo " " > $outfile
echo "dbcc log:${SERVER}: exiting at `date`." > $outfile
echo " " > $outfile
echo " " > $outfile2
echo " " > $outfile2
echo "dbcc log:${SERVER}: exiting at `date`." > $outfile2
echo " " > $outfile2
echo " " > $outfile2
echo "*********************************************************" >
  $outfile2
cat $outfile > $outfile2
# ***** you must edit the recipient of the email
/usr/ucb/mail -s "${SERVER}: dbcc cronjob complete"
  psychoDBA@dbahost < $outfile2
exit
```

SCANNING SERVER ERRORLOG
(SCAN_ERRORLOG)

 This script will scan the server error log for the specified server. The script will e mail the number of errors found and the error log line for each error as well as the number of time the server has been restarted within the current error log.

```
#!/bin/sh
#
# Bourne shell script to scan the server errorlog and
# email the list of errors found
#
# 11/25/96 Brian Hitchcock
#
if [ $# -lt 1 ]
then
echo $0: invalid format: $# argv parameters provided, 1 required
echo $0: required format: $0 '<SERVER>'
exit 1
fi
#
# setup parameters
#
# ***** you must edit the path for the server errorlog file
# ***** this means you must edit the path for filea and
errorlog_filename
# ***** we assume filename is errorlog_<servername>
filea=/export/home/sybase/install/errorlog_
SERVER=$1
errorlog_filename=${filea}${SERVER}
# ***** you must edit the path for the outdir output directory
outdir=/export/home/dbdump
outfile=${outdir}/${SERVER}_scan_errorlog.out
outfile2=${outdir}/${SERVER}_server_errors.out
outfile3=${outdir}/${SERVER}_server_restarts.out
#
# begin scanning
#
echo "scan server errorlog:${SERVER}: started at `date`." > $outfile
echo " " > $outfile
```

```
#
# looking for any errors
#
Error_count=`grep Error ${errorlog_filename} | wc -l`
grep Error ${errorlog_filename} > ${outfile2}
echo "server Errorlog Errors found =    ${Error_count}" > $outfile
#
# Looking for server restarts
#
Restart_count=`grep 'SQL Server/' ${errorlog_filename} | wc -l`
grep 'SQL Server/' ${errorlog_filename} > ${outfile3}
echo "server Errorlog Restarts found = ${Restart_count}" > $outfile
#
# email output of errorlog scan
#
echo " " > $outfile
echo "scan server errorlog:${SERVER}: exiting at `date`." > $outfile
echo " " > $outfile
echo "*********************** Errors ***********************" >
$outfile
cat $outfile2 > $outfile
echo " " > $outfile
echo "*********************** Restarts ***********************" >
$outfile
cat $outfile3 > $outfile
# ***** you must edit the recipient of the email
/usr/ucb/mail -s "${SERVER}: scan errorlog job complete"
  psychoDBA@dbahost < $outfile
exit
```

DUMPING SERVER CONFIGURATION (DUMP_SERVER_CONFIG)

This script will dump to a disk file the configuration information about the specified server. Note that this is much more than simply the output of **sp_configure**. This script dumps all the information regarding the server, the databases in the server, and the users of each database. This information allows you to completely rebuild the server and the databases in the event of a failure, or when you need to re-create the server on another server machine.

This script dumps the information regarding named caches in the server. Since named caches are unique to System 11, this script would generate errors if you run it against a System 10 or 4.9.2 Server. Note that the file used to start the server (RUN_<servername>) and the configuration file(s) used by the server are important sources of server configuration information as well, but these files are already on disk. This script will dump configuration information that is stored in the server to a disk file. The disk files are captured by the UNIX-level tape backups of the server machine. This ensures that all the information needed to rebuild the server is on tape in a form that you can read.

```sh
#!/bin/sh
#
# Bourne shell script to dump the configuration of the specified SQL
  Server
#
# 12/02/96 Brian Hitchcock
#
if [ $# -lt 1 ]
then
echo $0: invalid format: $# argv parameters provided, at least 1
  required
echo $0: required format: $0 '<SERVER>'
exit 1
fi
#
# setup parameters
#
# ***** you must edit the path for SYBASE and PWD environment
  variables
SYBASE=/export/home/sybase
SERVER=$1
PWD=`cat /export/home/sybase/.kparm`
# ***** you must edit the path for the dumpdir file directory
dumpdir=/export/home/dbdump
outfile=${dumpdir}/${SERVER}_config_dump.out
outfile2=${dumpdir}/${SERVER}_config_dump.out2
tempfile=${dumpdir}/${SERVER}_config_dump.temp1
#
chmod 700 $outfile
chmod 700 $outfile2
#
# begin dumping server configuration
#
```

```
echo "dump server config:${SERVER}: started at `date`." > $outfile
echo "dump server config:${SERVER}: started at `date`." > $outfile2
echo " " > $outfile
echo " " > $outfile2
#
# dump overall server configuration
#
$SYBASE/bin/isql -Usa -S${SERVER} -P${PWD} -I$SYBASE/interfaces -e >
  ${outfile} << finish_sql1
use master
go
select * from sysusages
go
select * from sysdevices
go
select * from sysdatabases
go
select * from sysservers
go
select * from sysremotelogins
go
select * from syslogins
go
sp_configure
go
sp_helpdevice
go
sp_helpdb
go
sp_helpcache
go
sp_cacheconfig
go
sybsystemprocs..p_mirror
go
sybsystemprocs..p_devspace
go
sybsystemprocs..p_servermap
go
finish_sql1
#
# setup list of databases in server
#
$SYBASE/bin/isql -Usa -S${SERVER} -P${PWD} -I$SYBASE/interfaces -e >
  ${tempfile} << finish_sql2
use master
```

```
go
select name from sysdatabases order by name
go
finish_sql2
#
# output list of databases
#
echo " " > $outfile
echo "@@@@@@@@@@@@@@@@@@@@@@@@" > $outfile
echo "all databases in server $SERVER...." > $outfile
echo "@@@@@@@@@@@@@@@@@@@@@@@@" > $outfile
echo " " > $outfile
cat ${tempfile} > $outfile
echo " " > $outfile
#
# cut out the first 4 and last 2 lines of the listing of all
# databases in this server
# see the dump_db_create script discussion for details of the
# following part of the script
#
num_lines=`wc -l ${tempfile} | cut -c1-9`
last_line=`expr $num_lines - 4`
first_line=`expr $last_line - 2`
databases_list=`tail -$last_line ${tempfile} | head -$first_line`
rm -f ${tempfile}
#
# now we dump configuration information for the database
#
for database_name in $databases_list
do
#
echo "@@@@@@@@@@@@@@@@@@@@@@@@@@@@@@@@@@@@@@@@@@@@" > $outfile
echo "dumping configuration information for database $database_name
  in $SERVER" > $outfile
echo "@@@@@@@@@@@@@@@@@@@@@@@@@@@@@@@@@@@@@@@@@@@@" > $outfile
echo " " > $outfile
#
$SYBASE/bin/isql -Usa -S${SERVER} -P${PWD} -I$SYBASE/interfaces -e >
  ${outfile} << finish_sql2
use $database_name
go
sp_helpdb $database_name
go
sp_helpsegment
go
sybsystemprocs..p_dbcreate $database_name
```

671

```
go
sp_helpuser
go
select * from sysusers
go
select * from sysalternates
go
finish_sql2
#
# the done is for the loop for each database
#
done
#
# append full output file to summary output file
# email output
#
echo " " > $outfile
echo "dump server config:${SERVER}: exiting at `date`." > $outfile
echo " " > $outfile
echo "dump server config:${SERVER}: exiting at `date`." > $outfile2
echo " " > $outfile2
echo " " > $outfile2
echo "********************************************************"
  > $outfile2
cat $outfile > $outfile2
# ***** you must edit the recipient of the email
/usr/ucb/mail -s "${SERVER}: dump server config cronjob complete"
  psychoDBA@dbahost < $outfile2
exit
```

MONITOR REPORT
(MONITOR_REPORT)

This script monitors the users of the specified server. This is a minimal monitoring tool but is very useful for tracking how many users are on the server, how much blocking is going on, and what server resources are being used. Since this script does a minimal amount of server activity, it can be run more often without interfering with the server users. If your server is experiencing performance problems, you can run this script every 15 minutes and track which users are blocking and what tables are locked, and so forth. This information can tell you a lot about transitory performance problems.

```
#!/bin/sh
#
# Bourne shell script to monitor the activity of the specified
# SQL Server
#
# 12/03/96 Brian Hitchcock
#
if [ $# -lt 1 ]
then
echo $0: invalid format: $# argv parameters provided, at least 1
  required
echo $0: required format: $0 '<SERVER>'
exit 1
fi
#
# setup parameters
#
# ***** you must edit the path for SYBASE and PWD environment
# variables
SYBASE=/export/home/sybase
SERVER=$1
PWD=`cat /export/home/sybase/.kparm`
# ***** you must edit the path for the dumpdir file directory
dumpdir=/export/home/dbdump
outfile=${dumpdir}/${SERVER}_monitor_report.out
outfile2=${dumpdir}/${SERVER}_monitor_report.out2
#
# begin monitor report
#
echo "monitor report:${SERVER}: started at `date`." > $outfile
echo "monitor report:${SERVER}: started at `date`." > $outfile2
echo " " > $outfile
echo " " > $outfile2
#
$SYBASE/bin/isql -Usa -S${SERVER} -P${PWD} -I$SYBASE/interfaces
  -e > ${outfile} << finish_sql1
use master
go
select @@servername, getdate()
go
sp_who
go
sp_lock
go
select * from sysprocesses
go
```

```
sp_monitor
go
finish_sql1
#
# append full output file to summary output file
# email output
#
echo " " > $outfile
echo "monitor report:${SERVER}: exiting at `date`." > $outfile
echo " " > $outfile
echo " " > $outfile2
echo "monitor report:${SERVER}: exiting at `date`." > $outfile2
echo " " > $outfile2
echo " " > $outfile2
echo "*******************************************************" > $out-
file2
cat $outfile > $outfile2
# ***** you must edit the recipient of the email
/usr/ucb/mail -s "${SERVER}: monitor report cronjob complete"
  psychoDBA@dbahost < $outfile2
exit
```

EXECUTE SP_SYSMON (EXECUTE_SP_SYSMON)

This script simply executes **sp_sysmon** and e-mails the output. The stored procedure **sp_sysmon** is new to SQL Server System 11 and the output provides a great deal of performance monitoring information. This script will work only with SQL Server System 11. While **sp_sysmon** is very useful, it does consume server resources while it runs. Unlike the script monitor_report, which can run at any time, **sp_sysmon** should be run only when it is worthwhile. For that reason, the execution of **sp_sysmon** is put into a separate script so you can schedule it separately from other scripts in the crontab list of cron jobs. When you are tuning the server, you may want to run **sp_sysmon** regularly. When you are done you may want to run it only once a day to monitor the overall performance trend.

```
#!/bin/sh
#
# Bourne shell script to execute sp_sysmon on the specified
# SQL Server
```

```
#
# 12/03/96 Brian Hitchcock
#
if [ $# -lt 1 ]
then
echo $0: invalid format: $# argv parameters provided, at least 1
  required
echo $0: required format: $0 '<SERVER>'
exit 1
fi
#
# setup parameters
#
# ***** you must edit the path for SYBASE and PWD environment
  variables
SYBASE=/export/home/sybase
SERVER=$1
PWD=`cat /export/home/sybase/.kparm`
# ***** you must edit the path for the dumpdir file directory
dumpdir=/export/home/dbdump
outfile=${dumpdir}/${SERVER}_monitor_report.out
outfile2=${dumpdir}/${SERVER}_monitor_report.out2
#
# begin executing sp_sysmon
#
echo "execute sp_sysmon:${SERVER}: started at `date`." > $outfile
echo "execute sp_sysmon:${SERVER}: started at `date`." > $outfile2
echo " " > $outfile
echo " " > $outfile2
#
$SYBASE/bin/isql -Usa -S${SERVER} -P${PWD} -I$SYBASE/interfaces -e
  > ${outfile} << finish_sql1
use master
go
select @@servername, getdate()
go
sp_sysmon 1
go
finish_sql1
#
# append full output file to summary output file
# email output
#
echo " " > $outfile
echo "execute sp_sysmon:${SERVER}: exiting at `date`." > $outfile
echo " " > $outfile
```

```
echo " " > $outfile2
echo "execute sp_sysmon:${SERVER}: exiting at `date`." > $outfile2
echo " " > $outfile2
echo " " > $outfile2
echo "*********************************************************"
  > $outfile2
cat $outfile > $outfile2
# ***** you must edit the recipient of the email
/usr/ucb/mail -s "${SERVER}: execute sp_sysmon cronjob complete"
  psychoDBA@dbahost < $outfile2
exit
```

SERVER AUTO-RESTART

This script will start the SQL Server when the server machine is rebooted. This script is normally located in /etc/rc3.d. You should check with your server machine SA for the details of how to install this script. Note that this script also starts the components of Sybase Replication Server. This is shown simply to demonstrate that you need to wait (in this example 300 seconds) to allow the SQL Server to start up and recover its databases before you try to start up other components.

```
#!/bin/sh
####################################################################
#   Entry to start sybase data server          #
####################################################################
if [ -f /export/home/sybase/install/startserver ] ;then
  su sybase -c "/bin/sh" << Here
        SYBASE=/export/home/sybase; export SYBASE
        /export/home/sybase/install/RUN_SPOTUS &
        /export/home/sybase/install/RUN_SPOTUS_BCK &
  sleep 300
  /export/home/sybase/install/RUN_SPOTUSRS &
  /export/home/sybase/install/RUN_SPOTUS_SPOTUSRS_RSSD_ltm &
  /export/home/sybase/install/RUN_SPOTUS_spotdb_ltm &
  /export/home/sybase/install/RUN_SPOTUK_spotdb_ltm &
Here
fi
```

CRONTAB ENTRIES FOR SCRIPTS

This output shows a typical set of crontab entries to execute the set of System 11 production server scripts. In this example, the databases are being dumped every night at 11PM (23:00) and the transaction logs are being dumped 30 minutes later at 23:30. Then, for the databases master and *sybsystemprocs*, the transaction log is truncated at 23:45. Note that master and *sybsystemprocs* do not have their transaction logs on a separate server device. That is why their logs must be truncated. Also notice that these same two databases do not appear in the crontab entry for dump transaction logs.

Removing dump files that are more than two days old is scheduled for 1 AM. Note that all files in directory /export/home/dbdump with a file-name of SPOTUS_*.dmp that are more than two days old will be removed. This is how you tell the script which file to remove—by specifying the directory and the file names. The **dbcc** runs happen at 2 AM followed by updating all table statistics for the specified databases at 3 AM, scanning the server error log at 4 AM, and dumping the server configuration at 5 AM.

The simple server performance monitoring script (monitor_report) runs at 9AM, 12 noon, and 3PM while the full monitoring script (execute_sp_sysmon) runs only once a day at 12:30PM. This example crontab listing should help you set up the cron jobs for your production server.

```
0 23 * * * /export/home/sybase/local/bin/dump_listof_dbs
SPOTUS spotdb SPOTUSRS_RSSD master sybsystemprocs

30 23 * * * /export/home/sybase/local/bin/logdump_listof_dbs
SPOTUS spotdb SPOTUSRS_RSSD

45 23 * * * /export/home/sybase/local/bin/trunclog_listof_dbs
SPOTUS master sybsystemprocs

0 1 * * * /export/home/sybase/local/bin/remove_old_files
"/export/home/dbdump/SPOTUS_*.dmp" 2

0 2 * * * /export/home/sybase/local/bin/dbcc_listof_dbs SPOTUS
spotdb SPOTUSRS_RSSD master sybsystemprocs
```

```
0 3 * * * /export/home/sybase/local/bin/update_listof_dbs
SPOTUS spotdb

0 4 * * * /export/home/sybase/local/bin/scan_errorlog SPOTUS

0 5 * * * /export/home/sybase/local/bin/dump_server_config
SPOTUS

0 9,12,15 * * * /export/home/sybase/local/bin/monitor_report
SPOTUS

30 12 * * * /export/home/sybase/local/bin/execute_sp_sysmon
SPOTUS
```

Index

LICENSE AGREEMENT AND LIMITED WARRANTY

READ THE FOLLOWING TERMS AND CONDITIONS CAREFULLY BEFORE OPENING THIS CD PACKAGE. THIS LEGAL DOCUMENT IS AN AGREEMENT BETWEEN YOU AND PRENTICE-HALL, INC. (THE "COMPANY"). BY OPENING THIS SEALED CD PACKAGE, YOU ARE AGREEING TO BE BOUND BY THESE TERMS AND CONDITIONS. IF YOU DO NOT AGREE WITH THESE TERMS AND CONDITIONS, DO NOT OPEN THE CD PACKAGE. PROMPTLY RETURN THE UNOPENED CD PACKAGE AND ALL ACCOMPANYING ITEMS TO THE PLACE YOU OBTAINED THEM FOR A FULL REFUND OF ANY SUMS YOU HAVE PAID.

1.   GRANT OF LICENSE: In consideration of your purchase of this book, and your agreement to abide by the terms and conditions of this Agreement, the Company grants to you a nonexclusive right to use and display the copy of the enclosed software program (hereinafter the "SOFTWARE") on a single computer (i.e., with a single CPU) at a single location so long as you comply with the terms of this Agreement. The Company reserves all rights not expressly granted to you under this Agreement.

2.   OWNERSHIP OF SOFTWARE: You own only the magnetic or physical media (the enclosed CD) on which the SOFTWARE is recorded or fixed, but the Company and the software developers retain all the rights, title, and ownership to the SOFTWARE recorded on the original CD copy(ies) and all subsequent copies of the SOFTWARE, regardless of the form or media on which the original or other copies may exist. This license is not a sale of the original SOFTWARE or any copy to you.

3.   COPY RESTRICTIONS: This SOFTWARE and the accompanying printed materials and user manual (the "Documentation") are the subject of copyright. The individual programs on the CD are copyrighted by the authors of each program. Some of the programs on the CD include separate licensing agreements. If you intend to use one of these programs, you must read and follow its accompanying license agreement. If you intend to use the trial version of Internet Chameleon, you must read and agree to the terms of the notice regarding fees on the back cover of this book. You may not copy the Documentation or the SOFTWARE, except that you may make a single copy of the SOFTWARE for backup or archival purposes only. You may be held legally responsible for any copying or copyright infringement which is caused or encouraged by your failure to abide by the terms of this restriction.

4.   USE RESTRICTIONS: You may not network the SOFTWARE or otherwise use it on more than one computer or computer terminal at the same time. You may physically transfer the SOFTWARE from one computer to another provided that the SOFTWARE is used on only one computer at a time. You may not distribute copies of the SOFTWARE or Documentation to others. You may not reverse engineer, disassemble, decompile, modify, adapt, translate, or create derivative works based on the SOFTWARE or the Documentation without the prior written consent of the Company.

5.   TRANSFER RESTRICTIONS: The enclosed SOFTWARE is licensed only to you and may not be transferred to any one else without the prior written consent of the Company. Any unauthorized transfer of the SOFTWARE shall result in the immediate termination of this Agreement.

6.   TERMINATION: This license is effective until terminated. This license will terminate automatically without notice from the Company and become null and void if you fail to comply with any provisions or limitations of this license. Upon termination, you shall destroy the Documentation and all copies of the SOFTWARE. All provisions of this Agreement as to warranties, limitation of liability, remedies or damages, and our ownership rights shall survive termination.

7.   MISCELLANEOUS: This Agreement shall be construed in accordance with the laws of the United States of America and the State of New York and shall benefit the Company, its affiliates, and assignees.

8.   LIMITED WARRANTY AND DISCLAIMER OF WARRANTY: The Company warrants that the SOFTWARE, when properly used in accordance with the Documentation, will operate in substantial conformity with the description of the SOFTWARE set forth in the Documentation. The Company does not warrant that the SOFTWARE will meet your requirements or that the operation of the SOFTWARE will be uninterrupted or error-free. The Company warrants that the media on which the SOFTWARE is delivered shall be free from defects in materials and workmanship under normal use for a period of thirty (30) days from the date of your purchase. Your only remedy and the Company's only obligation under these limited warranties is, at the Company's option, return of the warranted item for a refund of any amounts paid by you or replacement of the item. Any replacement of SOFTWARE or media under the warranties shall not extend the original warranty period. The limited warranty set forth above shall not apply to any SOFTWARE which the Company determines in good faith has been subject to misuse, neglect, improper installation, repair, alteration, or damage by you. EXCEPT FOR THE EXPRESSED WARRANTIES SET FORTH ABOVE, THE COMPANY DISCLAIMS ALL WARRANTIES, EXPRESS OR IMPLIED, INCLUDING WITHOUT LIMITATION, THE IMPLIED WARRANTIES OF MERCHANTABILITY AND FITNESS FOR A PARTICULAR PURPOSE. EXCEPT FOR THE EXPRESS WARRANTY SET FORTH ABOVE, THE COMPANY DOES NOT WARRANT, GUARANTEE, OR MAKE ANY REPRESENTATION REGARDING THE USE OR THE RESULTS OF THE USE OF THE SOFTWARE IN TERMS OF ITS CORRECTNESS, ACCURACY, RELIABILITY, CURRENTNESS, OR OTHERWISE.

IN NO EVENT, SHALL THE COMPANY OR ITS EMPLOYEES, AGENTS, SUPPLIERS, OR CONTRACTORS BE LIABLE FOR ANY INCIDENTAL, INDIRECT, SPECIAL, OR CONSEQUENTIAL DAMAGES ARISING OUT OF OR IN CONNECTION WITH THE LICENSE GRANTED UNDER THIS AGREEMENT, OR FOR LOSS OF USE, LOSS OF DATA, LOSS OF INCOME OR PROFIT, OR OTHER LOSSES, SUSTAINED AS A RESULT OF INJURY TO ANY PERSON, OR LOSS OF OR DAMAGE TO PROPERTY, OR CLAIMS OF THIRD PARTIES, EVEN IF THE COMPANY OR AN AUTHORIZED REPRESENTATIVE OF THE COMPANY HAS BEEN ADVISED OF THE POSSIBILITY OF SUCH DAMAGES. IN NO EVENT SHALL LIABILITY OF THE COMPANY FOR DAMAGES WITH RESPECT TO THE SOFTWARE EXCEED THE AMOUNTS ACTUALLY PAID BY YOU, IF ANY, FOR THE SOFTWARE.

SOME JURISDICTIONS DO NOT ALLOW THE LIMITATION OF IMPLIED WARRANTIES OR LIABILITY FOR INCIDENTAL, INDIRECT, SPECIAL, OR CONSEQUENTIAL DAMAGES, SO THE ABOVE LIMITATIONS MAY NOT ALWAYS APPLY. THE WARRANTIES IN THIS AGREEMENT GIVE YOU SPECIFIC LEGAL RIGHTS AND YOU MAY ALSO HAVE OTHER RIGHTS WHICH VARY IN ACCORDANCE WITH LOCAL LAW.
ACKNOWLEDGMENT

YOU ACKNOWLEDGE THAT YOU HAVE READ THIS AGREEMENT, UNDERSTAND IT, AND AGREE TO BE BOUND BY ITS TERMS AND CONDITIONS. YOU ALSO AGREE THAT THIS AGREEMENT IS THE COMPLETE AND EXCLUSIVE STATEMENT OF THE AGREEMENT BETWEEN YOU AND THE COMPANY AND SUPERSEDES ALL PROPOSALS OR PRIOR AGREEMENTS, ORAL, OR WRITTEN, AND ANY OTHER COMMUNICATIONS BETWEEN YOU AND THE COMPANY OR ANY REPRESENTATIVE OF THE COMPANY RELATING TO THE SUBJECT MATTER OF THIS AGREEMENT.

Should you have any questions concerning this Agreement or if you wish to contact the Company for any reason, please contact in writing at the address below.
Robin Short
Prentice Hall PTR
One Lake Street
Upper Saddle River, New Jersey 07458